Issues and Perspectives

Issues and Perspectives

READING AND WRITING IN COMMUNITIES

Richard P. Batteiger
Oklahoma State University

ALLYN AND BACON

Boston   London   Toronto   Sydney   Tokyo   Singapore

Series Editor: Joseph Opiela
Series Editorial Assistant: Amy Capute
Production Administrator: Marjorie Payne
Editorial-Production Service: Editorial Inc.
Cover Administrator: Linda Dickinson
Composition Buyer: Linda Cox
Manufacturing Buyer: Louise Richardson

Library of Congress Cataloging-in-Publication Data

Batteiger, Richard P.
   Issues and perspectives : reading and writing in communities /
Richard Batteiger.
      p. cm.
    ISBN 0-205-13396-7 (alk. paper)
    1. College readers. 2. English language—Rhetoric. I. Title.
   PE1417.B378   1991
   428.6—dc20   91-30182
                                        CIP

This book is printed on
recycled, acid-free paper.

Acknowledgments

Chapter 1
Page 8. From *Newsweek,* July 10, 1989. Copyright © 1989, Newsweek, Inc. All rights reserved. Reprinted by permission.
Page 14. From *Commonweal,* August 11, 1989. Reprinted by permission of Commonweal Foundation © 1989.

Credits continued on page 587, which constitutes an extension of the copyright page.

Printed in the United States of America

10 9 8 7 6 5 4 3 2 1   97 96 95 94 93 92

Contents

3 Children, Toys, and Play 52

9 Taking Out the Trash 447

Alternative Tables of Contents

Rhetorical

Narration

Description

Exposition

Argument

Classification

Arranged by Perspective and/or Discipline

Legal/Social

Business

Health and Medicine

Preface

THE DESIGN FOR *ISSUES AND PERSPECTIVES* originated in my conviction that reading and writing are closely related, that success in one is necessary for success in the other, and that success in both is required for success in college. Much academic writing is based on reading, on using information that is already available, rather than on developing new information. The writer's job is to take control of that information, integrate it into what she or he already knows, evaluate it, consolidate it with other information, and use it to make a point or support a conclusion. For these reasons, George Hillocks's inquiry method, which provides students with a ready-made data base of information, has been an important inspiration for the text's apparatus. The reading selections in each chapter provide a base of information and ideas that students can use as a resource for their own writing. The questions and activities at the end of each selection and each chapter ask students to understand, summarize, consolidate, compare, and verify the information from the reading selections, and then incorporate it into their own writing. Students can do this by writing about the subject of the chapter, or by extending the ideas, methods, and data from that chapter into other areas of inquiry. For example, after reading about birds in chapter 6, students can apply the methods and insights to the study of adaptive behavior in other animals and humans.

But information is never simply information. People approach the world from a variety of perspectives, and these perspectives influence the way they see the world and their views of what is right or wrong, good or bad, and true or false. In some cases these perspectives may coincide with academic disciplines, but they may also be based on ethical, political, religious, social, or other consideration. Being an effective critical reader and writer requires an understanding both of the information itself and the way various perspectives can affect that information.

Because people see the world from a variety of perspectives, readers need to be aware of how these perspectives shape the way writers approach the world and present information. To help students understand this, chapters 1 and 2 are devoted to explaining methods of critical reading and writing. Using reading selections to illustrate the main points, these chapters take students through the processes of reading critically and analytically, taking notes, writing summaries, and incorporating information from their reading into their own writing. Both chapters provide frequent writing exercises and activities that allow students to practice the skills being presented.

THE READING SELECTIONS

Each chapter of *Issues and Perspectives* treats a single subject from a variety of different personal and disciplinary perspectives, including science, social science, business, the humanities, history, law, and politics. The subjects themselves were chosen for a variety of reasons, ranging from personal idiosyncrasy to their social significance. Most of the writers represented here have not been widely anthologized in texts of this type. Their newness may help both students and teachers respond to them with a freshness and unconventionality that more familiar subjects and reading selections might not permit.

For example, chapter 5 considers the present situation of young African-American men in the United States. Briefly stated, that situation is not good. Young black men seem to provoke considerable hostility among other groups in the population. In addition, they are more likely than members of any other group to be in trouble of some kind, to be incarcerated, to be the victims of violent crime, to be unemployed or underemployed, or to live in poverty. But there are no simple explanations or solutions for this situation. The writers in this chapter illustrate the complexity of the problems involved by approaching the subject from a variety of directions. Donna Britt tells of her brother's death at the hands of police officers; Harry Edwards analyzes the role of black men in college and professional sports. Shelby Steele writes from the perspective of a successful black man about what he calls "race holding," i.e., using race as an excuse. Novelist John Edgar Wideman writes about himself and his brother who is serving a life sentence for murder. Combined, these perspectives deprive students of easy answers and invite analysis, discussion, and debate. Each chapter takes the shape of an extended, sometimes digressive discussion that may have been under way for some time. After reading the selections in the chapter, students should be prepared to join the discussion on their own terms.

THE APPARATUS

The apparatus is designed to encourage students to respond critically and thoughtfully to the reading selections. Each chapter of reading selections begins with a set of prereading exercises to help students establish what they already know and believe about the subject. These questions are designed to encourage students to make their own knowledge of a subject explicit and to use that knowledge to form a context for the new information they will encounter in the readings that follow.

Questions at the end of each selection and chapter do not ask for simple recall of information. Instead, they focus on the critical reading and thinking skills presented in chapters 1 and 2. Students are asked to summarize and analyze the central concepts in each selection and chapter. "Questions for Critical Readers," which occur at the end of each selection, ask students to demonstrate their understanding of the selection's central concepts, the major support or illustration the writer provides for those concepts, and the perspective from which the writer views the subject. Next, the questions for "Analysis and Discussion" ask students to use the information and ideas from the selection as the basis for an analysis and discussion of the writer's subject or a related subject. Finally, a suggested writing assignment asks students to apply the ideas and information they have encountered in each selection.

At the end of each chapter, "Suggestions for Writing and Research" invite students to draw on the entire chapter and compare the information, ideas, and methods of the various selections with each other, and then provide suggestions for writing and research. Writing assignments may relate directly to the chapter itself or may ask students to apply the methods and concepts of the chapter to issues and questions in their own lives.

ACKNOWLEDGMENTS

A number of people helped me as I thought about and assembled this text. Joe Opiela of Allyn and Bacon responded enthusiastically to my initial proposal and has provided important insight and encouragement along the way. His assistant, Amy Capute, has been a constant source of help and information. Debbie Clark, my secretary, helped with permissions and assembled the manuscript. She also keeps me organized from day to day, which is no small task. Karen Morris of the Edmond Low Library at Oklahoma State University helped me locate a number of the reading selections. Coleen Davis did most of the work with permissions, and without her there would be no book. Emily McKinley wrote much of the Instructor's Manual. The following reviewers also provided important insight, encouragement, and correction at crucial points: Philip Arrington, Eastern Michigan University; Kathleen Shine Cain, Merrimack College; Jay Funston, James Madison University; C. Jeriel Howard, Northeastern Illinois University; Nevin K. Laib, Franklin and Marshall College; Carolyn Miller, North Carolina State University; Louise Z. Smith, University of Massachusetts, Boston; Irwin Weiser, Purdue University; and Richard Zbracki, Iowa State University.

Reading and Writing in Communities of Belief

WHILE YOU ARE IN SCHOOL, reading and writing will be your primary means of learning. Through your reading you will learn about important ideas and information, and when you write you will learn to express your own ideas and to use what you know to argue for positions and solve problems. Once you get beyond the most elementary level of any subject, however, you will discover that disagreements about information and ideas are at the heart of most academic discussions. Writers will disagree about how to solve problems and answer questions. They will also disagree about how to understand or interpret facts. They will even disagree about whether facts exist.

Some people react to disagreements among experts by concluding that the experts are wrong. These people are usually looking for a single, all-encompassing truth. When they do not find it, they retreat into their own preconceived ideas about what the world is like or what it should be like. And they go further. Other people are fascinated when experts disagree. Instead of retreating in confusion, they get excited.

In chapter 1 you will read about a recent controversy over burning the United States' flag. There is much to disagree about on this subject. Some believe burning the flag is an act of desecration. Others take it as an act of political protest and say it should be protected as free speech. Instead of allowing these disagreements to confuse you or make you angry, try to see them as opportunities to explore the world from several different perspectives and learn about it in new ways. If you can accept the different perspectives you encounter as part of the richness of the intellectual world, then you are ready to learn, and you will discover that learning can be exciting, even if it is a bit bumpy along the way.

Consensus and Dissent

Most societies value consensus, just as most people believe that life is just easier if people can agree with each other. Social units such as families, churches, and clubs, and political units such as cities and nations find it easier to maintain themselves if most of their members agree about important issues. Current controversies about flag burning and abortion have led to intense conflicts about the basic principles that govern the nation's life, such as privacy and freedom of speech. In the face of these conflicts, it may become increasingly difficult to maintain agreement about the beliefs that citizens of the United States hold in common. Consensus usually helps preserve group cohesion by limiting or preventing discussion of potentially divisive questions that might threaten the group's survival. When consensus is valued in this way, people tend to discourage dissent and disagreement. People who challenge accepted ways of thinking and acting often find themselves being ignored, treated rudely, or dismissed as cranks, as though their ideas were silly or stupid. Sometimes they are even threatened.

It is true that some people disagree with others just for the fun of it. Perhaps they enjoy being difficult. But many disagreements arise from fundamental differences in the ways people look at and make sense of the world. These disagreements cannot be made to disappear by simply reviewing the facts or enforcing consensus. They require extensive inquiry, discussion, and debate if the people involved are to agree or even understand why they disagree. Most people now recognize that the earth is a sphere that revolves around the sun, not a flat surface that sits at the center of the universe. And most also know that diseases are caused by bacteria and other microorganisms, rather than evil spirits. To question these facts may seem silly today, but they have not always been accepted as facts. People believed in a flat earth or evil spirits for what they regarded as important reasons, and they believed that those who disagreed with them posed a threat to society—even to the survival of the earth itself. In some cases, people who disagree with widely accepted views have been put to death.

Although questions about the shape of the earth and the existence of bacteria were resolved long ago (for most people—there is still a Flat Earth Society), other questions remain and new ones come up all the time. For example, should burning the U.S. flag be protected as an exercise of free speech or prosecuted as a crime? Should advertising be banned from children's television programs? Should English be declared the official (or only) language in the United States? People often disagree profoundly about how to answer these questions because they have come to look at and make sense of the world in radically different ways; they belong to different communities of belief.

Communities of Belief

The world does not make sense by itself. People confer meaning on events and objects through their actions and interpretations. Making sense of the world appears to be a peculiarly human need and activity. But individuals do not have to face this task alone; much of it is done for them by the social, cultural, and intellectual groups in which they live. These communities of belief teach their members a way of making sense of the world. Individuals come to understand the world by learning the sense-making and meaning-giving strategies of the communities of belief in which they live.

The family is the first community of belief that most people encounter. Parents, grandparents, and siblings teach children practical lessons, such as to avoid fire, to stay out of the street, and to brush their teeth. They also teach them about what is right and wrong. As children grow, they encounter other communities of belief, many of which differ from the family and its way of looking at the world. Peers, schools, and the adult world present people with increasingly diverse views. Each new person one encounters presents a potentially new community of belief. College students encounter a bewildering array of new and different communities of belief as they learn about cultures, academic disciplines, and ideas that they have never encountered before.

Each new community of belief brings with it potential conflicts, as people attempt to reconcile their established ways of looking at the world with the new ones they have encountered. A child who has been taught to be patriotic and to support elected officials may experience anger and shock when other people question the government's actions. These conflicts are not simply between individual behaviors but between communities of belief.

It is possible to belong to several communities of belief without experiencing inconsistencies or contradictions that cannot be reconciled. Many people live simultaneously within the frameworks of religion, politics, and business without conflicts. And sometimes they can do this even when it seems that conflicts are inevitable. For example, many scientists find that science and religion are not incompatible, despite the many issues on which these communities of belief appear to disagree. But some conflict is inevitable, because communities of belief have rules of membership. They require those who belong to them to believe certain things and make sense of the world in certain ways. For example, psychology is an academic discipline, and it is also a community of belief. Psychologists believe that behavior can be explained rationally through systemic, empirical observation and experimentation. People who believe that behavior is caused by demons or divine intervention, or that it cannot be explained at all, simply cannot be psychologists. They do not belong to the community of belief that constitutes psychology as an academic discipline.

Individuals experience internal conflict when they cannot reconcile the inconsistencies between the communities of belief to which they belong. Scientists who accept theories of evolution and the biblical creation story have found some way to resolve the obvious inconsistencies between these two ways of making sense of the world. Perhaps they see one as an explanation of the other, or perhaps they do not see them as inconsistent. But not everyone can do this, and not all communities of belief can be reconciled with one another. For example, a community of belief that accepts and advocates white supremacy cannot be reconciled with one that promotes racial equality and civil rights for all.

Some people resolve their internal conflicts over different communities of belief by adopting the rules and point of view of a single community and using it as their primary or only reference point in making sense of the world. They conform to what that community says is right or appropriate, and they may dismiss the views of other communities as misguided or wrong. This provides a comfortable, consistent world view, and it may remove their immediate discomfort, but it may not solve the problem that brought the inconsistency to light.

Communities of Belief in the Academic World

In the academic world, communities of belief tend to be aligned with academic disciplines. Thus, physicists will seek scientific explanations for events and behaviors, while philosophers may seek logical or ethical explanations, and artists may explain the world in terms of aesthetics rather than logic or science. Several different communities may study the same thing, and each discipline will present its own interpretations of how the world works. Thus, what most of us see as identical events may have several different, but quite plausible, explanations. For example, human behavior is endlessly fascinating, and it has been studied in many different ways. Though it may seem the private preserve of psychology, it has also been examined by philosophers, sociologists, novelists, poets, scientists, economists, and many others. Each of these sees human behavior somewhat differently than the others. Each one asks different questions and reaches conclusions in terms acceptable to its own community of belief.

For example, in attempting to understand alcohol abuse, a philosopher might write from an ethical perspective. A psychologist might discuss the issue as a compulsive or addictive behavior. A biologist would look for physiological or genetic causes for the behavior. Economists and sociologists would explore the causes and consequences of alcohol abuse within the setting of society at large. A novelist might write about one alcoholic, the relationships with the family and others, and the effects of drinking on the alcoholic's own life.

Like other communities of belief, academic disciplines impose rules on those who would belong to them. That is, they ask their members to think and act in certain ways. The foundation of membership in the academic world is the belief that problems can be solved and the world can be understood through knowledge. Knowledge is an alternative to ignorance and narrow-mindedness, and it is the product of inquiry. To understand something, we must examine it carefully and thoroughly, from many different perspectives by observing, experimenting, and questioning. Knowledge gained through inquiry is subject to testing and verification in various ways. Those who question or doubt conclusions can repeat observations and experiments for themselves under the same and different conditions. They can ask for evidence and proof, and they can subject that evidence to rigorous examination. Evidence is then subject to discussion and debate. Once the debate and discussion are over, and knowledge has been accepted, it becomes part of the sense-making procedures of a community of belief.

Beyond the Academic World

Teachers can be very forceful and intense about what they know and believe because, like everyone else, they belong to communities of belief. They do not necessarily want to impose *what* they believe on others. They do hope that their students will learn to make sense of the world in a thoughtful, systematic way through inquiry, knowledge, and discussion. They also want their students to realize that those who belong to other communities of belief are not necessarily wrong, but simply different, and that there are reasons for their differences.

1

Becoming a Critical Reader

CRITICAL READING, WHICH IS THE KIND of reading your professors will expect of you in college, involves more than simply understanding the words on a page or memorizing facts that might be useful on a test. In most of the courses you take in college your teachers will give reading assignments and will expect you to perform in three broad areas:

1. *Understanding.* Do you comprehend what you have read? Do you understand the terms, information, and ideas? Can you evaluate what you have read to determine whether it is accurate and reliable?

2. *Analysis and Discussion.* Can you summarize complex information and concepts, and relate facts and ideas to each other and to larger contexts? Do you recognize different points of view and understand their differences? Can you construct a composite or synthesis that includes relevant points of view and relates them to each other?

3. *Application.* Can you use terms, information, and concepts from your reading in new situations, such as to support or illustrate your own ideas and opinions? Can you choose among competing and/or contradictory versions of the same events or ideas and explain the reasons for your

1

choice? Very often, application will involve writing papers in which you report results of your research and explain your own ideas and positions.

Critical reading is an important academic skill because the information we get from reading (or any other source) is never a direct representation of truth or reality. It is always someone's version of truth or reality. Information is always filtered through the person who provides it, through language, through culture and society, and through the medium that conveys it to us (writing, television, etc.). Unfortunately, texts, films, speeches, and other presentations do not come with labels that vouch for their truth or reliability. It is your job as a critical reader to sort out and evaluate different versions in order to arrive at a version that you can accept and that everyone (or almost everyone) can agree to.

For example, all attorneys know that eyewitness accounts of a crime or traffic accident can vary so drastically from each other that they may be the least reliable source of information about what actually happened. The problem is not that the witnesses lie or deliberately attempt to deceive, but they are affected by their own preconceptions and perceptions, as well as by the confusion of events. Witnesses report not what happened, but what they think happened. In court, what is often most important is not the version of a single witness, but the collective weight of a number of witnesses as they tell their versions. Attorneys seldom attempt to discover a single truth; they use the witnesses' different accounts to construct a single version that a judge and jury can accept as most likely to represent the truth.

Successful critical readers are like attorneys, judges, and jurors who are trying to figure out which version of an event to believe. They realize that different sources will present different versions of reality and that they must analyze, evaluate, compare, and question those versions in order to arrive at a version that seems to make sense. The following checklist provides an overview of what to think about as you prepare for critical reading.

A Checklist for Critical Reading

Context. What is the general background for the subject you are reading about? What other subjects are related to it? What is your personal connection with this subject?

Purpose. What is the writer's reason for writing? What does the writer want you to know, do, or believe when you have finished reading? What is your purpose for reading?

Main Ideas. What is the writer's central point, and what are the major subordinate points that supplement and support it?

Positions. What position has the writer taken about the subject? What is your own position about the subject?

Assumptions. What assumptions has a writer made about the subject or the world in general? What are your own assumptions about this subject?

Data and Information. Does the writer provide complete and accurate information? Do the examples and illustrations really apply to the subject? How is the writer using statistics?

Conclusions. What is the writer's conclusion? Does it follow from the information provided? What other conclusions are possible?

Reviewing. Review what you have learned and summarize it in the context of other knowledge you have about the subject.

Of course, attempting to pay attention to all of these questions and activities at the same time would be impossible. Instead, organize your critical reading into stages.

Before You Read. Prepare yourself to read effectively by previewing the subject and your own knowledge.

As You Read. Use reading strategies appropriate to the text and your purpose, and keep track of your reading by marking the text and taking notes.

After You Read. Review, summarize, and synthesize to increase your retention and understanding.

The next section explains each of these stages in detail.

Prereading: Preparing to Read Effectively

Take time to prepare yourself before you begin reading. It will help you read more effectively and remember more of what you read. The following questions will help you preview your subject and your own knowledge about it.

1. *Why Are You Reading?* Are you reading because you have a specific goal to accomplish, or are you simply curious about the subject? Has a teacher made an assignment? Do you need the information to solve a problem or answer a question? Your reason for reading will affect the way you read. For example, you can probably satisfy a general curiosity by reading quickly, identifying central concepts, and working for an overview. However, if you know that you need to remember specific infor-

mation for some reason, you will attempt to identify important ideas and information and devise ways of remembering them. If you are attempting to answer a specific question, you will look for an answer, and you may not need an overview of the whole subject.

For example, if you want general information about a subject such as global warming, you can consult a general source such as a news story and skim the information you find there to satisfy your curiosity. However, if you want to find specific information about the role of chlorofluoro-carbons (CFCs) in global warming, you will need to consult expert sources, such as scientific journals, and read them very carefully.

2. *What Do You Already Know?* You will almost always know something about the subjects you read about, even when you think you don't know anything about them. Your knowledge might consist of very general information that you have accumulated over the years, or you may have quite detailed knowledge as the result of careful study or firsthand experience. You will often know things that you are not aware of knowing until you survey your knowledge in detail. Reviewing your knowledge before you read will give you a foundation for the new information you will encounter when you read.

3. *What Is the Context for Your Subject?* No subject exists in isolation. Every subject has a context, and you will read more effectively if you are aware of that context. For example, any discussion of nuclear energy exists in multiple contexts. These include safety, costs, pollution from fossil fuels such as oil, natural gas, and coal, the prospect of running out of those fuels, and the economics of changing the way we produce and supply energy.

4. *What Are Your Attitudes and Beliefs About the Subject?* Your attitudes and beliefs will affect how, and how well, you read. Strong positive or negative feelings about a subject may prevent you from paying full attention to what you are reading. As a result, you may jump to conclusions too quickly and accept or reject what a writer says, rather than withhold judgment until you have enough information. If you have already made up your mind about a subject, you may not be receptive to others' attitudes and beliefs, especially if these are different from your own.

For example, if you have strong beliefs that commit you to accepting scientific theories of evolution, you will probably have a difficult time reading about creationism and suspending your judgment until you have attempted to understand the creationist explanation of how life on earth began.

Activities Before You Read

The activities that follow will help you do a careful and systematic job of exploring your subject and your own knowledge about it before you read. Cultivate the habit of doing each activity in a notebook or reading journal. As you read, your journal will become a permanent record of your learning and thinking. When you are asked to apply what you have learned, or write, your journal will refresh your memory and help you find ideas to write about.

1. *Write a brief paragraph* in which you explain why you are reading a specific selection and what you hope to learn from it.

2. *Make a list* or write a summary of what you already know about a subject.

3. *Identify the contexts* for your subject. Make a list or write a paragraph in which you identify related subjects.

4. *Describe your attitudes* and beliefs about the subject and state any positions you have taken about it. Attempt to identify the sources and reasons for your attitudes and beliefs. Evaluate how your feelings might affect your reading.

Reading: Use Appropriate Strategies

As you read, concentrate on using reading strategies that are appropriate to your purpose. Different kinds of texts require different kinds of reading. A chemistry text may require close reading and memorization. Newspapers, however, are meant to be read quickly. And remember that you will read differently depending on your purpose. It would be inappropriate to read slowly and carefully, attempting to remember minor details, if your purpose is to gather general information. The appropriate strategy would be to skim the text, moving rapidly rather than dwelling on one page or section, no matter how interesting it might appear. Gathering exact information, on the other hand, usually requires slow, careful reading.

As you read, look for key words, headings, summaries, charts and graphs, and other clues that will help you locate and understand the information you want. Read introductions and conclusions carefully. When you encounter important concepts or information, keep track of them in some way; either mark your text or take notes in your reading notebook or journal.

Mark the Text

Marking a text as you read is one of the best ways of keeping track of the ideas and information that you encounter. Underline central ideas, key words, and definitions. Make notes in the margins to briefly expand or qualify what a writer says, or to define new or important words. Put question marks next to passages that puzzle you. If you disagree with something a writer says, make a note about that in the margin. Put brackets around important passages or paragraphs. Label key examples, illustrations, and data.

Do not mark in books or magazines that you do not own. Instead, you will need to use other methods to keep track of ideas and information. The easiest, but most expensive, is to photocopy an entire article or chapter of a book, or at least the important passages. You can mark the copy because it belongs to you. Some readers make notes on half-sheets of paper and insert them in books or clip them to pages to mark important passages. Use small pads of "sticky" notes that you can attach temporarily to most surfaces. If you make notes on these sheets and attach them to the pages in your reading, they become highly visible "flags" that help you locate important passages quickly.

Take Notes

Most successful critical readers keep notes when they read, and many people keep reading journals, so that their notes are always in the same place. These notes need not be elaborate or extensive. They may include lists of key words, important definitions, summaries, lists of important evidence, and reactions to what you have read. Many times people spend valuable time copying long passages from their reading. It's probably best not to do this until you are certain that having an exact copy of the passage is essential to your purpose. You may, for example, think you want to quote that passage later in something you are writing. It's usually best to avoid this time-consuming copying until much later, when you are certain that it will be worth it. If you do decide that you need a copy of a specific passage, making a photocopy may be a better use of your time and money than copying that passage by hand into your notes.

But don't spend all of your time taking notes or copying what you read. Your primary job is reading, and taking too many notes may distract you from that. Keep in mind that taking notes while you read is not a matter of looking for "good quotes" or dredging for facts and statistics that you might be able to use in a paper. You are reading for a specific purpose, perhaps to get an overview of the subject, or to answer a specific question, and your note-taking should serve that purpose.

When you take notes about your reading, always record the title, author, date, and other publication data about each source that you consult. Nothing is more frustrating than having a valuable note and not knowing its source. Recording the information as you read will save you time and effort in the future.

You may find it helpful to have a consistent way of keeping your reading notes. You can use a spiral notebook, a loose-leaf binder, a stack of 5 × 8 inch cards (3 × 5 cards are too small), or a folder to hold loose sheets of paper. The simpler your system, and the easier it is to carry, the more likely you will be to carry it and use it while you read.

After You Read: Review and Synthesize

When you have finished reading, take time to review and consolidate what you have learned. The time you spend reviewing will reward you with greater retention and understanding of what you have read. The following activities will help you conduct a thorough review:

Review your prereading notes and answer the following questions.

1. What new concepts and information did you discover in your reading?
2. How do new concepts and information fit into what you already know?
3. Have your attitudes toward the subject changed as a result of your reading? If so, how? If not, why not?
4. Has your position changed as a result of your reading? How?
5. What questions do you have now that you did not have before your reading?

Write a brief summary. As you review, compose a mental summary of what you have just read. What is its context? What is its central point? What conclusion has the writer given? Is there an especially telling fact or example? Once you have composed this mental summary, write it in your reading notes.

Critical Reading: An Example

On the following pages are three articles that were published as a result of the 1989 U.S. Supreme Court decision declaring that burning the U.S. flag is protected as free speech. The first article is marked to show how a reader might mark it during reading. Following it are sample notes and a summary. After you have read the first article and the examples, you should read, mark, and take notes on the other two articles on your own. Then read the discussion that follows them.

Begin with prereading. Review the questions for prereading on pages 3–5, and make notes in your reading journal about:

- what you know about the subject of flag burning or desecration
- the general and personal contexts for this subject
- your attitudes about the flag and flag burning (or flag burners)
- any positions you have taken about flag desecration

The first article comes from *Newsweek*, a weekly news magazine with a wide circulation.

A Fight for Old Glory

THE JUSTICES KNEW the ruling would be provocative, as offensive to many Americans as the disputed act itself. Most U.S. Supreme Court decisions are announced in a few terse sentences, but last week two justices in the tense courtroom took the unusual step of reading at length from their opinions. In a 5-4 ruling that shuffled the justices' usual ideological alliances, the court established that First Amendment guarantees of free speech protect those who burn the American flag in political protest. The landmark ruling, said Justice Anthony M. Kennedy, was simply "a pure command of the Constitution."

The nation's reaction was stunned outrage. Veterans' groups across the country denounced the ruling. "Nobody, but nobody, should ever deface the American flag," said American Legion member Charles Inglis of Houston, who fought in both World War II and Korea. "I don't give a damn whether it's [the protester's] civil right or not. I fought to protect the American flag, not to protect him."

How do they Know this? Veterans are not "the Nation"

why do we fight wars?

President George Bush said burning the flag was "wrong, dead wrong." Radio listeners flocked to the phones to complain on local talk shows. A few angry citizens even took to the streets, with one group gathering on the steps of the Supreme Court to burn a mock justice's robe. A NEWSWEEK Poll found that 65 percent of Americans disagreed with the ruling.

The response on Capitol Hill was equally heated. By a vote of 97-3, the Senate passed a resolution expressing "profound disappointment" with the ruling. Congressmen from both parties marched to the floor to defend the flag. Members of both houses called for a constitutional amendment overruling the court (according to NEWSWEEK'S Poll, 71 percent of the public supports such a move). On Friday the Senate took steps to pass a new federal law that would ban flag-burning. "I'm mad as hell," said Democratic Rep. Douglas Applegate of Ohio. "We've witnessed the greatest travesty in the annals of jurisprudence . . . Are there any limitations? Are they going to allow fornication in Times Square at high noon?" Among the few senators to question the raging mood, Republican Gordon J. Humphrey of New Hampshire called it "an exercise in silliness [and] hypocrisy."

Not a law

Comparison not to the point

"We spit on you." It's hard to imagine a more uncomfortable test of the provision for free speech: both the speaker and the "speech" in this case were deeply unsympathetic to most Americans. An avowed communist committed to "world revolution." Gregory L. Johnson traveled to Dallas in 1984 to demonstrate outside the Republican National Convention. Fellow protesters tore down a

nearby flag; he doused it with lighter fluid and set
it on fire. Onlookers chanted "America, the red,
white and blue, we spit on you." Johnson was found
guilty under a Texas law against defiling the flag.
The high court has overturned the conviction, sparing Johnson a one-year prison term and a $2,000
fine. But the ruling did not make Johnson a believer
in the American system. "It's a sham to talk about
freedom of expression in the U.S." he told NEWS-
WEEK. "This is still an oppressive Supreme Court
and an oppressive Constitution." In the same spirit,
fellow members of the Revolutionary Communist
Youth Brigade gathered last week in Berkeley,
Calif., to repeat Johnson's act. "I think it's important to burn flags," said one protester.

    Although the ruling was in line with high-court   *What are these?*
precedents on First Amendment cases, the decision
was not an easy one for the justices; they are no less
appalled than ordinary Americans by the ugly spectacle of a burning flag. "The hard fact," said Kennedy, a conservative who supported the majority,
"is that sometimes we must make decisions we do
not like . . . It is poignant but fundamental that
the flag protects those who hold it in contempt."
Constitutional protection is all the more important
for speech that is repellent, argued Justice William
Brennan, who led the majority: this is the "bedrock
principle underlying the First Amendment." Justices Harry Blackmun, Thurgood Marshall and
conservative Antonin Scalia also voted with the majority. Chief Justice William Rehnquist dissented
along with Sandra Day O'Connor, John Paul Stevens and Byron White.

    To virtually all Americans, the flag embodies   *Flag as symbol*
national values—but *which* values? Defining the
particular role of the flag provoked sharp disagree-

ment both in the courtroom and the public debate about the case. Many veterans see the flag as an emblem of patriotism, to be treated with the respect accorded a comrade in arms. Dissenting Justice Stevens, a Navy veteran who won the Bronze Star in World War II, described Old Glory as a symbol of the strength and courage that made America a great power. "If those ideas are worth fighting for," he wrote, "it cannot be true that the flag that uniquely symbolizes their power is not itself worthy of protection." One man who agrees is Korean War veteran Daniel Walker, who happened to be passing by the 1984 protest just as Johnson put his match to the flag. Seeing the remains of the banner smoldering on the pavement, Walker scooped them up and took them home to bury in his yard. He thinks Johnson deserves to be punished. "This guy did not salute the flag," Walker said last week. "He had not served the country . . . He had no equity in the flag. He burned something he didn't respect."

Was this legal?

?

Liberty banner   To other Americans, including the majority of justices, the flag's importance is less as a banner of heroism than as a symbol of freedom—including the freedom to make a flag into a bikini, to sew it on the seat of one's pants and, now, even to set it on fire. As Johnson's leftist lawyer, William Kunstler, argued before the court in March: "I understand that this flag has serious, important meanings, real meaning to real people out there. But that does not mean that it may [not] have different meanings to others and they may not— under the First Amendment—show their feelings." Justice Brennan upheld that view. "We do not consecrate the flag by punishing its desecration," he wrote, "for in doing so we dilute the freedom that this cherished emblem represents." To those who agreed with Brennan, the flag has now been strengthened as a symbol of Americans' almost unbounded liberty to disagree. And so long as displaying the colors does not lead to what the court calls "imminent" violence, there can be no limits to its use—or abuse—in an act of political protest.

Of the great body of precedent that backed up last week's ruling, none is more apt than Justice Robert H. Jackson's point made in a landmark case in 1943. The "freedom to differ," Jackson wrote,   *precedent* "is not limited to things that do not matter much." The nation's flag matters; that fact was underlined last week. The sentiments of the nation's people matter, too, and many are looking for recourse against the court. It would not be hard to pass a law against flag-burning: 48 states and the federal government had such measures on the books before the court ruled. The problem is that even a new law would have little effect, since the justices' finding is based on the Constitution, which trumps all other law. This leaves the option of a constitutional amendment. An amendment to the First Amendment is an outlandish idea, and even those congress-   *why?* men who supported the notion last week know just how hard it would be to garner the support of two-thirds of both houses and 38 state legislatures. Still—fortunately—there's nothing to stop them from trying. The First Amendment guarantees their right.

—*Newsweek*, July 10, 1989
TAMAR JACOBY *with* ANN MCDANIEL *in Washington.*
PETER MCKILLOP *in New York and
bureau reports*

Sample Notes

A critical reader might make the following notes while reading "A Fight for Old Glory." These notes make no attempt to reproduce the whole article, but include just enough information to help a reader recall what the article says. Notice that the notes include the article's title, source, and date for easy reference. Later, this will be all the information you need to cite the source in a paper.

> Gregory L. Johnson, 1984 Texas case, burned flag outside Republican National Convention. Convicted. 1 yr. jail, $2000 fine. Supreme Court overturned, 1989, says Constitution guarantees right to burn flag as exercise of free speech, political protest. 65% of poll disapproves; 71% would amend Constitution to make flag-burning illegal.

Writing a Summary

The summary that follows provides an overview of the article, including the reasons that people want to make flag burning illegal. Write summaries in your own language, rather than using sentences from the article itself. If you do quote sentences or phrases from the article, enclose them inside quotation marks. Later on this will keep you from using the quotations in your own writing without acknowledging them. Doing this could result in your being accused of plagiarism.

> "A Fight for Old Glory"
> Newsweek, 7/10/89, pp. 18-20

> **Summary**
>
> In 1989 the Supreme Court (by a 5-4 vote) overturned the Texas conviction of Gregory L. Johnson for burning the American flag outside the Republican National Convention in 1984. The Court ruled that burning the flag is protected under the first amendment's guarantee of freedom of speech. Many citizens disapprove of the ruling (65% in a Newsweek poll) and 71% (same poll?) want a constitutional amendment to outlaw flag burning. Apparently they believe the flag is an important symbol of American values and an emblem of patriotism. Despite this disagreement, the ruling follows precedents set by other Supreme Court rulings (cites 1943 case).

Summaries do not need to be long or elaborate. This one is only 105 words long (including the note about the title and source), but it includes the essential facts of the action that led to the court case and the public's reaction to the Supreme Court ruling. Writing a summary like this one will help you remember what you have read.

Flag Burning and the Supreme Court

The following articles are responses to the Supreme Court's decision that burning the American flag is protected by the First Amendment's guarantee of free speech. The first, "Guarding Old Glory" by James Garvey, first appeared in *Commonweal*. The second, "Notes and Comment, a Letter to the New Yorker," was originally published in the "Talk of the Town" section of the *New Yorker*. As you read, be aware of the items on the Checklist for Critical Reading on page 2. Mark and underline the texts, take notes, and write a brief summary of each article. Then read the discussion that follows.

Guarding Old Glory

—————— JOHN GARVEY ——————

A RECENT SUPREME COURT DECISION, the one which made flag burning in the act of political protest a form of protected free speech, set off a wave of embarrassing behavior. It was initiated by our president, and was joined by our always cowardly Congress. If Bush's move for a constitutional amendment to protect the flag from the actions of those very few people who want to burn it passes through all the states, as it might, it could have terrible constitutional consequences. If ever there were a political equivalent of what Bonhoeffer called "cheap grace," this is it.

The nation will probably survive. But the erosion of the Bill of Rights is not something we should take lightly. It shouldn't be so easily subjected to our most passionate feelings about symbols which we are right to take seriously; what should worry us is that politicians are so eager to look for politically popular ways to qualify our freedom to explore what that seriousness means.

We Americans have always had trouble distinguishing between legality and morality, between behavior we accept as appropriate and the behavior we must tolerate in a society which considers liberty essential. The Court has not ruled it entirely illegal to bite the heads off living chickens, but this does not mean, as some demagogues have suggested, that either the Court or society regards it as "all right."

To rule, as the Court did, that offensive behavior may not in some circumstances be prosecuted is not to say that the behavior is any less offensive. One of democracy's greatest strengths is an ability to live with certain grey areas; to rely on persuasion, rather than coercion; to allow an area of argument and discourse, and even grave offense, rather than limit speech and action beyond the absolutely necessary requirements of civil order.

I worry about tampering with this. Let me take the argument in favor of banning flag burning a step farther along the road (or slippery slope) that seems to be its natural course. I am a Christian, and regard the cross as a serious and sacred symbol, much more a serious symbol than the flag could ever be. I do not want to live in a society where the flag cannot be desecrated, but the cross can be. However, this is precisely what will happen if Bush's amendment is passed. Am I not right to find this offensive? I propose extending the ban on desecration to include the cross; and because we live in a pluralistic society, I am not only willing but eager to see the ban extended to include (that is to say, to exclude from any desecration) such symbols as the Star of David, the Islamic Crescent, the image of the Buddha, and the Mormon representation of the angel Moroni. I am not sure whether the Masonic compass and square should be included, but I am willing to see the issue debated.

Of course, religious symbols are not the only ones whose violation wounds many sensibilities. Children could be scandalized, upset, and wounded deeply by depictions of Santa in compromising situations (drunk, say, or lecherous). Let's ban those, too.

The point is that I can either make the flag more sacred, in law, than the cross—clearly an act of idolatry directed either toward the flag or the law—or I must reflect on what the law and its limits are, and what law is meant to do. It is the exclusion of much of what we regard as important from state oversight that has made our society a free one. The importance of symbols I willingly accept, even celebrate. But our symbols are acknowledged as weak where they need the sort of law Bush proposes to shore them up. I do not want the cross protected by law; I don't think the law will make it a stronger symbol. Though I do not compare the two symbols in importance, I think it is not healthy for Americans, Christians or otherwise, to think of the flag, any more than the cross, as a symbol which requires the help now recommended.

All the easily hysterical reactions to this issue, both liberal and conservative, surfaced recently at a student art exhibit in Chicago when a student at the Art Institute placed a flag on the floor and invited observers to walk on it, and then record their reactions. This is the sort of thing that bores me even when it isn't trying to be offensive, but it caused a predictable reaction.

In the midst of the expectable fog, there was one serious and important question raised. Some state funds are voted for support of the Art Institute. To what extent should citizens have a right to refuse such funding, where it supports something they consider outrageous?

The reaction of a lot of people—some of whom, sadly, think of themselves as liberals—is that the denial of this funding amounts to censorship. The same argument was raised when the Corcoran Gallery canceled an exhibition of photographs, explicitly homoerotic and sadomasochistic, by the late photographer Robert Mapplethorpe. The exhibit was partially financed by the National Endowment for the Arts.

My hunch is that I would not have liked the exhibit at all. But even if it had been in honor of every act of mercy ever performed in history, or an homage to grandmothers everywhere (my hunch is that I wouldn't like those exhibits either), it seems to me (a) that no exhibit is entitled to government funding, no matter what its subject, and (b) that a gallery cancellation, even in fear of an anticipated reaction, does not amount to censorship. We should use our language (and maybe our public funding) more carefully than that.

Some liberals have argued that, because taxpayers passively fund many things with which they may not agree, the arts are entitled to a piece of the potentially offensive pie. There is a rather ugly persuasiveness to this: I am now forced to spend a good deal of my income on governmentally financed things which offend me, ranging from weapons systems to the salaries of tax auditors; why not (now that the gun is at my chest) make me fork over even more? Andy Warhol said that art is what you can get away with; so is one approach to government. My own argument is that people should be less passive. I am not unhappy when agitation of any sort makes it harder for politicians to channel my money toward the funding of abortions, nuclear weapons, or the infliction of the death penalty. Refusing support at the level of taxation is as appropriate, as democratic, as the boycott. It is as right to withhold tax money from something you object to (in the arts or in public policy) as it is to refuse to buy table grapes.

What is interesting here is the conjunction of these visual symbols, the flag on fire and on the floor, and the offensive Mapplethorpe pictures. They are allowed to stand for something, without our having to think very much about what they mean. Some people insist that funding offensive things should be compulsory, in the name of freedom. And the flag, as a symbol of freedom, is made to violate its own intended meaning—

a sad irony which reminds me of a case which should instruct us now, in which a state court insisted (it was overruled by the Supreme Court) that a couple accept the slogan "Live Free or Die" on their license plates or lose their freedom.

Notes and Comment

A Letter to the New Yorker

LETTER FROM A MAN we know:

When I was a lot younger (I'll turn seventy next year: can't believe it), there were fewer stars in the flag and a lot fewer flags in sight. Courthouses, department stores, hotels, and summer camps flew Old Glory—one each, on the whole—but not gas stations, movie theatres, shopping malls (we didn't have any), roadside vegetable stands, dry cleaners, garbage trucks, or the moon. We sang the anthem less often but perhaps with more feeling, for that reason. We didn't sing it before ballgames, for instance—that came along during the Second World War, I believe. (When we did stand up and sing, what we sang was "My Country 'Tis of Thee," not "The Star-Spangled Banner.") I can't help noticing that the standing and sometimes singing crowds at the ballpark nowadays always include some men and boys who have forgotten to take their caps off during the anthem. This irritates me, but not for patriotic reasons: I don't like inattention, which is what you get when everybody's doing something without much meaning.

I think we noticed flags more when I was younger, because there weren't so many of them. They turned up everywhere, of course, on Memorial Day, and before and during the Fourth of July; it was nice to see them—on front porches, in kids' hands, on bicycle handlebars, near fireworks stands, and in parades—and their festive presence sometimes made you think for a couple of seconds about what the holiday stood for and maybe what the flags stood for.

I can also remember times in my life when our country—its future and everything it stood for—seemed to be in terrible danger. But I can't recall ever feeling that our *flag* was imperilled; at those times, the flag almost seemed to mean less, rather than more. I served in the Air Force for three and a half years in the Second World War, most of that time out in the Pacific theatre, and I guess I was within sight of an American flag nearly every day then. I came to like the retreat ceremony (whenever there was time to hold one), when everybody on the base stopped and stood at attention and saluted while taps was sounded and the flag was lowered; the moment made you feel calm, and sometimes it reminded you of home, or even of why you were there, far away from home. Some of the friends I stood next to during one retreat or another didn't make it back from that war, but I imagine their feelings about the flag were just about the same as mine. I can't be sure, though, because we never talked about it. Most of all, those feelings were private; you could make the flag stand for whatever seemed appropriate, in your mind, or you could just stand there and think about nothing at all. That privacy, that little space in time that you had to yourself, was almost the best part for me, because the whole idea about the flag—about patriotism, if you will— is that you can decide for yourself what it stands for, what it means. In this country, you can.

When I was younger, you saw more street orators than you do today: I guess there are fewer now because everybody has decided that if you can't say something on television it's hardly worth saying at all. But back then you'd see a man come along carrying a grocery carton and an armful of pamphlets. He'd stop and climb up on the crate, and before he began speaking he'd unroll an American flag and attach it to a stick next to him on the crate or drape it on another box, which he'd put up on end to make a rostrum. Then he'd start his spiel—for vegetarianism, for Radical Syndicalism, for Prohibition or against Prohibition, for the Farmer-Labor movement, for Father Coughlin, for Bolshevism or Trotskyism, for anarchy (for no flags, that is), for God and country, whatever. Listening to him, I'd smile a little to myself about the presence of that flag beside him, because it stood for freedom, right there and then. It was his flag and mine, but he was using it for his own private purposes, which often turned out to include his wish to end our system of things as quickly as possible. I could see that the flag was part of his act; he hoped to win me over to his line of thinking simply because we both stood under, or alongside, the Red, White, and Blue. I was never swayed by such a trifling subterfuge; I don't think anybody was. Yet it never occurred to me to think that the speaker was abusing the flag by wrapping himself up in it that way, no matter how much I scorned his message, for that was one of the flag's purposes, after all. It was a symbol.

The Supreme Court said some of this the other day (almost in fewer words), when it affirmed Gregory Lee Johnson's right to burn the flag if he so desired, because the act was protected under the First Amendment. I think the Court was saying what I've been trying to get at here: that the flag is a symbol not of something simple but of something complicated, and that its uses can be various—even wildly so or infuriatingly so, to some of us—because they are private in the end. Now President Bush wants to amend the Constitution to make flag-burning illegal. He wants the flag to stand for one thing, or just a few things, and he wants our feelings about it to be public and dutiful instead of private and free. He wants the cheerful old workaday symbol declared an icon. But I suspect that most people in this country never really think about the flag at all, because it's already so public that it's just about used up. It belongs to advertisers and politicians and public patriots (including the President, the designated patriot), and what's being burned up now is me, because I once thought it was mine.

—*New Yorker* July 10, 1989

Reading Critically About Flag Burning

The following discussion is organized according to the Checklist for Critical Reading on page 2. As you read each section of the discussion, compare it with the notes you made as you read the articles.

WHAT IS THE CONTEXT?

Every subject exists in a context. This context supplies information about the subject itself, explains why the subject is important and who thinks it is important, and what the major issues are. The immediate context for present discussions the Supreme Court's ruling that flag burning is protected as free speech under the First Amendment consists of at least the following:

- knowledge that the flag is a national symbol
- visual images of flag-draped coffins of soldiers who have died in combat
- feelings of patriotism connected with the flag
- photographs of the statue showing Marines raising the flag on Iwo Jima during World War II
- experiences of singing the national anthem at public events and in school
- memories of saying the pledge of allegiance to the flag
- precedents set by earlier Supreme Court decisions about freedom of speech, patriotic behavior, and dissent
- long-term discussions about the role and limits of free speech and dissent in American society

The articles printed here also connect the discussion of flag burning with other issues that may, at first, appear unrelated to the subject of flag burning itself. Among them are:

- questions about other free speech issues, such as the boundary between art and pornography
- questions about using government funds to pay for activities (such as art exhibits) that people find offensive
- definitions of patriotism
- questions about the role and meaning of symbols in a society
- historical examples of patriotic behavior and free speech

All of these issues, and others as well, form the context of any discussion of flag burning or desecration. And all of them suggest potential subjects to write about.

PURPOSE

Because *Newsweek* is a news magazine rather than a journal of opinion, readers might expect the purpose of "A Fight for Old Glory" to be to provide an objective or neutral explanation of the Supreme Court decision about flag burning, the events that brought it about, and how people have reacted to that decision. In order to explain the angry reaction to the Court's decision, the article also has to explore Americans' attitudes toward free speech and their beliefs about what their national symbols mean. This exploration is also part of the article's purpose.

In "Guarding Old Glory," Garvey's purpose appears to be to argue against a constitutional amendment to protect the flag. He also wants to raise questions about art, pornography, and public funding for events and activities that people might not approve of. The anonymous author of the *New Yorker* article also disapproves of a constitutional amendment. But his larger purpose appears to be to contrast present attitudes toward the flag and patriotic behavior with different attitudes that he has experienced in years past.

MAIN IDEAS

Think of main ideas as the central concepts or blocks of information that a writer wants to present.

The *Newsweek* writers call the Court's decision "provocative," describe the variety of negative reactions to it, and then explain that the decision follows some specific legal precedents.

Garvey acknowledges that the Court's decision is unpopular but says that it is appropriate. To justify this he distinguishes between behavior that Americans may disapprove of and behavior that their political beliefs compel them to tolerate. He insists that the law has limits, and that some issues must be left to discussion and persuasion rather than coercion.

The central point of the *New Yorker* essay is that things have not always been as they are now, or as some people insist they should be now. The writer believes that patriotism is a matter of private decisions rather than public displays.

POSITIONS

Positions are judgments or claims about whether something is right or wrong, good or bad, true or false, or whether something ought to be done or not done.

News magazines are supposed to present objective reports of facts, so readers would not expect a *Newsweek* article to take a position about a controversial question like flag burning. While the authors do carefully avoid taking a position on the issue of flag burning itself, they do state several other positions. For example, the authors say that "an amendment to the First Amendment is an outlandish idea." This is a position, for it makes a value statement about whether the U.S. Constitution should be amended to prohibit flag burning. The writers also say that "to virtually all Americans, the flag embodies national values." This is a position because it is a claim about what Americans think. The writers also imply other, more subtle, positions. For example, they label Gregory Johnson an "avowed communist" and his attorney a "leftist." They also identify two justices who voted for the decision as conservatives. Together, these labels suggest that the issue can be understood in terms of liberal and conservative politics, rather than requiring a more complex assessment. So, even in what appears to be a straightforward news story, writers take positions.

Garvey announces his position against amending the constitution to protect the flag when he asserts that such an amendment would have "terrible constitutional consequences." He says this early, and spends the rest of the article explaining why he has taken this position. In the *New Yorker* article, the writer allows his positions to emerge slowly from the personal experiences he tells about. Thus, near the end, he agrees with the Supreme Court and says that an amendment to the Constitution would take away his private patriotism and replace it with a public and, in his view, less sincere or valuable patriotism.

ASSUMPTIONS

The *Newsweek* writers make a number of assumptions. For example, when they use labels like "conservative," "leftist," and "avowed communist," they assume that these labels have fixed meanings and that their readers will know those meanings. The writers do not acknowledge that these labels may have a variety of meanings to different readers and writers. In a rather subtle way, this use of simple labels to describe complex concepts works against William Kunstler's argument that the flag may have different meanings to different people. They also assume that their readers will agree that a burning flag is an "ugly spectacle." According to the polls the writers cite, most of their readers would, in fact, agree.

Garvey's statement that a constitutional amendment to protect the flag would "erode the Bill of Rights" assumes that such an effect would be bad, and so assumes the superior status of the Bill of Rights itself. When he calls the Congress "cowardly," he assumes that his readers will understand and agree with him. When he refers to "what law is meant to do" or the flag's "intended meaning," he is suggesting his assumption that laws, symbols, and words may not have different meanings to different people, but only one acceptable meaning. But Garvey never tells his readers what those intended meanings and purposes might be. The writer of the *New Yorker* article seems to assume that too much of anything is not good, and that we might use up the flag if we use it too much, as though patriotism were a consumable item rather than an abstraction.

DATA AND INFORMATION

The *Newsweek* writers present a variety of data and information, and readers need to analyze and evaluate that data carefully. Twice the writers cite the results of a *Newsweek* poll to show public disapproval of the Supreme Court decision about burning the American flag. A sidebar that accompanies the article states that the Gallup organization, a respected polling company, conducted this poll of 500 people and that the results are expected to be accurate within 5 percentage points. That means that somewhere between sixty and seventy percent of the public disagreed with the Court at the time the poll was taken.

Some of the information is incomplete. The writers report a Senate resolution against the decision, but do not explain that this does not have the force of law. They mention a "landmark" 1943 free speech decision, but do not name it, so it will be difficult for us to locate more information about it. To describe reactions to the decision, the writers quote a number of people, but most of these are Supreme Court justices, senators, congressmen, and veterans. The one common citizen quoted is the man who witnessed the burning and took the flag home to bury it.

Garvey includes some information important to this discussion, especially his description of a controversial exhibit at the Art Institute of Chicago and the information that public funds were used to support both that display and a controversial photography exhibit.

The writer of the *New Yorker* article notes that the national anthem has not always been sung before baseball games. This is something that can be investigated, as are his accounts of street orators. However, his assertion that fewer flags were displayed in the past than now seems nearly impossible to investigate. Still, it is an assertion about data, and something that readers should pay attention to.

CONCLUSIONS

When you attempt to review or evaluate conclusions, think of where the writer leaves you and of the dominant ending impression or thought you receive as you finish reading.

The *Newsweek* writers summarize the situation effectively, explaining that laws against burning the flag will be ineffective because the Constitution takes precedence. They correctly point out that just as the Constitution protects those who wish to burn the flag, it also protects those who would propose an amendment making flag burning illegal. And this, according to the writers, is "fortunate." With this word, the writers appear to be concluding that the First Amendment, and the disagreements we have about freedom of speech, are good things.

Garvey does not really end "Guarding Old Glory" where he began it. He moves from flag burning to public funding of activities that many people disapprove of. If there is a conclusion, it is probably that, because of their political beliefs, Americans must at least tolerate many views and actions that they disapprove of. The *New Yorker* writer concludes that the flag is a symbol of something complex rather than of something simple, and that any attempt to make it stand for one thing, rather than many, will diminish its value.

Synthesizing

After you have read a number of selections about a single subject, it's always useful to construct a synthesis, a kind of super-summary of the discussion that includes points of view, ideas, and information from several writers. A synthesis allows you to:

1. See an overview of the subject
2. Establish a context for your own ideas, so you can see where they fit into the extended discussion of the subject represented by your collection of sources
3. Provide an accurate summary of the subject for your own readers when you shift your attention from reading to writing

An effective synthesis will reflect the overall shape of the discussion or debate that you have surveyed in your reading. It should:

1. Point to the major issues that writers have raised about the subject

2. Show how these ideas or issues are related to each other

3. Point to major areas of consensus or disagreement

A synthesis does not have to account for everything that each writer or source has said. Instead, it needs to represent the major issues, facts, opinions, and data.

Writing a Synthesis

This section will demonstrate writing a synthesis using the three articles about flag burning that you read earlier in the chapter. The procedure will be to:

- List the main ideas, facts, and positions
- Organize these into some sort of sequence or hierarchy
- Summarize these ideas as concisely as possible, including only what is essential

(If you later decide to use this synthesis in something you write about flag burning, you can include additional details. For now, concentrate on the overview.)

A synthesis of the flag burning articles would include the following minimum information.

FROM THE NEWSWEEK ARTICLE

- The U.S. Supreme Court has ruled that flag burning as a political protest is protected under the First Amendment.
- President Bush and many veterans disagree with this ruling.
- Sixty-five percent of people surveyed in a poll disagree with the ruling.
- Senators and congressmen, among others, are calling for a constitutional amendment that would make flag burning illegal.
- The ruling was prompted by the arrest and conviction of Gregory Johnson, an "avowed communist," who burned an American flag outside the Republican National Convention in 1984.

- The most recent ruling is consistent with earlier Supreme Court rulings (precedents) concerning the First Amendment.
- Part of the reaction is a result of the flag's value as a symbol, though not everyone agrees about what it symbolizes.

FROM THE COMMONWEAL ARTICLE

- Legality vs. morality; behavior we accept vs. behavior we must tolerate.
- Democracy relies on persuasion rather than coercion.
- Protecting the flag may require protecting other objects that have symbolic value.
- Weak symbols need laws to protect them.
- The situation has parallels with controversies over artistic expression.

FROM THE NEW YORKER

- Flags and national anthem (visible patriotism) were less prominent before World War II.
- In the past, no one attempted to enforce a single idea of what the flag meant or what patriotism was.
- The flag is a symbol, but of something complex, not something simple.
- Attempts to amend the Constitution to make flag burning illegal are attempts to make the flag mean one thing rather than many.

An Activity. Review the articles about flag burning and identify any ideas or information not included here that you think should be part of a synthesis. Then organize that information, along with what you find listed here, and write a synthesis of the three articles.

A synthesis, like a summary, cannot be right or wrong. It is more appropriate to speak of it as complete or incomplete.

A Class Activity. Share your synthesis with several classmates; read theirs at the same time. Critique each synthesis for completeness. What information should be included and what should be left out of each synthesis?

Readings Between the Acts

PAUSE HERE for a moment to review and practice your critical reading skills before you move on to chapter 2, where you will learn to use your reading as a basis for writing. The three brief articles printed here are all about the subject of how people stop smoking. The first, from *The Washington Post*, summarizes the Surgeon General's 1990 annual report about the health consequences of smoking. The second article, "Smoking: Find the Right Way to Quit," is from *Changing Times* magazine and is written for general readers who may be trying to find a way to quit smoking. The third article is from *The Journal of the American Medical Association (JAMA)*. Its purpose is to give physicians medical information that they can use to help their patients choose among the various methods of stopping smoking. Read all three articles using the critical reading strategies explained in chapter 1.

Before You Read

Begin with prereading. Make some notes in which you identify your attitudes toward smoking and state what you know about stopping smoking.

Read Each Selection Carefully

Mark important passages in each article, and take notes about key ideas and information.

After You Read

Write a brief summary of each article, and then a brief synthesis of all three.

You will use these notes in chapter 2, where the articles about how to stop smoking will be the basis of examples and illustrations of how to use reading as a basis for writing.

Quitting Time

SUSAN OKIE

QUITTING SMOKING YIELDS "major and immediate health benefits," regardless of a smoker's age, according to the surgeon general's annual report on the health consequences of smoking.

Smoking-related illnesses cause more than one out of every six deaths in the United States, according to the report.

Although heart disease, stroke, chronic lung disease, many cancers and a variety of other disorders are more common in smokers than in nonsmokers, the report found that the risk of these health problems begins to decline as soon as a smoker quits.

Someone who stops smoking before age 50 is only half as likely to die within the next 15 years as a person who continues to smoke, according to the report, which is the first to focus entirely on smoking cessation.

"The earlier one quits, the greater the benefits," says Surgeon General Antonia C. Novello. But, she adds, "even people who quit smoking at older ages can expect to enjoy a longer and healthier life compared with those who continue to smoke."

More than 38 million Americans have quit smoking, and 90 percent of those did so on their own, according to the report. But private health insurance plans, state Medicaid programs and perhaps the federal Medicare program should cover the cost of smoking cessation programs for smokers who need extra help, says William L. Roper, director of the federal Centers for Disease Control.

Most insurance plans do not currently pay for such programs.

The 628-page report summarized the results of hundreds of studies on smoking-related illnesses and on how their frequency is affected by quitting. It concluded that, for some diseases, an ex-smoker's risk of illness declines rapidly, while for others, it takes as long as 15 years to drop to that of a nonsmoker. For example, smokers are twice as likely to die of heart disease as nonsmokers, but about half of this excess risk disappears within the first year after quitting.

The reduction in cancer risk is more gradual. A male smoker is 22 times as likely to die of lung cancer as a man who has never smoked. Ten years after quitting, a man who formerly smoked is still 6 to 11 times more likely to die of lung cancer than is a lifelong nonsmoker.

The report also called smoking the most important modifiable cause of infant mortality and premature births in the United States. Smoking during pregnancy slows the growth of the fetus and increases the chances of premature delivery, bleeding and other complications. The report said that, despite these well-recognized risks, about 25 percent of pregnant women in the United States smoke throughout pregnancy.

It concluded that if all women could be persuaded not to smoke during pregnancy, about 5 percent of infant deaths and 20 percent of low-birthweight births could be prevented. It said that even if a woman quits smoking as late as the third or fourth month of pregnancy, her risk of having a low-birthweight baby becomes the same as that of a woman who never smoked.

Even smokers who already have developed serious illnesses such as heart disease or cancer can improve their health by quitting, the report concluded. For instance, those with heart disease can reduce their chances of a heart attack by 50 percent or more. Someone who stops smoking after having been diagnosed with cancer has a smaller risk of developing a second cancer than a person who continues to smoke.

The report said the weight often gained by smokers who quit poses far less risk to health than continuing to smoke.

Smoking—
Find the Right Way to Quit

AGAINST THE ODDS, Gayle Lollgen at age 30 accomplished what some 50 million other Americans only wish they could. More than three years ago at her home in Lyndhurst, N.J., Lollgen, a two-pack-a-day puffer, crushed out a cigarette and has not smoked since. She was able to conquer the habit cold turkey with no help from a quit-smoking group or counselor. "It took me a few tries," she says, "but I finally realized that if I ever wanted to breathe normally again, I had to quit."

As encouraging as Lollgen's triumph is, it really lights up a dark statistic. Whether they've quit on their own or with help, reformed smokers are a tiny band next to the battalions who are fighting a losing battle with the habit.

If your own intentions are stronger than your will, new inducements are springing up. Smoke-free zones in office buildings and restaurants are now commonplace and many employers are making smokers feel distinctly uncomfortable on the job.

Programs promising to get you off cigarettes abound, offering aid that ranges from five-day cessation programs for less than $35 to weeks-long courses costing several hundred dollars. You can try to beat the habit by joining a mutual support group whose members cheer each other on, or you can go one-on-one with a hypnotist or sign up for aversion therapy, which conditions you to loathe cigarettes.

Are such quit-smoking programs worth the time and, in some instances, the sizable price? If so, which kind is most likely to be the one that actually enables you to break the habit for good? The outcome will be influenced by your own personality, the degree of your addiction and the seriousness of your decision to quit.

DO-IT-YOURSELF HELP

Most people get hooked on cigarettes partly because of the stimulation from nicotine, with outright chemical dependency developing as tolerance to the drug builds up. The trouble starts when an addicted smoker who tries to quit experiences the familiar pains of withdrawal, symptoms that run the gamut from nervousness to headache and poor concentration.

One way to avoid such physical and mental distress, researchers now know, is to get a measured amount of nicotine from a source other than tobacco. A prescription preparation in chewing gum form called Nicorette does just this, giving would-be quitters the nicotine "fix" they crave without tobacco's deleterious effects.

The difference is that users, rather than getting the short, repeated bursts of nicotine experienced in smoking, receive a steady but lower dose that satisfies their craving. This buys time while the smoker battles to overcome psychological dependence on cigarettes. The recommendation for most smokers is to start with about ten sticks of gum a day (the manufacturer warns that you should never use more than 30 pieces a day). After one month, a return visit to the doctor is advised to determine whether you should continue to use the gum. Use of the gum usually tapers off and is ultimately eliminated by the fourth or sixth month. The cost is about $24 for a box of 96 pieces.

Experimentally, nicotine gum works well enough, as much as doubling the likelihood of success for a person trying to quit who is also getting counseling or attending a group program. But in real life, partly because doctors and patients don't always use the product properly, success appears to be less predictable.

Says Nina Schneider, a research psychologist at the University of California at Los Angeles, "Some doctors fail to realize that patients don't get the abrupt jolt with gum that they do with a cigarette, so they may underprescribe and the patient doesn't get the base level needed to avoid withdrawal." Incidentally, a new formulation of Nicorette, doubling the potency of each stick, will be submitted to the FDA next month and is already available in Canada and some other countries.

Some practitioners, says Schneider, make the mistake of placing a priority on weaning the smoker from cigarettes themselves, rather than the nicotine. Another caveat, she says: "To work, the gum has to be used in the absence of smoking, since smoking will trigger a desire to relapse."

Effective as it may be in helping to break the chain of nicotine dependency, the gum is not for everyone, particularly heart patients. People suffering from TMJ, a painful disorder of the temporomandibular joint in the jaw, should avoid the gum, as should nursing mothers and women who are pregnant or planning to be. In some users, nicotine gum has caused nausea, hiccups, and jaw and throat soreness, and has worsened dental problems.

Nicotine gum comes with a fairly explicit set of instructions on how to use it. But you'll probably get better results if you use it under the care of a doctor who regularly prescribes it and follows up on patients' results.

Even in the best of hands, nicotine gum is no cure-all. "Nicotine is only half of the problem," says Dr. Alan Lipschitz, a psychiatrist at

New York Medical College and Metropolitan Hospital in New York City. "You still have to do battle with all the psychological cues that remind you to light up—the cup of coffee or the stressful situation."

Help along these lines is available in a host of publications, including a 119-page book, *How to Quit Smoking Permanently*, by Walter S. Ross (Little, Brown; $4.95 paperback), which graphically explains nicotine addiction and incorporates nicotine gum into the approach. Other manuals to help you recognize and avoid the situations that prompt you to light up and to remind you of the financial and health costs of smoking are available from the federal government and nonprofit organizations (see the box).

AVERSION THERAPY

Taking the fun out of smoking and making it repugnant is the idea behind aversion therapy. In the most common form the participant draws on a cigarette every six seconds until smoking actually becomes more unpleasant than relaxing. One form of rapid smoking called reciprocal aversion has each member of a group light up each time any other member reaches for a cigarette. In one study using this method, about 61% of the participants were still off cigarettes after six months.

Aversion therapy is combined with exercise, relaxation techniques and weight control in a quit-smoking strategy called the Schick program, developed by the Schick Center for Control of Smoking. Available mainly in the Western U.S., the therapy costs around $500 for one-hour sessions that run for five days. According to the company, some 58% to 60% of its graduates are not smoking at the end of the first year. An early form of aversion therapy that consists of giving a smoker mild electric shocks has fallen from grace with most practitioners. Some patients with heart or lung disease are advised to avoid aversion therapy.

HYPNOSIS AND ACUPUNCTURE

Nearly everyone with a bad habit sooner or later wonders whether it is possible to break it under a hypnotist's spell. Maybe. But you should first understand, says the International Society for Professional Hypnosis, that the hypnotist doesn't put you in a trance, as many people expect, but rather lulls your conscious mind into a "passive condition." Then, the theory goes, your subconscious is free to accept the positive suggestion of the hypnotist.

Not everyone is a candidate for hypnosis, but if you think you might be, start by picking a qualified professional. You can save yourself some grief by steering clear of practitioners advertising themselves as Doctor of Hypnology; there is no such degree. You can further narrow your choices by picking from a list of physicians and psychologists who are trained in hypnosis and have been approved by the American Society of Clinical Hypnosis.

Nobody has hard numbers on how successful hypnosis is likely to be, notes the American Council on Science and Health, though prospects improve for patients who are undergoing more than one session. "I have used hypnosis with some patients," says Lipschitz, "but I suggest it only as part of a varied approach that uses other techniques, like group therapy."

Fees for hypnosis start at $35 for a single session. To get the names of society-approved practitioners in your area, write to the American Society of Clinical Hypnosis, 2250 E. Devon Ave., Suite 336, Des Plaines, Ill. 60018, and include a self-addressed, stamped envelope.

Acupuncture is a procedure in which long thin needles are inserted under the skin to treat pain at points distant from the place that hurts. Advocates also attribute to it abilities to manipulate the body's internal energy forces. Whatever the reason, it appears to help some smokers unhook from cigarettes, especially if it is used together with behavior modification therapies. In one form, would-be quitters agree to leave a set of needles in place in their outer ear between treatment sessions. When the urge to smoke strikes, they are told to simply manipulate the needles and the cigarette will develop an undesirable taste.

GROUP PROGRAMS

During his 42 years as a heavy smoker, Nicolo Pietropaolo of Nanuet, N.Y., had tried again and again to shake the habit. His longest abstention lasted just three months. Believing that there had to be a way, he signed up in desperation for FreshStart, a four-week course offered at his New York City office by the American Cancer Society. It turned out to be his salvation. "I think what worked for me was the support of the other group members," he recalls. "Whenever we felt like smoking, we called each other."

Like Pietropaolo, thousands of well-meaning smokers sign up each year in a host of group programs that promise to help them quit and even to keep off weight while wrestling with the urge to smoke. Participants share the misery of quitting and lend each other moral support in weekly sessions that typically run one to six weeks. Organizations as diverse as the American Lung Association, the Seventh Day Adventist Church and commercial enterprises like Smokenders offer their services in many communities. You'll pay as little as $25 (or even nothing) for five or so sessions with a nonprofit group to as much as $295 for six weekly two-hour sessions with Smokenders. Hospitals, universities and agencies of state and local governments increasingly sponsor quit-smoking clinics.

MEASURING SUCCESS

How effective are programs in getting people to quit? Most studies of long-term results are imprecise because researchers usually must accept what former participants report instead of having access to purely objective information. If there is no control group against which to gauge results, the deficiency will be magnified.

Carole Tracy Orleans, a clinical psychologist at the University of Pennsylvania School of Medicine, has extensively evaluated the reported success rates of various quit-smoking programs. Overall, she found that between 15% and 25% of participants are still off cigarettes a year after therapy.

More impressive success rates (as high as 80%) are claimed by some commercial programs. One reason for these high rates, says Orleans and other researchers, is that participants willing to pay the hefty fees of commercial programs tend to be highly motivated and thus likely to quit smoking regardless of the program they select.

If a program boasts a rate that seems too good to be true, Orleans advises, ask how it was determined. If the studies rely on voluntary responses to a written questionnaire, those still abstaining from cigarettes are more likely to respond than those who relapsed. Were there any blood, urine or breath tests to verify abstinence? Is the rate at least a one-year rate, measured from the beginning rather than the end of the program? Does the rate include all who began the program, not just those who completed it?

Ultimately, selecting the approach that works for you may be a trial-and-error proposition. "There's little scientific evidence to show what works and doesn't work for a given individual," explains Dr. Paul Montner, who is a specialist in smoking cessation with New York's Interfaith Medical Center. "You have to start with what seems best for you. But don't give up if you try something and it doesn't work. Remember that most ex-smokers went through repeated efforts."

Whatever course you choose, by augmenting it with the following actions, you can boost your chances of success.

- Make an agreement with a smoking friend or spouse to quit together.
- Ask to move to a nonsmoking part of your workplace so that the temptation to light up is reduced.

- Form a support group of people you can call any time you get the urge to smoke. Adds Schneider, "Even if you're in a group program, form a subgroup and exchange phone numbers." Lifting the phone to call a compatriot may be the effort that begins to get you off the smoking hook.

Methods of Smoking Cessation— Finally, Some Answers

THOMAS J. GLYNN

FORTY MILLION LIVING AMERICANS have quit smoking.[1] While not as catchy, perhaps, as "Fifty million Frenchmen can't be wrong" or "Millions have read the book, now see the movie," the principle is the same—this is a massive number of people focused on one activity.

Unfortunately, until now we have known very little, or have had to surmise, *how* so many smokers have achieved their goal of quitting. The article by Fiore et al[2] in this issue of THE JOURNAL, however, finally provides some answers and, even more important, guidance on this issue.

Among the important findings presented by Fiore et al are the following:

• More than 90% of successful quitters do so on their own, without participation in an organized cessation program.

• Quit rates (defined as smoking abstinence for $\geq$ 1 year) are twice as high for those who quit on their own compared with those who participate in a cessation program. However, this finding is not based on randomly allocating smokers to one method or the other. Rather, smokers who enter cessation programs may be those who were unable to quit on their own.

• Smokers who quit "cold turkey" are more likely to remain abstinent than those who gradually decrease their daily consumption of cigarettes, switch to cigarettes with lower tar or nicotine, or use special filters or holders.

• Quit attempts are nearly twice as likely to occur among smokers who receive nonsmoking advice from their physicians compared with those who are not advised to quit.

• Heavy ($\geq$25 cigarettes a day), more addicted smokers are much more likely to participate in an organized cessation program than persons who smoke less.

These data, and the conclusions derived from them, are a movable feast—they provide a wide variety of health professionals, and smokers themselves, with specific actions each can take to help reduce smoking prevalence. Among the groups who can benefit from the information are the following:

Physicians.   The primary message for physicians is that their advice is a key element in motivating smokers to make quit attempts. Even if smokers do not quit the first or second time they receive their physician's advice to do so—and most data suggest this is the case—the advice of the physician can help move smokers from one stage to another in the quitting process,[3,4] eventually leading to successful abstinence from smoking.

In keeping with these data, the National Cancer Institute recently developed a simple protocol to help physicians provide advice about smoking cessation.[5] The National Cancer Institute suggests that the physician's office or clinic be smoke free, that all smokers in the practice be identified, and that the physician (and other office support staff) *ask* about smoking at each patient visit; *advise* smokers to stop at every opportunity; *assist* smokers in stopping by helping them set a quit date, providing self-help material, and prescribing pharmacological adjuncts as appropriate; and *arrange* follow-up contact with the patient to prevent relapse.

Public Health Planners/Practitioners.   Among the messages for those involved in public health planning or practice are the following: (1) Efforts should be directed at *motivating* more smokers to make serious quit attempts; rather than developing new programs; (2) existing self-help cessation materials should be made more widely available; increased availability will be more successful than developing new materials or "fine tuning" existing materials; and (3) consideration should be given to focusing on the heavier, more severely addicted smoker in organized cessation programs. Similar recommendations were made recently by a National Cancer Institute expert advisory panel, which also encouraged projects that will provide self-help materials to high-risk populations, especially blacks, Hispanics, and pregnant women, whose particular needs have often been neglected in our smoking-cessation efforts.[6]

Smoking-Cessation Researchers.   In addition to finally providing evidence for the widespread belief that the majority of smokers who quit do so on their own, the findings of Fiore et al call our attention to several potential research questions. What determines relapse, and how can it be prevented? How can we motivate more smokers to make *serious* quit attempts? What are the most effective means of dissemination and adoption of successful cessation methods?

Smokers.   Important messages for smokers in this article are (1) they *can* quit; (2) they can successfully stop smoking if they do so on their own (especially by setting a specific quit date and stopping cold turkey on that date); (3) smoking-cessation programs are helpful for some, especially heavier, more addicted smokers; and (4) permanent quitting from a first or second attempt is unusual; the smoker may suffer an initial relapse and need to learn from that experience in order to make another, successful, quit attempt.

A major conclusion that may be drawn from these data, then, is that we do not need to expand our efforts to involve more smokers in formal cessation programs. Nevertheless, we should not abandon these programs,[7] as some, such as the American Lung Association's "Freedom From Smoking" clinic program, are successful, and we need to maintain a variety of approaches to cessation. This is especially true for heavier smokers who wish to try to quit with the more formal methods. We do need to focus on the broad *public health* implications of our smoking-cessation efforts, and our agenda should include the following goals:

• *To motivate more smokers to make serious quit attempts.* While physicians are in a unique position to motivate smokers, it is equally important to motivate the smoker on a *society-wide* basis, so that nonsmoking cues, such as increased tobacco taxes, restrictive smoking policies, and counteradvertising campaigns, become "persistent and inescapable." The National Cancer Institute and the American Cancer Society, through their upcoming American Stop Smoking Intervention Study for Cancer Prevention, will provide a major demonstration of this strategy.[8]

• *To increase success rates among those smokers who make quit attempts.* As detailed by Fiore et al, about 30% of smokers make a quit attempt each year, but only about 8% of those are successful, suggesting unacceptably high relapse rates.

Several factors may account for this, including the seriousness of the attempt (ie, a willingness to undergo the discomfort associated with quitting), the strength of nicotine addiction, and the degree of support the smoker receives after quitting. The physician can help ameliorate these factors by (1) motivating smoking patients to make serious, *sustained* quit attempts; (2) helping patients learn, prior to the quit attempt, about the severity and duration of potential withdrawal symptoms; (3) prescribing, for heavily addicted smokers (eg, first cigarette within 30 minutes of waking or a cigarette habit of more than a pack a day), a nicotine replacement product, after careful explanation of its proper use; and (4) advising patients to seek the support, even if quitting "on their own," of a spouse, friend, or someone else in a position to help reinforce their decision to quit. Finally, recent research suggests that, while training physicians to give advice about smoking cessation can increase patient quit *attempts*, it will take greater effort—perhaps several follow-up visits or contacts—to reduce the high relapse rates experienced.[4,9,10]

• *To provide those involved in reducing smoking prevalence with the most expedient means of doing so.* Too often, those charged with reducing smoking prevalence, such as physicians, nurses, dentists, public health officers, and smoking-cessation program coordinators, are not provided with or aware of the most appropriate information available to help smokers stop, especially on their own.[11] For physicians, this may mean not being aware of effective cessation strategies[5] or the proper use of nicotine gum (or the transcutaneous nicotine patch that may soon be available). It could also mean being unaware of the special help for heavy smokers that organized cessation programs can provide. For public health officers and smoking-cessation program directors, it could be not realizing the importance of providing simple self-help materials to as many smokers as possible and not limiting their efforts to those who have already expressed an interest in giving up tobacco. The importance of a variety of providers and a menu of methods becomes more important as more smokers are motivated to make serious quit attempts.

With the knowledge that there will be more than 2 million tobacco-related deaths worldwide from tobacco this year, it is obviously necessary to expand our efforts to reduce smoking prevalence not only in the United States and other industrialized countries but, especially, in the developing world, where the tobacco industry is increasing its markets and the rates of tobacco-related death are rising. Next week's World No-Tobacco Day (May 31), sponsored by the World Health Organization, provides an excellent opportunity to embark on a renewed effort to help those who want to quit smoking to do so, and to help those who do not now smoke, especially in developing countries, to remain nonsmokers.

ENDNOTES

1. Pierce JP, Fiore MC, Novotny TE, Hatziandreu EJ, Davis RM. Trends in cigarette smoking in the United States: projections to the year 2000. *JAMA* 1989;261:61–65.
2. Fiore MC, Novotny TE, Pierce JP, et al. Methods used to quit smoking in the United States: do cessation programs help? *JAMA*. 1990;263:2760–2765.
3. Prochaska JO, DiClemente CC. Stages and processes of self-change of smoking: toward an integrative model of change. *J Consult Clin Psychol* 1983; 51:390–395.
4. Wilson DM, Taylor DW, Gilbert JR, et al. A randomized trial of a family physician intervention for smoking cessation. *JAMA*. 1988;260:1570–1574.
5. Glynn TJ, Manley MW. *How to Help Your Patients Stop Smoking: A National Cancer Institute Manual for Physicians.* Bethesda, Md: National Cancer Institute; 1989. National Institutes of Health publication 89–3064.
6. Glynn TJ, Boyd GM, Gruman JC. Essential elements of self-help/minimal

intervention strategies for smoking cessation. *Health Educ Q.* 1990;17. In press.

7. Chapman S. Stop-smoking clinics: a case for their abandonment. *Lancet* 1985;1:918–920.
8. Pechacek TF, Erickson AC. ASSIST—The American Stop Smoking Intervention Study for Cancer Prevention. In: Daube M, ed. *The Global War Proceedings of the Seventh World Conference on Tobacco and Health.* In Press.
9. Cohen SJ, Stookey GK, Katz BP, Drook CA, Smith DM. Encouraging primary care physicians to help smokers quit: a randomized, controlled trial. *Ann Intern Med.* 1989;110:648–652.
10. Cummings SR, Coates TJ, Richard RJ, et al. Training physicians in counseling about smoking cessation: a randomized trial of the 'Quit for Life' program. *Ann Intern Med.* 1989;110:640–647.
11. Glynn TJ, Boyd GM, Gruman JC. *Self-Guided Strategies for Smoking Cessation: A Program Planner's Guide.* Bethesda, Md: National Cancer Institute. In press. National Institutes of Health publication 90-3104.

2

From Reading to Writing

MANY OF THE WRITING ASSIGNMENTS you encounter in college will rely on reading in some way. Teachers may ask you to respond to what you have read, to agree or disagree, to evaluate, to summarize or explain, to synthesize. Or, they may ask you to use examples, illustrations, and information from your reading to support your own ideas. Effective critical reading is the foundation for completing these kinds of writing assignments successfully.

Reading and Writing: The Conversation

Reading is much like listening to (or even overhearing) a conversation in progress in which writers are talking to each other, to you, to decision makers, and to anyone who is interested or will pay attention. Writers are attempting to inform and persuade each other, the uninformed, and the uninterested. No one but the most thorough scholar or researcher will attempt to read the entire conversation, and in many cases there is no need to do so. In most cases you will be able to write effectively if you are familiar with only part of this conversation, especially if your reading has provided an overview of the subject and introduced you to the major issues. In fact, it is generally easy to get such an overview of the major issues in a specific subject. The three articles that you have read about quitting smoking were easy to locate in the library, requiring a computer search that took only a few minutes. Specialized information, for example, about the precise demographics of smoking, is generally much more difficult to find.

Writing: Joining the Conversation

When you are asked to write something based on your reading, you are being asked to join the conversation and contribute something to it. Sometimes teachers will expect you to summarize the conversation, to demonstrate that you have done the required reading. More often, teachers and employers will expect and reward your own contribution. You can make your own contribution in several ways:

• *You can provide new information.* For example, you might decide to do original research such as surveying your classmates to determine whether they smoke, how they stopped smoking, or some other information.

• *You can construct an interesting or unusual synthesis.* For example, the Surgeon General's report is a synthesis of information about the health consequences of smoking. It does not present original research, but collects information from a variety of places and presents it in one place.

• *You can evaluate or critique the subject, or part of it, from your own perspective, or from a disciplinary point of view not used before.* For example, you might look at smoking, and quitting, from a legal rather than a medical perspective, perhaps exploring whether there should be legal consequences for those who do not stop smoking.

• *You can write about your own experience.* For example, perhaps you have attempted to stop smoking. You can contribute your own experience to the conversation, perhaps offering details that no one else has noticed, or explaining why you succeeded or failed.

RULES OF THE GAME

When you join a continuing conversation (whether it is written or spoken), there are certain things you *must* do and certain things you *must not* do.

You must:

• Show knowledge of what has been said so far in the conversation

• Join in at a level of sophistication that suits your readers

• Give others credit for the ideas and information that they have introduced

• Add something new to the conversation; that is, do something more than repeat what others have said

• Provide enough context to show your readers how and why you got into the conversation

• Establish your own authority to be in the conversation, and give your readers some reason to listen to you

You must not:

• Simply summarize, synthesize, or repeat what others have said unless that is your assignment or your purpose

• Construct a paper made entirely of quotations and paraphrased passages that you stitch together loosely with a few of your own words. This is simply another way of repeating what others have said, although the research apparatus of quotations, footnotes, and lists of sources makes it look like you are doing something other than repeating the conversation. That is, it may look like real writing, but it isn't.

BEGIN WITH YOUR OWN IDEAS

All successful writing begins with a writer who has an idea, and useful ideas come from active, thoughtful engagement with a subject. Because of this, successful writers are also often successful readers, people who have listened carefully to the conversation. It is difficult to have ideas of one's own without knowing the ideas others have had, which of those have been rejected, and which are still under discussion.

For example, at one time people believed that smoking was not harmful, or that the damage it does cannot be reversed. But the reading selections show that both of these ideas have been rejected, so neither one would be a solid foundation for a paper. You could, of course, write about how those ideas were rejected, giving a historical account of the research that led to the discovery that smoking is harmful, or that stopping leads to almost immediate improvements. The historical approach would be an interesting perspective and might result in discovering information that most people have been unaware of.

It can be intimidating to read informed, well-written articles and books about any subject. The writers may seem so smart and well-informed, their coverage of the subject so thorough, that they appear to have said everything there is to say about a subject. This may leave the impression that the conversation is over and that there is no room for anyone else to enter it.

But it is unlikely that all of the interesting ideas about any subject have been used up, leaving you nothing left to say. Writers manage to contribute new ideas about a great many subjects that would seem to have been thoroughly covered by others. Witness the yearly crop of new books, films, and television programs about subjects such as the Civil War, biblical topics, nature, and others. While much is repeated, much is new as well. Sometimes the most refreshing treatment of a subject comes not from new information, but from a new perspective. In the case of smoking, for example, medical authorities have spent years telling smokers to quit, that smoking is harmful. As the article from *Changing Times* indicates, many programs have become available to help smokers quit smoking, and these must have had some success, since forty million have quit. But the article from the *Journal of the American Medical Association* suggests that smokers need motivation more than they need programs. This is a new perspective.

FINDING YOUR OWN IDEAS

You will be able to enter the conversation about a subject only if you engage that subject seriously and thoughtfully. At the heart of that engagement is an exploration of your personal authority over the subject. Your authority is based on a combination of your personal experiences, your attitudes, your beliefs, and your knowledge.

Your personal experience is part of what gives you authority over any subject. For example, your experience with smoking might take any of the following forms:

- You are a smoker.
- You have tried to quit smoking and failed.
- You have quit.
- You know smokers.
- You know someone who has quit, or tried to quit.
- You know someone who died of the effects of smoking, or who is very ill.
- You know someone who has smoked for years with no ill effects.
- You may be allergic to smoke.

Each of these experiences is rich with information about smoking and how people stop smoking, and this information forms part of your personal authority over the subject.

An Activity. In your reading journal, write about your personal experiences with smoking. Describe these in as much

detail as you can manage and then look closely at your descriptions. What has surprised you? What do you feel strongly
about? What did you have the most to say about? What did
you write most easily about? These subjects are probably strong
points in your experience. They are potential subjects for
writing.

Because of your personal experiences you may have strong attitudes,
beliefs, or emotional reactions to smokers and smoking. You might be
strongly opposed to smoking because of friends or relatives who have
become ill or died as a result of smoking, or simply because you find the
smell or appearance of smoking distasteful. Your religious beliefs may
predispose you to disapprove of smoking. Or, you may be a smoker who
believes that anti-smoking rules and campaigns are infringing on your
rights.

An Activity.   Describe your emotional reactions to smoking,
or your beliefs and attitudes about it. Try to explain where
these attitudes and beliefs came from and evaluate how strong
they are. Also, try to tie your emotional reactions to specific
events in your experience.

Knowledge is also part of your authority over a subject. While some
of your knowledge comes from personal experiences, you also acquire
knowledge both deliberately and casually through reading and other media: newscasts, magazines, newspapers, and talking with other people.

An Activity.   Make a list of what you know about smoking.
Try to get beyond your prereading notes. Be exhaustive. Try
for a list that includes seventy-five to one hundred items.

DISCOVERING WHAT YOU KNOW AND BELIEVE

Your personal experiences, attitudes, beliefs, and knowledge about
a subject are rich sources of ideas for writing. Begin your search for ideas
by examining what you know and believe about a subject. The following
questions and activities will help you do this. Answer the questions or
do the activities in your reading journal so that you will have a permanent
record of your thinking. It's possible that much of what you write here
will be useful as part of a paper.

1. Look at your prereading notes. Review what you knew about
the subject before you began reading. What were your opinions and reactions? Does your reading support or challenge your attitudes and beliefs?

2. Review your sources carefully. What do they say that you disagree with? Explain why you disagree. Give reasons and be precise. Disagreements are often key points of departure for writing.

3. What is your interest in your subject? Explain it in detail.

4. How does the subject connect to your own studies, or your life in general?

5. What part of the subject do you want to know more about? What interests you most? Why?

6. What position or conclusion does your reading suggest?

7. What do you wish your sources had told you more about? That is, are there parts of the subject where you thought the writers stopped short of giving you as much information as you wanted or needed? Describe the information you want.

8. Could your sources have provided more complete or more convincing evidence for some position, point, or conclusion? Describe the evidence you believe is needed, and explain why you believe it is not adequate.

9. What do you know that has not been mentioned in your reading?

TURNING IDEAS INTO WRITING

Once you have reviewed your own knowledge and beliefs about a subject, you should be able to identify several ideas that might serve as subjects for a writing assignment. This section will present and show you how to evaluate several possible ideas for writing about smoking.

For example, you might begin with the following statement: *"People should stop smoking."* There's nothing wrong with this statement. It's true, and your reading will certainly have supported it. The trouble is, it's also obvious. It is either implicit or explicit in virtually everything you will read about smoking. Few people would question it, and it gives you little to do besides repeat what other writers have already said. Even hard-core smokers know they should quit. A more interesting approach might be to follow up on the suggestion in the *JAMA* article that people who are helping smokers stop smoking should concentrate on providing motivation.

"Smoking is hazardous to your health" might seem like a possible subject for writing, but it suffers from many of the same problems as the first one: a similar statement has been printed on cigarette packages for more than twenty years. It's not news, and few people would take issue with it. There is very little to say about this subject that does not involve repeating what every other writer on the subject has said.

Interesting subjects for writing sometimes come from unusual directions, and they almost always require that you do something with the information you possess, not simply repeat it. The following subjects have some potential.

1. Let's assume that you are interested in policies about smoking in public. It's common knowledge that restaurants must provide non-smoking areas, and that smoking is now banned on most domestic airline flights. Numerous airports do not permit smoking in public, and an increasing number of businesses, schools, and other institutions are instituting or considering non-smoking policies. It would be pointless to write a paper advocating policies that already exist.

A more interesting approach would be to place smoking in the context of other activities that society regulates, such as crime, and to explore whether prohibiting smoking is a greater infringement on smokers' rights than smoking is on non-smokers' rights. A comparable situation might be the protection of flag burning as free speech: it may not be popular, but to prohibit it goes against well-established principles. This would not necessarily be an easy paper to write, or even a popular one, but it would certainly be an interesting approach to the subject.

2. Let's assume that you are interested in the obvious hazards of smoking, but you want to do more than just repeat those hazards. In this case, it might occur that the hazards that seem obvious to you and the Surgeon General are not equally obvious to everyone else. People continue to smoke, and tobacco companies continue to defend their products. Occasionally a smoker, or a survivor, sues a tobacco company, attempting to collect a judgment by proving that the company knew it was selling a dangerous product.

A couple of subjects present themselves here. You could explore the reasons that people continue to smoke, despite ever-mounting evidence that it will probably kill them and that it is harming those around them. You could probably find some published information about this subject, but it also offers an opportunity to do extensive interviews with smokers. Of course, people do all sorts of things that are not good for them, and this kind of behavior might be part of the context for your subject.

As an alternative, you could explore why tobacco companies insist that there is no conclusive evidence to show that their products are harmful. This would require that you examine and evaluate the evidence, looking at it from both sides, and that would take you beyond mere repetition.

An Activity.   Using the examples in this section as models, describe two or three ideas for papers about smoking or quitting smoking.

BEING AN AUTHORITY

Having and writing about your own ideas, rather than repeating those that belong to someone else, will affect your stance as a writer in positive and useful ways. As a student you often write to prove that you have completed reading assignments or to demonstrate your mastery of a specific body of information. In both cases you write to an audience that knows what you are going to say before you say it.

When you write about your own ideas, you write from a position of knowledge. You are not the novice writing to prove what you know, and your audience will not know what you are going to say before you say it. Instead, you are asking your readers to pay attention to the point you are making about your subject. Thus, when you write about your own ideas you write with an authority that is impossible to claim when you simply summarize or repeat what others have said. This authority is the result of your careful and thoughtful engagement with your subject.

AUDIENCE: WHO WILL READ WHAT YOU WRITE?

In most cases your immediate audience for academic writing will be a teacher. Teachers read what you write in order to prepare you to write for other audiences. They will appreciate it if you attempt to envision and write for real readers. In all cases, real readers are people who need or want to know the ideas and information you are writing about. They are interested in the subject, or they can be convinced to be interested in it.

Some decisions about your audience are obvious. You won't write about the hazards of smoking or the reasons for quitting for an audience of people who do not smoke. But many people might be interested in why smokers continue to smoke, despite the hazards, or whether restrictions on smoking infringe on smokers' rights. For example, you might attempt to get non-smokers, who probably favor restrictions, to understand why those restrictions are unfair and possibly illegal. Or, you might attempt to show smokers how they can assert their rights to fair treatment.

When you are attempting to determine who your audience might be, ask the following questions:

- Who needs or wants to know the information you are writing about?
- Who will be interested in this question or issue?
- Why will the readers you envision be interested in your subject?
- How will your subject affect the readers you envision?
- How will your audience react to what you say about the subject?

- Can you accomplish your purpose with the audience you have in mind?

An Activity.   For each of the ideas for papers about smoking that you described earlier, describe an audience that you would like to write for.

WHAT IS YOUR PURPOSE?

You will write more effectively if you know what you want to accomplish by writing about a particular subject for a specific audience. The following questions will help you think productively about your purpose. Write your responses in your reading journal.

- What do you want to accomplish by writing about this subject?

For example, if you write about why smokers continue to smoke, despite the hazards, your audience might be the very people you are writing about, and your purpose might be to motivate them to quit by showing them how they are avoiding the question of quitting.

Or, you might write for people who know smokers who will not or cannot quit, and your purpose may to be help them understand why smokers persist, or to give them some ideas about how to motivate smokers to make a serious effort to quit smoking.

- Can you accomplish your purpose or goal with the audience you have chosen to write for (or the one you must write for)?

It's not possible to accomplish some purposes with some audiences. That's why you need to choose a reader appropriate to your purpose, or a purpose appropriate to your reader. Smokers are not likely to support restrictions on smoking. Tobacco company executives are not likely to respond favorably to arguments that they should be liable for the health consequences of smoking.

An Activity.   Using the subjects and audiences you described earlier, explain the purpose you would attempt to accomplish in each paper.

Supporting Your Ideas

Once you have identified the idea you will write about and settled the questions of your audience and purpose, you need to think about how you will support the idea. What information will you use as evidence, examples, or illustrations to help your audience understand and convince them to believe what you say? Which sources will you quote to strengthen your case and enhance your own authority? Providing adequate support is not simply a matter of collecting data and quotations and throwing them into your own writing wherever they seem to fit. Support is most effective when it is unobtrusive and does not distract from your own writing and ideas. You can use sources for support in the following ways:

SOURCES PROVIDE INFORMATION

From your reading you obtained information that you could not get on your own. For example, you would not know that forty million people have quit smoking, or that most people who quit successfully do so on their own, unless the reading selections at the start of this chapter gave you that information. Using this kind of information in your own writing will help you make a point or help your readers understand what you are saying.

SOURCES ENHANCE YOUR AUTHORITY

Using the best available sources as intelligently and carefully as you can will enhance your authority by showing your readers that you are in control of your subject. When you take a position or interpret information, you can make your position or interpretation stronger by showing your readers that others who are authorities agree with us. For example, when you discuss the hazards of smoking, citing or quoting the Surgeon General's report carries greater weight than citing an individual smoker's personal experiences. The report is based on scientific observations of a great many smokers, not just one.

GIVE CREDIT TO SOURCES

When you use information or ideas that come from what someone else has said or written, you need to tell your readers where you got it. In fact, a good guideline for deciding whether you need to give credit to a source is to ask yourself how you came to know the information you are using. If it came from your own observations or experiences, you can use it freely without citing a source. If it did not originate with you, then you need to give credit to its source.

For example, if you say that forty million people have quit smoking, you need to cite a source for that information unless you counted the forty million yourself.

Once you know the information that you want to use from your reading, you need to decide how you will use it. Writers usually include information from their sources as isolated data, summaries, paraphrases, or quotations.

Isolated data.   This usually consists of a fact, an observation, a statistic, or some other piece of information that you have taken from a source. For example, you might want to report that ninety percent of those who have quit smoking have done so on their own.

To include this data in your own writing, you simply incorporate it into one of your own sentences. If you want to name the source right there, you might do it this way:

> According to the Surgeon General's annual report on health and
> smoking (quoted in the *Washington Post*), one out of every six deaths
> in the United States is related to smoking.

Summaries.   Sometimes, in order to make your own point or explain a complicated concept, you may need to summarize what someone else has said. It may provide important background information, or it may make your own explanation clearer. A summary presents a concise version of a writer's information or position without repeating everything that writer has said. Summaries make a point or provide information quickly and concisely, taking as little space and time as possible. When you use summaries in this way, you will not always summarize an entire article or book; instead, you will summarize only that portion of your source that applies to the point you are making. The summaries you wrote as part of your critical reading should help you do this now if you revise them to fit the context, style, and purpose of your paper.

Paraphrase.   When you paraphrase a passage from a source, you re-state it in your own words. A paraphrase is different from a summary chiefly because it presents the information in a single phrase or statement, and it attempts to present all of the information in the original. Summaries, in contrast, present selected information from the original source. A paraphrase is appropriate when you want to present more than an isolated fact but less than a full summary, and you do not need to quote the source directly. (A quotation might be too long for your purpose or contain information that you do not need.)

For example, the article from *Changing Times* contains the following statement: "Most people get hooked on cigarettes partly because of the stimulation from nicotine, with outright chemical dependency developing as tolerance to the drug builds up."

A paraphrase of this statement might read as follows: Most smokers develop a chemical dependency on nicotine as they become tolerant of the drug.

Quotations. When you quote from a source, you use the writer's exact words, just as you found them in the original. Use a direct quotation when you believe the writer's words are more effective than any paraphrase you could write, or when you want your readers to experience the full effect of the writer's voice. This is usually the case when the writer (or speaker) is well known and has a special authority over the subject. For example, you would not paraphrase Patrick Henry's "Give me liberty or give me death," nor would you paraphrase Martin Luther King, Jr.'s "I Have a Dream" speech. You would quote both, because of their uniqueness and forcefulness.

When you use a direct quotation, always enclose it in quotation marks to indicate that you are using someone's exact words. And always double check to be sure that you have copied those words exactly. Try to make the quotations you use relate to their immediate context in your own writing. Introduce quotations by using words and phrases that attach them to the sentences that surround them. Review the article from *Changing Times* and note how the quotations in it are introduced.

3

Toys, Children, and Play

TOYS, GAMES, AND PLAY have different meanings for different people. Children may regard them as sources of endless hours of amusement. Some adults see toys as a means of preparing children for adulthood: educational toys teach children the information they will need in school and beyond; competitive games help children develop the motivation that will enable them to survive in a competitive adult world.

Other people see toys, play, and games as sources of information about beliefs and values. In the hands of anthropologists, historians, or psychotherapists, toys become a kind of book in which it is possible to read about the material, intellectual, psychological, and spiritual culture of the people who use them. The presence or absence of toys and games, or of certain kinds of toys and games, can say much about a culture and its view of childhood. A society in which children play with computers and fashion dolls is much different from one in which the main toys are marbles, rag dolls, and yo-yos. A culture that uses homemade toys of wood is much different from one that uses mass-produced plastic toys.

Finally, toys and games can reveal a great deal about what adults think of children and childhood, because adults design, manufacture, and sell most toys.

The selections in this chapter examine toys, games, and play from these various perspectives. John Brewer writes about the history of toys and play, treating toys and games as cultural artifacts that provide information about societies and people. Bruno Bettelheim, a child psychiatrist, explores how children learn about rules. Brian Sutton-Smith approaches toys as an anthropologist who is interested in what they might mean and how they might affect those who play with them. David Owen writes about the toy industry and the way it develops and markets toys; he is especially interested in the role of television in promoting toys. Margaret Donaldson, a psychologist, focuses on how children learn, and she suggests that they may do so for fun rather than for other reasons. Johnathan Holden, a poet and essayist, writes about his boyhood fascination with toy guns and real explosions. Marie Winn voices her concern that watching television has replaced other forms of play, and that children are poorer for the substitution.

Before you begin reading, take a few minutes to review your memories and attitudes about toys and play. The questions and activities in the next section, "Before You Read," will help you focus your attention on the subject and prepare you for reading. Use your reading journal to compose thorough answers to each of the prereading questions.

Before You Read

1. What do you remember about the toys you had as a child? Describe a toy you owned and how you played with it.
2. When you remember playing, what images come to mind? What scenes do you see? What games or activities are you involved in? What toys are you and other children playing with? Choose a specific scene or event and describe it in detail.
3. If you had to define or explain the concept of "toy" to someone who knew nothing about toys, what would you say?
4. Describe a favorite toy and explain what was special about it.
5. Describe a time when you played without toys. What did you do, and how did the absence of toys affect your play?
6. Describe a toy that you didn't like, that you thought was stupid or useless as a toy. Explain why you didn't like it.
7. What toys did you own that, as you think about them now, helped prepare you for adulthood? What were they, and what did they contribute to your development?
8. What kinds of toys were you not allowed to play with as a child? Why were they prohibited?
9. How have toys changed since you were a child?

The Genesis of the Modern Toy

——————— JOHN BREWER ———————

Brewer is a historian. His interest in this article is in tracing both the historical development of toys and the growth of the idea of play itself. This essay first appeared in History Today *(December 1980).*

IT IS A COMMONPLACE that a culture can be understood by an examination of its artifacts. Yet the history of 'material culture', as opposed to the history of a society's finest works of sculpture, art and architecture, is still an embryonic science. Costume, the tools of a man's (or woman's) trade, household utensils, furnishings, playthings—all of these, especially those that did not belong to the elite or leaders of a society, have not received the attention devoted to 'high' culture. Yet many aspects of everyday life exhibit the beliefs and social experience of the bulk of a nation's people. Costume can tell us how the members of a society are ranked and ordered, how sexes are differentiated (if at all), and what qualities are least or most admired. Toys are equally revealing for they almost always contain statements made by adults (often though not invariably parents) either about the culture in which they live and/or the values that they think desirable. Toys mirror a culture—or at least, aspects of it; conversely, if we wish to understand the significance of an individual toy or game, we must set it within a broad context, looking at it in the light of prevailing attitudes towards work and play, the psychology of man, the nature of learning and the place of the child in both family and society. Toys are cultural messages—sometimes simple, occasionally complex and ambiguous, but invariably revealing.

Yet the idea of the 'educational toy'—indeed, even the concept of the toy as a plaything peculiar to children—is a relatively recent one. Before the eighteenth century there were virtually no toy manufacturers nor toyshops in Europe and America; equally, there were almost no books written or produced especially for children, who shared most games and recreations with adults. The world of the child was not precisely separated from the realm of the adult; no special sector or segment of the culture was devoted exclusively to children. Thus Dr. Johnson defined 'toy' in his famous *Dictionary* as 'a petty commodity; a trifle; a thing of no value; a plaything or bauble'. There was absolutely no mention of children. The term 'toy' meant any small inexpensive object or trinket sold to young and old alike. The travelling pedlar or chapman, the town's 'toyman', offered cheap jewellery, buckles, bangles and hairpins; his wares were those of the modern Woolworth's. Even 'dolls' were not intended for children but were in fact miniature mannequins clothed to display the latest fashion, fad or frippery. There were therefore almost no toys in the modern sense. This did not, of course, mean that children had no playthings; it simply meant that they had to fall back on the things that they shared with their elders. They improvised and invented toys and games. Domestic utensils, the resources of field and forest, the debris of the urban environment: all of these contributed towards imaginative and open-ended play.

How do we explain this almost total absence of toys in the sixteenth and seventeenth-century English and colonial American household? Historians have advanced several explanations, nearly all of which attribute the lack of toys to parental attitudes towards children and social attitudes towards play. Judged by modern standards, it is argued, parents treated their children either with an indifference that verged on callousness or were actively brutal towards them, beating them with monotonous frequency. The world of the Anglo-American child before the modern era is therefore often portrayed as cruel, cold, unemotional and lacking in the sort of family affection that might encourage play. These attitudes are usually explained as a reaction to the horrifying rates of infant and child mortality which militated against a close parent-child bond, and by the prevailing contemporary view that when children came into the world they were, like all human creatures, tainted with original sin against which a constant and brutal war had to be waged.

Those historians who look on the history of childhood as the gradual emancipation of the child from this callous and cruel régime have used several types of evidence to demonstrate the harshness of seventeenth-century childhood. English infants, they point out, were swaddled, bound so tightly that they could not move their legs and arms. This does not, however, seem to have been the practice in the thirteen colonies of America where babes wore loose-fitting garments. Nevertheless in both cultures parental breast-feeding was far from universal, and the infant was often packed off to a wet-nurse, where quite commonly neglect and ill-treatment resulted in the child's death. From the age of two corporal punishment seems to have been the staple of the child's educational diet. Schoolmasters ('my system is to whip, and to have done with it') as well as parents and tutors rarely spared the rod to spoil the child. Punishment, corporal or otherwise, was generally severe: one unfortunate colonial child who wet his bed was forced 'to drink a pint of piss'. The time between infancy and gainful employment was mercilessly brief: service, apprenticeship or labour in the family began as early as seven, and all children were put to work before they were twelve or thirteen. Children died in such numbers that they left very little trace of their lives behind them. Even in the communities on the colonial frontier, where infant mortality rates were lower than in the coastal towns or back in Europe, the death of a child— your child—was a frequent occurrence.

This picture of the heartless and cruel world inhabited by children needs some qualification. Nearly all of the evidence that appears to demonstrate parental indifference towards the child in fact shows simply that his *individuality* was not strongly recognised. We tend to assume that parental affection cannot flourish unless children are regarded as individuals. But this is essentially a modern (and Western) assumption that in part stems from our elevation of the bond between the parent (or, at least, the mother) and the individual child above almost all other forms of attachment. The chief affective bonds of the pre-modern American and English parent were probably to the family as a whole rather than to its individual members; this does not mean that they never showed affection to their children, only that they cared for them as a 'brood'.

Other evidence of lack of affection is either ambiguous or can be matched by examples of affection. The pervasive presence of infant and child mortality undoubtedly helped generate psychological mechanisms for parents to cope with and distance themselves from the inescapability of deaths within the family. But many of the statements made by the bereaved parents speak more of an attempt to flee from and suppress grief than of a genuine indifference. Moreover parental attitudes towards children began to change even though a dreadfully high rate of infant mortality persisted. There is therefore some reason to doubt that its effect on parent-child relations was quite as strong as some historians have suggested.

But what are we to make of the frequent beatings and floggings of young colonial children? Some of the parents who appear to have been the most brutal certainly thought of themselves as being cruel in order to be kind. Brought up as (usually Calvinist) Protestants, their fierce religiosity required them to curb their children. Since the human (and therefore children's) proclivity for wickedness, sloth and indolence was known to be extraordinarily strong, and because sin constantly threatened to engulf a child, the caring, attentive and loving parent was obliged— almost compelled—to impose a harsh, punitive régime of the strictest discipline to keep children on the straight and narrow. The terrors of corporal punishment were necessary to produce a good citizen and Godly person who was industrious and virtuous. Paradoxically, therefore, and because nearly all parents assumed that the only way to socialise and educate their children was by overpowering and overcoming their inherent propensity for sin and sloth, the harshest parents were often the most caring. It is a tribute to many parents' remarkable sense of religious duty that they persisted in being cruel to be kind, despite the considerable psychological toll—the extraordinary domestic tension—which emanated from the conflict between parental desire and parental obligation.

This is not to condone the systematic physical punishment of children, nor is it to deny that in the sixteenth and seventeenth centuries children, as weak and subordinate members of society, were sometimes the victims of capricious and senseless violence, but it is to emphasise that this 'no toy' culture was radically different from our own, and cannot be understood by the application of modern social and moral standards.

The play of both adults and children in the seventeenth-century American colonies was almost never regarded as being instructive, purposeful or educationally useful. Rather it was condemned by puritans and zealots as a sinful and idle pursuit, or justified as a catharsis—a periodic and exuberant release from the rigours of work that refreshed body and soul. Most communities had a calendar of recreations tied to important local events, the seasonal rhythms of work or, in western Europe, to saints' days. In colonial Williamsburg, for example, recreations were concentrated in April and in autumn, when the town was crowded because the courts and assemblies were sitting. Such occasions verged on the Brueghelesque. They were often boistrous and sometimes violent—cockfighting and wrestling (which, with its eye-gouging, horrified English visitors to the colonies) accompanied cudgelling and boxing. The audiences for these 'rude' recreations were often as violent as the sports themselves. The pattern of these celebrations varied from colony to colony in format and degree of restraint, but most of them, if their critics are to be believed, involved gargantuan feasting, prodigious drinking and sexual licence. Instructive play was almost entirely absent; games of chance—dice and cards—and gambling (in the South particularly on horse-racing) were extremely popular. Nevertheless such recreations did serve important functions: old and young, rich and poor were all expected to participate in events that gave symbolic expression to the ideal of community and solidarity. The customary distinctions of age, wealth and power were briefly swept aside in the maelstrom of egalitarian celebration. As one fastidious observer of a Virginia cockfight disapprovingly observed, the cockpit was 'surrounded by many genteel people, promiscuously mingled with the vulgar and debased'. Children were also present. It was thought neither necessary nor desirable to distinguish 'child's play' from the recreations of others.

Play occurred publicly, often out-of-doors and usually with other members of the community. It was therefore not especially associated with the domestic environment, except in the most prosperous households. Rather the household was associated with work: there was a 'family economy' to which all of its members, of every age, were expected to contribute. The family that worked together in the home also played together, but they did so not within the confines of the household but in the community at large.

The 'no toy' culture, which scarcely seems to have recognised the special state of childhood, was gradually but radically transformed between the late seventeenth and early nineteenth centuries. The most significant changes were the development of a new conception of man, and a parallel recognition of new processes of human learning. Man came to be seen as a malleable and manipulable creature who entered the world with a mind that was not primed with evil but was a *tabula rasa*, like a blank sheet of paper, on which appropriate sense impressions could imprint knowledge and learning. Man, in other words, was capable of moral improvement provided that he was nurtured in the right environment. This view was accompanied by the relatively novel theory of the human psyche that emphasised man's innate tendency to eschew pain and pursue pleasure. From this perspective the widespread use of brutal corporal punishment was clearly counterproductive: by associating learning and pain it was more likely to discourage an interest in learning than to teach or socialise. Such crude practices, it was argued, should be replaced by a much more subtle psychological manipulation of the child, one that used the propensity for play to make learning stimulating and pleasurable.

These educational theories are traditionally associated with the English philosopher, John Locke, whose *Some Thoughts concerning Education* (1693), which went through numerous editions in several languages and on both sides of the Atlantic, made him the Dr. Benjamin Spock of his age. Locke was not the first philosopher to realise that play could be used didactically, nor was his psychology unique but, as an intellectual of prodigious repute in both North America and Europe, he lent considerable weight to the 'environmentalist' theory of learning. Moreover, the book was timely. Like childcare manuals such as Dr. William Cadogen's *Essay on the Nursing and Management of Children* and Dr. William Buchan's *Domestic Medicine* (twenty editions between 1769 and 1819), Locke's *Thoughts* was read chiefly by the affluent and middling classes of America and England who had the time, the leisure, the money, and the social predisposition to lavish attention on their children.

We should not, of course, assume that these ideas swept all before them. Their acceptance varied from place to place and class to class. They were taken up predominantly by middle-class parents eager to 'improve' their children. But the old attitudes and practices continued: many children were still whipped and flogged, and imaginative learning rarely ousted the more traditional method of rote memorisation. Indeed, for many children the situation deteriorated at the end of the eighteenth century, when evangelicals on both sides of the Atlantic returned to the older view of infant depravity and renewed the practice of wholesale flogging.

Nevertheless Lockean theory marks the growing acceptance in North America of the idea that education was a matter of carrot rather than stick. It also heralds the genesis of the toy both as a plaything peculiar to children and as an educational device. Locke and his eighteenth-century followers were adamant that play was the key to successful learning: 'the chief Art is to make all that they have to do, Sport and Play too . . . Learning anything, they should be taught, might be made as much a Recreation as their Play, as their Play is to their learning'. Both play and playthings, which had previously been regarded either as an obstruction to learning or as matters of no didactic consequence, became crucial to the educational process. As Locke remarked about playthings (in sentiments remarkably similar to those of Froebel over 100 years later), 'nothing that may form adult's minds, is to be overlook'd and neglected, and whatsoever introduces Habits, and settles Customs in them, deserves the Care and Attention of their Governors, and is not a small thing in its Consequences'. Toys and games were recognised as being very important. Indeed Locke was responsible for popularising one of the earliest 'educational' toys, the so-called 'Locke blocks', whose role in teaching the alphabet he lovingly describes in his *Thoughts on Education*.

Locke's theories seem remarkably modern, and certainly they approximate much more closely to present-day views of learning than to the régime of flogging that he so vehemently opposed. Nevertheless his concept of play and of the role of toys and games was remarkably circumscribed. In his desire to establish a controlled environment for the child, he recommended education at home under a private tutor; schools and schoolboys, he believed, conveyed 'the contagion of Rudeness and Vice' which threatened a young man's 'Innocence and Virtue'. By seeking to locate education primarily in the home, Locke contributed towards the concern with domesticity that was such a marked feature of genteel and bourgeois life in the eighteenth and nineteenth centuries. The idea of the home as a sanctum, a haven in the heartless world, developed largely through the dissociation of the dwelling-place from the place of work, and because of the transformation of the middle-class woman from an important figure in the family economy to the mother and guardian of children kept in the home. Prosperity and the desire for gentility produced a growing leisured class of women whose chief tasks were to adorn themselves and their homes and to superintend the moral welfare of their progeny. For the middle classes of America 'work', which had once been associated both with the home and with the entire family, became a predominantly masculine activity conducted beyond the domestic horizon. Play, especially children's play, became restricted to the domestic environment in which parental (especially maternal) control could be most successfully exercised. On those occasions when bourgeois children went out to visit the circus, the theatre or some improving public exhibit, they went *en famille* to an occasion attended by other families. There was no question of children venturing forth, even in the cause of self-improvement, without a nurse or parent in tow.

This desire to control the play of children stemmed from notions of play itself. Neither Locke nor the aspiring middle-class parent thought of play as a means by which children could learn from *each other;* nor, though they saw play as a means of teaching individuals social and moral precepts, did they envisage play itself as a form of socialisation. Rather they regarded it as a tool of the tutor or parent, a *means* by which children could be educated. Play, therefore, was looked on as an individualistic endeavour, even when it involved other children, and as being didactic in a rather narrow sense.

Judged by these criteria a great many traditional forms of recreation were found wanting. It is not surprising, therefore, that the very classes which encouraged child's play and bought their children educational toys simultaneously attacked both the traditional conception of play and the recreations themselves. During the course of the eighteenth century rumbustious community events were increasingly criticised for their barbarity, their indiscriminate intermingling of classes and ages (now regarded as a reprehensible rather than desirable aspect of leisure), and their encouragement of depravity. Community festivals and popular 'rough' sports were either domesticated, controlled or actively suppressed. Thus Christmas was transformed into the family festival *par excellence,* admission to sports events was regulated by admission charges, and 'cruel' or 'rude' recreations were attacked by reform groups and through legislation. Games of chance were flatly condemned as 'incroaching Wasters of useful Time'. Play and recreation, both for adult and child, now either had to be 'profitable' and productive, a workhorse harnessed to the load of earning, or to be suppressed as a nuisance.

These attitudes and values were clearly expressed in the earliest toys and games for children. Marketed in North America in the last quarter of the eighteenth century, they were almost all remorselessly didactic: they taught skills, they moralised, they imparted knowledge. The old and well-loved games of chance—cards, dice and a board game known as the Game of Goose (the precursor of snakes and ladders)—were transformed into educational aids. Card packs, for instance, were designed to teach geography, history, spelling and astronomy; board games with such titles as 'The Cottage of Content; or, Right roads and Wrong ways', 'The New Game of Human Life' and 'Virtue rewarded and Vice punished' combined a quite extraordinary unctuousness with competitive play. Packets of puzzles and riddles, the Chinese tangram (a figure of seven pieces), the rhebus, where images and pictures were substituted for words, and the jigsaw (invented in the 1760s by an Englishman named Spillsbury) all demanded calculation, patience, application, skill, ingenuity and a modicum of imagination. Such toys, together with a burgeoning children's literature, were advertised, bought and sold for their 'Lockean' qualities. Liza Lucas Pinckney asked a friend in England to help her young son by buying him 'the new toy, the description of which I enclose, to teach him according to Mr Locke's methods—which I have carefully studied—to play himself into learning'. The early toy manufacturers and entrepreneurs were fully aware of the marketability of this concept: their advertising emphasised 'improving toys' that inextricably combined 'entertainment, amusement and instruction'. Educational games, however tedious and demanding, were packaged in bright boxes and decorated in gay colours to catch the youthful eye.

In certain respects the lot of children—especially of the middle-class child whose parents could afford the new toys and games—seems to have improved. Parents were encouraged to take their children to the circus, pantomime and theatre, and to visit museums. There were brightly coloured and sensibly worded spelling, reading and elementary science books. Toyshops bulged not only with strictly didactic playthings, but with mechanical devices (of varying degrees of delicacy and complexity) for young boys, and with the inevitable dolls and dolls' houses, complete with fashionable furniture, for the female child whose future, as far as her parents were concerned, could be summarised in one word—motherhood. 'Role-model' toys, with their mimetic preparation for adult life, even toys intended simply to entertain were developed and marketed by the same manufacturers who had seen the commercial advantage of linking play and learning. By the early nineteenth century there was an international toy market, centred primarily on England and Germany which, for the first time, made widely available the sort of playthings that we take for granted today.

But the purveyors of such toys were selling much more than attractive objects; they were marketing a particular social morality—one that emphasised competitiveness, industry, probity, and *individual* endeavour. Nearly all of the toys that countenanced interaction between children emphasised competitiveness to the exclusion of other types of social intercourse. And most of the games, with their emphasis on general progressive accumulation of either 'points' or an equivalent of money, could hardly have been more appropriately designed to teach delayed gratification. Several others stressed respectability, placing emphasis on 'appearances', 'making a good impression', as the key to success: 'Habit', as one game succinctly put it, 'makes the Man'. These toys and games— educational or otherwise—also helped children develop a sense of private property. Previously most children's playthings had not belonged to them;

they had been everyday objects whose use was often shared with the rest of the family. Toys—objects given by parents or adults to children to play with—were for a child's exclusive use. He or she *owned* toys, whereas they had formerly *shared* playthings. In sum, play had been transformed from the imaginative and unstructured pursuit of the 'no toy' culture into a rigorous training in social duties and family obligations. The new toys and games, which left so little to the imagination, epitomised the bourgeois attributes necessary for commercial industrial and social success in adult life. They were not only puzzles and problems but the concrete expression of a strict morality.

The birth of toys—and of the educational toy in particular—therefore marks an important moment in our cultural history. It commemorates the recognition that both social behaviour and scholarly learning are best assimilated by the judicious use of encouragement, praise, shame and blame, rather than by the indiscriminate use of the rod, and marks the point at which an individualistic, competitive ethic came to dominate the social thinking of the middle and upper classes of American society. This development, as I have tried to emphasise, was a mixed blessing. Certainly it did not, as some historians have assumed, constitute a 'liberation' for children; rather it involved the exchange of one set of parental and social controls for another—less brutal, no doubt, but more successful in bridling the child. Toys were the frosting on a cake that was designed to look delicious but which might well prove unpalatable.

The subsequent history of the educational toy after its period of gestation in the eighteenth and its birth in the early nineteenth century was marked by two developments: the escape of the toy out of the household and, via the kindergarten, into the school; and the progressive liberalisation of the concept of play. Both of these changes stemmed largely from the adoption in the second half of the nineteenth century of the educational ideas of the German, Friedrich Froebel. Like many of his predecessors Froebel saw play and the creation of an appropriate environment as the keys to learning. His approach, however, was more 'permissive' than almost all of his precursors: parents and teachers were not to determine or interfere with children's play, but gently to guide the child on a voyage of self-discovery which would simultaneously reveal the richness of his environment. Imagination, exploration, self-development, all of these were emphasised as never before: child-centred education became acceptable. And Froebel and his followers, most notably Elizabeth Peabody, created a new controlled environment, neither home nor school, in the form of the kindergarten where children could learn by playing with Froebel's specially designed (and highly abstract) toys—the sphere, the cube and coloured rods. These simple playthings, almost devoid of a local cultural context, were the symbols of a highly integrated system of learning that saw self-development socialisation and the exploration of the environment as complementary facets of the growth of human knowledge.

It is difficult to overestimate the influence of Froebel. His ideas were assimilated in the United States and Britain and even became institutionalised parts of the school system. His methods and his toys were used to teach both rich and poor; and it is very largely as a result of his followers that almost every modern daycare centre, nursery-school, kindergarten and primary school has its building blocks and modular toys. Certainly by the late nineteenth century the conception of play and of its role in education was altogether more flexible than it had been at the end of the eighteenth century, and was more readily accepted as a didactic tool outside the home. Today the belief that children can 'play themselves into learning' is tantamount to an unquestioned orthodoxy.

The history of the educational toy (as of toys in general) can therefore be seen as going through three stages: the first, to which most of my discussion has been devoted, saw the gradual emergence in the eighteenth century of the toy as we know it today; the second phase, between *c.* 1760 and 1840, witnessed the widespread marketing of such playthings, and was also characterised by a rather narrow definition of both play and learning. The final phase, which began in the mid-nineteenth century, has seen the gradual liberalisation of play and an enormous diversification of playthings.

A society with many different (sometimes conflicting) values will produce many different kinds of toys. But when we look at the modern Cindy-doll,[1] at the spin-off playthings from the successful cinema or television series, we should ask ourselves exactly the same questions that we ask of the earliest toys: What does this aspect of our material culture tell us about our society? What values do the toys seek to sustain? What do they reveal of the world of parents and children, and of the world of work and play? If we can go some way towards answering these questions we may well learn not only about 'child's play' but also uncover many of our own assumptions which are at once a part of our modern culture and a comment upon it.

NOTES ON FURTHER READING

1. Lloyd de Mause (ed.), *The History of Childhood* Harper (New York, 1975).
2. Theodore K. Rabb and Robert I. Rotberg (eds.), *The Family in History, Interdisciplinary Essays* Harper (New York, 1973).
3. Philippe Aries (trans. Robert Baldick), *Centuries of Childhood: A Social History of Family Life* (New York, 1962).

[1] A doll that can be dressed up, known in America as a barbie-doll.

4. Edmund S. Morgan, *The Puritan Family* (New York, 1966; first edition, 1944).
5. John Demos, *A Little Commonwealth: Family Life in Plymouth Colony* (New York, 1970).
6. Jane Carson, *Colonial Virginians at Play* (Williamsburg, 1965).
7. J. H. Plumb, 'The New World of Children in Eighteenth-Century England', *Past and Present*, 67 (May, 1975).
8. Lawrence Stone, *The Family, Sex and Marriage in Early Modern England* (New York, 1978).

QUESTIONS FOR CRITICAL READERS

Remembering and Understanding

1. Summarize Brewer's discussion of toys, giving his main points.
2. Briefly summarize the changes that occurred during the eighteenth century in the way people viewed childhood and play.
3. Briefly summarize the influence of moral and religious ideas on the history of toys and play.

Analyzing and Discussing

4. Brewer says that toys "almost always contain statements made by adults (often though not invariably parents) either about the culture in which they live and/or the values that they think desirable." Select a single toy or type of toy and explain the statement that it makes about your culture and/or its values.
5. Brewer points out that before the eighteenth century children did not have separate play activities, but participated in adult recreations. If this were still true, what would children do for play?

Writing

6. Brewer says that by the end of the nineteenth century toys were thought to provide "rigorous training in social duties and family obligations." Select two or three toys you are familiar with and write a paper in which you explore whether they continue to conform to this attitude.
7. Use any standard reference work or encyclopedia to gather information about John Locke. In addition to his views on education, what other ideas and accomplishments are credited to Locke? How many of these do you recognize as still popular or current? Write a brief summary of the information you find.

Play, Games, and Rules

——————— Bruno Bettelheim ———————

Bruno Bettelheim, a well-known psychotherapist, survived the Nazi death camps during World War II and then settled in the United States. He wrote extensively about children, and his best-known book may be The Uses of Enchantment. *He committed suicide in 1990. In this selection he discusses how children come to understand play and games and how they learn to follow rules and accept winning and losing.*

MOST ADULTS FIND IT EASIER to involve themselves directly in complex, adult games, such as chess or baseball, than in play on simpler levels, such as stacking blocks or riding a hobbyhorse or a toy car. Although the words *play* and *game* may seem synonymous, they in fact refer to broadly distinguishable stages of development, with *play* relating to an earlier stage, *game* to a more mature one. Generally speaking, *play* refers to the young child's activities characterized by freedom from all but personally imposed rules (which are changed at will) by free-wheeling fantasy involvement, and by the absence of any goals outside the activity itself. *Games,* however, are usually competitive and are characterized by agreed-upon, often externally imposed, rules, by a requirement to use the implements of the activity in the manner for which they are intended and not as fancy suggests, and frequently by a goal or purpose outside the activity, such as winning the game. Children recognize early on that play is an opportunity for pure enjoyment, whereas games may involve considerable stress. One four-year-old, when confronted with an unfamiliar play situation, asked, "Is this a fun game or a winning game?" It was clear that his attitude toward the activity depended on the answer he was given.

Piaget stresses how important learning the rules of the game is in the process of socialization; a child must become able to control himself in order to do so, controlling most of all his tendency to act aggressively to reach his goals. Only then can he enjoy the continuous interaction with others that is involved in playing games with partners who are also opponents. But obeying the rules and controlling one's selfish and aggressive tendencies is not something that can be learned overnight; it is the end result of long development. When he begins playing games, a child tries to behave as he could in his earlier play. He changes the rules to suit himself, but then the game breaks down. In a later stage he comes to believe that the rules are unalterable. He treats them as if they were laws handed down from time immemorial, which cannot be transgressed under any circumstances, and he views disobeying the rules as a serious crime. Only at a still later stage—often not until he has become a teenager and sometimes even later than that—can he comprehend that rules are voluntarily agreed upon for the sake of playing the game and have no other validity, and that they can be freely altered as long as all participants agree to such changes. Democracy, based on a freely negotiated consensus that is binding only after it has been formulated and accepted, is a very late achievement in human development, even in game-playing.

When children are free to do as they like in games not supervised by adults, more often than not arguments over which game they will play and how, and what rules they should follow, take up most of their time, so that little actual playing gets done. Left to their own devices, children may require hours of fruitful deliberation before they agree on the rules and related issues, such as who should begin the game and what role each child is to have in it. And this is how it ought to be, if playing games is to socialize children. Only by pondering at great length the advantages and disadvantages of various possible games, their relative appropriateness to the conditions at hand—such as the size of the group, the available playing area, and so forth—and what rules should apply and why, will children develop their abilities to reason, to judge what is appropriate and what is not, to weigh arguments, to learn how consensus can be reached and how important such consensus is to the launching of an enterprise. Learning all this is infinitely more significant for the child's development as a social human being than is mastering whatever skills are involved in playing the game itself. Yet none of these socializing skills will be learned if adults attempt to control which games are played, or if they prevent experimentation with rules (out of fear that this may lead to chaos), or if they impatiently push for the game to get started without further delay.

When thinking about an organization like Little League, we should keep in mind that the most important function of play and games for the well-being of the child is to offer him a chance to work through unresolved problems of the past, to deal with pressures of the moment, and to experiment with various roles and forms of social interaction in order to determine their suitability for himself.

A freely organized ball game looks very ragged, and it is very ragged. The children use the game to serve their individual and group needs, so there are interruptions for displays of temper, digressions for talking things over or to pursue a parallel line of play for a time, surprising acts of compassion ("give the little guys an extra turn")—all acts outside adult game protocols. If adults want to see a polished game of baseball played according to the rule books, they can turn on their television sets. John Locke wrote that "because there can be no *Recreation* without Delight, which depends not always on Reason, but oftener on Fancy, it must be permitted Children not only to divert themselves, but to do it after their own fashion." How wonderful it would be for our children if we adults would heed the advice of this great philosopher!

For years the growing child moves back and forth among the many demands that playing games imposes on him. When all goes well, a child can do full justice to the game's requirements. But when things become psychologically too bewildering or frustrating for him, he may revert to spontaneous play. Although he may understand the rules governing the game—even insist that others follow them—he himself will be unable to obey them and may assert that they do not apply to him. For example, a young child may know perfectly well how to play checkers. All will go smoothly until he realizes, or believes, that he will lose. Then he may suddenly request, "Let's start over." If the other player agrees and the second game goes more in the child's favor, all is well. But if things look bleak for the child the second time around, he may repeat his request for a fresh start, and he may do so repeatedly. This can be frustrating to an adult, who may decide that the child should learn to finish a game once he has started it, even if he is about to lose. But if the adult is able to be patient and agree to repeated new beginnings, even though the checker game may never be concluded the child will eventually learn to play better.

If the adult insists that the child continue playing when he is likely to lose, he will be asking too much of the child's still weak controls. If the child could articulate his position, he might say, "Obeying the rules when it seems I'm going to lose is just too much for me. If you insist that I go on, I'll just have to give up on games and return to fantasy play, where I can't be defeated." Then the checker, which had been accepted as a marker to be moved only according to established rules, will suddenly be moved as the child's fancy determines, or in a way that seems to assure his winning. If this is not accepted, the marker may become a missile, to be hurled off the board or even at the winning opponent.

The reasons for the child's behavior are not difficult to understand. Feeling himself momentarily defeated by the complex realities of the game—he is losing, and thus his extremely tenuous self-respect is about to be damaged, something to be avoided at all costs—he reverts to a play level at which the rules no longer pertain, in order to rescue his endangered feeling of competence. If the opponent is also a child, he will intuitively understand (although not applaud) his companion's action. The child opponent may say in response, "Come on, now, you're acting like a baby," as if recognizing—probably from his own experience in similar situations—that what has taken place is a regression to an earlier stage of development, because the higher stage has proved too painful to be worth the effort to maintain. Or he may suggest, "Let's play something else," knowing that checkers has become too difficult.

If the opponent is an adult, however, such intuitive understanding may be missing. Some parents, unfortunately, are eager to see their child behave maturely before he is ready to do so. They become unhappy with his behavior when he reverts to simple, unstructured play. But criticism and insistence on mature behavior just when the child feels most threatened merely aggravate his sense of defeat. We ought to recognize that a child may be forced by as-yet-uncontrollable pressures to disregard, or even to pervert, the rules of the game in an instant, and that if he does so, he does it for compelling reasons.

Again we must remember that for a child, a game is not "just a game" that he plays for the fun of it, or a distraction from more serious matters. For him, playing a game can be, and more often than not is, a serious undertaking: on its outcome rest his feelings of self-esteem and competence. To put it in adult terms, playing a game is a child's true reality; this takes it far beyond the boundaries of its meaning for adults. Losing is not just a part of playing the game, as it is for adults (at least most of the time), but something that puts the child's sense of his own competence in question and often undermines it.

What makes it all so confusing is that now and then the child is easily able to finish a game even though he is aware that he is losing. So if he can accept defeat sometimes, why not always? Because he could act mature yesterday, adults expect him to do so today, and they try to hold him to this maturity or are critical if he does not. What they overlook is that they themselves act similarly in real life. They are able to accept defeat with relative equanimity when they feel secure in other important respects; at other times defeat temporarily disintegrates them, makes them depressed and unable to function. Since game-playing is for the child a real-life experience, he behaves accordingly: when feeling relatively strong and secure, he can accept defeat in a game without falling apart, but when insecure, he cannot. Because a child's inability to accept defeat in a game is a sign that at that moment he is quite insecure, it becomes even more important that we do not add to this feeling by criticizing him.

Some children—and most children at some stages in their lives—simply cannot afford to lose. So they correct their fortune in order to win—wanting to move a checker more spaces than they are entitled to, for example, or asking for an extra turn (as opposed to making a move while an opponent is out of the room). It is then wrong to hold them to the rules of the game, because they may give up playing altogether and become utterly dejected, deeply disappointed in themselves. If, instead of objecting to their insisting on changing the rules, we silently accept it and in this way make it possible for them to win, they will enjoy the game and continue playing it. As a child continues to play—and to cheat in this way—he slowly becomes more experienced in playing the game and needs to cheat less often, and less outrageously. This is why it is especially important for parents to play games with their child, because others are not so ready to let him change the rules at will without at least remarking on it. But improving his chances of winning may be necessary if the child is to play often enough to become sufficiently expert to win playing by the rules. Winning makes him more and more secure about his ability to hold his own in the game, and soon he will give up changing the rules altogether, although he will by no means win every time. The ability to win fair and square will provide him with enough security in playing the game that an occasional loss will no longer be experienced as such a severe defeat that he must avoid the game altogether. And the parent's pleasure in playing will increase with the child's.

QUESTIONS FOR CRITICAL READERS

Remembering and Understanding

1. Explain the distinction that Bettelheim makes between play and games.
2. According to Bettelheim, how do children learn to understand, accept, and follow rules?
3. Bettelheim believes that games will teach children important skills and values. What does he believe children will learn, and what evidence does he provide to support his belief?

Analyzing and Discussing

4. Bettelheim says children eventually learn that rules in games are voluntarily agreed to and have no other validity. Describe an occasion on which you and others negotiated rules or changes to rules, and describe how those negotiations proceeded.
5. Bettelheim says that when children become frustrated they attempt to change the rules of games. Recall a time when you were involved in such an attempt (or perhaps did it yourself) and describe what happened.
6. How does Bettelheim's professional position as a psychotherapist influence the ways he understands and describes toys, games, and play?

Writing

7. What have games contributed to your socialization as an adult? Identify
   several ways in which learning to observe the rules and procedures of games
   has helped you learn adult behaviors or affected the way you acted in a
   social situation. Write a paper in which you describe the games and explain
   how and what you learned from them.

The Mad Hatter Kingdom of Toys

—————— BRIAN SUTTON-SMITH ——————

Sutton-Smith, an anthropologist, is a professor in the graduate school of education at the University of Pennsylvania. He is interested in whether toys have any effects at all on those who use them, and if so whether those effects might be positive or negative. He also sees toys as a source of information about individuals and cultures. He is interested in what toys say about the culture that uses them, and what a culture expresses through its concerns about toys. This selection is the first chapter of his book Toys as Culture *(New York: Gardner Press, 1986).*

MY FIRST PUBLIC EXPERIENCE with toys occurred on a television guest trip. I was doing a circuit as a television co-author of a book my wife, Shirley Sutton-Smith, and I had written called *How to Play with Your Children (and When Not To)*. This was the early seventies, and we were enthused about the discoveries of a number of psychologists, which seemed to show that being playful and being creative were connected. So we wrote the book to advocate that parents should pay more attention to young children's play and also spend more time playing with them. However, most readers seemed to like most the "when not to" piece. It was apparently a relief to be told not to interfere too much with the children's ability to develop independently through their own play.

Up until this time I had not had any special experience with toys, except what a parent of five children nowadays inevitably gets. My own childhood was in the Depression years, so my personal experience with toys, although not absent, was hardly relevant to the modern era of toy supermarkets and billion-dollar industries. I had, however, been studying children's play and children's games for some 20 years and written a number of books about them. So I was intrigued by the problem of how toys fitted into all of this. They were supposed to be connected with children's play in one way or another, but there was very little written about toys that demonstrated anything that would convince a skeptic.

71

The origin of this book, then, was my search for an answer to the question of what difference toys made to children.

Although it is possible that they make very little difference at all, we know that some 800 companies sell about 150,000 different kinds of toy products (with about 4,000 new items every year), involving about 250,000 tons of plastics, 200,000 tons of metal at 150,000 retail outlets, and employ about 60,000 people. This means that toys make a big difference to these workers, economically at least. It is true that the most cynical speculators about toys suppose them to do nothing but provide exercises for children in becoming expert mobile consumers. "We are training little children," such a person might say, "to be excited by novel childish things, which, after a brief period of exploration, they can discard. Like their parents with furniture, or clothing, or household gadgets, or automobiles, children are learning how to consume, how to enjoy objects momentarily or at some length and then to throw them away or give them to the Salvation Army and get a tax deduction. People who learn these habits know also that they must work hard to make money in order to be able to throw away the gadgets they buy. This cycle of consumption and planned obsolescence is good for business, good for the government. It indicates a new kind of human nature." In this view, toys play an essential role: they are the possessions with which children can learn the materialistic culture habits of late-twentieth-century, American civilization.

Meanwhile, on the media circuit, I was finding that radio and television interviewers and the listeners and viewers who called in to ask questions were often passionate believers in the effects of toys on children. Most of them made it sound as if toys were vitally important to the future of the human race. Very strong opinions were voiced on whether or not sex-role stereotyping in toys had an effect on how boys and girls developed; on whether toy guns were good or bad for children; on whether there should be dolls or toys which showed the whole body as it actually is, with sex organs and all; on whether toys were ever of any educational value; on whether they were dangerous; on whether they stifled the imagination; and on whether advertising manipulated parents by putting pressure on children. It seems to have been television advertising, in particular, that had forced these issues to surface and, as a result, generated consumer groups concerned with protecting children from new and alien forces in modern society.

These, then, were some of the questions raised, and, although the answers to them were often wildly different, everyone seemed to assume that toys were having a powerful effect. But I often came away from these sessions, wishing I could summon a psychiatrist and give him some of the phone numbers of the callers or even the address of the television-station announcer. I remember one such TV gentleman, who had in his head the single notion that toys were dangerous. It was his *one* idea. No matter what I said about play or about toys, he kept returning to the theme: "But they are dangerous, aren't they?" In front of us at the time we had some soft dolls, some wooden blocks and a small plastic train set on plastic tracks. I agreed with him several times that toys could be dangerous on occasion. For example, the most dangerous toy of all is the bicycle. I broke my two front teeth falling off mine at the age of eleven years. I was racing down the street with my next door neighbor, and our bikes clashed together in such a way as to pitch me over the handlebars onto my face. Anyway, my announcer persisted, and I looked helplessly at the relatively inoffensive blocks, plastic train and soft dolls in front of me. Finally, in some exasperation, I admitted, "Well, I suppose if I take this plastic train set and hit you hard enough over the head with it, I might hurt you a bit." That finished his line of questioning.

What I am getting at is, that it's a mad-hatter world out there. There's a great deal of public involvement with toys and many opinions expressed in a vehement way, although there is often no hard evidence about any of it. I was riding home from work one day and I heard a conversation on the radio about the *Cabbage Patch Dolls*. (These are the famous line of soft and homely dolls mass-marketed by Coleco in the Christmas season of 1983, all of which were sold with adoption papers and with the prospect of continuing birthday cards. All were supposedly different in some small detail from each other. The line of dolls developed from an expensive hand-made line sold in the same fashion and, because of shortages, created incredible consumer eagerness.) The conversation went something like this:

> *First speaker:* "I think these dolls are an insult to everyone in the adoption profession. Adoption is a matter of heartbreak for the natural parents in having to give away their child. It is a contract full of pain and unhappiness. And these dolls trivialize the whole matter and treat it as some kind of fun for children. The dolls themselves are ugly, suggesting that children who are put up for adoption are ugly. I don't think it is right that children should be introduced to adoption issues in this way."
>
> *Second speaker:* "On the contrary, I think for the first time the idea of adoption has become something more universally understood. The fact that the dolls look ordinary is good, because most people are ordinary, and children should not expect anything special of adoption either."

About the only way to comment on this kind of dialogue is to offer another which might go something like this:

> *First speaker:* "I don't believe children should be allowed to play with toy motor cars. These are such small objects and nothing like

the real ones. Children will get a totally wrong idea of the size, dimensions and danger of real motor cars from playing with these miniature ones. It seems probable that many children will be run over because they will think that real motor cars are as harmless as the ones they play with."

Second speaker: "On the contrary, play with such motor cars introduces children to the principles of motor control, to the directionality of right and left, and to the rules of the road. They are a buffered form of learning, where one can participate in some of the functions of the automobile world without any of its dangers."

Or consider this imaginary dialogue:

First speaker: "I don't believe children should be allowed to play with dolls, because they often put them under water in the bath and drag them around on the floor behind them, thus not learning a proper respect for life and predisposing them to dangerous forms of behavior, which they might carry over into motherhood."

Second speaker: "I think by looking after the dolls, by feeding and washing and clothing them, they are introduced to the principles of mother care."

Now, all of these speakers seem to believe that playing with a toy has a direct relationship to real-life behavior. The First Speaker in each dialog seems to believe that the relationship is a literal one. What you do to the toy or learn from the toy is what you will do in real behavior. The Second Speaker in each dialog seems to be working at some other level, suggesting that children are not so much learning specific behaviors as principles of behaving. That is, the first, in each instance, sees the child as a dumb willing Hans who will automatically carry over behavior from the world of toys to the world of everyday life. The second sees children as sophisticated enough to ignore what doesn't fit everyday life, but nevertheless to apply the positive principles of socialization learned in play to everyday reality. Neither First Speaker nor Second Speaker explains how any of this happens, only asserts that it does. One may ask, for example, whether a child who plays with a toy gun is stupid enough to assume, when s/he gets a real gun, that, if used in the same way, no one will get killed. Or one may ask, alternatively, are children really intelligent enough to learn that toy guns don't kill but real ones do? Whether you take the dumb view of children or the bright view, in both cases toys are assumed to have profound effects.

And there appear to be valid positions on both sides. "We have case after case of children being shot by other children or by other people with real guns they thought were toys," says Barbara Lautman, communications director of Handgun Control Incorporated. "A conservative estimate would be 100 children a year who are killed or seriously injured." This group supports a ban on the manufacture and sale of toy guns.

The National Coalition to Ban Handguns, however, does not have a formal position on toy guns. According to the Executive Director, Michael K. Beard: "There's simply no reliable research on the subject, and we're not willing to go out on a limb and say there's a relationship that we're able to prove. I played with guns as a kid, and I don't think there's a male on my staff that didn't. It would be ridiculous to make a statement."

On the other hand the International Playground Association has taken a position against War Toys (tanks, soldiers, action dolls, weapons)—not against children playing at war, only against adults aiding and abetting that play by providing the toys, as if implicitly supporting the activity. They argue that, after all, children are not given toys to help them become thiefs, or drug addicts, or pimps, and they should not, therefore, be given toys, which, at the very least, sanction the notion that war at some level (even the toy level) is acceptable.

Others, on the contrary, take for granted that little boys have always played at war, and will always continue to do so as long as we live in a world where there has been a war almost every year somewhere on this globe for the past 2,000 years. Playing war is playing patriotism, playing John Wayne, playing Darth Vader, they say.

There is, however, no end to these "voices" about toys. Consider advertising aimed at children. A 1978 report by the Federal Trade Commission staff argued that the $600 million spent annually by advertisers on children's TV programs deceive children who are too unsophisticated to understand the messages or to judge the products. A Boston group called Action for Children's Television, which represents a coalition of various health and consumer organizations, had urged the FTC to set guidelines limiting advertising on children's programs. The 1978 report by the FTC staff said that the "possibility of unfairness or deception in children's advertising was sufficiently great to justify a rule-making procedure to explore the issue further." Some of the proposed alternatives were to ban all advertising directed at children under the age of eight years, to ban only advertising for highly sugared cereal foods directed to children under 12 years and to require substantial warnings for products containing substantial amounts of sugar. It was said also that young children do not have the ability to discern whether the toys as advertised are the toys they get.

But as the hearings dragged on, it became clear once more that, as far as toys were concerned, there was again little reliable evidence that young children could or could not make discriminations in such a way that would inevitably do them harm. There were those who argued that indeed the evidence showed that, certainly by ten or eleven years, most children become very cynical about television advertising, and thus are by then well prepared to be skeptical consumers in the marketplace. Of course, when the tremendous pressure brought by the industries that had the most to lose by such a ban was brought to bear on Congress and ultimately on the Federal Trade Commission itself (and with Ronald Reagan in the White House), it was announced on September 30, 1981, that the FTC had dropped its attempt to set up rule-making procedures about whether advertising to children was unfair or deceptive. The commission said, "It could not justify sacrificing other important priorities in continuing its inquiry." And as Fred Furth, a lawyer for Kellogg, said: "Those consumer groups wanted the commission to become a national nanny who would decide what could be advertised on children's programs."

But if the matters at stake here—how dangerous toys are, whether children's war-play should be promoted through war toys, and whether advertisers should have free access to children—are of considerable importance, many other issues of perhaps less moment have also angered the public. One continuing controversy has concerned the worth of various novel kinds of dolls: glamor dolls, action dolls, and anatomically correct dolls. As one parent said in an interview: "I can stand anything but I can't stand those dolls that crap." And on one of my television interviews someone on the phone raved about the "filth that comes out of the bottom of 'Baby Alive'." For others, it was the sheer horror of having their fingers in the mouth of a baby doll that could suck. For writer Rose Goldsen, it was the promised anatomy that was not realized.

> Yet, even a cursory inspection of the dolls promoted as 'anatomically correct' reveals that the term promises more than it delivers. The little boys have penis and scrotum, to be sure, but there's not a single navel among the lot, not an anus, nor are their nipples pigmented. These dolls have no tongue, no gums, not a tooth or suggestion of a tooth; their painted lips rim a gaping hole. Ears are molded in a piece with the head, eyebrows are painted on. Eyelids, eyelashes, they have none. No anatomically correct nostrils. Their arms and legs are not articulated. Fingers are not jointed nor are toes. Poor Li'l Ruthie's vagina lacks what might be called labial flexibility."

Asked one of my interviewers, "If children get to play with dolls like this when they are infants, won't they want to be playing 'doctors' earlier than they should? And why put genitals on Baby Joey, in any case? Isn't it better to leave something to the imagination?"

The all-time anathema for many professional women, however, as well as the all-time best-selling doll in the modern era and the basic reason for the success of Mattel Toys is the doll *Barbie* with her various cohorts, her male companion Ken and her hundreds of dress and leisure accessories. Even after the era of women's liberation she is often perceived as a symbol of empty glamor. There is also the objection, again, to having a doll with—in part—realistic sex anatomy, this time breasts, although the realism is perceived as partial. Rose Goldsen writes: "They [the breasts] make no pretense of being anatomically correct, of course; no nipples, no pigmentation, no network of veins. Those breasts are strictly to drape clothes around, to suggest fantasies having to do with self-decoration. They have nothing to do with fantasies about providing milk for infants, nothing to do with succorance and nurturance of babies . . . "

Some years ago a new version of Barbie was created, called Growing up Skipper, who could be made to grow up from a flat-chested child to a bosomed teenager by rotating the left arm. A writer in *Ms.* magazine wrote: "The mind reels at the possibilities for 'creative' play—eight-year-old girls trying to grow their own (breasts) and thereby twisting one another's arms into a mass of torn ligaments, small boys staging neighborhood porno exhibits. . . . One wonders whether men would tolerate a comparable male toy. Can't you see it: Growing up Buster—twist his leg, his penis grows and his testicles descend."

The boy action-dolls (G.I. Joe, etc.) also come in for their share of criticism. Janet Weaver, Director of the National Child Research Center in Washington, says, "They suggest to children that all problems can be solved with action . . . There are no steps to reach a solution, just 'pow' and there's your answer." She was also concerned that grown-up dolls encourage children to "rush out of childhood, finding boyfriends and girlfriends at the age of six." Even Margaret Mead felt cause to be concerned that real-life dolls might affect children very differently from fictional dolls. "It's fine," she says, "for children to play with Sesame Street dolls, Winnie the Pooh bears or miniature Waltons who are three dimensional extensions of favorite stories or programs. But if we give children a doll of the President's wife we really don't know enough about what we are doing."

Her statement is true of all the quotations and dialogues of the preceding pages. No one knows enough about what they are either saying or doing. Those who are making millions of dollars out of toys put their money into making toys that will sell better, not into finding out through research what toys do or do not do to or for children. This does not mean that many of their toys are not well made, nor that there hasn't been industry-wide concern about such matters as improving toy safety. But on the other hand, social scientists have not paid much research attention to toys either. In their hundreds of thousands of research studies over the past fifty years on children, they have devoted very few to toys as such. Educators, for their part, are typically involved with controlling or getting rid of play rather than understanding it. There are some important exceptions to this generalization, however, as the concept of the "play way" in education implies. Despite the fact that the most important thing to young children is their play, and that a great deal of that has to do with playing with toys, there is nevertheless little study of the matter. *Play continues to be the most neglected and has now become the most exploited arena of child life:* neglected by those who appoint themselves scientists of childhood or educators of children, and exploited by companies who make toys and build playgrounds for children. The question for this book is how one might begin to think seriously and systematically about the subject matter of toys. How might one develop a social science of toys, seeing none as yet exists?

QUESTIONS FOR CRITICAL READERS

Remembering and Understanding

1. Identify Sutton-Smith's central point, and use your restatement of that point as the beginning of a summary of his discussion of toys.
2. What does Sutton-Smith mean by the reference to a "mad hatter kingdom" in his title?
3. How does Sutton-Smith establish his authority to write about toys, and how does he disclose his qualifications to his readers?

Analyzing and Discussing

4. Sutton-Smith says that the question is "how one might begin to think seriously and systematically about the subject matter of toys." How would you begin such a project or investigation? What information would you gather? What questions would you ask?
5. One writer has disclosed that, in the 1970s, Sutton-Smith was a consultant to toy manufacturers. How does this information affect your assessment of his conclusions?
6. Select two or three toys and speculate about either what they say about their culture, or what effects they might have on the children who use them.

Writing

7. Select a specific toy that you have owned, perhaps one that you remember as a particular favorite. Write a paper in which you describe the toy and how you played with it, and discuss whether playing with it had any effect on you, and what that effect was.

Where Toys Come From
The Influence of Television

DAVID OWEN

This selection is an excerpt from Owen's article "Where Toys Come From,"
which first appeared in the Atlantic Monthly, *where he is a contributing*
editor. Owen's focus here is on toy manufacturers and the way they develop
and market new toys. He is especially concerned with the role of television
in the development and promotion of toys.

BERNARD LOOMIS WAS BORN in the Bronx in 1923. His father was
a Russian immigrant who dabbled in show business and generally failed
to make a living as an itinerant salesman of woolen goods. "Ours was a
family whose economics were always confused," Loomis says. There was
no money for toys; among young Bernard's few playthings were a Lionel
train catalogue, which he knew backward and forward, and a vivid imagination. One year he played a full American League baseball season using
a deck of cards. He had developed an elaborate system in which every
card he turned over meant something specific: a ball, a strike, a double,
a pop fly. In fat notebooks he kept track not only of scores but also of
pitching records and batting averages. By the time the World Series rolled
around, he had played every game in the schedule.

Loomis attended New York University at night and held down a
succession of dead-end jobs. "I fooled around in a lot of things in some
kind of search that even I didn't understand," he says. By the late 1950s
he was working in New York as a toy manufacturer's representative,
having lately retired from the hardware business. At the 1961 Toy Fair
he met Ruth and Elliot Handler, of Mattel (who had bought out Harold
Matson and now ran the company together). He liked the Handlers and
their colleagues immediately, and accepted the offer of a job.

Mattel was a small company at the time, but it was on the verge of
becoming the driving force in the industry. "Much of what the toy business
is today started with Mattel in the late 1950s," Loomis says. "That was

when the industry changed from being a customer-driven business where the customer decided what he wanted, to being a consumer-communication business."

In a word, television. The first step had come in 1955, before Loomis arrived, when Mattel had bought half a million dollars' worth of commercial time on the new Mickey Mouse Club show. It was, according to lore, the first time that toys—beginning with an item called a Mouse Guitar—were advertised on national television. (The first to be advertised on local TV may have been Hasbro's Mr. Potato Head, which was pitched in California in 1952.)

Television expanded the market for new toys and made it possible for manufacturers to spend more money on new products. It also enabled retailers to cut their prices, since the increased customer traffic permitted narrower profit margins. The new way of life evolved further in 1960, with the introduction of Chatty Cathy, the world's first talking doll and a toy whose marketing strategy Loomis helped devise. Chatty Cathy could never have been produced in the days before television; the potential market would have been too small to justify the cost of developing the doll's talking mechanism. With television, the demand for Chatty Cathy was so great that some retailers began to sell it at less than cost in order to steer the crowds into the stores—a radical step in a business where merchandise had traditionally sold for double its wholesale price.

In 1969 Loomis and others at Mattel undertook what would eventually be seen as an epochal step in the marriage of toys and television. Mattel had introduced a line of miniature cars called Hot Wheels. Instead of simply advertising them on television, why not give them an entire show of their own? The thirty-minute *Hot Wheels* cartoon show joined ABC's Saturday-morning lineup. The show, developed in close collaboration with Mattel, featured cars from the Hot Wheels line.

The new show didn't catch the attention of children only. It was also noticed by Topper Corporation, a now defunct competitor of Mattel's. Topper complained to the Federal Communications Commission that *Hot Wheels* violated FCC regulations concerning the separation of programming and advertising. The FCC agreed, and asked stations to log part of the show as advertising time—a move that seemed to deter the formation of any similar alliances between broadcasters and toy companies.

Loomis and Mattel, it turned out, had merely been ten years ahead of their time. During the decade it took their time to catch up, Loomis left Mattel to become the president of the foundering Kenner Products, which was owned by a division of General Mills. Loomis turned the company around with a string of hit toys, including a licensed "action figure" (as most dolls for boys are known) based on the television series *Six Million Dollar Man.*

The Six Million Dollar Man doll was a big success, and Loomis began looking for other properties to license. One day in 1976 he noticed a brief item in the *Hollywood Reporter* about a movie that was being made. Loomis had never heard of the director, but he liked the title: *Star Wars.* "I circled the item and sent a copy to a man in our marketing group, and I said, 'Find out about this.' " A short time later he and Twentieth Century Fox Film Corporation signed an agreement giving Kenner exclusive rights to manufacture crafts, games, and toys based on the motion picture.

The agreement didn't cost much. Toys based on movies had seldom sold well, and outer space was thought to be a poisonous theme. But Loomis wasn't interested in the movie; all he cared about was the characters. "I contend that George Lucas is one of the world's great toy designers," he says today. Kenner's line wasn't scheduled to appear until roughly a year after *Star Wars* had been released. The characters, Loomis assumed, were strong enough to stand alone.

He never had a chance to find out if he was right. From the day it opened, *Star Wars* was a phenomenal success. Children were sitting through it a dozen, two dozen times. "We had a tiger by the tail," Loomis says today. Christmas was just around the corner, and Kenner wouldn't be able to ship toys until spring; the *Star Wars* line had been planned for the *following* Christmas. The toys were being manufactured overseas, and there was no way to speed up production. Could anything be done?

Loomis pondered the problem for a long time, and then had an idea: why not sell the toys before they existed? Kenner could print a certificate promising to deliver toys by a certain date and package it with a picture of the *Star Wars* characters. Parents would have something to put under the Christmas tree, and kids could at least hang the picture in their rooms until spring. Loomis presented the idea to his staff. They all thought he was crazy.

Loomis says that he was taken aback. "But I believed that one of my duties as head of a toy company was to lose at least a million dollars a year on things that didn't happen," he says. "So I went ahead." The promotion turned out to be a huge success. Children were happy to receive the pictures. When their toys finally arrived by mail, they took them to school and sent jealous friends rushing to toy stores. *Star Wars* eventually generated more than $750 million in toy sales.

Star Wars confirmed what the *Six Million Dollar Man* had first shown, which was that licensed characters could be the basis for very lucrative toys. But *Star Wars* also showed that the logistics of producing such toys could be complicated: there were many factors beyond the toy company's control. If only it were somehow possible to manage the package from beginning to end.

By 1978 Loomis had become the head of the General Mills Toy Group (which included Kenner and Parker Brothers). One day he met with representatives of American Greetings Corporation, a maker of greeting cards. American Greetings owned the licensing rights to a popular cartoon character called Ziggy and wondered whether Loomis might be interested in producing a Ziggy toy.

Loomis said no. Ziggy was already established in the marketplace, with greeting cards, a syndicated comic strip, and other tie-ins. Loomis wasn't interested in simply tagging along. "But I told them, sort of casually, 'If you ever have a project where you want a partner from day one, come back and see me again.' As it happened, the men had copies of the American Greetings line for the following year. Loomis flipped through the cards, and then stopped. There was a character on one greeting card that looked promising. Loomis pointed to the picture and said, "Mark the time and date. We're going to make history."

Actually, there are several versions of this story. In another one, Jack Chojnacki, who was the director of licensing for American Greetings, discovered that an element common to a lot of successful greeting cards and other products was strawberries. An art director heard this and remembered that one of American Greeting's most successful cards featured a little girl with strawberries on her bonnet. He had an artist add more strawberries. Then a doll was made. Chojnacki and Ralph Shaffer, the director of new-product development, took the card and the doll to Loomis, who looked at them and said, "This is going to be the next major phenomenon in merchandising."

All versions of the story have the same ending: the little girl in the greeting card became a bustling industry called Strawberry Shortcake. What was remarkable was not the character—just a little girl with berries on her clothes—but the marketing plan built around it. Loomis had been thinking about the uncertainties of the toy business and had decided that the way to protect against them was to concentrate on lines of toys rather than on individual products. An important reason that Barbie was successful year after year, he believed, was that Mattel had made the doll part of an imaginary environment that, with careful management, could be extended indefinitely. The key was giving the customer a reason to keep buying.

What Loomis had discovered was, in a sense, the 10 Lego Characteristics. Like GKC, he believed that the secret of producing a successful toy lay in finding a concept broad enough for more than one season. Such concepts tend to be simple: plastic building blocks, a dress-up doll, stick-on faces for vegetables. Of course, Lego, Barbie, and Mr. Potato Head (now thirty-five years old) were created through inspiration and luck, not the application of a formula. But the formula could be a useful guide in the development and marketing of humbler toys. Every toy a company produced, Loomis believed, could be a line; indeed, it should be.

For Strawberry Shortcake, Loomis, Shaffer, and Chojnacki envisioned just such a line, with lots of characters and a story tying them together. (Strawberry Shortcake's friends have names like Lime Chiffon and Raspberry Tart; they live in Strawberryland and join together to combat a limited form of evil that manifests itself in things like disappointing fruit crops.) Loomis also wanted to involve the entire Toy Group. The girl on the greeting card would be translated into toys, games, television shows, and hundreds of licensed products, and everything would be created from scratch and centrally controlled. Loomis's idea about the importance of lines would quickly become the conventional wisdom of the industry.

The first Strawberry Shortcake television special, which aired in 1980, revived a controversy that many believed had been laid to rest. *Welcome to the World of Strawberry Shortcake* was as much a program-length commercial as the old *Hot Wheels* had been. But the regulatory mood in Washington had changed, and the Strawberry Shortcake special opened the way for what sometimes appears to be the transformation of children's television into a promotional arm of the toy industry.

There are now about twenty toy-based television series. A recent Saturday morning lineup included shows based on GoBots, Wuzzles, Snorks, M.A.S.K., Popples, and others. The shows are typically financed directly by toy companies or their licensing partners, who also control the scripts. Last year the FCC in effect gave its blessing to the new shows by refusing to hold hearings on product-based TV for children.

Shortly after the FCC decision Peggy Charren, the president of a consumer group called Action for Children's Television (ACT), told *Newsweek*, "We think the FCC has now completely disowned the nation's children." Charren, whose name is almost invariably preceded in print by adjectives like *indefatigable*, has been fighting broadcasters, breakfast-cereal manufacturers, toy companies, and others since the late 1960s. Her organization has been instrumental in bringing about a number of changes in children's television, including a reduction in the number of minutes devoted to advertising in programs aimed at kids.

ACT's main argument against the toy-based shows is that young children draw no distinction between commercial and editorial content and are thus easy targets for manipulative marketing. Toys based on popular movie and television characters have been around for years (for example, Mickey Mouse dolls); but in the past, ACT has said, the movies and programs always came first. Now the toys often precede the programs, whose scripts are conceived of as promotional tools. Furthermore, according to ACT, the toy-based shows have prevented better programming from reaching children.

ACT has proposed a number of remedies over the years, including the banning of toy advertising from children's television, and the banning of *all* advertising from children's television. More recently, as the prospects for new regulation have dimmed, ACT has retreated to a much tamer demand—that toy-based television shows be sprinkled with announcements reminding children that they are being pitched.

The toy companies more or less concede that their new programs are commercials; boastful sales pitches to retailers describe the shows in almost the same terms that Peggy Charren uses. When criticized, though, the toy companies also say that being on TV doesn't guarantee success for a toy; three of the most popular children's shows at the moment are the three segments of the ninety-minute cartoon series *Smurfs*, yet Smurfs toys don't sell well. Toy companies also say that toys are such a big part of the lives of children that there isn't all that much else to make shows about. Furthermore, they say, the question of which comes first, the toy or the show, is irrelevant.

There are many, many other arguments and counterarguments. The ones cited just sketch the general outline of the debate. In that debate right-thinking people tend to come down fairly quickly on the side of ACT: who can help but be appalled by all that crass commercialism? But the real issues are not as simple as Charren and her supporters make them out to be.

First of all, ACT's proposed reforms seem naive. Banning advertising from children's shows has a certain surface appeal, but the idea is unrealistic. Why not also require toy companies to give their products away? Removing all the money from children's television would not prompt producers to create better shows. ACT's proposal last January that toy-based shows be required to contain disclaimers identifying them as promotions seems counterproductive. If young viewers really can't distinguish between shows and commercials, then the toy companies could probably *increase* sales by reminding kids that the toys they're watching can also be bought.

Another possibility might be to prohibit toy companies from creating television programs. But how do you banish Strawberry Shortcake and Care Bears without also banishing Muppets? The Muppets' creator, Henson Associates, is on almost everyone's (including Peggy Charren's) list of top-quality producers, but the Muppets support a profitable stable of more than 500 licensed products, many of them toys. Henson even has its own New York toy store, called Muppet Stuff. Henson Associates, whatever else it is, is an extremely successful toy business, and Henson's shows, whatever else they are, are program-length commercials. Children's Television Workshop, home of the widely acclaimed series *Sesame Street*, earns back two thirds of the show's production costs from the licensing of toys and other products.

Nor is it possible to make meaningful distinctions according to whether the toys or the shows were thought of first. To young viewers, Mickey Mouse and Strawberry Shortcake are contemporaries. What's more, there's no pattern to the order in which toys and shows appear. Companies now often find it profitable to introduce toy-based shows well in advance of the toys on which they are based.

The real question has to do not with toy companies but with the quality of children's television, which is abysmal. Sitting through a full Saturday or Sunday morning of kidvid, as I dutifully did several times in the course of researching this article, is a pretty horrifying experience. "Speaking of Girza, it's time to move on to Bandasar and take care of Tormac," and so on and so on, hour after hour. Much of ACT's support, I suspect, comes from people who feel the same way: the kids' shows are horrible, so let's do something about the people who make them.

But program quality is a quicksand subject for people who, like Peggy Charren, believe in the First Amendment. ACT's January petition to the FCC, Charren has stressed, "does not seek to ban or impede the presentation" of the toy-based shows but merely to make explicit to young viewers the programs' commercial intent. ACT has also been quick to condemn various right-wing groups that periodically call for the elimination of television shows they find offensive. To confront directly what is genuinely bothersome about children's television—its mindlessness—is to come uncomfortably close to advocating censorship.

ACT addresses the quality issue only obliquely, by claiming that having to satisfy the requirements of toy manufacturers stifles the creativity of the producers and that children's programming would improve if the toy companies cleared out. In an article last year in *PTA Today*, ACT's director of development quoted a television producer as saying, "I would love to create shows rather than have someone come in and say, 'This is the golden ashtray everyone's buying; give me a show about it.'" Charren has said, "It's a shame we don't have diversity of producers for children's TV. Certainly they'd like to be there, but it's the money powers that are playing the ratings game who keep them out."

"Money powers" and "ratings game" are buzz phrases calculated to heat the blood of caring persons, but unless one rejects the idea of commercial TV, there's nothing sinister about the people they signify (respectively, advertisers and viewers). In fact, commercial television is one of the few truly democratic institutions around: viewers "vote" by watching, and the shows that don't get enough votes don't stay on the air. Charren has said that the networks could field better programs if they wanted to, because "broadcasters know what quality programming is." Good programs, she says, "are the ones they submit for awards." This is a specious argument. Book publishers must know what good books are (the ones they submit for awards); why don't they print more of them?

The solution to the kidvid problem—the real kidvid problem—is simple: if parents prevented their children from watching the shows, they wouldn't be on. Parents complain about the quality of the shows but don't prevent their children from gluing themselves to the boob tube. In the end, the garbage on TV is probably a fairly accurate representation of what the audience (parents included) really wants. There was a vast outpouring of public protest when CBS canceled *Captain Kangaroo*, in 1981, but the show's ratings had been microscopic for years. No one wanted to see it go, but no one wanted to see it, either.

The well-known discrepancy between what parents say and what they do arises in this case from a deep ambivalence about television. On the one hand, almost everyone at least pays lip service to the idea that watching a lot of TV is bad; on the other hand, television has become a sort of national babysitting service. According to the A.C. Nielsen Company's 1986 Report on Television, children between the ages of two and five watch an average of twenty-eight hours and fifteen minutes of television a week. Their most active viewing period is weekdays between ten in the morning and four-thirty in the afternoon. Busy parents (or the sitters they hire) are using television to keep their children quiet. This is a great tragedy. But the responsibility for it belongs to parents.

Most of the toy-based shows are crummy, but so are most of the other shows. *Scooby Doo,* a cartoon show created before the toy companies invaded Saturday morning, is not a better program than *Snorks. Sesame Street* is reflexively admired by almost everyone, but I suspect that adults would praise it less if they watched it more. *Sesame Street* may not be schlock, but kids often watch it the way they watch schlock: like zombies. Four hours of television a day is much too much, even if it's Bert and Ernie. ACT for years has paradoxically called upon the networks to provide *more* television shows aimed at children during *more* hours of the week. Kids might be better off if broadcasters got rid of children's shows and substituted the one kind of programming most kids can't stand: news.

To fail to be appalled by the connection between toy companies and children's television is not to endorse the shows. But it is possible to find a few nice things to say about them. First, toy-based programs at least encourage children to spend some of their waking hours away from the television set: a child who wheedles his parents into buying him a toy he's seen on TV will presumably play with it once in a while. Second, the new shows have a number of features missing from a lot of other shows—particularly widely admired cartoon "classics" such as *Popeye* and *Tom and Jerry:* for example, racial balance, uplifting sentiments, and, for the most part, a conspicuous lack of violence. Third, the substantial cost of creating television shows has encouraged toy companies to favor products that are well thought out, well designed, and not likely to disappear overnight: fad toys don't earn back multimillion-dollar television investments. Fourth . . .

Well, three is pretty many.

STAYING POWER

If Bernard Loomis helped invent the strategy of concentrating on expandable lines of toys, Hasbro has come close to perfecting it. In an industry where violent, unruly expansion and contraction is the rule, Hasbro's rise to pre-eminence has been impressive. The company has lately become a darling of the nation's financial analysts and business magazines, which have praised it for unusually sound management.

Most observers give credit for Hasbro's success to the company's young chairman, Stephen Hassenfeld. Hassenfeld, forty-four, and his brother, Alan, thirty-seven, who is Hasbro's president, represent the family's third generation in the toy business. Unlike Charles Lazarus and Bernard Loomis, Stephen and his brother had lots and lots of toys when they were growing up. Their father, Merrill, was widely admired in the industry, and executives of other companies often showed their affection by showering the Hassenfeld boys with their toys. The head of the company that manufactured Lionel trains even added young Stephen's name to his list of salesmen, which meant that every time a new train or accessory came out, Stephen received a sample. Directing one of the world's most spectacular toy trains around his basement, he knew from a very early age what he wanted to do when he grew up.

Over the past ten years or so Stephen has gone far toward making Hasbro what all toy companies yearn to be: a rational enterprise. Selling toys has always been a fashion business. Companies have scored inebriating successes alongside sobering failures, all subject to the largely unpredictable whims of children. The goal, seldom achieved, has been to minimize the failures without killing off the creativity that produces successes.

Hasbro's strategy for growth without trauma has focused on diversification within the toy industry. It has done this partly by acquiring other companies (it bought the Milton Bradley Company and its Playskool subsidiary, in 1984, for $350 million) and partly by expanding steadily into new toy categories. The strategy is now nearly universal, or universally aspired to, in the industry. Tonka Corporation, formerly known only as an unflashy manufacturer of high-quality toy trucks, now offers a greatly expanded selection that includes GoBots, a Cabbage Patch-inspired line of stuffed dogs called Pound Puppies, and Rock Lords, transformable figures described on their cartoon show as "powerful living rocks." Tonka's expansion has been successful. As of last year the company was the sixth-largest toy manufacturer in the country.

Stephen Hassenfeld's first big hit was the 1982 reintroduction of G.I. Joe. Originally marketed, in 1964, as a Second World War-era infantryman, G.I. Joe was turned into a cadre of quasi-military "adventurers" in 1970. In succeeding years the line was expanded to include a figure with what Hasbro called a "Kung-Fu grip," a bionic warrior, a superhuman, and a spaceman. The line was discontinued altogether in 1978, when it was done in by a combination of high oil prices—which made its large plastic body and accessories expensive to manufacture—and a proliferation of smaller, less expensive action figures. When G.I. Joe resurfaced four years later, the line had shrunk (from just under a foot to just under four inches, a size made popular by *Star Wars* toys), changed its slogan (from "a fighting man from head to toe" to "a real American hero"), and multiplied itself into an anti-terrorist "strike force" consisting of sixteen separate characters (one of which was female and none of which was actually called G.I. Joe).

The redesigned toy did $49 million in business in 1982, and became the nation's best-selling toy in the second half of the year. Hassenfeld's first reaction to the toy's success was one of joy; his second was one of concern. Forty-nine million dollars represented 36 percent of Hasbro's revenue at the time, making the company dangerously vulnerable to a drop in the toy's popularity. Perhaps the most important lesson Hassenfeld had learned during his lifelong tutelage in the toy business was that profit often goeth before a fall. The mistake that other toy-makers had habitually made, he felt, was in believing that they were immune to the syndrome of booms going bust.

This is not to say that Hassenfeld abandoned his popular new toy. Quite the contrary. But he made plans for the future of the company which didn't depend on G.I. Joe's continued success. Profits from the toy's first year were reinvested in the company's future, primarily as part of the package that financed the Milton Bradley acquisition.

As it happens, G.I. Joe has shown no sign of weakness. The line brought in $86 million in 1983, $132 million in 1984, and $136 million in 1985. But at the same time Hasbro has grown so much that by last year $136 million represented just 11 percent of its total business. The toy's profitability had increased while simultaneously becoming less important.

As sound as it may seem from the sidelines of the toy business, Hassenfeld's healthy skepticism about the longevity of best-selling toys has sometimes not been in evidence in the management of other toy companies. The fastest-selling toy of all time, Coleco's line of Cabbage Patch Kids, surprised almost everyone by remaining a hit toy for three full years (and bringing Coleco more than $1.2 billion in sales from 1983 to 1985). But by the end of 1985 Cabbage Patch still accounted for an astonishing 74 percent of Coleco's business. Last spring analysts were predicting that Cabbage Patch sales for 1986 might decline by as much as 35 percent of what they had been in 1985. Since Coleco's 1986 catalogue is still weighted heavily toward Cabbage Patch, the company could be in serious trouble.

Coleco's hopes for 1986 and beyond may hinge on the performance of its latest excursion into the now crowded male-action-figure category, where it will compete with G.I. Joe, Masters of the Universe, and many, many others. Coleco's entry is a licensed line of toy soldiers based on the R-rated Rambo movies, in which Sylvester Stallone plays a vengeful Vietnam veteran. Coleco has toned down the movie character in the cartoon it has created (the cartoon Rambo doesn't kill anyone), but, like the movie, the cartoon and the toy line appeal to the nation's recent anxiety about terrorism.

Parents and others sometimes complain about the prevalence of lines, and the emphasis on repeated purchases, in the toy business today. Yet the modern way has much to recommend it. Nothing looks more forlorn to the person who bought it than a toy that is used a time or two and then forgotten. For a toy line to remain viable year after year, children have to continue playing with it. When line extensions predominate at the Toy Fair, it means the playroom is safe from revolution for another year. Nobody throws away Lego. The emphasis on lines can help keep prices down, by giving manufacturers longer to earn back their investments. It also helps keep quality up. A line doesn't last simply because it's a line. Children go back for more only if the central concept appeals to them in some enduring way.

Enduring appeal is an idea that covers a lot of territory, of course. Whereas Cabbage Patch sales may slip considerably this year, Barbie may have her biggest year ever, after more than a quarter of a century on the shelf. Toy analysts wonder if her new competitor, Jem, will have anything like that staying power.

Hasbro executives discovered Jem, or rather ur-Jem, several years ago, when an independent toy designer showed them a male rock-star doll. The doll looked promising, and Hasbro took an option on the rights.

MTV, the rock-music television channel, had grown enormously popular. MTV is aimed primarily at teenagers and young adults, but Hasbro knew that a lot of younger kids were watching it as well. Rock videos had introduced little girls to a whole new way of thinking about fashion: eight-year-olds were asking their moms if they could dye their hair pink and cut holes in their sweatshirts and do a lot of other things that Barbie didn't do. It occurred to people at Hasbro that there might be a market for a fashion doll that looked less like Barbie and more like the people on MTV.

The Hasbro executive most responsible for keeping the project going was Maurene Souza, the vice-president of marketing for girls' toys. One of the first things that Souza did was work out a "back story" for the new doll. When my wife was growing up, she had a favorite doll she called Leprosy—the most beautiful-sounding word she had encountered up to that point. Nowadays dolls come not only with ready-made names but also with full-blown biographies. In time the optioned male rock star became Jem/Jerrica, "a woman with a mysterious dual identity," to quote from Hasbro's publicity:

> She's Jerrica Benton, a savvy Eighties career woman, co-owner of Star Light Music Company and benefactor of Starlight House, a shelter for homeless girls. But, with the magic of "Synergy," a super-holographic computer that filters power through her Jem Star earrings, Jerrica becomes Jem, a truly outrageous rock singing sensation.
>
> With the help of little sister Kimber and friends Aja and Shana, the four become "Jem and the Holograms," the hottest girl group since the Supremes. Exciting adventures unfold as Jerrica competes for control of Starlight [sic] Music against evil co-owner Eric Raymond, while Jem and the Holograms come up against the mischievous "bad-girl" rock band, "The Misfits."

There's also Rio, Jerrica's boyfriend, who, unlike Barbie's Ken, has a snappy wardrobe (the *Miami Vice* look) and combable hair.

"Changing from Jem to Jerrica gives the toy a great deal of depth," Souza says. "There are clothes for being Jem; there are clothes for being Jerrica. There are things Jerrica can do; there are things Jem can do. Barbie has really been locked into the mainstream American life-style. Jerrica is part of that too, although she's more a woman of the world. Jem becomes the fantasy. It gives us a lot of places to go with both of them." "Synergy" is Jem's key to longevity. If MTV goes out of style, the holographic computer can change Jerrica into something else: Jem, attorney-at-law.

To spread the word about Jem, Hasbro began including seven-minute Jem segments in its syndicated Sunday-morning cartoon show *Super Sunday*. The segments were so successful that Jem was spun off into her own regular series. Each show contains original songs presented in the form of "videos."

Mattel's response was immediate. Before the Toy Fair, and long before Jem's debut on *Super Sunday*, Hasbro had begun to run teaser ads of the "Jem—Coming Soon" variety in the trade press. Not long after the first ad appeared, Mattel introduced Barbie and the Rockers (featuring Dee Dee, Dana, Diva, and Derek) and prepared to slug it out. Hasbro had been expecting a rock band, but they hadn't been expecting Barbie to be a member. Truly outrageous! Mattel says that it thought of Barbie and the Rockers before it heard about Jem and the Holograms, but most people I talked to were skeptical. Mattel has always rejected the idea of a cartoon series for Barbie, whose principal strength is that she is Everygirl, but who knows?

Hasbro's hopes for Jem are fairly modest. "We want a piece," Souza says. "There's no way we're going to put Barbie out of business."

I can't make up my mind about Jem. She's a bit taller than Barbie (they can't wear each other's clothes), and she's significantly smaller in the bosom. Rio is more appealing than Ken, who has molded plastic hair and what looks like a thyroid problem. Jem has a radio in her Rockin' Roadster, but Barbie has a shower. Hmmmm.

Then again, it isn't up to me, is it?

QUESTIONS FOR CRITICAL READERS

Remembering and Understanding

1. What is Owen's central point about the relationship of television to the toy industry? Re-state it in your own words, and summarize the evidence Owen cites to support that point.
2. Summarize the arguments for and against television programs that are essentially commercials for toys.
3. Describe Owen's attitude toward the toy industry's use of television and cite statements from the article to support your description.

Analyzing and Discussing

4. Owen devotes considerable attention to product-based television shows for children. Can you envision a similar concept for adults? What would it be like?
5. What would be accomplished by banning advertising from children's television, or prohibiting programming based on toys?
6. Does advertising really affect what you buy? Do a survey of the foods you eat and the products you use. How many of them did you buy as a result of advertising? What other criteria did you use?

Writing

7. Spend a Saturday or Sunday morning watching children's television. Take notes as you watch, and write a paper in which you describe and evaluate either the programming or the advertising that you see, and make suggestions for changes.

The Desire to Learn

———— Margaret Donaldson ————

Donaldson, a child psychologist, teaches at the University of Edinburgh in Scotland. Her special interest is the study of children's language and thinking. In addition to her professional writing about children, she has also written a number of books of stories for children. In this chapter from her book Children's Minds *her subject is how children learn. She is interested not in how children learn specific facts or behaviors, but in the general processes of learning. How, for example, do children learn what the world around them is like and how it functions? Though Donaldson is not directly interested in toys and play, it is not difficult to apply her insights to the experiences children have at play.*

At a very early age, human babies show signs of a strong urge to master the environment. They are limited in what they can do by the slow development of their skill in controlling their own movements. Thus it is fair to call them "helpless" in the sense that they cannot manage the environment well enough to survive unaided. This makes it all the more interesting to discover that the urge to manage the environment is already there at this time of helplessness and that it does not appear to derive from anything else or to depend on any reward apart from the achieving of competence and control.

For some time past it has been widely accepted that babies—and other creatures—learn to do things because certain acts lead to "rewards"; and there is no reason to doubt that this is true. But it used also to be widely believed that effective rewards, at least in the early stages, had to be directly related to such basic physiological "drives" as thirst or hunger. In other words, a baby would learn if he got food or drink or some sort of physical comfort not otherwise.

It is now clear that this is not so. Babies will learn to behave in ways that produce results in the world with no reward except the successful outcome. For an example of work which shows this clearly we may turn to some studies carried out by Hanus Papoušek.

Papoušek began by using milk in the normal way to "reward" the babies he studied and so teach them to carry out some simple movements, such as turning the head to one side or the other. Then he noticed that an infant who had had enough to drink would refuse the milk but would still go on making the learned response with clear signs of pleasure. So he began to study the children's responses in situations where no milk was provided. He quickly found that children as young as four months would learn to turn their heads to right or left if the movement "switched on" a display of lights—and indeed that they were capable of learning quite complex sequences of head turns to bring about this result. For instance, they could learn to make alternating turns to left and right; or to make double alternating turns (two left, two right); or to make as many as three consecutive turns to one side.

Papoušek's light display was placed directly in front of the infants and he made the interesting observation that sometimes they would not turn back to watch the lights closely although they would "smile and bubble" when the display came on. Papoušek concluded that it was not primarily the sight of the lights which pleased them, it was the success they were achieving in solving the problem, in mastering the skill. If he is right in this—and there is a considerable amount of other confirming evidence—then we may conclude that there exists a fundamental human urge to make sense of the world and bring it under deliberate control.

Papoušek argues further that what his babies are doing as they try to achieve this control is matching incoming information about the world against some sort of inner "standard." And this amounts to saying that they are already engaged in building some kind of "model" of bits of the world—some mental representation of what it is like. They then experience satisfaction when the fit between the model and the world is good, dissatisfaction when it is bad—that is, when the expected result fails to occur, when the lights do not go on. Papoušek reports "increased tension and finally upsetness and signs of displeasure" in the latter case.

Now on even the simplest notion of what is involved in adaptation, it can come as no surprise that dissatisfaction arises when prediction fails. As soon as a species abandons reliance on instinctual patterns of behavior and begins to rely instead on building inner representations and making predictions then it becomes critical for survival to get the predictions right. Thus the realization of incongruity between our notion of the world and what it turns out to be like should naturally lead us to want to understand it better. And many different theories about the growth of intelligent thought stress that this kind of cognitive conflict is unacceptable to us, that it is something we try to get rid of. After the early stages, the conflict may be between different parts of our world model. If we come to face the fact that we hold two inconsistent beliefs we find this uncomfortable. And so we should. For it is axiomatic that the different parts of a model must fit together.

This argument obviously harks back to what was said in the last chapter about the educational value of becoming aware of error. But there are two further considerations which now need to be added. Firstly, it is not only when incongruities are forced on us by events that we try to resolve them. Sometimes we positively seek them out, as if we liked having to deal with things that we do not understand, things that challenge us intellectually. But secondly we may, on the contrary, become afraid of meeting incongruity, afraid of realizing that we are wrong, and we may then take steps to defend ourselves against this recognition by avoiding situations that are likely to give rise to it. We may withdraw.

These are sharply contrasted responses and the difference between them is of crucial educational importance. Education should aim to encourage the readiness to come to grips with incongruity and even to seek it out in a positive fashion, enjoying challenge. Equally, it should aim to discourage defense and withdrawal. But often it seems in effect to do exactly the opposite. The reasons for this cannot become clear without consideration of another topic: the development of the self-image.

We are beings who ask questions; we are beings who make value judgments, holding some things good and important, others bad or worthless; and we are beings who build models of the world. In the course of time, these models come to include some representation of ourselves as part of the world. It is thus inevitable that we should arrive at the question: of what value am I? And it is also inevitable that the answer should matter to us a great deal.

When a child first asks this question, how is he to get the answer? One obvious way will be to try to discover what value other people place upon him. With increasing maturity, when he has perhaps managed to develop a more independent value system of his own, the judgments of others may come to matter less. But while he is still a young child they are bound to exert powerful influence on his self-esteem.

I have been arguing that there is a fundamental human urge to be effective, competent, and independent, to understand the world and to act with skill. I am reminded of a little girl of eighteen months, verbally somewhat precocious, who, when she was offered help with anything, was given to saying firmly: "Can man'ge." To this basic urge to "manage" there is added in our kind of culture very strong social approval of certain kinds of competence. It is arguable that in some ways we do *not* encourage competence—that we keep our children too dependent for too long, denying them the opportunity to exercise their very considerable capacity for initiative and responsible action. This is perhaps hard to avoid in a complex urban society with a highly developed technology. Yet within the educational system at least there is certainly strong social approval of competence in the more disembedded skills of the mind. So the child who succeeds in coping with these new challenges when he enters school will be highly valued by his teachers—and all too often the one who initially fails will not. In either case the child will quickly discover how he is judged to be doing. That he has often made up his mind about his cognitive competence even before he comes to school is emphasized by Marion Blank, who reports the occurrence of remarks like "I'm dumb," "I can't," "I'm stupid," and "I don't know how to do things" from certain kindergarten children faced by some cognitive demand.

There can be no doubt that if we decide we cannot cope with a particular kind of challenge we tend to give up and avoid it. Bruner draws a sharp distinction between "coping" and "defending" which he likens to the distinction between "playing tennis on the one hand and fighting like fury to stay off the tennis court altogether on the other." People do of course differ in the extent to which they persevere in the teeth of persistent failure. Robert the Bruce is said to have observed the tenacity of a spider and resolved to try again. But a spider has presumably no self-image to disturb it, and Robert the Bruce was a mature man who doubtless had a strong and resilient one.

Szasz has this to say on the subject:

> Definers (that is, persons who insist of defining others) are like pathogenic microorganisms: each invades, parasitizes, and often destroys his victim; and, in each case, those whose resistance is low are the most susceptible to attack. Hence, those whose immunological defenses are weak are most likely to contract infectious diseases; and those whose social defenses are weak—that is, the young and the old, the sick and the poor, and so forth—are most likely to contract invidious definitions of themselves.
>
> If the child is defined as a failure he will almost certainly fail, at any rate in the things which the definers value; and perhaps later he will hit out very hard against those who so defined him.

So we know at least something to avoid. But we must contrive to avoid it not merely at the surface of our behavior. If we do not genuinely respect and value the children, I am afraid they will come to know.

Yet important as it is to avoid infecting the children with "invidious definitions," it is not enough. More than this is called for. When it comes to self-esteem, not even a young child depends entirely for his judgments on the views of others. For he can often see quite well for himself how he is doing. Paquita McMichael, in an interesting study of the relation between early reading skills and the self-image, concluded that there was a good deal of objective truth in the children's assessments of their competence. "When they agreed that they were not able to do things as well as some other children they were admitting to a reality."

Thus a very important part of the job of a teacher—or of a parent in a teaching role—is to guide the child towards tasks where he will be able objectively to do well, but not too easily, not without putting forth some effort, not without difficulties to be mastered, errors to be overcome, creative solutions to be found. This means assessing his skills with sensitivity and accuracy, understanding the levels of his confidence and energy, and responding to his errors in helpful ways.

Most teachers would accept this, I daresay, but it is not at all easy to achieve in practice and there is no general formula for success. However, a valuable discussion of teaching episodes where just this kind of thing is being attempted is given in Marion Blank's book: *Teaching Learning in the Preschool*. She argues that it is essential to permit errors to occur but that the effectiveness of any teaching critically depends on how the wrong responses are then handled by the teacher. She makes many specific practical suggestions about this but she acknowledges that it is not possible at the moment to give rules for the exact application of her technique— it remains an art. Obviously much depends on the child's personality. Ways that work with a passive withdrawn child will not work with a hyperactive impulsive one. And if the child is functioning very poorly it is necessary to concentrate on helping him over his difficulties without too much delay.

It should be noted that Blank developed her techniques for use in a one-to-one teaching situation. She fully recognizes the difficulties of applying them with a group. It remains true that the kinds of teaching decision with which she is concerned are of pervasive importance and that there must surely be gain from any enhanced awareness of them.

The traditional way of encouraging children to want to learn the things that we want to teach is by giving rewards for success: prizes, privileges, gold stars. Two grave risks attend this practice. The first is obvious to common sense, the second much less so.

The obvious risk is to the children who do not get the stars, for this is just one way of defining them as failures. The other risk is to all of the children—"winners" and "losers" alike. There is now a substantial amount of evidence pointing to the conclusion that if an activity is rewarded by some extrinsic prize or token—something quite external to the activity itself—then that activity is less likely to be engaged in later in a free and voluntary manner when the rewards are absent, and it is less likely to be enjoyed.

This has now been demonstrated in numerous experiments with people of ages ranging from three or four years to adulthood.

One study, by M. R. Lepper and his colleagues, was carried out in a nursery school. Some of the children were given materials to draw with and were told that they would get a prize for drawing, which they duly did. Other children were given the same materials but with no prizes or talk of prizes. Some days afterwards all of the children were given the opportunity to use these same materials again in a situation where lots of other toys were also available to them. The question was: would the groups differ in the amount of time which they spent in drawing? One might have expected that those who had been rewarded would return more eagerly to the situation which had been "reinforced." But the opposite happened. The children who had been rewarded spent a smaller proportion of their time drawing.

If one takes as criterion not the time freely spent on an activity but the person's own statement of how much it has been enjoyed, the same sort of thing is found: extrinsic material reward tends to decrease enjoyment. Children (and adults) who have been given prizes for doing something tend to say that they like it less well than children who have been given none. And there is even some evidence to suggest that the quality of what is produced may decline.

These findings obviously lead on at once to a further question: if you tell a child he is doing well, are you also rewarding him and hence perhaps running the same sort of risk as if you give him a prize? For, after all, verbal approval is a kind of prize. And certainly, like a material object, it is extrinsic to the activity itself—something added on at the end.

The available evidence suggests that the effects of telling someone he has done well are not the same as those of giving him a prize. For instance, R. Anderson, S.T. Manoogian and J. S. Reznick carried out a study very similar to the one by Lepper and his colleagues (see above) except that there were two extra conditions, in one of which the children were praised for their drawings. The results from Lepper's study were confirmed: the giving of material rewards was related to a decrease in time spent on the activity later. But the giving of verbal encouragement had the opposite effect. And this is just as well. If it were not so, teachers would have to face a disconcerting dilemma. For the children must know how they are doing. As we have seen, they often have a shrewd idea of this themselves—and some tasks make it very evident. The young children who were given the task of balancing blocks on a narrow bar could see for themselves whether the blocks stayed in place or fell off. So they could develop theories, discover the inadequacies of these theories, and develop better theories, all without external reward of any kind. This is part of the justification for "discovery learning." But it is not equally possible in all kinds of learning to contrive situations where the child will see for himself the outcome of his efforts. Frequently he must be told. He must be told: "Good, you've got that right!" or: "No, that's wrong.* Try again."

---

*Notice that, if the child is told "That's good!" whether he has really done well or not, the informational value of the comment is destroyed. It is a subtle art to give genuine information and to encourage at the same time.

Such comments do more, of course, than merely give objective knowledge of results. They are unquestionably not neutral. But perhaps it is relevant to an understanding of the difference between words of praise and gold stars to draw a distinction between reward and recognition and to acknowledge how strong a need we have to communicate achievement to our fellow men and see it confirmed in their eyes. Thus Gerard Manley Hopkins, who considered that his vocation as a Jesuit was incompatible with the publication of his poetry in his lifetime, reveals in his letters— especially his letters to Robert Bridges—how hard this was for him: "There is a point with me in matters of any size when I must absolutely have encouragement as much as crops rain . . . " He goes on bravely, " . . . afterwards I am independent." But many of us do not reach this kind of independence ever. And young children are certainly unlikely to have done so.

The final condition which Anderson and her colleagues included in their study (see page 122) is relevant here. In this condition the experimenter began by declaring an interest in "how boys and girls draw pictures"—and thereafter firmly refused to manifest this interest in any way. A child might show a picture, trying, as the report of the study puts it, "to elicit some recognition or validation." But he got none. The experimenter ignored all such overtures, turning his face away and saying: "I've got work to do." It is not surprising to learn that the children who received this treatment showed the greatest drop of all in the time which they later spent in drawing.

This still leaves us with the question of why extrinsic material rewards tend to produce effects of damaging kinds. The explanation which fits the known facts most nearly would seem to be that we enjoy best and engage most readily in activities which we *experience as freely chosen*. We do not like being controlled, we like controlling ourselves. Insofar as reward is seen as a means of controlling our behavior, it tends to diminish our interest and our pleasure. Of course we may work hard to get the reward at the time and for so long as we expect more reward to be forthcoming, but we will be less likely to go on with the activity when the reward is withdrawn.

This is strikingly illustrated by the following story (quoted by E. L. Deci in his book *Intrinsic Motivation*).

In a little Southern town where the Klan was riding again, a Jewish tailor had the temerity to open his little shop on the main street. To drive him out of the town the Kleagle of the Klan set a gang of little ragamuffins to annoy him. Day after day they stood at the entrance of his shop. "Jew! Jew!" they hooted at him. The situation looked serious for the tailor. He took the matter so much to heart that he began to brood and spent sleepless nights over it. Finally out of desperation he evolved a plan.

The following day, when the little hoodlums came to jeer at him, he came to the door and said to them, "From today on any boy who calls me 'Jew' will get a dime from me." Then he put his hand in his pocket and gave each boy a dime.

Delighted with their booty, the boys came back the following day and began to shrill, "Jew! Jew!" The tailor came out smiling. He put his hand in his pocket and gave each of the boys a nickel, saying, "A dime is too much—I can only afford a nickel today." The boys went away satisfied because, after all, a nickel was money, too.

However, when they returned the next day to hoot at him, the tailor gave them only a penny each.

"Why do we only get a penny today?" they yelled.

"That's all I can afford."

"But two days ago you gave us a dime, and yesterday we got a nickel. It's not fair, mister."

"Take it or leave it. That's all you're going to get!"

"Do you think we're going to call you 'Jew' for one lousy penny?"

"So don't!"

And they didn't.

All of this leads to a central dilemma for those who want to teach the young. There is a compelling case for control. The young child is not capable of deciding for himself what he should learn: he is quite simply too ignorant. And he needs our help to sustain him through the actual process of learning. Whitehead puts it vividly: "After all the child is the heir to long ages of civilization and it is absurd to let him wander in the intellectual maze of men in the Glacial Epoch."

On the other hand, we should never forget the children who, having learned to shout "Jew" for a dime, would not then shout it when the payment came to an end. And there is clear evidence that if we try to exercise the control not by reward but by punishment the negative effects are even greater. If, when they leave us, our pupils turn away from what we have taught them, the teaching has surely been in vain.

Those who are most keenly aware of this latter danger tend to call themselves "progressive" and to advocate "freedom." Those who are most keenly aware of the former danger—the danger of leaving children to wander in the intellectual mazes of prehistory—are the advocates of "formal education" and of "discipline."

I can see only one way out of this dilemma: it is to exercise such control as is needful with a light touch and never to relish the need. It is possible after all for control to be more or less obtrusive, more or less paraded. Also a great deal will depend on what the teacher sees the aim of the control to be. If the ultimate aim of the control is to render itself unnecessary, if the teacher obviously wants the children to become competent, self-determining, responsible beings and believes them capable of it, then I am convinced that the risk of rejection of learning will be much diminished. We come back thus to the question of whether the teacher truly respects the children and lets them see it. If this condition is met, then the guidance of learning within a structured environment will not be seen as the action of a warder behind prison bars.

QUESTIONS FOR CRITICAL READERS

Remembering and Understanding

1. Re-state Donaldson's central point and summarize the evidence she cites to support that point.
2. Explain why Donaldson refers to and summarizes experiments by Papoušek. What does this information contribute to her own point?
3. According to Donaldson, what is the role of incongruity in learning?

Analyzing and Discussing

4. Donaldson says that learning results from the "realization of incongruity between our notion of the world and what it turns out to be like." Describe an occasion on which you experienced the kind of incongruity Donaldson refers to, and explain what you learned from it.
5. Donaldson writes about the need to base our behavior on accurate predictions of what the world is like. To what extent do toys, play, and games provide an accurate representation of the world?
6. What does Donaldson mean when she says that humans are beings who build models of the world?

Writing

7. Donaldson says that extrinsic rewards are not important to learning, and may in fact interfere with learning. Explore the role of reward in your own learning experiences. Describe rewards that you have received for specific learning or behavior, and then explain why you believe those rewards were or were not important.

Guns and Boyhood in America

JONATHAN HOLDEN

Holden is a poet. In this essay, which appeared originally in The Georgia Review *(1988), Holden explores his childhood fascination with guns and pyrotechnics, an interest that is often dismissed or deplored as "macho" and silly. Holden uses his own experiences with guns as a child and an adult to attempt to get beyond the usual clichés about guns.*

FOR ME, AS A BOY, certainly the most beautiful sound in the world, more beautiful than Mozart or Bach, was the sound of an explosion—the report of a firecracker or a rifle shot. I studied such sounds—their complicated, collapsing echoes—in the vain hope that I could capture them by somehow reproducing them, either with my own palate and saliva (Kkkkk!) when playing with Tommy Emory, Jimmy Connon, and the other neighborhood kids the open-ended game that we called "Guns," or by some kind of word, some verbal expletive like BANG. If I'd been allowed by my parents to own and shoot guns, or if such magical entities as firecrackers had been legal in New Jersey and therefore readily available, I probably wouldn't have dwelt upon such sounds in the almost prurient way that I did—and that, if my thirteen-year-old son and his pals are any indication, most American boys are doing still and have probably always done. But we were forbidden by state law (and, in my case, also by parental law) from indulging in the expediency of the literal, so we had to go to almost fantastic trouble to steal little voyeuristic peeks into those flash/bang mysteries which, on the radio and in comic books and movies, were so ubiquitous that shooting seemed part of the American landscape itself. It was the Colt .45 six-shooter, after all, that had "won" the West, had secured for us our ongoing daydream of boyhood, paradise—that ideal "territory," the frontier for which Huck Finn had once lit out. We sensed, all of us, that if one were born American and male, then mastery of such sounds, together with ownership and control of the machinery to make them, was our birthright.

I and the other boys on Pleasantville Road prepared regularly, systematically almost, to lay claim to this birthright. We prepared for it after school as well as on weekends and, of course, all summer, every afternoon. We prepared for it with the same unquestioning seriousness with which we made revving noises as we pushed toy dump trucks and bulldozers through the sand, the same, unquestioning fervency with which Pat Burke's four sisters played with dolls. We even practiced being wounded by gunshots the way they did it in the movies. I don't know whether or not little boys in Europe do this; but neither time that I've been there have I ever noticed kids playing "guns." Maybe, after two world wars, they've had enough. Maybe playing "guns" is no fun for them anymore. But as an American boy, playing in a countryside that has never been invaded, I reveled in the sanctimonious emotion—a kind of deep solemnity—that I felt when Tommy Emory or Pat Burke would make a gunshot noise and I decided to be wounded, and so would clutch my arm and, grunting, stagger back, doubling up finally to crumple to the ground. Sometimes I would emit low moans. When dying in make-believe, I felt profoundly righteous. I felt mature. I think I imagined being wounded as like being sick. Whenever I had to stay home from school with a headache or a sore throat, and my mother took my temperature and smoothed my brow and spoiled me, placing tall glasses of chocolate milk beside my bed, I became dramatically, incontestably important.

I had the biggest and the most variegated collection of cap pistols on Pleasantville Road. The more of them I bought, the more particular I got. A toy handgun had to pass two criteria. It had to resemble, physically, any of the countless pistols I had seen in movies or that I mooned over in the sporting-goods section of the Sears catalogue. And it had to produce audio or visual phenomena like those of a real gun. All of us boys squandered our allowances on rolls of caps as readily as, years later, we'd spend our money on beer. But caps were never loud enough to shock us the way we wanted to be shocked unless you placed a whole new roll on the flagstone by the back door and flattened it with a framing hammer. The most imaginative cap pistol I owned was a pretty good replica of a Colt .45. It was called a ".45 Smoker" and had a little door on one side. You'd open the door, pour flour or cornstarch in, shut it again. When the toy was thus loaded, the barrel would emit pale puffs of cornstarch dust when you fanned the hammer.

One day, for reasons I don't recall, I lit a candle and was fanning the hammer furiously, volleying puffs into the candle-flame, when to my astonishment there was a low "whoosh!" and a modest fireball rolled out. I repeated this experiment successfully enough times that it became predictable. The fireball was a measly one anyway, so I cut a two-foot length from a garden hose, poured some cornstarch into one end, held it up to the candle, and blew. My first try blew the candle out, but finally, through persistent trial and error, I produced some larger "whooshes." It's in the nature of pyrotechnic play that as the limit of each stage of development is reached, it gets familiar and thus boring. But the play is addictive, and a player is continuously, inexorably tempted toward trying to make a bigger bang—something that will truly surprise him, a bang big enough to sober him up once and for all.

My father was a chemist at the Bell Telephone labs in Murray Hill. To encourage my interest in science, my parents got me, one Christmas, a Gilbert Chemistry Set. Most of the experiments in the little manual looked boring, but one stood out: a recipe for gunpowder, the first and only chemical experiment that ever interested me. It called for the classic ingredients: potassium nitrate, sulfur, and powdered charcoal. I don't remember the proportions, but I do remember looking up "Gunpowder" in *The Encyclopaedia Britannica* and learning that many different proportions had been tried over hundreds of years, as if civilization itself had always been composed of bloodthirsty little boys scheming together, conducting experiments about how to make the biggest bang. The residents of ancient China had been every bit as absorbed in the problem as we were in A.D 1955 in New Jersey.

The encyclopedia entry on gunpowder was my first inkling that every single one of the destructive arts that so fascinated us as boys had equally fascinated ancient peoples. Such arts, when they didn't require any modern technology—I learned this later when studying karate—had been perfected thousands of years ago. Young men had thought up every possible method of dirty fighting (apparently it was one of the first things so-called civilized people worried about), and they refined these methods and the means of teaching them *en masse* to soldiers so efficiently that no more improvement, no further "progress" in the art, was possible.

As I stared at the pitifully small bottle of saltpeter provided me by the Gilbert Chemistry Set, almost my first thought was how to get more. Order another whole chemistry set to get one bottle? The problem of how to get saltpeter, though I didn't know it then, also had a history. As gunpowder became known (and, of course, popular) in Europe, old barns and old buildings—all places where bird-droppings had accumulated conspicuously—were scoured for the precious substance, just as landscapes are scoured for uranium today.

The gunpowder I made was a disappointment. It fizzled meekly. So, for a bang, I fell back on the staple I was used to, kitchen matches. I'd found that if I whanged Ohio Bluetips with a hammer on the backdoor flagstone, the matchhead might emit a little snap. Science is a collective enterprise. It had been discovered by us neighborhood boys that the pale-blue pimple at the tip of a kitchen match was the magic part, providing initial ignition which would spread down through the slower igniting navy-blue crust that jacketed the rest of the matchhead. On a kitchen cutting board, using my mother's best kitchen knife, we'd saw or chop the live tips off the matches, hundreds of them, boxes of them. We worked with the purposeful patience of adults, collecting the tips on a crisp sheet of typing paper that was creased by a single fold, along which I could jiggle them into an empty aspirin bottle. Then, because we'd been taught to be neat and always pick up after ourselves, we'd throw the useless sticks, like the stripped carcasses of so many tiny wooden chickens, in the garbage.

Not only would the matchtips snap when smashed; they flared with enough gusto that, perhaps, you could use them to fuel a rocket or to make your own cannon cracker. But these projects failed. The rockets I designed out of rolled typing paper were tilted heavenward inside a launcher of galvanized stovepipe and, when set off, strained to move, flaring with brief hope before the propellant fizzled and left the little paper husk like a stranded car burning peacefully. There were also formidable problems in our design of matchhead bombs, not unlike an engineering problem faced in World War I: how to synchronize the fire of a cockpit machine gun with the monoplane's propeller so that in a dogfight the pilot could shoot straight ahead without shooting his own propeller off. You had to have a fuse that would pass through the seal to the explosive without either destroying the seal or going out.

In his charming memoir, the Nobel Prize-winning physicist Richard Feynman describes the difference between science and superstition, proposing a concept that he calls "Cargo Cult Science":

> In the South Seas there is a cargo cult of people. During the war they saw airplanes land with lots of good materials, and they want to make the same thing happen now. So they've arranged to make things like runways, to put fires along the sides of the runways, to make a wooden hut for a man to sit in, with two wooden pieces on his head like headphones and bars of bamboo sticking out like antennas—he's the controller—and they wait for the airplanes to land. They're doing everything right. The form is perfect. It looks exactly the way it looked before. But it doesn't work. No airplanes land. . . ."★

Like the South Sea Islanders Feynman describes, we were ignorant of the principles that go into making a good fuse; but we knew what a fuse should look like. We'd seen them in the movies and occasionally first hand when we were lucky enough to handle the few real fireworks our buddies smuggled into New Jersey. Fuses looked a lot like string, so we tried string. But the string did not burn with a hiss. It didn't progress grimly toward its destination with the sparkling intensity of any of the

---

★*Surely You're Joking, Mr. Feynman* (New York: W. W. Norton, 1985), pp. 310–11.

Hollywood fuses we'd seen eating their way toward a powder keg. To be sure, they *looked* like fuses, like tails of demons snaking out of cylinders, coiling along the ground with ominous portent. But when we lit them, an inch or so of string would burn and the ash would break off, leaving the rest of the string dormant, inert—just a length of stupid household string.

My father mistook my experiments with gunpowder for an interest in science, and he made a dangerous mistake. To encourage me, he brought back from the labs a bottle of potassium nitrate (KNO_3), and when I *still* couldn't make lively enough gunpowder, he brought back a bottle of potassium chlorate ($KClO_3$). As he knew, $KClO_3$ was a much more efficient and faster oxidizing agent than KNO_3. Father, who was a good chemist and had developed a crystal used in SONAR antisubmarine detection in World War II, had the sense to warn me that, whereas grinding the three ingredients for gunpowder together with the back of a tablespoon was probably not too dangerous when using KNO_3, he wouldn't advise doing that with $KClO_3$. So I poured the powders together into a little cardboard box which, a Christmas before, had housed my first tie clip, taking care to pluck out the cotton lining and save it for bomb seals. Then I fit the lid back on, squeezed tight, and shook. The final mixture was an unnatural grayish green—the same color we see in the backdrop to the line-squall of a really ugly thunderstorm as it rolls up over the trees—and it proved to burn much faster than the old. But I still couldn't get it to go off by hitting it. Because of the fuse problem, I still couldn't make a bomb that would explode.

My determination was nowise diminished. Our neighbors, the Walters, had built a shooting range up in the woods. It was only a few hundred yards away, and sometimes on a Saturday or Sunday we could hear, for an hour or so, the tantalizing echo of a .22 tear again and again through those rickety woods. It was a mysterious sound, because it was many possible sounds at once: it was as if somebody had dropped an armload of dry shingles; it was as if some ghostly express train were racing through the trees at an impossible speed, going east and west at the same time. The thin, dry echoes bristled from different points at once. Now and then, when I heard the shooting start, I'd wander up the bridle path to the clearing where old Fred Walter and his son, Richard, had set up their range—a wall of railroad ties backed by dirt. I'd just stand there with the hangdog, solemn politeness of a little boy requesting candy, a boy embarrassed by the obviousness of his own greed but determined to cover it. I'd stand there whiffing the blue tang of the gunsmoke (the scent seemed as elusive and full of longing as the color blue itself, full of adult seriousness and withheld knowledge), and I'd muse upon the heft and texture and force of each shot, trying to gauge it, trying not so much to understand it as to get a sense of it, and loving almost as much as the stroke of each shot the complex clack of the rifle's bolt action ejecting a shell—loving, as I put it years later in a poem,

> that slick, exact way
> the steel sleeves of the breech
> unlock, retract, consolidate
> shut. . . .

The Walters left the shells in the dirt where they landed. I would collect them and take them home. I had found a use for them.

There was a way around the "fuse problem." You could fill the brass shell of a .22 long about half full of my improved potassium chlorate powder and pack the end with cotton. Then you could take a full double-page from the classified section of the Sunday *New York Times*, place the .22 shell on it, bunch the paper around it into a loose ball, place this ball out on the ash patch near the defunct corncrib where my family burned brush, and apply a match. A modest cage of flame would engulf the shell, heating it up until: Eureka!

One summer afternoon Mother was weeding the family garden about thirty feet southeast of my little proving ground, where I was conducting another test. As she bent to grip a weed, CRACK!—the bomb test succeeded, and something sang past her left ear. That afternoon marked the end of my supply of chemicals.

In an effort to grasp more fully the gunshot sounds I pined for, I studied and evaluated the words for these sounds in the hundreds of comic books I owned. I studied them as seriously as I studied and rehearsed Stan "The Man" Musial's coiled, stealthy batting stance. The basic formulas—BANG! CRACK! POW! BAM! BLAM! and RAT-A-TAT-TAT!—I thought to be wholly inadequate. They weren't especially accurate. They didn't capture the mysterious essence of a shot. They were clichés. I vowed that when I became a comic-book artist I would give serious attention to this matter. I would correct the problem.

Our neighbors the Remsens had visited Belgium, and the Remsen boys, Tony and Derek, brought back a Belgian comic-book version of The Red Rider. The text was in French, and the report of a rifle was denoted by the word "PAN!" Not knowing any French, I didn't know enough to nasalize the pronunciation, to omit the *n*-sound; but even had I known enough to do that, I would have found the resulting *"P-agh!"* inadequate. It did not capture the elusive beauty of echoes. (I was rehashing these issues recently with the poet Robert Pinsky, who proposed an enviable invention—one which, thirty years ago, I would have used dozens of times a day. He pointed out that POW! could be improved with an extra P hyphenated as a prefix: P-POW!— a sophisticated improvement on the KA-POW! of the Walters' .22 shots in the woods, shots far enough away that the echo reached you before the initial report. P-POW! put one right up at the shooting range again.)

In the early fifties there was one comic book that not only took seriously the sounds of specific gunshots but also took pains to represent weapons, uniforms, planes, and all other military equipment with documentary accuracy. This was *Two-Fisted Tales,* a war comic from a line of publications that, for aficionados, has become legendary: E.C. Comics, edited by William F. Gaines. *Two-Fisted Tales* presented mainly Korean War stories, but unlike other comics it wasn't propagandistic. It didn't present war as fantasy. It wasn't, like *G.I. JOE,* nostalgic. It was realistic in its presentation of war, and its tone was, if anything, ironic. *Two-Fisted Tales* depicted mortars that went PONG! and PONK! When the Red Chinese infantry assaulted American GI's in human waves, the Communist submachine guns, known as "burp guns" emitted a noise that I had never seen in a comic before, a nasty BRRRR-APPP!

As the Korean War ended, *Two-Fisted Tales* looked for new material and, needing a war, began depicting famous battles from history—especially Civil War battles. As usual, the illustrators took pains to render everything—climate, topography, uniforms, and weapons—with documentary authenticity. I remember two episodes in particular. The duel between the *Monitor* and the *Merrimack* was memorable because it was there I learned that cannonballs could be skipped like stones over great spans of water. The other was "The Battle of Lexington and Concord," as presented by the artist Al Williamson. Williamson came up with the single best gunshot noise I have ever encountered, in comics or out. As the front rank of British regulars marched in cadence toward the Colonists (who were crouched behind a low, crumbling stone wall, waiting until, as our social studies teacher said, they could "see the whites of their eyes"), Williamson's task was to come up with a word for the voluptuous sound of a fusillade of flintlocks and matchlocks. He did, and I remember it virtually letter by letter, both small caps and large: FAP! PAD-A-BOW!

One of the comic-book gunshot sounds that I'd dismissed at the time as a cliché was much more accurate than I had realized. It was only thirty years later, after firing a .357 magnum at a limestone outcrop, that I discovered how seriously I had underrated BAM! "BAM!" is almost exactly the sound which a magnum makes. BAM! As both your hands lift off, the blast not only leaves your ears ringing, it seems almost to numb the whole right hemisphere of your head. It *is,* as the cliché would have it, "earsplitting." I'd shot a .22 revolver once, but never a handgun of this horsepower. I found it amazing.

Most new experiences—if they pack any wallop, any danger or fear or guilt—retain a certain mysteriousness until one gets used to them. It's this mysteriousness that calls one back to replay them, to dwell upon them. The most artful way of dwelling on such elusive moments is verbal—by trying to describe them in words and adjusting the words in tiny, hairsplitting ways like calipers until they fit the experience exactly. To get the right fit, to "capture" the experience, is one reason people practice "creative writing," but it's not the main one. The main reason is that as one is indulging in the serious playfulness of trying to find "the right words," one comes to learn much more about the essence of the experience than one had expected. The great, implicit axiom that underlies imaginative writing is the plausible assumption that the only way to begin to understand matters of any subtlety is to tinker around with possible words for them. Good writing is a heuristic method of investigation.

Even before I tried to describe shooting the magnum, I knew that everything I'd ever heard about Americans and guns, like H. Rap Brown's infamous dictum that "Violence is American as apple pie," was true. But until I started writing, what I knew—and believed—had only the force of a truism; as I envisioned curling my fingers around the handle of the magnum, I recalled the feel of all the cap pistols I used to tote as a boy. My whole, trigger-happy boyhood began to crystallize again, and I understood, with real force and with a sudden, deep chagrin, just how profoundly and insidiously my own boyhood aesthetic fascination with guns was implicated in the very fabric of American culture and history.

I thought back to the times I had pretended to be wounded by gunfire as a boy, to the corny swoon I entertained as I would topple to the grass and lie, moaning, waiting for some maternal nurse to descend and fuss over me. And I realized that this is how boys in America are encouraged—from the moment they're handed their first, plastic, toy automatic—to give their bodies to the military. Combat is presented to them as exciting and beautiful, pain as make-believe. I thought of how thoroughly weaponry is woven into the American landscape itself, so ubiquitous that we scarcely notice it. Where I live, the daily artillery practice fifteen miles away at Ft. Riley is fitful summer thunder, weekday hatching of malefaction acknowledged only once a year, on the Fourth of July.

I think that the average, middle-class American accepts the condition of living in such a heavily armed environment mainly because movie and TV gunfighting is presented with an aesthetic veneer as the natural, manly way to conduct a dispute. But the presentation of guns as aesthetic is a seductive lie. I once saw handguns used in a civilian argument that validated James Dickey's *Deliverance* as anything but fantasy. The incident took place on a canoe trip in southeastern Missouri, when one of our party got into an argument with two rednecks known as the Brown brothers, who lived in a trailer overlooking Courteois Creek. I drew on the experience later, near the end of a poem of mine called "River Time":

And two men, two fat retarded twins
in bib-overalls, two comical men,
humpty-dumpties with rotted mouths
were circling my Minnesota friend,
spitting words, gesticulating at him,
arguing he better move his goddamn
hippie van because this floodplain
here belonged to *them*, while Tom,
from the cab, glared down with a stiff
slightly puzzled stare, white-knuckled
in the face. And the look the architect
slipped me meant something dirty
he knew about, it meant *Move off*.
We walked our canoe across the ford,
shoved it up on mud. The rain
returned, through the rain
we watched one brother squat
behind Tom's camper to jot the plate.
Tom's truck wallowed, bucking in reverse
like a dog digging, spewing back rocks.
But the fat guy expected it. He lurched
the gap to his pick up's cab,
and the long .22 automatic he pulled
discharged its six dried-twig snaps
at the back where Tom's boy bounced
as the rear of the fleeing camper
leapt over the crest and out of sight.

In fistfights the hate-scent can be so strong
it gets the tightening circle half incensed.
But anger, in a shot, goes so abstract
at first you can't even recognize it.
Just this detached small-kindling spark.
Could it be some practical joke
over which both brothers on the opposite bank
now chortled and whooped like Laurel and Hardy,
they were slapping their knees, congratulating
each other with whops on the back. *What time
was it?* All I knew was how wet and cold
and pathetic we looked, searching
for footholds in the mud, slipping,
digging in our heels again and heaving
our canoes up the bank—
how sick of this desolate river and the rain.

There was an ugly, aimless quality to the scene. The *snaps* of the
shots sounded trivial. The Brown brothers were unpredictable, grotesque.

Yet, when I wrote later about firing my friend's magnum, I found myself
reliving the aesthetic swoon of wielding a revolver as heavy, businesslike,
and shiningly machined as anything I had ever touched. It was like sitting
down behind the wheel of an incredible new sports car. As I wrote, I
found myself describing not just the report of a magnum, but the feel of
it in my hand—its potential, its heft, and the shocking naturalness of it.
Even though real guns had not been allowed by my parents into our
house, it seemed, now, that during my whole boyhood I had, unbeknown
to me, been trained to relish and to find reassurance—even a kind of
phony confidence, a bravado—in the feel of a rifle snugged up against
the crook of my shoulder, or the feel of a six-gun making my right hand
vital like a wand. For an American boy, aiming a toy rifle or wielding a
toy six-gun (along with all the fantasies they set off) is almost as fundamental as swinging a baseball bat. The feel of a firearm in his hands
extends well beyond all rational considerations. It touches upon his identity:

Some Basic Aesthetics

Out past the motels where town ends
and all the weather starts and the windy
grasses rattle their dried bracelets
Greg swung his pick-up off the county road
and we wobbled westward over ruts, looking
for some place safe to shoot.
What does being "American" feel like?
Steering the sights of his .357 magnum
from lucky rock to rock, I could feel
the solid handshake of its grip adjusting
me again in the comfortable old stance
that cap pistols set us in as boys.
Our trigger fingers light, whimsical,
we'd point, peremptory, directing
that hypothesis from tree to rock to darting
Indian to Kraut. This stance redoubled us
as in the batter's box, bats cocked.
Drop your guns. Keep your hands up. I expected
someday to own guns, to wear a tie.
Steering the magnum's trustworthy weight, sparing
a bush, sparing a dry patch, sparing a tree,
I parked my sights in front of a rock
where, on flatter ground, third base might be.
If it's possible to "feel" America
it was the first *Bam* boxing both my ears,
        numbing
half my face as, *Bam*, the limestone flared
a whiff of smoke, went out. *Bam*.

The valley harvested another crop of echoes
broadening into luxurious redundancy
upon redundancy. It was the thrill
of having your hands on so many cylinders
at once, all of them extra,
more capability than I would ever need.

QUESTIONS FOR CRITICAL READERS

Remembering and Understanding

1. In addition to telling a story, Holden is also making a point about boys (men) and their fascination with guns. What is that point, and what evidence does Holden offer to support it?
2. List the information that this essay provides about gunpowder, and then write a brief description/summary based on that information.
3. Holden explains why he spends so much time discussing the proper word(s) for the sound of an explosion. What is his reason?

Analyzing and Discussion

4. Holden says that boys are encouraged to give their bodies to the military. Identify and describe examples of toys, games, and other aspects of play that might encourage young boys to be fascinated with the military.
5. Holden calls his fascination with guns "aesthetic." This is unusual and requires explanation. What might he mean?
6. Holden says a fascination with guns is part of the "fabric of American culture and history." Agree or disagree with this statement, and explain your position.

Writing

7. Select a toy, activity, or idea that fascinated you as a child (and may continue to fascinate you) as guns fascinated Holden. Describe the toy or activity and provide details of your fascination with it. What did you do to pursue your interest? Why were you interested? Explain that interest by placing it in a variety of contexts, as Holden does with guns.

The End of Play

—————— MARIE WINN ——————

Marie Winn is a freelance writer who has spent most of her career writing for and about children. She has been especially concerned about the effects of television on children. In this selection from her book, Children Without Childhood, *she argues that children's play has disappeared, mostly because of the influence of television.*

TELEVISION AND PLAY

OF ALL THE CHANGES that have altered the topography of childhood, the most dramatic has been the disappearance of childhood play. Whereas a decade or two ago children were easily distinguished from the adult world by the very nature of their play, today children's occupations do not differ greatly from adult diversions.

Infants and toddlers, to be sure, continue to follow certain timeless patterns of manipulation and exploration; adolescents, too, have not changed their free-time habits so very much, turning as they ever have towards adult pastimes and amusements in their drive for autonomy, self-mastery, and sexual discovery. It is among the ranks of school-age children, those six-to-twelve-year-olds who once avidly filled their free moments with childhood play, that the greatest change is evident. In the place of traditional, sometimes ancient childhood games that were still popular a generation ago, in the place of fantasy and make-believe play—"You be the mommy and I'll be the daddy"—doll play or toy-soldier play, jump-rope play, ball-bouncing play, today's children have substituted television viewing and, most recently, video games.

Many parents have misgivings about the influence of television. They sense that a steady and time-consuming exposure to passive entertainment might damage the ability to play imaginatively and resourcefully, or prevent this ability from developing in the first place. A mother of two school-age children recalls: "When I was growing up, we used to go out into the vacant lots and make up week-long dramas and sagas. This was during third, fourth, fifth grades. But my own kids have never done that sort of thing, and somehow it bothers me. I wish we had cut down on the TV years ago, and maybe the kids would have learned how to play."

The testimony of parents who eliminate television for periods of time strengthens the connection between children's television watching and changed play patterns. Many parents discover that when their children don't have television to fill their free time, they resort to the old kinds of imaginative, traditional "children's play." Moreover, these parents often observe that under such circumstances "they begin to seem more like children" or "they act more childlike." Clearly, a part of the definition of childhood, in adults' minds, resides in the nature of children's play.

Children themselves sometimes recognize the link between play and their own special definition as children. In an interview about children's books with four ten-year-old girls, one of them said: "I read this story about a girl my age growing up twenty years ago—you know, in 1960 or so—and she seemed so much younger than me in her behavior. Like she might be playing with dolls, or playing all sorts of children's games, or jump-roping or something." The other girls all agreed that they had noticed a similar discrepancy between themselves and fictional children in books of the past: those children seemed more like children. "So what do *you* do in your spare time, if you don't play with dolls or play make-believe games or jump rope or do things kids did twenty years ago?" they were asked. They laughed and answered, "We watch TV."

But perhaps other societal factors have caused children to give up play. Children's greater exposure to adult realities, their knowledge of adult sexuality, for instance, might make them more sophisticated, less likely to play like children. Evidence from the counterculture communes of the sixties and seventies adds weight to the argument that it is television above all that has eliminated children's play. Studies of children raised in a variety of such communes, all television-free, showed the little communards continuing to fill their time with those forms of play that have all but vanished from the lives of conventionally reared American children. And yet these counterculture kids were casually exposed to all sorts of adult matters—drug taking, sexual intercourse. Indeed, they sometimes incorporated these matters into their play: "We're mating," a pair of six-year-olds told a reporter to explain their curious bumps and grinds. Nevertheless, to all observers the commune children preserved a distinctly childlike and even innocent demeanor, an impression that was produced mainly by the fact that they spent most of their time playing. Their play defined them as belonging to a special world of childhood.

Not all children have lost the desire to engage in the old-style childhood play. But so long as the most popular, most dominant members of the peer group, who are often the most socially precocious, are "beyond" playing, then a common desire to conform makes it harder for those children who still have the drive to play to go ahead and do so. Parents often report that their children seem ashamed of previously common forms of play and hide their involvement with such play from their peers. "My fifth-grader still plays with dolls," a mother tells, "but she keeps them hidden in the basement where nobody will see them." This social check on the play instinct serves to hasten the end of childhood for even the least advanced children.

What seems to have replaced play in the lives of great numbers of preadolescents these days, starting as early as fourth grade, is a burgeoning interest in boy-girl interactions—"going out" or "going together." These activities do not necessarily involve going anywhere or doing anything sexual, but nevertheless are the first stage of a sexual process that used to commence at puberty or even later. Those more sophisticated children who are already involved in such manifestly unchildlike interests make plain their low opinion of their peers who still *play*. "Some of the kids in the class are real weird," a fifth-grade boy states. "They're not interested in going out, just in trucks and stuff, or games pretending they're monsters. Some of them don't even *try* to be cool."

VIDEO GAMES VERSUS MARBLES

Is there really any great difference, one might ask, between that gang of kids playing video games by the hour at their local candy store these days and those small fry who used to hang around together spending equal amounts of time playing marbles? It is easy to see a similarity between the two activities: each requires a certain amount of manual dexterity, each is almost as much fun to watch as to play, each is simple and yet challenging enough for that middle-childhood age group for whom time can be so oppressive if unfilled.

One significant difference between the modern pre-teen fad of video games and the once popular but now almost extinct pastime of marbles is economic: playing video games costs twenty-five cents for approximately three minutes of play; playing marbles, after a small initial investment, is free. The children who frequent video-game machines require a considerable outlay of quarters to subsidize their fun; two, three, or four dollars is not an unusual expenditure for an eight- or nine-year-old spending an hour or two with his friends playing Asteroids or Pac-Man or Space Invaders. For most of the children the money comes from their weekly allowance. Some augment this amount by enterprising commercial ventures—trading and selling comic books, or doing chores around the house for extra money.

But what difference does it make *where* the money comes from? Why should that make video games any less satisfactory as an amusement for children? In fact, having to pay for the entertainment, whatever the source of the money, and having its duration limited by one's financial resources changes the nature of the game, in a subtle way diminishing the satisfactions it offers. Money and time become intertwined, as they so often are in the adult world and as, in the past, they almost never were in the child's world. For the child playing marbles, meanwhile, time has a far more carefree quality, bounded only by the requirements to be home by suppertime or by dark.

But the video-game-playing child has an additional burden—a burden of choice, of knowing that the money used for playing Pac-Man could have been saved for Christmas, could have been used to buy something tangible, perhaps something "worthwhile," as his parents might say, rather than being "wasted" on video games. There is a certain sense of adultness that spending money imparts, a feeling of being a consumer, which distinguishes a game with a price from its counterparts among the traditional childhood games children once played at no cost.

There are other differences as well. Unlike child-initiated and child-organized games such as marbles, video games are adult-created mechanisms not entirely within the child's control, and thus less likely to impart a sense of mastery and fulfillment: the coin may get jammed, the machine may go haywire, the little blobs may stop eating the funny little dots. Then the child must go the storekeeper to complain, to get his money back. He may be "ripped off" and simply lose his quarter, much as his parents are when they buy a faulty appliance. This possibility of disaster gives the childs play a certain weight that marbles never imposed on its light-hearted players.

Even if a child has a video game at home requiring no coin outlay, the play it provides is less than optimal. The noise level of the machine is high—too high, usually, for the child to conduct a conversation easily with another child. And yet, according to its enthusiasts, this very noisiness is part of the game's attraction. The loud whizzes, crashes, and whirrs of the video-game machine "blow the mind" and create an excitement that is quite apart from the excitement generated simply by trying to win a game. A traditional childhood game such as marbles, on the other hand, has little built-in stimulation; the excitement of playing is generated entirely by the players' own actions. And while the pace of a game of marbles is close to the child's natural physiological rhythms, the frenzied activities of video games serve to "rev up" the child in an artificial way, almost in the way a stimulant or an amphetamine might. Meanwhile the perceptual impact of a video game is similar to that of watching television—the action, after all, takes place on a television screen—causing the eye to defocus slightly and creating a certain alteration in the child's natural state of consciousness.

Parents' instinctive reaction to their children's involvement with video games provides another clue to the difference between this contemporary form of play and the more traditional pastimes such as marbles. While parents, indeed most adults, derive open pleasure from watching children at play, most parents today are not delighted to watch their kids flicking away at the Pac-Man machine. This does not seem to them to be real play. As a mother of two school-age children anxiously explains, "We used to do real childhood sorts of things when I was a kid. We'd build forts and put on crazy plays and make up new languages, and just generally we *played*. But today my kids don't play that way at all. They like video games and of course they still go in for sports outdoors. They go roller skating and ice skating and skiing and all. But they don't seem to really *play*."

Some of this feeling may represent a certain nostalgia for the past and the old generation's resistance to the different ways of the new. But it is more likely that most adults have an instinctive understanding of the importance of play in their own childhood. This feeling stokes their fears that their children are being deprived of something irreplaceable when they flip the levers on the video machines to manipulate the electronic images rather than flick their fingers to send a marble shooting towards another marble.

PLAY DEPRIVATION

In addition to television's influence, some parents and teachers ascribe children's diminished drive to play to recent changes in the school curriculum, especially in the early grades.

"Kindergarten, traditionally a playful port of entry into formal school, is becoming more academic, with children being taught specific skills, taking tests, and occasionally even having homework," begins a report on new directions in early childhood education. Since 1970, according to the United States census, the proportion of three- and four-year-olds enrolled in school has risen dramatically, from 20.5 percent to 36.7 percent in 1980, and these nursery schools have largely joined the push towards academic acceleration in the early grades. Moreover, middle-class nursery schools in recent years have introduced substantial doses of academic material into their daily programs, often using those particular devices originally intended to help culturally deprived preschoolers in compensatory programs such as Headstart to catch up with their middle-class peers. Indeed, some of the increased focus on academic skills in nursery schools and kindergartens is related to the widespread popularity among young children and their parents of *Sesame Street*, a program originally intended to help deprived children attain academic skills, but universally watched by middle-class toddlers as well.

Parents of the *Sesame Street* generation often demand a "serious," skill-centered program for their preschoolers in school, afraid that the old-fashioned, play-centered curriculum will bore their alphabet-spouting, number-chanting four- and five-year-olds. A few parents, especially those whose children have not attended television classes or nursery school, complain of the high-powered pace of kindergarten these days. A father whose five-year-old daughter attends a public kindergarten declares: "There's a lot more pressure put on little kids these days than when we were kids, that's for sure. My daughter never went to nursery school and never watched *Sesame,* and she had a lot of trouble when she entered kindergarten this fall. By October, just a month and a half into the program, she was already flunking. The teacher told us our daughter couldn't keep up with the other kids. And believe me, she's a bright kid! All the other kids were getting gold stars and smiley faces for their work, and every day Emily would come home in tears because she didn't get a gold star. Remember when we were in kindergarten? We were *children* then. We were allowed to just play!"

A kindergarten teacher confirms the trend towards early academic pressure. "We're expected by the dictates of the school system to push a lot of curriculum," she explains. "Kids in our kindergarten can't sit around playing with blocks any more. We've just managed to squeeze in one hour of free play a week, on Fridays."

The diminished emphasis on fantasy and play and imaginative activities in early childhood education and the increased focus on early academic-skill acquisition have helped to change childhood from a play-centered time of life to one more closely resembling the style of adulthood: purposeful, success-centered, competitive. The likelihood is that these preschool "workers" will not metamorphose back into players when they move on to grade school. This decline in play is surely one of the reasons why so many teachers today comment that their third- or fourth-graders act like tired businessmen instead of like children.

What might be the consequences of this change in children's play? Children's propensity to engage in that extraordinary series of behaviors characterized as "play" is perhaps the single great dividing line between childhood and adulthood, and has probably been so throughout history. The make-believe games anthropologists have recorded of children in primitive societies around the world attest to the universality of play and to the uniqueness of this activity to the immature members of each society. But in those societies, and probably in Western society before the middle or late eighteenth century, there was always a certain similarity between children's play and adult work. The child's imaginative play took the form of imitation of various aspects of adult life, culminating in the gradual transformation of the child's play from make-believe work to *real* work. At this point, in primitive societies or in our own society of the past, the child took her or his place in the adult work world and the distinctions between adulthood and childhood virtually vanished. But in today's technologically advanced society there is no place for the child in the adult world. There are not enough jobs, even of the most menial kinds, to go around for adults, much less for children. The child must continue to be dependent on adults for many years while gaining the knowledge and skills necessary to become a working member of society.

This is not a new situation for children. For centuries children have endured a prolonged period of dependence long after the helplessness of early childhood is over. But until recent years children remained childlike and playful far longer than they do today. Kept isolated from the adult world as a result of deliberate secrecy and protectiveness, they continued to find pleasure in socially sanctioned childish activities until the imperatives of adolescence led them to strike out for independence and self-sufficiency.

Today, however, with children's inclusion in the adult world both through the instrument of television and as a result of a deliberately preparatory, integrative style of child rearing, the old forms of play no longer seem to provide children with enough excitement and stimulation. What then are these so-called children to do for fulfillment if their desire to play has been vitiated and yet their entry into the working world of adulthood must be delayed for many years? The answer is precisely to get involved in those areas that cause contemporary parents so much distress: addictive television viewing during the school years followed, in adolescence or even before, by a search for similar oblivion via alcohol and drugs; exploration of the world of sensuality and sexuality before achieving the emotional maturity necessary for altruistic relationships.

Psychiatrists have observed among children in recent years a marked increase in the occurrence of depression, a state long considered antithetical to the nature of childhood. Perhaps this phenomenon is at least somewhat connected with the current sense of uselessness and alienation that children feel, a sense that play may once upon a time have kept in abeyance.

QUESTIONS FOR CRITICAL READERS

Remembering and Understanding

1. Re-state Winn's central point in your own words and then use your re-statement as the starting point of a summary of her discussion.
2. Describe Winn's notions of how children should play and the activities

their play should consist of. What image of childhood do these activities project?

3. List the questions you would like to ask Winn, and for each one explain why you want an answer.

Analyzing and Discussing

4. Why (in addition to the reasons she gives) might Winn value certain activities over others?
5. Using Winn's discussion of marbles and video games as your starting point, defend video games as a form of "real play."
6. Winn quotes a mother who says, "We used to do real childhood sorts of things when I was a kid." She seems to believe that certain kinds of play activities are natural to all children. Compare her examples with your experience and that of your classmates. Make your own list of what you consider "real childhood sorts of things." Does your list agree or disagree with the examples Winn gives? Explain the similarities and differences.

Writing

7. Based on what you know about yourself and your peers, write a paper in which you agree or disagree with Winn's argument about television and her fears for the future. Give reasons for your own position.

Synthesizing and Consolidating

1. Apply Bettelheim's ideas about games, rules, and play to one of the other articles in this section. For example, how do Bettelheim's observations apply to Winn's position on television and play?
2. How does Sutton-Smith's perspective differ from Bettelheim's? How are the two similar?
3. Sutton-Smith observes that many educators do their best to eliminate play rather than understand it, apparently because they believe play is out of place in school. What would the other writers in this chapter say to these teachers?
4. Compare the views of Owen and Sutton-Smith on regulating advertising directed at children.
5. Donaldson cites research that implies that children learn for the satisfaction of learning. Relate this to the concepts of play and games as the other writers in this chapter explain them. Is it possible that children learn because they see learning as play?
6. Winn seems concerned that children imitate adults too much, but other writers in this section have suggested that play is a kind of preparation for adult life. What would Bettelheim, Brewer, and Sanders say in response to Winn's concern?
7. Winn says that "the diminished emphasis on fantasy and play and imaginative activities in early childhood education and the increased focus on early academic-skill acquisition have helped to change childhood from a play-centered time of life to one more closely resembling the style of adulthood: purposeful, success-centered, competitive." Using Brewer's article for background, respond to Winn's statement.

Suggestions for Research and Writing

1. Describe a time when you (or someone you knew) disregarded or perverted the rules of a game to avoid losing. What happened, and what might have been the reasons for that behavior?
2. Brewer traces the divergence of children's play from adult recreations and the creation of separate toys and games for children. Winn says that "today, children's occupations do not differ greatly from adult diversions." Based on your experience as a child and as an observer of children at play, explain which of these two views seems more accurate to you.
3. Re-read Winn's discussion of marbles and video games, and then research her assertions about video games. If your research shows that her assertions are correct, defend her statements by adding examples and data that you have gathered. If your research shows that she is incorrect, write a paper in response to her discussion in which you present the results of your research.
4. Design the ideal toy. Base your design on your reading in this chapter and any additional research that you do. Describe the toy and explain why you

believe it is the ideal toy. In your explanation you should make some effort to respond to the requirements of the authors in this chapter.

5. Make a list of the toys you played with (as many as you can think of). Then interview several classmates of the opposite sex about the toys they played with. How are your lists similar or different? Describe the similarities and differences, and evaluate the effects toys might have had on the development of gender identity in you and the classmates you interviewed.

6. Was there a toy that you wanted but never owned? What was it? Describe the toy and explain why you wanted it, why it was special, and how it would have affected your life.

7. Several writers in this chapter criticize toys and games for emphasizing competition. Using your knowledge of all kinds of games that you have played, try to design a game in which winning requires that players cooperate with each other. (This would be a good group activity.) When you have designed the game, describe it so that others will want to play it.

4

Remembering Vietnam

DURING THE RECENT WAR against Iraq in the Persian Gulf, it was
not unusual to hear people talk about the war in Vietnam. Americans
were assured that the Gulf War would not be "another Vietnam." Military
commanders took care to distance themselves from the Vietnam War. At
the end of the Gulf War, President Bush declared the end of what he
called the "Vietnam syndrome." The public seemed determined to treat
veterans of the Gulf War quite differently than they had treated Vietnam
veterans. It would seem that the war in Vietnam, which lasted from 1960
to 1975, has maintained a peculiar grip on Americans even fifteen years
after it ended.

There are many ways of understanding the role of the Vietnam War
in American culture and history, and its continuing hold on the American
people. A complete understanding of the war would require that it be
viewed from a variety of perspectives: political, economic, historical, ideological, strategic, and tactical, among others. But it is often the personal
perspective that makes war accessible and understandable to those who
have not experienced it. The personal perspective does not, of course,
provide a complete understanding of the Vietnam War. It is far too limited
for that. But it has produced some of the most powerful and interesting
writing about the war.

The writers whose work is presented in this chapter examine the Vietnam War from a personal perspective. They write about their own experiences or about the individual experiences of others. They generally ignore questions of policy, ideology, strategy, and economics in order to understand and explain how the war affected individuals at the time and how it continues to affect them. Stanley Karnow provides a historical overview of the gradual increase in the number of American combat soldiers in Vietnam and of the typical soldier's life. Tim O'Brien writes of his own experiences in a combat unit. Michael Herr, who was in Vietnam as a war correspondent, takes his readers through one of the bloodiest events of the war, the battle for Hue during the 1968 Tet Offensive. Myra McPherson writes about women who served in Vietnam, a group that has received little attention through the years. Gloria Emerson, taking "blood" as her subject and theme, writes about protests against the war. Kurt Anderson writes of the experience of visiting the Vietnam Memorial in Washington, D.C. Fred Reed, another veteran, takes exception to the notion that Vietnam veterans regret their war experiences. Howard Morland, also a veteran, responds to what he sees as a growing nostalgia for the Vietnam War, as men who did not serve or did not see combat now regret their lack of involvement, as though they had been excluded from something important.

The writers here will sometimes disagree about the war, what it was like, and what it means. They have in common an honest attempt to understand how individuals experience war. Some of these selections contain language and descriptions that many people would find crude or offensive. However, it is also possible to see this language as part of what these writers want to say, as the result of conscious and deliberate decisions that they have made about how to best say what they have to say about war.

Before You Read

Before you read the selections in this chapter, respond to at least three of the following exercises in your reading journal.

1. What do you know about the Vietnam War? Make a list or write an account of the war that displays your knowledge.
2. Describe the most vivid or memorable scene or description of war that you have encountered in film or reading. Explain why you found it memorable.
3. Do you believe the films you have seen or the books you have read portray war realistically? Explain why or why not, giving specific examples and reasons.

4. Do you know anyone who has been in a war? Who? What do you know about their experiences, and how do you know it?
5. Describe the sights, sounds, and smells you would expect to encounter on a battlefield.
6. Describe the way you think you would react to being in combat.
7. Explain what you know about the way the American public reacted to the Vietnam War.

Escalation

——— STANLEY KARNOW ———

*Stanley Karnow began his career as a reporter in 1950. He reported from
Southeast Asia from 1959 to 1971 for* Time, Life, *and* The Washington
Post. *He was the chief correspondent for the Public Broadcasting System's
documentary* Vietnam: A Television History. *This selection is from his
book,* Vietnam *(New York: Viking, 1983), which is a companion to the
television series.*

THERE WAS NO "TYPICAL" U.S. SOLDIER in Vietnam, despite the
stereotype of the "grunt" promoted by the news media, politicians, and
even veterans themselves. The three million Americans who served there
went through many varied experiences—partly because the quality of the
war varied in different areas of the country, and partly because its nature
changed over time.

American units in the Mekong delta slogged week after week across
paddies, occasionally tangling with Vietcong guerrillas, while other units
clashed with North Vietnamese regiments in big engagements in the highlands. Still others were continually peppered by snipers as they patrolled
the perimeters of sprawling U.S. installations at Danang and Bienhoa and
Camranh, and many more spent seemingly endless periods at lonely hilltop
batteries, firing artillery shells at real or presumed enemy concentrations.
Air force pilots could return from dangerous missions over North Vietnam
to the relative comfort of their bases, and some lucky GIs drew assignments
in Saigon, where the military bureaucracy resembled a miniature Pentagon.

But Vietnam was unique among American wars in at least two respects: under a rotation schedule, draftees were committed for only a
year—which meant, for many, that survival became their main preoc-
cupation; but in a war without front lines, few could feel safe anywhere.
A survey conducted for the Veterans Administration and published in
1980 underscored the point statistically: of the veterans sampled, most
had been exposed to "combat," which meant that they had come under
some kind of attack. But in reality, only a minority had actually clashed
with large North Vietnamese units or Vietcong irregulars, run into mines

or booby traps, or been ambushed. Yet 76 percent had been on the receiving end of enemy mortars or rockets, and 56 percent had seen Americans killed or wounded. While infantrymen obviously faced greater risks, headquarters typists were also vulnerable.

In many ways, the American troops sent to Vietnam were no less ideological than their North Vietnamese and Vietcong adversaries. Exhorted by Kennedy and Johnson to join in the crusade to halt the spread of global Communism, they firmly believed in the sanctity of their cause. Also, their fathers had fought in World War II, and they felt it was their generation's turn to do its duty. They knew the United States had never been defeated in a war, and their impulses were stimulated and dramatized by the exploits of movie and television heroes—a factor that emerges repeatedly in their personal recollections. William Ehrhart, a former marine sergeant, emphasized the influence on him of what he called the "John Wayne syndrome," and another veteran, Dale Reich, imagined himself to be "a soldier like John Wayne, a dashing GI who feared nothing and either emerged with the medals and the girl, or died heroically." In *Born on the Fourth of July*, an account of his service, Ron Kovic recalled his decision to enlist in the marines after two recruiters had stirringly addressed his senior high school class: "As I shook their hands and stared up into their eyes, I couldn't help but feel that I was shaking hands with John Wayne and Audie Murphy."

According to the 1980 Veterans Administration study, most Vietnam veterans did not lose their patriotic pride after the conclusion of the war. Looking back, 71 percent of those polled said that they were "glad" to have gone to Vietnam; 74 percent claimed to have "enjoyed" their tour there; 66 percent expressed a willingness to serve again. But these responses, although astonishing, do not necessarily contradict the more familiar notion that ordinary U.S. soldiers became increasingly disillusioned as the war dragged on. For as the prospect of victory dimmed, their zeal was eroded by frustration, and they sought to attribute blame for their disappointment. In the retrospective survey, 82 percent complained that they had been sent into a conflict which "the political leaders in Washington would not let them win"—a sentiment shared by Americans as a whole, which has doubtless contributed to their declining faith in their public institutions. Yet no nation, least of all the United States, readily admits to failure. So the veterans and civilians who viewed the war as a tragedy could also subscribe to President Reagan's description of its purpose as "noble."

As they waged the war, however, U.S. troops were gradually disenchanted less by grand strategic flaws than by the accumulation of their own experiences. I have compiled dozens of these experiences, either from direct interviews or from memoirs, and the stories could fill volumes. But perhaps the bits and pieces that follow add up to a credible set of impressions.

Most GIs sent to Vietnam after the first American forces arrived in 1965 went as individual replacements rather than in units. Consequently, from the start many of them were overcome by loneliness. When he reached one of the American division headquarters along with a handful of other men, Dale Reich was randomly assigned to a company whose members accepted him without comment: "The old clichés about camaraderie under fire did not seem to apply. . . . I was crushed by the combination of slipping one step closer to combat, and finding no one to pat me on the back and assure me that I would survive. Instead, I found that even my fellow soldiers had no real interest in my welfare."

The solitude was intensified by a feeling that they were in an alien and probably hostile environment. William Ehrhart had fantasized before leaving home that it would be like the scenes of World War II he had seen in the movies—French girls and Italian kids spilling into the streets to hail their liberators with wine and flowers. But Vietnam was taut and tense. Charles Sabatier, a draftee from Texas, had scarcely landed in Saigon when he noticed that the windows of the green U.S. army bus that transported him to his camp were screened with wire mesh as a precaution against grenade assaults. "I thought we were in a friendly country, and now I'm told that people might run up and throw grenades into the bus. And I thought, Oh my God, they're going to try to kill me. There I was, twenty years old, and suddenly I realized that I might not live to be twenty-one or twenty-two."

Vietnam confused and confounded innocent young Americans. Many, persuaded they were there as saviors, sincerely treated the Vietnamese with concern and kindness, providing them with hygiene, roads, wells, and other benefits as part of programs that one U.S. general called the velvet glove. But they were also chronically apprehensive and rightly suspected that any Vietnamese might be hostile. They were told that some areas belonged to the Vietcong and others to the Saigon regime, but they never trusted such flimsy intelligence, as a former marine captain, E.J. Banks, recalled:

> You never knew who was the enemy and who was the friend. They all looked alike. They all dressed alike. They were all Vietnamese. Some of them were Vietcong. Here's a woman of twenty-two or twenty-three. She is pregnant, and she tells an interrogator that her husband works in Danang and isn't a Vietcong. But she watches your men walk down a trail and get killed or wounded by a booby trap. She knows the booby trap is there, but she doesn't warn them. Maybe she planted it herself. It wasn't like the San

Francisco Forty-Niners on one side of the field and the Cincinnati Bengals on the other. The enemy was all around you.

Soon after taking over the region around Danang in the spring of 1965, the U.S. marines embarked on "cordon-and-search" missions, later to be given the quaint title of "country fair" operations. In theory, they were supposed to surround a group of hamlets, then distribute food and dispense medical care to the inhabitants while probing for Vietcong cadres. In practice, as Ehrhart described them, the operations were less benign: "We would go through a village before dawn, rousting everybody out of bed, and kicking down doors and dragging them out if they didn't move fast enough. They all had underground bunkers inside their huts to protect themselves against bombing and shelling. But to us the bunkers were Vietcong hiding places, and we'd blow them up with dynamite—and blow up the huts too. If we spotted extra rice lying around, we'd confiscate it to keep them from giving it to the Vietcong."

As the peasants emerged, Ehrhart continued, they were "herded like cattle into a barbed wire compound, and left to sit there in the hot sun for the rest of the day, with no shade." Meanwhile, several South Vietnamese policemen with an American interrogator and his interpreter would pass through the crowd, selecting people to be taken to a nearby tent for questioning about the Vietcong presence in the vicinity: "If they had the wrong identity card, or if the police held a grudge against them, they'd be beaten pretty badly, maybe tortured. Or they might be hauled off to jail, and God knows what happened to them. At the end of the day, the villagers would be turned loose. Their homes had been wrecked, their chickens killed, their rice confiscated—and if they weren't pro-Vietcong before we got there, they sure as hell were by the time we left."

These were routine missions, not outrageous atrocities like the Mylai massacre that occurred in March 1968. Yet, in village after village, a fear of the unknown engulfed American soldiers. Mark Smith, a veteran of the First Cavalry Division, was fascinated by Vietnam's beauty from the start. In coastal Binh Dinh province north of Saigon, his operational area, the lush green mountains rose from a plain of rice fields divided with such geometrical precision as to suggest that the peasants who had land-scaped the scene were natural mathematicians. But he felt intimidated by the "subtle, incomprehensible" villages—"whole societies right in front of us, yet impenetrable even after we had entered them, never under-standing anything or seeing anything understandable, the people staring at us as if we were from Mars."

Approaching a hard-core Vietcong village could be explosive, how-ever, as two marine companies discovered in early 1967 at Thuybo, a complex of hamlets straddling an intersection of rivers about a dozen miles south of Danang. Captain E. J. Banks, commanding the sweep, had expected only a minor engagement, even though the sector had been designated as "unfriendly." But, on that hot and humid morning, the enemy fire intensified as his men advanced slowly across rice fields toward the tree line shrouding the village. By dark, they had suffered heavy casualties, and only one helicopter managed to get through to evacuate the wounded. What began as a small-scale operation would degenerate into three murderous days of fighting, as so many operations in Vietnam did. A marine private, Jack Hill, later recollected his own experience during the encounter: "They started with snipers, and then their thirty calibers opened up, sounding like ten or fifteen jackhammers going off at the same time. Our guys were falling everywhere. We spread out and dug in, waiting for the word to go forward. But we couldn't move. We were pinned down, all day and all night. It was raining something pitiful, and we couldn't see nothing. So we just lay there, waiting and waiting and hearing our partners dying, big guys dying and crying for their mothers, asking to be shot because they couldn't take it no more."

Hill's squad finally entered the village at dawn. The enemy had evaporated, leaving not even a cartridge shell. The peasants, mostly old men and women, were running around in panic, screaming and denying any connection with the Vietcong. Disregarding them, the marines combed the place, burning huts and blowing up underground shelters: "Our emotions were very low because we'd lost a lot of friends. The death rate was ridiculous for such an operation. So when we went through those hutches, we gave it to them, and whoever was in a hole was going to get it. And whatever was moving was going to move no more—especially after three days of blood and guts in the mud."

Interviewed in Thuybo after the war, a local Communist cadre depicted the episode as a holocaust, claiming that the marines had deliberately slaughtered one hundred and forty-five civilians, including women and children. Captain Banks rejected the charge, contending that not more than fifteen peasants had been killed—"as if it had been a robbery and gunfight on a city street and several bystanders were hit." The truth will never be known. The only reality about death in Vietnam was its regularity, not its cause.

Another reality that frustrated U.S. troops in Vietnam was the enemy's ability to return to villages that had supposedly been cleaned out. They could never "liberate" territory, but found themselves going back again and again to fight the same battles in the same areas with the same unsatisfactory results. Their repeated offensives during 1967 in Binh Dinh province, a Communist stronghold since the French war, illustrated the problem. They conducted at least four massive drives into the region— operations with names like Masher, White Wing, and Pershing—and inflicted nearly eleven thousand casualties on the North Vietnamese and Vietcong. But apart from its principal towns, the province remained in Communist hands.

For most GIs in combat zones, patrols with no fancy operational names were a daily ordeal. Ehrhart recollected the normal experience of his marine unit as it plodded across rice fields and through jungles in the region near Danang: "You carried fifty to seventy pounds of equipment, and it was tough going, particularly in forested areas. Often you'd have to pull yourself along from one tree branch to the next, or we'd have to help each other by gripping hands. And you couldn't see anything, so you didn't know what was there around you. Of course, squads were sent out to flank the main column, but they would disappear from sight. Nobody wanted an assignment to the flanking squads because it was pretty hairy."

The heat and rain and insects were almost worse than the enemy. Drenched in sweat, the men waded through flooded paddies and plantations, stopping from time to time to pick leeches out of their boots. They might reach for a cigarette only to find the pack soaked. And at the end of the day, as Ehrhart recalled, they had nothing to look forward to except the next day.

> You dug a hole right beside where you were going to sleep, and put up a one-man poncho tent. Unless something happened, you'd wake up in the morning with your mouth tasting rotten and your clothes still wet. You'd eat, maybe for a half hour or forty-five minutes, and then you'd be off again, not thinking very much. In retrospect, it amazes me how ordinary that kind of life became. You're sitting there at six o'clock in the morning, a cigarette hanging out of your mouth, pulling on your boots, and you're in the middle of nowhere. Suddenly you realize, I'm not supposed to live this way, but then you're surprised that it seems so natural.

American combat units often patrolled for months without drawing even stray Vietcong sniper fire, and as Mark Smith remembered thinking at the time, "It was better to get into a fight than just walk around sweating." To him, indeed, battle was exhilarating.

> When you made contact with the enemy, you went from the most horrible boredom to the most intense excitement I've ever known in my life. You couldn't remain detached. Someone was trying to kill you and you were trying to kill someone, and it was like every thrill hitting you all at once. If I felt safe in a fight, below the line of fire, I almost didn't want it to end. But even in a severe fight, when I didn't feel safe, there was a distinct beauty to it—a sense of exultation, the bullets cracking around your head and the tracers flying so close that they would blind you for a moment.

But there was none of that romantic agony for many GIs as the unseen enemy harassed them with mines, booby traps, and mortars. Ronald J. Glasser, an army doctor, compiled some of their combat experiences in a book entitled *365 Days*, describing the kind of search-and-destroy mission that killed and crippled American soldiers every day in Vietnam— without bringing the United States any nearer to its vague and elusive goal of victory.

By early morning, a suffocating dry heat hung over the rice fields, making it nearly impossible to breathe. The men chewed salt tablets as they walked, trying as well as they could to shelter the metal parts of their weapons from the sun. "A little before noon, the point man, plodding along a dusty rise, sweating under his flak vest, stepped on a pressure-detonated 105-mm shell, and for ten meters all around the road lifted itself into the air, shearing off his legs as it blew up around him. The rest of the patrol threw themselves on the ground." That evening, the company was mortared—only two rounds, but enough to keep the men awake despite their exhaustion. The heat continued to hang over them as they lay on the ground, smoking marijuana or just looking vacantly up at the empty sky. It was the fifth night that week they had been hit. They would suffer more losses the next morning, when they began sweeping again.

> They moved out on line, humping through the gathering heat, chewing salt pills as they had the day before, looking out over the same shimmering landscape. A little after ten o'clock, they began moving through a hedgerow. A trooper tripped a wire and detonated a claymore set up to blow behind him. It took down three others, killing two right off and leaving the third to die later. The survivors rested around the bodies till the dust-offs came in and took out the casualties, then started up again.

Soon afterward, one of the platoons entered a tangled jungle area. The thick overhead foliage filtered out almost all the sunlight, making it difficult to see, while the matting of vines and bushes held onto the heat, magnifying it until the men felt that they were moving through an airless oven. The sweat poured off them as they trod cautiously. At places the growth was so thick that they slung their weapons and pulled the vines apart with their bare hands. Thorns caught onto their fatigues and equipment, and they had to tear themselves loose. Scratched and bleeding, they pushed on.

> Three quarters of the way through the tangle, a trooper brushed against a two-inch vine, and a grenade slung at chest height went off, shattering the right side of his head and body. The medic, work-

ing down in the dim light, managed to stop the major bleeders, but could do nothing about the shattered arm and the partly destroyed skull. Nearby troopers took hold of the unconscious soldier and, half carrying, half dragging him, pulled him the rest of the way through the tangle.

The Communists invented an extraordinarily lethal arsenal of mines and booby traps. The "Bouncing Betty" was so called by GIs because it leaped out of the earth, exploding as its firing device was triggered. More destructive were mortar and artillery shells hung from trees, nestled in shrubbery, or buried under the mud floors of Vietnamese huts. Others included booby-trapped grenades tripped by wires and fragmentation mines detonated by enemy guerrillas crouched in the jungle; and there were primitive snares, like sharpened bamboo staves hidden in holes. Cautious and fearful, GIs constantly attempted to second-guess the mines, as Tim O'Brien wrote in his memoir of the war, *If I Die in a Combat Zone:*

Should you put your foot to that flat rock or the clump of weeds to its rear? Paddy dike or water? You wish you were Tarzan, able to swing with the vines. You try to trace the footprints of the man to your front. You give it up when he curses you for following too closely; better one man dead than two. The moment-to-moment, step-by-step decision-making preys on your mind. The effect is sometimes paralysis. You are slow to rise from rest breaks. You walk like a wooden man . . . with your eyes pinned to the dirt, spine arched, and you are shivering, shoulders hunched.

It was less a fear of death that nagged the American soldiers, as one of O'Brien's buddies put it, than the absurd combination of certainty and uncertainty—the certainty that the mines were everywhere, and the uncertainty about how to move or sit in order to avoid them. The Vietcong had so many ways to plant and camouflage mines, he mused. "I'm ready to go home," he added.

So were many GIs as the war floundered, and their original sense of purpose became clouded by doubt. Looking back, Ehrhart spoke for others:

After a few months, it began to seem crazy, but you didn't dare to draw conclusions that might point in terrifying directions. Maybe we Americans weren't the guys in white hats, riding white horses. Maybe we shouldn't be in Vietnam. Maybe I'd gotten my ass out in these bushes for nothing. Still, it never occurred to me to lay down my rifle and quit. Instead, you develop a survival mentality. You stop thinking about what you're doing, and you count days. I knew that I was in Vietnam for three hundred and ninety-five days, and if I was still alive at the end of those three hundred and ninety-five days, I'd go home and forget the whole thing. That's the way you operated.

QUESTIONS FOR CRITICAL READERS

Remembering and Understanding

1. Write a summary of Karnow's account of American escalation in Vietnam.
2. Using the information that Karnow provides, write a profile of the American soldier in Vietnam.
3. According to Karnow, what circumstances did American soldiers face in Vietnam? List as many as you can find and then use them to write a profile or summary.
4. Karnow's first paragraph is quite general. After you have read all of this selection, write a new opening paragraph that you believe introduces the subject more effectively.

Analyzing and Discussing

5. Karnow says that "in many ways, the American troops sent to Vietnam were no less ideological than their North Vietnamese and Vietcong adversaries." What does he mean by the term "ideological," and what evidence does he provide for this statement?
6. Karnow mentions the "John Wayne Syndrome," but he does not explain it in detail. Find out enough about John Wayne to explain why soldiers would base their behavior on him.

Writing

7. Karnow says American soldiers in Vietnam were disenchanted by their experiences. He then gives a number of examples of this. Review these examples and then write an explanation of the reasons for their disenchantment.

Arrival

———— TIM O'BRIEN ————

Tim O'Brien served as a combat infantryman in Vietnam. His novel about the war, Going After Cacciato, *won the National Book Award in 1978. This selection is from* If I Die In A Combat Zone *(1973), which is a nonfiction account of his tour of duty. This book has been praised for its brilliant evocation of the footsoldier's daily life. O'Brien's most recent book is* The Things They Carried, *a collection of short stories about the Vietnam War.*

FIRST THERE IS SOME MIST. Then, when the plane begins its descent, there are pale gray mountains. The plane slides down, and the mountains darken and take on a sinister cragginess. You see the outlines of crevices, and you consider whether, of all the places opening up below, you might finally walk to *that* spot and die. Or that spot, or that spot. In the far distance are green patches, the sea is below, a stretch of sand winds along the coast. Two hundred men draw their breath. You feel dread. But it is senseless to let it go too far, so you joke: there are only 365 days to go. The stewardess wishes you luck over the loudspeaker. At the door she gives out some kisses, mainly to the extroverts.

From Cam Ranh Bay another plane takes you to Chu Lai, a big base to the south of Danang, headquarters for the Americal Division. You spend a week there, in a place called the Combat Center. It's a resortlike place, tucked in alongside the South China Sea, complete with sand and native girls and a miniature golf course and floor shows with every variety of the grinding female pelvis. There beside the sea you get your now-or-never training. You pitch hand grenades, practice walking through mine fields, learn to use a minesweeper. Mostly, though, you wonder about dying. You wonder how it feels, what it looks like inside you. Sometimes you stop, and your body tingles. You feel your blood and nerves working. At night you sit on the beach and watch fire fights off where the war is being fought. There are movies at night, and a place to buy beer. Carefully, you mark six days off your pocket calendar; you start a journal, vaguely hoping it will never be read.

134

Arriving in Vietnam as a foot soldier is much like arriving at boot camp as a recruit. Things are new, and you ascribe evil to the simplest physical objects: You see red in the sand, swarms of angels and avatars in the sky, pity in the eyes of the chaplain, concealed anger in the eyes of the girls who sell you Coke. You are not sure how to conduct yourself—whether to show fear, to live secretly with it, to show resignation or disgust. You wish it were all over. You begin the countdown. You take the inky, mildew smell of Vietnam into your lungs.

After a week at the Combat Center, a truck took six of us down Highway One to a hill called LZ Gator.

A sergeant welcomed us, staring at us like he was buying meat, and he explained that LZ Gator was headquarters for the Fifth Battalion, Forty-Sixth Infantry, and that the place was our new home.

"But I don't want you guys getting too used to Gator," he said. "You won't be here long. You're gonna fill out some forms in a few minutes, then we'll get you all assigned to rifle companies, then you're going out to the boonies. Got it? Just like learning to swim. We just toss you in and let you hoof it and eat some C rations and get a little action under your belts. It's better that way than sitting around worrying about it.

"Okay, that's enough bullshit. Just don't get no illusions." He softened his voice a trifle. "Of course, don't get too scared. We lose some men, sure, but it ain't near as bad as '66, believe me, I was in the Nam in '66, an' it was bad shit then, getting our butts kicked around. And this area—you guys lucked out a little, there's worse places in the Nam. We got mines, that's the big thing here, plenty of 'em. But this ain't the Delta, we ain't got many NVA, so you're lucky. We got some mines and some local VC, that's it. Anyhow, enough bullshit, like I say, it ain't all that bad. Okay, we got some personnel cards here, so fill 'em out, and we'll chow you down."

Then the battalion Re-Up NCO came along. "I seen some action. I got me two purple hearts, so listen up good. I'm not saying you're gonna get zapped out there. I made it. But you're gonna come motherfuckin' close, Jesus, you're gonna hear bullets tickling your asshole. And sure as I'm standing here, one or two of you men are gonna get your legs blown off. Or killed. One or two of you, it's gotta happen."

He paused and stared around like a salesman, from man to man, letting it sink in. "I'm just telling you the facts of life, I'm not trying to scare shit out of you. But you better sure as hell be scared, it's gotta happen. One or two of you men, your ass is grass.

"So—what can you do about it? Well, like Sarge says, you can be careful, you can watch for the mines and all that, and, who knows, you might come out looking like a rose. But careful guys get killed too. So what can you do about it then? Nothing. Except you can re-up."

The men looked at the ground and shuffled around grinning. "Sure, sure—I know. Nobody likes to re-up. But just think about it a second. Just say you do it—you take your burst of three years, starting today; three more years of army life. Then what? Well, I'll tell you what, it'll save your ass, that's what, it'll save your ass. You re-up and I can get you a job in Chu Lai. I got jobs for mechanics, typists, clerks, damn near anything you want, I got it. So you get your nice, safe rear job. You get some on-the-job training, the works. You get a skill. You sleep in a bed. Hell, you laugh, but you sleep in the goddamn monsoons for two months on end, you try that sometime, and you won't be laughing. So. You lose a little time to Uncle Sam. Big deal. You save your ass. So, I got my desk inside. If you come in and sign the papers—it'll take ten minutes—I'll have you on the first truck going back to Chu Lai, no shit. Anybody game?" No one budged, and he shrugged and went down to the mess hall.

LZ Gator seemed a safe place to be. You could see pieces of the ocean on clear days. A little village called Nuoc Mau was at the foot of the hill, filled with pleasant, smiling people, places to have your laundry done, a whorehouse. Except when on perimeter guard at night, everyone went about the fire base with unloaded weapons. The atmosphere was dull and hot, but there were movies and floor shows and sheds-ful of beer.

I was assigned to Alpha Company.

"Shit, you poor sonofabitch," the mail clerk said, grinning. "Shit. How many days you got left in Nam? 358, right? 357? Shit. Your poor mother. I got twenty-three days left, twenty-three days, and I'm sorry but I'm gone! Gone! I'm so short I need a step ladder to hand out mail. What's your name?"

The mail clerk shook hands with me. "Well, at least you're a lucky sonofabitch. Irish guys never get wasted, not in Alpha. Blacks and spics get wasted, but you micks make it every goddamn time. Hell, I'm black as the colonel's shoe polish, so you can bet your ass I'm not safe till that ol' freedom bird lands me back in Seattle. Twenty-three days, you poor mother."

He took me to the first sergeant. The first sergeant said to forget all the bullshit about going straight out to the field. He lounged in front of a fan, dressed in his underwear (dyed green, apparently to camouflage him from some incredibly sneaky VC), and he waved a beer at me. "Shit, O'Brien, take it easy. Alpha's a good square-shooting company, so don't sweat it. Keep your nose clean and I'll just keep you here on Gator till the company comes back for a break. No sense sending you out there now, they're coming in to Gator day after tomorrow." He curled his toe around a cord and pulled the fan closer. "Go see a movie tonight, get a beer or something."

He assigned me to the third platoon and hollered at the supply sergeant to issue me some gear. The supply sergeant hollered back for him to go to hell, and they laughed, and I got a rifle and ammunition and a helmet, camouflage cover, poncho, poncho liner, back pack, clean clothes, and a box of cigarettes and candy. Then it got dark, and I watched Elvira Madigan and her friend romp through all the colors, get hungry, get desperate, and stupidly—so stupidly that you could only pity their need for common sense—end their lives. The guy, Elvira's lover, was a deserter. You had the impression he deserted for an ideal of love and butterflies, balmy days and the simple life, and that when he saw he couldn't have it, not even with blond and blue-eyed Elvira, he decided he could *never* have it. But, Jesus, to kill because of hunger, for fear to hold a menial job. Disgusted, I went off to an empty barracks and pushed some M-16 ammo and hand grenades off my cot and went to sleep.

In two days Alpha Company came to LZ Gator. They were dirty, loud, coarse, intent on getting drunk, happy, curt, and not interested in saying much to me. They drank through the afternoon and into the night. There was a fight that ended in more beer, they smoked some dope, they started sleeping or passed out around midnight.

At one or two in the morning—at first I thought I was dreaming, then I thought it was nothing serious—explosions popped somewhere outside the barracks. The first sergeant came through the barracks with a flashlight. "Jesus," he hollered. "Get the hell out of here! We're being hit! Wake up!"

I scrambled for a helmet for my head. For an armored vest. For my boots, for my rifle, for my ammo.

It was pitch dark. The explosions continued to pop; it seemed a long distance away.

I went outside. The base was lit up by flares, and the mortar pits were firing rounds out into the paddies. I hid behind a metal shed they kept the beer in.

No one else came out of the barracks. I waited, and finally one man ambled out, holding a beer. Then another man, holding a beer.

They sat on some sandbags in their underwear, drinking the beer and laughing, pointing out at the paddies and watching our mortar rounds land.

Later two or three more men straggled out. No helmets, no weapons. They laughed and joked and drank. The first sergeant started shouting. But the men just giggled and sat on sandbags in their underwear.

Enemy rounds crashed in. The earth split. Most of Alpha Company slept.

A lieutenant came by. He told the men to get their gear together, but no one moved, and he walked away. Then some of the men spotted the flash of an enemy mortar tube.

They set up a machine gun and fired out at it, over the heads of everyone in the fire base.

In seconds the enemy tube flashed again. The wind whistled, and the round dug into a road twenty feet from my beer shed. Shrapnel slammed into the beer shed. I hugged the Bud and Black Label, panting, no thoughts.

Charlie was zeroing in on their machine gun, and everyone scattered, and the next round slammed down even closer. More giggling and hooting.

The lieutenant hurried back. He argued with a platoon sergeant, but this time the lieutenant was firm. He ordered us to double-time out to the perimeter. Muttering about how the company needed a rest and that this had turned into one hell of a rest and that they'd rather be out in the boonies, the men put on helmets and took up their rifles and followed the lieutenant past the mess hall and out to the perimeter.

Three of the men refused and went into the barracks and went to sleep.

Out on the perimeter, there were two dead GI's. Fifty-caliber machine guns fired out into the paddies, and the sky was filled with flares. Two or three of our men, forgetting about the war, went off to chase parachutes blowing around the bunkers. The chutes came from the flares, and they made good souvenirs.

In the morning the first sergeant roused us out of bed, and we swept the fire base for bodies. Eight dead VC were lying about. One was crouched beside a roll of barbed wire, the top of his head resting on the ground like he was ready to do a somersault. A squad of men was detailed to throw the corpses into a truck. They wore gloves and didn't like the job, but they joked. The rest of us walked into the rice paddy and followed a tracker dog out toward the VC mortar positions. From there the dog took us into a village, but there was nothing to see but some children and women. We walked around until noon. Then the lieutenant turned us around, and we were back at LZ Gator in time for chow.

"Those poor motherfuckin' dinks," the Kid said while we were filling sandbags in the afternoon. "They should know better than to test Alpha Company. They just know, they *ought* to know anyhow, it's like tryin' to attack the Pentagon! Old Alpha comes in, an' there ain't a chance in hell for 'em, they ought to know *that*, for Christ's sake. Eight to two, they lost six more than we did." The Kid was only eighteen, but everyone said to look out for him, he was the best damn shot in the battalion with an M-79.

"Actually," the Kid said, "those two guys weren't even from Alpha. The two dead GI's. They were with Charlie Company or something, I don't know. Stupid dinks should know better." He flashed a buck-toothed smile and jerked his eyebrows up and down and winked.

Wolf said: "Look, FNG, I don't want to scare you—nobody's trying to scare you—but that stuff last night wasn't *shit*! Last night was a lark. Wait'll you see some really *bad* shit. That was a picnic last night. I almost slept through it." I wondered what an FNG was. No one told me until I asked.

"You bullshitter, Wolf. It's never any fun." The Kid heaved a shovelful of sand at Wolf's feet. "Except for me maybe. I'm charmed, nothing'll get me. Ol' Buddy Wolf's a good bullshitter, he'll bullshit you till you think he knows his ass from his elbow."

"Okay, FNG, don't listen to me, ask Buddy Barker. Buddy Barker, you tell him last night was a lark. Right? We got mortars and wire and bunkers and arty and, shit, what the hell else you want? You want a damn H bomb?"

"Good idea," Kid said.

But Buddy Barker agreed it had been a lark. He filled a sandbag and threw it onto a truck and sat down and read a comic. Buddy Wolf filled two more bags and sat down with Buddy Barker and called him a lazy bastard. While Kid and I filled more bags, Wolf and Barker read comics and played a game called "Name the Gang." Wolf named a rock song and Barker named the group who made it big. Wolf won 10 to 2. I asked the Kid how many Alpha men had been killed lately, and the Kid shrugged and said a couple. So I asked how many had been wounded, and without looking up, he said a few. I asked how bad the AO was, how soon you could land a rear job, if the platoon leader were gung-ho, if Kid had ever been wounded, and the Kid just grinned and gave flippant, smiling, say-nothing answers. He said it was best not to worry.

QUESTIONS FOR CRITICAL READERS

Remembering and Understanding

1. Based on the information O'Brien provides, describe briefly the experience of being a new replacement in Vietnam.
2. What are the most vivid or memorable details of O'Brien's description? Explain what makes them memorable for you.
3. Describe the physical sensations that O'Brien experienced on his arrival in Vietnam.

Analyzing and Discussing

4. O'Brien seems puzzled by the way his fellow soldiers react to the attack during his first night at LZ Gator. Were you puzzled? How do you think they should have reacted?
5. What is your response to the proposal that a soldier could have a safe job

away from the fighting if he reenlisted in the Army? O'Brien does not explain why he refuses to reenlist. Can you offer an explanation?

6. What is O'Brien's attitude toward his new experiences? How does he use tone to convey this attitude?

Writing

7. Recall a time when you were in a situation that was entirely new to you. Describe that experience, and explain how it made you feel. Try to capture details the way O'Brien does when he says, "Things are new, and you ascribe evil to the simplest physical objects: You see red in the sand, swarms of angels and avatars in the sky, pity in the eyes of the chaplain, concealed anger in the eyes of the girls who sell you Coke."

Hell Sucks

——— MICHAEL HERR ———

Michael Herr went to Vietnam in 1967 as a correspondent for several American publications. He has been praised for his ear for dialogue, and you might read some of his dialogue out loud to get its flavor. The selection printed here describes the intense battle for the city of Hue during the 1968 Tet Offensive. In that offensive, North Vietnamese and Viet Cong soldiers staged a coordinated attack throughout South Vietnam against Americans and South Vietnamese soldiers. It comes from his book, Dispatches, which some readers called "stunning" and "convulsively brilliant." Herr's title is a reference to Civil War general William T. Sherman's statement, "War is hell."

DURING THE FIRST WEEKS OF THE TET OFFENSIVE the curfew began early in the afternoon and was strictly enforced. By 2:30 each day Saigon looked like the final reel of *On the Beach,* a desolate city whose long avenues held nothing but refuse, windblown papers, small distinct piles of human excrement and the dead flowers and spent firecracker casings of the Lunar New Year. Alive, Saigon had been depressing enough, but during the Offensive it became so stark that, in an odd way, it was invigorating. The trees along the main streets looked like they'd been struck by lightning, and it became unusually, uncomfortably cold, one more piece of freak luck in a place where nothing was in its season. With so much filth growing in so many streets and alleys, an epidemic of plague was feared, and if there was ever a place that suggested plague, demanded it, it was Saigon in the Emergency. American civilians, engineers and construction workers who were making it here like they'd never made it at home began forming into large armed bands, carrying .45's and grease guns and Swedish K's, and no mob of hysterical vigilantes ever promised more bad news. You'd see them at ten in the morning on the terrace of the Continental waiting for the bar to open, barely able to light their own cigarettes until it did. The crowds on Tu Do Street looked like Ensor processioners, and there was a corruption in the air that had nothing to do with government workers on the take. After seven in the evening,

141

when the curfew included Americans and became total, nothing but White Mice patrols and MP jeeps moved in the streets, except for a few young children who raced up and down over the rubbish, running newspaper kites up into the chilling wind.

We took a huge collective nervous breakdown, it was the compression and heat of heavy contact generated out until every American in Vietnam got a taste. Vietnam was a dark room full of deadly objects, the VC were everywhere all at once like spider cancer, and instead of losing the war in little pieces over years we lost it fast in under a week. After that, we were like the character in pop grunt mythology, dead but too dumb to lie down. Our worst dread of yellow peril became realized; we saw them now dying by the thousands all over the country, yet they didn't seem depleted, let alone exhausted, as the Mission was claiming by the fourth day. We took space back quickly, expensively, with total panic and close to maximum brutality. Our machine was devastating. And versatile. It could do everything but stop. As one American major said, in a successful attempt at attaining history, "We had to destroy Ben Tre in order to save it." That's how most of the country came back under what we called control, and how it remained essentially occupied by the Viet Cong and the North until the day years later when there were none of us left there.

The Mission Council joined hands and passed together through the Looking Glass. Our general's chariot was on fire, he was taking on smoke and telling us such incredible stories of triumph and victory that a few high-level Americans had to ask him to just cool it and let them do the talking. A British correspondent compared the Mission posture to the captain of the *Titanic* announcing, "There's no cause for alarm, we're only stopping briefly to take on a little ice."

By the time I got back to Saigon on the fourth day a lot of information from around the country had settled, and it was bad, even after you picked out the threads of rumor: like the one about the "Caucasians," obviously Americans, fighting for the VC, or the one about thousands of NVA executions in Hue and the "shallow graves" in the flats outside the city, both of which proved true. Almost as much as the grunts and the Vietnamese, Tet was pushing correspondents closer to the wall than they'd ever wanted to go. I realized later that, however childish I might remain, actual youth had been pressed out of me in just the three days that it took me to cross the sixty miles between Can Tho and Saigon. In Saigon, I saw friends flipping out almost completely; a few left, some took to their beds for days with the exhaustion of deep depression. I went the other way, hyper and agitated, until I was only doing three hours of sleep a night. A friend on the *Times* said he didn't mind his nightmares so much as the waking impulse to file on them. An old-timer who'd covered war since the Thirties heard us pissing and moaning about how *terrible* it was and he snorted, "Ha, I love you guys. You guys are beautiful. What the fuck did you think it was?" We thought it was already past the cut-off point where every war is just like every other war; if we knew how rough it was going to get, we might have felt better. After a few days the air routes opened again, and we went up to Hue.

Going in, there were sixty of us packed into a deuce-and-a-half, one of eight trucks moving in convoy from Phu Bai, bringing in over 300 replacements for the casualties taken in the earliest fighting south of the Perfume River. There had been a harsh, dark storm going on for days, and it turned the convoy route into a mudbed. It was terribly cold in the trucks, and the road was covered with leaves that had either been blown off the trees by the storm or torn away by our artillery, which had been heavy all along the road. Many of the houses had been completely collapsed, and not one had been left without pitting from shell fragments. Hundreds of refugees held to the side of the road as we passed, many of them wounded. The kids would laugh and shout, the old would look on with that silent tolerance for misery that made so many Americans uneasy, which was usually misread as indifference. But the younger men and women would often look at us with unmistakable contempt, pulling their cheering children back from the trucks.

We sat there trying to keep it up for each other, grinning at the bad weather and the discomfort, sharing the first fear, glad that we weren't riding point or closing the rear. They had been hitting our trucks regularly, and a lot of the convoys had been turned back. The houses that we passed so slowly made good cover for snipers, and one B-40 rocket could have made casualties out of a whole truckload of us. All the grunts were whistling, and no two were whistling the same tune, it sounded like a locker room before a game that nobody wanted to play. Or almost nobody. There was a black Marine called Philly Dog who'd been a gang lord in Philadelphia and who was looking forward to some street fighting after six months in the jungle, he could show the kickers what he could do with some city ground. (In Hue he turned out to be incredibly valuable. I saw him pouring out about a hundred rounds of .30-caliber fire into a breach in the wall, laughing, "You got to bring some to get some"; he seemed to be about the only man in Delta Company who hadn't been hurt yet.) And there was a Marine correspondent, Sergeant Dale Dye, who sat with a tall yellow flower sticking out of his helmet cover, a really outstanding target. He was rolling his eyes around and saying, "Oh yes, oh yes, Charlie's got his shit together here, this will be *bad*," and smiling happily. It was the same smile I saw a week later when a sniper's bullet tore up a wall two inches above his head, odd cause for amusement in anyone but a grunt.

Everyone else in the truck had that wild haunted going-West look that said it was perfectly correct to be here where the fighting would be the worst, where you wouldn't have half of what you needed, where it was colder than Nam ever got. On their helmets and flak jackets they'd written the names of old operations, of girlfriends, their war names (FAR FROM FEARLESS, MICKEY'S MONKEY, AVENGER V, SHORT TIME SAFETY MODE), their fantasies (BORN TO LOSE, BORN TO RAISE HELL, BORN TO KILL, BORN TO DIE), their ongoing information (HELL SUCKS, TIME IS ON MY SIDE, JUST YOU AND ME GOD—RIGHT?). One kid called to me, "Hey man! You want a story, man? Here man, write this: I'm up there on 881, this was May, I'm just up there walkin' the ridgeline like a movie star and this Zip jumps up smack into me, lays his AK-47 fucking right *into* me, only he's so *amazed* at my *cool* I got my whole clip off 'fore he knew how to thank me for it. Grease one." After twenty kilometers of this, in spite of the black roiling sky ahead, we could see smoke coming up from the far side of the river, from the Citadel of Hue.

The bridge was down that spanned the canal dividing the village of An Cuu and the southern sector of Hue, blown the night before by the Viet Cong, and the forward area beyond the far bank wasn't thought to be secure, so we bivouacked in the village for the night. It had been completely deserted, and we set ourselves up in empty hootches, laying our poncho liners out over broken glass and shattered brick. At dusk, while we all stretched out along the canal bank eating dinner, two Marine gunships came down on us and began strafing us, sending burning tracers up along the canal, and we ran for cover, more surprised than scared. "Way to go, motherfucker, way to pinpoint the fuckin' enemy," one of the grunts said, and he set up his M-60 machine gun in case they came back. "I don't guess we got to take *that* shit," he said. Patrols were sent out, guards posted, and we went into the hootches to sleep. For some reason, we weren't even mortared that night.

In the morning we crossed the canal on a two-by-four and started walking in until we came across the first of the hundreds of civilian dead that we were to see in the next weeks: an old man arched over his straw hat and a little girl who'd been hit while riding her bicycle, lying there with her arm up like a reproach. They'd been lying out like that for a week, for the first time we were grateful for the cold.

Along the Perfume River's south bank there is a long, graceful park that separates Hue's most pleasant avenue, Le Loi, from the riverfront. People will talk about how they'd sit out there in the sun and watch the sampans moving down the river, or watch the girls bicycling up Le Loi, past the villas of officials and the French-architected University buildings. Many of those villas had been destroyed and much of the University permanently damaged. In the middle of the street a couple of ambulances from the German Mission had been blown up, and the Cercle Sportif was covered with bullet holes and shrapnel. The rain had brought up the green, it stretched out cased in thick white fog. In the park itself, four fat green dead lay sprawled around a tall, ornate cage, inside of which sat a small, shivering monkey. One of the correspondents along stepped over the corpses to feed it some fruit. (Days later, I came back to the spot. The corpses were gone, but so was the monkey. There had been so many refugees and so little food then, and someone must have eaten him.) The Marines of 2/5 had secured almost all of the central south bank and were now fanning out to the west, fighting and clearing one of the major canals. We were waiting for some decision on whether or not U.S. Marines would be going into the Citadel itself, but no one had any doubts about what that decision would be. We sat there taking in the dread by watching the columns of smoke across the river, receiving occasional sniper rounds, infrequent bursts of .50-caliber, watching the Navy LCU's on the river getting shelled from the wall. One Marine next to me was saying that it was just a damned shame, all them poor people, all them nice-looking houses, they even had a Shell station there. He was looking at the black napalm blasts and the wreckage along the wall. "Looks like the Imperial City's had the schnitz," he said.

The courtyard of the American compound in Hue was filled with puddles from the rain, and the canvas tops of the jeeps and trucks sagged with the weight of the water. It was the fifth day of the fighting, and everyone was still amazed that the NVA or the Cong had not hit the compound on the first night. An enormous white goose had come into the compound that night, and now his wings were heavy with the oil that had formed on the surface of the puddles. Every time a vehicle entered the yard he would beat his wings in a fury and scream, but he never left the compound and, as far as I knew, no one ate him.

Nearly 200 of us were sleeping in the two small rooms that had been the compound's dining quarters. The Army was not happy about having to billet so many of the Marines that were coming through, and they were absolutely furious about all the correspondents who were hanging around now, waiting until the fighting moved north across the river, into the Citadel. You were lucky to find space enough on the floor to lie down on, luckier if you found an empty stretcher to sleep on, and luckiest of all if the stretcher was new. All night long the few unbroken windows would rattle from the airstrikes across the river, and a mortar pit just outside fired incessantly. At two or three in the morning, Marines would come in from their patrols. They'd cross the room, not much caring whether they stepped on anyone or not. They'd turn their radios on and shout across the room to one another. "Really, can't you fellows show a bit more consideration?" a British correspondent said, and their laughter woke anyone who was not already up.

One morning there was a fire in the prison camp across the road from the compound. We saw the black smoke rising over the barbed wire that topped the camp wall and heard automatic weapons' fire. The prison was full of captured NVA and Viet Cong or Viet Cong suspects, the guards said that they'd started the fire to cover an escape. The ARVN and a few Americans were shooting blindly into the flames, and the bodies were burning where they fell. Civilian dead lay out on the sidewalks only a block from the compound, and the park by the river was littered with dead. It was cold and the sun never came out once, but the rain did things to the corpses that were worse in their way than anything the sun could have done. It was on one of those days that I realized that the only corpse I couldn't bear to look at would be the one I would never have to see.

It stayed cold and dark like that for the next ten days, and that damp gloom was the background for all the footage that we took out of the Citadel. What little sunlight there was caught the heavy motes of dust that blew up from the wreckage of the east wall, held it until everything you saw was filtered through it. And you saw things from unaccustomed angles, quick looks from a running crouch, or up from flat out, hearing the hard dry rattle of shrapnel scudding against the debris around you. With all of that dust blowing around, the acrid smell of cordite would hang in the air for a long time after firefights, and there was the CS gas that we'd fired at the NVA blowing back in over our positions. It was impossible to get a clean breath with all of that happening, and there was that other smell too that came up from the shattered heaps of stone wherever an airstrike had come in. It held to the lining of your nostrils and worked itself into the weave of your fatigues, and weeks later, miles away, you'd wake up at night and it would be in the room with you. The NVA had dug themselves so deeply into the wall that airstrikes had to open it meter by meter, dropping napalm as close as a hundred meters from our positions. Up on the highest point of the wall, on what had once been a tower, I looked across the Citadel's moat and saw the NVA moving quickly across the rubble of the opposing wall. We were close enough to be able to see their faces. A rifle went off a few feet to my right, and one of the running figures jerked back and dropped. A Marine sniper leaned out from his cover and grinned at me.

Between the smoke and the mist and the flying dust inside the Citadel, it was hard to call that hour between light and darkness a true dusk, but it was the time when most of us would open our C rations. We were only meters away from the worst of the fighting, not more than a Vietnamese city block in distance, and yet civilians kept appearing, smiling, shrugging, trying to get back to their homes. The Marines would try to menace them away at rifle point, shouting, "Di, di, *di*, you sorry-ass motherfuckers, go on, get the hell away from here!" and the refugees would smile, half bowing, and flit up one of the shattered streets. A little boy of about ten came up to a bunch of Marines from Charlie Company. He was laughing and moving his head from side to side in a funny way. The fierceness in his eyes should have told everyone what it was, but it had never occurred to most of the grunts that a Vietnamese child could be driven mad too, and by the time they understood it the boy had begun to go for their eyes and tear at their fatigues, spooking everyone, putting everyone really uptight, until a black grunt grabbed him from behind and held his arm. "C'mon, poor li'l baby, 'fore one a these grunt mothers shoots you," he said, and carried the boy to where the corpsmen were.

On the worst days, no one expected to get through it alive. A despair set in among members of the battalion that the older ones, the veterans of two other wars, had never seen before. Once or twice, when the men from Graves Registration took the personal effects from the packs and pockets of dead Marines, they found letters from home that had been delivered days before and were still unopened.

We were running some wounded onto the back of a half-ton truck, and one of the young Marines kept crying from his stretcher. His sergeant held both of his hands, and the Marine kept saying, "Shit, Sarge, I ain' gone make it. Oh damn, I'm gone die, ain't I?" "No, you ain't gonna die, for Christ's sake," the sergeant said. "Oh yeah, Sarge, yeah, I am." "Crowley," the sergeant said, "you ain't hurt that bad. I want you to just shut the fuck up. You ain't done a thing except bitch ever since we got to this fucking Hue City." But the sergeant didn't really know. The kid had been hit in the throat, and you couldn't tell about those. Throat wounds were bad. Everyone was afraid of throat wounds.

We lucked out on our connections. At the battalion aid station we got a chopper that carried us and a dozen dead Marines to the base at Phu Bai, and three minutes after we landed there we caught a C-130 to Danang. Hitching in from the airfield, we found a Psyops officer who felt sorry for us and drove us all the way to the press center. As we came in the gate we could see that the net was up and the daily volleyball game between the Marines assigned to the press center was on.

"Where the hell have *you* guys been?" one of them asked. We looked pretty fucked up.

The inside of the dining room was freezing with air-conditioning. I sat at a table and ordered a hamburger and a brandy from one of the peasant girls who waited tables. I sat there for a couple of hours and ordered four more hamburgers and at least a dozen brandies. It wasn't possible, just not possible, to have been where we'd been before and to

be where we were now, all in the same afternoon. One of the correspondents who had come back with me sat at another table, also by himself,
and we looked at each other, shook our heads and laughed. I went to my
room and took my boots and fatigues off and got into the shower. The
water was incredibly hot, for a moment I thought I'd gone insane from
it, and I sat down on the concrete floor for a long time, shaving there,
soaping myself over and over. I dressed and went back to the dining room.
The net was down now, one of the Marines said hello and asked me if I
knew what the movie was going to be that night. I ordered a steak and
another long string of brandies. When I left the correspondent was still
sitting alone. I got into bed and smoked a joint. I was going back in the
morning, it was understood, but why was it understood? All of my stuff
was in order, ready for the five-o'clock wake-up. I finished the joint and
shuddered off into sleep.

By the end of the week the wall had cost the Marines roughly one casualty
for every meter taken, a quarter of them KIA. 1/5, which came to be
known as the Citadel Battalion, had been through every tough battle the
Marines had had in the past six months, they'd even fought the same
NVA units a few weeks before between Hai Vanh Pass and Phu Loc, and
now three of its companies were below platoon strength. They all knew
how bad it was, the novelty of fighting in a city had become a nasty joke,
everyone wanted to get wounded.

At night in the CP, the major who commanded the battalion would
sit reading his maps, staring vacantly at the trapezoid of the Citadel. It
could have been a scene in a Norman farmhouse twenty-five years ago,
with candles burning on the tables, bottles of red wine arranged along
damaged shelves, the chill in the room, the high ceilings, the heavy ornate
cross on the wall. The major had not slept for five nights, and for the
fifth night in a row he assured us that tomorrow would get it for sure,
the final stretch of wall would be taken and he had all the Marines he
needed to do it. And one of his aides, a tough mustang first lieutenant,
would pitch a hard, ironic smile above the major's stare, a smile that
rejected good news, it was like hearing him say, "The major here is full
of shit, and we both know it."

Sometimes a company would find itself completely cut off, and it
would take hours for the Marines to get their wounded out. I remember
one Marine with a headwound who finally made it to the Battalion CP
when the jeep he was in stalled. He finally jumped out and started to
push, knowing it was the only way out of there. Most of the tanks and
trucks that carried casualties had to move up a long straight road without
cover, and they began calling it Rocket Alley. Every tank the Marines
had there had been hit at least once. An epiphany of Hue appeared in

John Olson's great photograph for *Life*, the wounded from Delta Company hurriedly piled on a tank. Sometimes, on the way to the aid station the more seriously wounded would take on that bad color, the gray-blue fishbelly promise of death that would spread upward from the chest and cover the face. There was one Marine who had been shot through the neck, and all the way out the corpsmen massaged his chest. By the time they reached the station, though, he was so bad that the doctor triaged him, passed him over to treat the ones that he knew could still be saved, and when they put him into the green rubber body bag there was some chance that he was clinically alive. The doctor had never had to make choices like that before, and he wasn't getting used to it. During the lulls he'd step outside for some air, but it was no better out there. The bodies were stacked together and there was always a crowd of ARVN standing around staring, death-enthralled like all Vietnamese. Since they didn't know what else to do, and not knowing what it would look like to the Marines, they would smile at the bodies there, and a couple of ugly incidents occurred. The Marines who worked the body detail were overloaded and rushed and became snappish, ripping packs off of corpses angrily, cutting gear away with bayonets, heaving bodies into the green bags. One of the dead Marines had gone stiff and they had trouble getting him to fit. *"Damn,"* one of them said, "this fucker had big feet. Didn't this fucker have big feet," as he finally forced the legs inside. In the station there was the youngest-looking Marine I'd ever seen. He'd been caught in the knee by a large piece of shrapnel, and he had no idea of what they'd do with him now that he was wounded. He lay out on the stretcher while the doctor explained how he would be choppered back to Phu Bai hospital and then put on a plane for Danang and then flown back to the States for what would certainly be the rest of his tour. At first the boy was sure that the doctor was kidding him, then he started to believe it, and then he knew it was true, he was actually getting out, he couldn't stop smiling, and enormous tears ran down into his ears.

It was at this point that I began to recognize almost every casualty, remember conversations we'd had days or even hours earlier, and that's when I left, riding a medevac with a lieutenant who was covered with blood-soaked bandages. He'd been hit in both legs, both arms, the chest and head, his ears and eyes were full of caked blood, and he asked a photographer in the chopper to get a picture of him like this to send to his wife.

But by then the battle for Hue was almost over. The Cav was working the northwest corner of the Citadel, and elements of the 101st had come in through what had formerly been an NVA re-supply route. (In five days these outfits lost as many men as the Marines had in three weeks.) Vietnamese Marines and some of the 1st ARVN Division had been moving the remaining NVA down toward the wall. The NVA flag that had flown for so long over the south wall had been cut down, and in its place an American flag had been put up. Two days later the Hoc Bao, Vietnamese Rangers, stormed through the walls of the Imperial Palace, but there were no NVA left inside. Except for a few bodies in the moat, most of their dead had been buried. When they'd first come into Hue the NVA had sat at banquets given for them by the people. Before they left, they'd skimmed all the edible vegetation from the surface of the moat. Seventy percent of Vietnam's one lovely city was destroyed, and if the landscape seemed desolate, imagine how the figures in that landscape looked.

There were two official ceremonies marking the expulsion of the NVA, both flag-raisings. On the south bank of the Perfume River, 200 refugees from one of the camps were recruited to stand, sullen and silent in the rain, and watch the GVN flag being run up. But the rope snapped, and the crowd, thinking the VC had shot it down, broke up in panic. (There was no rain in the stories that the Saigon papers ran, no trouble with the rope, and the cheering crowd numbered thousands.) As for the other ceremony, the Citadel was thought by most people to be insecure, and when the flag finally went up there was no one to watch it except for a handful of Vietnamese troops.

Major Trong bounced around in the seat of his jeep as it drove us over the debris scattered across the streets of Hue. His face seemed completely expressionless as we passed the crowds of Vietnamese stumbling over the fallen beams and powdered brick of their homes, but his eyes were covered by dark glasses and it was impossible to know what he was feeling. He didn't look like a victor, he was so small and limp in his seat I was afraid he was going to fly out of the jeep. His driver was a sergeant named Dang, one of the biggest Vietnamese I'd ever seen, and his English was better than the major's. The jeep would stall on rubble heaps from time to time, and Dang would turn to us and smile an apology. We were on our way to the Imperial Palace.

A month earlier the Palace grounds had been covered with dozens of dead NVA and the burned-over leavings of three weeks' siege and defense. There had been some reluctance about bombing the Palace, but a lot of the bombing nearby had done heavy damage, and there had been some shelling, too. The large bronze urns were dented beyond restoring, and the rain poured through a hole in the roof of the throne room, soaking the two small thrones where the old Annamese royalty had sat. In the great hall (great once you'd scaled it to the Vietnamese) the red lacquer work on the upper walls was badly chipped, and a heavy dust covered everything. The crown of the main gate had collapsed, and in the garden the broken branches of the old cay-dai trees lay like the forms of giant insects seared in a fire, wispy, delicate, dead. It was rumored during those days that the Palace was being held by a unit of student volunteers who had taken the invasion of Hue as a sign and had rushed to join the North Vietnamese. (Another rumor of those days, the one about some 5,000 "shallow graves" outside the city, containing the bodies from NVA executions, had just now been shown to be true.)

But once the walls had been taken and the grounds entered, there was no one left inside except for the dead. They bobbed in the moat and littered all the approaches. The Marines moved in then, and empty ration cans and muddied sheets from the *Stars and Stripes* were added to the litter. A fat Marine had been photographed pissing into the locked-open mouth of a decomposing North Vietnamese soldier.

"No good," Major Trong said. "No good. Fight here very hard, very bad."

I'd been talking to Sergeant Dang about the Palace and about the line of emperors. When we stalled one last time at the foot of a moat bridge, I'd been asking him the name of the last emperor to occupy the throne. He smiled and shrugged, not so much as if he didn't know, more like it didn't matter.

"Major Trong is emperor now," he said, and gunned the jeep into the Palace grounds.

QUESTIONS FOR CRITICAL READERS

Remembering and Understanding

1. What is the central point that Herr is making with his descriptions and stories of combat in Hue during the Tet Offensive?
2. Herr says that during Tet Saigon looked like the last reel of *On The Beach*. Find a review or summary of that film, or watch the film itself if you can, and find out what it is about. Explain how this information helps you understand Herr's allusion to it.
3. Using Herr's stories about the Marines he is with, describe what these men were like.
4. Using details that Herr provides, describe what the city of Hue looked like during the siege.

Analyzing and Discussing

5. Herr says that the Mission Council "joined hands and passed together through the Looking Glass." The allusion here is to Lewis Carroll's *Through the Looking Glass*. Refer to Carroll's book and find out what Herr means by applying it to those in charge of the U.S. Command in Vietnam.
6. Choose several passages that seem to communicate Herr's attitude toward

the scenes he describes and the war itself, and use these as the basis of a description of his attitude.

Writing

7. What is your reaction to Herr's language? Does his language contribute to his descriptions and make them more effective, or does it get in the way? Is Herr's language necessary to the point he is making, or is he simply engaging in gratuitous obscenity? Using specific examples from Herr's description, write an explanation of your response.

The Women Who Went

———— MYRA MCPHERSON ————

McPherson did not serve in Vietnam. After the war was over she became interested in the experiences of those who had served and collected their stories in her book Long Time Passing, *from which this selection is taken.*

LYNDA VAN DEVANTER TELLS HER STORY with the flair of an actress now. Since 1980, when she became a national VA spokeswoman for Vietnam women veterans, Van Devanter has told it on television shows and in congressional hearings and for journalists. To those who have heard it often, there is a staginess to the tremble, the tears, the melodramatic catch in her voice. And yet for years it was not this way. Buried deeply, locked away were her memories of Vietnam. From 1969 to 1970 Van Devanter was an operating room nurse in Pleiku. Years later Van Devanter sought psychiatric help. She never dreamed of mentioning Vietnam as a cause of any emotional problems. That, she thought, would be "over-dramatizing. Vietnam was years ago. It must just be me." Today, she recalls that in those "closet-veteran" years, "I had a recurring nightmare that scared the absolute shit out of me. There are tons and tons of black, napalm-burned skin about to crash down on me. The dream always starts with this 'plop, plop, plop,' and I always think it is rain. And then I look up and everything over me is covered with black, bloody, *stinking*—I can still smell it—burned flesh. And it's all coming down and I think I'm going to drown in it. I would wake up screaming and realized I better get into therapy real fast—but I sure better not tell the doctor about *this* because he might think I'm crazy, might commit me."

Her real stories were hardly different from the nightmares. "Napalm burn just reeks—*reeks*. If you try to brush napalm off, it continues to roll down, it just oozes fire along the skin. Burning flesh smells are so beyond description. Add to that the smell of napalm, a petroleum distillate, *and* the infection, which happens with really bad burns. The infection gives off a very distinct odor, a little bit like a sewer. The combination of these three smells you will *never ever* lose the memory of."

153

Another memory, so a part of Van Devanter now that it is told by rote, in present tense, is of the death of one young man. "It is the largest trail of blood leading to the table that I have ever seen. I slip in it because my eyes are drawn to the gurney [a stretcher]. As they move him to the operating table, I watch in horror as the lower portion of his jaw, teeth exposed, dangles from what is left of his face." She chokes. "I have to catch myself to keep from getting sick. He is drowning in blood. I grab a tray of instruments. For the sake of speed, we perform the tracheotomy without donning gloves . . . The surgeon grabs instruments from the tray to clamp off the largest bleeders in the face and jaw. The soldier is bleeding so fast that it is necessary to start four large needles in his leg, neck, and both arms and to pump blood into all of them simultaneously." For several hours Van Devanter does this, moving around the body, continuously pumping blood into those four large needles. "During one of my circuits around the table, I kick his clothes to one side, to get them out of the way, and a snapshot falls out of the pocket of his fatigues." It is a picture of the soldier and his girl—dressed for a prom. He is straight, blond, and tall in his tuxedo. She has shining dark hair and is wearing a long pastel gown. The tears come to Van Devanter again. "Love for him shines in her eyes."

For months, Van Devanter had tried to feel as little as possible. "There had been that veneer of unreality," she says, shifting to the past tense. "Suddenly now, he was *real* to me.

"Finally, after six hours of surgery, the surgeon decided it was hopeless. He packed his head in pressure dressings and sent him to the post-op intensive care unit to die. As I cleaned up the room, I kept telling myself that a miracle could happen. I came upon the photograph again, picked it up, and stared. He was a young man who could love and think and plan and dream—and now he was lost to himself, to her, and to their future. I sat on the floor and sobbed. After making the room ready for the next casualty, I walked over to the post-op ICU to see him. His bandages had become saturated with blood several times over, and the nurses reinforced them with more rolls of bandages, and now his head was grotesquely large under the swath of white." Still, the red stains seeped through. Van Devanter held his hand and asked if he was in pain. He squeezed her hand weakly. Van Devanter called for pain medication. "I held his hand until the life just literally drained out of him. He literally bled to death . . .

"That boy has been a constant nightmare. I can see everything about him, every single blood vessel of his face. There is another nightmare. Lines and lines and lines of mothers sobbing and crying, not knowing: 'Why did he die? How did he die? What was it like for him? Who was there? Did our government really not take care of him?' "

Van Devanter's quest today is to find the thousands of nurses who came back from Vietnam with their own troubled memories, only to receive the same hostility and indifference she and many others found. These women are truly the forgotten Vietnam veterans nobody knows.

And, like male veterans, they have diverse feelings about the war. In 1983 Van Devanter wrote the first account of the war by a woman veteran, *Home Before Morning*. Her autobiography sparked an emotional debate among nurses who said she exaggerated and distorted conditions to bolster her antimilitary political views. Van Devanter denied the distortions, attributing much of the criticism to her strong antiwar tones and political activism. She was among the VVA delegation who made a controversial trip to Hanoi in 1982.

Van Devanter vividly describes grueling seventy-two-hour shifts by medical personnel "falling into an almost deathlike sleep at the operating tables," working under a barrage of rocket attacks, standing in mud and blood while tending to a "steady flow of casualties."

Colonel Mary Grace, who was a nursing supervisor in the evacuation hospital where Van Devanter worked, commented, "I certainly don't recognize that. I'd say she's been watching too much 'M*A*S*H.' " "This book makes us look like a bunch of bed-hopping, foul-mouthed tramps," blasted retired Colonel Edith Knox, a former head nurse of the 67th Evacuation Hospital in Qui Nhon. Jo Ann Webb, former Army nurse, said Van Devanter "fictionalized" the work load. "She talks about this endless flow of casualties, and official Army figures show the hospital was 50 percent full. I'm incensed that she's become a professional veteran and now she's making money off it." However, Webb's husband, James Webb, who wrote the bestselling *Fields of Fire*, is regarded as a professional veteran and a financially successful one, in many veteran circles. His wife shares Webb's view that the war was a right cause and wants to portray veterans in the best possible light. During one conversation with me, she insisted that the majority of the men on her ward had used heroin before coming to Vietnam, although official statistics contradict such anecdotal evidence.

"These people would obviously prefer that I had written a book that said we were saints and angels and everything was wonderful," said Van Devanter. "They're trying to write revisionist history. It's absolute bullshit for Jo Ann Webb to spout these figures, which don't tell you anything about the magnitude of the casualties. This is not a book about numbers. This is also not a big sex book. I mentioned exactly two relationships in Vietnam, both of which illustrated the need to hold onto another human being in a situation of complete insanity."

Her descriptions of Vietnam are substantiated by other women veterans, including her former roommate, Army nurse Lynn Calmes Kohl. Now a housewife in Appleton, Wisconsin, Kohl, like Van Devanter, suffered a breakdown after the war.

"Actually," said Kohl, "what Lynda wrote was mild."

For the public who long ignored Vietnam, Van Devanter's experiences were shocking but important revelations.

One reader, William Baffa, following one published account in the Los Angeles *Times*, wrote a letter representative of most. "I read with horror the article about the young soldier who bled to death of head wounds . . . the tiny children with arms and legs blown off . . . the pregnant woman and her child who entered the world with a gunshot wound in his belly. *It ruined my day!* My hope is that it ruined the day for many readers . . . Can anything short of ridding our civilization of the periodical insanity of war really honor the sacrifices that countless millions have made to do what remains a 'to-be-continued' cause? How long can we continue to demand this devastating sacrifice of the young and innocent?"

Kathy Gunson, who was stationed at the 85th Evacuation Hospital in Phu Bai was an emergency room nurse. She also was the evaluator of the cause of death for the Killed in Action (KIA). "One minute I had a friend, and the next minute I was determining his cause of death." She was also a triage officer, presiding over those who had been "triaged out"—left to die because they were so far gone. There were only so many nurses and doctors to work on those who might be saved.

"I desperately want my childhood back—with its innocence and ignorance. I want to go back to Vietnam and make it different," she wrote in 1979. "I want to come home to a marching band and a red carpet. I want to hear a 'thank you.' I want to hear 'I'm sorry.' " The nurse could no longer nurse. "I love nursing, but the sight of pain, suffering, and blood makes me ill, and I grieve because I can no longer cope with my feelings when I'm working." Above all, Gunson wanted to "feel at peace with myself."

"What haunts me," says Van Devanter, "is that nobody knows of the contribution of these women. The major legacy study of Vietnam veterans does not include *one* woman. The mother of the boy who lost his face has no idea that somebody was standing and holding her son's hand. Even the ones who were triaged out, the 'expectant ones,' were not just shunted over to a corner. Somebody would always go and take their hand and speak to them quietly, just in case they *could* hear. The people of this country have no concept of that. Their sons might have died in vain for a cause that was horrendous—but they didn't die alone."

So little is known about the nurses of Vietnam that there are not even accurate statistics on how many were there. Official "guesstimates" range anywhere from 7,500 to 55,000. Like so many who had direct experience, Van Devanter decries Pentagon statistics, especially the DOD "official" numbers of women who served in Vietnam. "It is *absolutely inaccurate.* The Air Force doesn't even know, and the Army states 234 nurses. I know that for the one year I was in Vietnam there were a *minimum* of 500. For the years 1969 and 1970, the DOD shows a total of six in all of Pleiku! There were seven in my quarters *alone* in one year. There were a total of at least fifty-five or sixty just at my hospital, and that doesn't include any other outfits in Pleiku."

"Although animal studies show that females are more susceptible to the reproductive side effects of dioxin, not one female has been included in Agent Orange studies," adds Van DeVanter.

"In each town I visited, I've made a point of calling the VA hospital and stating clearly that I am a service-connected veteran of Vietnam and I require gynecological care. I was told by nearly every location that they did not have a GYN clinic or a GYN physician." The response of the VA is that since women comprise such a small number of veterans, it would not be feasible to provide such services—but that the women were entitled to receive government-paid service with a private gynecologist. Yet, Van Devanter claims, "In no case save one was I told that I was entitled to receive that care by contract service with a private physician— and that was only because I pushed it."

That was in 1981. Two years later, in March of 1983, for the first time there was finally a congressional hearing and a GAO report which indicted the VA for its lack of services and outreach for women.

Countless nurses did not know they had been entitled to GI education benefits. Unfortunately for most, the ten-year time period for qualification after leaving the service had expired.

Women who have served in the military have historically been ignored.

"When women tried to join veterans' groups, they were told they couldn't be full-time members," said Van Devanter. Not until 1978 did the VFW finally agree to permit women veterans to join as members. Some might surmise after such treatment, "Why would anyone want to join them?"—but women veterans should have the right to *refuse*, not be told they *can't* join.

World War II movies portrayed nurses as bravely waiting for their gallant lovers to return, with intermittent forays to the operating table. Or they were given saintly roles—epitomized in one movie where Veronica Lake walks toward a nest of hated Japs, a grenade inside her blouse, a sacrificial *kamikaze* blonde beauty who would save the rest of the hospital.

In actuality, World War II's massive mobilization brought 350,000 women into the service as well as many others who served in quasi-military support units such as the WASP, whose 800 women pilots ferried war planes around the world. They drove trucks, changed tires, repaired planes, and rigged parachutes; were gunnery instructors, air traffic controllers, naval air navigators, and nurses. The first WAC unit landed in Normandy thirty-eight days after D-Day. And sixty-five women were taken captive as POWs on Corregidor. Nurses were on the beachhead at Anzio. Studies of World War II women in the service showed that they developed psychological disorders less frequently than men, their venereal disease rate was one sixth that of men, the WAC pregnancy rate was negligible, and their disciplinary rates were much lower.

During Korea, and then again during Vietnam, the unpopularity of the wars brought far fewer women into the military.

In all wars, women have been killed, maimed, disabled, and injured psychologically. No Vietnam nurses argue that they have a corner on this. However, Vietnam had its special characteristics. Nurses often suffered a more severe emotional mauling than soldiers who had respites in combat, as has been mentioned. They saw waves of the mutilated fresh from the battlefield, who in previous wars would never have been saved that long.

In this war, long on booby traps, gore was the norm.

Peggy DuVall, a New York State Vietnam veteran, remembers pumping blood into an eighteen-year-old who stepped on a mine. "Both eyes were removed, and his face was totally chewed up. He lost an arm and a leg. A shell fragment tore a hole in his trachea. When you finally saved a life," she said, "you wondered what kind of life you had saved. We could never have been prepared for that kind of nursing. We saw football-hero types with their legs blown off. We saw boys go home as vegetables because of crazy tropical diseases." DuVall repeats the words used by a remarkable number of former Vietnam nurses, "We put their bodies back together *as best we could.*"

Many nurses tended to overinvest emotionally in their patients, even when the patients' chances of living were poor. Du Vall, who worked in hospitals in Da Nang and Long Binh, recalls that on a 7 P.M. to 7 A.M. shift, two nurses and two medics would take care of seventy-eight men. Exhaustion and trying to build a wall around their emotions led to deep depressions for many.

"People don't want to hear about the blood and guts," said Cissy Shellabarger, "but that's all I know about, the grief. It was the first time I've ever been that frightened." In the emergency room of an evacuation hospital in Cu Chi, she worked around the clock during the Tet Offensive of 1968.

The morning in 1968 that the Tet Offensive began, mortar-rocket attacks thundered on the hospital. Still, the medical corps continued to work. Nurses saw soldiers with legs blown off who were in so much shock they registered no pain. Another Vietnam nurse, Sharon Balsey, says, "In U.S. emergency rooms you hardly ever see blast injuries. I just freaked out. Nothing prepares you for it. I never got to the point where the mutilation of bodies didn't bother me."

Many Vietnam nurses still recall how affected they were about working on men so young, in this teenage war, where the average age was nineteen.

During Tet "I've never seen so many wounded in my life. It reminded me of that scene in *Gone with the Wind* where all the wounded are lined up for miles around the railroad station," says Shellabarger. "And the rumors were so bad—that Saigon had fallen, things like that . . . Not knowing the truth was the worst."

There are seven nurses' names on the Vietnam Veterans Memorial, but that small a number of dead does not fully convey a sense of the daily fear of death or injury. There were no front lines and few rear areas. Although the antiwar movement made much of American pilots bombing North Vietnam hospitals, enemy mortar-rocket attacks on U.S. hospitals were by and large overlooked in the States and formed no part of antiwar rhetoric. For nurses, mortar attacks meant the nightmare of trying to get the wounded under cots, of working in horrifying conditions, of not knowing if they would be hit.

"In the central highlands, the physical danger was there all the time. The VC would sometimes bomb the hospitals just out of harassment," said Van Devanter. "Oftentimes, they would bomb the hospitals intentionally, trying to kill a high-ranking POW who had been taken, who was injured and in the hospital. You knew if you had any NVA over the rank of major, you could *count* on rocket attacks all night long."

Many of the women went because they believed in their government, because they believed in a Florence Nightingale role, or for adventure, for the sense of helping. Many seem to have been Roman Catholics trained to believe in authority. "If our government said we were helping to stop communism," said one, "who were we to question?" Many returned pacifists; others upheld the view that the war was right but that the toll was terrible. "I was very hawkish at first, but later I was ready to say it wasn't a prosperous war. The cost in terms of life was terrible. The Vietnamese weren't willing to fight their own war. We should have left Vietnam earlier," said ex-nurse Sharon Balsey. No matter the viewpoint, disillusionment was there.

A rather typical reaction was from a nurse who cannot recall whether she was for or against the war when she went. "I just wanted to go and nurse." After her second day in the emergency room, she said, "You looked at one more of those boys, and you knew we were in the wrong place." She is still tormented. "Vietnam was really hard on me. I did not bounce well." She refuses still to confront her emergency room memories.

Certain differences separate the women from the men who served in Vietnam. First and foremost was the already mentioned ordeal of facing shattered casualties. "Medics had more in common with us than combat soldiers," said one nurse. The women often felt isolated because they were relatively so few in number. And there was a confusion of roles. On the one hand, women have been taught from childhood that it is okay to express emotions. This sometimes helped them. Together, the nurses could get drunk and cry. However, most of the time they had to negate those emotions in order to function. Most nurses recall, almost astonished, their toughness, the wall they were forced to build. However, they were also expected, as Shad Meshad explained it, "to be warm fuzzies."

A former Army psychologist in Vietnam, Meshad pioneered the Vietnam veterans psychological readjustment counseling outreach program. "Nurses had to be a wounded soldier's mother, wife, girlfriend. They saw these beautiful young eighteen- and nineteen-year-old kids, coming in every day with sucking chest wounds and ripped-off flesh, and they had to hold their hands and tell them everything was okay."

Like the soldiers who shot back, they wanted revenge.

For all the pain, nurses also recall a terrible nostalgia for the most intensely emotional time in their lives. Romances were often an attempt for a moment of closeness and tenderness; of escape, in a world gone mad.

As officers, they were not supposed to date enlisted men. However, most male officers were older and married. "I don't know how many times a doctor would tell me he couldn't bear to say goodbye to Jeannie, who was maybe twenty-two or twenty-three and deeply in love," recalls Meshad, who has, since Vietnam, counseled some 200 ex-nurses. "They'd ask me to do it for them."

"Above all," said Meshad, "the nurses, brought up to nurture and protect others, felt like failures because no matter what they did the GIs kept dying."

QUESTIONS FOR CRITICAL READERS

Remembering and Understanding

1. Describe the recognition that women Vietnam veterans have received for their service.
2. What do Vietnam War nurses claim is special about their experiences?
3. Summarize McPherson's account of the number of women who served in Vietnam.

Analyzing and Discussing

4. McPherson reports serious disagreements among Vietnam nurses about the conditions in which they served. Identify specific points of disagreement

and try to explain what causes them. How would you go about attempting to resolve these differences?

5. McPherson says that "women who have served in the military have historically been ignored." Why should this be so?

6. The nurses McPherson describes speak of nurturing, but also of wanting revenge. How can these two emotions be reconciled?

Writing

7. After doing the necessary research, write a paper in which you describe the role of women in the Persian Gulf war against Iraq in 1991. You should be able to find most of the information you need in standard newspaper and magazine indexes.

Blood

GLORIA EMERSON

In this excerpt from her book Winners and Losers, *Emerson uses blood as her subject and theme. She discusses the blood of soldiers who fought, and the symbolic blood that those who protested against the war poured on buildings, draft records, and themselves to dramatize their protest. While many of those who protested against the war did not fight in the war itself, their experiences are important to an understanding of how individuals reacted to and were affected by the war.*

BLOOD: SOMETIMES A GI would complain that the Vietnamese fighting him did not bleed enough. One man from North Carolina told me that when he cut himself shaving, he bled more than a "dink." There were soldiers puzzled by this; it seemed to bother a few. The reason was the Vietnamese did not have as much blood, for they were much slighter, they did not consume the vast amounts of food the Americans do. In the field, it was not special for infantrymen to be supplied by helicopters with hot lunches every three days, whose odd diet for the tropics included barbecued beef, cabbage, potatoes, two kinds of soft drinks, milk and two kinds of ice cream. Some units were allowed beer; others were not. It was too hot for the men to often want second helpings, and too much food made them sleepy. They had so much to carry: packs that weighed sixty-five pounds or more, nine quarts of water meant another eighteen pounds, one hundred rounds of ammunition were another six. The Vietnamese never ate like that, could not have as much blood in their smaller bodies, which did not bulge or thicken as ours do.

The blood of the soldiers and civilians never looked the same red. The shade changed with the wounds. Sometimes blood coming from the eyes or the skull looked a bright, fresh pink, but the blood was dark and browner if the wound was in the stomach. In the heat the blood seemed to dry in greenish ribbons on the clothes of the Vietnamese. After a while the blood did not matter unless a man drowned in his own; it was the wounds the blood concealed which were worse. Once in a ward of the provincial hospital of Quang Ngai, where the Vietnamese went, where the smell was that of a wet and rotting rag pressed over the face, among the patients was a man with no blood on him at all, although so red were his eyes, which he never seemed to blink, that blood might have been inside them. He sat on the edge of a cot in that darkened room, wearing undershorts, no inch of his skin as it once had been. He was covered with small black marks—ears, lips, hands, neck, wrists—made by shrapnel, almost as if he had been a target in a shooting gallery, unable to get away, being moved forward again and again to be hit by steel. He was waiting for a doctor, but two days later a doctor had not yet come.

In New York nothing worked like a liver. Jill Seiden Mahoney found out that if you mushed the liver on bandages, it made stains that looked like seeping, untreated head wounds. It looked ghastly and the smell was repulsive, which was fine. The liver was useful for the "die-ins," the name for reenactments by the antiwar movement of Vietnamese villagers receiving brutal injuries from American weapons, chemicals, bombs.

Mrs. Mahoney, who was single then, and her friends made up what they called the Emma Goldman Brigade, in honor of the anarchist. Before they demonstrated, the Brigade went to some trouble to make their faces look as if they had been scarred in the war. Their favorite method was to use a mixture of oatmeal, ketchup and liquid make-up foundations, which they put on their faces after twisting their skin with strips of Scotch tape. The effect was exactly what they wished: shocking.

The targets of their protests were often business corporations; in the spring of 1972 it was the ITT Building on Park Avenue. The ten women in the Brigade, dressed in black pajamas, with the liver-stained bandages on their heads and their faces deformed, rushed into the lobby when it was crowded in the morning with people coming to work. The first thing they did was to put up posters of wounded Vietnamese children on the marble walls.

"Then we started dying, we started our blood bath. We threw Baggies which had red stuff in them. We were screaming, yelling, dying, very dramatically. Here's the sick part: the janitors started ripping down the posters of those fucked-up hurt little babies. After fifteen minutes the police came. They seemed sort of scared of us," she said. "We were rolling on the floor; it was all they could do to get us to stand up and shut up. Each of us had a flare for drama and we were trying to imagine what it would be like for a Vietnamese woman under bombs. We had fun. It sounds childish to say that now, but it was exhilarating. That day we felt we were in control. If you're rolling on the floor, screaming, nobody wants to get near you. When we finally limped out, some people applauded.

"I never knew if they applauded because they enjoyed the show or because we were leaving or they thought they were brave," she said. "It was meant to disrupt; everybody was talking about us. Energy that might have been used in their jobs that day was going into talking about our demonstration.

"Oh, sure, I know that it is said that doing things like that alienated people. But look, any action will alienate somebody. You have to expect it."

In the sixth grade in P.S. 104 in New York, she knew that her IQ was over 130. Her parents were not surprised. After graduating from the University of Pennsylvania in 1967, she worked for an advertising agency, Cunningham & Walsh, in the city. "I was a Jewish princess," she said.

In the streets young people were passing out pamphlets denouncing the war in Vietnam, and from them she learned about it.

"I would take time off to go to antiwar demonstrations; it shocked some people, who called me a Communist. The antiwar movement was personally and socially fulfilling and it was lots of fun. I miss it very much but I'm glad the war is over. I miss the commitment and the urgency—the commitment to selflessness. When it happened I thought we were all just the greatest, as a group certainly more generous than the people in the advertising agency."

In those days she often wore a T-shirt saying "The East is Red, the West is Ready," while her friend Coke, an unusually pretty blonde, wore one saying "The Vietnamese People Are Not the Enemy." Both women did not care if people stared at their ample chests; they wanted the T-shirts to be read.

Some of their exploits were daring: ten of them bought tickets, at fifteen dollars apiece, to attend and disrupt the National Women's Republican Club lunch in March 1972, which honored Patricia Nixon as the Woman of the Year. It was crucial for them to look like ladies. They obliged.

"Everybody still had one good dress," Mrs. Mahoney said, who wore a pink-and-brown suit from Saks Fifth Avenue. Coke even had a fur coat which she had stopped wearing; it was skunk. The plan of the Emma Goldman Brigade was for five of them to release the rats they were carrying with them, healthy rats that had been secured from laboratories so no one could accuse them of using animals that might spread disease. They were always careful about small things like that. It went wrong in the lobby: a man she calls John Finnigan of the New York Red Squad, who was watching radicals, stopped seven of the women from going into the ballroom. Three of the rats had to be released in the lobby. Inside, Mrs. Mahoney, who did not have a rat, rose and in a strong voice spoke against the war, saying nothing—on the advice of a lawyer—that was either treasonous or obscene. Then she left, leaving the ladies at her table, who were Republicans from Westchester County, in an unpleasant, if not agitated, state of mind. Two more rats were released in the ballroom, causing some consternation, but the lunch and ceremony continued.

"The antiwar movement made a difference in me and in everybody who participated. I think if there had not been such a movement, they might have nuked Vietnam off the face of the earth," she said. "It forced people to recognize what was going on or to become totally, unnaturally, blind."

It still puzzles her why other people do not understand very much, do not even know that GVN meant the Government of Vietnam in Saigon, that DRVN meant the north, or the Democratic Republic of Vietnam, that ARVN was the army in the south.

"They can tell you someone's batting average from 1948, or who hit the big homer in the 1932 World Series, but they don't know the difference between the NLF and the NFL."

The blindness, as she called it, always surprised her. On the day of the Emma Goldman Brigade's die-in in the lobby of the ITT Building, it was raining. The group worried that the rain might wash off some of the mess they had put on their faces. It was decided to take taxis.

"We were totally mutilated. None of us were recognizable," she said. "We got into two cabs at Fifty-third and Third. In each cab one person had to sit in front, so the drivers had to see what we looked like. We told them where we wanted to go and they didn't say a word. Remember how we looked and what we wore, and besides that, we all smelled, it was the oatmeal and the other stuff. We smelled horrible. Neither driver said a word, or even did a double-take. And in one newspaper, I think it was the *Daily News,* they described us as 'slovenly hippies.' They just thought we were dirty."

The Emma Goldman Brigade did not hold together but the women have stayed friends. Her marriage in September 1973 to Peter Paul Mahoney peeled apart. They had met in the antiwar movement, gone through the hard days before and during the Gainesville trial, endured all of it, only to find out how different they were. In those days she saw him as a valiant fellow who stood out for her among all the other veterans going to war against the war.

Even when the war ended and she needed a job, Mrs. Mahoney was not one to jump over her principles. She now works for a small trade magazine, having refused to consider better-paying jobs related to the military-industrial complex, the stock market, or the manufacture of foods or consumer items she thinks are dangerous. She does not want to ever contribute in any way to the misery of any people.

She will not eat bacon or frankfurters because they contain nitrates. She is even beginning to cut back on pastrami. She will not eat canned tuna fish because she deplores the killing of the porpoises caught in the tuna nets and she thinks the waters are filthy. She is quite specific about insect parts and rodent hairs in some American chocolate. When she has time she makes her own cosmetics, but she hardly wears any.

There are no regrets, just a tiny afterthought.

"The Brigade should have used indelible red ink for blood," she said, "instead of Rite-Dye."

It became quite commonplace in the antiwar movement for bags of "blood"—red tempera paint—to be thrown at structures which symbolized the war, or whose offices made the war possible. They were thrown, over and over and over again, in the names of the people of Vietnam and Cambodia and Laos and their victims. On a Good Friday, April 20, 1973, to commemorate the shedding of the blood of Jesus Christ, bags of blood were thrown at five Boston institutions. Four people who threw blood inside the JFK Federal Building were charged with willful destruction of government property before a federal magistrate. The government claimed it took five men working for three hours to clean off the paint. The defendants were allowed five minutes for a summation statement. One of them, Madeleine Cousineau, pointed out that Pope Paul VI, in his encyclical "On the Development of Peoples," stated that property must never take precedence over the common good of people, that peace is not merely the absence of war—and that she felt Americans who continued to commemorate Good Friday and to call themselves "one nation under God" had to reexamine "our way of dealing with our fellow human beings . . ." She was fined thirty-five dollars.

Then the paint seemed trivial and false, so the blood of humans was used. On a Saturday at the end of April in 1973, six vials of it were splashed on the tables and walls of the State Dining Room during an ordinary public tour of the White House.

"Claire got the tables and I got the walls," Steve Cleghorn said. The woman was his wife. Both were in their twenties, described as Christian/Catholics who wanted to serve humanity. The couple both worked in a soup kitchen operated by the Community for Creative Non-Violence. Friends donated the blood to fill the vials. Nearly fifty people were in the room where White House dinners are given when the couple went to work. Some screamed out "Please don't, please don't, you awful people," "Kooks" and "Bastards!"

The man and the woman each said the same thing as they emptied the vials. It was: "This is the blood of your victims." Their manner was unperturbed and thoughtful.

"The blood is seeping through the walls and the blood is coming from underneath the varnish of the tables. It's not that we have put it there. It's already there," the woman said later.

"In some sense, what we did is cast in Gospel terms," Mr. Cleghorn, who had once studied in a Paulist seminary, explained. "The table of state is where the buying and selling goes on, internationally."

In a handwritten statement that was only published in *The Daily*

Rag, a community newspaper in Washington, D.C., which ran a long interview with them, the couple said: "There is no sanctuary from this blood. This is the blood of our brothers and sisters. We affirm this blood and life. We resist waste and death. We mark these walls and this table with the blood of your victims."

In the White House, when the State Dining Room was blood-splashed, they were arrested by Secret Service agents. One of them asked Mrs. Cleghorn if she meant to embarrass the President.

"That wasn't my intention; my intention was to speak the truth. If that embarrasses the President, let it be," she said.

QUESTIONS FOR CRITICAL READERS

Remembering and Understanding

1. Summarize the reasons that the women Emerson writes about protested against the war.
2. Describe the different ways protesters made themselves appear to be bleeding.
3. How did other people react to the protesters described here?

Analyzing and Discussing

4. Emerson uses blood as a synecdoche for the war, a part that represents the whole. What other images could serve as synecdoches for the Vietnam War, or for war in general?
5. What was the point of war protesters making themselves look like casualties of war? Does their use of real or imitation blood on themselves have symbolic value?
6. What appears to have been the purpose of the protests described here?

Writing

7. Identify a situation in which you believe you would feel compelled to protest an official policy that you disagreed with. Write a paper in which you describe that situation and method you would choose for your protest.

Hush, Timmy—
This Is Like a Church

—————— Kurt Andersen ——————

This article originally appeared in Time *magazine. It gives some background information about the origin of the Vietnam Memorial in Washington, D.C., and describes the experience of visiting that memorial. The Vietnam Memorial has become for many people a place that has a special atmosphere, and some veterans believe it has a special power to heal their own psychological wounds.*

THE VETERAN AND HIS WIFE had already stared hard at four particular names. Now the couple walked slowly down the incline in front of the wall, looking at rows of hundreds, thousands more, amazed at the roster of the dead. "All the names," she said quietly, sniffling in the early-spring chill. "It's unreal, how many names." He said nothing. "You have to see it to believe it," she said.

Just so. In person, close up, the Viet Nam Veterans Memorial—two skinny black granite triangles wedged onto a mound of Washington sod—is some kind of sanctum, beautiful and terrible. "We didn't plan that," says John Wheeler, chairman of the veterans' group that raised the money and built it. "I had a picture of seven-year-olds throwing a Frisbee around on the grass in front. But it's treated as a spiritual place." When Wheeler's colleague Jan Scruggs decided there ought to be a monument, he had only vague notions of what it might be like. "You don't set out and *build* a national shrine," Scruggs says. "It *becomes* one."

Washington is thick with monuments, several of them quite affecting. But as the Viet Nam War was singular and strange, the dark, dreamy, redemptive memorial to its American veterans is like no other. "It's more solemn," says National Park Service Ranger Sarah Page, who has also worked at the memorials honoring Lincoln, Washington and Jefferson. "People give it more respect." Lately it has been the most visited monument in the capital: 2.3 million saw it in 1984, about 45,000

168

a week, but it is currently drawing 100,000 a week. Where does it get its power—to console, and also to make people sob?

The men who set up the Viet Nam Veterans Memorial Fund wanted something that would include the name of every American killed in Viet Nam, and would be contemplative and apolitical. They conducted an open design competition that drew 1,421 entries, all submitted anonymously. The winner, Maya Ying Lin, was a Chinese-American undergraduate at Yale: to memorialize men killed in a war in Asia, an Asian female studying at an old antiwar hotbed.

Opposition to Lin's design was intense. The opponents wanted something gleaming and grand. To them, the low-slung black wall would send the same old defeatist, elitist messages that had lost the war in the '60s and then stigmatized the veterans in the '70s. "Creating the memorial triggered a lot of old angers and rage among vets about the war," recalls Wheeler, a captain in Viet Nam and now a Yale-trained Government lawyer. "It got white hot."

In the end, Lin's sublime and stirring wall was built, 58,022 names inscribed. As a compromise with opponents, however, a more conventional figurative sculpture was added to the site last fall (at a cost of $400,000). It does not spoil the memorial, as the art mandarins had warned. The three U.S. soldiers, cast in bronze, stand a bit larger than life, carry automatic weapons and wear fatigues, but the pose is not John Wayne-heroic: these American boys are spectral and wary, even slightly bewildered as they gaze southeast toward the wall. While he was planning the figures, sculptor Frederick Hart spent time watching vets at the memorial. Hart now grants that "no modernist monument of its kind has been as successful as that wall. The sculpture and the wall interact beautifully. Everybody won." Nor does Lin, his erstwhile artistic antagonist, still feel that Hart's statue is so awfully trite. "It captures the mood," says Lin. "Their faces have a lost look." Out at the memorial last week, one veteran looked at the new addition and nodded: "That's us."

But it is the wall that vets approach as if it were a force field. It is at the wall that families of the dead cry and leave flowers and mementos and messages, much as Jews leave notes for God in the cracks of Jerusalem's Western Wall. Around the statue, people talk louder and breathe easier, snap vacation photos unselfconsciously, eat Eskimo Pies and Fritos. But near the wall, a young Boston father tells his rambunctious son, "Hush, Timmy—this is like a church." The visitors' processionals do seem to have a ritual, even liturgical quality. Going slowly down toward the vertex, looking at the names, they chat less and less, then fall silent where the names of the first men killed (July 1959) and the last (May 1975) appear. The talk begins again, softly, as they follow the path up out of the little valley of the shadow of death.

For veterans, the memorial was a touchstone from the beginning, and the 1982 dedication ceremony a delayed national embrace. "The actual act of being at the memorial is healing for the guy or woman who went to Viet Nam," says Wheeler, who visits at least monthly. "It has to do with the felt presence of comrades." He pauses. "I always look at Tommy Hayes' name. Tommy's up on panel 50 east, line 29." Hayes, Wheeler's West Point pal, was killed 17 years ago this month. "I know guys," Wheeler says, "who are still waiting to go, whose wives have told me, 'He hasn't been able to do it yet.' " For those who go, catharsis is common. As Lin says of the names, chronologically ordered, "Veterans can look at the wall, find a name, and in a sense put themselves back in that time." The war has left some residual pathologies that the memorial cannot leach away. One veteran killed himself on the amphitheatrical green near the wall. A second, ex-Marine Randolph Taylor, tried and failed in January. "I regret what I did," he said. "I feel like I desecrated a holy place."

The memorial has become a totem, so much so that its tiniest imperfections make news. Last fall somebody noticed a few minute cracks at the seams between several of the granite panels. The cause of the hairlines is still unknown, and the builders are a little worried.

Probably no one is more determined than Wheeler to see the memorial's face made perfect, for he savors the startlingly faithful reflections the walls give off: he loves seeing the crowds of visitors looking simultaneously at the names and themselves. "Look!" he said the other day, gesturing at panel 4 east. "You see that plane taking off? You see the blue sky? No one expected that."

QUESTIONS FOR CRITICAL READERS

Remembering and Understanding

1. Summarize Andersen's account of what the Vietnam Memorial looks like and how this design was selected.
2. Based on the information Andersen provides, explain how the Vietnam Memorial is different from other war memorials.
3. Effective writers can often convey information without seeming to. Andersen gives information about the memorial's physical appearance, but he gives no separate description. Assemble the details he gives and write a description of the memorial using only the information that Andersen provides. Then, locate a photograph of the Memorial and test your description (and Andersen's details).

Analyzing and Discussing

4. What purpose is served by constructing monuments and memorials to wars and veterans?
5. What is it that gives the Vietnam Memorial a special quality that, Andersen says, vets approach as though it were a force field?

Writing

6. Recall a time when you visited a monument, memorial, battlefield, or other historic place. Try to remember what you experienced there. What was the atmosphere? How did people act? List as many details as you can remember, and then write a description of that place. Explain its special quality and its relationship to the people or events that it memorializes.

A Veteran Writes

——— FRED REED ———

Fred Reed, a former U.S. Marine, was a reporter for Army Times *in Southeast Asia during the fall of Saigon and Phnom Penh. In this essay, first published in* Harper's, *Reed takes issue with the notion that all veterans regret or resent their service in Vietnam, or that their tour there was a time of unremitting horror.*

I BEGIN TO WEARY of the stories about veterans that are now in vogue with the newspapers, the stories that dissect the veteran's psyche as if prying apart a laboratory frog—patronizing stories written by style-section reporters who know all there is to know about chocolate mousse, ladies' fashions, and the wonderful desserts that can be made with simple jello. I weary of seeing veterans analyzed and diagnosed and explained by people who share nothing with veterans, by people who, one feels intuitively, would regard it as a harrowing experience to be alone in a backyard.

Week after week the mousse authorities tell us what is wrong with the veteran. The veteran is badly in need of adjustment, they say—lacks balance, needs fine tuning to whatever it is in society that one should be attuned to. What we have here, all agree, with omniscience and veiled condescension, is a victim: the press loves a victim. The veteran has bad dreams, say the jello writers, is alienated, may be hostile, doesn't socialize well—isn't, to be frank, quite right in the head.

But perhaps it is the veteran's head to be right or wrong in, and maybe it makes a difference what memories are in the head. For the jello writers the war was a moral fable on Channel Four, a struggle hinging on Nixon and Joan Baez and the inequities of this or that. I can't be sure. The veterans seem to have missed the war by having been away in Vietnam at the time and do not understand the combat as it raged in the internecine cocktail parties of Georgetown.

Still, to me Vietnam was not what it was to the jello writers, not a ventilation of pious simplisms, not the latest literary interpretation of the

172

domino theory. It left me memories the fashion writers can't imagine. It was the slums of Truong Minh Ky, where dogs' heads floated in pools of green water and three-inch roaches droned in sweltering back-alley rooms and I was happy. Washington knows nothing of hot, whore-rich, beery Truong Minh Ky. I remember riding the bomb boats up the Mekong to Phnom Penh, with the devilish brown river closing in like a vise and rockets shrieking from the dim jungle to burst against the sandbagged wheelhouse, and crouching below the waterline between the diesel tanks. The mousse authorities do not remember this. I remember the villa on Monivong in Phnom Penh, with Sedlacek, the balding Australian hippie, and Naoki, the crazy freelance combat photographer, and Zoco, the Frenchman, when the night jumped and flickered with the boom of artillery and we listened to Mancini on shortwave and watched Nara dance. Washington's elite did not know Nara. They know much of politicians and of furniture.

If I try to explain what Vietnam meant to me—I haven't for years, and never will again—they grow uneasy at my intensity. *My God*, their eyes say, *he sounds as though he liked it over there. Something in the experience clearly snapped an anchoring ligament in his mind and left him with odd cravings, a perverse view of life—nothing dangerous, of course, but. . . . The war did that to them*, they say. *War is hell.*

Well, yes, they may have something there. When you have seen a peasant mother screaming over three pounds of bright red mush that, thanks to God and a Chicom 107, is no longer precisely her child, you see that Sherman may have been on to something. When you have eaten fish with Khmer troops in charred Cambodian battlefields, where the heat beats down like a soft rubber truncheon and a wretched stink comes from shallow graves, no particular leap of imagination is necessary to notice that war is no paradise. I cannot say that the jello writers are wrong in their understanding of war. But somehow I don't like hearing pieties about the war from these sleek, wise people who never saw it. It offends propriety.

There were, of course, veterans and veterans. Some hated the war, some didn't. Some went around the bend down in IV Corps, where leeches dropped softly down collars like green sausages and death erupted unexpected from the ungodly foliage. To the men in the elite groups—the Seals, Special Forces, Recondos, and Lurps who spent years in the Khmer bush, low to the ground where the ants bit hard—the war was a game with stakes high enough to engage their attention. They liked to play.

To many of us there, the war was the best time of our lives, almost the only time. We loved it because in those days we were alive, life was intense, the pungent hours passed fast over the central event of the age and the howling jets appeased the terrible boredom of existence. Psychologists, high priests of the mean, say that boredom is a symptom of maladjustment; maybe, but boredom has been around longer than psychologists have.

The jello writers would say we are mad to remember fondly anything about Nixon's war that Kennedy started. They do not remember the shuddering flight of a helicopter high over glowing green jungle that spread beneath us like a frozen sea. They never made the low runs a foot above treetops along paths that led like rivers through branches that clawed at the skids, never peered down into murky clearings and bubbling swamps of sucking snake-ridden muck. They do not remember monsoon mornings in the highlands where dragons of mist twisted in the valleys, coiling lazily on themselves, puffing up and swallowing whole villages in their dank breath. The mousse men do not remember driving before dawn to Red Beach, when the headlights in the blackness caught ghostly shapes, maybe VC, thin yellow men mushroom-headed in the night, bicycling along the alien roads. As nearly as I can tell, jello writers do not remember anything.

Then it was over. The veterans came home. Suddenly the world seemed to stop dead in the water. Suddenly the slant-eyed hookers were gone, as were the gunships and the wild drunken nights in places that the jello writers can't picture. Suddenly the veterans were among soft, proper people who knew nothing of what they had done and what they had seen, and who, truth to be told, didn't much like them.

Nor did some of us much like the people at home—though it was not at first a conscious distaste. Men came home with wounds and terrible memories and dead friends to be greeted by that squalling she-ass of Tom Hayden's, to find a country that viewed them as criminals. Slowly, to more men than will admit to it, the thought came: *These are the people I fought for?* And so we lost a country.

We looked around us with new eyes and saw that, in a sense the mousse people could never understand, we had lost even our dignity. I remember a marine corporal at Bethesda Naval Hospital who, while his wounds healed, had to run errands for the nurses, last year's co-eds. "A hell of a bust," he said with the military's sardonic economy of language. "Machine gunner to messenger boy."

It wasn't exactly that we didn't fit. Rather, we saw what there was to fit with—and recoiled. We sought jobs, but found offices where countless bureaucrats shuffled papers at long rows of desks, like battery hens awaiting the laying urge, their bellies billowing over their belts. Some of us joined them but some, in different ways, fled. A gunship pilot of my acquaintance took to the law, and to drink, and spent five years discovering that he really wanted to be in Rhodesia. Others went back into the death-in-the-bushes outfits, where the hard old rules still held. I drifted across Asia, Mexico, Wyoming, hitchhiking and sleeping in ditches a lot until I learned that aberrant behavior, when written about, is literature.

The jello writers were quickly upon us. We were morose, they said, sullen. We acted strangely at parties, sat silently in corners and watched with noncommital stares. Mentally, said the fashion experts, we hadn't made the trip home.

It didn't occur to them that we just had nothing to say about jello. Desserts mean little to men who have lain in dark rifle pits over Happy Valley in rainy season, watching mortar flares tremble in low-lying clouds that flickered like the face of God, while in the nervous evening safeties clicked off along the wire and amtracs rumbled into alert idles, coughing and waiting.

Once, after the GIs had left Saigon, I came out of a bar on Cach Mang and saw a veteran with a sign on his jacket: VIET NAM: IF YOU HAVEN'T BEEN THERE, SHUT THE FUCK UP. Maybe, just maybe, he had something.

QUESTIONS FOR CRITICAL READERS

Remembering and Understanding

1. Re-state Reed's central point in your own words.
2. List the words and phrases Reed uses to describe other writers who have written about Vietnam veterans. What do these words and phrases tell you about his attitude toward these other writers? What is he trying to accomplish by using these words?
3. What, exactly, did Reed find enjoyable about war?

Analyzing and Discussing

4. Do you think Reed's descriptions of other writers are effective? That is, does his language produce in you the attitude or reaction that you think Reed intends?
5. How does Reed establish his own authority to write about this subject? How does he distinguish himself from others who have written about Vietnam veterans?
6. How do people gain the right to speak or write about an event or experience? What do they have to do to establish their authority?

Writing

7. Do you agree with Reed's point? Explain why or why not, and give your reasons.

Why War Is Ignoble

HOWARD MORLAND

Morland, who flew Air Force transports during the Vietnam War, wrote this "My Turn" column for Newsweek *in response to hearing a man express regret that he had not fought in Vietnam. Specifically, he is questioning what he perceives as a nostalgia for war. Morland is a free-lance writer who describes himself as an "anti-nuclear pacifist humanist musician."*

WHENEVER YOUNG AMERICANS DEPART for overseas battlefields, older men seem to envy them the adventure. On the eve of the Vietnam War, my college dean told me he was sorry he had not come under fire during his wartime service in the Pacific. He wanted to know how he might have responded to the test of combat. He assumed I would understand, and his regrets may have led me to later join the Air Force rather than seek a draft deferment.

Today, because of the crisis in the Mideast, a new generation of young people hears of the salutary effects of the battlefield from their Vietnam-era elders. In September, liberal essayist Roger Rosenblatt told a national television audience that he now wishes he had fought in Vietnam. He said that even though he "disapproved of our being in Vietnam," he feels "deep regret" that he never experienced the "dependent connection to one another" of soldiers "thrown into an incomprehensible horror." Watching him on the MacNeil/Lehrer News-Hour sent me searching through my own Vietnam experiences for a clue to this curious longing for memories of combat.

My job in 1968 was to pilot C-141 transport planes of the type now hauling U.S. soldiers and gear to Saudi Arabia. Except for one close call when a battle-damaged Phantom jet crashed and exploded near my plane at Da Nang Air Base, I never came in harm's way. My own knowledge of combat comes from the stories soldiers told as I airlifted them from the battlefield zone. One night, on a flight from Cam Ranh Bay to California, a young veteran the age of today's tennis champion Pete Sampras sat between the pilot seats and told the flight crew about his year in Vietnam. He described a photograph in his duffel bag, of an American

GI holding the severed heads of two Viet Cong prisoners. The hapless prisoners were grabbed and beheaded as revenge for the death of an American, killed when another Viet Cong prisoner turned himself into a human bomb by detonating a concealed grenade in his own armpit. In the eerie darkness seven miles above the Pacific, our narrator described the sound a bullet made as it plowed through a friend's body two feet away. He thought it wise not to make close friends in combat. His homecoming plan: lock himself in the bathroom, sit on the john, smoke cigarettes and shake for several hours.

Pondering this survivor's tale, I entered the cargo bay and sat with the coffins of a dozen veterans who had undergone the ultimate combat experience. The young soldier on the flight deck may have embellished his war stories, I thought, but the boys in the boxes were testament to the truth. I was struck by how lonely one feels in the company of the dead.

Two years later in Thailand, a Thai veteran made a point of showing me snapshots of Vietnamese bodies stretched out in a row. He had helped kill them. A fresh haircut on the corpse closest to the camera caught my eye; I wondered if the man with the haircut had sensed it would be his last. My host seemed to invite me to explain the meaning of the carnage, but I was still young enough to believe people should live forever, and like the then young Mr. Rosenblatt, I saw no sufficient reason for that particular war.

'Bloody shreds': Combat is unique in the way it celebrates untimely death at the hand of fellow human beings. Mark Twain saw the horror in this, and, in a poem called "The War Prayer" wrote of a ghostly old man who disrupts a church service as the preacher delivers a patriotic war prayer. The old man offers his own grim version. "O Lord our God, Help us to tear their soldiers to bloody shreds with our shells . . . to drown the thunder of the guns with the shrieks of their wounded, writhing in pain . . . to lay waste their humble homes with a hurricane of fire." Persuaded that it could be considered sacrilegious, Twain had his poem published posthumously. In his bitter assessment, " . . . Only dead men can tell the truth in this world." But his warning, when it appeared, was widely ignored.

War is like other human activities in that people who enjoy it the most will do it the best, and be chosen to run it. Obviously, not everyone enjoys it, but there is a common notion that all combatants should somehow love war, and benefit from it. The premise of the typical Hollywood action movie is that real men love each other most when locked in a deeply fraternal exercise designed to demonstrate how short life can be. If war is such an ennobling experience, why does it bring out the worst in people, not the best?

I have always believed that I might kill or die for a worthy enough cause. It's the way boys were raised in my native South, as in most other places, and for good reason. During much of history, a successful army was the most important institution a people could possess. A bad day on the battlefield meant extinction for a number of ancient civilizations. However, this country has never faced extinction in any of its wars. Our recent wars have all been exercises in foreign policy, and for such wars the worthiness of the cause must justify the slaughter. Are we convinced that the war now brewing in the Persian Gulf is worthy of the bloodshed it would entail?

In my view, no American should ever be required to kill or die simply as a test of manhood—particularly if that test involves some politician's perception of manhood. And certainly no American should die simply because as a nation our imagination is too poverty stricken to figure out how to live without cheap oil. For lethal force to have any legitimate role, we must strictly and dispassionately confine it to legitimate questions about international law and homeland defense. War is too brutal to be used as a rite of passage for a college dean, for an essayist, or even for a U.S. president.

I don't know why Roger Rosenblatt feels the way he feels, but I'm glad he didn't fight in Vietnam. I wish nobody had.

QUESTIONS FOR CRITICAL READERS

Remembering and Understanding

1. Explain what Morland means when he says that war is ignoble.
2. Summarize the reasons that Rosenblatt wishes he had experienced war and combat.
3. What is Morland's response to Rosenblatt's particular variety of nostalgia?

Analyzing and Discussing

4. Morland says he has always believed that he might kill or die for a worthy enough cause. What, in your opinion, would be a worthy enough cause to kill or die for?
5. Rosenblatt and Morland present two different views of war. Summarize each one and discuss their differences.
6. Morland suggests that the people who enjoy war will conduct it best. What kind of person would find war enjoyable? Under what circumstances would war be enjoyable?

Writing

7. Morland mentions the impressions of war given by Hollywood films. Recall the film versions of war that you have seen, and write a paper in which you describe the impression of war that those films gave.

Synthesizing and Consolidating

1. Review the journal entries that you did for prereading at the beginning of this chapter.

   a. What *new* information have these writers added to what you already knew about the Vietnam War or war in general?
   b. Have the readings here *changed* any of your preconceptions or attitudes about the Vietnam War or soldiers and combat in general? If so, choose one change and explain it. If not, explain how these readings have confirmed what you already thought or believed.

2. Choose one of the selections from this chapter and list at least five follow-up questions that you would like to ask the writer.
3. Is there some question or issue that these writers did not raise but you think they should have? What is it? State it and explain why you believe it is important.
4. The writers here obviously have different kinds of authority about war. Describe the different kinds of authority you find here and, if you find one type of authority more effective or convincing than the others, explain why.
5. Do any of the writers represented here make statements that you disagree with or that challenge your attitudes and beliefs. Find two or three of those statements, summarize them accurately, and then state your own position.
6. Review Karnow's descriptions of American soldiers in Vietnam and then compare what he says with the accounts of O'Brien, Herr, and Reed. Do these descriptions agree or disagree with Karnow? Explain the similarities and differences that you find.
7. Do the writers in this chapter reach a consensus about what war is like? Divide them into groups based on their descriptions of what combat is like and then summarize the position you think each group would take. (A group may consist of only one writer.)
8. Choose a passage from one selection in this chapter in which you thought the language or the description was needlessly offensive. Re-write the passage in language that you think is more acceptable. Then compare the two versions and decide which one you believe is more effective.

Suggestions for Research and Writing

1. Several writers have pointed out that the Vietnam War was controversial in the United States. Review newspaper and magazine accounts of the period from 1965–1970 and write a paper in which you explain the controversy.
2. Have you ever pretended to be a soldier? Describe the experience and then explain how war as the writers here have described it is different from what you imagined.

3. Locate a veteran of Vietnam or some other war. Interview that person about his or her experiences, and then write an account of those experiences. First, write this account in the first person, as it was told to you, then re-write it as though you were a historian writing a biography of the person.
4. Research the role of American servicewomen in the Vietnam War.
5. The Vietnam War had a language of its own, sometimes not understandable to those who were not there. Using the selections printed here and any other resources you can find, assemble as much of that special language as you can, and explain its function for those who used it.
6. Throughout this chapter the writers mention atrocities. Research the history of atrocities in the Vietnam War or in some other war of your choice. As part of your research, you will need to establish how the world defines atrocities.

5

Young Black Men In America

DURING THE PAST FORTY YEARS the United States has made considerable progress toward racial equality. The Supreme Court has ruled that separate schools for blacks are unequal, and thus illegal. The Congress has passed several civil rights laws. The progress that has been made might suggest that racism has been eliminated, that all racial and ethnic groups now compete on an equal footing for the resources that are necessary to survive and succeed in America. But such a conclusion would ignore the very real inequalities and difficulties that a number of groups in the United States continue to face.

One group in particular, young black men, continues to live on the margins of American society. As a group, young black men are more likely to be unemployed, to be undereducated, to be victims of violent crime (including homicide), to commit suicide, or to be in jail, especially on death row, than members of any other group in American society.

Some people might say that the black man's marginality in society must be his own fault, that he is marginal by choice, preferring unemployment and violence to a steady job and a stable life. Certainly, these people might say, anyone who has failed to take advantage of the progress of the past forty years must be living on society's margins voluntarily.

But most of the available information about young black men suggests that they have been pushed to the margins of society by a pervasive pattern of social and economic racism that is so deeply ingrained in society that it is almost invisible. Only when someone separates black men from the general background of society and studies them as a group does it become apparent that they are not participating fully, that something is wrong.

The selections in this chapter explore the situation of young black men from a variety of social, economic, and political perspectives. Together, the writers in this chapter describe a problem of major proportions. And they suggest that it is a problem with more questions than answers. Donna Britt writes of her brother, shot by policemen. Jewelle Gibbs reviews social, economic, and historical factors that affect the present status of young black men. Harry Edwards evaluates professional sports as a factor in the lives of black men. In his discussion of race and crime, Robert Staples redefines race and crime as political facts, which leads to some unusual conclusions. Shelby Steele advances a theory of what he calls "race holding," and asks that blacks be judged, and judge themselves, on some basis other than their race. John Edgar Wideman describes the exciting events that overtook his younger brother Robby in the racial violence of 1968, after Martin Luther King, Jr. was assassinated.

People are not simply the statistics others use to describe them. They are also the images that others have of them. The chapter begins by asking you to explore your images of young black men and of members of other ethnic and racial groups.

Before You Read

Before you read the selections in this chapter, answer the following questions in your reading journal.

1. Why should young black men be perceived as different from other blacks or members of other minority groups?
2. What are the myths and stereotypes that surround black men?
3. How are black men typically portrayed in the news media, film, and television? Make a list of as many examples as you can think of, and describe two or three of these in detail.
4. Describe your most memorable experience with members of racial or ethnic groups other than your own. Do you remember them as positive or negative experiences? Why?
5. How have your experiences with members of other races or ethnic groups confirmed or contradicted your preconceptions of what those people would be like?

6. What is your own perception of the situation of young black men in America, and what are the sources of your information?

7. What aspects of American life offer blacks and other minority groups the greatest opportunities for success and equality? Where do they find the most limited opportunities?

The Death of a Black Man: My Brother

Donna Britt

Donna Britt is a reporter for The Washington Post, *where this article first appeared. As she writes about her brother's death at the hands of white police officers, she is attempting not only to describe what happened, but also to understand and make sense of it, and communicate its meaning to others. Britt occupies multiple positions here. She is black. She is the victim's brother. She is a reporter. All of these positions influence what she says.*

ACCORDING TO THE POLICE REPORT, the patrolmen who peered into the ravine that morning saw a man who was black, barefoot and wearing an aluminum cooking pot on his head. A witness who'd been observing the man said that he was crouched "like a native hunter" while chanting something unintelligible. Then the man stood and said to no one in particular, "Take me higher."

Police had been called to this wooded, sparsely populated section of Gary, Indiana, on Sept. 29, 1977, because the man reportedly had tried to slip his hand into the window of a stranger's truck. The truck's owner had confronted him and asked what he was doing. "I've got to get home," the man said, trembling. "Will you take me home?"

He never made it. Convinced that the man was on drugs, the truck owner told him to wait while he called the police to take him home. He then phoned the cops, telling them he was "holding" someone who was trying to steal his truck.

The two white patrolmen who responded, Officers Jerry Cyprian and Daniel Mattox, said they found the man in the nearby gully, a tire clutched in one hand, a broken bottle top in the other. Minutes later the policemen pumped one .357 magnum bullet into the man's chest and another into his left thigh when, the report says, he shouted, "I'm going to kill you," and charged at one of them with a chain, a brick, a plastic baseball and a three-foot length of pipe. Within minutes, he was dead.

Twelve years after my brother Darrell died in that ditch, I couldn't recall the headline of the story describing his killing. Then an editor friend at the Gary *Post Tribune* sent me a clipping.

Unidentified man shot by Gary policemen.

Even back then, part of me—detached from the tunnel of pain that roared within me after I heard the news—was struck by the headline's impersonal tone. *Unidentified man shot by Gary policemen.* What hit me was that the event it announced—the halt of another anonymous Gary man's life by local police—seemed an event of only minor surprise, hardly "news" at all. I realized that if this particular death had not been Darrell's, I might easily have flipped by it on my way to something I could relate to—the women's pages, maybe, or the comics.

My family will never know what happened on that September morning. Darrell, who had attended Indiana University and was working as a laborer at Bethlehem Steel, had no history of mental problems. The autopsy found no alcohol or narcotics in his blood. An inquest investigating the shooting exonerated the two policemen. But they were hardly "Gary's finest." Both later left the police force in disgrace—Cyprian in 1979 after his conviction for child molestation; Mattox in 1987 following a burglary conviction.

Darrell was 26 when he died. That I am now older than my beloved big brother seems an error of cosmic proportion. Somehow, I have traveled beyond the man whose advanced age—three mighty years older than I— and mysterious "older-man" experiences—high school, dating—made him seem exotically mature. Since he died, a marriage and its breakup, childbirth and an evolving career have deepened and defined me. How could I have grown so without him?

Some things haven't changed. In the years since Darrell's death, I've seen hundreds of headlines announcing the violent end of a life. After grad school, I took a newspaper job in Detroit, the pre-District of Columbia murder capital, and sometimes reported on the carnage.

Ten years and two jobs later, I moved to Washington from Los Angeles, where muggings and gang-related shootings are so common that one local woman bought a pit bull for her preteen son and told him never to leave home without it. I found I'd landed in a place where the skyrocketing murder rate prompted the mayor to proclaim to reporters, "This is not Dodge City." A place where in January, the month I arrived, 50 men, women and children were murdered. *Fifty.*

Fifty is exactly the number of bodies that can comfortably sit on a large District bus; twice what many experts feel is an acceptable number of students in an elementary school classroom; more than seven times the number who perished when space shuttle Challenger exploded in 1986. In Washington, D.C., 50 people who assumed they'd see Valentine's Day were murdered in the first month of this year.

Forty-seven of them were black.

We know black life is tenuous. We know that Americans whose skins are dark have much higher odds than their pale neighbors of one day smiling from the pages of their local newspapers as statistics. We read that more black men aged 18 to 25 are murdered than are killed by accidents or disease; that in 1987, 61 percent of the 15- to 19-year-old boys murdered in the United States were black, despite blacks constituting only 12 percent of the population.

I suspect that most people confronted by these numbers, even while they cluck their tongues over their morning coffee, secretly don't care overmuch. They think, "What can you do about druggies and dope dealers and low-lifes who insist on blowing each other away?" They feel, in hidden places few of them are willing to acknowledge or excavate, that anyone who has the bad luck to be born black in America takes his chances. Much the way I—an African American woman who considered herself profoundly sensitive to the lives of African Americans—wouldn't have cared much about that body in the ditch if it hadn't been my brother's.

The issue, it seems, can be reduced to a question: What is the value of a black life?

When Darrell died, I listened to a reporter friend's vague promise to look into the bizarre circumstances of his shooting and my brother Mellick's suggestion that we push the police to provide explanations, reparation. I—commonly considered the pushiest Britt around—just sat, mute in my assumption that the universally apparent wrongness of Darrell's killing would be recognized and dealt with. Even little kids cry foul when two gang up on one.

Part of me knew better. Because the bottom line was clear: Another black man who'd apparently been caught doing something he shouldn't have was dead. No big deal.

Life went on. The day after his bullet punctured Darrell's thigh, Officer Mattox hit and kicked a handcuffed Hispanic suspect before shooting up the man's car; he was sentenced to three years' probation for violating the man's civil rights. On Nov. 18, in Alabama, Robert Edward Chambliss, a 73-year-old retired auto mechanic, was sentenced to life in prison for killing four little girls in a Birmingham church bombing 14 years earlier. In December, the U.S. Department of Health, Education and Welfare reported that in 1976, black men in the United States lived 5.6 fewer years than white men, due to poorer nutrition, housing and medical care and "a higher rate of violence"—accidents, suicides, homicides. Business as usual.

But nothing was as usual. My mother saw Darrell everywhere: in young men with his coloring or haircut, in guys who sported similar jackets. For a moment she'd think, "Why, there's Darrell," and reach out to him and it would be the most natural thing in the world.

Back at the University of Michigan, I finished the semester in a fog. As the months passed, I wondered if I could possibly live long enough to experience an afternoon, an hour or even five minutes free of the heavy, breathless hurt crowding my chest.

Something so incomprehensible had happened that I had to repeat it to myself to digest it. Trying on a new dress, I'd stare in the mirror and think, "Darrell is dead." In the midst of savoring a slice of perfect cheesecake, I'd remember, "Oh, yes, Darrell's gone." Just at the delicious moment before sliding into hilarity over a Mary Tyler Moore rerun, I'd think, "That's right. My brother died," and listen to my laugh trill on without me.

The man who I am to believe spent his last moments charging at a couple of badge-wearing strangers who'd just fired two warning shots at him was, in my childhood opinion, the finest human being on the planet.

Gentle where I was feisty, effortlessly humorous where I was clumsy with a joke, Darrell was everything that I wasn't—and still he adored me. The guy was a riot. My younger brother Bruce and I would be sitting in the living room, watching TV, and Darrell would "sneak" into the room, apparently bent on frightening us. In plain sight, he'd sidle past us in a burlesque tiptoe, "hiding" his 180-pound frame behind a slender vase. Inching closer, he'd crouch behind a completely inadequate footrest. Then he'd jump out at us with a loud "Boo!" We'd scream with laughter.

Darrell was my knight, one of the few people I've known who seemed reflexively good. When he and Mellick played cowboys as toddlers, Mellick invariably used his older-brother status to force Darrell to be the villain. My mother says Darrell sobbed for her to make him stop. "Bad guys," he told her, "always lose."

He's the one who, when I was 5 and he found me sniffling in the closet, told me that the grown-ups were wrong for snickering when I brought the wrong hat to one of my parents' guests. When I was a flat-chested preteen, he soothed the sting of Mellick's put-downs of my "pear-shaped" body by saying he hoped to marry a girl just like me.

Perhaps more than anyone except my mother, Darrell shaped me. His implied lack of respect for "bad girls" convinced me that I should guard my virginity fiercely; his friends' hesitant flirting taught me volumes about the power of sexual attraction. He set the standard for what still most beguiles me in men: the ability to dig deep enough to answer my questions. His unwavering acceptance—even of my weakness for hope-lessly uncool Broadway musicals—showed me that someday, a man who wasn't a relative might love me.

He wasn't perfect. Slow to anger, he'd occasionally erupt memo-rably. Fascinated by the mystical, he—like many in his generation—

experimented with marijuana and other drugs in the 1970s when he went away to college.

I hated it when he left for Indiana, fearful that our closeness couldn't survive the distractions of college life. An avid basketball player, he tried out for Coach Bobby Knight's freshman team. To everyone's surprise, Darrell—5 feet 10½ and cut from his high school team—made the squad after a walk-on tryout.

"He told me he was so hot that day, hitting bombs from the three-point line, outplaying quality people like George McGinnis [now a former NBA star]," Mellick recalls. "So hot that they couldn't cut him." But he didn't make varsity the next season. Darrell was deeply disappointed.

Hoping to cash in on his humor, he left school after his sophomore year, traveling to Los Angeles in search of fame. He returned home after six months, broke, chastened but still mesmerizing with his tales of Hollywood egos and nights spent under starry Arizona skies.

Back in Gary, he moved to a beachfront neighborhood on Lake Michigan and worked as a drug counselor. Later he was dropped by the program's new funders, who decreed that every staffer had to have a college degree. Soon after, he took a job in the steel mill.

I knew it was temporary—a man of Darrell's intellect could never settle for manual labor. But his jokes became moodier, more pointed. "Darrell is changing," I told my mom during a visit home. "What's happening to him?"

He called me three days before he was shot. He missed our childhood closeness, he said—couldn't we try to recapture it? Touched almost beyond speech, I sputtered something like, "I want that, too." Then he told me he was thinking of becoming a minister.

Long ago, he said, our mother had told him that when he was an infant, our near-blind great-grandmother had laid hands on him and announced, "This boy is going to be a preacher." Darrell chuckled.

"I resisted that my whole life, but it was always there."

For my family, Darrell's sudden transformation was startling. Mellick, himself quite devout, recalls that a month earlier he'd talked to his younger brother about the beauty of "living in the Word." Darrell had rebuffed him. "He told me that his feeling was that if you got into the Bible, you'd die. That God would just take you. He told me, 'I'm going to have fun, live *my* life.' "

But, inexplicably, a few weeks later, he seemed totally changed. "The last time I saw him, he was a Christian," says Mellick. "He had such a glow, a peace. It was obvious that he'd undergone a very sincere conversion, almost to the point where he wasn't dealing with religion as we know it. It wasn't like, 'I'm going to start going to church.' Darrell was transformed in the spirit.

"I said, 'Slow down a little bit, you have the rest of your life for this.' He just said that he loved me and he loved God and he was all right. He really had been touched."

Maybe he always had been. In that last conversation, he said to me, so quietly, "When I was 6 or 7, I used to talk to Jesus. I *heard* Him; felt so close to Him. . . . But I never told anybody because I knew people would think I was nuts."

Nuts? I thought. Never you.

Back then, so much was impossible. It was unthinkable that words like those from the coroner's report of the shooting scene—"Rigor mortis and lividity are absent and steam is rising from the [victim's] blood as it hits the cooler air"—could ever be related to my brother. So unthinkable that after his death, I shuffled and reshuffled the evidence: Darrell's ashen face in his coffin; my father's disbelief at watching a morgue staffer roll his nude body out from among an assortment of naked black corpses; *Unidentified man shot by Gary policemen.*

I have told myself that these things happen. That my brother's being blown away on a cool fall morning had nothing to do with the fact that he was black and the shooters were not. That a *white* man who cursed and threatened a pair of marginal cops, who came at one of them with a pipe and a chain and threw a plastic baseball at him, would have been dispatched just as efficiently. And I don't believe it.

I don't believe it because I know that if *I* could question the value of black life, if I could, for 20 years, unconsciously feel that a black body in a ditch could in no way be connected to me, then why should Cyprian and Mattox have felt any kinship to the suspected thief in that gully? If I could be so blind, it is depressingly predictable that lots of other folks, some of them bearing guns and the license to use them, should be, too. Blind enough that in a life-and-death pinch, they'd shoot first and, maybe, think later.

But then, I saw Darrell as special, totally unlike those whose speech, dress, bearing or lack of education brand them as expendable. He wasn't one of those for whom the possibility of ending up an anonymous corpse on a morgue slab was real. But Cyprian and Mattox didn't see that. They must have seen black. And I can't help thinking that was enough.

My search for a scapegoat always brings me to the same place. But in 1989, racism is an outmoded notion, something—like bubonic plague, child labor and public hangings—that we feel we've moved past. And frankly, we've had enough of it. We're damned sick of blacks' and Latinos' and Native Americans' and Jews' and women's and gays' and even white men's whining about discrimination. Even the best of us are circling the wagons, disconnecting the antenna that links us to every one of the ax-grinders.

It nicks me when I watch "L.A. Law" and realize that, until late last season, the only major character whose personal life wasn't examined, indeed wasn't even referred to, is black. *You are not,* the beast whispers, *important enough, interesting enough, real enough to warrant examination.*

It slices deeper when my 3-year-old son, Darrell's namesake, announces that he doesn't want to return to his preschool because "there are too many black people there." Day after day, I hold him and his big brother close, tell them, "You are so handsome, so smart, so special just as you are." My 7-year-old stares at me sadly, knowing how much this means to me. "But I want *blue* eyes, Mom," he says. "Superman has blue eyes."

It scrapes bone when I remember that, despite the circumstances of my brother's killing, most of the black people murdered in this country are killed by other blacks.

African Americans, black Harvard psychologist Alvin Poussaint recently told me, have always vented their wrath at racism on each other, on themselves. We've never been known for assassinating the bigots who trumpet our supposed worthlessness. "But here we are," he said, "systematically gunning each other down. It's as if we've internalized the old Klan notion that the only good nigger is a dead one."

But this has to end. Nobody should live as I have, feeling the beast at my heels, continually phoning my younger brother ("Hi—just checking in,") to verify he's safe. Nobody should ever have to pray, as one of my best friends recently did, that his pregnant wife wouldn't bear a son because "I couldn't stand for a son of mine to deal with what I, as a black man, have dealt with. I've been stopped by police a dozen times in my life and I have never committed a crime."

I do have sons. They *are* bright and beautiful and special. They deserve to believe it. They deserve to live it.

Most days, I'm now able to talk about Darrell without a sob closing my throat. Most days. Earlier this year, I was on an Indianapolis-bound plane when a thirtyish woman asked if I ever had attended Indiana University. No, I said, but I occasionally visited my brother, Darrell Britt, when he was a student there.

"Darrell Britt? I *know* him," she said. "Tell him you met Chicken— he knows me by my nickname." I sat, eyes stinging, a bright smile smashed on my face. Darrell, she said, is so funny. "Won't you give him my regards?"

I nodded, incapable of announcing that her hilarious classmate had been dead for a decade; unwilling to witness one more person's shock at the news. But I also was silenced by my pleasure at hearing Darrell discussed so delightedly; by how apt it was, hearing him alive and funny again.

Later, marveling at how I maintained that fiction, I realized that on some level, it has ceased to *be* fiction. Just as the world has moved on—the Gary police cooperated with me on this story; officers assure me that fewer Cyprians and Mattoxes are on the force—Darrell and I have moved on as well.

He comes to me in dreams, tweaks me when I get complacent, smiles at me from other brothers' faces on the street. Just as I now take tremendous pleasure in great food and new dresses, I've begun to feel joy, clear and uncomplicated, about my brother.

It helps, knowing that he has indeed been taken higher. It helps, knowing, as Darrell always did, that the bad guys inevitably will lose.

QUESTIONS FOR CRITICAL READERS

Remembering and Understanding

1. List the statistics Britt provides and then present them in a paragraph that makes a point.
2. In addition to the story of her brother's death, Britt is also making a point about black men in general and their situation in American society. Restate her main point, and summarize her discussion.
3. Is Britt totally mystified by her brother's reported behavior on the night he was killed? Where does she suggest that there were things in her brother's life that she did not understand but that may explain his behavior?

Analyzing and Discussing

4. How does the fact that Britt is writing about her brother affect what she sees and reports? Does that relationship make her story more or less believable?
5. Britt discloses that the police officers who shot her brother "later left the police force in disgrace." How does this information affect your perception of the story she tells? Does police misconduct in other situations necessarily mean that the police acted wrongly in killing her brother?
6. Britt says that she "wouldn't have cared much about that body in the ditch if it hadn't been my brother's." How does this statement affect how you perceive her?

Writing

7. Using the information Britt supplies, and any inferences you can draw from what she says, tell the story of Darrell Britt's death from the perspectives of the police officers who shot him and a newspaper reporter or investigator attempting to reconstruct and report what happened.

Young Black Males in America

———— JEWELLE T. GIBBS ————

Gibbs is on the faculty of the School of Social Welfare at the University of California, Berkeley. In this essay, which originally appeared in Young, Black, and Male in America: An Endangered Species, *Gibbs analyzes the social factors that she believes contribute to what she calls the deteriorating situation of black youth and black males in America.*

CONTRIBUTING FACTORS TO THE DETERIORATING STATUS OF YOUNG BLACK MALES

Four major sets of factors can account for this downward spiral of black youth, and particularly black males, since 1960: historical, socio-cultural, economic, and political. These factors are briefly discussed below.

Historical Factors. Black youth today are the ultimate victims of a legacy of nearly 250 years of slavery, 100 years of legally enforced segregation, and decades of racial discrimination and prejudice in every facet of American life. Countless authors have documented the brutality of slavery, the cruelty of segregation, and the injustice of discrimination. Generations of blacks have endured inferior schools, substandard housing, menial jobs, and the indignities of poverty. Yet, through all of these travails, each generation of blacks made some progress and believed that their children would eventually merge into the mainstream of American society. These beliefs were infused with new life by the New Deal programs of the 1930s, nurtured by the economic opportunities of World War II, and fostered by the postwar policies of the Truman administration. By 1960, many blacks were optimistic that "Jim Crow" was in a terminal stage, that opportunities were increasing for minorities, and that black youth would finally be able to share in the American dream. No one could have anticipated that the tremendous civil rights and economic gains of the 1960s would have been seriously eroded and ideologically challenged by the mid-1980s, leaving black youth in a worse economic and social

193

situation than they had experienced since before President John F. Kennedy initiated his New Frontier.

The past two and one-half decades since 1960 have been one of the most turbulent periods in American history, encompassing the rise of the civil rights movement, the urban riots, the women's movement, the Vietnam War, the war on poverty, and major political and economic changes in the society. The era began with a liberal Democratic administration committed to increasing opportunities for minorities, but it has gradually evolved into a conservative Republican administration which has aggressively dismantled or diluted many of the most effective civil rights and social welfare programs.

Black youth, who lived through a period of heightened expectations and increased opportunities in the 1960s and early 1970s, began to see their dreams of major social change gradually fade as the economy stopped expanding and other groups (e.g., women, immigrants) began competing for the same limited resources. While much of the civil rights legislation and many of the anti-poverty programs primarily benefited working and middle-class blacks (who were in a better position to take advantage of them), the unanticipated effect of these changes was to create a wider gap between middle-class and poor blacks. Middle-class blacks moved out of the inner cities into integrated urban and suburban areas, leaving poor blacks behind in blighted neighborhoods without effective leadership, successful role models, or the supportive institutions and social networks that provided social stability, economic diversity, and traditional values to the community (see Clark, 1965; Glasgow, 1981). Thus, with increased isolation from the black middle class and alienation from the white community, black inner-city ghettos have gradually become "welfare reservations" where black youth have few, if any, positive role models; where they lack access to high-quality educational, recreational, and cultural facilities; where they do not have job opportunities or adequate transportation to locate jobs; and where they are confronted daily with adult role models who are openly involved in drugs, prostitution, gambling, and other forms of deviant behavior.

Sociocultural Factors.   These recent historical and demographic developments have undoubtedly contributed to sociocultural changes in the black community. As the black middle class has drifted away from the inner cities, it has left a vacuum not only in terms of leadership but also in terms of values and resources. For example, in these transformed ghettos, the black church, which had formerly been the center of activity in the black community, has lost much of its central function as a monitor of norms and values. The power of political organizations has been diminished, as their constituencies no longer include the better educated and wealthier blacks who are more likely to participate actively in the political process. In cities with shrinking tax bases, civic and social organizations have fewer resources to improve neighborhoods, initiate youth programs, or provide incentives to attract external sources of support.

With the breakdown or weakening of these traditional institutions within inner-city communities, there has been a parallel breakdown of the traditional black community values of the importance of family, religion, education, self-improvement, and social cohesion through extensive social support networks. Many blacks in inner cities no longer seem to feel connected to each other, responsible for each other, or concerned about each other. Rather than a sense of shared community and a common purpose, which once characterized black neighborhoods, these inner cities now reflect a sense of hopelessness, alienation, and frustration. It is exactly this kind of frustration that exploded in the urban riots of the 1960s from Watts, California, to Detroit, Michigan, to Washington, D.C.

It is also this kind of frustration that erupts into urban crime and violence, family violence, and self-destructive violence. Thus, we see situations in which young black men sell drugs openly on major thoroughfares without fear of apprehension; teenage girls have multiple out-of-wedlock pregnancies without fear of ostracism; youthful gangs terrorize neighborhoods without fear of retaliation; and young teenagers loiter aimlessly at night on street corners without fear of reprobation.

The poverty and the powerlessness of black youth are inextricably linked to the safety and security of the rest of the society, since the frustration-bred violence will ultimately spill over the invisible walls of the ghetto. The violence which young black males now direct mainly against the black community (black-on-black crime), against relatives and friends (homicide), and against themselves (suicide), will inevitably erupt and spread throughout urban and suburban America, leaving behind damage, destruction, and distrust in its wake. In anxious anticipation of this rising tide of black rage, urban dwellers now put bars on their doors and windows, shopkeepers turn their stores into fortresses, and politicians build new prisons. The causes of these antisocial behaviors are ignored, denied, or blamed on the black youth, who are written off as being intellectually deficient, culturally deprived, and pathologically deviant. Short-term remedies are devised for the consequences of their behaviors, with little understanding that these Band-Aid solutions are very temporary, very perishable, and very ineffective to cure the underlying causes of frustration and anger in these black youth.

Economic Factors. The post–World War II economic revolution in the United States is the third major factor contributing to the problems of black youth. Two parallel developments created chronic unemployment among black males, both young and old: the structural change in the economy from a predominantly manufacturing and industrial base to a predominantly high-technology and service base, and the movement of these newer jobs from the central cities to the suburbs and peripheral areas (Kasarda, 1985; Sum, Harrington, and Goedicke, 1987). Black youth did not have the skills to compete in the new industries; nor did they have the transportation to follow the jobs to the suburbs. As these jobs moved away from the central cities to the suburbs and exurbs, new services were developed to supply the needs of employers in these industrial and technical companies. These new employment opportunities were increasingly filled by white women and young immigrant workers. After the urban riots of the 1960s, many of the "Mom-and-Pop" stores were forced to close or moved away from the inner cities, removing another source of employment for black youth. As these convenience stores have gradually been replaced, the new owners are predominantly Asian, Hispanic, and Middle-Eastern immigrants who tend to employ family members rather than black youth from the community. Some black leaders have accused these immigrant shopkeepers of commercial exploitation of the black community without returning any economic benefits to the community by hiring black youth.

Black youth, who once had the monopoly on menial service and domestic jobs in restaurants, airports, and department stores, are increasingly being displaced by Asian and Hispanic youth. Although there is some controversy about the displacement theory, statistics indicate that black youth employment rates have decreased as the employment rates of other nonwhite youth have increased. In any case, whether the competition for jobs between black and immigrant youth is perceived or actual, interethnic tensions have increased between blacks and these other minority groups in many urban areas. However, some employers have suggested that immigrant youth are more cooperative, less aggressive, and willing to work for lower wages than black youth. In their analysis of the employment problems of poor youth in America, Sum and his colleagues (1987) conclude that "it is poor black teens who were experiencing the most severe employment problems in March 1985 in both an absolute sense and relative to whites and Hispanics in similar family income positions." Clearly, there are some "noneconomic" factors operating in the severe employment problems of young black males—problems which reflect discriminatory hiring practices as much as they reflect economic and technological changes.

Political Factors.   The fourth major factor which has exacerbated already existing problems for black youth is the conservative political climate in this country, which began with the election of Richard Nixon in 1968 and has been strongly reinforced by the Reagan administration. Many political analysts interpret this growing conservatism as a backlash to the antipoverty programs and affirmative action policies of the Johnson and Carter administrations, a not-so-subtle protest of the "middle-American majority" to the civil rights and economic gains of minority groups (Omi and Winant, 1986). Threatened with the loss of their special status, these "middle Americans" have been manipulated by politicians and lobbyists for their own self-serving goals. Framing their rationale in neoconservative dogma, these policymakers have shifted the emphasis from the goal of providing all citizens with a decent standard of living through federally subsidized health and welfare programs to the need to blame the poor and disadvantaged for their perceived lack of motivation, their "dysfunctional" family systems, and their dependency on welfare programs. By shifting the focus from society's responsibility for its most vulnerable citizens to an emphasis on the so-called "social pathology" of minority youth and their families, advocates of this view (such as Murray, 1984) have quite deliberately and effectively transformed the national debate from a proactive emphasis on policies of prevention and early intervention to a reactive emphasis on retrogressive policies and punitive programs. As a result, politicians who support cuts in social programs aimed primarily at disadvantaged and minority families have found increasing favor with the voters in the past 20 years; thus programs with a direct impact on black youth, such as CETA, the Job Corps, federally subsidized loans for college, and youth employment programs, all have been severely cut back or eliminated.

The impact of these political and economic changes has resulted in direct negative consequences of fewer educational and employment opportunities for young black males. It has also affected their perceptions of opportunity and their access to the American dream of social and economic mobility. Several national surveys and opinion polls have shown that black families believe they are worse off economically and politically in the 1980s than they were in the 1970s. Consequently, black youth have responded by withdrawing from the labor market, reducing their applications to four-year colleges, and increasing their involvement in self-destruction and deviant behavior. Peak suicide rates of black youth are also correlated with periods of political conservatism in the past two decades. Thus, there is a reciprocal relationship between the political backlash against minority gains and the social indicators for black youth; that is, these youth respond in a *rational manner* to perceived prejudice and socioeconomic barriers to their mobility by dropping out of the labor market and choosing not to attend college. This reciprocal relationship suggests a self-fulfilling prophecy, which could be reversed if policies and programs were to change, as suggested in later chapters of this book.

IMPLICATIONS OF THE PROBLEMS OF YOUNG BLACK MALES

This summary of the major social and economic problems of young black males clearly demonstrates that they are an endangered group and a population "at risk" for an escalating cycle of deviance, dysfunction, and despair. What are the implications of these problems, if they are left unsolved, for black youth, black families, and the larger society? The major implications can be projected in four areas: economic, social, sociocultural, and political.

QUESTIONS FOR CRITICAL READERS

Remembering and Understanding

1. Write a brief summary of each of the four sets of factors Gibbs explains.
2. Choose what you believe to be the most important factor from each set, and use these four to write a synthesis/summary.
3. Gibbs gives few statistics. What other information does she offer in support of her conclusions?

Analyzing and Discussing

4. Gibbs says that black youths react "in a *rational manner* to perceived prejudice . . . by dropping out of the labor market and choosing not to attend college." Why is this a rational response?
5. Gibbs says that peak suicide rates of black youth are correlated with periods of political conservatism. If this is so, does it mean that there is a cause and effect relationship? Why would Gibbs want to claim or suggest such a relationship?
6. How has Gibbs's perspective as a social scientist affected her analysis here? For example, how would her discussion be different if she were writing about individuals rather than groups?

Writing

7. Identify a specific problem that Gibbs describes, and write a paper in which you explain how you would solve that problem.

Race in Contemporary
American Sports

———— HARRY EDWARDS ————

Harry Edwards is a black sociologist who teaches at the University of California, Berkeley. He has devoted his career to the scholarly study of sports and the status of black athletes in American life. He organized a protest by black athletes at the 1968 summer Olympic games, and he has continued to work actively for the welfare of black athletes. He has worked as a consultant to television networks and to professional sports leagues. The article printed here examines the widespread assumption that blacks have been especially successful in professional sports. This article was originally published more than ten years ago. Professor Edwards graciously agreed to update the statistics for the present publication.

LONG ESTABLISHED MYTH to the contrary notwithstanding, sports are inextricably intertwined and interdependent with—not isolated or insulated from—the most serious, deeply rooted and tenacious, ideological values and structural relationships existing in society. More formally stated—far from being activities appropriately consigned to the "toy department" of human affairs, sports reflect, reaffirm, and reinforce the prevailing character of human and institutional relationships within and between societies and the ideological foundations buttressing those relationships. Today the implications of this proposition are nowhere more clearly evident or more profound than with regard to the subject of *race and sport in America.*

Since Jackie Robinson ostensibly shattered the color barrier in professional baseball, sports have accrued a reputation for having achieved extraordinary, if not exemplary, advances in the realm of interracial relations. To some extent, this reputation has been deliberately fostered by skilled "sports propagandists" eager to project "patriotic" views consistent with America's professed ideals of racial justice and equality of opportunity. To a much greater extent, however, the portrayal of sport as an arena of interracial beneficence has been spawned and propagated by less-calculating observers of the sporting scene: people who simply have been naive and critically ignorant about the dynamics of sports and its relationship to society generally and about the race-related realities of American sports in particular.

The sources of many misconceptions about race and sport can be traced to developments in sport which would appear on the surface to validate such ill-informed views. For instance, though Blacks constitute only eleven percent of the U.S. population, in 1991 just over 63 percent of the players in the National Football League were Black. Similarly *forty six* of the first fifty collegiate football players taken in the 1990 National Football League player draft were Black, while *twenty-seven* of the twenty-eight first round NFL draft choices in 1990 were Black. As for the other two major professional team sports, 76 percent of the players making National Basketball Association rosters in the 1990–91 season were Black, while Blacks comprised 15 percent of America's major league baseball players at the beginning of the 1991 season.

Black representation on sports honor rolls has been even more disproportionate. For example, 12 of the last 13 Heisman Trophy awards have gone to Black collegiate football players. In the final rushing statistics for the 1990 NFL season, *thirty-eight* of the top forty running backs were Black. And, of course, boxing championships in the heavier weight divisions and "most valuable player" designations in both collegiate and professional basketball have been dominated by Black athletes since the 1960s.

But, though figures never lie, the meanings of figures are never self-evident. And a judicious interpretation of these and related figures points toward conclusions quite different from what is generally believed. In short, the evidence tends to suggest that in both sport and society, America has "progressed" from a "Jim Crow" pre-Jackie Robinson era to a post-Robinson era characterized by what I would term "Mr. James Crow, Esquire"—a system whereby the traditional inequities and hypocrisies of interracial relationships are camouflaged and sustained through more subtle and sophisticated means.

Since Jackie Robinson's debut, Blacks have made virtually *no* progress beyond the athlete role in major American sports. And, even as athletes in these sports, Blacks often enjoy far less than total equality of opportunity. Consistent with America's traditional view of Blacks as intellectually inferior, for example, Black athletes are virtually excluded from so-called "thinking positions" in football and baseball. In the NFL, therefore, at the beginning of the 1990 season, only three of twenty-eight starting quarterbacks were Black. Similarly, Black representation among professional baseball pitchers, catchers, and in other infield positions is very low relative to their numbers in outfield positions.

Furthermore, in the three major team sports of football, basketball, and baseball, Blacks have been virtually excluded from both front-office and on-the-field positions of authority at both the collegiate *and* the professional levels.

At the collegiate level, racial discrimination limits Black access to jobs as head coaches and athletic directors. A pervasive rationalization throughout major (usually meaning predominantly White) American colleges and universities is that a Black head coach would not be acceptable to "alums," athletic "boosters," white students and players, and/or that Blacks do not have the intelligence and leadership qualities to manage a major collegiate sports program successfully. Only two schools in a Major Division I NCAA Conference had Black head football coaches in 1990— (at Stanford and Northwestern University). The real significance of this situation can be truly understood only when it is considered within the context of the fact that there was a 92 percent turnover in head football coaches at Major Division I universities over the decade of the 1980s. But, then, *it was not until 1980 that a Black head coach was hired.* In collegiate basketball, there are only 31 Black head coaches at major universities in the U.S. and no Black head baseball coaches.

In the professional ranks, Black access to front-office and authority positions is more limited than at the collegiate level.

In the National Football League:

a. There is only one head coach;

b. There is only one offensive coordinator out of twenty-eight;

c. There are no defensive coordinators;

d. Only 4 percent of the assistant coaches in the NFL are Black;

e. There are only five Blacks holding executive positions with NFL teams;

f. There are no Black general managers;

g. There are no Black owners;

h. There are three Black persons working out of NFL Commissioner Paul Tagliabue's office.

Yet 63 percent of the players in the NFL are Black!

In professional baseball:

a. There have been only three Black managers over the entire history of professional baseball. Only two Black managers, Cito Gaston and Frank Robinson, are managing in the majors today.

b. Of 123 coaches in major league baseball, there are 17 Blacks, none of whom is a third-base coach—the individual generally considered next to the manager in rank and authority.

c. Blacks own no professional baseball franchises outright, and only one Black person owns even a piece of a franchise.

Yet 17 percent of the players in professional baseball are Black!

In the National Basketball Association, a similar statistical picture emerges. Given the tremendous power of the mass media in influencing perceptions of reality and disseminating ideological definitions, it is perhaps to be expected that the pressbox would be no less characterized by race-related Black underrepresentation than other aspects of American sport. So, at the start of the 1990 season, not a single major league baseball team had a Black "play-by-play" announcer on its broadcast staff. In fact, with the exception of a few widely scattered Black sportscasters and reporters on media staffs serving areas with substantial Black populations and two Black network "color commentators" or sports "anchors", Blacks are conspicuously absent from the major sports media both in public roles and in authority positions behind the scenes.

The less-publicized figures cited above on Black involvement in media roles and executive capacities in sports are quite consistent with the realities of Black circumstances generally in America. For example, a survey commissioned by members of the U.S. Congressional Black Caucus in 1972 found minorities to be most underrepresented in the media industry among major industries in eighteen American cities having substantial minority populations. Similarly, in 1981, a California State Commission on the Status of Minorities in the Media reported that 97 *percent* of the print and broadcast media in the state (a state that will be over 50 percent minority by 1990) is today owned, controlled, and overwhelmingly staffed by White males.

So just as Blacks are underrepresented in authority positions and are overrepresented in the lower occupational statuses in the broader American labor force, Blacks in sport also function in a semicaste system, relegated as they are to the least powerful, least secure, most expendable, and most exploited role in the sports institution—that of the athlete.

And lest the fact be overlooked, it should be mentioned that even as athletes, Blacks have substantial access to positions in only four or five sports. Less than half-a-dozen Black athletes have risen to the top echelons of sports other than boxing, basketball, baseball, football, and track. All other sports—perhaps 90 percent of all the organized sports activities pursued in America—remain for the most part "lily white."

But if American sports and society are so thoroughly afflicted by racism, how does one account for the disproportionate number of Black athletes in even four or five sports and the widely acknowledged excellence of their athletic performances? From the outset it should be stated that the level of Black representation and the quality of Black performances in sports have no demonstrable relationship to any race-linked genetic, biological, or physiological characteristics. Every study purporting to demonstrate some such relationship has exhibited critical deficiencies in methodological, theoretical, or conceptual design. Secondly, the factors determining the caliber of sports performance are so complex and disparate as to render ludicrous any attempt to trace athletic excellence to some singular category of human features.

I contend that racism—particularly within the sports institution—is the major force blocking Black access to most American sports and to "thinking" and authority roles in accessible sports. But I also believe that racism throughout the *larger society* accounts for the disproportionately high presence of Black athletes in some sports and their dominance, if not demonstrable superiority, in all sports activities to which they have access in numbers.

Traditional myths and popular beliefs about Black athletes persist: they are alleged to be "natural" athletes, physically superior to athletes from other groups. However, the evidence tends to support cultural and social—not biological—explanations of Black athletic success and overrepresentation in the athlete role.

Briefly:

a. Thanks to the mass media and long-standing traditions of racial discrimination in American society, the Black athlete is much more visible to Black youths than, say, Black doctors or Black lawyers. Therefore, unlike the white child who sees many different potential role models in the media, Black children tend to model themselves after the Black athlete. The Black athlete is the one prevalent and positive Black success figure they are exposed to regularly year in and year out in America's white, male-dominated mass media.

b. The Black community tends to reward athletic achievement much more and at an earlier stage of career development than any other activity. This also fosters sports-career aspirations in greater numbers of young Blacks than the actual opportunities for sports success would warrant.

c. Because over 90 percent of American sports activities are still devoid of any significant Black presence, the overwhelming majority of aspiring Black athletes emulate established Black sports role models and seek careers in only four or five sports—basketball, football, baseball, boxing, and track. The brutally competitive selective process that ensues eliminates all but the most-skilled Black athletes by the time they reach the collegiate and advanced amateur ranks. It is estimated that just under 2 percent of college varsity athletes ever sign a professional sports contract. The competition for available positions in sports offering opportunities to Blacks is made all the more intense because, as mentioned earlier, even in these sports, some positions are relatively closed to Blacks.

d. And, finally, sport is seen by many Black male youths as a means of "proving" their manhood. This tends to be extraordinarily important to Blacks because the Black male in American society has been relegated institutionally to the status of "boy" for generations.

These factors contribute to channeling disproportionately high numbers of highly talented and motivated young Black males into American sports. By contrast, white male youths are exposed to countless role models and occupational opportunities. Thus, there is probably what was potentially a white "O.J." or "Dr. J." piloting a plane, drawing up engineering plans for a bridge, or a skyscraper, or managing a corporation, somewhere in America.

As soon as someone discovers that one Black child has greater athletic potential than his peers—usually in junior high school if not before—that child all too often is separated from his peers in the minds of many "significant others"—teachers, counselors, coaches, administrators and even parents. He becomes "something special"—which is to say that, among other things, beyond maintaining the academic minimums necessary to athletic eligibility, he is exempt from the educational expectations placed upon his nonathlete peers. Far too many people simply assume that the future of an individual of outstanding athletic potential lies with the single-minded development of a sports career. *Thus by the time the Black scholarship athlete enters college, so little has been expected of him academically at least since junior high school that he has frequently come to demand virtually nothing of himself intellectually beyond maintaining athletic eligibility.* And the results are as predictable as they are inevitable.

An estimated 25–35 percent of high school Black athletes qualifying for scholarships on athletic grounds cannot accept them due to accumulated academic deficiencies. Of those who are eventually awarded collegiate athletic scholarships, 75 percent *never* graduate from college.

Of the 25–35 percent who do eventually graduate, an estimated 75 percent of them graduate either with physical education degrees or in majors specifically created for scholarship athletes and generally held in very low repute. The problem with these "jock" majors is that they have a very poor record as acceptable credentials in the job market.

Seventy-four percent of the players—Black and White—who made a NFL roster in 1990 had not earned their college degrees, although nearly all had exhausted their four years of collegiate eligibility. Similarly, an estimated 80 percent of NBA players have no college degrees.

By several accounts, the overwhelming majority of Black scholarship athletes and professional athletes have no post-career occupational plans; former Black scholarship athletes and professional athletes are unemployed more often and make less when they do have jobs than their nonathlete peers; and former Black scholarship athletes and professional athletes are likely to switch jobs more often, to hold a wider variety of jobs, and to be less satisfied with the jobs they hold primarily because the jobs tend to be "dull," dead-end, or minimally rewarding.

In short, due to educational deficiencies, the average accomplished Black athlete not only fails to achieve expectations of lifelong affluence, but he frequently falls far short of the levels typically achieved by his nonathletic peers.

What has not been thoroughly understood in Black America is that for all these reasons the overwhelming majority of Black youths seeking sports stardom are foredoomed to be shuttled back into the Black community as noncontributors, undercontributors, and all too often as "mal-contributors" lacking access to any legitimate means of sustaining themselves or their self-respect. It is simply not generally appreciated that despite 76 percent of Blacks in professional basketball, 63 percent Blacks in professional football, and 15 percent Black people in professional baseball, *there are still just over 1,600 Black people making a living as professional athletes in these three major sports today. And if we added to this number all the Black athletes making a living as professionals in all other American sports, all the Blacks making a living in minor and semi-professional sports leagues, and all the Black trainers, coaches, and doctors making a living in professional sports, there would still be less than 2,600 Black Americans total making a living in professional athletics today!*

In the international arena, the challenges to intelligent Black sports involvement are no less prevalent than in domestic sports. The fact that sports recapitulate prevailing structural and ideological relationships both *within* and *between* societies portends the clash of competing social systems and ideologies in the international sports arena. With the decline of colonialism and the rise of sovereign new nations complete with their own distinct structural and ideological features during the last half of the twentieth century, there has been a quickening and intensification of the transformation of international sports events into global political and ideological struggles camouflaged under the pageantry of athletic competition. World-class athletes have been reduced to the status of little more than "foot soldiers" in recurrent battles for sports supremacy—the generally acknowledged presumption being that demonstrated athletic superiority at least implies ideological and societal superiority.

Black Americans of course have a stake in all international political developments—whether within or outside of sports. But within the international sports realm the issue of South African sports participation is of particular relevance. In international sports, it is this issue—because of the racial considerations involved—that is likely to weigh most heavily upon the moral and political integrity of Black America. Governing apartheid regimes in South Africa have traditionally offered exorbitant sums of money to foreign athletes—especially Black athletes—and foreign sports organizations in an effort to regain international sports legitimacy and respectability. Black Americans were challenged to become acutely sensitive to sport's role in international politics as a propaganda vehicle in order to avoid playing the "dupe" in what was a racist ploy orchestrated by those inside and outside of South Africa who would make apartheid respectable.

In conclusion, then, I do not advocate that Black society discourage its youths from either domestic or international sports participation. To the contrary, I am thoroughly convinced that Black achievements in sports have benefited Afro-American society in many ways. On a spiritual level, the performances of outstanding Black athletes have bolstered Black pride and self-esteem. On a practical level, sports have been a means to higher-education opportunities for many Black youths (myself included) who have moved on to establish productive careers in other fields. Further, by virtue of their enormous accomplishments in sports, Black athletes have demonstrated that the greatest obstacle to Black achievement in *all* areas of American life has not been a lack of capability or competitiveness, but a lack of opportunity. By every measure, therefore, I believe that Black involvement in sport is as legitimate as Black pursuit of career opportunities in any other field—law, medicine, science, education, or whatever—and therefore is to be encouraged. But as with all careers, Blacks pursuing a sports career must approach the task *intelligently*. And first, foremost, and above all else *this means recognizing that sport inevitably recapitulates society and that, therefore, it would be as impossible for a substantially racist society to have a substantially nonracist sports institution as it would be for a chicken to lay a duck egg.*

This is not to suggest that, in the American case, Jackie Robinson and the countless others who have struggled for racial progress both inside and beyond the sports arena have done so in vain. They have most certainly made enormous contributions. But human relations across the spectrum of institutions in American society have historically been bent, twisted, and contorted out of shape in order to deny Black people—among others—

opportunities supposedly theirs by birthright. We had best keep in mind that despite all myths to the contrary, sport is no exception.

QUESTIONS FOR CRITICAL READERS

Remembering and Understanding

1. What is Edwards's main point? Re-state it in your own words and then use your statement as the basis of a summary of Edwards's discussion of black athletes.
2. List the information Edwards offers to support his point.
3. What conditions would have to change for Edwards to agree that sports are no longer racist?

Analyzing and Discussing

4. How does Edwards's dual perspective as a black and an athlete affect his presentation and/or his credibility? (i.e., Does this make him more credible than he might otherwise be?)
5. Despite statistics showing that blacks are overrepresented as athletes in most major sports, Edwards claims that American sports are racist. How does he support this claim? Do you accept his conclusion? Explain why or why not.
6. Edwards says that "sports recapitulate prevailing structural and ideological relationships both *within* and *between* societies."

   a. What do you think this statement means? Explain how Edwards applies it to his argument.
   b. How do sports in the university "recapitulate prevailing structural and ideological relationships" within and between universities?

Writing

7. Using Edwards's methods and perspective, analyze some other well-known cultural institution, such as television, film, the university, or business.

Race, Masculinity and Crime

———— ROBERT STAPLES ————

Robert Staples is a sociologist. He teaches at the University of California, San Francisco, and he has written extensively about black men, women, and families. In his writing, Staples is no doubt influenced by his professional training as a sociologist and his personal status as a black male. The selection printed here, from his book Black Masculinity *(The Black Scholar Press, 1982), examines the relationship between race and crime from a political and economic perspective.*

IN THE PAST HUNDRED YEARS criminologists have shown great interest in the relationship between race and crime. Various theories have been put forth to explain the association between racial membership and criminal activity. These theories have ranged from Lombroso's discredited assertion that certain groups possess inherent criminal tendencies to the now widely accepted theory that certain racial groups are more commonly exposed to conditions of poverty which lead them to commit crimes with greater frequency. The purpose of this chapter is to examine the relationship of race and crime in a theoretical framework which will permit a systematic analysis of racial crime within the political-economic context of American society.

The approach used here to explain race and crime is the colonial model. This framework has been formulated and used in the writings of Fanon, Blauner, Carmichael and Hamilton and Memmi and others. It is particularly attributed to Fanon, whose analysis of colonial relationships in Africa has been used to explain the American pattern of racial dominance and subjugation. While there are many criminologists who will summarily dismiss this model as lacking any relevance for understanding the relationship between race and crime, it behooves us to give it a hearing since many blacks, especially those presently incarcerated, give it considerable credence. In fact, it is their definition of themselves as political prisoners that has motivated many prison protests in recent years.

Basically, the colonial analogy views the black community as an underdeveloped colony whose economics and politics are controlled by leaders of the racially dominant group. In this framework, it is useful to view race as a political and cultural identity rather than to apply any genetic definitions. Race is a political identity because it defines the way in which you are to be treated by the political state and the conditions of your oppression. It is cultural in the sense that white cultural values always have ascendency over black cultural values. Thus, what is "good" or "bad," "criminal" or "legitimate" behavior is always defined in terms favorable to the ruling class. The result is that black crime in America evolves according to the relationship of blacks to the colonial structure, in which racial inequality is perpetuated by the political state.

Obviously, there are some imperfections in the colonial analogy as a sole explanatory model to explain race and crime. We must have more theoretical and empirical research before mechanically applying the structural forms characteristic of classical colonialism to the complexities of crime in America. Yet, the essential features of colonialism are manifest in American society. Black men have been, and remain, a group subjected to economic exploitation and political control; they lack the ability to express their cultural values without incurring serious consequences. While other colonial factors such as the geographical relationship of the colonial masters to the colonized, the population-ratio, and the duration of colonization may be missing, they do not profoundly affect the form or substance of black and white relations in America which are based on white superordination and black subordination.

In using this model I am not discounting the complications of class often interjected into the issue of crime and race. However, domestic colonialism is as much cultural as economic. While members of the white working class are more victimized by their class location than other whites, they are not subjected to the dehumanized status of blacks of all social classes. The racist fabric of white America denies blacks a basic humanity, which permits the violation of their right to equal justice under the law. In America the right to justice is an inalienable right; but for blacks it is still a privilege to be granted at the caprice and goodwill of whites, who control the machinery of the legal system and the agents of social control.

The colonial model may also be used to explain the relationship between black masculinity and criminal behavior. When we speak of crime, it is automatically assumed that these are acts of men. Statistically, that is still the case. Although the incidence of criminal acts by women is on the rise, they still represent only four percent of the prisoners in the United States. Under a system of internal colonialism, black men will be more likely to commit criminal acts or be arrested for such because the society denies them access to its goals. For example, women, at least those with children, may receive welfare assistance in order to support themselves. Failing that, they may turn to prostitution, a more lightly punished crime. Conversely, the colonized man must often turn to serious crime in order to satisfy the basic needs for food, clothing and shelter. Hence crime is, for some black men, a matter of sheer survival.

LAW AND ORDER

One of the key elements in securing the obedience of the citizenry to a nation's laws is their belief that the laws are fair. A prevalent view of the law among blacks is summed up in Lester's statement that "the American black man has never known law and order except as an instrument of oppression. The law has been written by white men, for the protection of white men and their property, to be enforced by white men against blacks in particular and poor folks in general. "Historically, a good case can be made for the argument that the function of law was to establish and regulate the colonial relationship of blacks and whites in the United States. Initially, the domestic colonial system was established by laws which legitimized the subordination of the black population.

The legalization of the colonial order is best seen in the Constitution itself. While the Constitution is regarded as the bulwark of human equality and freedom, it originally denied the right to vote to Afro-Americans and made the political franchise an exclusive right of white property owners. In fact, blacks were defined as a source of organic (or human) property for white slave holders in the notorious "3/5" clause. The clause allowed the slave owner to claim 3/5 constituency for each slave that he possessed. Since non-citizens are beyond the pale of legal equality, the Dred Scott decision in 1857 affirmed that slaves were not citizens and could not bring suit in the courts. The ultimate blow to black aspirations occurred in 1896 when the Supreme Court upheld racial segregation in its "separate but equal" decision in the Plessy v. Ferguson case.

In a contemporary sense, black men are not protected by American law because they have no power to influence those laws. They have no laws of their own and no defense against the laws of the colonizer. Thus, the power to define what constitutes a crime is in the hands of the dominant group and is another means of racial subordination. How crime is defined reflects the relationship of the colonized to the colonizer. The ruling caste defines those acts as crimes which fit its needs and purposes to be defined as such and characterizes as criminals those individuals who commit certain kinds of illegal acts, while other such acts are exempted from prosecution and escape public censure because they are not perceived as criminal or a threat to society.

As a result of the colonial administration's power to define the nature of criminality, white collar crimes which entail millions of dollars go unpunished or lightly punished, while those of the colonized involving nickels and dimes result in long jail sentences. The chief executive of the political state can wage a war that takes thousands of lives in direct violation of the Constitution, while the colonized are sent to gas chambers for non-fatal crimes such as rape. It is no coincidence that the two criminal acts for which politicians once wanted to preserve the death penalty were kidnapping and airline hijacking; the former a crime committed mainly against the wealthy, while the latter is most often a political crime against the state.

Crime is often seen as a racial issue in the United States because a majority of the violent crimes committed in urban areas involve black males. In particular, the type of crimes they commit such as robbery, burglary and assaults, are the ones which create the most public fear and concern. Yet, the greatest amount of money stolen is through white collar crime such as employee thefts, embezzlement, financial fraud, etc. Most white collar criminals are white males. It is estimated that white collar crime costs the nation as much as $200 billion dollars a year compared to $88 billion for street crime. And, the greatest sources of violence in this country are unsafe automobiles and consumer products. Over thirty million Americans are injured and thirty thousand killed each year because of unsafe consumer products other than automobiles. The call for law-and-order, however, is aimed mostly at the crimes of the poor and blacks. The findings of Bennett and Tuchfarber are instructive: the hardliners on law-and-order were Republican, middle class, white and elderly. Blacks, in spite of the fact that they were more likely to live in crime infested areas, preferred to identify and alleviate the conditions that breed crime and violence.

AGENTS OF SOCIAL CONTROL

In any colonial situation, there must be agents to enforce the status quo. A classical colonial world is dichotomized into settlers and natives, and the policeman acts as the go-between. Fanon describes it in colonial Africa:

> In the colonies it is the policeman and the soldier who are the official instituted go-betweens, the spokesman of the settler and his rule of oppression . . . by their immediate presence and their frequent and direct action, they maintain contact with the native and advise him by means of riflebutts and napalm not to budge. It is obvious here that the agents of government speak the language of pure force. The intermediary does not lighten the oppression, nor seek to hide the domination; he shows them up and puts them into practice with the clear conscience of an upholder of the peace, yet he is the bringer of violence into the home and into the mind of the native.

One could hardly find a more perfect example of the role of the policeman than in the findings of the United States Commission on Civil

Rights in the 1960s. Police brutality was discovered to be a fact of daily existence for Afro-Americans and a primary source of white abuse against any black challenge to the status quo. In essence:

> Police misconduct often serves as the ultimate weapon for "keeping the Negro in his place," for it is quite clear that when all else fails, policemen in some communities can be trusted to prevent the Negro from entering a "desegregated" school or housing project, a voting booth, or even a court of law. They may do it merely by turning their backs on private lawlessness, or by more direct involvement. Trumped up charges, dragnet roundups, illegal arrests, the "third degree" and brutal beatings are all part of the pattern of "white supremacy."

Many white officers covet an assignment in the black community because it is financially lucrative. They find it easier to collect extortion money from petty ghetto criminals and are less likely to be detected, investigated or convicted since blacks believe it to be futile to report corrupt police officers. They also have a greater opportunity to receive outstanding merit citations based on the number of arrests they make or "crimes" that they solve. These awards allow them to achieve more rapid promotion, greater authority and higher salaries.

In order to enforce colonial rule, the policeman must have certain traits. First and foremost, he must be a member of the dominant racial group. Almost every major urban area has a police force that is predominantly white, although the cities themselves may be populated mostly by blacks. It is not only that the police force is composed mostly of members of the colonizer's group, but they also represent the more authoritarian and racist members of that sector. One survey disclosed that the majority of white police officers hold anti-black attitudes. In predominantly black precincts, over 75 percent of the white officers expressed highly prejudiced feelings towards blacks and only 1 percent showed sympathy toward the plight of blacks. A series of public hearings on police brutality in Chicago revealed that candidates who do poorly on the psychological tests or who demonstrate personality problems while undergoing training in the police academy are assigned to "stress areas" in Chicago's black and brown ghettos.

Considering the characteristics of policemen assigned to the black ghetto, it is no surprise to find that for the years 1920–1932, out of 479 blacks killed by white persons in the South, 54 percent were slain by white police officers. In more recent periods, according to a Police Foundation study, 75 percent of the civilians killed by police in seven cities between 1973–74 were black males. They concluded that many police shootings did not appear to have served any compelling purpose. They fell into a "middle ground" where it was difficult to determine if the shooting was justified or not. In nine out of ten cases, police who shot civilians were not punished.

Even less surprising are the studies which indicate that blacks believe that policemen are disrespectful, that police brutality exists in their areas, and that blacks are treated worse than whites by the police. These beliefs are based on two basic types of complaint besides the abuse suffered at the hands of the white police officer. One is that the police are more tolerant of illegal activities, such as drug addiction, prostitution, and street violence, that they would not permit in white communities. The other is that the police see as much less urgent the calls for help and complaints from black areas than from white areas.

Distrust of white policemen is widespread in the black community. Even black police officers have expressed a distrust of them. A study of black policemen in Washington, D.C. revealed that a majority of them were not inclined to trust their fellow white officers. In New York City about 3,000 black police officers quit the predominantly white policeman's association in protest over the union's support of a white officer accused of killing a black youth. Further evidence of racism among white policemen comes from the former Sheriff of San Francisco, Richard Hongisto, who states, "I believe that I literally heard thousands of racially derogatory remarks cited by white police officers during the course of my ten years in the police department." Almost every survey taken reveals that a larger number of blacks than whites hold unfavorable attitudes toward the police. Such a situation once led Louis Lomax to comment: "I don't know a single Negro who doesn't get a flutter in his stomach when approached by a white policeman."

Such complaints about the police force stem from its functional role in colonial society. The police are not placed there to protect the indigenous inhabitants, but to protect the property of the colonizers who live outside that community and to restrain any black person from breaking out of the colonial wards in the event of violence. No amount of "proper" behavior on the part of the police, therefore, nullifies the fundamental colonial machinery which imposes law and order according to the definitions of the colonizer. The law itself constitutes the basis for colonial rule and the ideology of white supremacy shapes the police force, the courts, and the prisons as instruments of continued colonial subjugation.

CRIMES BY BLACK MEN

The colonial character of American society tends to structure the racial pattern of crime. In the urban areas where most blacks live, major crimes against property are committed by whites (68.3 percent white, 32.7 percent black). More blacks (47.9 percent) than whites (47.8 percent) are arrested for serious crimes of violence such as murder, rape, and aggravated assaults. These crimes of violence by blacks are most often committed against other blacks. One survey reported that black males had a victimization rate of 85 per 1,000 population as compared with that of 75 per 1,000 for white males. It concluded that "the typical crime victim is black. He is a young black male—and a poor, uneducated black male at that." The poorer a person is, the more likely it is that he or she will become a victim of crime.

The above statistics follow the typical pattern in the colonial world. The violence with which the supremacy of white values is affirmed, and the aggressiveness which has characterized the victory of these values over the lives and thoughts of the colonized man, means that his challenge to the colonial world will be to claim that same violence as a method of breaking into the colonizer's forbidden quarters. According to Fanon, colonized men will initially express this internalized aggressiveness against their own people. This is the period when the colonized terrorize each other, while the colonizer or policeman have the right to assault the colonized male with impunity. This pattern of intra-racial violence allows the colonized man to negate his powerlessness, to pretend that colonialism does not exist. Ultimately, this behavior, Fanon states, should lead to armed resistance to colonialism.

The cultural values of white supremacy place little premium on the lives of blacks in the United States. The death of a colonized man is of little importance to the continuation of colonial rule, except that it may deprive a particular colonizer of the labor of a skillful worker. Hence, while blacks are generally given longer prison terms than whites for the same crime, they get shorter sentences for murdering other blacks.

QUESTIONS FOR CRITICAL READERS

Remembering and Understanding

1. Identify what you believe to be Staples's main point and re-state it in your own words.
2. Write a brief summary of Staples's discussion.

Analyzing and Discussing

3. Staples explains that he will use a "colonial model" to explain race and crime. Why would it be useful to treat the United States as though it were a colonial power within its own borders?
4. Staples says that he considers race as a political and cultural identity rather

than a genetic one. What does he mean by this distinction, and how does it change the relationship between race and crime?

5. Staples's perspective here is political. How does this perspective yield results different from those we would get from a biological or psychological perspective?

6. Staples argues that black men turn to crime for survival because they have been excluded from society's benefits. Under what circumstances is crime justifiable?

Writing

7. Staples says that "what is 'good' or 'bad,' 'criminal' or 'legitimate' behavior is always defined in terms favorable to the ruling class." Write a paper in which you apply this statement to any social situation you are familiar with (for example, home, school, or work). Identify and discuss established standards for conduct in this situation in terms of how those standards favor those who are in charge.

Blacks in College

Differences by Race and Sex

———— JACQUELINE FLEMING ————

In this selection from her book, Blacks in College *(San Francisco: Jossey-Bass, 1988), Fleming examines differences in students' academic performances in relation to their sex and race. Fleming's approach is that of a social scientist. She is interested in how circumstances affect* groups *of people rather than individuals. Thus, in this excerpt, when she discusses the college performance of blacks, whites, males, and females, her observations will not apply to all individuals, but only to the performance of a group as a whole.*

FOR MOST OF THIS BOOK, we have been concerned with the accumulating evidence that black students show better development in predominantly black colleges. Beyond the broad findings of this study, there are issues specific to each of the sexes within each of the races that should be highlighted. In this chapter, we ask, "Who gets the most out of college?" Even in this arena, it turns out to be a man's world. Women usually bring up the rear. In predominantly black colleges, black men gain the most, and in predominantly white colleges, white men take first prize.

The idea that men, on their own turf, dominate the scene is hardly a new one. It is a truism in every area of extrahome life. We know that dominance has many rewards. And we now know that on college campuses those rewards include intellectual gains. Dominance implies competition, and it is certainly true that women and minorities do not compete well in college when there are white men present. It is also true that black women do not compete well when there are large numbers of black men present. But why? Is it that men are simply the villains of the world, from whom everyone else needs protection? Or is there some tacit agreement between the sexes and the races that allows men in general, or white men in particular, to take control and keep it? Does competition for the unique rewards of education begin with the inequities in the childrearing process? Or are we dealing with some vestige of primitive territoriality that evolution has not allowed us to escape?

Do the analyses presented in this book help us learn any more about the obvious battle between the sexes and between the races? Our data certainly confirm that male dominance in general and white male dominance in particular are facts of life even on college campuses. We learn that the college environment is a critical factor in terms of which group it supports most. But we also learn that the current college environment is not the whole answer. There is evidence of cross-pressures, contradictory messages, and motivational conflicts that are a part of the early learning students bring with them to the college setting. When early learning, traditions, and the press of the college environment convey similar messages, the motivational potential of students is more available for use. When those early conflicts are reactivated by nonsupportive college settings, the ability to get the most out of college is compromised.

THE WHITE MALE

It is the traditional role of men to dominate life outside the home. Indeed, we expect this of men. Through centuries of mutual agreement between the sexes, men have been granted the world at large as their special territory. It is only recently that the occupation of different spheres of activity by men and women has become a competitive issue. The world outside the home has continued to enlarge, offering more and more opportunities for the development of social and cognitive capacities. The world inside the home has shrunk to minute, unsatisfying proportions that leave little room for the critical manipulation of things and people. Despite the battle over women's (and minorities') rights to participate in the world of men, the current trends are still dictated by expectations so old that they are no longer conscious. It is completely in accordance with these expectations that white men take first prize for college development on predominantly white campuses.

In a real sense, the longevity of traditional expectations for men acts as a kind of support system for them and their dominance activities. This system helps yield intellectual gains. Indeed, the ways in which social expectations are supportive of the white male are evident in their college development. It is not that intellectual development per se is vastly better for white men than for others; the fact is that the college environment seems more supportive of their overall development. The actual cognitive improvements for men during the college years were not that much better than for other groups. Improvement on grade averages was better for whites than blacks in only one out of three samples. In the Texas sample, improvement on the measures of cognitive growth was better for whites on only one of three indices. In the study of competitive performance, also carried out in Texas, whites showed no more improvement than blacks.

Thus, actual cognitive development is not the unique advantage of white males. Yet the general developmental profile for white males is always better, because the intellectual and psychosocial sides of college life complement one another and give the impression of good adjustment to a supportive environment. Furthermore, in two out of three samples, well-rounded personality development is accompanied by increasing energy—a sign of good personality integration. White males also have the ability to translate cognitive functioning into unambivalent educational, vocational, and career ambitions. They seem relatively free from downward pulls on their aspirations and from motivational conflicts that douse ambition. The difference between white males and other groups was especially clear in direct competition. Here, white males were able to call up stronger reserves of positive achievement and power motivations that help them enjoy their tasks and sustain a higher level of performance at any given time. Perhaps more than anything else, it seems that stronger positive motivations are the legacy of consistent expectations for the white male's dominant role in the world.

This is not to say that the white male role does not have its share of strains. According to social scientists such as Nancy Chodorow (1978) and Joseph Pleck (1981), the male role strains begin all too early. The characteristic male inability to achieve satisfying intimacy in relationships may begin with too much mothering and not enough fathering. Males then come to deny their dependence on women, devalue them, and become driven by needs to be superior to them. At the same time, they become inclined toward competitive rather than cooperative relationships with other males. Remnants of this early dilemma were, of course, evident in the college profiles. Lack of mutuality, avoidance of social involvements, and conflicts between intellectual and affiliative demands were features of male college development. Yet, in a world that has come to value male activities to the extent that it has, these costs of masculinity may go unnoticed.

THE BLACK MALE

It seems safe to continue saying that males dominate and that their dominance activities have a payoff in developmental gains during the college years. If this is true of white males, are black males any different? Certainly, black males behave similarly on their own turf in black colleges and reap similar gains. But on predominantly white college campuses, black male development suffers most. Clearly, black males are hardest hit by the stress of interracial educational environments. What is it that happens to their dominance tendencies, and what happens to their intellectual gains? The idea that racist influences hit black males the hardest is not new. However, the phenomenon is such an interesting one that it invites at least several levels of analysis. On the most immediate level, the fact that black students must matriculate in an atmosphere that feels hostile arouses defensive reactions that interfere with intellectual performance. But the element of interpersonal hostility does not explain why black males are the hardest hit.

A second level of analysis leads us to suspect that male-male interactions are the most laden with hostility. We recall from our discussion of early learning that males are the victims of insufficient fathering, so that they learn to be competitive rather than cooperative with other males. Since black, as well as white, males are similarly deprived, they are predisposed to interact competitively. The racial difference serves to intensify the basically hostile nature of male-male interactions. Black males are then excluded from participation in a wide range of activities and restricted to small groups of all-black social and political organizations. Apparently, the restricted role that black males play, both within the classroom and without, acts to constrict the intellectual gains that issue from being an actor in campus goings-on.

Upon entering what is in some sense alien territory, black males fall into the category of subdominant males by virtue of their visibility and small numbers. Interestingly, observers of primate dominance hierarchies such as Robert Rose and his colleagues (Rose, Holaday, and Bernstein, 1971; Rose, Gordon, and Bernstein, 1972) find that subdominant males lapse into a nonconfrontational, lethargic state of behavior that can only be described as depression. In many ways, the developmental profiles of black males in white colleges can also be described as depressed. They become unhappy with college life. They feel that they have been treated unfairly. They display academic demotivation and think less of their abilities. They profess losses of energy and cease to be able to enjoy competitive activities. To be sure, there are ways in which these males do not act depressed, inasmuch as they become assertive and may participate energetically in certain campus activities. Nonetheless, these developments are defensive and do little to remedy their plight.

Black males on black campuses exhibit behavioral profiles that are indistinguishable from those of white males. Though they are sometimes disenchanted with the classroom atmosphere, they maneuver around their dissatisfaction by forming informal attachments to faculty and by participating in extra-classroom activities. They experience cognitive growth as well as a release of their assertive energies. Their competitive abilities improve as they come to enjoy competition and find expression for their power motivation in black settings. In short, they display a social and intellectual ascendance that looks like great fun.

The role strains from which black males suffer are in the same interpersonal arena as those influencing white males. But the strains among black males are more visible, perhaps because we are able to observe their behavior in two vastly different settings. In the supportive environments of black colleges, where black men feel accepted, interpersonal issues become almost irrelevant to them. They show far less concern for others. They use the many opportunities for comforting relationships to reach a state of interpersonal detachment. Thus, in a warm environment where there are many opportunities for relatedness, black males strive to remain unaffected by people. Perhaps this maneuver helps them feel in control of their emotional needs for intimacy.

But in stressful environments such as white colleges, where they do not feel warmly received or secure in the comfort of many relationships, black males are unable to maintain controlled feelings of detachment. Their feelings of being surrounded by a hostile environment hit them where they hurt the most, in the denied needs for friendship and intimacy. The threat to needs for relatedness creates a vast interpersonal void that they must spend time and energy trying to fill—energy that has to be siphoned off from intellectual pursuits. Black men often try to work the problem out through their interpersonal lives. They may attempt to attain dominance over women or to live through children. In each of these important relationships, they are striving to become central or indispensable in the lives of others. This may be a way of trying to establish new interpersonal anchors to offset the feelings of being rejected. First and foremost, then, black men on white campuses are responding to feelings of competitive rejection that have consequences for their capacity to muster intellectual motivation. Although black males in white colleges suffer intellectual losses, the problem is not essentially an intellectual one. The problem for black males in white settings is very much an interpersonal issue that rearouses the usually unnoticed strains of being male. The hostile reception given to them on white campuses acts to trigger interpersonal vulnerabilities and initiates a depressive withdrawal from the situation. In black settings, which offer so many opportunities for social ascendance, these interpersonal strains can be ignored.

QUESTIONS FOR CRITICAL READERS

Remembering and Understanding

1. Identify Fleming's central point, and re-state it in your own words.
2. Summarize Fleming's analysis of the differences in the academic performance of black and white males in college.

Analyzing and Discussing

3. Early in her discussion, Fleming says that "despite the battle over women's (and minorities') rights to participate in the world of men, the current trends are still dictated by expectations so old that they are no longer conscious." Make those expectations explicit by listing what you believe to be society's unconscious expectations of women and/or minorities.
4. Identify specific situations on your campus that will support Fleming's assertion that the college environment seems more supportive of the overall development of white men. Make a list of these situations and then use them in a brief explanation of how the college environment is more supportive of white men than of other groups.
5. Fleming says that blacks who attend white campuses do so in an atmosphere of hostility. Observe events on your own campus carefully, and try to make a list of the situations that black students may perceive as hostile.
6. Fleming's approach is that of a social scientist, and her results apply to groups rather than individuals. How could you apply her findings to the behavior of individuals?

Writing

7. Fleming says that black males on white campuses are "excluded from participation in a wide range of activities and restricted to small groups of all-black social and political organizations." Examine your own campus for evidence that this statement is true. Observe activities and organizations on your campus carefully and then write a brief paper in which you describe the level of black participation in activities and organizations.

Race Holding

————— **SHELBY STEELE** —————

In this chapter from his book The Content of Our Character, *Steele speaks first-hand about his experiences as a successful black man. His position may be unusual and even unpopular, especially among blacks and those who consider themselves liberals on matters of race. Rather than attribute all failures to racism, Steele writes about the ways that blacks (and, by extension, members of other groups) can use race, legitimately or not, to support their own lack of success.*

I AM A FORTYISH, MIDDLE-CLASS, black American male with a teaching position at a large state university in California. I have owned my own home for more than ten years, as well as the two cars that are the minimal requirement for life in California. And I will confess to a moderate strain of yuppie hedonism. Year after year my two children are the sole representatives of their race in their classrooms, a fact they sometimes have difficulty remembering. We are the only black family in our suburban neighborhood, and even this claim to specialness is diminished by the fact that my wife is white. I think we are called an "integrated" family, though no one has ever used the term with me. For me to be among large numbers of blacks requires conscientiousness and a long car ride, and in truth, I have not been very conscientious lately. Though I was raised in an all-black community just south of Chicago, I only occasionally feel nostalgia for such places. Trips to the barbershop now and then usually satisfy this need, though recently, in the interest of convenience, I've taken to letting my wife cut my hair.

I see in people's eyes from time to time, and hear often in the media, what amounts to a judgment of people like myself: You have moved into the great amorphous middle class and lost your connection to your people and your cultural roots. You have become a genuine invisible man. This is a judgment with many obvious dimensions, many arrows of guilt. But, in essence, it charges me with selfishness and inauthenticity.

At one point I romanticized my situation, thought of myself as a marginal man. The seductive imagery of alienation supported me in this.

But in America today racial marginality is hard to sell as the stuff of tragedy. The position brings with it an ugly note of self-insistence that annoys people in a society that is, at least officially, desegregated.

For better or worse, I'm not very marginal. In my middle-American world I see people like myself everywhere. We nod coolly at stoplights, our eyes connect for an awkward instant in shopping malls, we hear about one another from our white friends. "Have you met the new doctor at the hospital . . . the engineer at IBM . . . the new professor in history?" The black middle class is growing. We are often said to be sneaking or slipping or creeping unnoticed into the middle class, as though images of stealth best characterized our movement. I picture a kind of underground railroad, delivering us in the dead of night from the inner city to the suburbs.

But even if we aren't very marginal, we are very shy with one another, at least until we've had a chance to meet privately and take our readings. When we first meet, we experience a trapped feeling, as if we had walked into a cage of racial expectations that would rob us of our individuality by reducing us to an exclusively racial dimension. We are a threat, at first, to one another's uniqueness. I have seen the same well-dressed black woman in the supermarket for more than a year now. We do not speak, and we usually pretend not to see each other. But, when we turn a corner suddenly and find ourselves staring squarely into each other's eyes, her face freezes and she moves on. I believe she is insisting that both of us be more than black—that we interact only when we have a reason other than the mere fact of our race. Her chilliness enforces a priority I agree with—individuality over group identity.

But I believe I see something else in this woman that I also see in myself and in many other middle-class blacks. It is a kind of race fatigue, a deep weariness with things racial, which comes from the fact that our lives are more integrated than they have ever been before. Race does not determine our fates as powerfully as it once did, which means it is not the vital personal concern it once was. Before the sixties, race set the boundaries of black life. Now, especially for middle-class blacks, it is far less a factor, though we don't always like to admit it. Blacks still suffer from racism, so we must be concerned, but this need to be concerned with what is not so personally urgent makes for race fatigue.

I have a friend who did poorly in the insurance business for years. "People won't buy insurance from a black man," he always said. Two years ago another black man and a black woman joined his office. Almost immediately both did twice the business my friend was doing, with the same largely white client base.

Integration shock is essentially the shock of being suddenly accountable on strictly personal terms. It occurs in situations that disallow race as an excuse for personal shortcomings and it therefore exposes vul-

nerabilities that previously were hidden. One response to such shock is
to face up to the self-confrontation it brings and then to act on the basis
of what we learn about ourselves. After some struggle, my friend was
able to do this. He completely revised his sales technique, asked himself
some hard questions about his motivation, and resolved to work harder.

But when one lacks the courage to face oneself fully, a fear of hidden
vulnerabilities triggers a fright-flight response to integration shock. Instead of admitting that racism has declined, we argue all the harder that
it is still alive and more insidious than ever. We hold race up to shield
us from what we do not want to see in ourselves. My friend did this at
first, saying that the two blacks in this office were doing better than he
was because they knew how to "kiss white ass." Here he was *race-holding*,
using race to keep from looking at himself.

Recently I read an article in the local paper that explored the question
of whether blacks could feel comfortable living in the largely white Silicon
Valley. The article focused on a black family that had been living for
more than a decade in Saratoga, a very well-to-do white community. Their
neighborhood, their children's schools, their places of employment, their
shopping areas and parks—their entire physical environment—were populated by affluent whites. Yet during the interview the wife said they had
made two firm rules for their children: that they go to all-black colleges
back east and that they do "no dating outside the race, period."

I have pushed enough black history and culture on my own children
to be able to identify with the impulse behind the first of these rules.
Black children in largely white situations must understand and appreciate
their cultural background. But the rigidity of these rules, not to mention
the rules themselves, points to more than a concern with transmitting
heritage or gaining experience with other blacks. Rigidity arises from fear
and self-doubt. These people, I believe, were afraid of something.

What was striking to me about their rules, especially the one prohibiting interracial dating, was their tone of rejection. The black parents
seemed as determined to reject the white world as to embrace the black
one. Why? I would say because of integration shock. Their integrated
lives have opened up vulnerabilities they do not wish to face. But what
vulnerabilities? In this case, I think, a particularly embarrassing one. On
some level, I suspect, they doubt whether they are as good as the white
people who live around them. You cannot be raised in a culture that was
for centuries committed to the notion of your inferiority and not have
some doubt in this regard—doubt that is likely to be aggravated most in
integrated situations. So the rejecting tone of their rules is self-protective:
I will reject you before you have a chance to reject me. But all of this is
covered over by race. The high value of racial pride is invoked to shield
them from a doubt that they are afraid to acknowledge. Unacknowledged,
this doubt gains a negative power inside the personality that expresses

itself in the rigidity and absolutism of their rules. Repressed fears tend always to escalate their campaign for our attention by pushing us further and further into irrationality and rigidity.

The refusal to see something unflattering in ourselves always triggers the snap from race fatigue to race-holding. And once that happens, we are caught, like this family, in a jumble of racial ironies. The parents in Saratoga, who have chosen to live integrated lives, impose a kind of segregation on their children. Rules that would be racist in the mouth of any white person are created and enforced with pride. Their unexamined self-doubt also leaves them unable to exploit fully the freedom they have attained. Race fatigue makes them run to a place like Saratoga, but integration shock makes them hold race protectively. They end up clinging to what they've run from.

Once race-holding is triggered by fear, it ensnares us in a web of self-defeating attitudes that end up circumventing the new freedoms we've won over the past several decades. I have seen its corrosive effects in my own life and in the lives of virtually every black person I've known. Some are only mildly touched by it, while others seem incapacitated by it. But race-holding is as unavoidable as defensiveness itself, and I am convinced that it is one of the most debilitating, yet unrecognized, forces in black life today.

I define a *holding* as any self-description that serves to justify or camouflage a person's fears, weaknesses, and inadequacies. Holdings are the little and big exaggerations, distortions, and lies about ourselves that prop us up and let us move along the compromised paths we follow. They develop to defend against threats to our self-esteem, threats that make us feel vulnerable and that plant a seed of fear. This fear can work like wind on a brushfire, spreading self-doubt far beyond what the initial threat would warrant, so that we become even more weakened and more needy of holdings. Since holdings justify our reticence and cowardice, they are usually expressed in the form of high belief or earthy wisdom. A man whose business fails from his own indifference holds an image of himself as a man too honest to be a good businessman—a self-description that draws a veil over his weakness.

For some years I have noticed that I can walk into any of my classes on the first day of the semester, identify the black students, and be sadly confident that on the last day of the semester a disproportionate number of them will be at the bottom of the class, far behind any number of white students of equal or even lesser native ability. More to the point, they will have performed far beneath their own native ability. Self-fulfilling prophesy theory says that their schools have always expected them to do poorly, and that they have internalized this message and *done* poorly. But this deterministic theory sees blacks only as victims, without any margin of choice. It cannot fully explain the poor performances of these black students because it identifies only the forces that *pressure* them to do poorly. By overlooking the margin of choice open to them, this theory fails to recognize the degree to which they are responsible for their own poor showing. (The irony of this oversight is that it takes the power for positive change away from the students and puts it in the hands of the very institutions that failed them in the first place.)

The theory of race-holding is based on the assumption that a margin of choice is always open to blacks (even slaves had some choice). And it tries to make clear the mechanisms by which we relinquish that choice in the name of race. With the decline in racism the margin of black choice has greatly expanded, which is probably why race-holding is so much more visible today than ever before. But anything that prevents us from exploiting our new freedom to the fullest is now as serious a barrier to us as racism once was.

The self-fulfilling prophesy theory is no doubt correct that black students, like the ones I regularly see, internalize a message of inferiority that they receive from school and the larger society around them. But the relevant question in the 1990s is why they *choose* to internalize this view of themselves. Why do they voluntarily perceive themselves as inferior? We can talk about the weakened black family and countless other scars of oppression and poverty. And certainly these things have much to do with the image these students have of themselves. But they do not fully explain this self-image because none of them entirely eliminates the margin of choice that remains open. Choice lives in even the most blighted circumstances, and it certainly lives in the lives of these black college students.

I think they *choose* to believe in their inferiority, not to fulfill society's prophesy about them, but for the comforts and rationalizations their racial "inferiority" affords them. They hold their race to evade individual responsibility. Their margin of choice scares them, as it does all people. They are naturally intimidated by that eternal tussle between the freedom to act and the responsibility we must take for our actions. To some extent all of us balk in the face of this. The difference is that these students use their race to conceal the fact that they are balking. Their "inferiority" shields them from having to see that they are afraid of all-out competition with white students. And it isn't even an honest inferiority. I don't think they really believe it. It is a false inferiority, *chosen* over an honest and productive confrontation with white students and with their real fears—a strategy that allows them to stay comfortably on the sidelines in a university environment that all but showers them with opportunity.

"I'm doing okay for a black student," a student once told me. "I'm doing well considering where I came from," I have told myself. Race allows us both to hide from the real question, which is, "Am I doing what I can, considering my talents and energies?"

I see all of this as pretty much a subconscious process, fear working on a subterranean level to let us reduce our margin of choice in the name of race. Consciously, we tell ourselves that we are only identifying with our race, but fear bloats our racial identity to an unnatural size and then uses it as cover for its subversive work. The more severe the integration shock, the more fear cover is needed.

Doesn't race enhance individuality? I think it does, but only when individuality is nurtured and developed apart from race. The race-holder, inside the bubble of his separate self, feels inadequate or insecure and then seeks reassurance through race. When, instead, a sense of self arises from individual achievement and self-realization. When self-esteem is established apart from race, then racial identity can only enhance because it is no longer needed for any other purpose.

The word *individualism* began to connote selfishness and even betrayal for many blacks during the sixties. Individualism was seen as a threat to the solidarity blacks needed during those years of social confrontation. Despite the decline in racism, these connotations have lingered. Race-holding keeps them alive because they serve the race-holder's need to exaggerate the importance of race as well as to justify a fear of individual responsibility. Race-holding makes fluid the boundary between race and self, group and individual identity, so that race can swing over at a moment's notice and fill in where fears leave a vacuum.

This is a worse problem than is at first apparent because the individual is the seat of all energy, creativity, motivation, and power. We are most strongly motivated when we want something for ourselves. When our personal wants are best achieved through group action, as in the civil rights movement, we lend our energy to the group, and it becomes as strong as the sum of our energies. When the need for group action recedes, more energy is available to us as individuals. But race-holding intercedes here by affixing the race-holder too tightly to this racial identity and by causing him to see the locus of power in race rather than in himself. In this way race-holding corrupts the greatest source of power and strength available to blacks—the energy latent in our personal desires.

One of my favorite passages in Ralph Ellison's *Invisible Man* is his description of the problem of blacks as:

> not actually one of creating the uncreated conscience of [our] race, but of creating the *uncreated features of [our] face*. Our task is that of making ourselves individuals. . . . We create the race by creating ourselves and then to our great astonishment we will have created something far more important: we will have created a culture.

These lines hold up well, more than thirty years after they were written. They seem to suggest a kind of Adam Smith vision of culture:

When the individual makes himself, he makes culture. An "invisible hand" uses individual effort to define and broaden culture. In the 1990s we blacks are more than ever in a position where our common good will best be served by the determined pursuit of our most personal aspirations.

I think the means to this, and the answer to race-holding generally, is personal responsibility, a source of great power that race-holding does its best to conceal.

Some years ago I made a mistake at a neighbor's cocktail party that taught me something about personal responsibility. I went to the party for the thinnest of reasons—mere politeness—though the afternoon was hot and I was already in a peevish mood. The event would have been problematic even if I weren't the only black at the party. But I was, and on this afternoon I *chose* to make note of the fact, though it was hardly a new experience for me. As I strolled around the sun-baked patio, avoiding people more than engaging them, I held this fact more and more tightly until I came to believe it had a profound meaning I needed to understand. After a while I decided that others needed to understand it, too.

In the sixties, blacks and white liberals often engaged in something that might be called the harangue-flagellation ritual. Blacks felt anger, white liberals felt guilt, and when they came together, blacks would vent their anger by haranguing the whites, who often allowed themselves to be scourged as a kind of penance. The "official" black purpose of this rite was to "educate" whites on the issue of race, and in the sixties this purpose may sometimes have been served. But in the eighties, after a marked decline in racism and two decades of consciousness-raising, the rite had become both anachronistic and, I think, irresponsible. Nevertheless, it suited my mood on this hot afternoon, so I retrieved it from its dusty bin and tried to make it fashionable again.

A woman at the party said how much she liked Jesse Jackson's rhetorical style. Was "style" the only thing she liked? I asked, with an edge to my voice. The woman gave me a curious and exasperated look, but I pushed on anyway. Soon I was lecturing the six or seven people around me: I told them that racism had been driven underground in the sixties and seventies, where more insidious strategies for foiling the possibilities of black people had evolved. I pointed to the black unemployment rate, the continued segregation of many schools, housing discrimination, and so on. Soon I saw that the old harangue-flagellation ritual was firmly back in place. I was shaming these people, and they nodded at what I said in a way that gratified me.

But at home that night I felt a stinging shame, and even weeks later the thought of that afternoon made me cringe. Eventually I saw why. For one thing, I was trading on my race with those people, using the very thing I claimed to be so concerned with to buy my way out of certain anxieties. Like the Saratoga family, I was race-holding in response to the integration shock I felt in this integrated situation. I had begun to feel vulnerable, and I hit those people with race before they could hit me with it. My vulnerabilities, of course, were essentially the same as the Saratoga family's. On some level I doubted myself in relation to these whites, and my insecurities drove me into an offense that was really a defense. The shame I began to feel, though I could not identify it at the time, was essentially the shame of cowardice. I felt as though I'd run away from something and used race to cover my tracks.

This shame had another dimension that was even more humiliating than the cowardice I had felt. On that patio I was complaining to white people, beseeching them to see how badly blacks were still treated, and I was gratified to see their heads nod as though they understood. My voice contained no audible whine, but at least some of what I said amounted to a whine. And this is what put the sting in my shame. Cowardice was a common enough fault, but whining was quite another thing.

The race-holder whines, or complains indiscriminately, not because he seeks redress but because he seeks the status of victim, a status that excuses him from what he fears. A victim is not responsible for his condition, and by claiming a victim's status the race-holder gives up the sense of personal responsibility he needs to better his condition. His unseen purpose is to hide rather than fight, so the anger and, more importantly, the energy that real racism breeds in him is squandered in self-serving complaint. The price he pays for the false comfort of his victim's status is a kind of impotence.

The difference between the race-holder who merely complains and the honest protester is that the latter keeps the responsibility for his condition in his own hands. The honest protester may be victimized, but he is not solely a victim. He thinks of himself as fully human and asks only that the rules of the game be made fair. Through fairness, rather than entitlement, he retains his personal responsibility and the power that grows out of it. But he also understands that he must keep this responsibility whether or not society is fair. His purpose is to realize himself, to live the fullest possible life, and he is responsible for this, like all men, regardless of how society treats him.

Personal responsibility is the brick and mortar of power. The responsible person knows that the quality of his life is something that he will have to make inside the limits of his fate. Some of these limits he can push back, some he cannot, but in any case the quality of his life will pretty much reflect the quality of his efforts. When this link between well-being and action is truly accepted, the result is power. With this understanding and the knowledge that he is responsible, a person can see his margin of choice. He can choose and act, and choose and act again, without illusion. He can create himself and make himself felt in the world. Such a person has power.

I was neither responsible nor powerful as I stood on my neighbor's patio complaining about racism to these polite people. In effect I was asking them to be fully responsible for something that blacks and whites *share* responsibility for. Whites must guarantee a free and fair society. But blacks must be responsible for actualizing their own lives. If I had said this to the people at the party, maybe they would have gone away with a clearer sense of their own responsibilities. But I never considered it because the real goal of my complaining was to disguise a fear I didn't want to acknowledge.

The barriers to black progress in America today are clearly as much psychological as they are social or economic. We have suffered as much as any group in human history, and if this suffering has ennobled us, it has also wounded us and pushed us into defensive strategies that are often self-defeating. But we haven't fully admitted this to ourselves. The psychological realm is murky, frightening, and just plain embarrassing. And a risk is involved in exploring it: the risk of discovering the ways in which we contribute to, if not create, the reality in which we live. Denial, avoidance, and repression intervene to save us from this risk. But, of course, they only energize what is repressed with more and more negative power, so that we are victimized as much by our own buried fears as by racism.

In the deepest sense, the long struggle of blacks in America has always been a struggle to retrieve our full humanity. But now the reactive stance we adopted to defend ourselves against oppression binds us to the same racial views that oppressed us in the first place. Snakelike, our defense has turned on us. I think it is now the last barrier to the kind of self-possession that will give us our full humanity, and we must overcome it ourselves.

QUESTIONS FOR CRITICAL READERS

Remembering and Understanding

1. What is race fatigue?
2. Explain integration shock.
3. Re-state Steele's central point, and use it as the basis of a summary of his essay.
4. Explain Steele's concept of holding.

Analyzing and Discussing

5. Steele contrasts two visions of the self. In one, he says, people tell themselves that they are doing well considering what they are or where they came from. In the other, they ask, "Am I doing what I can, considering my talents and energies?" What is the difference between these two statements.

6. Steele suggests that successful blacks may perceive other successful blacks as threats to one another's uniqueness. What does he mean by this? How does his own position as a successful black influence his conclusion here?

Writing

7. Steele applies his theory of "holding" to blacks, but it is certainly not restricted to any one group. Most groups and many individuals have some device or defense mechanism that allows them to avoid looking at themselves. Identify such a strategy that you use, or that someone or some group that you know uses, and explain how it functions for them, just as Steele explains how race holding functions for blacks.

Brothers and Keepers

———— JOHN EDGAR WIDEMAN ————

Wideman is best known as a novelist. He grew up in Pittsburgh's ghetto, Homewood, played basketball for the University of Pennsylvania, and attended Oxford University as a Rhodes Scholar. The selection here is from Brothers and Keepers, *a memoir in which he writes about himself, his brother, and their relationship. Wideman's brother, Robby, is serving a life sentence for murder. The book grew from conversations they had during Wideman's visits to Robby in prison, and is really a cooperative venture. As you read you will notice that Wideman uses both of their voices.*

IT WAS A CRAZY SUMMER. The summer of '68. We fought the cops in the streets. I mean sure nuff punch-out fighting like in them Wild West movies and do. Shit. Everybody in Homewood up on Homewood Avenue duking with the cops. Even the little weeny kids was there, standing back throwing rocks. We fought that whole summer. Cop cars all over the place and they'd come jumping out with night sticks and fists balled up. They wore leather jackets and gloves and sometimes they be wearing them football helmets so you couldn't go upside they heads without hurting your hand. We was rolling. Steady fighting. All you need to be doing was walking down the avenue and here they come. Screeching the brakes. Pull up behind you and three or four cops come busting out the squad car ready to rumble. Me and some the fellas just minding our business walking down Homewood and this squad car pulls up. Hey, you. Hold it. Stop where you are, like he's talking to some silly kids or something. All up in my face. What you doing here, like I ain't got no right to be on Homewood Avenue, and I been walking on Homewood Avenue all my life an ain't no jive police gon get on my case just cause I'm walking down the avenue. Fuck you, pig. Ain't none your goddamn business, pig. Well, you know it's on then. Cop come running at Henry and Henry ducks down on one knee and jacks the mother-fucker up. Throw him clean through that big window of Murphy's five-and-dime.

232

You know where I mean. Where Murphy's used to be. Had that cop snatched up in the air and through that window before he knew what hit him. Then it's on for sure. We rolling right there in the middle of Homewood Avenue.

That's the way it was. Seem like we was fighting cops every day. Funny thing was, it was just fighting. Wasn't no shooting or nothing like that. Somebody musta put word out from Downtown. You can whip the niggers' heads but don't be shooting none of em. Yeah. Cause the cops would get out there and fight but they never used no guns. Might bust your skull with a nightstick but they wasn't gon shoot you. So the word must have been out. Cause you know if it was left to the cops they would have blowed us all away. Somebody said don't shoot and we figured that out so it was stone rock 'n' roll and punch-up time.

Sometimes I think the cops dug it too. You know like it was exercise or something. Two or three carloads roll up and it's time to get it on. They was looking for trouble. You could tell. You didn't have to yell pig or nothing. Just be minding your business and here they come piling out the car ready to go ten rounds. I got tired of fighting cops. And getting whipped on. We had some guys go up on the rooves. Brothers was gon waste the motherfuckers from up there when they go riding down the street but shit, wasn't no sense bringing guns into it long as they wasn't shooting at us. Brothers didn't play in those days. We was organized. Cops jump somebody and in two minutes half of Homewood out there on them cops' ass. We was organized and had our own weapons and shit. Rooftops and them old boarded-up houses was perfect for snipers. Dudes had pistols and rifles and shotguns. You name it. Wouldna believed what the brothers be firing if it come to that but it didn't come to that. Woulda been stone war in the streets. But the shit didn't come down that way. Maybe it woulda been better if it did. Get it all out in the open. Get the killing done wit. But the shit didn't hit the fan that summer. Least not that way.

Lemme see. I woulda been in eleventh grade. One more year of Westinghouse left after the summer of '68. We was the ones started the strike. Right in the halls of good old Westinghouse High School. Like I said, we had this organization. There was lots of organizations and clubs and stuff like that back then but we had us a mean group. Like, if you was serious business you was wit us. Them other people was into a little bit of this and that, but we was in it all the way. We was gon change things or die trying. We was known as bad. Serious business, you know. If something was coming down they always wanted us wit them. See, if we was in it, it was some mean shit. Had to be. Cause we didn't play. What it was called was Together. Our group. We was so bad we was having a meeting once and one the brothers bust in. Hey youall. Did youall hear on the radio Martin Luther King got killed? One the older guys running the meeting look up and say, We don't care nothing bout that ass-kissing nigger, we got important business to take care of. See, we just knew we was into something. Together was where it was at. Didn't nobody dig what King putting down. We wasn't about begging whitey for nothing and we sure wasn't taking no knots without giving a whole bunch back. After the dude come in hollering and breaking up the meeting we figured we better go on out in the street anyway cause we didn't want no bullshit. You know. Niggers running wild and tearing up behind Martin Luther King getting wasted. We was into planning. Into organization. When the shit went down we was gon be ready. No point in just flying around like chickens with they heads cut off. I mean like it ain't news that whitey is offing niggers. So we go out the meeting to cool things down. No sense nobody getting killed on no humbug.

Soon as we got outside you could see the smoke rising off Homewood Avenue. Wasn't that many people out and Homewood burning already, so we didn't really know what to do. Walked down to Hamilton and checked it out around in there and went up past the A & P. Say to anybody we see, Cool it. Cool it, brother. Our time will come. It ain't today, brother. Cool it. But we ain't really got no plan. Didn't know what to do, so me and Henry torched the Fruit Market and went on home.

Yeah. I was a stone mad militant. Didn't know what I was saying half the time and wasn't sure what I wanted, but I was out there screaming and hollering and waving my arms around and didn't take no shit from nobody. Mommy and them got all upset cause I was in the middle of the school strike. I remember sitting down and arguing with them many a time. All they could talk about was me messing up in school. You know. Get them good grades and keep your mouth shut and mind your own business. Trying to tell me white folks ain't all bad. Asking me where would niggers be if it wasn't for good white folks. They be arguing that mess at me and they wasn't about to hear nothing I had to say. What it all come down to was be a good nigger and the white folks take care of you. Now I really couldn't believe they was saying that. Mommy and Geral got good sense. They ain't nobody's fools. How they talking that mess? Wasn't no point in arguing really, cause I was set in my ways and they sure was set in theirs. It was the white man's world and wasn't no way round it or over it or under it. Got to get down and dance to the tune the man be playing. You know I didn't want to hear nothing like that, so I kept on cutting classes and fucking up and doing my militant thing every chance I got.

I dug being a militant cause I was good. It was something I could do. Rap to people. Whip a righteous message on em. People knew my name. They'd listen. And I'd steady take care of business. This was when Rap Brown and Stokely and Bobby Seale and them on TV. I identified with those cats. Malcolm and Eldridge and George Jackson. I read their books. They was Gods. That's who I thought I was when I got up on the stage and rapped at the people. It seemed like things was changing. Like no way they gon turn niggers round this time.

You could feel it everywhere. In the streets. On the corner. Even in jive Westinghouse High people wasn't going for all that old, tired bullshit they be laying on you all the time. We got together a list of demands. Stuff about the lunchroom and a black history course. Stuff like that and getting rid of the principal. We wasn't playing. I mean he was a mean nasty old dude. Hated niggers. No question about that. He wouldn't listen to nobody. Didn't care what was going on. Everybody hated him. We told them people from the school board his ass had to go first thing or we wasn't coming back to school. It was a strike, see. Started in Westinghouse, but by the end of the week it was all over the city. Langley and Perry and Fifth Avenue and Schenley. Sent messengers to all the schools, and by the end of the week all the brothers and sisters on strike. Shut the schools down all cross the city, so they knew we meant business. Knew they had to listen. The whole Board of Education came to Westinghouse and we told the principal to his face he had to go. The nasty old motherfucker was sitting right there and we told the board, He has to go. The man hates us and we hate him and his ass got to go. Said it right to his face and you ought to seen him turning purple and flopping round in his chair. Yeah. We got on his case. And the thing was they gave us everything we asked for. Yes . . . Yes . . . Yes. Everything we had on the list. Sat there just as nice and lied like dogs. Yes. We agree. Yes. You'll have a new principal. I couldn't believe it. Didn't even have to curse them out or nothing. Didn't even raise my voice cause it was yes to this and yes to that before the words out my mouth good.

We's so happy we left that room with the Board and ran over to the auditorium and in two minutes it was full and I'm up there screaming. We did it. We did it. People shouting back Right on and Work out and I gets that whole auditorium dancing in they seats. I could talk now. Yes, I could. And we all happy as could be, cause we thought we done something. We got the black history course and got us a new principal and, shit, wasn't nothing we couldn't do, wasn't nothing could stop us that day. Somebody yelled, Party, and I yelled back, Party, and then I told them, Everybody come on up to Westinghouse Park. We gon stone party. Wasn't no plan or nothing. It all just started in my head. Somebody shouted party and I yelled Party and the next thing I know we got this all-night jam going. We got bands and lights and we partied all night long. Ima tell you the truth now. Got more excited bout the party than anything else. Standing up there on the stage I could hear the music and see the niggers dancing and I'm thinking, Yeah. I'm thinking bout getting high and tipping round, checking out the babes and grooving on the sounds. Got me a little reefer and sipping out somebody's jug of sweet wine and the park's full of bloods and I'm in heaven. That's the way it was too. We partied all night long in Westinghouse Park. Cops like to shit, but wasn't nothing they could do. This was 1968. Wasn't nothing they could do but surround the park and sit out there in they cars while we partied. It was something else. Bands and bongos and niggers singing. *Oh bop she bop* everywhere in the park. Cops sat out in them squad cars and Black Marias, but wasn't nothing they could do. We was smoking and drinking and carrying on all night and they just watched us, just sat in the dark and didn't do a thing. We broke into the park building to get us some lectricity for the bands and shit. And get us some light. Broke in the door and took what we wanted, but them cops ain't moved an inch. It was our night and they knew it. Knew they better leave well enough alone. We owned Westinghouse Park that night. Thought we owned Homewood.

In a way the party was the end. School out pretty soon after that and nobody followed through. We come back to school in the fall and they got cops patrolling the halls and locks on every door. You couldn't go in or out the place without passing by a cop. They had our ass then. Turned the school into a prison. Wasn't no way to get in the auditorium. Wasn't no meetings or hanging out in the halls. They broke up all that shit. That's when having police in the schools really got started. When it got to be a regular everyday thing. They fixed us good. Yes, yes, yes, when we was sitting down with the Board, but when we come back to school in September everything got locks and chains on it.

We was just kids. Didn't really know what we wanted. Like I said. The party was the biggest thing to me. I liked to get up and rap. I was a little Stokely, a little Malcolm in my head but I didn't know shit. When I look back I got to admit it was mostly just fun and games. Looking for a way to get over. Nothing in my head. Nothing I could say I really wanted. Nothing I wanted to be. So they lied through their teeth. Gave us a party and we didn't know no better, didn't know we had to follow through, didn't know how to keep our foot in they ass.

Well, you know the rest. Nothing changed. Business as usual when we got back in the fall. Hey, hold on. What's this? Locks on the doors. Cops in the halls. Big cops with big guns. Hey, man, what's going down? But it was too late. The party was over and they wasn't about to give up nothing no more. We had a black history class, but wasn't nobody eligible to take it. Had a new principal, but nobody knew him. Nobody could get to him. And he didn't know us. Didn't know what we was about except we was trouble. Troublemakers; and he had something for that. Boot your ass out in a minute. Give your name to the cops and you couldn't get through the door cause everybody had to have an I.D. Yeah. That was a new one. Locks and I.D.'s and cops. Wasn't never our school.

They made it worse instead of better. Had our chance, then they made sure we wouldn't have no more chances.

It was fun while it lasted. Some good times, but they was over in a minute and then things got worser and worser. Sixty-eight was when the dope came in real heavy too. I mean you could always get dope but in '68 seems like they flooded Homewood. Easy as buying a quart of milk. Could cop your works in a drugstore. Dope was everywhere that summer. Cats ain't never touched the stuff before got into dope and dope got into them. A bitch, man. It come in like a flood.

Me. I start to using heavy that summer. Just like everybody else I knew. The shit was out there and it was good and cheap, so why not? What else we supposed to be doing? It was part of the fun. The good times. The party.

We lost it over the summer, but I still believe we did something hip for a bunch of kids. The strike was citywide. We shut the schools down. All the black kids was with us. The smart ones. The dumb ones. It was hip to be on strike. To show our asses. We had them honkies scared. Got the whole Board of Education over to Westinghouse High. We lost it, but we had them going, Bruh. And I was in the middle of it. Mommy and them didn't understand. They thought I was just in trouble again. The way I always was. Daddy said one his friends works Downtown told him they had my name down there. Had my name and the rest of the ringleaders'. He said they were watching me. They had my name Downtown and I better be cool. But I wasn't scared. Always in trouble, always doing wrong. But the strike was different. I was proud of that. Proud of getting it started, proud of being one of the ringleaders. The mad militant. Didn't know exactly what I was doing, but I was steady doing it.

The week the strike started, think it was Tuesday, could have been Monday but I think it was Tuesday, cause the week before was when some the students went to the principal's office and said the student council or some damn committee or something wanted to talk to him about the lunchroom and he said he'd listen but he was busy till next week, so it could have been Monday, but I think it was Tuesday cause knowing him he'd put it off long as he could. Anyway, Mr. Lindsay sitting in the auditorium. Him and vice-principal Meers and the counselor, Miss Kwalik. They in the second or third row sitting back and the speakers is up on stage behind the mike but they ain't using it. Just talking to the air really, cause I slipped in one the side doors and I'm peeping what's going on. And ain't nothing going on. Most the time the principal whispering to Miss Kwalik and Mr. Meers. Lindsay got a tablet propped up on his knee and writes something down every now and then but he ain't really listening to the kids on stage. Probably just taking names cause he don't know nobody's name. Taking names and figuring how he's gon fuck over the ones doing the talking. You. You in the blue shirt, Come over here. Don't none them know your name less you always down in the office cause you in trouble or you one the kiss-ass, nicey-nice niggers they keep for flunkies and spies. So he's taking names or whatever, and every once in a while he says something like, Yes. That's enough now. Who's next? Waving the speakers on and off and the committee, or whatever the fuck they calling theyselves, they ain't got no better sense than to jump when he say jump. Half of them so scared they stuttering and shit. I know they glad when he wave them off the stage cause they done probably forgot what they up there for.

Well, I get sick of this jive real quick. Before I know it I'm up on the stage and I'm tapping the mike and can't get it turned on so I goes to shouting. Talking trash loud as I can. Damn this and damn that and Black Power and I'm somebody. Tell em ain't no masters and slaves no more and we want freedom and we want it now. I'm stone preaching. I'm chirping. Get on the teachers, get on the principal and everybody else I can think of. Called em zookeepers. Said they ran a zoo and wagged my finger at the chief zookeeper and his buddies sitting down there in the auditorium. Told the kids on the stage to go and get the students. You go here. You go there. Like I been giving orders all my life. Cleared the stage in a minute. Them chairs scraped and kids run off and it's just me up there all by my ownself. I runs out of breath. I'm shaking, but I'm not scared. Then it gets real quiet. Mr. Lindsay stands up. He's purple and shaking worse than me. Got his finger stabbing at me now. Shoe's on the other foot now. Up there all by myself now and he's doing the talking.

Are you finished? I hope you're finished cause your ass is grass. Come down from there this instant. You've gone too far this time. Wideman. Get down from there. I want you in my office immediately.

They's all three up now, Mr. Lindsay and Miss Kwalik and Meers, up and staring up at me like I'm stone crazy. Like I just pulled out my dick and peed on the stage or something. Like they don't believe it. And to tell the truth I don't hardly believe it myself. One minute I'm watching them kids making fools of theyselves, next minute I'm bad-mouthing everything about the school and giving orders and telling Mr. Lindsay to his face he ain't worth shit. Now the whiteys is up and staring at me like I'm a disease, like I'm Bad Breath or Okey Doke the damn fool and I'm looking round and it's just me up there. Don't know if the other kids is gone for the students like I told them or just run away cause they scared.

Ain't many times in life I felt so lonely. I'm thinking bout home. What they gon say when Mr. Lindsay calls and tells them he kicked my ass out for good. Cause I had talked myself in a real deep hole. Like, Burn, baby burn. We was gon run the school our way or burn the motherfucker down. Be our school or wasn't gon be no school. Yeah, I was yelling stuff like that and I was remembering it all. Cause it was real quiet in there. Could of heard a pin drop in the balcony. Remembering everything I said and then starting to figure how I was gon talk myself out this one. Steady scheming and just about ready to cop a plea. I's sorry boss. Didn't mean it, Boss. I was just kidding. Making a joke. Ha. Ha. I loves this school and loves you Mr. Lindsay. My head's spinning and I'm moving away from the mike but just at that very minute I hears the kids busting into the balcony. It's my people. It's sure nuff them. They bust in the balcony and I ain't by myself no more. I'm hollering again and shaking a power fist and I tells Mr. Lindsay:

You get out. You leave.

I'm king again. He don't say a word. Just splits with his flunkies. The mike starts working and that's when the strike begins.

Your brother was out there in the middle of it. I was good, too. Lot of the time I be thinking bout the party afterward, my heart skipping forward to the party, but I was willing to work. Be out front. Take the weight. Had the whole city watching us, Bruh.

QUESTIONS FOR CRITICAL READERS

Remembering and Understanding

1. Wideman says his brother could have told him what he needed to hear about what was happening to black people. Summarize what Robby tells him.
2. How is Wideman different from his brother?
3. What was Robby's goal in the strike? What did he want to change?

Analyzing and Discussing

4. Contrast Robby's view of himself and the school officials' view of him during the strike that he organized.
5. How does Robby's participation in the strike help him redefine his own character?
6. What changes in black consciousness does Robby's story portray?

Writing

7. Identify and describe a particularly volatile or exciting time in your life, as Robby describes the strike. Work to convey the experience in vivid details, as Robby does, and to suggest your feelings about the experience through your tone.

Synthesizing and Consolidating

1. Review the prereading notes you made in your reading journal before you read this chapter. Identify one idea or position that has changed as a result of the readings. Describe that change, and explain what caused it.
2. In your reading journal, make a list of the most memorable *new* information you have acquired from reading this chapter. What do you know now that you did not know earlier?
3. How do the selections in this chapter support or undermine the popular stereotypes about young black men?
4. How would Steele respond to Staples or Fleming?
5. Several writers in this chapter mention role models. How do role models influence our behavior? Make a list of the people you consider role models, and then describe how you have consciously or unconsciously modeled your behavior after them.
6. Make a list of the role models available in American society for young black men, then use your list to classify these role models and write a brief description of each one.
7. How are the role models available to young blacks similar to or different from the role models available to whites?
8. Use Staples's ideas to interpret or explain the death of Darrell Britt.
9. Several of the writers here discuss images of blacks, but almost all of these images have been produced by whites. What images do blacks project of themselves, independent of those that whites have created? Describe an image of blacks that originates with blacks, and explain how it is different from the images produced by whites. (For example, consider the images that blacks project of themselves through their dress, hair styles, and music.)

Suggestions for Writing and Research

1. Staples says that crimes committed by blacks create the most fear and concern among whites, but that white-collar crime results in a greater loss of money. Investigate this assertion by gathering statistics about both types of crime. What is the average annual cost of each type? Do blacks in fact commit more crimes of violence or crimes against property than whites do? To what extent are blacks involved in white-collar crime? Write a paper in which you present and explain the statistics you have gathered and argue whether one type of crime is more serious than the other.
2. Police involved in drug enforcement have developed profiles of likely drug offenders and used these profiles to stop and search or question people who fit the profiles. Investigate these profiles. Explain what the profiles are and how they are used, and discuss whether they are legal.
3. Investigate the integration of a major-league sport and write a paper in which you describe how blacks gained access to this sport as players.

4. Research and explain the 1954 Supreme Court decision *Brown vs. Board of Education.*
5. In recent years organizations that do not admit blacks, women, Jews, or members of other groups have received much attention. Many have been ordered by courts to change their membership practices. What is your position on this issue? Should organizations such as golf clubs, service clubs, and others be forced to accept members regardless of race or sex? Or should membership restrictions be allowed? Explain your position. (You may also need to do some research into this issue.)

6

Birds

Adapting for Survival

BIRDS ARE PRESENT ON ALL CONTINENTS, and thus have successfully adapted physically and behaviorally to a wide range of conditions,
from arctic cold to desert and tropical heat. In addition, many birds
migrate thousands of miles each spring and fall in order to locate conditions
in which they can live. Despite their obvious ability to survive such a
wide variety of conditions, birds are also quite sensitive to environmental
pressures. They are quick to respond to pollution, pressure from other
populations (including humans), and degradation of their habitat. Some
researchers, in fact, have suggested that birds provide an early warning
of what is in store for humans if the quality of the environment continues
to deteriorate.

Because birds live virtually everywhere on earth, they are among
the easiest wild animals to observe in their natural surroundings. This
accessibility has made them very popular. Millions of people around the
world spend significant amounts of their time watching and studying birds,
and they spend significant amounts of money on binoculars, books, tape
recordings, and bird seed. They do this because they believe birds are
interesting to study and aesthetically pleasing. At least one researcher has
suggested that it may be psychologically important for people to have
birds around.

Because they are easy to observe and study, birds have provided scientists with considerable information about evolution, and have even been crucial in the formation of evolutionary theories. Several varieties of finches in the Galapagos Islands were crucial to Darwin's formulation of his theory of evolution (not surprisingly, they have come to be known as Darwin's finches). Birds also offer a relatively convenient focus for nature study. To learn about birds in any depth or detail involves learning about most of the plants and animals that share their habitat.

The writers in this chapter include birdwatchers, biologists, a poet, and a historian. All of them are close observers and careful students of birds and nature. All are concerned in some way with how birds adapt to their environment in order to survive. This interest in adaptation commits them to understanding the role of evolution in shaping both behavior and physical characteristics.

Connor, a dedicated birdwatcher, writes about migration and the effects of habitat destruction on migratory bird populations. Wilcove takes a historical approach as he reevaluates the causes for the passenger pigeon's extinction, seeing extinction as a failure to adapt. Heinrich, a zoologist, explains egg colors as evolutionary adaptations. Kim Harris explains how birds are adapted to survive in cold weather. Carrighar provides a composite description of the behavior of swans. Vander Wall and Balda report their observations of how Clark's nutcrackers and certain trees in the mountains have evolved into mutually dependent organisms. Austin describes ravens, vultures, and other scavengers of the desert, analyzing how they live in a harsh climate. Baker spent ten years observing peregrine falcons in England and writes about his observations, which include how peregrines are adapted to their habitat and to their role as predators. Galvin, in his poem about young owls, suggests that people who observe birds need not confine themselves to a scientific response.

Before You Read

Before you begin to read the selections in this chapter, answer the following questions in your reading journal.

1. Make a list of as many facts about birds as you can think of.
2. Describe your emotional response to birds. How do you react when you see a bird, or a special bird?
3. How many species of birds can you identify? List them.
4. Explain what you know about the relationship between birds and the environment.
5. Describe a specific interesting experience you have had with birds.
6. What special symbolic or mythic meanings do birds have? List and explain as many as you can think of.

Empty Skies

—————— JACK CONNOR ——————

Connor is a teacher, free-lance writer, and dedicated birdwatcher. In this article he explores what happens to birds that migrate to the tropics each year only to find that their winter habitats are being destroyed. Connor is the author of The Complete Birder, *which contains a wealth of information about birds and how to observe and study them.*

8:30 a.m. Cape May Point, New Jersey, April 16, 1988

"**Anything there?**" "**Nothing. Nada. Zip. Zero. Zilch.**" "**Come on, warblers.**" "**Hold it. What's this?**" "**A bird?**" "**A leaf. Sorry.**" "**Come on, warblers!**"

BIRD BANDER PATTI HODGETTS and Paul Kerlinger, the director of the Cape May Bird Observatory, are walking Hodgetts's net lane, a line of 15 black-mesh nets strung for 175 yards through what is ordinarily ideal habitat for migrant songbirds, a thick forest of oaks, pines and tangled undergrowth on the edge of Cape May State Park. Hodgetts stops every few steps to adjust a panel of netting or to disentangle the briers and branches that have been blown into the mesh. Kerlinger scans ahead with his binoculars. "I haven't even seen a migrant all day," he says.

The day is cool but bright. Sunlight descends in shafts from the forest canopy, and birds that have wintered in these woods—cardinals, titmice, chickadees and white-throated sparrows—are singing all around.

"Too much wind today for warblers," Hodgetts says.

"Maybe," Kerlinger says. "Anything that came in last night could be sitting tight, resting up."

Hodgetts was on the scene at 7 o'clock to open the nets and has walked the lane each quarter hour. She has caught only two birds all morning, both ruby-crowned kinglets. Kinglets are not one of the species she is studying, but she banded, measured and weighed the birds before

244

opening her hand and letting each fly away. "That's because I band everything. I don't like the idea of catching a bird and just letting it go."

The target species for Hodgetts's study are long-distance migrant songbirds—the warblers, thrushes, vireos, orioles and tanagers, which overwinter in the Caribbean and Central and South America and come north in April and May to nest in the United States and Canada each summer. Her study is part of a larger project Kerlinger has been coordinating for several years with bird-banding stations on islands off the Gulf Coast of Louisiana, Mississippi and Florida.

"We're measuring the fat on these birds," Kerlinger explains, "which means what we're really doing is studying how healthy they are. We band them, weigh them and then look under the feathers on their breasts to measure how much fat they have left. Their fat is their fuel. What we want to know is how stressed they are. A warbler without fat isn't going to make it to the breeding grounds, unless it can feed, rest and put on weight.

"What we'd like to do eventually is study the birds before they try to cross the Gulf. It's a nonstop, 500-mile flight, at minimum. How many birds leaving from the Central American coast are healthy enough to make it across?"

Hodgetts's work station is a large desk tucked under a tree at the end of the net lane. On it are the tools of the bander's trade: a logbook, two field guides, half a dozen strings of coded bands on coat hangers, three sets of pliers, a plastic ruler, a spring scale and a holding box. Hodgetts points to the holding box, which stands up like a dollhouse and has 40 numbered compartments so, theoretically at least, the bander could capture and hold 40 different birds at once. "We aren't going to need *that* today," Hodgetts says. "I can't imagine I'm going to use it this *year*."

Kerlinger sits down and sighs, "Talk to any bander you want. They all say the same thing. Warbler numbers are down, vireo numbers are down, tanagers, thrushes—all the groups that winter in the Caribbean and Central America. The tropical forests are disappearing and so are the birds.

"The scariest part is that the birds are too spread out up here on their nesting territories to be counted. If we ordinarily have 10 million pairs of one species of songbird breeding over an area of a million square miles and one summer the number dropped by 2 or 3 million pairs, I don't think we would even notice. You certainly couldn't prove they were lost.

"Think of how it happens locally. Let's say there are usually four pairs of wood thrushes that nest in the woods behind your backyard. One year, only three pairs come back. Unless you're a very careful observer, I doubt you're even going to notice the difference. You'd still be hearing that wood thrush song, and you'd probably just assume everything's OK. Now another year goes by, and only two pairs come back. That's a 50 percent loss in a couple of years, and you still might not notice. Multiply that by several million backyards, and you've got a disaster. A sneaky, insidious, nearly invisible *disaster*."

There are two equally short, equally valid answers to the question, "Why do birds migrate?"

Because they can. Because they must.

About half of the world's species of birds and more than three-quarters of all North American species are migratory in all or parts of their ranges. Their seasonal movements are arguably the most spectacular natural phenomenon on Planet Earth. A common estimate of the number of birds that head south from North America each fall is 5 billion, and on any given clear night, spring or fall, the skies over North America can be filled by hundreds of millions of birds on migration. Clemson University researchers once captured on radar the image of 2 million songbirds migrating over a single South Carolina airport.

Migration is a successful strategy for so many birds because it enables them to use temporary food sources. Most of our insect-eating migrants have descended from species that lived year-round in the tropics. As the ancestral species expanded their warm-weather ranges northward into temperate areas, they found insect prey that was underexploited by the resident species during the summer months but not available during the winter. Most theorists believe these species first learned to move short distances back and forth from the edges of their original ranges. In time, evolutionary selection accentuated and fine-tuned these movements by rewarding those species and individuals that developed characteristics— longer wings, stronger flight muscles, sharper orientation abilities—that adapted them for long-distance travel.

Even for the best-designed travelers, however, migration is a seasonal life-or-death test of health and adaptation. Each species has had to develop its own specific routes to its own particular wintering and nesting grounds. The blackpoll warbler, for example, flies nonstop for 80 hours and 1,400 miles over the Atlantic Ocean, from New England to Venezuela. Many blackpolls must die each year by drowning when ocean winds blow in the wrong direction; others die when they reach their destination because they arrive too exhausted to search out their insect prey. Still, the species' migration strategy is obviously a successful one. If it weren't, evolution would not have developed it in the first place.

Now, however, the blackpoll and other tropical migrants are facing a problem for which evolution could not have prepared them.

The Nature Conservancy has estimated that 74,000 acres of tropical forest are cleared worldwide every day. That would be a loss of 40,000 square miles annually, an area equal to the size of the state of Virginia. Botanist Peter Raven, during his keynote address to the 1987 meeting of the American Association for the Advancement of Science, announced his estimate for the loss of tropical forests each year: 80,000 square miles, an area the size of Nebraska.

No one claims these estimations can be precise—the clearing is going on piecemeal all around the equatorial belt of the world, and much of it is happening far from the eyes of anyone interested in measuring it—but no one disputes that the loss is large and accelerating. Burned and bulldozed clear-cuts are evident in forests and jungles everywhere throughout the tropics; waterfalls of once pristine rivers now gush mud, the wash from erosion upstream; and smoke from fires in the Amazon can be seen in photographs from weather satellites.

Human populations are growing rapidly in most tropical countries, especially in the Caribbean and Central America. The ever increasing need for more roads, more farmland, more houses, more pasture and more firewood leads inevitably to less and less standing forest. Ninety-five percent of the tree cover that once made Haiti lush and green is now gone, and the last few trees on the now brown hillsides are disappearing as peasants fell them for charcoal. With a per capita income of less than $500 annually, Haiti is the poorest of all countries in the region, but other countries are nearly as impoverished. The per capita income in Guatemala is less than $1,200 a year; in Nicaragua it's less than $1,000; in Honduras and El Salvador it's less than $800.

Much of the deforestation in these countries develops from the interests of North American companies and from the general dependence of all economies in the region on exports to the U.S. The enormous American consumption rate of coffee, bananas, sugar and beef makes them major exports, and the production of each has required the clearing of vast tracts of forest.

Cattle farming, especially, is a rapidly expanding industry in South America. Cattle raised there are leaner and cheaper than cattle raised in the U.S. A hamburger made from South American beef costs producers five cents less than a hamburger made from the beef of North American cattle—and both are USDA approved. In Brazil, the country with the largest remaining tropical jungle in the world, one official estimated that 38 percent of the forests lost there between 1960 and 1975 were cleared to make pastureland for cattle. Rainforest Alliance has estimated that one acre of tropical forest must be cleared for every five pounds of beef produced each year.

"It's a counterfeit paradise," says Daniel Katz of Rainforest Alliance.

The soil in the lush rain forest paradoxically is terribly thin and will support cattle grazing for only a few years before the soil is depleted.

The wildlife usually mentioned as threatened by this deforestation are animals most North Americans have encountered only in zoos or museums—jaguars, tapirs, howler monkeys, quetzals, macaws and harpy eagles. Seldom discussed are the animals that can be heard and seen every summer in any neighborhood in the U.S.: our migrant songbirds. Yet tropical forests are as vital to the protection of the ovenbird as they are to the howler monkey; as important to the scarlet tanager as to the scarlet macaw.

Open your field guide to its approximate midpoint and you'll see why. Nearly half of all species of birds (and more than three-quarters of all individual birds) that live in North America are songbirds, of the order Passeriformes. Most songbirds survive each year only because they can migrate to warmer habitats south of our borders.

Forty-seven of our 52 warblers and 22 of our 32 flycatchers retreat to wintering grounds in Mexico or farther south to feed on insects from October to March. The flycatchers include the eastern kingbird, the vermilion flycatcher, the scissor-tailed flycatcher, the olive-sided flycatcher, and both the eastern and western wood pewees. The warblers include the ovenbird, the redstart, Wilson's warbler, the northern parula, the hooded and the black-and-white warblers. The blackpoll winters in the Brazilian jungle, a habitat that shrinks by an estimated 3.6 million acres every year.

Nine of our 11 vireos, 4 of our 5 native orioles and all 4 of our tanagers winter in the Caribbean islands, Mexico and Central America.

Of our 5 spot-breasted thrushes, the group many birdwatchers consider the sweetest singers of all birds, only one—the hermit thrush—is a year-round resident in North America. The wood thrush, the gray-cheeked thrush, Swainson's thrush and the veery all fly south across the Gulf of Mexico each fall to find food and protection.

Many nonsongbirds also must retreat to warmer latitudes each winter, of course. Fourteen of our 15 hummingbirds and all 4 of our swifts (black, Vaux's, white-throated and chimney) are long-distance migrants that depend on tropical habitats for winter survival. Swainson's hawk, the broad-winged hawk, the swallow-tailed kite and the Mississippi kite are four raptors that feed primarily on insects and so also must retreat south each year.

It is the songbirds the experts seem most worried about, however, and the research information most point to first is that being compiled by Chandler Robbins, wildlife biologist at the U.S. Fish and Wildlife Service's Patuxent Wildlife Research Center in Laurel, Maryland.

Robbins has been coordinating the national Breeding Birds Survey and analyzing its data for 22 years. Each summer since 1966, approximately 2,000 ornithologists, both professional and amateur, have been taking a census of nesting birds throughout the U.S. and reporting their counts to Patuxent. Each participant is assigned a route 24.5 miles long with 50 stops, one each half mile. The observer looks and listens for three minutes at each stop, counting the birds seen or heard, and then moves on. Since some species are more easily counted than others, it is the relative numbers that are considered most meaningful. The piercing "wheeeep!!" of the great crested flycatcher can be heard from a quarter of a mile away. The quiet "tepick" of the least flycatcher, by contrast, carries about as far as a muffled sneeze.

"There are other variables too," Robbins says. "The weather patterns differ from year to year, and some observers are more experienced birders than others. Sometimes a route gets taken over by a less experienced birder, and the count might go down there. Or a less experienced birder may turn his route over to a better one, and the count along that route might go up. Even though those variables tend to average out over the whole country, we don't like to make much of year-to-year changes. We look for longer-term trends, and we're seeing one now: a continuous drop in the number of long-distance migrant songbirds over the last seven years.

"There were signs of a downturn in the summer of 1979, and since 1980, it's been a steady decline. That drop has continued every summer through 1986, which is the most recent year we've analyzed, and we're expecting it to continue. The trend is clear for whole groups of songbirds that winter in the tropics: thrushes, warblers, vireos, tanagers. For certain species, there's been as much as a 30 percent decline.

"Some of the birds we're talking about are among the best-known backyard birds in North America—the wood thrush, the red-eyed vireo, the scarlet tanager. Those and others seem to be having serious problems now and are probably headed for worse."

Robbins is careful to note that the Breeding Birds Survey data cannot be used to measure the exact correlation between deforestation and declining numbers of songbirds. "Different species of birds nest and winter in different areas and encounter different problems in each area and en route. It's not as if all the birds that nest in New Jersey winter in Guatemala. Depending on which species they are, they're going back to Guatemala, Cuba, Mexico, Panama, Venezuela, Brazil. We've been anticipating a decline in tropical migrants since we started the Breeding Birds Survey because of the tremendous loss of habitat down there, but it's very tough to isolate a single cause of mortality and decline."

Biologist John Terborgh, whose book *Where Have All the Birds Gone?* will be published next year by Princeton University Press, has been studying the ecology of tropical forests for 20 years. He currently shuttles between his office at Princeton University and the research station he directs in Manu National Park in southeastern Peru. Like Robbins, he is pessimistic about the future of our migrant songbirds and feels certain that deforestation on the wintering grounds is a leading cause of their recent decline.

"The Bachman's warbler is probably extinct now. No one has seen one in 10 or 15 years, to my knowledge. It nested in the southeastern U.S., but it wintered exclusively in Cuba. I haven't had the opportunity to work in Cuba, but flying over it, all I see from one coast to the other are sugarcane plantations. Bachman's warblers can't live in sugarcane.

"The Kirtland's warbler is probably next in line. In my opinion, it's pretty much a lost cause already. There are only a couple of hundred pairs left, and apparently they all winter in the northern Bahamas. That habitat is being rapidly altered by development for the tourist industry."

Terborgh has suggested in his research that the clearing of a given area of land on the migrants' wintering grounds may be far more detrimental than clearing the same total area on the breeding grounds. The reason: songbird populations are much more tightly packed on their wintering grounds. Almost the entire population of the magnolia warbler, for example, a species that breeds across Canada from the Yukon to Newfoundland and across the U.S. from Minnesota east and south to North Carolina, squeezes itself into the islands of Hispaniola and Cuba and the eastern third of Mexico during the winter. It shares this territory with more than a hundred other North American migrant species and several hundred resident species. Other populations of migrant songbirds are even more closely spaced. Most chestnut-sided warblers, a species that breeds over much of the same territory as the magnolia warbler, live from October to March in just three small countries at the narrowest section of Central America—Nicaragua, Costa Rica and Panama.

This dense concentration of birds is partially due to the rich variety of plant and animal life found in the tropics all around the world. In Costa Rica, which is smaller than West Virginia, more than 800 species of birds have been recorded, equal to the total recorded for all of the continental U.S.

Another reason for the particularly high density of birds in the Central American tropics is the chance alignment of land and water in the Western Hemisphere. If you look at a map of the Americas, concentrating on the rectangular area that can be drawn south from San Diego to the Equator, east through the Galápagos Islands to the coast of South America, north through the Panama Canal to Jacksonville, and back west to San Diego, you'll see that open ocean is by far the most common habitat due south of the U.S. Evolution has designed some migrant landbirds— the blackpoll, the Connecticut warbler, the blackburnian warbler and a few others—to make the long flight all the way to South America. Most species, however, are genetically programmed to find winter shelter in the relatively limited land masses between the two continents. Even before man began clearing the forests in the Caribbean and Central America, the birds there must have been very tightly packed.

"As far as our migrants are concerned," Terborgh observes, "the area that is especially crucial is what I call the near tropics. Half of all landbirds that breed in North America winter in just five countries—the Bahamas, Cuba, Mexico, Haiti and the Dominican Republic. Clearing one hectare of forest there is probably the equivalent of clearing five to eight hectares up here."

One point songbird researchers make again and again is that it is a misconception to think of warblers, vireos, thrushes, orioles and tanagers as "our" birds because they breed here and only winter in the south. It is more accurate to think of them as tropical birds that move north briefly each year only to nest.

Ornithologist Allen Keast of Queen's University in Kingston, Ontario, conducted a study in which he compiled banding data, nesting records and records of arrival dates on wintering territory for 14 species of warblers to demonstrate that all 14 spend much less time on their breeding grounds than on their winter territory. The American redstart and the yellow warbler are typical. Each arrives in Ontario in late May, and then mates, nests, fledges its young and departs within 10 to 12 weeks. Migration back and forth requires 5 or 6 weeks each way. Both have returned to their wintering territory by September and stay there until March. They spend 6 to 7 months on their wintering grounds in the tropics and only about 3 months up here. The timetable for other warblers, and many other insect-eating songbirds, is similar. These birds are visitors to our latitudes; their homes are in the tropics.

Another common misconception, evident in a thousand cartoons and postcards, is that birds are taking a kind of vacation during the winter months.

The truth is that for most tropical migrants, like migrant species everywhere, survival on the wintering grounds is at least as difficult as it is on the breeding grounds. In fact, the first winter is the most difficult period in most birds' lives, and the majority do not survive. Far fewer individuals of all species of songbird come north each spring than fly south each fall.

In the winter of 1984, during the second year of a banding project in Jamaica, Chandler Robbins was thrilled to recapture 10 of the 20 black-and-white warblers and 4 of the 9 worm-eating warblers he had banded on the same sites the previous winter. "When you realize those birds are crossing the ocean and migrating hundreds of miles north, and that the ordinary mortality rate for such small birds is about 50 percent anyway, it's amazing that you can find so many of the very same individuals back on the very same winter territories."

Ornithologist John Kricher, chairman of the biology department at Wheaton College in Norton, Massachusetts, has had similar experience banding migrants in Belize. In 1983, Kricher and his fellow workers recaptured individuals of nine different species they had banded on the same site the previous winter. The birds included wood thrushes, yellow-bellied flycatchers, catbirds, ovenbirds, chats, Kentucky warblers and hooded warblers. Many of them were caught in the same net they'd been trapped in 12 months earlier. One wood thrush was recaptured on the same site three years in a row.

This winter-site fidelity is further evidence of the value of winter habitats. Individual birds return to the same parcel of land because they have managed to survive there. "Wood thrushes, hooded warblers and many other species are actually territorial on their wintering grounds," Kricher notes. "They don't sing, but they do use chip notes, wing flicks and other subtle threats to defend their territory against others of the same species. In winter, it's the females as well as the males that defend territory. Female hooded warblers, for example, are just as capable of driving off invading males as other males are."

What happens to those birds who return to their winter territory to find it clear-cut or burned? The answer is unknown, since these are the individuals that are seldom recaptured, but undoubtedly their chances for survival drop significantly. The few banding records that are available suggest that birds that lose their winter territory become "floaters." Unable to find an unoccupied territory, they move from area to area, feeding wherever they can before being driven out by the resident individual.

"You can only stress a bird so much," Kricher observes. "And even when things are going right, songbirds are subjected to stress the whole year long, wherever they are. There's stress on the wintering grounds in finding and defending territories. Migration itself is enormously difficult. The birds have to build up their fat resources before they leave, and many cross the Gulf only to die from exhaustion on the other side. And the birds that do make it to the nesting grounds successfully are subject to all the rigors of nesting: they have to find protected nesting areas, defend against predators, deal with cowbirds and find enough food to feed their young."

The increasing number of cowbirds and the dwindling number of unfragmented forest tracts are the two problems songbird researchers most often name as reasons for nest failure on the breeding grounds.

The two problems are interrelated. The brown-headed cowbird is a nest parasite that lays its eggs in the nests of other songbirds, usually after removing one of the hosts' eggs. The brown-headed cowbird young grows faster than the hosts' young, pushes them aside to get the food brought by the nesting parents and in the end is usually the nest's single survivor.

The brown-headed cowbird is a bird that requires open spaces and once was limited to the Great Plains of the U.S. The clearing and fragmenting of the forests in North America have enabled it to expand its range enormously, and it now occurs in every state in the Lower 48 and all provinces of Canada except the Yukon. This range explosion has brought it into contact with many songbirds that have not yet evolved the countermoves necessary to defend themselves. The Kirtland's warbler, which nests only in the jack-pine forests of Michigan, is now plagued by the cowbird—although field-workers in Michigan are working hard to capture cowbirds in that area. Other less celebrated songbirds are also severely parasitized. The worm-eating warbler, whose population seems to be declining rapidly in the East, is so frequently a host that researchers in Virginia and elsewhere have been hard pressed to find any nests at all without cowbird young. In the West, the species declining most rapidly is probably the black-capped vireo. Cowbirds are a major cause of its decline, parasitizing its nests at rates from 70 percent up to 100 percent in some sites. The black-capped vireo has been entirely eliminated in Kansas and reduced to just four counties in Oklahoma.

The bronzed cowbird, a Western species and nest parasite, is also expanding its range; and in June 1985, a third cowbird species reached the U.S., the shiny cowbird, *Molothrus bonariensis*, another nest parasite. It was first recorded on the Florida Keys and has since been seen in several areas in South Florida.

"Tropical deforestation is what brought it here," John Terborgh explains. "It was limited to the South American mainland until the 1960s, but the land clearing for cattle enabled it to expand there. Then it moved off the coast to Grenada, found more cleared cattle land, and then it just went right up the island chain—up the Antilles to Puerto Rico and to Cuba, and finally here. The yellow-shouldered blackbird has practically disappeared in Puerto Rico since the cowbird invaded. Who knows what it's going to do in Florida?"

The naturally short lives of all songbirds make them particularly sensitive to nest failures and habitat loss. The birds simply don't live long enough to survive a few seasons of hardship. The population of the dusky seaside sparrow, a nonmigratory race of the seaside sparrow that once lived on the east coast of Florida, declined from an estimated 1,000 individuals in 1970 to 0 in 17 years. The last dusky died in captivity on June 17, 1987.

What can we do to help our songbirds?

"First and foremost," John Terborgh says, "we have to educate our own politicians. They have to know that we realize our government has been basically ignoring this problem. I think people should write their Congressmen and ask, 'Where are the birds?' and 'What are we doing to protect the ones we have left?' We do have treaty arrangements with Latin American countries for the protection of migratory birds, but they aren't being backed up except by token expenditures—and most of that goes to ducks and other game birds. We need to enforce the treaties.

"Also, we're not protecting our own forests as well as we should be. Even in National Parks, the large forest tracts are being fragmented."

Stanley Senner, executive director of Hawk Mountain Sanctuary in Pennsylvania and chairman of the U.S. section of the International Council for Bird Preservation, has been sharply critical in past years of the way Congress has funded the U.S. Fish and Wildlife Service and of the way the Service has spent the money. "This year, I saw some signs of a change in attitude," he says. "We did persuade Congress to put an add-on of $1 million in fiscal year 1988 for research on migratory nongame birds, and the Service seems to be making a good faith effort to spend that money. A million dollars is a drop in the bucket, and much more money than that is spent on ducks, but at least it's a start.

"Rosalie Edge, the woman who founded Hawk Mountain Sanctuary, had a saying I try to repeat whenever possible: 'The time to save a species is when it's still common.' We need to spend money on migratory nongame birds now, before they reach the stage where they must be officially declared endangered species. If a species is reduced to 200 or 300 individuals, the war is lost."

The Nature Conservancy, Rainforest Alliance, World Wildlife Fund and other nongovernmental conservation organizations are working in the Caribbean and Central America to help protect and manage forest habitats. Ruth Norris, director of nongovernmental services for the Latin American division of the Nature Conservancy, believes the key to saving tropical habitats is making conservation economically profitable. "Many of these countries are consumed by debt crises and political crises. We need to do what we can to help them develop limited and appropriate tourist activities, sustainable forestry practices and community education programs so that the people who live in and near these areas will support conservation—not out of some high and mighty ideal, but because saving habitat generates some real income for them."

"One of the easiest ways to participate in the effort to save tropical forests," John Terborgh says, "is to take your vacation in Mexico or Central America. Visit the National Parks there, and make sure the tourist agencies know you're going there to look for birds. We have to persuade the Latin American countries that there are financial reasons to preserve habitats."

Chandler Robbins adds, though, "It's a very delicate political problem. We can't just buy up property to preserve pristine areas. The people there need land and jobs. A lot of them are living in abject poverty, just scratching for survival. We have to support the conservation agencies that are working so hard down there to find economic ways to preserve forest habitats and to educate the people in the areas to see that their wildlife is a national heritage. Even in a place like Haiti, where practically all the forest is gone anyway, there are some people working very hard to try to educate administrators and other people about conservation. These people need whatever support we can give them."

"What it will take to save the tropical forests," says Ruth Norris of the Nature Conservancy, "is the same sort of thing it took to get our own environmental movement started here in the United States: a few dedicated, hard-working, local people who have widespread outside support. I do see some glimmering rays of hope. There's been some discussion recently, for instance, about changing the ways international lending agencies and the international assistance agencies provide for projects in Third World countries."

The World Bank, for example, has been severely criticized in the past by conservation organizations for funding projects that have destroyed wildlife habitats and led to only short-term profits for local economies. In recent months, however, the Bank seems to be responding to these criticisms. The number of environmentalists on its staff has grown from half a dozen only two years ago to a current total of 48, and representatives from the Bank now regularly speak of considering environmental consequences of all prospective projects.

"Another glimmering ray of hope," Ruth Norris says, "is the growing movement of national conservation in Central and South America. In recent years, more and more local organizations are becoming involved in community education and in the very tough job of developing comprehensive management plans. They're not just trying to put up fences to keep people out. They're involving the local community in work that conserves the resource and helps them.

"I think the Spaceship Earth concept, that we have to take care of the life-support systems of the planet, is a growing trend up here in North America too. Something I always like to tell people is that you don't have to be able to give a personal check for $50,000. In recent years, a lot of people in our own local chapters and in so many other local and state organizations have been collecting money for conservation projects in Latin America, sponsoring tours down there, giving educational programs about these areas and going out of their way to help people take responsibility for the protection of the biological diversity in the tropics. René Dubos has a wonderful phrase: 'Think globally; act locally.' More and more people seem to be coming to share that attitude."

12:30 p.m. Cape May Point, New Jersey, April 16, 1988

Patti Hodgetts walks down her net lane one last time and closes down her nets. Paul Kerlinger returned to the paperwork in his office two hours ago. 12:30 is earlier than Hodgetts expects to quit ordinarily, but in 5½ hours she has banded only 13 birds—10 ruby-crowned kinglets and 3 cardinals. Neither species is a long-distance migrant, and she has not heard or seen a single one of Kerlinger's target species.

At the end of the lane, Hodgetts pulls a plastic sheet over her work station and weighs it down with rocks. The data she has compiled on the 13 birds she has caught barely fill a page in her logbook and are not relevant to her project, but she is undiscouraged. She will be banding here seven days a week for six more weeks and feels sure she will have better luck. "Today was only one day," she says. "We'll see what happens tomorrow."

QUESTIONS FOR CRITICAL READERS

Remembering and Understanding

1. Write a brief explanation of why birds migrate.
2. State Connor's central point as concisely as you can, and then describe the evidence Connor supplies to support that point.
3. Why is deforestation in the neo-tropics a problem? What specific conditions and problems does deforestation cause?

Analyzing and Discussing

4. Using Connor's information, explain how the United States and other developed countries contribute to deforestation.
5. How are we to balance the legitimate economic concerns of Third World developing countries with the desire of people who live in the United States to prevent the extinction of birds?

6. Connor writes as an amateur birdwatcher who is a citizen of the United States. How might his conclusions be different if he were responsible for economic development in a developing country?

Writing

7. Using the information Connor provides, write an explanation of how migration and evolution influence each other.

In Memory of Martha
and Her Kind

—————— DAVID WILCOVE ——————

Wilcove is a senior ecologist for the Wilderness Society. In this article he engages in what might be called "historical ecology" to reevaluate the reasons that the passenger pigeon, once the most numerous bird in North America, became extinct. The traditional explanation has been that the passenger pigeon was hunted to extinction, but Wilcove finds other reasons by taking an ecological approach to the question.

First the legend. It is September 1, 1914, a hot, muggy day in Cincinnati. Summoned by telegram and letter, eminent ornithologists from across the country have gathered at the city's zoo, where they now cluster in front of a large, metal aviary. Joining them are a handful of reporters and a crowd of onlookers. Their hushed voices are almost lost amidst the incessant droning of the summer cicadas. Inside the aviary, a lone bird—a pigeon—lies huddled on the floor, a small, listless ball of feathers. The pigeon is Martha, the world's last passenger pigeon, and she is dying. The grand old men of ornithology have gathered to witness the passing of her race. The oldest among them remember a time when clouds of wild pigeons swept across the skies of a wilder nation. Now, in Martha's final hours, they sense their own impending mortality. Martha is motionless, but the steady blinking of her beady, dark eyes betrays life. The blinks grow longer, until the eyes no longer open. An elderly gentleman extracts a pocketwatch from his vest. It is 1:00 P.M.

Now the reality. Martha was indeed the last passenger pigeon, and she died on September 1, 1914. But her death was witnessed not by a gathering of eminent graybeards, but by her keeper and his son. The press essentially ignored the event, save for a short obituary in the Cincinnati Enquirer. *A day or two after her death, she was taken to the Cincinnati Ice Company plant, suspended in a tank of water, and frozen in a three-hundred-pound block of ice. Martha was then shipped to the Smithsonian and promptly stuffed. She resides there today, sharing her glass case in the Hall of Birds with a great auk, a Carolina parakeet, and other spectral companions.*

EXACTLY SEVENTY-FIVE years have passed since Martha's death, and while other species have vanished in the interim, none has seemed so tragic and inexplicable a loss as that of the passenger pigeon, once the most abundant bird on Earth. The passenger pigeon remains a subject of lively speculation and research among scientists. In fact, we probably know more today about the reasons for its extinction than did ornithologists at the turn of the century, who witnessed the process with little more than bewilderment. It is finally time to give Martha the obituary she deserved.

Martha was part of a small colony of passenger pigeons at the zoo. The colony had been started in 1878 or 1879 (the record is unclear) with the purchase of four pairs of wild pigeons from Michigan. What prompted the zoo to buy pigeons in the first place will never be known, but it paid handsomely for them—$2.50 a pair at a time when dead ones were selling for thirty-five to forty cents a dozen in the markets of Chicago. The decision proved to be a wise one, for within two decades, the passenger pigeon was extinct in the wild. The Cininnati Zoo housed its pigeons in an outside aviary where, it was hoped, they would prosper. They didn't. A few young were produced, but never enough to make up for the loss of older birds, and over time the colony dwindled. Other zoos were even less successful at breeding passenger pigeons, and by the spring of 1909 the Cincinnati flock, now totaling just three individuals, was all that remained. A year later, only one, Martha, was left.

She would live for four more years, an aging dowager sharing her aviary with a handful of mourning doves, probably placed there to keep her company. During the last months of her life, Martha was too weak to fly up to her perch, and she spent her time huddled on the floor of her cage. Now a celebrity, she drew crowds of onlookers who were probably disappointed by the inert little bird they saw. On Sundays, in fact, the keepers had to rope off the area around the cage to keep the public from throwing sand at her to make her move. At the time of her death she was reputed to be twenty-nine years old, a remarkably advanced age for a pigeon.

Captive propagation has been used to save other species, most notably the Socorro dove of Mexico and the pink pigeon of Mauritius, so why didn't it work with the passenger pigeon? No one knows for certain, but the most plausible explanation is simply ignorance. Zoos today go to extraordinary lengths to maintain healthy bloodlines among their animals. Stud books, DNA "fingerprinting," computer simulations, and the like are routinely used to minimize inbreeding and genetic bottlenecks among zoo animals. A century ago, however, captive propagation was more a matter of benign neglect than science: Put a few pigeons of both sexes in a cage, feed them, protect them, and let nature take its course. Nature did, but one suspects the end result was increasingly unfit pigeons.

Far more difficult to comprehend is how the passenger pigeon ever ended up in such a precarious state, from billions of wild birds at the start of the nineteenth century to a handful of captive ones at the close. Observers who witnessed the great flocks were convinced the species was all but indestructible, and the answers usually put forth to explain its demise—overhunting and the clearing of forests—simply don't add up. True, millions of pigeons were killed, but the numbers taken were at best a small fraction of the total population. And while forest destruction certainly contributed to the extinction of the passenger pigeon, the birds disappeared far more rapidly than the trees. To understand why the pigeons vanished, one must first understand how they lived and, in particular, their unique relationship with beech, oak, and hickory trees, whose mast they devoured.

Prior to the arrival of European settlers, most of eastern North America was covered by these mast-producing trees. Their large, nutritious nuts sustained the great flocks of pigeons. Both the trees and the pigeons shared a common survival strategy, a faith in the old adage of safety in numbers. As anyone with an oak or hickory in the backyard soon learns, these trees do not produce a steady crop of nuts year after year. Instead, all of the oaks, hickories, or beeches in a given area produce an enormous crop of nuts only once every few years. This synchronous and unpredictable production of mast is designed to overwhelm hungry squirrels, bears, blue jays, and other seed predators, giving at least a few beechnuts, acorns, and chestnuts the chance to grow up to be saplings.

The passenger pigeon responded to this trick by adopting a nomadic lifestyle. During the fall and winter, flocks wandered through the eastern forests in search of masting trees, sometimes traveling hundreds of miles a day. With the coming of spring, they formed immense nesting colonies in areas where large crops of nuts from the previous autumn remained on the ground. Like their food trees, the pigeons were following a strategy of overwhelming abundance: nesting aggregations so vast that local predators could not wipe them out. One such colony in Wisconsin was estimated to cover more than 750 square miles and contain some 136 million birds. Because the colonies were such an ephemeral phenomenon, switching location from year to year and dispersing as soon as nesting was over, pigeon predators were never able to build their numbers to the point where they could have a serious impact on the birds.

Against hawks, raccoons, foxes, and opossums, the passenger pigeon's strategy was a spectacular success. Against *Homo sapiens*, it was a fatal mistake. The colonies were a magnet for professional hunters eager to supply urban markets with pigeon meat. The resulting carnage has been described and redescribed many times, but it bears repeating. Young birds were knocked from their nests with poles; "stool pigeons," tethered birds whose eyelids had been sewn shut, were used to lure other pigeons to the ground where they could be netted; trees filled with nests were cut down or set afire; and sulfur was burned beneath nesting birds to suffocate them. From a single nesting colony near Grand Rapids, Michigan, hunters shipped 588 barrels—more than 100,000 pounds—of pigeons to market.

By the 1700s observers along the eastern seaboard could see something was amiss. The flocks were thinning, the nesting colonies were disappearing. "Some years past they have not been in such plenty as they used to be," wrote one naturalist in 1770. "This spring I saw them fly one morning, as I thought in great abundance; but everybody was amazed how few there were; and wondered at the reason." The last major nesting in New England occurred near Lunenburg, Massachusetts, in 1851. A decade later the big flocks were gone from coastal New York State and Pennsylvania. And though such declines did not go unnoticed, little was done to save the wild pigeons. A few states passed laws to protect nesting colonies from harassment, but they were rarely enforced.

By the latter half of the 1800s the northern Lake States had become the last stronghold of the passenger pigeon. Here the birds fell victim to two seemingly unrelated advances in technology: the expansion of the railroad and the invention of the telegraph. In 1830 there were only twenty-three miles of railroad track in the United States; by the Civil War, the total had risen to more than 30,000 miles. This railroad network allowed commercial pigeon hunters to reach even the most distant colonies and ship birds to urban markets hundreds of miles away. The telegraph enabled hunters everywhere to learn quickly of the discovery of new nesting colonies. Exposed and vulnerable, the wild pigeons evaporated like ether. In 1878 their total population was estimated at fifty million birds (give or take a few million). By 1887 only one large nesting aggregation was left, located in Wisconsin. The birds abandoned this colony just two weeks after starting to nest, probably because of hunters. A few scattered pigeons were sighted here and there throughout the 1890s, but they were little more than the dying embers of an extinguished firestorm. On March 24, 1900, the last wild passenger pigeon was killed in Pike County, Ohio, leaving only Martha and her aging zoo colleagues.

Why the pigeons disappeared so rapidly—from tens of millions in 1878 to virtually none twenty years later—has long puzzled natural historians. Recently, two ornithologists from the University of Minnesota, David E. Blockstein and Harrison B. Tordoff, came up with a compelling explanation for the demise of the passenger pigeon. During this critical twenty-year period, they argue, hunters managed to disrupt or destroy every major nesting colony. The birds were prevented from breeding for a period of time exceeding several pigeon generations, and the population crashed as entire cohorts died without replacing themselves.

Although the vast majority of passenger pigeons nested in a few immense colonies, a small proportion regularly chose to nest solitarily or in little groups. These birds were never exploited as ruthlessly as those in the colonies, yet they too disappeared. Blockstein and Tordoff believe that without the numerical protection provided by the large colonies, these lone pairs and little groups rarely produced fledglings. Their conspicuous twig nests and fat squabs were easy targets for a host of predatory animals.

The loss of the passenger pigeon was an ecological event of profound significance, altering the lives of predators and prey, shifting and changing the pathways of nutrients and energy flow in ways we will never fully understand. With the great flocks gone, the very oaks and hickories whose limbs once snapped under the weight of feasting pigeons now stood empty. Nuts once destined to be turned into pigeons fell to the ground, where they were eagerly hoarded by squirrels and blue jays. And for animals accustomed to dining on squab, the end of the nesting colonies meant a long, difficult search for other foods.

The passenger pigeon was a phenomenon of numbers. "Yearly the feathered tempest roared up, down, and across the continent," wrote Aldo Leopold, "sucking up the laden fruits of forest and prairie, burning them in a traveling blast of life." From an ecological perspective, the extinction of the passenger pigeon is best defined not by the death of the last individual (a lone, decrepit bird in a metal cage) but by the disappearance of the flocks. Thus, if ecologists rather than historians were in charge of such things, we would know 1887—the year of the last great nesting aggregation—as the true date of extinction for the passenger pigeon.

There is no one alive today who remembers the autumn skies as they appeared darkened by pigeons, no one who can recall the flashes of blue and russet as the flocks wheeled and turned before diving into the trees. The captive birds, however, lasted long after the wild flocks were gone, and as this seventy-fifth anniversary approached, I began to wonder whether anyone alive today remembered Martha, whether that tenuous and final link between us and the living bird still endured. Was there a young child growing up in Cincinnati in the early years of this century, a boy or girl with an incipient curiosity about birds, who might have visited the local zoo? Would seeing the very last passenger pigeon stick in a child's memory, and persevere through the ups and downs of seventy-plus years?

In the winter of 1987 I published a notice in several ornithological journals, asking anyone who had seen Martha before her death to contact me. I received only one reply, a brief letter from a gentleman named Merrill Wood. He wrote:

> *I remember when I was six years old, my parents took me to the Cincinnati Zoo in the summer of 1914 (June, July, or August, probably August) to see the last living Passenger Pigeon, kept in a large enclosure*

with some Mourning Doves. My mother (no orthnithologist) said she did
not see much difference in the two species of doves. In September my
father read to me from a newspaper that this famous bird had died.

Mr. Wood identified himself as a retired professor of zoology "now age seventy-eight and probably will soon join that bird."

I wish Professor Wood good health for many years to come, but I also know he is right: There cannot be many people left who have seen a living passenger pigeon, and sometime in the not-too-distant future there will be none. And once again the passenger pigeon will face extinction, this time in memory.

By the year 2014, the centennial of Martha's death, our only remaining links to the passenger pigeon will be a handful of historical accounts and the mounted specimens that stare vacantly into space from the security of their museum showcases.

The land itself will show no signs the wild pigeon was ever here, or was even meant to be here, except perhaps in the names we have bestowed upon a few landmarks—places like Pigeon Creek in Pennsylvania or Pigeon Swamp in New York. If there are alternative explanations for these names, I prefer not to know them. We name bridges and buildings after famous people. We can also name a few creeks and swamps after the remarkable bird we destroyed.

QUESTIONS FOR CRITICAL READERS

Remembering and Understanding

1. What are the usual reasons given for the passenger pigeon's extinction?
2. Explain how Wilcove's explanation differs from the usual explanation. How does his explanation rely on his perspective as an ecologist?
3. How did passenger pigeon habits change as a result of hunting pressure?
4. How did the telegraph and the railroad contribute to the extinction of the passenger pigeon?

Analyzing and Discussing

5. What ecological lessons can be found in the passenger pigeon's extinction?
6. Compare the two versions of Martha's death. Which do you prefer? What purpose does the legend serve?

Writing

7. Using the information Wilcove supplies, write a paper in which you explain how the passenger pigeon's disappearance must have affected its environment.

Fuel Efficiency

The Economical Heating Systems of Our Winter Birds

KIM HARRIS

Harris teaches agricultural economics. Like Connor, his interest in birds is an avocation. His favorite bird is the wild turkey. In this article he writes about the physical and behavioral adaptations that allow birds to survive very cold temperatures in the winter.

WINTER IS A HARSH SEASON in the snow-belt. The days are short, cold, strong. Winds drive through this region bringing the wake of the whole frigid north behind them, and the bounties of warmer seasons disappear. Snow and ice often cover seeds and berries. Most airborne insects have been killed, while others have taken refuge, waiting in slumber for the first warm kiss of spring. Trees and shrubs stand naked, and the supply of protective cover is far exceeded by its demand.

On the bitterest of days not one track, not even a rabbit's, tells of mammals stirring. But the birds are out—they flock to feeders, busier than a whole lodge of beavers.

Why all the bustle? Small birds can perish overnight in such weather. That many of them survive, not just through one sub-zero night or one long winter, but perhaps through six or seven winters, is one of the great wonders of nature. Such mysteries have captured the curiosity of scientists for decades.

Birds have numerous adaptations to survive cold, and some birds are better equipped than others. One adaptation—migration—is an obvious solution. Few could dispute the wisdom of flying south in the winter. But migration is more than a strategy to avoid cold weather. And it is not without perils.

By mid-October most summer residents have departed or are preparing to depart for points south. In their place come the winter birds: Dark-eyed Juncos, White-throated Sparrows, American Tree Sparrows and White-crowned Sparrows, to name several. The migratory winter residents mingle with the year-rounders like the Tufted Titmice, Black-capped Chickadees, Blue Jays, Cardinals, House Sparrows, and the few species for whom migration is an individual matter, some going, some not. Song Sparrows and American Robins belong to this indecisive group.

It typically is the seed-eating birds that winter in our backyards and dine on our offerings of food, while the insect-loving birds migrate south-ward, although there are some insectivores that stay and some seed-eaters that go. The insectivores that remain, like the woodpeckers, for instance, are equipped to extract choice morsels from behind and between the bark of trees, and also generally display the ability to adapt their diets to a menu of seeds during the winter.

Another adaptation birds use to beat the cold is a favorite method used by people—huddling and snuggling together. If several well-fed birds are able to find a sheltered roost, such as a tree cavity free from wind, cold and wet, the heat from their bodies can warm them through the coldest winter nights. In a trio of birds holed-up together for the night, each bird may reduce its heat loss by one-third. The drier and snugger the perch, and the more feathered friends, the better.

All warm-blooded animals generate heat by converting nutrients and stored fats into energy, to some degree defying the cold by consuming more calories. Birds are no exception. To keep warm in cold weather, birds, especially smaller ones, increase their consumption of food. During the winter a bird like the Chickadee, a small bundle of enthusiasm weigh-ing only a scant more than the average first-class letter, may devour its own weight in food each day, doubling or tripling its heat and energy production. By constantly stoking its furnace with seeds during the day, the Chickadee manages to survive even sub-zero nights.

A few birds, like Hoary and Common Redpolls, stash seeds in a special storage pouch in the esophagus, then snack on the high energy morsels during the night. For their ingenuity, the redpolls win first prize in the songbird kingdom for being the birds most able to withstand the coldest temperatures.

Larger birds are at an advantage over their smaller brethren when it comes to heat conservation. Because of their greater body size, larger birds retain heat more effectively and therefore don't have to eat as much. Smaller birds compensate in part by having more feathers relative to their body size than larger birds.

All birds have a built-in advantage over mammals when it comes to withstanding cold—their body temperatures are higher. They run what for us would be called a high fever. A bird's normal body temperature percolates between 100 and 112 degrees Fahrenheit, with small songbirds at the higher end of the range.

Anyone who lives in the cold-belt knows that good insulation, for both home and person, is key to staying warm. The most important insulator for a bird is its feathers. A bird may have 25 to 30 percent more feathers in winter than it does in mid-summer. Down—the tiny, soft, tuft-like feathers that usually grow beneath the contour feathers—is one of the world's most effective heat traps. Humans have long recognized the highly effective insulating properties of down, using it in everything from hats to foot warmers.

A bird's body feathers trap a layer of air next to the skin, greatly limiting the outward escape of precious body heat. These feathers, controlled by tiny muscles, can be fluffed to trap more insulating air next to the body. This explains that familiar cold-weather scene, when birds with their feathers fluffed look as fat as tennis balls.

To waterproof this specialized overcoat, a bird uses its beak to collect fresh oil from the oil gland located at the base of its tail and waxes its outer layer of feathers. This protects its inner layer of down against cold, wet and blowing wind. In wintertime a bird spends great lengths of time preening, keeping its portable windbreaker cleaned, combed and well oiled.

The methods of heat conservation discussed so far are considered to be *passive* in that they have a very small energy cost. Another important mechanism that helps maintain body temperature by generating heat is shivering. Birds shiver just as humans do by involuntarily contracting their muscles in rapid and unsynchronized movements. But shivering requires a larger energy cost. The energy expended in shivering must be regained, which is accomplished by feeding.

What about the exposed areas—a bird's eyes, bill and feet—don't they get cold? The eyes aren't at great risk, since they are sunken almost completely inside the head. A bird's head, along with the inner part of its chest, makes up its *core*, that part of the body that maintains the most constant heat.

At the center of the core is its heart, which pumps heat throughout the body via a network of blood vessels. Smaller birds with higher metabolic rates usually have relatively larger hearts than do bigger birds. Their hearts also beat faster, on the order of four hundred beats or more per minute. The tiny Chickadee's heart beats five hundred times a minute when it's asleep, and when awake and active, the heartbeat is double its resting rate.

A bird's bill is more exposed than its eyes, but far less sensitive to the cold, being made of horn, not skin. It can always be neatly tucked under its feathers if conditions warrant, a behavior that both warms the beak and, possibly, allows the bird to breath air that is already warmed by the body.

The same applies to its feet. A bird can tuck one foot in its belly feathers and balance, one-legged, on the other. How about the exposed foot? A bird's feet are fleshless. They have very little of the softer muscle tissue that surrounds our legs and feet and just enough tendons to perform the necessary flexings and bendings. Many birds have an anti-freeze adaptation known as the "counter-current heat exchange system." For these birds, the arteries and veins in their feet and legs run side-by-side, allowing the cold returning blood to be warmed by the arteries, and keeping their feet, if not toasty, at least unfrozen.

Given all these adaptations, some birds would still freeze during a fifteen-hour night if they didn't have some mechanism for conserving their precious bedtime energy supply.

Some birds can decrease their need for food, water and oxygen, permitting energy conservation and enhancing their chances of awakening to dawn's early light. The mechanism they use is a kind of controlled hypothermia, or overnight hibernation. In some birds, like the Chickadee, the body temperature may drop as much as twenty degrees, which means the bird's oxygen consumption may be reduced by as much as 75 percent. Bodily needs for food are correspondingly reduced, making fifteen hours in the cold of a winter's night possible.

How much cold can a bird endure? The limits depend on its species, its age and its health. John K. Terres writes in *The Audubon Society Encylopedia of North American Birds* that in tests with House Sparrows it was discovered "they could go longest without food in summer—for sixty-seven hours at about eighty-five degrees. With a drop in air temperature to about fifty degrees, there was a rapid decline in the ability of the Sparrows to resist starvation. At five degrees, the Sparrows could live without food for fifteen hours—the length of a winter night. At twenty degrees below zero, they could live only about ten hours without food, and at thirty degrees below, they lived only about seven hours."

In the end, a bird's capacity for survival comes down to food and shelter. The warm glow from the body of a well-fed bird, snug from cold and dampness, will keep it alive in temperatures as low as thirty to forty degrees below zero.

So the next time the mercury hitches a ride on the Siberian express, and bitter north winds howl through the trees and swirl through your shrubbery, remember the birds beyond your kitchen window. These feathered dynamos live life on the edge, constantly searching out food to supply their enormous energy needs. To feed them and to provide them with shelter is to wager a bet on their chances of survival—a wager that pays handsome dividends. They will bring a spot of life and color into the most drab of winter days and a lively reassurance that life outlasts all winters.

QUESTIONS FOR CRITICAL READERS

Remembering and Understanding

1. List several physical or behavioral adaptations that allow birds to survive extreme cold. Then write a brief summary that includes them all.
2. Summarize the information that Harris gives about bird anatomy and physiology.
3. How does Harris establish his authority? What does he say to encourage you to believe what he says?

Analyzing and Discussing

4. Why don't birds just hibernate?
5. Why would larger birds be better able to conserve heat then small birds?
6. Birds need to take on enough food to last them through the night. Why not simply eat through the night? What prevents this?

Writing

7. Write a paper in which you explain how humans adapt to adverse conditions. Include physical and behavioral adaptations as well as methods that humans have invented to protect themselves.

Why Is a Robin's Egg Blue?

———— BERND HEINRICH ————

Bernd Heinrich is a professor of zoology at the University of Vermont. His chief professional interest is in bumblebees, and he has also had a lifelong interest in birds. In this article, which first appeared in Audubon *magazine, Heinrich investigates the reasons that some birds' eggs are colored. As a scientist, Heinrich is committed to an explanation of egg coloration that is consistent with evolutionary theory. From this perspective, egg coloration is yet another way in which birds are adapted to their environment.*

THE FOUR TINY EGGS that were cradled on feathers in a nest of moss, lichens, and spider webs were decorated more beautifully than any I had ever seen before. They were greenish-blue, marked with purple and lavendar blotches and black scratchy squiggles. A cascading chaffinch song rang from the surrounding beech forest on that beautiful spring morning and heightened the sensations I felt when I discovered the eggs.

I was then eight years old, and in the following years I became obsessed with collecting the nests and eggs of other species. The more I found, the greater the obsession became. Each find rewarded me with revelations about the species' intricacies and its individualities.

Later, while in grammar school and high school in central Maine, I continued to collect songbird nests and eggs. I did not dare let the authorities at my boarding school know, in part perhaps because my pleasure was so great that it did not seem it could be morally right. I spent endless days in the woods watching birds and hunting for nests. I kept my carefully tended illicit collection hidden under the floorboards of an abandoned shed. (At that time I did not know anything about wildlife laws.) Now, thirty-five years later, this collection of ninety-six species of Maine land bird eggs with their nests is still in excellent condition, in the museum and teaching collections of the University of Vermont. Although I long ago stopped collecting wild bird eggs, my fascination and enthusiasm have not been erased. I still collect these jewels, but only on film. The main excitement now is in trying to find a coherent system of filing it all in the mind. And as I am a biologist, the filing system I use is based on evolution.

First one sees the diversity. The four eggs of the scarlet tanager, in a cup of loose twigs lined with dark rootlets, are sky blue and spotted with light brown in a ring at the larger end. The four eggs of the eastern peewee are a light cream, with a wreath of reddish-brown and lavendar spots about the larger end. These colors are set against a perfectly round nest-cup decorated with gray-green lichens. Woodpecker and kingfisher eggs, from holes excavated in trees and sandbanks, respectively, are translucent white without any trace of markings. The different colors, or lack of them, are products of evolution. What were the selective pressures that produced them?

Although the eggs of many species of songbirds have characteristic colors that are fairly uniform within a clutch, I noticed that those of most hawks differed radically within the same nest, even more than they differed between species. One egg of a broad-winged hawk, for example, had distinct dark brown or purple splotches. Another in the same clutch had chocolate brown spots and squiggles. A third had purple or brown washes, and still another might be almost colorless. The same variety of colors— but in greens, blues, grays, and browns—was present in any one clutch of common raven's and common crow's eggs.

These combinations of markings and colors on bird eggs seemed like creativity gone berserk. Why should the color of an eggshell matter to a bird? Why, indeed, have any color at all? There must have been reasons to add the color, or else specialized glands to apply color would not have evolved. So why are robins' eggs pale blue, flickers' eggs pure white, and loons' eggs dark olive green?

Birds' eggs are marked by pigments secreted from the walls of the oviduct. The egg remains uncolored until just before being laid, when it traverses the region of the uterus. The pressure of the egg squeezes the pigment out of the uterine glands onto the eggshell, and the motion of the egg affects the color patterns. It is as if innumerable brushes hold still while the canvas moves. If the egg remains still there are spots, and if it moves while the glands continue secreting, then lines and scrawls result.

Egg color is under genetic control, and there is considerable genetic plasticity. Strains of domestic chickens have been developed that lay eggs tinted blue, green, and olive, as well as the more familiar white and brown.

It is not surprising that Charles Darwin, with his wide-ranging interests, also thought about the adaptive significance of the coloration of birds' eggs. Since coloration is generally absent in hole-nesters such as woodpeckers, parrots, kingfishers, barbets, and honey guides, he supposed that the pigmentation on the eggs of open-nesters acts as a sunscreen to protect the embryo. The British ornithologist David Lack, in turn, believed the white coloration of eggs of hole-nesters allowed the birds to see their eggs in the dark. Even if it is advantageous for birds to see their eggs in the dark (which I doubt), we are still left to explain the tremendous differences in colors and patterns found, especially in the species that do not nest in holes. Why isn't one sunscreen best? And if so, why don't all use it? And why are some hole-nesters' eggs spotted? Perhaps, as Austin L. Rand, former chief curator of zoology at the Field Museum in Chicago, has said: "Like some of the specific differences in nest-building, variations in egg color are simply expressions of the general tendency of birds toward diversity." This idea, too, might be right, but if so it is only a small part of the proverbial elephant that the six blind men try to describe by touch. With regard to egg coloring, we are still blind, and we all touch the elephant in different places.

One summer when I was motoring across the country with my family, we stopped in Yellowstone National Park. My most vivid memory was of walking across a sedge meadow bordered by stunted black spruce. I was captivated by the sound of a sandhill crane trumpeting, and the song of the Wilson's snipe high in the air. Looking down, I saw a nest in the mossy sedge. It contained four olive green eggs generously marked with blackish-brown. It was the nest of the Wilson's snipe, and the eggs blended beautifully with the dark green vegetation of this boggy meadow. Later on, we camped in numerous gravel pits and along roadside turnoffs by steambeds and sandy parking lots—habitat where killdeers nest. A killdeer perched on the ground over its eggs is not difficult to spot. But the adult slips off the nest when anyone comes near, and the bare eggs are something else. Colored a drab buff and profusely spotted with black, the four eggs are not easy to make out in a depression filled with pebbles.

Experiments confirm that the color of some birds' eggs conceals them from predators. In a famous experiment, Niko Tinbergen distributed equal numbers of naturally spotted eggs of black-headed gulls, uniformly khaki-colored eggs, and white eggs near a gull colony and then recorded the predation by carrion crows and herring gulls on these unguarded eggs. The natural eggs suffered the least predation.

We might reasonably assume that the color of snipe, killdeer, and gull eggs is adaptive for camouflage, and that it evolved under selective pressure from visually oriented egg predators. But why then do other ground-nesting birds—most ducks and many grouse—have unmarked eggs that cannot be considered camouflaged by any stretch of the imagination? Perhaps part of the answer is that most of these birds hide their nests in dense vegetation, and the incubating female's own body is a camouflage blanket.

So far so good. But there is a hitch. Ducks and grouselike birds usually lay more than a dozen eggs per clutch. If the female started to sit on the eggs as soon as the first ones were laid, in order to hide them, the chicks would then hatch out over a period of up to two weeks. It is necessary for the eggs to hatch synchronously, and to accomplish this, the hen must not sit on the eggs until the last one is laid. So how are the eggs protected from predators? A pet mallard hen gave me a hint. She built a nest by scraping leaves together under a bush by the front window. Being well fed, she layed enormous clutches of creamy pale green eggs. But I never saw the eggs directly. Each morning before she left, after laying an egg, she used her bill to pull leaves from around the nest to cover the eggs completely. The leaves were better camouflage than spots on the eggs or her own body could ever be. I do not know if all ducks and grouse cover their eggs in a similar manner, but their nests are usually mere depressions, with loose vegetation that could serve as a cover. Not all grouse have uncamouflaged eggs, though. Those of the willow and rock ptarmigans, for example, are heavily blotched and marbled with blackish-brown. (I wager that ptarmigans leave their eggs uncovered.)

Many birds with nests that have no loose material with which to cover the eggs also have unmarked, uncamouflaged eggs. They include hummingbirds, pigeons, and doves. But these birds only lay two eggs per clutch, and they incubate as soon as the first egg is laid. Perhaps because none of their eggs are normally left uncovered, there has been no need to color them for camouflage.

The best explanation for the lack of color and markings on hole-nesters' eggs and those of birds that lay small clutches is probably simply that there was no need for color, so none evolved. Yet, as already mentioned, there are birds that nest in holes and also lay spotted eggs. All of these birds, however, build nests inside the holes. (True hole-nesters excavate their own holes and lay white eggs without adding any nest material.) I suspect, therefore, that the spots are evolutionary baggage. They tell us that these birds had previously been open-nesters who switched to hole-nesting. But they retained the habit of building nests, as well as the coloration of their eggs, because there was no great selective pressure for change.

While coloring and markings are primarily for camouflage, they can also function to make something stand out like a red flag. Along the coast of Maine the harbors and inlets are dotted with the floats of thousands of lobster traps. There are green floats, red floats, white floats, striped red-white floats, and so on. The large numbers of traps and the featureless environment of the open water make it impractical for a lobsterman to find his traps by remembering their precise locations. Each fisherman uses a different color pattern for his floats so he can quickly home in on his own traps.

On our Atlantic and Pacific coasts, on adjacent islands, and in Europe, there are murres that nest on the ledges and sea cliffs in colonies of hundreds of thousands. Several species of colonial cliff-nesting murres (as well as the extinct great auk) have eggs that vary endlessly in colors and markings. The ground color of the eggs varies from creamy to white, reddish, warm ocher, pale bluish, or even deep greenish-blue. The markings upon this ground color, in turn, may be blotches, spots, or intricate interlacing lines of yellowish-brown, bright red, dark brown, or black. Some eggs are totally unmarked. (When a murre loses the one egg—its entire clutch—it lays another, and this one is colored like the first.) In contrast, the eggs of the closely related auklets of various species, which nest in burrows or rock crevices, have few or no markings.

Chester A. Reed, one of the early oologists during the heyday of egg collecting in the last century, says of the murres: "The eggs are laid as closely as possible on the ledges where the incubating birds sit upright, in long rows like an army on guard. As long as each bird succeeds in finding an egg to cover on its return home, it is doubtful if the bird either knows, or cares, whether it is its own or not." Thanks to experiments some twenty-five years ago by Beat Tschantz of the Zoological Institute of the University of Bern, Switzerland, we know that Reed was wrong. The murres no more incubate each other's eggs than the lobstermen tend each other's traps. Both use color and markings to identify their property. Tschantz switched eggs in nests and found that if an egg of a different color or marking pattern was substituted for the bird's own egg, that egg was rejected, but another egg with a similar pattern was accepted. The birds don't have innate recognition of their own eggs. For example, if a murre's egg is marked with white feces in small increments, the bird learns the new color pattern and will reject eggs of its own pattern. This fine discrimination by murres stands in strong contrast to the behavior of some birds—herring gulls, for example—which accept almost anything of any color even remotely resembling an egg.

Recognition of eggs by their color pattern has evolved in some other birds under an entirely different set of selective pressures: the need to detect and destroy the eggs of parasites.

Reproductive success in murres is enhanced if the females can pick out their own uniquely colored eggs. In contrast, under the selective pressure of brood parasitism, a bird's reproductive success is enhanced if it can recognize the eggs of other birds in its clutch and discard them. The possibility of parasitism would place selective pressure on the host bird to detect the odd-colored eggs. This would, in turn, put pressure on the parasite to produce eggs resembling those of its host.

The European cuckoo and its hosts may have evolved the most sophisticated egg-color matching. The European cuckoo never builds a nest of its own. Among the various birds it victimizes are wagtails, which have white eggs densely spotted in gray; bramblings, whose pale blue

eggs have heavy reddish spots; and European redstarts, with blue un-
spotted eggs. The cuckoo eggs found in these nests usually match closely
those of their hosts. The accuracy of the imitations is sometimes so good
that even the human eye has difficulty in distinguishing the eggs of the
parasite from those of the host.

It was long a mystery how such color matching could occur, for
surely cuckoos do not paint their eggs to match those of their intended
victims. The real answer, however, is almost as bizarre: in any given area
the cuckoos are made up of reproductively isolated subgroups called
"gentes," whose females restrict their parasitism to particular hosts. It is
believed that the gentes arose through geographic isolation, although at
the present time two or more gentes may occupy the same area. A given
female always lays the same-colored eggs, and almost always with the
same host species.

In European passerine birds heavily parasitized by cuckoos, there
has been potent selective pressure to foil the parasitism. Hosts have developed a strong attention to egg color code, abandoning many nests with
cuckoo eggs or throwing the cuckoo eggs out. This puts stronger pressure
on the cuckoos to produce even better egg mimicry. Only the well-matched
eggs are accepted.

Parasitism in North America is no less severe, but the principal
parasite of songbirds, the brown-headed cowbird, thus far has not evolved
egg-color mimicry. Nevertheless, the cowbird is a highly successful parasite. It is one of the most common of our native passerine birds, and it
is also one of the most widely distributed. According to Herbert Fried-
mann, a long-time student of avian brood parasitism, it parasitizes more
than 350 species and subspecies of birds. Some species suffer heavily. Up
to 78 percent of all song sparrow nests in some areas have been victimized
by this parasite. The cowbird, however, also lays eggs occasionally in the
nests of such unlikely potential hosts as the spotted sandpiper and ruby-
crowned kinglet, as well as in many other nests where its eggs regularly
get damaged or evicted. In short, it wastes many eggs. The cowbird is
partial to open habitat, having spread east from the short-grass prairies
in the Midwest only in the last two or three centuries.

At this point in the evolutionary race, only some of the potential
victims of the brown-headed cowbird have evolved appropriate egg-rejection
responses. Stephen I. Rothstein of the University of California at Santa
Barbara determined this by making plaster of paris eggs and painting
them to mimic cowbird eggs. He deposited these in a total of 640 nests
of forty-three species. He found that two-thirds of the passerine birds
accepted the parasite eggs, while only one-fourth consistently rejected
them. Some birds, like the red-winged blackbird, yellow warbler, phoebe,
and barn swallow, consistently accepted both fake and real parasite eggs,
while others, like the catbird, robin, and kingbird, consistently rejected

them. Since the birds were either consistent "acceptors" or "rejectors," he speculated that once the rejection behavior was genetically coded, it was of such great advantage that it spread rapidly and became fixed.

Early on in the relationship between parasite and potential host, a lack of color matching of the eggs is probably not necessary to ensure the parasite's success. However, eventually, as with the European cuckoo, similarity becomes important. It is doubtful if rejection can occur if—initially by chance and ultimately by evolution—the parasite and host eggs are exactly alike. Indeed, song sparrows and brown-headed cowbirds have eggs that are similar in size and dense brown spotting; and this sparrow rarely rejects the cowbird eggs. Both robins and catbirds, which have immaculate blue eggs, on the other hand, almost always do. In contrast, the phoebe, which lays pure white eggs, readily accepts cowbird eggs. But does a phoebe, nesting under a ledge or on a beam under a barn, ever notice the color of its eggs at all?

Since a key component of defense against parasitism involves egg recognition, one would predict that means of detecting foreign eggs would evolve. For example, it would be easier to recognize a stranger's egg if all the eggs within a clutch were similar. Does this help explain the fact that songbirds subject to parasitism have uniform egg coloring, while birds such as hawks, ravens, and crows have a variety of egg colorations in one clutch?

Some sixty years ago Bernhard Rensch, studying mimicry of cuckoo eggs in Germany, wondered whether songbirds could recognize their own eggs. In one experiment he replaced the first three eggs in a nest of the garden warbler with lesser whitethroat eggs. The warbler then ejected its own fourth egg! Rensch concluded that egg rejection was not on the basis of true recognition of a bird's own eggs, but on the basis of the discordance in appearance relative to the other eggs in the nest. But recent experiments by Rothstein show that there is more to the story. Like the murres studied by Tschantz, some songbirds also *learn* the appearance of their own eggs, becoming imprinted on the first egg they see in their nest. In an experiment that showed this most clearly, Rothstein removed all eggs in a catbird nest each day as they were laid, replacing them with cowbird eggs. Although catbirds normally reject cowbird eggs placed in with their own, this catbird accepted a whole clutch of cowbird eggs. Then a single catbird egg added to the cowbird eggs was rejected.

Why don't more birds practice the art of parasitism? As with many historical questions, we don't have an ironclad answer, but we may identify some of the selective processes at work. One possibility is that after a parasite has become established, and through millions of years improved its strategy, the hosts will have such good methods of egg detection that another bird just starting out would have no success. For example, I doubt that the brown-headed cowbird could become established in Europe, because the European birds, under the selective pressure of the cuckoo, have already evolved such a sophisticated egg-recognition system that they would not be fooled by the crude tactics of the cowbird.

There are other implications. For example, a parasite would have a great advantage if it could utilize a variety of hosts. And multiple parasitism would be easy if all the parasite's victims had similar eggs. Any bird lucky enough to have distinctively marked eggs should most easily spot and reject a parasite's eggs. In other words, to avoid parasitism a bird should have eggs that are different from those whose nests the parasite already uses. This would make for variety among different species but uniformity within clutches. And in general these are the patterns we see in nature.

Perhaps there is, after all, an evolutionary reason for the "general tendency of birds toward diversity." Perhaps catbirds' eggs, by being blue, are less camouflaged, but they gain instead by providing a sharp contrast so cowbirds' eggs can be detected and evicted.

It will likely not be possible ever to say with any degree of precision why a robin's egg is blue or a kingbird's egg is white and splotched with dark brown and purple. However, the diversity of patterns shows that there are different selective pressures at work. The coloration of birds' eggs reflects a long interplay of forces, in the face of randomness and chance, to produce organization in many parallel evolutionary paths that we now see in different stages. This, in turn, "colors" the mind as well as the eye, and gives eggs an additional beauty that no person's brush could ever impart.

QUESTIONS FOR CRITICAL READERS

Remembering and Understanding

1. Give one of the possible functions of egg coloration, and summarize the arguments for and against it.
2. Summarize the selective evolutionary pressures that produced egg coloration.
3. Explain brood and nest parasitism.

Analyzing and Discussing

4. Heinrich mentions "diversity" several times. What is it, and why is it an evolutionary advantage?
5. Heinrich is a scientist committed to explanations that rely on evolutionary theory. What other perspectives does he mention that might lead to different explanations for egg coloration?

6. What does egg coloration help birds know or do that would be impossible without it?

Writing

7. Formulate a question about a particular animal attribute, such as "Why do reptiles have scales?" or "Why do humans have fingernails?" Research your question and write an answer.

Call to a Trumpeter

SALLY CARRIGHAR

Carrighar has had a long and successful career as a writer and naturalist. She wrote for various motion picture studios in the 1920s, and published a book about whales in 1978. This description of a family of swans is from her classic 1947 book, One Day At Teton Marsh. *She also wrote the screenplay of this book, which was produced by Walt Disney in 1966. Rather than providing a scientific or strictly behavioral account, Carrigher conveys information in the form of a composite narrative of events that might have happened on a particular day.*

THE LATE, YELLOWING SUN shot its rays through the willow brush. The willows grew out of the water in clusters like giant fistfuls. They met at the top in a wide glinting blur. Below was the lucent brown gloss, now frosted lightly with autumn dust. In flowing water the dust had wrinkled against the stems. On sheltered bays swimming animals had left shining paths.

The Trumpeter Swan was gliding beneath the wilderness of the brush. Where the overhead boughs spread apart, his breast broke a pale blue sheen. Under the leaves that joined, he was scattering green-gold flakes. He was crossing reflections of the stems, red with a violet bloom on the bark. But all the willows were not bursts of color. Among them were dead thickets, bare and silvered by the sun so that they looked ice-coated, tangles with the crystal magic of winter. Any day the sheaths of ice would become real, and the tremulous water no longer would yield to a white feathered bow.

Here the willows became so dense that the Swan must keep swinging to wind among them. He paddled faster, with his throat tensely upright. He could not relax when he felt so enclosed, although he was more concerned for his family, following him, than for himself. A moose and her calf were browsing near on the leaves. They were out of sight, but the plunge of their hoofs was disquieting. And he could hear their talk, rough murmurs that may have seemed a violence to the Swan, whose own voice was a ringing clear channel for his emotions.

278

The thickets beyond were spaced thinly, and he came out on a small lagoon. His throat fell into a flow of curves, a tranquil sway forward and back over his wings, a lift to capture a mayfly, a downward folding to layer a feather, a revolving to scan the shoreline. The fly and feather and shore may have been only excuses for the elegant pleasure of motions so slowly graceful. He seemed more quiet than if he had not moved at all.

Now, late in the afternoon, little wind touched the responsive water. It was a stillness quick to stir, like the Swan's awareness. But a flock of mergansers splashed into the bay. They were learning how to drive fish to the shallows. The one they pursued dodged away to the willow canals, and several of the ducks dived. The Swan returned to the willows himself. Mergansers, with their habit of swimming underwater, made him nervous. For no one could tell where they would come up again. The Swan had a poise so sensitive, controlling such immense power, that lively animals often were subdued by it. Much of the time he lived in a peace he partly created; but no duck respected it. Nor did the winds. And the snows would not, and even more disastrously human beings had entered it.

He was leading his family to the beaver pond, a width from which they could rise in flight. Since the day drew to its end, his mate might follow him into the sky, if she ever would. Rounding a thicket, he missed the silent movement behind, of the others. He strengthened the stroke of one foot to pivot, and paddled back. His three cygnets had stopped to dabble for insects in floating leaves. Their mother was not with them.

The Swan was patient. He held his place with a weaving pressure of one web and the other and watched the fledglings. Their winter plumage was nearly complete. At first they had been all violet-gray, but their heads now were pinkish rust. Their bills were violet, mottled with rose. And did their colors please their father, whose eyes could distinguish them but were used to adult swans' vivid white?

The cygnets were two-thirds grown, larger than ducks but doubtless small to him. Their necks were shorter-proportioned than they would be later, and their heads were fluffier. One was beating his wings, a stretching that half-lifted him into the air, with his olive-brown feet patting the water. The other two also began to flap—little mimics still. In many ways they were not mature, needing yet to be watched. See how heedlessly they are switching their bills through the leaves, concerned only with food. They have not learned a swan's exquisite caution. At their age most birds were meeting the world by themselves, but in those species the new generation numbered thousands, even millions. The Swan was protecting his cygnets as if he had known that less than a hundred new broods of trumpeters had hatched this year, throughout the world.

Their mother should not expose them to danger by lingering so. Surely she was not far behind, concealed by the brush, but why not here? Her manner lately had made the Swan uneasy. She had seemed separate, most of the time near the family but not careful to guard the cygnets on one side while he guarded them on the other, not balancing her moves with his, with a matching grace as harmonious as a single swan's; not coming into the air with the others, not once since the young had begun to fly.

The mother had not been in the air since the flightless weeks of her summer molt. But the Swan's own wing feathers were grown out now; hers should be too. This was the season when swans should be making expeditions around the valley, around the peaks cupping the sky, up the Snake to its highest rill. Always on other years he and his mate had taken their young on autumn flights.

A swan's nature widened as the fall of leaves widened horizons. And these short family tours were the only ones they would make. No trumpeters anywhere migrated southward now. Once they did; even the grandparents of these two had been in the spindrift of wings scudding down the continent to the marshes that do not freeze. But human beings had come to those marshes to shoot swans for their down. And some of the ponds had been drained. Wildness was gone from the south—knowledge that older swans seemed to have given the recent ones. This Jackson Hole pair never had seen the devastation of the wintering grounds; yet their impulse to go was checked.

Actually human beings had stopped killing trumpeters everywhere. They had found that their spirits were lifted by the resonant voices and the great translucent wings. And so they had made a law that no one might destroy these birds. But how could that news be conveyed to the wild discouraged instincts?

The birds' down kept them warm in the northern winters, but too often their food was lost. They would stay on the narrowing ponds until the underwater plants were glazed over completely; then would starve. So quickly a species can die: of the immense flocks of trumpeters less than a thousand birds, anywhere, now remained alive.

These two had been fortunate. They had been reared on the Red Rock Lakes, where there was permanent open water. Then on one of their fall flights they had found this Teton Marsh, even warmer, and had stayed. Men had come here to kill ducks however, and some of their shot had fallen into the shallows. The mother swan had found several and had swallowed them, believing them snails perhaps. By this time the shot had eroded away, but she was sick of lead poisoning—sick of civilization really, as much as the swans who starved.

The father and the cygnets rounded the island and walked up into the sedges. The mother stayed in the water. She no longer spent the nights on their hillock; that was one of her strange new ways. The young ones let themselves down on the spongy roots. Sleepiness soon dazed their eyes. The Swan too folded his feet beneath him. He plucked a few sedge seeds and turned his neck backward so that his head lay at the upper edge of one wing. Most of his bill was under the feathers, but his eyes were out.

His mate appeared tense. He raised his head, for she was pushing against the island. With fumbling, broken motions she was trying to come ashore. But her legs were not strong enough to support her, and she sank back in the water.

She slept. For a long time the Swan stayed awake, watchful and now with a deep uneasiness. The sky was a merging of faded daylight and coming moonlight, a bright dust that anywhere might be stars. The yellow and green of the shoreline grasses still faintly showed. Their reflection was touched by the shine on the pond, which gave them the delicacy of grasses in spring, when they were tremulous, with their stirrings yet uncertain. Below the vertical blurs the water was mauve and blue-silver, the shades in the sky. A dragonfly passed, drained of his color. The grasses grayed. Overhead then was only a dark immensity, pricked by stars.

As soon as the sun was up, the cygnets began to stir. Piping a soft impatience, they slipped down in the water and filed away toward the willow thickets. Their father overtook them; more slowly their mother followed. The family passed other sedge hillocks and a corner of the meadow. The sun, coming in levelly, filled the grasses with light, and glanced off the water, striking the swans' plumage twice.

Even the father's own feeding was an aid to his young. The willow channels were ice-bordered this morning, but he paddled along the open center, watching the liquid brown depths. Some plants grew too deep, but finally he found a bed of clasping-leaf pondweed that he could reach. He swung down his head and first raked in the muck. The sensitive skin on his bill touched a dragonfly nymph. He nibbled it up and probed for more. Meanwhile, in brushing between the rippled leaves, he had broken off some of them. They floated up, nourishment for the cygnets. And when he pulled up a whole spray, waterboatmen and scuds were dislodged, and the young swans caught them. Several ducks—mallards and the consistent little thieves, baldpates—sped up to share the food. The Swan did not object. He cleared the channel of the weeds, satisfying his own hunger, the cygnets', and that of various smaller birds.

When the meal was finished, the cygnets paddled off to the meadow. They were sleepy, climbed out into the grass, and cuddled down. Their mother had stayed in the willows, but their father joined them.

He laid his head between his wings and closed his eyes. He also wished to sleep, for his day's vigilance had begun too early. Late in the night the beaver had been moving with sounds that were harmless, but toward morning a slap of his tail had sent a warning over the marsh. Peering up from the sedges, the Swan had discovered an otter.

The enemy swam about, underwater or sculling through the surface.

Moonlight silvered his wakes, and the ripples swished into the sedge blades of the swans' roost. Finally he went away, but he might return. The Swan had felt too alarmed to relax again.

Even now, in the reassuring light of day, he could not sleep. For the weather was making all the creatures restless. It made the swans, too, nervous, but they did not hop, flutter, or call continually, or fight. They showed their discomfort by letting the others' movements unsettle them. The cygnets were aroused by a varying hare, thumping her own tension.

At once they wished to be somewhere else. The Swan was disturbed at the prospect of taking them out alone. He called to his mate, but she did not come. Perhaps he could lead the young ones to the backwash, usually a quiet place. No; they would go past the dam. Two parents might have distracted them. They ignored their father's urging. He paddled faster and swung in advance.

Beyond the dam was the wooded bank with the beaver's canal cut into it and his house built against it. The adult swans never had brought the young here; an enemy could steal toward them too secretly through the grove. Now the cygnets swung up the shore, piping their pleasure in the new place. They stopped near the canal and jabbed for water-skaters in the debris drifted against the bank.

The current, draining toward the dam, was a swifter movement against the Swan's feet than the flow in the sedge beds or thickets. But his webs could detect another, uneven surge, no doubt stirred by the otter. An otter might swim up under a cygnet and pull it down. He was likely to do it only if he could find no fish, and this pond fairly swayed with fish; yet an otter's caprice was not to be trusted.

The Swan's eyes strained across the pond. The otter was submerged and not visible through the surface, dazzled with sunlit ripples. The smallest cygnet, a female, sensed her father's alarm. She showed the first stilling of her impulsiveness, the first touch of a swan's caution. While her brothers hunted more insects, she moved farther along the shore, where she could take flight more easily.

The heavy irregular surge became stronger. No more waiting; the father must take his young ones into the air. He called and had made the first leaping strokes with his feet when a marsh hawk swung over the grove.

The Swan could outdistance the hawk in flight, but the cygnets could not. Here then they must stay. The harrier had seen them. He would torment them—a prospect that put a more sensuous grace in his wingbeat. This was one of his great days. The swift wind had given him opposition, and that he loved. Here could be more of it.

With a shrill cry he turned down and straightened out, hanging above the young female. His yellow claws dropped. His hovering face would be terrible to a cygnet; ruffed and flat, it combined the look of a hawk and an owl.

The father was down-wind of the harrier. He could rise only by turning his back on the cygnets. He paddled instead to the little one's side, whipping a violent spray with his wings. The hawk cried another taunt, and the Swan replied with a louder warning. His neck was drawn back and his beak was open, ready for a murderous lunge if the hawk should drop lower.

At a sag in the wind the harrier swayed, lost his position, and circled above the pond to advance again over the cygnet. With that brief break the father sped into the wind, was soon off the water and pursuing the hawk. The harrier swept away, across the meadow and river and on over the sagebrush plain. The Swan was close behind, calling threats. The harrier went into a steep dive, a winding ascent, and another dive—sinuous turns that the larger Swan could not closely follow. But in fleeing, the hawk had admitted that he was vanquished. The father hastened back toward the pond and the greater threat of the otter.

The young ones had been subdued by their fright. Now they would be obedient. The marsh no longer beat with the otter's swimming, but the family filed to the sedge beds and their roost. There, secluded behind the tall, upright blades, they would wait out this tumultuous morning.

Soon after noon the wind blew down a dead tree that anchored the beavers' dam. It crashed on the pond with the high, metallic clatter of shattered water. Ducks exploded from the surface. The pelican sailed away. The great blue heron flopped up with a *quonck* in a loud collapsing voice. And out from the willows, like mosquitoes from beaten grass, rose smaller birds, incredible numbers seen together, of magpies, and mourning doves, belted kingfishers, yellow warblers, mountain and black-capped chickadees, pink-sided juncos, and tree swallows. Only the swans did not fly. Over their hillock the white and gray wings briefly waved; then were folded.

Soon the fears, too, were folded. The boldest birds came down, each leading a flock of excited followers.

The storm was close to Jackson Hole. Now the winds whirling around its center had passed on east. The water lay heavy and still, repeating with darkened colors every shoreline twig and root, every russet, cream, or brown-striped breast of a floating duck.

The Swan's mate spread the clearest outline on the surface. Below her perfectly was reflected the white sway of her side. It ended in the black knob of her knee, high because her legs were pulled up in discomfort. The Swan came off the roost to float beside her, and the cygnets followed. The family drew together, seeming to sense a crisis. A strange new sound was roughening the air.

The first hint of its meaning came to the Swan when he found that his toes touched the muck. They never had done that here. Now his webs were flat on the bottom, and he stood. Then the cygnets' feet touched, as their mother may have seen, for she lowered her own webs. At once she started toward the pond. Not being able to walk, she must stay on water deep enough so that she could paddle. She stopped at the outer border of the sedge beds, and the others with her. But she soon had to move again.

The dam had not been visible from the sedge roost. When the swans came out into the pond they discovered a break in the beaver's masonry. Around the roots of the upset tree the water was pouring down to the creek below. This was the reason for the roar they were hearing. The shores of the pond were drawing inward; its size was shrinking. Behind the swans were channels and slopes of bare mud.

Several times the family let the shallow water drive them on. Then they went to the center of the pond and huddled there near the end of the fallen tree. The father was facing the backwash, but into his sidewise vision a shadow flowed. It was the otter, topping the dam with his lilting step.

The mother too saw him. They swung together, enclosing the cygnets. The otter dived in the pond. But he emerged and began to tour the borders. No switch of his tail-tip and no toss of his arrogant head was missed by the eyes of the Swan.

The otter tumbled and swam in the draining pond. He rode the cascade through the break and caught a fish and climbed up on the prostrate trunk of the tree to eat it. The swans went out on the open surface.

A second otter came. The lively creatures were splashing together. The swans turned toward the shore, then back on the pond again, for the otters went out on the silt. The father Swan shifted about, tense and frantic.

Over the earth swept a sudden darkening, and a quick wind stirred the leaves. The air was oppressive. It lay in the Swan's lungs so heavily that each breath must be pushed out. Limpness lowered the arch in the mother's throat.

Down from the sky fell a soft tumult of snow. The flakes dissolved on the water; on the shores, the dam, and the brush they spread a cover. The downy mist thickened. An enemy could pounce from it. The swans heard the otters' cries but they could not see them. They could not see, in fact, to the other side of the pond. They heard also the brutal hoarseness of ravens, brawling over something, somewhere out there in the close white shower.

But loudest for the father may have been the calls of competing instincts. Surely he should be loyal first to his sick mate. He should stay here and protect her, helpless, needing him so desperately. His devotion to her was a lifelong emotion; his concern for the cygnets would pass before another brood could hatch.

Yet his full care of the young ones, recently, had strengthened his sense of responsibility for them. To save them, he should leave this vanishing marsh. He should take them to a new home, probably on the Red Rock Lakes, where he had spent his own years as a cygnet. Safety and food depended on water, and soon apparently none would be here.

To protect his mate or his fledglings—both calls rose from the deepest instincts in his nature. And the conflict may have been no less an anguish because conscious reasoning did not weigh it. Decided either way, one almost-irresistible urge must be denied.

He knew which call he would answer when he felt his wings lift. Into the dense enveloping snow he sped. He trumpeted to the cygnets and then slowed his flight, listening for the skitter of their feet, the air thrashed by their wings. When all three were aloft, a different note came into his voice. It spoke to his mate, though not with a summons. He was aware now that she could not rise. But he sent down his cry, for her to understand if she could. Twice he led the cygnets in low circles above the marsh, trumpeting to the white bird, so quiet upon the black pond. Finally her throat straightened, her bill lifted upward, and she trumpeted one answering call.

He turned his course west toward the Teton slope. Along the base of the mountains was a row of lakes, familiar enough so that he could find them in blind flying. He held his speed to the cygnets' and constantly urged them on, so that none would be lost. He was taking them to the smallest lake, on Mount Moran, near the northern tip of the range. It could not be a home, for these lakes froze from shore to shore. But on its breadth were the tops of several muskrat lodges. One would be a roost where the family could await the end of the storm.

He still was awake when the storm broke up. The mountain and the long range south took shape. The overhead thickness began to lift and shred. For a while clouds, luminous with moonlight, continued to cross the frosted blue of the dark night sky. Their shining passage seemed the only happening, now that the earth was covered by the wide monotony of the snow. As smoothly as swans the clouds appeared from over the Teton crest, to stream above the valley and beyond the eastern range. With a lingering hold one pulled away from another . . . lost the touch . . . moved on alone. Two united . . . blended . . . started to separate . . . clung . . . tore apart. Always they were changing, but their world did not change. It was a world of inviolate wildness.

A new wind swept the clouds away, and in the sky was only the moon, a hanging ball of light that dimmed the stars.

The bugling of an elk awakened the cygnets in the morning. He stood on a granite cliff above the lake and sent his challenge over the valley with a rising flow of notes almost as clear and vibrant as the Swan's.

The early light was coloring the snowy peaks with the nacreous pink of sea shells. Coming down the slope, the sunshine gilded the ivory crown upon the elk's head. It passed the pines and spruces at the shore and stretched back over the misty surface of the lake to the lodge.

The Swan allowed the cygnets to feed for a brief time. Soon he called them and rose from the pond to start their flight to the Red Rock Lakes. The sky felt crisp and electric, for with the storm's departure ozone from above the stratosphere was raining earthward. The pressure of the air was heightened, heightening in turn each animal's vitality. Never had the cygnets flown so swiftly.

Everything seemed changed, and for the better. That may have been the reason why the Swan reversed his course. Or possibly the danger to his mate was, after all, the stronger call. He circled back at the head of the valley, turning south instead of north. Setting an almost-adult speed for the young swans, he was following the Gros Ventre crest.

The indigo river shone between the white flats of the valley floor. One of its curves, there, held the marsh. The pond was smaller than before the tree fell, but it was not empty. The Swan was spiraling down.

His glide along the water stopped him near the dam. During the night the beaver partly had repaired it, and the inflow of the brook had filled the marsh up to the level of the dam's unfinished top. The willow channels still were drained, but the surface spread back past the sedge beds, past the Swan's roost. Floating near the hillock was his mate.

He hastened toward the roost, so eagerly that now the ripples did not melt out from his sides but splashed away. The cygnets stopped at a bed of milfoil, which the lowering of the pond had brought within their reach.

The mother watched her family's return. Her eyes were more intense this morning, with a more accessible look. And there were other proofs that she was slightly stronger. Her wings lay higher on her back, and her throat was swinging slowly. Her head was turning in the sunlight. If she had swallowed more of the shot, she might not have recovered. She might not if the weather had remained depressing. But its most invigorating benefits had come together at her crisis. She would live, though never again to mother cygnets, for the poison had made her barren.

As the Swan approached, he thrust his head beneath the surface, tossed it back with a shower of crystal drops upon his wings. He beat the wings and half-rose from the water. Slowing the stroke, he let himself down but again reared, framed in his wings' great pulsing gleam of white.

The motion may have been stirred by instinct's memory of the autumn when they plighted their devotion. The ritual had been a kind of dance, in which the two, advancing toward each other, lifted from the water, breast to breast. This later day his mate could only once and briefly raise her wings—the merest opening along her sides, yet a wish expressed.

He tilted his bill as if to trumpet, but swung it down and glided closer to her. Both birds turned their attention to the sunny day, the cygnets, and the life that they would share once more, beginning with this new and silent clasping of their spirits.

QUESTIONS FOR CRITICAL READERS

Remembering and Understanding

1. Extract from the narrative as much information about swans as you can. Then use this information to write a description of the Trumpeter Swan as a species.
2. Carrighar frequently anthropomorphizes the swans she is describing. List the anthropomorphic statements she makes and then summarize Carrighar's description based on these features.
3. What point is Carrighar making? Re-state it in your own words.

Analyzing and Discussing

4. To what extent do Carrighar's anthropomorphic statements make her account of the swans more or less believable?
5. Locate a standard reference work about birds and read about Trumpeter Swans. How accurate is the information that Carrighar provides?
6. Does Carrighar's use of a narrative format make her description more or less effective for you?

Writing

7. Choose an animal or person you are familiar with and write a story in which you include as much information as you can about behavior, life cycle, and habitat.

Remembrance of Seeds Stashed

————— STEPHEN VANDER WALL —————

and

RUSSELL P. BALDA

This article, which originally appeared in Natural History *magazine, reports a collaborative research project in which Vander Wall, an undergraduate at the time, and Balda, a professor of zoology, observed the foraging behavior of several species of mountain birds. Because they are scientists, they base their conclusions on extensive observations and experiments. Also, they understand behavior within the framework of evolutionary biology.*

For several species of birds in the American Southwest, and for the pines on which they feed, survival and reproduction hinge on the birds' remarkable memory

MOST CONIFEROUS TREES rely on the wind to disperse their winged seeds, which are kept tightly sealed in cones until maturity to protect them from birds and other potential predators. But in many mountainous regions of the western United States, certain pine trees have actually come to depend on seed-eating birds for seed dispersal. This mutualistic relationship profoundly influences the natural history of both the birds and the trees.

Over the millennia, the pines, which include piñon pines, whitebark pine, southwestern white pine, and limber pine, developed a number of characteristics that make them attractive to foraging birds. Cones are often conspicuously positioned on branches, and as summer turns to fall and the cones on many of the trees begin to open, the seeds within them are visible for several yards. These wingless seeds are much larger than the seeds of most other conifers, and to some extent, their quality can be determined at a distance: edible (and viable) piñon pine seeds, for example, are dark chestnut brown; inedible (infertile) seeds are usually paler.

Many mammals are also drawn to the prominently displayed seeds,

288

and piñon seeds were a staple in the diet of several American Indian tribes. No seedlings can grow from consumed seeds, so why did these trees evolve such an apparently maladaptive set of traits?

The answer to this question lies in the foraging behavior of the four species of birds, all in the family Corvidae, that harvest most of the seeds from these pines: Clark's nutcracker (*Nucifraga columbiana*); piñon jay (*Gymnorhinus cyanocephalus*); Steller's jay (*Cyanocitta stelleri*); and scrub jay (*Aphelocoma coerulescens*). Our studies have demonstrated that while these birds collect impressive numbers of seeds in the fall, they do not eat all the seeds right away; they bury most in the soil as reserves against the lean winter and spring months, when other food is unavailable. The ability of the seeds to remain viable—and edible—for many weeks in the cold ground holds the key to the mutually beneficial relationship between tree and bird.

The most proficient harvester of pine seeds is the Clark's nutcracker, a close relative of the Eurasian nutcracker (*N. caryocatactes*), which is well known for its extensive collecting of the seeds of European and Asian pines. Clark's nutcracker breeds throughout the western United States and southwestern Canada in mixed coniferous forests of high, rugged mountains. A strong, skillful flier, it often ranges great distances, especially in fall and winter, to lowland valleys.

Two structural features contribute to the nutcracker's efficiency at gathering seeds. It has a long, sturdy, sharply pointed bill that it uses as a chisel to pry open cone scales. The length of the bill allows the bird to poke deep between the scales while keeping its facial feathers free of the pitchy surface of the cone. The second structure, unique to nutcrackers, is the sublingual pouch, a specialized expandable sac in front of and below the tongue. The evolution of this pouch involved only slight modification of other features of the mouth, but it led to sweeping changes in the nutcracker's life history.

In late August, the nutcrackers leave their breeding grounds and move down the mountainsides to areas where pine cones are beginning to ripen. They remove green, tightly closed cones from the trees either by twisting them loose or by pecking at the cone's point of attachment to the tree. Each detached cone is carried to a tree stump or the crotch of a sturdy limb where, holding the cone by its feet, the nutcracker forcefully chisels between the cone scales with its bill and extracts seeds. In mid-September, piñon, southwestern white, and limber pine cones mature and begin to open while still on the trees, and the nutcrackers change their foraging behavior, using their bills as forceps to remove seeds directly from attached cones.

After extracting a seed, the nutcracker rattles it in its bill. How the seed sounds and how much it weighs apparently enable the bird to distinguish inedible seeds from edible ones. Inedible seeds are discarded, while edible seeds, if not eaten immediately, are placed in the sublingual pouch. Of the more than seven hundred seeds we have removed from pouches, all have been edible and potentially viable. Nutcrackers rarely make mistakes, even though more than half the seeds in a crop may be unfertilized or diseased.

When fully expanded, the sublingual pouch can hold about ninety Colorado piñon pine seeds or about twice as many of the smaller whitebark pine seeds. Holding seeds in its pouch does not prevent the nutcracker from vocalizing, eating, or testing the quality of more seeds. Because it accommodates so many seeds without interfering with the rest of the bird's activities, the pouch enables the nutcracker to forage widely and to transport seeds long distances to favored storage sites.

Part of our fieldwork in the San Francisco Mountains of north-central Arizona involved learning where the birds were taking their seeds. After hours of following birds through forests, across canyons, and up mountainsides, we discovered their destination: a south-facing slope high in the mountains. To reach this location, some birds flew up to fourteen miles.

We found that a dozen or more nutcrackers may store their seeds in a communal caching area, often working as little as three feet apart. The cache areas are usually windswept ridges, south-facing slopes, and rocky cliff edges—places where snow is lacking or melts early in the spring and where seeds are, therefore, accessible in the wintertime. Such sites are rare, which probably explains why cache areas are communal. After selecting an appropriate site, a bird jabs its bill into the soil once or twice to make a small hole. It then puts from one to fourteen seeds into the hole, holding them one at a time in the tip of its bill and inserting them to a depth of from one-half to one inch. When finished with a particular hole, the bird first rakes soil or litter over it with its bill and then places a small object, such as a twig, pebble, pine cone, or even a lump of snow, on top of the spot to help hide it.

Studies of piñon, Steller's, and scrub jays reveal that they too invest considerable time and energy each fall collecting, transporting, and caching pine seeds but that they differ from the nutcracker, and among themselves, in many aspects of their behavior. Many of these differences are related to differing morphologies. Like the nutcracker, the piñon jay has a long, sharply pointed bill with which to chisel into closed, green cones, but the Steller's and scrub jays do not. They must wait for cones to ripen or open naturally before they can harvest seeds. Before cones open, these jays harass foraging nutcrackers in an attempt to get them to drop seeds or the cones they are working on.

None of the three jays has a sublingual pouch. Piñon and Steller's jays transport seeds in an expandable esophagus, while the scrub jay simply uses its mouth and bill. The piñon jay can carry up to fifty-six piñon seeds, the Steller's jay eighteen, and the scrub jay only five—in each case considerably fewer than the ninety seeds carried by the nutcracker.

The maximum distance that birds carry seeds also varies: about six miles for the piñon jay; two for the Steller's; and half a mile for the scrub jay. Again, all are less than the nutcracker's fourteen miles. Distance is thus positively correlated with the quantity of seeds transported. Interestingly, those species that travel farther are also swifter fliers.

All the jays store seeds in the soil in much the same manner as does the nutcracker, but the habitats in which seeds are buried differ. When harvesting piñon pine seeds, for example, Steller's jays carry seeds upslope to ponderosa pine forests. Piñon and scrub jays cache extensively in piñon-juniper woodlands, although in some areas of their range, the piñon jays also store seeds at higher elevations, in the ponderosa pine forests, and farther downslope, in grasslands. Thus, the birds transport seeds to several habitats over a wide elevational range.

Caching systems also vary. Steller's and scrub jays cache seeds on their breeding territories and actively defend the supplies against intruders, whereas nutcrackers and piñon jays cache in areas used communally by many individuals. Nutcracker cache areas may be completely unassociated with breeding areas.

An active nutcracker can store a prodigious quantity of seeds. During years of abundant cone production, nutcrackers will engage in seed storage for about fifty days. If the cache site is, say, three miles from the seed-collecting area, each nutcracker could make about ten round trips per day. At the mean rate of 65 piñon pine seeds per trip, one bird could conceivably store 32,500 seeds each fall in more than 8,000 separate caches.

Perhaps even more impressive than how many seeds the nutcracker buries is how many it manages to recover, often months later. Experiments with captive birds in large enclosures have demonstrated that both the Clark's nutcracker and the Eurasian nutcracker can remember the location of individual caches. In one experiment, nutcrackers found only seeds that they had hidden even though hundreds of caches made by other birds were present. In another, a bird was taken out of the enclosure temporarily and one-half of its caches were removed. When this bird later searched for seeds, it dug at both full and empty cache sites. The results of these and other experiments indicate that seed recovery is not dependent on the sense of smell and, since nutcrackers generally probed with an accuracy of from 60 to 90 percent, that the searches were not random (the predicted accuracy of a random search would be less than one percent).

In an experiment to test their memory more directly, nutcrackers were allowed to cache seeds in soil in the midst of large rocks, logs, and shrubs, objects they might use as landmarks. Then, the birds were removed, and all the large objects on one-half of the enclosure were shifted eight inches in the same direction without disturbing the caches. The other, control half of the enclosure was unchanged. As expected, when the nutcrackers were returned, they recovered seeds on the control half with their usual success rate. On the half with the shifted objects, however, they probed eight inches away from the actual caches but in the "correct" sites with respect to the objects. Apparently, nutcrackers remember the arrangement of objects surrounding each cache.

But what happens if snow obliterates surface objects? Despite the birds' preference for snow-free sites, snow does sometimes cover caches, and the birds routinely dig through six inches of snow. The effect of snow was tested indirectly in a large room with logs and other objects on a sandy floor. After a nutcracker made several caches, it, along with all objects on the sand, was removed from the room. When the bird was placed back in the room thirty-one days later, the accuracy with which it located buried seeds decreased from about 90 to 50 percent. Removal of the surface objects greatly reduced the bird's efficiency. What success it did have was probably due to such aboveground objects as walls, light switches, and perches, cues that may be analogous to tree trunks, branches, and boulders not obscured by snow.

The observation that in experiments nutcrackers rarely find seeds cached by other birds indicates that although seeds are stored in communal areas, each bird has its own seed reserve. In the wild, nutcrackers and jays have been observed searching for the stored seeds of other birds, but this usually occurred when the searching bird had seen the cache being made. Caching birds frequently thwart attempted thefts by digging up their seeds and moving them. Sometimes, a thief is successful, but in general, stealing is an ineffective strategy. In the autumn, when seeds are abundant and easily accessible, harvesting and storing one's own supply is more efficient than attempting to steal from another bird, which may take pains to prevent the theft.

Clark's nutcrackers begin recovering buried seeds in the late fall, as the supply of seeds in cones becomes depleted. During the winter months, stored seeds make up the bulk of the diet, which is supplemented with overwintering insects and an occasional mouse or chipmunk. In years when pine trees produce few or no cones, nutcrackers are forced to leave their alpine haunts in search of other foods. When the shortage of conifer seeds is severe, the birds wander far outside their normal range and habitat; in years past, they have been recorded in the Great Plains, southwestern deserts, and Pacific coastal areas.

Nutcrackers continue to draw on their stored seed reserves during the breeding season. Among the earliest nesting birds in North America, they may lay eggs in late February. The cached pine seeds provide the adults with the extra energy necessary for winter breeding. When eggs hatch, in March or April, pine seeds also make up almost the entire diet of the nestlings. Feeding seeds to young is a rare behavior among birds, even granivorous ones, because most seeds do not provide enough protein and fats for rapid growth of young birds. Young nutcrackers have apparently evolved the ability to develop on a diet of pine seeds; more important, the seeds fed to them by their parents are unusually high in lipids and proteins.

Early breeding is advantageous for the young birds because it gives them more time to gain weight and foraging experience before the onset of winter. After the young leave the nest, they follow their parents to a cache site. While adults search for seeds, groups of siblings usually wait in nearby trees, although young birds occasionally hop along the ground behind their parents, giving high-pitched hunger calls. After a cache is located, the adults shell seeds and feed them whole to the young. Fledglings are fed by parents until mid-July; by early August, they are foraging for themselves on the ripening cones.

The three jays vary in their dependence on stored seeds. Piñon jays rely on them heavily in the winter and, like the nutcrackers, will erupt from their normal range if seeds are not available for storage. In years of good cone crops, piñon jays may also breed as early as late February, but they differ from nutcrackers in that stored seeds constitute only about 10 percent of the nestling diet; the other 90 percent is made up largely of insects. Steller's and scrub jays used stored seeds to supplement their winter diet but do not usually undergo eruptive movements when pine seeds are not available. Both species breed late in the spring and, like most birds, feed mainly insects to their young.

These four species form a graded series of behavioral and morphological specializations for seed collecting, transportation, and storage in the order, from least to most specialized, of scrub jay, Steller's jay, piñon jay, and Clark's nutcracker. The gradation can provide insights into how the remarkable specializations found in the nutcracker today might have evolved in tandem. Modifications in bill morphology and foraging technique that allowed more efficient foraging, for example, were accompanied by the development of food-transporting structures and strong, swift flight, which permitted the birds to range greater distances and exploit widely scattered resource patches. As adaptations evolved that increased the total quantity of seeds cached, other aspects of the nutcracker's life history changed: it became an early breeder; its nestlings adapted to a seed diet; and its increased dependency on seeds obliged it to emigrate when seed crops failed.

The advantages to the pines in this apparently coevolved system derive from the failure of the birds to recover all the cached seeds. Nutcrackers and piñon jays, especially, seem to have an insatiable drive to store pine seeds and frequently bury two to three times more than they could possibly consume, perhaps as insurance against spoilage and cache-robbing rodents. Cached seeds that survive the winter and that were placed in a good seedbed may germinate. Identifying seedlings that originated from nutcracker or jay caches is generally easy since they often grow in clusters. In many whitebark and limber pine forests, clusters of mature trees can frequently be found, evidence of a long history of caching.

This seed-dispersal system is superior to the wind dispersal of most other conifers in several ways. First, because the large seeds of bird-dispersed pines have more stored energy and nutrients, seedling establishment is more likely to be successful. Second, by burying the seeds in the soil, the birds provide them with far better microsites than could random scattering by the wind. Third, nutcrackers, piñon jays, and to a lesser extent Steller's and scrub jays transport seeds over long distances, which makes them excellent vehicles of colonization. In mountainous regions, suitable habitat for pines is usually patchily distributed, and the distances between patches are often too great to be bridged by a seed dependent on the wind. For a strong flier like the nutcracker, however, traveling across canyons and between mountaintops is easy.

The location of suitable habitat for the trees may also change over time, and there is evidence that seed-caching birds affected the distribution of these pines in the past. Since the Pleistocene, the vegetation zones of the West and Southwest have undergone marked geographical and elevational fluctuations. These changes have been well documented by pollen analysis and by the discovery of fossilized pine needles in packrat dens. During the last glaciation, for example, single-leaf piñon pine, which today is found primarily in the foothills and low mountain slopes of the Great Basin of Utah and Nevada, was restricted to an area now occupied by the Mojave Desert in southern California. This species' large, wingless seeds probably could not have moved such distances assisted only by the wind and gravity, even over a period of several thousand years. Most likely, birds ancestral to the seed-caching nutcrackers and jays were the vehicles by which this and other such pines came to occupy their present ranges. Thus, when climatic conditions shift, causing inhospitable areas to become suitable for plant growth and reproduction, these birds may help the pines to colonize new locations.

Such effective and far-ranging seed dispersal does not come cheap. The birds' dependence on the pines has required the trees to invest, so to speak, in the expensive production of high-energy seeds, many of which will be eaten and never have a chance to germinate. For the birds, too—especially the nutcrackers and piñon jays—dependence has its costs. When seed production is poor and the birds are forced to emigrate, their breeding success drops and many emigrants die. Thus, the coevolutionary relationship between tree and bird cannot be considered a perfect or finished product. It is a living process, constantly subjected to factors tending toward greater specialization and factors penalizing overspecialization. The point of balance between these two conflicting influences determines how dependent on stored seeds birds in a particular environment may become.

QUESTIONS FOR CRITICAL READERS

Remembering and Understanding

1. Summarize the mutualistic relationship between birds and pine trees that the authors describe.
2. The authors derive some of their information from experiments. Describe the procedures and results of one of their experiments.
3. List the words, phrases, and other features that identify this article as the work of scientists. What do these features tell you about what the authors expect of their audience?

Analyzing and Discussing

4. How does the information presented here contribute to a more thorough understanding of relationships between species in an ecosystem?
5. What other cooperative relationships exist in nature? Describe at least one that you are aware of.
6. How has their perspective as scientists allowed the authors to notice and understand things about their subject that others might not see?

Writing

7. The discoveries described here began with the authors' curiosity about something they observed. Describe several observations that have made you curious. Choose one of these, and explain how you would go about investigating.

The Scavengers

MARY AUSTIN

Mary Austin wrote essays, poems, novels, and books about Native American culture. She was a feminist, and her nature writing has been compared with that of Thoreau and John Muir. She was born in Illinois in 1868 and moved to California in 1888. She lived in the desert near Bakersfield for a number of years and in 1903 published The Land of Little Rain, *which has been called a classic of western American nature writing. Austin was concerned with the relationship of people to their natural and social environments, and she was especially interested in the role of environments in conditioning individuals and cultures.*

FIFTY-SEVEN BUZZARDS, one on each of fifty-seven fence posts at the rancho El Tejon, on a mirage-breeding September morning, sat solemnly while the white tilted travelers' vans lumbered down the Canada de los Uvas. After three hours they had only clapped their wings, or exchanged posts. The season's end in the vast dim valley of the San Joaquin is palpitatingly hot, and the air breathes like cotton wool. Through it all the buzzards sit on the fences and low hummocks, with wings spread fanwise for air. There is no end to them, and they smell to heaven. Their heads droop, and all their communication is a rare, horrid croak.

The increase of wild creatures is in proportion to the things they feed upon: the more carrion the more buzzards. The end of the third successive dry year bred them beyond belief. The first year quail mated sparingly; the second year the wild oats matured no seed; the third, cattle died in their tracks with their heads toward the stopped watercourses. And that year the scavengers were as black as the plague all across the mesa and up the treeless, tumbled hills. On clear days they betook themselves to the upper air, where they hung motionless for hours. That year there were vultures among them, distinguished by the white patches under the wings. All their offensiveness notwithstanding, they have a stately flight. They must also have what pass for good qualities among themselves, for they are social, not to say clannish.

296

It is a very squalid tragedy—that of the dying brutes and the scavenger birds. Death by starvation is slow. The heavy-headed, rack-boned cattle totter in the fruitless trails; they stand for long, patient intervals; they lie down and do not rise. There is fear in their eyes when they are first stricken, but afterward only intolerable weariness. I suppose the dumb creatures know nearly as much of death as do their betters, who have only the more imagination. Their even-breathing submission after the first agony is their tribute to its inevitableness. It needs a nice discrimination to say which of the basket-ribbed cattle is likeliest to afford the next meal, but the scavengers make few mistakes. One stoops to the quarry and the flock follows.

Cattle once down may be days in dying. They stretch out their necks along the ground, and roll up their slow eyes at longer intervals. The buzzards have all the time, and no beak is dropped or talon struck until the breath is wholly passed. It is doubtless the economy of nature to have the scavengers by to clean up the carrion, but a wolf at the throat would be a shorter agony than the long stalking and sometime perchings of these loathsome watchers. Suppose now it were a man in this long-drawn, hungrily spied upon distress! When Timmie O'Shea was lost on Armogossa Flats for three days without water, Long Tom Basset found him, not by any trail, but by making straight away for the points where he saw buzzards stooping. He could hear the beat of their wings, Tom said, and trod on their shadows, but O'Shea was past recalling what he thought about things after the second day. My friend Ewan told me, among other things, when he came back from San Juan Hill, that not all the carnage of battle turned his bowels as the sight of slant black wings rising flockwise before the burial squad.

There are three kinds of noises buzzards make—it is impossible to call them notes—raucous and elemental. There is a short croak of alarm, and the same syllable in a modified tone to serve all the purposes of ordinary conversation. The old birds make a kind of throaty chuckling to their young, but if they have any love song I have not heard it. The young yawp in the nest a little, with more breath than noise. It is seldom one finds a buzzard's nest, seldom that grown-ups find a nest of any sort; it is only children to whom these things happen by right. But by making a business of it one may come upon them in wide, quiet cañons, or on the lookouts of lonely, table-topped mountains, three or four together, in the tops of stubby trees or on rotten cliffs well open to the sky.

It is probable that the buzzard is gregarious, but it seems unlikely from the small number of young noted at any time that every female incubates each year. The young birds are easily distinguished by their size when feeding, and high up in air by the worn primaries of the older birds. It is when the young go out of the nest on their first foraging that the parents, full of a crass and simple pride, make their indescribable chucklings of gobbling, gluttonous delight. The little ones would be amusing as they tug and tussle, if one could forget what it is they feed upon.

One never comes any nearer to the vulture's nest or nestlings than hearsay. They keep to the southerly Sierras, and are bold enough, it seems, to do killing on their own account when no carrion is at hand. They dog the shepherd from camp to camp, the hunter home from the hill, and will even carry away offal from under his hand.

The vulture merits respect for his bigness and for his bandit airs, but he is a sombre bird, with none of the buzzard's frank satisfaction in his offensiveness.

The least objectionable of the inland scavengers is the raven, frequenter of the desert ranges, the same called locally "carrion crow." He is handsomer and has such an air. He is nice in his habits and is said to have likable traits. A tame one in a Shoshone camp was the butt of much sport and enjoyed it. He could all but talk and was another with the children, but an arrant thief. The raven will eat most things that come his way—eggs and young of ground-nesting birds, seeds even, lizards and grasshoppers, which he catches cleverly; and whatever he is about, let a coyote trot never so softly by, the raven flaps up and after; for whatever the coyote can pull down or nose out is meat also for the carrion crow.

And never a coyote comes out of his lair for killing, in the country of the carrion crows, but looks up first to see where they may be gathering. It is a sufficient occupation for a windy morning, on the lineless, level mesa, to watch the pair of them eying each other furtively, with a tolerable assumption of unconcern, but no doubt with a certain amount of good understanding about it. Once at Red Rock, in a year of green pasture, which is a bad time for the scavengers, we saw two buzzards, five ravens, and a coyote feeding on the same carrion, and only the coyote seemed ashamed of the company.

Probably we never fully credit the interdependence of wild creatures, and their cognizance of the affairs of their own kind. When the five coyotes that range the Tejon from Pasteria to Tunawai planned a relay race to bring down an antelope strayed from the band, beside myself to watch, an eagle swung down from Mt. Pinos, buzzards materialized out of invisible ether, and hawks came trooping like small boys to a street fight. Rabbits sat up in the chaparral and cocked their ears, feeling themselves quite safe for the once as the hunt swung near them. Nothing happens in the deep wood that the blue jays are not all agog to tell. The hawk follows the badger, the coyote the carrion crow, and from their aerial stations the buzzards watch each other. What would be worth knowing is how much of their neighbor's affairs the new generations learn for themselves, and how much they are taught of their elders.

So wide is the range of the scavengers that it is never safe to say, eyewitness to the contrary, that there are few or many in such a place. Where the carrion is, there will the buzzards be gathered together, and in three days' journey you will not sight another one. The way up from Mojave to Red Butte is all desertness, affording no pasture and scarcely a rill of water. In a year of little rain in the south, flocks and herds were driven to the number of thousands along this road to the perennial pastures of the high ranges. It is a long, slow trail, ankle deep in bitter dust that gets up in the slow wind and moves along the backs of the crawling cattle. In the worst of times one in three will pine and fall out by the way. In the defiles of Red Rock, the sheep piled up a stinking lane; it was the sun smiting by day. To these shambles came buzzards, vultures, and coyotes from all the country round, so that on the Tejon, the Ceriso, and the Little Antelope there were not scavengers enough to keep the country clean. All that summer the dead mummified in the open or dropped slowly back to earth in the quagmires of the bitter springs. Meanwhile from Red Rock to Coyote Holes, and from Coyote Holes to Haiwai the scavengers gorged and gorged.

The coyote is not a scavenger by choice, preferring his own kill, but being on the whole a lazy dog, is apt to fall into carrion eating because it is easier. The red fox and bobcat, a little pressed by hunger, will eat of any other animal's kill, but will not ordinarily touch what dies of itself, and are exceedingly shy of food that has been manhandled.

Very clean and handsome, quite belying his relationship in appearance, is Clark's crow, that scavenger and plunderer of mountain camps. It is permissible to call him by his common name, "Camp Robber": he has earned it. Not content with refuse, he pecks open meal sacks, filches whole potatoes, is a gormand for bacon, drills holes in packing cases, and is daunted by nothing short of tin. All the while he does not neglect to vituperate the chipmunks and sparrows that whisk off crumbs of comfort from under the camper's feet. The Camp Robber's gray coat, black and white barred wings, and slender bill, with certain tricks of perching, accuse him of attempts to pass himself off among woodpeckers; but his behavior is all crow. He frequents the higher pine belts, and has a noisy strident call like a jay's, and how clean he and the frisk-tailed chipmunks keep the camp! No crumb or paring or bit of eggshell goes amiss.

High as the camp may be, so it is not above timber-line, it is not too high for the coyote, the bobcat, or the wolf. It is the complaint of the ordinary camper that the woods are too still, depleted of wild life. But what dead body of wild thing, or neglected game untouched by its kind, do you find? And put out offal away from camp over night, and look next day at the foot tracks where it lay.

Man is a great blunderer going about in the woods, and there is no other except the bear makes so much noise. Being so well warned beforehand, it is a very stupid animal, or a very bold one, that cannot keep safely hid. The cunningest hunter is hunted in turn, and what he leaves of his kill is meat for some other. That is the economy of nature, but with it all there is not sufficient account taken of the works of man. There is no scavenger that eats tin cans, and no wild thing leaves a like disfigurement on the forest floor.

QUESTIONS FOR CRITICAL READERS

Remembering and Understanding

1. In several places Austin attributes human characteristics to the birds she writes about. Find these and then summarize what these characteristics imply about the birds.
2. Choose one of the scavengers Austin describes. Make a list of the information she provides, and write a summary of its behavior and role in the desert.
3. Summarize the evidence that the species Austin describes are interdependent.

Analyzing and Discussing

4. Think of the vultures as a riddle. What question does their presence in the desert pose for Austin? How does solving the riddle lead to information about the desert environment?
5. What is Austin's view of the place of people in nature?
6. Why do people consider scavengers to be more gruesome than other species?

Writing

7. Using information that Austin provides, write a description of life in the desert.

Peregrines

J. A. BAKER

Baker, an Englishman, spent ten years observing peregrine falcons near the east coast of England. His observations became the basis of his book The Peregrine, *from which this selection is taken. In the book, Baker compresses his ten years of observations into one winter season. He is a close, careful, patient observer. As a result, he sees things that others might not notice. One reviewer described Baker's language as "brutal, hard, Saxon" and as "poetic prose."*

THE HARDEST THING OF ALL to see is what is really there. Books about birds show pictures of the peregrine, and the text is full of information. Large and isolated in the gleaming whiteness of the page, the hawk stares back at you, bold, statuesque, brightly coloured. But when you have shut the book, you will never see that bird again. Compared with the close and static image, the reality will seem dull and disappointing. The living bird will never be so large, so shiny-bright. It will be deep in landscape, and always sinking farther back, always at the point of being lost. Pictures are waxworks beside the passionate mobility of the living bird.

Female peregrines, known as falcons, are between seventeen and twenty inches long; roughly the length of a man's arm from elbow to fingertip. Males, or tiercels, are three to four inches shorter, fourteen to sixteen inches long. Weights also vary: falcons from 1¾ to 2½ pounds, tiercels from 1½ to 1¾ pounds. Everything about peregrines varies: colour, size, weight, personality, style: everything.

Adults are blue, blue-black, or grey, above; whitish below, barred crosswise with grey. During their first year of life, and often for much of their second year also, the younger birds are brown above, and buff below—streaked vertically with brown. This brown colour ranges from foxy red to sepia, the buff from pale cream to pale yellow. Peregrines are born between April and June. They do not begin to moult their juvenile feathers till the following March; many do not begin till they are more than a year old. Some may remain in brown plumage throughout their

301

second winter, though they usually begin to show some adult feathers from January onwards. The moult may take as long as six months to complete. Warmth speeds it, cold retards it. Peregrines do not breed till they are two years old, but one-year birds may select an eyrie and defend territory.

The peregrine is adapted to the pursuit and killing of birds in flight. Its shape is streamlined. The rounded head and wide chest taper smoothly back to the narrow wedge-shaped tail. The wings are long and pointed; the primaries long and slender for speed, the secondaries long and broad to give strength for the lifting and carrying of heavy prey. The hooked bill can pull flesh from bones. It has a tooth on the upper mandible, which fits into a notch in the lower one. This tooth can be inserted between the neck vertebrae of a bird so that, by pressing and twisting, the peregrine is able to snap the spinal cord. The legs are thick and muscular, the toes long and powerful. The toes have bumpy pads on their undersides that help in the gripping of prey. The bird-killing hind toe is the longest of the four, and it can be used separately for striking prey to the ground. The huge pectoral muscles give power and endurance in flight. The dark feathering around the eyes absorbs light and reduces glare. The contrasting facial pattern of brown and white may also have the effect of startling prey into sudden flight. To some extent it also camouflages the large, light-reflecting eyes.

The speed of the peregrine's wing-beat has been recorded as 4.4 beats per second. Comparative figures are: jackdaw 4.3, crow 4.2, lapwing 4.8, woodpigeon 5.2. In level flapping flight the peregrine looks rather pigeon-like, but its wings are longer and more flexible than a pigeon's and they curl higher above the back. The typical flight has been described as a succession of quick wing-beats, broken at regular intervals by long glides with wings extended. In fact, gliding is far from regular, and at least half the peregrine flights I have seen have contained few, if any, glides. When the hawk is not hunting, the flight may seem slow and undulating, but it is always faster than it looks. I have timed it at between thirty and forty miles an hour, and it is seldom less than that. Level pursuit of prey has reached speeds of fifty to sixty miles an hour over distances of a mile or more; speeds in excess of sixty m.p.h. were only attained for a much shorter time. The speed of the vertical stoop is undoubtedly well over a hundred miles an hour, but it is impossible to be more precise. The excitement of seeing a peregrine stoop cannot be defined by the use of statistics.

Peregrines arrive on the east coast from mid-August to November; the majority reach here in late September and the first half of October. They may come in from the sea in any weather conditions, but are most likely to do so on a clear sunny day with a fresh north-west wind blowing. Passage birds may stay in one area for two to three weeks before going south. Return passage lasts from late February to May. Winter residents usually depart in late March or early April. Juvenile falcons are the first peregrines to arrive in the autumn, followed by juvenile tiercels, and later by a few adult birds. Most adults do not come so far south, but remain as close as they can to their breeding territory. This order of migration, which prevails along the European coastline from the North Cape to Brittany, is similar to that observed on the eastern coast of North America. Ringing recoveries suggest that immigrants to the east coast of England have come from Scandinavia. No British-ringed peregrines have been recovered in south-east England. Generally speaking, all the juveniles that wintered in the river valley, and along the estuaries, were paler in color than juveniles from British nests; they had a distinctive wing pattern of light reddish-brown wing coverts and secondaries contrasting with black primaries, similar to that of a kestrel.

The territory in which my observations were made measures roughly twenty miles from east to west and ten miles from north to south. It was hunted over by at least two peregrines each winter, sometimes by three or four. The river valley and the estuary to the east of it are both ten miles in length. Together they formed a long narrow centre to the territory, where at least one peregrine could always be found. Why these particular places were chosen it is difficult to be sure. Most parts of England, including towns and cities, could provide a winter's keep for a resident peregrine, yet certain areas have always been regularly visited, while others have been ignored. Peregrines that have a definite liking for duck or shore birds will obviously be found on the coast, at reservoirs and sewage farms, or in fenland. But the birds that wintered in the valley took a wide range of prey, in which woodpigeons and blackheaded gulls predominated. I think they came here for two reasons: because this was a wintering place that had been used for many years, and because the gravelly streams of the valley provided ideal conditions for bathing. The peregrine is devoted to tradition. The same nesting cliffs are occupied for hundreds of years. It is probable that the same wintering territories are similarly occupied by each generation of juvenile birds. They may in fact be returning to places where their ancestors nested. Peregrines that now nest in the tundra conditions of Lapland and the Norwegian mountains may be the descendants of those birds that once nested in the tundra regions of the lower Thames. Peregrines have always lived as near the permafrost limit as possible.

Peregrines bathe every day. They prefer running water, six to nine inches deep; nothing less than two inches or more than twelve inches is acceptable to them. The bed of the stream must be stony and firm, with a shallow incline sloping gradually down from the bank. They favour those places where the colour of the stream-bed resembles the colour of their own plumage. They like to be concealed by steep banks or overhanging bushes. Shallow streams, brooks, or deep ditches, are preferred to rivers. Salt water is seldom used. Dykes lined with concrete are sometimes chosen, but only if the concrete has been discoloured. Shallow fords, where brown-mottled country lanes are crossed by a fast-running brook, are favourite places. For warning of human approach they rely on their remarkably keen hearing and on the alarm calls of other birds. The search for a suitable bathing place is one of the peregrine's main daily activities, and their hunting and roosting places are located in relation to this search. They bathe frequently to rid themselves of their own feather lice and of the lice that may transfer to them from the prey they have killed. These new lice are unlikely to live long once they have left their natural host species, but they are an additional irritation to which the hawk is most sensitive. Unless the number of lice infesting the hawk's feathers is controlled by regular bathing, there can be a rapid deterioration in health, which is dangerous for a juvenile bird still learning to hunt and kill its prey.

Though there can be many variations, a peregrine's day usually begins with a slow, leisurely flight from the roosting place to the nearest suitable bathing stream. This may be as much as ten to fifteen miles away. After bathing, another hour or two is spent in drying the feathers, preening, and sleeping. The hawk rouses only gradually from his post-bathing lethargy. His first flights are short and unhurried. He moves from perch to perch, watching other birds and occasionally catching an insect or a mouse on the ground. He reenacts the whole process of learning to kill that he went through when he first left the eyrie: the first, short, tentative flights; the longer, more confident ones; the playful, mock attacks at inanimate objects, such as falling leaves or drifting feathers; the games with other birds, changing to a pretence of attack, and then to the first serious attempt to kill. True hunting may be a comparatively brief process at the end of this long reenactment of the hawk's adolescence.

Hunting is always preceded by some form of play. The hawk may feint at partridges, harass jackdaws or lapwings, skirmish with crows. Sometimes, without warning, he will suddenly kill. Afterwards he seems baffled by what he has done, and he may leave the kill where it fell and return to it later when he is genuinely hunting. Even when he is hungry, and has killed in anger, he may sit beside his prey for ten to fifteen minutes before starting to feed. In these cases the dead bird is usually unmarked, and the hawk seems to be puzzled by it. He nudges it idly with his bill. When blood flows, he feeds at once.

Regular hunting over the same area will produce an increasingly effective defensive reaction from possible prey. It is always noticeable that the reaction of birds to a peregrine flying above them is comparatively slight in September and October, but that it steadily increases throughout the winter, till in March it is violent and spectacular. The peregrine has to avoid frightening the same birds too often, or they may leave the area altogether. For this reason he may be seen hunting in the same place for several days in succession, and then not be seen there again for a week or more. He may move only a short distance, or he may go twenty miles away. Individuals vary greatly in their hunting habits. Some hunt across their territory in straight lines five to fifteen miles long. They may suddenly turn about and fly back on the same course to attack birds already made uneasy. These hunting lines may run from estuary to reservoir, from reservoir to valley, and from valley to estuary; or they may follow the lines of flight from roosting places to bathing places. The territory is also effectively quartered by long up-wind flights, followed by diagonal down and cross wind gliding that finishes a mile or two away from the original starting point. Hunting on sunny days is done chiefly by soaring and circling down wind, and is based on a similar diagonal quartering of the ground. When an attack is made, it is usually a single vicious stoop. If it misses, the hawk may fly on at once to look for other prey.

In early autumn, and in spring, when days are longer and the air warmer, the peregrine soars higher and hunts over a wider area. In March, when conditions are often ideal for soaring, his range increases, and by long stoops from a great height he is able to kill larger and heavier prey. Cloudy weather means shorter flights at lower levels. Rain curtails the hunting range still further. Fog reduces it to a single field. The shorter the day the more active the hawk, for there is less time available for hunting. All its activities contract or expand with the shortening or lengthening of days on either side of the winter solstice.

Juvenile peregrines hover whenever the wind is too strong to allow them to circle sufficiently slowly above the area they are surveying. Such hovering usually lasts for ten to twenty seconds, but some birds are more addicted to the habit than others and will hover persistently for long periods. The hunting hawk uses every advantage he can. Height is the obvious one. He may stoop (stoop is another word for swoop) at prey from any height between three feet and three thousand. Ideally, prey is taken by surprise: by a hawk hidden by height and diving unseen to his victim, or by a hawk that rushes suddenly out from concealment in a tree or a dyke. Like a sparrowhawk, the peregrine will wait in ambush. The more spectacular methods of killing are used less often by juveniles than they are by adults. Some soaring peregrines deliberately stoop with the sun behind them. They do it too frequently for it to be merely a matter of chance.

Like all hunters, the peregrine is inhibited by a code of behaviour. It seldom chases prey on the ground or pursues it into cover, in the manner of other hawks, though it is quite capable of doing so. Many adults take only birds in flight, but juveniles are less particular. Peregrines perfect their killing power by endless practice, like knights or sportsmen.

Those most adaptable, within the limits of the code, survive. If the code is persistently broken, the hawk is probably sick or insane.

Killing is simple once the peregrine has the advantage of his prey. Small, light birds are seized in his outstretched foot; larger, heavier birds are stooped at from above, at any angle between ten and ninety degrees, and are often struck to the ground. The stoop is a means of increasing the speed at which the hawk makes contact with his prey. The momentum of the stoop adds weight to the hawk and enables him to kill birds twice as heavy as himself. Young peregrines have to be taught to stoop by their parents; captive birds have to be trained by falconers in a similar way. The action of stooping does not seem to be innate, though it is quickly learnt. The ability to stoop at birds in flight was probably a comparatively recent evolutionary development, superseding capture by follow-chase and the taking of ground-game. Most birds still fly up from the ground when a peregrine passes above them, though this may increase their vulnerability.

The peregrine swoops down towards his prey. As he descends, his legs are extended forward till the feet are underneath his breast. The toes are clenched, with the long hind toe projecting below the three front ones, which are bent up out of the way. He passes close to the bird, almost touching it with his body, and still moving very fast. His extended hind toe (or toes—sometimes one, sometimes both) gashes into the back or breast of the bird, like a knife. At the moment of impact the hawk raises his wings above his back. If the prey is cleanly hit—and it is usually hit hard or missed altogether—it dies at once, either from shock or from the perforation of some vital organ. A peregrine weighs between 1½ and 2½ lbs.; such a weight, falling from a hundred feet, will kill all but the largest birds. Shelduck, pheasants, or great black-backed gulls, usually succumb to a stoop of five hundred feet or more. Sometimes the prey is seized and then released, so that it tumbles to the ground, stunned but still alive; or it may be clutched and carried off to a suitable feeding place. The hawk breaks its neck with his bill, either while he is carrying it or immediately he alights. No flesh-eating creature is more efficient, or more merciful, than the peregrine. It is not deliberately merciful; it simply does what it was designed to do. The crow-catchers of Königsberg kill their prey in the same way. Having decoyed the crows into their nets, they kill them by biting them in the neck, severing the spinal cord with their teeth.

The peregrine plucks feathers from his prey before he begins to eat. The amount of plucking varies, not only with the hunger of the hawk, but also according to individual preference. Some hawks always pluck their prey thoroughly, others pull out only a few beakfuls of feathers. Peregrines hold the prey steady by standing on it, gripping it with the inner talon of one or both feet. Plucking takes two to three minutes.

Eating takes ten minutes to half an hour, depending on the size of the prey; ten minutes for a fieldfare or redshank, half an hour for a pheasant or mallard.

Prey may be eaten where it falls, if it is too heavy to carry off, or if it has landed in a suitable place. Many peregrines seem to be quite indifferent, feeding wherever they happen to make a kill. Others prefer a completely open place, or a completely secluded one. Seventy per cent of the kills I have found were lying on short grass, although most of the land here is arable. Peregrines like a firm surface to feed on. Small kills are often eaten in trees, especially in autumn. Birds reared in tree nests may eat their kills in trees whenever possible. On the coast, some peregrines prefer the top of the sea-wall for feeding, others eat at the foot of the wall, near the water line. The latter may have come from cliff eyries and be used to a steep slope above them as they eat.

A peregrine kill can be easily recognised. The framework of a bird is left on its back, with the wings untouched and still attached to the body by the shoulder-girdles. The breastbone and all the main bones of the body may be quite fleshless. If the head has been left, the neck vertebrae will usually be fleshless also. The legs and back are frequently left untouched. If the breast-bone is still intact, small triangular pieces will have been nipped out of it by the peregrine's bill. (This is not always true of very large birds, which have thicker bones.) When a kill is left with a good deal of meat still on it, the peregrine may return next day, or even several days later, to finish it up. Surplus meat from abandoned kills helps to support foxes, rats, stoats, weasels, crows, kestrels, gulls, tramps, and gypsies. The feathers are used by long-tailed tits in the construction of their nests. I have found an unusual concentration of such nests in areas where many kills have been made.

No other predator conflicts with the peregrine in the pursuit of prey, but it is sometimes prevented from hunting in certain places by the determined and concerted attacks of crows. When man is hunting, the peregrine goes elsewhere. It is remarkably quick to distinguish between an unarmed man and a man with a gun. There is a curious relationship between peregrines and kestrels that is difficult to define. The two species are often seen in the same place, especially in autumn and spring. I rarely saw one of them without finding the other close by. They may share the same bathing places, the peregrine may occasionally rob the kestrel of its prey, the kestrel may feed on kills the peregrine has left, the peregrine may attack birds that the kestrel unwittingly puts up for him. In September and October some peregrines seem to copy the kestrel's way of hunting, and I have seen the two species hovering together over the same field. In a similar way, I have seen a peregrine hunting near a short-eared owl, and apparently mimicking its style of flight. By March the relationship between kestrel and peregrine has changed; the peregrine has become hostile, and will stoop at, and probably kill, any kestrel hovering near him.

QUESTIONS FOR CRITICAL READERS

Remembering and Understanding

1. Using the information Baker provides, write a brief description of the peregrine, including its physical appearance and habits.
2. Describe how the peregrine uses its habitat to obtain food, shelter, and protection.
3. How does Baker establish his authority? Can you separate information based on observation from information he has taken from his reading?

Analyzing and Discussing

4. What does Baker mean when he says that "pictures are like waxworks beside the passionate mobility of the living bird"? Test his statement by comparing a photograph of a bird or some other animal with the living animal.
5. Does it strike you as odd to speak of a bird as having a personality? What does this statement tell you about the way Baker views peregrines?
6. Baker characterizes some of the peregrine's activities as playing. What does the behavior he describes have in common with human play?

Writing

7. Return to Baker's description of some peregrine behavior as play. Write your own description of this behavior without relying on play or other concepts as metaphors.

Young Owls

BRENDAN GALVIN

Galvin is a poet who lives and writes in New England. The poem printed here comes from his 1980 collection Atlantic Flyway. *Galvin sees the owls as the raw material of art rather than of science. He seems no less curious than the scientist, and he does provide information about owls. But his response is aesthetic rather than scientific. To write a poem about owls, rather than simply describe their behavior, is to suggest that they have a meaning beyond themselves, and that part of the business of the poet is to attempt to explain what that meaning might be.*

Now crows mill blackly above them,
yawking as though
something is stuck in their craws,
and a panic of baby white
floats off the nest as if
struck in midflight.

But they are there,
trying deficient wings
and feet like goalies' mitts
at the nest's brink,
trying a gargle of little bones
and a stare like corpse candles,
their black pupils fixed in yellow.

They sit it out,
or lean into the future,
waiting for their buff feathers
to straggle downhill through scrub
till they are dressed like bark.

Visitations of neither
luck nor wisdom, they mean
no frogs in the garden this year,

no hunting the slope under the nest
for lady slippers
langorous with spring.

Dropping to berry tangles
on feet that later, quicker,
will snatch June bugs from the air
and flip them like popcorn
to their beaks,
they waddle toward dusk

and clutches of young terns
in the hollows on Egg Island,
fuzzy about how shadows
drop out of the sun,
how nothing in this world
gets out of its life alive.

QUESTIONS FOR CRITICAL READERS

Remembering and Understanding

1. Summarize the physical and behavioral information Galvin presents about owls.
2. In the third stanza, what does the phrase "dressed like bark" mean?
3. Write a prose paraphrase of the poem, including as much information as you can, in the same order that Galvin uses.

Analyzing and Discussing

4. How does Galvin establish his authority?
5. What does Galvin mean by the phrase "neither luck nor wisdom?"
6. If Galvin were writing as a scientist, what information would he need to include that he has not included here?

Writing

7. Choose some place, person, or animal that may seem to you rather commonplace and mundane. Write a description in which you provide accurate information but also respond aesthetically to your subject.

Synthesizing and Consolidating

1. Use the information provided in the articles in this chapter to explain the concept of evolution as these authors understand it and use it in their descriptions of birds and their behavior.
2. Several of the selections in this chapter explain physical features and behaviors by citing evolutionary processes. Collect and review several of these explanations and use them as examples in an explanation of the role of evolution in the development of physical and behavioral adaptations.
3. Compare Carrighar's description of swans with Vander Wall and Balda's descriptions of foraging. How are these approaches to describing behavior similar? How are they different?
4. How would Carrighar or Austin have written Heinrich's article about eggs? What would have been different? What would have been the same?
5. Using information from several articles in this chapter, write a comprehensive description of the hazards that birds face.
6. Several of the writers in this chapter describe relationships in which birds and other animals or plants depend on each other for survival. Collect these examples and write a summary explanation of mutualistic or symbiotic behavior.
7. Many people fear the extinction of a particular species. But the disappearance of the passenger pigeon has not caused widespread disaster (so far as we know). What would be the result, though, if birds themselves should become extinct? Draw on all of the selections in this chapter as you speculate about this question.

Suggestions for Writing and Research

1. Research the problem of deforestation in the Amazon river basin of South America. How will this deforestation affect not only Brazil, but the rest of the world?
2. How is it possible to choose between trees for birds or development for Third World countries? Or is the choice that simple? Research the role of environmental awareness in developing countries. Does environmental protection automatically work against economic development?
3. There are several captive breeding programs for birds in the United States, for hawks and eagles, whooping cranes, and California Condors, among others. Read about one of these programs and write a summary explanation that includes why the program began, how it operates, and how successful it has been. (You should be able to begin your search for information in *Reader's Guide to Periodical Literature* or a comparable index.)
4. Select some animal other than birds and research its interactions with humans. What is the basis of its relationship with humans? For a subject you might consider such animals as the plains buffalo, mice and rats, or whitetail deer, all of which have had significant interactions with humans.

5. Go watch a bird. Find some local place where birds are plentiful or easy to observe—a pond, the edge of a field, a small patch of woods. Visit that place several times and each time sit quietly for at least forty-five minutes. Go early in the day, or just before sunset. Write a paper in which you report the number and kinds of birds you saw and describe their activities.

6. Write a paper in which you identify and describe at least three different ways of writing about animals. For example, Baker, Carrigher, and Austin represent significantly different approaches. How are these pieces different from each other? What are the differences in their language? What different assumptions do they make about animals?

7. Using the selections in this chapter as models, write two different descriptions of the same thing. You can choose a person or an animal (such as a pet that is readily available to you, or perhaps a farm animal).

    a. In the first description, present only observable details about behavior, physical features, habitats, and other aspects of your subject. Do not imply or infer anything that you cannot observe directly.

    b. For the second description, place the observable details in the context of a story, and/or write a description in which you freely anthropomorphize and imply or infer information that is not directly available by observation.

7

The City and the Country

A Sense of Place

MOST AMERICANS LIVE IN or near large cities, but that has not always been the case. For much of its early history the United States was an agricultural society, and most of the population lived in the country. The movement of people to the cities during the twentieth century was part of the larger change of the United States from a rural, agricultural society to an urban industrial and technological society.

Whether out of nostalgia for the pioneer past or for some other reason, many Americans have consistently romanticized the country, representing it as a near utopia. In this view, the country is a place where life is simple, the people are innocent and friendly, the air and water are clean, and traditional values and virtues reign. The city, in contrast, is an evil, dirty, crowded, and crime-ridden place where people pay no attention to one another and human relationships are difficult, if they exist at all. The city has no virtues; its values are greed and self-indulgence. Of course, not everyone agrees with these views. Some see the country and its people as backward, narrow-minded, and primitive, in contrast to the city, which is progressive, modern, and sophisticated, a place of high culture and excitement.

Debates about the relative advantages and disadvantages of the city and the country are usually part of discussions about which is the better place to live. For example, people may say they want to move to the country in order to get "back to the land" and experience a simple, virtuous country life. Such a statement implies that the place one lives is important because it has some effect on those who live there. People who move to the country because they believe country life and people are simple and virtuous, and country work honest, are hoping that the virtues and values they associate with the country will be available to them. People who take this view attribute the way they feel, or the quality of their lives, to the place they live rather than to their own actions. That is, they believe there is something intrinsic in the place itself, rather than the way they live there, that makes them feel good, or gives them a good or bad life.

The writers in this chapter address the issue of place in a variety of ways. Curtis Badger tells of the decision to sell the farm where members of his family have lived for more than a hundred years, and explores his own connection with that land. Sue Hubbell writes of a special place on her small Ozark farm where she can find spring in the middle of winter. Jeffrey Pasley challenges the romanticized vision of country life and offers a version that is, for him, more realistic and honest. Writing in response to Pasley, Henry Fairlie condemns the madness of city life. Richard Rhodes spent a year with a farm family in Missouri, and here he describes a rather typical farmer's day. Peter Shaw approaches urban population density from an unusual perspective; he likes it and believes it confers certain advantages on the city dweller. In contrast, Gretel Ehrlich writes of the peace of mind she can find living in Wyoming, where, on occasion, she can go for days and see no other living creatures except sheep. Donald McCaig, writing of sheep farming in the mountains of western Virginia, suggests that the "fast lane" is where you find it.

All of these writers are working against the larger background of the positive and negative myths and meanings that have become attached to the city and the country. As you read, you too will need to become aware of your own versions of these myths and of your ideas about the importance of place.

Before You Read

Before you begin reading, answer the following questions in your reading journal.

1. What specific values do you associate with the city and the country? Make a list for each one.

2. Describe specific experiences that you have had in the country or on a farm. Explain your reactions to these experiences. Did they leave you with positive or negative memories?

3. Describe a specific experience you have had in a city. Explain your reactions to this experience and whether it left you with positive or negative memories.

4. How important is it to you to live in a certain place (or kind of place) or to have specific surroundings, such as prairie, city, or desert? Identify and describe a specific place, and explain why it is important to you.

5. Describe a specific stereotype that you have of a person, place, or event in the city or the country, and then try to give a version that is more accurate or that does not rely on the stereotype.

Spring

SUE HUBBELL

Sue Hubbel gave up city life and moved to a farm in the Ozarks in 1973, where she keeps more than eighteen million bees for a living. The selection printed here is from her book A Country Year, published in 1986, in which she reflects on nature and her experiences during a year of living in the country. Hubbell is an active, intelligent, careful observer of her surroundings.

THERE WAS A DAY LAST WINTER when I badly needed springtime, and since it did not appear that spring was going to come to me I went to it. One of the good things about living here is that the lay of the land between river and creek and the steepness of the terrain create different climates and seasons all over the place.

No matter what the calendar says, a few sunbeams bring springtime to the south face of the creek hollow, and so on that sunny winter day I went there. I bundled up in insulated coveralls, insulated boots, scarf, woolen hat and two pairs of gloves, and set off with the dogs across the snow-covered field toward the southeast to the high rocky point where the creek and the river join.

Overhead a rough-legged hawk was quartering the field, hunting in vain for mice. By the calendar's springtime he would be in Canada on the way to his northern breeding grounds; so would the golden-crowned kinglets I discovered at the edge of the field in the cedar and pine trees. Tiny, cheerful, gray-green birds with a patch of brilliant yellow on the top of their heads, the flock of kinglets were inspecting twigs for insect eggs with such keenness that I bothered them not at all as I stood and watched. The cold began to seep in at my feet, however, so I walked on through the woods, breaking a path in the crusty snow.

The soil is poorer and thinner here, on the narrowing strip of land sloping southward. Hardwood trees give way to scrub, grasses and, finally, at the rocky cliffs several hundred feet above the juncture, to the modest plants of a limestone glade. The view from this rocky point is spectacular, and the walk to it is one of my favorites in the winter. With the leaves off the trees, the structure of cliffs along the river and creek and the hills

316

beyond are visible—all the foundations of this beautiful land are there to see.

Water melting from the snow above oozed through the low grasses and dripped from the cliff edge; there, in the sunshine, mosses and lichens were holding their own private but exuberant springtime. All were shades of tender, sweet and vibrant green, and several varieties of mosses were covered with fruiting bodies.

I was warm out of the wind, so I pulled off my heavy coveralls and scrambled down the cliffs to look for the blossoms of harbinger-of-spring which should be growing in the rich soil at the creek's edge. *Erigenia bulbosa* takes its genus name from the Greek *ery-geneia*, "early born," Homer's epithet for Eos, goddess of the dawn. Poking in the leaf mold at the foot of the cliffs, I found the early born, with its bulbous root and clusters of small white flowers.

The climb back up the steep cliffs was harder than my sliding descent, and I had to stop once to catch my breath and peel off my sweatshirt. At the top I found a sunny niche among the lichens and moss and sat down, taking off my heavy boots and socks. Across the creek, the snowy, shadowed woods on the north face of the hollow insisted that it was still winter.

That was in January; now, in April, it is springtime everywhere. The kinglets and the rough-legged hawks are gone. The woods are full of migrating warblers, and the hummingbirds have returned to the feeder by the windows. There are wildflowers everywhere, even on the north face of the river's gorge, on Pigeon Hawk Bluff, where spring comes last and most grudgingly of all. This slope is frosted with the feathery white blossoms of the small tree that as a child in Michigan I had known as shadblow. Ozarkers call it sarviceberry. The tree's botanic name is *Amelanchier arborea*. On the ground under the trees are the pink and white blossoms of rue anemone and the white-blossomed, liver-leafed hepaticas.

In the grass around the cabin the bees are eagerly working golden dandelions and ignoring the bluets and violets. The violets, purple, blue and white, are growing in such profusion that the air is scented with their fragrance. From the upland woods, the sweet odor of wild plum blossoms comes in on every breeze. The bees like wild plum blossoms, and so do I. They smell exactly like cherry Lifesavers taste.

The violets bloom along the dirt roads I drive down to get to my beeyards, and in one yard a special violet, the Johnny-jump-up, which looks like a little pansy, has taken over. I had fenced off these beehives, so that the cows cannot graze near the hives, and the Johnny-jump-ups have pushed out the pasture grasses and surrounded the hives with blossoms, blue and purple with yellow and white centers.

I have a friend, an amateur botanist, who carries a sketch pad with her and draws each flower she identifies. There is no surer way, she tells me, of learning a plant, simply because of the painstaking observation needed to put it on paper. She is right, and some day when I have fewer bees and more time I would like to do this too. But now I am so occupied with the bees that I have not even had time to walk back to the point at the juncture of the hollow and the river where I first found springtime. The season is well advanced there, and I know what I should find, for I have seen it in other years: the wildflower whose common name I like best of all, hoary puccoon. Puccoon is an Indian word. I do not know its meaning, but I like its sound. There are other puccoons, hairy and narrow-leaved, but mine, the hoary, has thick clusters of yellowish-orange blossoms. They are as pretty and showy as any cultivated flowers in a formal garden, and make the rocky glade overlooking the river and creek beautiful beyond telling.

This afternoon when I got back from the beeyards, Nancy was waiting for me. It was Thursday, she pointed out. Nancy works in the office of a small factory in town, and because she is competent she takes her job seriously and finds it hard to leave it behind when she locks the office door. Once, a few years ago, I was listening to her complaints about office politics, and pointed out to her that she was always in a bad mood by Thursday. I could remember what Thursday was like in an office. Friday is still ahead, and by Thursday work deadlines are overwhelming, co-workers have called in sick, and the stupidity of the boss and one's own clear crystalline good sense seem in sharpest contrast. I told her that a good thing about working in an Ivy League university had been that on Thursday there was always a sherry hour to be found somewhere on campus to help put things back in perspective.

Nancy has not lived in university circles and did not know about sherry hours, so I introduced her to them. I now keep a bottle of sherry on hand. Word has gone round, and sometimes we are joined by others for a late-afternoon Thursday sherry hour. But today she was the only one waiting for me, and we decided to walk down to the river first. She wanted to tell me about the really dumb thing the new vendor had done, the terrible mixup with an invoice, what her supervisor had said to her, what she had said to the supervisor and how irritating it was when the computer broke down for the third time.

I nodded and said Umn. I remember what it was like to work in an office, particularly in the springtime.

Before we got to the river, we found patches of Dutchman's-breeches, fern-leafed plants with pinkish-white blossoms shaped like a pair of tiny pantaloons. Nancy kneeled down to take a better look. The river's banks were covered with *Mertensia virginica*, one of the many wildflowers that are called bluebells. The clusters of sky-blue, bell-like flowers were growing so thickly that we could not walk among them without crushing them, so we simply stood and admired.

Back at the cabin we poured glasses of sherry and took lawn chairs to the deck of the barn loft. It is high up there, so we could still have sunshine.

We drank a toast to springtime. The low rays of the sun spread golden light across the greening fields. The breeze was fragrant with wild plum blossoms and violets. There was no more talk of invoices. Instead we sat silently, sipping sherry and watching the buds swell in the western woods until the sun went down behind them.

QUESTIONS FOR CRITICAL READERS

Remembering and Understanding

1. Contrast real spring with the early spring that Hubbell finds in December.
2. Collect Hubbell's use of the five senses in her description, and then describe the information she conveys through each one.
3. Summarize Hubbell's account of the differences between city ways and country ways.

Analyzing and Discussing

4. What are Hubbell's claims about the restorative powers of nature and the country, and how does she illustrate and support these claims? Do you believe these claims are true?
5. In addition to describing her surroundings, Hubbell is taking a position about the quality of life in the country as opposed to the city. Summarize her position, and then write your response to it.
6. Hubbell decides that if spring will not come, she will find it on her own. Apply this to your own life. How do you satisfy your needs even when the world is not especially willing to cooperate with you?

Writing

7. Like Hubbell's botanist friend, choose a place or an object (such as a flower) and sketch it as carefully as you can. Don't be concerned about the artistic merit of your work. Instead, concentrate on details. When you have finished your sketch, write an explanation of what you learned about the subject of your sketch as a result of making the sketch.

We're Selling the Family Farm

———— CURTIS BADGER ————

Curtis Badger has never been a farmer and has never actually lived on the family farm, but the land has been in his family for more than a hundred years. It represents for him a tangible connection with the past and with his family, and for this reason it has acquired special meanings for him.

. . . THERE'S A STRONG NOTE OF FINALITY to that statement, something that conjures up visions of foreclosures and fallow fields, of rusting tractors going to the highest bidder. But there is nothing quite so dramatic about this sale, nothing so immediate. There will be no foreclosure, no auction of equipment, no abdication of a dream. The tragedy lies not so much in human failure, or even the failure of a system. Instead, the failure is one of values and perception; it is a measure of how in the past century our relationship with the land has changed, how we have distanced ourselves from something fundamental and vital.

While a contemporary failed farm story may deal with economic issues, trade surpluses, embargoes, drought, interest rates, natural disasters, or international politics, our farm has fallen victim to a plight that is less specific but far more serious and deeply rooted. It is a small farm— a mixture of open fields, woodlands, and salt marsh—by nature an anachronism in the world of corporate agribusiness.

My uncle used to farm the land, and when he retired several years ago he rented it to another farmer. There is some marketable pine, but it is not good farmland, and the rents have seldom been high enough to pay the county real estate tax. The land is low, and there are only thirty-five cleared acres separated into three small fields.

The beauty of the farm is that it lies along Philips Creek, just west of Hog Island Bay and The Nature Conservancy's 35,000-acre reserve on the coast of Virginia. For years I've had a duck blind at a cedar point along the creek. From there I can see across a meadow of spartina grass— brittle and golden in the early sunlight of winter—to the bay and Hog

Island beyond, where a century ago there was a fishing village, long since claimed by the tides. Oysters grow along a muddy bar in the shallows of the seaside creek, which meanders through the salt marsh, forming property boundaries to the south and east. A small stream breaks off to define the northern boundary.

Sometimes a northeaster will push the tide over the low berm of cedar and groundsel and into the fields, not a pleasant prospect for a farmer who has just put in a fall crop of corn or soybeans. My uncle used to curse the tide and keep a hopeful, helpless vigil for lethal northeasters. As a farmer, he never cared much for the land. The cleared acreage was too small to make grain farming practical and was several miles from his homeplace, which meant driving tractor, combine, bush hog, and other equipment over busy public roads. He persisted out of habit, I guess, refusing to give in to the encroaching salt marsh, the bay myrtle and sheep bur, the capriciousness of the tides.

Since the death of my grandfather in 1953, my uncle and father have owned the farm jointly, sharing expenses and profit, when there was one. My father saw the farm from a different perspective than my uncle. He was an accountant and worked in an office, and the farm represented an escape. He hunted his setter around the field margins and greenbrier thickets where the quail coveyed. And he took delight in hiking the woodlots, assessing the size and health of the pines and tracing the western property boundary from a concrete marker to a notched oak tree. As long as you own land, he told me, you'll never have to worry about having a place to hunt.

My uncle has wanted to sell the farm for years; my father has stubbornly resisted. My uncle had better land to farm and hunt; my father never had to shadowbox a northeaster.

Two events brought my family to the reluctant decision to sell the farm. In 1977 the Virginia General Assembly passed a law requiring fair market value standards for real estate assessment. This meant that although the farm was of questionable agricultural value, it had development potential because it was on the water. Suddenly, by legislative magic, our land was transformed from a marginal farm to a marketable commodity, and it was assessed with the assumption that an RV part and a Putt Putt Golf Course could replace my duck blind on the cedar point at any time.

Although we had no intention then of selling the property, and certainly not to a builder of RV parks and Putt Putts, the annual assessment and tax bill quickly escalated. Soon, the rental income would not cover the taxes, and last year, in a season that broke many farmers, our renter could afford to pay nothing at all.

The second reason we are selling is that my uncle and father have gotten older. My uncle has emphysema, and my father had a slight stroke last winter and can no longer search out the popular quail coverts. To keep the farm would be an unaffordable luxury; to sell it would mean some degree of financial security for both men. There really was no decision.

The saga of our family farm is symptomatic of a disease that is quietly claiming much good land in rural America. It is not the failed farmer story or, more accurately, the story of farmer as victim. It will provoke no Farm Aid concerts, no movies with a social message. Although it lacks stage presence, what is happening to our farm is slow, insidious, and far more damaging than contemporary drama.

When a working farm faces foreclosure, it will probably be taken over by a larger working farm. It's not an attractive process, but the land will remain in agriculture. Our farm will never be a farm again. It is too small, too isolated, to be an efficient producer in the world of agribusiness. And its "commercially developable" tax bracket narrows the options uncomfortably. How many families could afford to subsidize marginal farmland, given the pressures of rising taxes and lucrative offers from developers?

Near our farm there are hundreds more like it, many owned by widows whose only income is from Social Security, supplemented by a modest land rental. Taxes have risen dramatically, especially on farms near the water, and many landowners have been forced to sell places that have been in the family for generations. And who can blame them? How can you live with the insecurity of a modest pension and uncertain rent income when faced with the prospect of a few hundred thousand tucked away in CDs and municipal bonds? The farms die, and the RV parks and waterfront retirement villas spread like a plague of locusts.

The sad irony is that a century ago our farm was a self-contained unit. My family lived in a large frame house in the center of the largest field. The only remnants of the house are two stark, crumbling chimneys and a brick foundation wreathed in honeysuckle. The scuppernong grapevine that grew on an arbor behind the house has gone feral; it has enveloped what remains of the rotting porch beams and is forever trying to make its way into the soybeans that surround the house lot.

The thirty-five acres were sufficient to provide a good living for my great-grandparents. They grew vegetables for the table and for the market, and the corn crop subsidized the livestock and poultry business, which in turn provided eggs, milk, cheese, butter, ham and bacon, sausage and scrapple, soap and lard, and a frying chicken for Sunday dinner. My father remembers tending a sweet potato crop on the pine island where my duck blind is. Many of my ancestors were born in the house; a small cemetery nearby makes the cycle of farm life complete.

During the past hundred years this small farm fed, clothed, and otherwise nurtured four generations of my family. Its profits helped my great-grandparents' sons buy farms of their own and sent their two daughters to college. In less than a lifetime, the farm has gone from a provider of life to a liability. And therein lies the tragedy.

What remains is the scrap heap of human history, the detritus of a time of innocence. We cling to these things as tenaciously as the scuppernong embraces its collapsed arbor. On the pine island is a small freshwater pool, a good place to see wildlife. Scrub cedars grow in thick folds around the pond, and one winter, when I was exploring the woods, I found beneath a tangled mound of greenbrier a pile of old, handmade bricks. It was here at the little pool that my ancestors dug the red clay to make the bricks that formed the foundation and fireplaces of the house. When my wife and I built a house a few years ago we went to the farm and carefully removed several hundred bricks from the grip of the honeysuckle and wild scuppernong. We carried them a few at a time across a muddy field to the car, and we took them home and built a walkway. We could have bought new bricks cheaply, or gotten some for free from other abandoned farmhouses nearer where we lived. But those bricks would have had no life.

The old house began to collapse when I was a boy, and my father and I removed the heart-pine flooring and stored it in a barn, raw material for a future woodworking project. That was twenty-five years ago, and we still are searching for a project noble enough for the wood.

A part of our family Christmas ritual was going to the farm to cut a cedar to decorate. The prickly texture of cedar, the rich aroma that fills the house, are part of the sensations of Christmas. Cedars are prolific at the farm, and we transplant seedlings to our yard, where they become special trees among the native cedars.

In glass jars I keep pottery shards collected from the bare fields of the farm. There are even a few arrow points among them. We found an old trash dump near what was once the farm's west entrance, and we have a collection of glass jars and bottles that were my family's kitchen discards generations ago.

Beneath the arbor were large rocks that my great-grandfather had used as ballast in his schooner. Captain John Badger, according to family history, joined the California Gold Rush in 1849, at age seventeen. After becoming ill with malaria in Panama, he made his way to San Francisco, where he slowly regained his strength and set out for the goldfields. He apparently had some success, and ten years later he returned to Virginia to operate a small fleet of merchant ships purchased with his Gold Rush bounty. Unfortunately, he had the poor judgment to run the Union blockade during the Civil War and lost his schooners in the process. After the war, he returned to the family tradition of farming, and the rocks are all that remain of his Gold Rush adventure.

Captain John's ballast stones are now in our yard. When we moved two years ago, they were among the first items in the moving van.

When a piece of land, no matter how modest, has been in your family for generations, you come to know it intimately. It is as familiar as your child's voice, your lover's touch. Although I never lived on the farm, I know it as I know the lines on my face. On many pre-dawn mornings in winter I have made my way without a light through the pine forest to my duck blind on the far side of the woods. Is it genetic navigation—the eyes of Captain John leading me through the cedar thickets and around the mounds of greenbrier?

The pines were harvested in the thirties, when my father was young. The subsequent generation has grown slowly. When the stand was young it was thick and verdant, and no one thought to thin it out so the timber could grow taller and faster. As a result, there are a lot of fairly old trees that look alike. But the trees that survived the harvest of the thirties are the venerable giants. They have stories to tell. My favorites are the old cedars that line the creekbank, their twisted roots laid bare by the tides. Their limbs have become contorted by storms sweeping in from the low marsh and the sea. They look painfully arthritic, but their foliage is green and lush. The roots sink deep into the clay soil and tap some ancient reservoir. These trees seem to have been here as long as the land, and their roots are so complex they seem to be part of it. They seem not so much to bore into the soil as to embrace it, to protect and preserve it.

The land and the trees and the salt marsh—the farm—have served my family similarly. The land is like a complex root structure that binds the generations. In our family scrapbook is a yellowed, faded photograph of my great-grandparents and their family on the porch of the old farmhouse. It is dated November 1901. Captain John wears a gray suit and vest and is standing in the center of the group. He was seventy when this photograph was taken, but he still appears lean and strong. His beard is long and untrimmed, and he holds a pipe in his left hand. His right hand is rather jauntily stuck in his pants pocket. To his left is his wife, Sue, wearing an austere black dress, her dark hair parted in the middle and pulled back tightly. Their children stand around them. The men are in suits, and the women wear their Sunday dresses. Seated on the porch is Aunt Easter Badger, a former slave freed by Captain John, a woman who became, in name and in spirit, a member of the family.

I can remember only one of the persons in the photograph. The young girl seated with Aunt Easter is my great aunt Susie, whom I saw only a few times before her death. Yet I know these people. We have held the land in common, and it binds us as surely as the blood of family.

In the land's eyes, of course, we were just passing through. There is comfort in knowing that the land endures, that there is something about this particular piece of property that will remain with our family for generations to come. The tragedy lies not in the sale of a single farm but in what the sale symbolizes. Three generations ago the farm gave sustenance to the members of a large family and lent their lives purpose and direction. Today it is not worth the trouble to strike plow to soil. Our land is no longer valued as a farm but as a commodity—real estate.

So what are we to do? Shall we clear the pine island and subdivide it into tiny parcels, each with its own water and electric hookup? Shall we bulldoze what remains of the old house and scuppernong and build a recreation center, complete with video game room and swimming pool? Shall we carve a marina out of the salt marsh? Build a dock and tackle shop?

The profits are seductive, but perhaps we are too intimidated by Captain John's shadowy frown, by his continued presence upon the land. What we need is a buyer who understands the importance of continuity with the land, someone who realizes that land, like a living thing, can never be owned. We need someone who understands the importance of old bricks and pottery shards, someone who knows that the roots of twisted cedars bind more than sandy soil.

QUESTIONS FOR CRITICAL READERS

Remembering and Understanding

1. Summarize the memories and associations Badger connects with the house and land he describes here.
2. Why does Badger want to prevent the farm from being sold to developers?

Analyzing and Discussing

3. Badger says the sale is symbolic. What does it symbolize?
4. Badger clearly attaches values to the land. What are those values? List them, and then write a summary in which you explain the values Badger relates to the land.
5. Is Badger, in your opinion, being overly nostalgic or romantic about the farm and its importance? To what extent might he be operating with stereotyped notions of the past, of farming, and perhaps even of his own family?
6. What does Badger mean when he calls artifacts of the farm "detritus of a time of innocence"?

Writing

7. Badger has kept pieces of the farm: bricks, stones, and lumber. Identify items that are mementos of your own family or some person who is important to you for some reason. Describe them and tell their story.

The Idiocy of Rural Life

———— JEFFREY L. PASLEY ————

Jeffrey Pasley grew up in Kansas and attended college in Minnesota. He has worked as a writer for the Washington Monthly *and* The New Republic, *where this selection first appeared. In this article he attacks what he believes to be the clichés and stereotypes of rural life and attempts to set them straight. In some ways he has the perspective and intensity of the convert, since he seems especially pleased to have left the country and moved to the city.*

The bourgeoisie has subjected the country to the rule of the towns. It has created enormous cities, has greatly increased the urban population as compared with the rural, and has thus rescued a considerable part of the population from the idiocy of rural life.

—MARX AND ENGELS, *The Manifesto of the Communist Party*

If we let Republican farm policies drive our family farmers off the land, then your food won't be grown by farmers whose names are Jones or Smith or Anderson. No, your food will be raised by Tenneco Corporation, or Chevron, or ITT.

—SENATOR TOM HARKIN, *Democrat of Iowa*

THE IDEA THAT PEOPLE STILL FARM for a living in 1986 is an alien and yet somehow romantic one, redolent of grandparents and "Little House on the Prairie." A 1986 *New York Times* poll reported that fifty-eight percent of Americans believe that "farm life is more honest and moral than elsewhere," and sixty-seven percent think that "farmers have closer ties to their families than elsewhere." Images of rural life dominate the "Americana" that passes for tradition in the United States. At a holiday like Thanksgiving, when we are supposed to give thanks to our Pilgrim ancestors and the "bounty" before us, we pay homage to the values embodied in the idea of the "family farm."

At one time, this reverence for farm life made sense. The United States began as an agricultural nation. In 1790, ninety-three percent of the American population worked on farms. Agricultural products made up eighty percent of exports. The Founders, knowing which side their breadbasket was buttered on, heaped extravagant praise on the nation's farmers. "Cultivators of the earth are the most valuable citizens," wrote Thomas Jefferson, "They are the most vigorous, the most independent, the most virtuous, & they are tied to the country & wedded to its liberty and interests by the most lasting bonds."

The "family farm" remained a powerful myth long after it ceased to be a political fact. "The great cities rest upon our broad and fertile prairies. Burn down your cities and leave our farms, and your cities will spring up again as if by magic; but destroy our farms and the grass will grow in the streets of every city in the country," thundered Populist leader William Jennings Bryan. Yet as the myth gained strength, Americans were actually leaving the farm by the millions. Though the number of farmers continued to grow until 1920, the cities grew much faster, and the percentage of the American population working in agriculture declined with every census after 1790. The figure dropped to thirty percent by 1910, and to three percent in 1985. As the country grew, it exposed its citizens to creature comforts and other opportunities to prosper more easily, which made it hard to keep the farmers down on the farm. As farmers sold out or quit, those who remained bought up their land. Average farm size increased from 152 acres in 1930 to 441 acres in 1985.

I grew up outside Topeka, Kansas, attended a rural high school that had an Ag-Science building but no auditorium, and graduated from a college in the Minnesota farm country. In my experience, the standard image of the farmer has more to do with urban romanticism than with reality. Yet when the most recent farm crisis hit the nation's front pages and movie screens in 1985, the "family farm" captured the national imagination. Journalists suddenly found the stuff of Greek tragedy in Ames, Iowa. "Beauty is a cruel mask," wrote Paul Hendrickson of the *Washington Post*, "when the earth rolls right up to the edge of the interstate, freshly turned. When the rosebud trees are bleeding into pinks and magentas. When the evening rain is soft as lanolin." And so on.

With the papers full of stories about farmers going out of business, committing suicide, or shooting their bankers, farm-state politicians and activists began to campaign for a program specifically to help "family" farms, a proposal that evolved into the "Save the Family Farm Act." Introduced in October by Harkin and Representative Richard Gephardt of Missouri, the bill would impose mandatory controls on the amount farmers could produce and the extent of land they could farm, and would force larger farmers to set aside a larger percentage of their acreage. The bill would roughly double commodity prices (followed by additional yearly increases), sharply increasing the cost of raw food products. A small price to pay, its proponents say, so that family farmers can afford to maintain their traditional way of life. For supporters of the bill, the question is not primarily economic. On humanitarian grounds, they want to preserve the family farm as a way of life. On social grounds, they want a Jeffersonian countryside of small, independent landowners. Yet when I asked Charles O. Frazier of the National Farmers Organization, which supports the Harkin bill, whether the measure might hurt farmers in the long run, he replied, "To hell with the long run, we're talking about running a business."

Farmers are just like everyone else. They want to make money and live better than their parents did—and better than their neighbors, if possible. Urbanites often confuse the folksy ways of some farmers with an indifference to material wealth and the refinements that it brings. The difference between farmers and city-dwellers lies not in a different attitude toward money, but in different choices about what to spend it on. Washington lawyers want to make money to buy a BMW and a vacation in Paris. The average farmer may prefer a big pickup truck with floodlights on top and a motor home he can take to Florida for the winter. Indeed, the young farmers who are in the most trouble today got that way by expanding their operations too quickly in the 1970s. Farmers aren't uniquely greedy, just ambitious like any other businesspeople.

In any case, family ownership of farms is not in danger. Nonfamily corporations operate only 0.3 percent of the nation's farms, own only 1.6 percent of the farmlands, and account for only 6.5 percent of total sales of farm products. Agriculture simply doesn't offer a big enough return to attract many large corporations. Though farmland has become concentrated in the hands of fewer landowners, more than half of the large farms are owned by families, in many cases organized as partnerships or family corporations. "The family farm today is grandpa, two sons, and some grandsons who all help manage the place. The family farm of the future is a family farm corporation. These are stronger operations than the old-style family farms," said Jim Diggins, vice president of Farmer's National Company, an Omaha farm management firm.

The USDA divides farms into five classes: rural residences ("hobby farmers"), small family, family, large family, and very large farms. The farm crisis has left the large and very large family farms relatively untouched. Because of their economies of scale, even when prices drop they can still make a profit. Large family farmers operate an average of 1,807 acres, hold an average of $1.6 million in assets, and clear an average income of around $78,000 a year; and they are located in areas where living costs are low. Families on very large farms hold an average of 3,727 acres and net an average annual family income in 1983 of almost $600,000.

What the Pa Ingalls fans have in mind are rural residences and small family farms, which usually occupy three hundred acres or less. Although these small farmers make up two-thirds of the total, however, they do not depend on agriculture for their living. According to the USDA, their "off-farm income" has exceeded their "on-farm income" ever since 1967. The yeomen of 1986 till the soil only as a sideline, and make ninety percent to one hundred percent of their income from jobs or businesses off the farm. So the "farm crisis" isn't impoverishing them.

In fact, just about the only ones really endangered by the current crisis are medium-sized family farmers. It is this group, which amounts to one-fourth of all farmers, whom the Save the Family Farm Act proposes to save. They are hardly what Jefferson had in mind. On average, they own about eight hundred acres with assets approaching $1 million. Despite their size, they are far from self-sufficient. These are the farmers, by and large, who depend on government subsidies. Their troubles lie in the basic economic facts of the institution. Unlike small farmers, who have other sources of income, or large farmers, who have diversified multimillion-dollar operations, the family farmer gets paid only when he sells his crops. In between harvests, he must borrow money if he is to stay in business and feed his family. In no other industry does a worker need to take out loans in order to keep his job. The farmer is at the mercy of the interest rate, as well the weather and the grain markets. They have the vulnerabilities of workers and businessmen with few of the benefits—neither employment security and benefits on the one hand, nor freedom and the possibility of lavish income on the other.

These family farmers occupy a precarious center between the larger and smaller operations. Their farms are big enough to require full-time work but not big enough to lower costs or allow them to take full advantage of new technology. In order to compete with the large farms, the family farmer has to invest in the same expensive machinery and chemicals. Because he has fewer assets, his debts are proportionately much higher. He often has to sell his crop when he needs to make a payment, rather than when the price is highest. His high costs relative to his size make his profit margin razor-thin when it exists at all.

Thus medium-sized family farmers rely heavily on the increasing value of their land to help them pay their debts and get new loans. While inflation plagued the rest of the country in the 1970s, family farmers experienced a boom, as food prices and especially land values climbed to unprecedented heights. When inflation slowed down in the 1980s, so did the farm economy, sending land values through the floor. The farmers who invested heavily in new land on the wave of rising values found themselves hopelessly trapped when the values fell. The moral of this tale cannot be missed: those family farmers' fortunes depended not on their farming abilities, but on land values, a factor out of their control. Their ownership of land made them only more dependent. According to the USDA, farmers that leased more land weathered the crisis better, since they had fewer debts to pay at inflated interest rates. The family farmer has always walked this economic treadmill. The United States had its first farm crisis, Shay's Rebellion in 1786, before it had a Constitution.

How then, did American family farmers become, in Harkin's words, "the most efficient and productive in the world"? Family farmers can keep labor costs very low because the family provides the bulk of the labor. Family farms operate under vastly different labor standards than the rest of American industry. "Child labor laws do not apply to family farms because family farms must have child labor to survive," wrote Minnesota politician and family farm alumnus Darrell McKigney. "Twenty or thirty years ago farm families commonly had ten or more children. [With automation] today five or six is a more common size." From a very early age, family farm children participate in every phase of the operation, from work with dangerous heavy equipment to close contact with carcinogenic chemicals and disease-carrying animals. In numerous farm areas, so many children are taken out of school at harvest time that the schools officially close until the harvest is finished. Practices that would be outrageous at a textile mill suddenly become all warm and cuddly when they appear on the family farm.

　　Family farmers also achieve efficiency through a draconian work schedule that no self-respecting union would allow. "The farm family does physically demanding and highly stressful work at least fourteen hours a day (often at least eighteen hours a day during harvest season), seven days a week, 365 days a year without a scheduled vacation or weekends off," wrote McKigney. "The farmer must endure all of this without the benefit of a health plan, safety regulations, a retirement plan, workmen's compensation, or any of the benefits that most U.S. labor unions demand." Psychologist Peter Keller, past president of the Association for Rural Mental Health, pointed out that many farmers are permanently tied to their farms. A dairy farmer, for instance, cannot just take off for a two-week vacation and not milk his cows. "Farmers lose perspective on the other things in life," said Keller. "The farm literally consumes them."

　　And the family farm physically consumes those who work on it, too. According to the National Safety Council, farming is the nation's most dangerous job—more dangerous even than working in a mine. In 1983 farming clocked in at 55 job-related deaths per 100,000 workers, or five times the rate for all major industries combined. In 1984 Tom Knudson of the *Des Moines Register* published a Pulitzer Prize-winning series that cataloged the myriad health and safety risks run by farmers. Farmers working with powerful farm machinery face death or maiming by crushing, chopping, asphyxiation, or electrocution. ("As he reached for a stalk of corn dangling from the corn picker, Vern Tigges of Dexter felt a jolt.

In the next moments in a fierce and frantic struggle with the machine, three fingers were ripped from his hand.") They may be poisoned by the nitrogen dioxide gas that accumulates in grain silos, or have their lungs permanently damaged from breathing the air in enclosed hog pens. They may be crippled by "farmer's lung disease," caused by moldy grain dust. They may develop leukemia from contact with herbicides used on corn. (Iowa farmers contract leukemia twenty-four percent more frequently than the average American.) Knudson wrote that recent health findings exploded "the myth of farming as the good life of fresh air and sunshine."

But what about the benefits of good-old-fashioned-lemonade values and the supportive friendliness of a rural community? Though hard data is difficult to come by, many small towns appear to suffer from teenage pregnancy, alcoholism, and other social maladies at rates that are higher than average. One New England study showed relatively high suicide rates among farmers during a period antedating the farm crisis. And rural communities haven't always stood by their financially troubled members. Sociologist Paul Lasley's Iowa Farm and Rural Life Poll reported that a majority of Iowa farmers felt they received little or no support from their churches, neighbors, schools, or local voluntary organizations. At a "town meeting" with Representative Tim Penny, Democrat of Minnesota, in New Market, Minnesota, I heard farmers ridicule the idea of slightly higher property taxes to improve the area's meager school system practically in the same breath that they demanded higher subsidies for themselves. These things never happened on "The Waltons."

The usual lesson gleaned from the facts of farm life is that there is nothing wrong with the family farm that higher commodity prices won't solve. Yet farm programs have come and farm programs have gone, and still farmers (and especially farmers' children) have left, for the simple reason that life is usually better off the farm. "It is a way of life, but so was the village blacksmith," says economist William H. Peterson. The urban "wage-slave" worker, for all his lack of "independence" and supposed alienation from his work, has some decided advantages over the rural yeoman. He has the security of a regular income, and definite hours set aside for his leisure. More often than not, the law guarantees the nonfarmer a safe place to work, and protects him from the whims of his employer. The urban wage-earner has daily contact with a wide variety of other people, and access to cultural events and decent public services.

Proponents of Harkin-Gephardt and similar measures worry about where farmers will go once they leave the land. Yet former farmers do not just fade away. They have skills and work habits that many employers find attractive. (If they sell their farms, they will also have several hundred thousand dollars.) Growing farm management companies hire experienced farmers to manage large rented operations, under much more favorable terms and conditions than they could get on their own. Farmers working for others would demand better working conditions. Many states now have retraining programs for those who give up farming and want to learn a new trade or profession.

I saw the movie *Country* on a rainy Monday night in Topeka. Two farmers and their wives and a group of teenage girls were the only other people in the theater. The farmers complained loudly throughout the first hour of the film, and then left, shaking their heads in disgust. The girls sat through the final credits, sniffling at the plight of Sam Shepard and Jessica Lange. At a farm protest rally in Minnesota, I heard a song that went like this:

> Now some folks say
> There ain't no hell
> But they don't farm
> So they can't tell.

We should take the singer at his word. Tyrants from Stalin to Mao to Pol Pot have subjugated their populations by forcing them to "stay on the land." Given the conditions of life on the family farm, if ITT or Chevron or Tenneco really does try to force some family farmers off their land, they might well be doing them a favor.

QUESTIONS FOR CRITICAL READERS

Remembering and Understanding

1. What is Pasley's main point about farm life? Re-state it and summarize the main evidence he uses to support that point.
2. Use the statistics Pasley provides to write a summary description of contemporary farming in the United States.
3. What does Pasley think is wrong with most descriptions of farm life, including those in popular films?

Analyzing and Discussing

4. What is at stake here? Why does Pasley want to demystify and de-mythify rural life? Why is it important to say the things he is saying?
5. How could misconceptions about farmers and farming contribute to what is commonly called "the farm problem"?
6. What would be lost if the family farm disappeared?

Writing

7. Explore the ways that some aspect of American life is usually represented by films or books, the media, advertising, and public opinion in general. Identify the clichés and stereotypes that people commonly use and then write a paper in which you criticize those myths and stereotypes and provide accurate information.

The Idiocy of Urban Life

Or The Cow's Revenge

——— HENRY FAIRLIE ———

Fairlie is an Englishman who has lived for many years in the United States. In recent years he has written a great deal about contemporary American politics for The New Republic, *where this article first appeared. He wrote this selection in response to Pasley's "The Idiocy of Rural Life." As you read, keep in mind Fairlie's usual perspective as a political writer. Fairlie also appears to have lived in cities all of his life. He has a reputation for having a sharp wit, and you may want to consider whether you should take everything he says at face value.*

BETWEEN ABOUT 3 A.M. and 6 A.M. the life of the city is civil. Occasionally the lone footsteps of someone walking to or from work echo along the sidewalk. All work that has to be done at those hours is useful—in bakeries, for example. Even the newspaper presses stop turning forests into lies. Now and then a car comes out of the silence and cruises easily through the blinking traffic lights. The natural inhabitants of the city come out from damp basements and cellars. With their pink ears and paws, sleek, well-groomed, their whiskers combed, rats are true city dwellers. Urban life, during the hours when they reign, is urbane.

These rats are social creatures, as you can tell if you look out on the city street during an insomniac night. But after 6 A.M., the two-legged, daytime creatures of the city begin to stir; and it is they, not the rats, who bring the rat race. You might think that human beings congregate in large cities because they are gregarious. The opposite is true. Urban life today is aggressively individualistic and atomized. Cities are not social places.

The lunacy of modern city life lies first in the fact that most city dwellers who can do so try to live outside the city boundaries. So the two-legged creatures have created suburbs, exurbs, and finally rururbs (rurbs to some). Disdaining rural life, they try to create simulations of it. No effort is spared to let city dwellers imagine they are living anywhere but in a city: patches of grass in the more modest suburbs, broader spreads in the richer ones further out; prim new trees planted along the streets; at the foot of the larger back yards, a pretense to bosky woodlands. Black & Decker thrives partly on this basic do-it-yourself rural impulse in urban life; and with the declining demand for the great brutes of farm tractors, John Deere has turned to the undignified business of making dinky toy tractors for the suburbanites to ride like Roman charioteers as they mow their lawns.

In the city itself gentrification means two tubs of geraniums outside the front door of a town house that has been prettified to look like a country cottage. The homes, restaurants, and even offices of city dwellers are planted thick with vegetation. Some executives have window boxes inside their high-rise offices; secretaries, among their other chores, must now be horticulturists. Commercials on television, aimed primarily at city dwellers, have more themes of the countryside than of urban life. Cars are never seen in a traffic jam, but whiz through bucolic scenery. Lovers are never in tenements, but drift through sylvan glades. Cigarettes come from Marlboro Country. Merrill Lynch is a bull. Coors is not manufactured in a computerized brewery, but taken from mountain streams.

The professional people buy second homes in the country as soon as they can afford them, and as early as possible on Friday head out of the city they have created. The New York intellectuals and artists quaintly say they are "going to the country" for the weekend or summer, but in fact they have created a little Manhattan-by-the-Sea around the Hamptons, spreading over the Long Island potato fields whose earlier solitude was presumably the reason why they first went there. City dwellers take the city with them to the country, for they will not live without its pamperings. The main streets of America's small towns, which used to have hardware and dry goods stores, are now strips of boutiques. Old-fashioned barbers become unisex hairdressing salons. The brown rats stay in the cities because of the filth the humans leave during the day. The rats clean it up at night. Soon the countryside will be just as nourishing to them, as the city dwellers take their filth with them.

The recent dispersal of the urban middle-class population is only the latest development in this now established lunatic pattern. People who work in Cleveland live as far out as lovely Geauga and Ashtabula counties in northeast Ohio, perhaps 30 or 50 miles away. A bank manager in Chardon, which used to be a gracious market town in Geauga, once explained to me how the city people who come to live there want about five acres of land. "But they want the five acres for themselves alone, and not for others who come to follow their example, though no one is going to supply the services—electricity, gas, sewerage, water—for a few people living on their five acres. So the place fills up, and soon they've rebuilt the urban life they said they were escaping. What is more, they don't like paying for those services, since the rich come out to escape the high city taxes." They also force up the price of land and old houses, so that real estate is put beyond the reach of farmers and others who must work there.

In the old industrial cities, people lived near their places of work. The mill hands lived around the cotton mill, and the mill owner lived close at hand, in the big house on the hill, looking down on the chimney stacks belching out the smoke that was the evidence they were producing and giving employment. The steelworkers and the steel magnate lived close to the steel mill. The German brewer Miller lived next to his brewery in Milwaukee. The city churches had congregations that were representative of both the resident population and the local working population. It wasn't so much that work gave meaning to life as that it created a community that extended into and enriched the residential community, and sustained a solidarity among the workers. It was the auto-makers, especially the ever revolutionary Henry Ford, who realized that their own product enabled them to build factories far from the dispersed homes of the workers, and not unconsciously they appreciated that a dispersed work force would be docile.

Work still gives meaning to rural life, the family, and churches. But in the city today work and home, family and church, are separated. What the office workers do for a living is not part of their home life. At the same time they maintain the pointless frenzy of their work hours in their hours off. They rush from the office to jog, to the gym or the YMCA pool, to work at their play with the same joylessness. In the suburbs there is only an artificial community life—look at the notice board of community activities in a new satellite town like Reston, outside Washington. They breathlessly exhort the resident to a variety of boring activities—amateur theatricals, earnest lectures by officers of the United Nations Association, sing-songs—a Tupperware community culture as artificial as the "lake" in the supposed center of the town. These upright citizens of Reston were amazed one day when they found that their bored children were as hooked on drugs as those in any ghetto.

Even though the offices of today's businesses in the city are themselves moving out to the suburbs, this does not necessarily bring the workers back closer to their workplace. It merely means that to the rush-hour traffic into the city there is now added a rush-hour traffic out to the suburbs in the morning, and back around and across the city in the evening. As the farmer walks down to his farm in the morning, the city dweller is dressing for the first idiocy of his day, which he not only accepts but even seeks—the journey to work.

This takes two forms: solitary confinement in one's own car, or the discomfort of extreme overcrowding on public transport. Both produce angst. There are no more grim faces than those of the single drivers we pedestrians can glimpse at the stoplights during the rush hour. It is hard to know why they are so impatient in the morning to get to their useless and wearisome employments; but then in the evening, when one would have thought they would be relaxed, they are even more frenetic. Prisoners in boxes on wheels, they do not dare wonder why they do it. If they take to public transit, there may still be the ritual of the wife driving the breadwinner to the subway station, and meeting him in the evening. Life in the suburbs and exurbs has become a bondage to the hours of journeying.

The car, of course, is not a vehicle suitable to the city. The problems of traffic in the city, over which urban planners have wracked their brains for years, could be simply eliminated if private cars were banned, or if a swinging tax were levied on those who drive into the city alone. The dollar toll in New York should be raised to five dollars—each way. There should be a toll on all the bridges crossing the Potomac from Virginia, and at every point where the rush-hour drivers cross the District line from Maryland. The urban dwellers in Virginia and Maryland make sure that their jurisdictions obstruct any legitimate way the District might force the suburban daytime users of the city to pay for its manifold services. But ten dollars a day to cross into Washington, in addition to parking fees, would soon cut down the urban idiocy of bringing a small room to work and parking it in precious space for eight hours.

On the bus or subway each morning and evening other urban dwellers endure the indignity of being crushed into unwelcome proximity with strangers whom they have no wish to communicate with except in terms of abuse, rancor, and sometimes violent hostility. The wonder is not that there is an occasional shooting on public transit, but that shootings are not daily occurrences. The crushing of people together on the subway can have unintended results. One of my memories is of being on a London tube at rush hour in my younger days, pressed against a young woman who was with her boyfriend. To my surprise, though not unwelcome, her hand slipped into mine. It squeezed. Mine squeezed back. Her expression when they got out at Leicester Square, and she found she'd been holding my hand, and even had begun pulling me off the train, has not been easy to forget in 35 years. But generally even eye contact on public transport is treated as an act of aggression or at least harassment.

This primary urban activity of getting to and from work has other curious features. As every Englishman visiting America for the first time remarks, the smell of deodorants on a crowded bus or subway in the morning is overpowering. Even the stale smell of the human body would be preferable. It must account for the glazed looks—perhaps all deodorants contain a gas introduced by the employers to numb the urban office workers to the fatuity of their labors.

But whether they have come by car or public transit, the urban office workers must continue their journey even after they have gotten to the city. They then must travel in one of the banks of elevators that often run the height of three city blocks or more. Once again they are herded into confined spaces. City people are so used to moving in herds that they even fight to cram themselves into the elevators, as they do into buses or subway cars, as if it mattered that they might get to their pointless occupations a minute later. The odd thing about the elevators themselves is that there are no fares for distances often longer than those between two bus stops. Office elevators are public transit, free to anyone who needs to use them—but there's no such thing as a free elevator ride, as the president will tell you. Banks of elevators occupy large areas of valuable city land on every floor. This and the cost of running and maintaining them is written into the rents paid by the employers. If the urban workers had not been reduced to a docile herd, they would demand that the employers who expect them to get to work subsidize all the public transport into the city, while leaving those who bring their rooms on wheels to pay for them themselves.

In the modern office building in the city there are windows that don't open. This is perhaps the most symbolic lunacy of all. Outdoors is something you can look at through glass but not touch or hear. These windows are a scandal because they endanger the lives of office workers in case of fire. But no less grievous, even on the fairest spring or fall day the workers cannot put their heads outside. The employers do not mind this, may have even conspired with the developers to dream up such an infliction, because the call of spring or fall would distract their employers. Thus it's not surprising that the urban worker has no knowledge of the seasons. He is aware simply that in some months there is air conditioning, and in others through the same vents comes fetid central heating. Even outside at home in their suburbs the city dwellers may know that sometimes it's hot, and sometimes cold, but no true sense of the rhythms of the seasons is to be had from a lawn in the back yard and a few spindly trees struggling to survive.

City dwellers can now eat the vegetables of their choice at almost any time of the year—always with the proviso that they will never taste a fresh vegetable, even though the best supermarkets have various ways to touch them up. Anyone who has not eaten peas picked that morning has never tasted a pea. The simple fact is that some frozen vegetables (frozen within hours of being picked) are fresher than the alleged fresh vegetables on the produce counter of the supermarkets. The suburbanite again struggles to simulate the blessings of rural life by maintaining a vegetable patch in the back yard. The main consequence of this melancholy pursuit comes in high summer, when office workers bring in their homegrown tomatoes to share with their colleagues, ill-colored, lump-faced objects with scars all over them, since they have not been staked correctly.

The city dweller reels from unreality to unreality through each day, always trying to recover the rural life that has been surrendered for the city lights. (City life, it is worth noticing, has produced almost no proverbs. How could it when proverbs—a rolling stone gathers no moss, and so on—are a distillation from a sane existence?) No city dweller, even in the suburbs, knows the wonder of a pitch-dark country lane at night. Nor does he naturally get any exercise from his work. When jogging and other childish pursuits began to exercise the unused bodies of city dwellers, two sensible doctors (a breed that has almost died with the general practitioner) said that city workers could get their exercise better in more natural ways. They could begin by walking upstairs to their office floors instead of using the elevators.

Every European points out that Americans are the most round-shouldered people in the world. Few of them carry themselves with an upright stance, although a correct stance and gait is the first precondition of letting your lungs breathe naturally and deeply. Electric typewriters cut down the amount of physical exertion needed to hit the keys; the buttons on a word processor need even less effort, as you can tell from the posture of those who use them. They might as well be in armchairs. They rush out to jog or otherwise Fonda-ize their leisure to try to repair the damage done during the day.

Dieting is an urban obsession. Country dwellers eat what they please, and work it off in useful physical employments, and in the open air, cold or hot, rainy or sunny. Mailmen are the healthiest city workers. When was your mailman last ill for a day? If one reads the huge menus that formed a normal diet in the 19th century, you realize that even the city dwellers could dispatch these gargantuan repasts because they still shared many of the benefits of rural life. (Disraeli records a meal at the house of one lordly figure that was composed of nine meat or game entrées. The butler asked after the eighth, "Snipe or pheasant, my lord?") They rode horseback to work or to Parliament even in the coldest weather, and nothing jolts and enlivens the liver more than riding. Homes were cold in the winter, except in the immediate vicinity of the hearth or stove. Cold has a way of eating up excess fat. No wonder dieting is necessary in a cossetted life in which the body is forced to do no natural heavy work.

Everything in urban life is an effort either to simulate rural life or to compensate for its loss by artificial means. The greatest robbery from the country in recent years has of course been Levi's, which any self-respecting farmer or farm worker is almost ashamed to wear nowadays. It was when Saks Fifth Avenue began advocating designer jeans years ago that the ultimate urban parody of rural life was reached. The chic foods of the city have to be called health foods, which would seem a tautology in the country. And insofar as there used to be entertainments in the city that enticed, these can now be enjoyed more than sufficiently on VCRs and stereos.

It is from this day-to-day existence of unreality, pretense, and idiocy that the city people, slumping along their streets even when scurrying, never looking up at their buildings, far less the sky, have the insolence to disdain and mock the useful and rewarding life of the country people who support them. Now go out and carry home a Douglas fir, call it a Christmas tree, and enjoy 12 days of contact with nature. Of course city dwellers don't know it once had roots.

QUESTIONS FOR CRITICAL READERS

Remembering and Understanding

1. What is Fairlie's central point about cities and urban life? Re-state it and give the chief reasons he has for his position.
2. Collect statements that indicate Fairlie's tone, his attitude toward his subject. Make a list of these statements and then describe his attitude.
3. Fairlie seems nostalgic for pre-industrial America. Using the details he provides, explain what he thinks pre-industrial America was like and contrast it with his view of the present.

Analyzing and Discussing

4. In what ways is Fairlie's commentary here influenced by his background as a political writer? That is, how might his statements be taken as political rather than strictly personal?
5. Fairlie says that television commercials have more themes of the countryside than of urban life. In addition to the examples of this that Fairlie provides, give examples of your own of both country and urban scenes, and discuss their effectiveness in selling products.
6. What image of the country does Fairlie invoke, directly through description and indirectly through his descriptions of a contrasting urban life? Do you believe his conception of country life is credible?

Writing

7. Respond to Fairlie's article by choosing some specific point that he makes with which you agree or disagree. Write a paper in which you use Fairlie's statement as your starting point. State your agreement or disagreement, and then explain your own position in detail.

Life in the Fast Lane

———— Donald McCaig ————

*Donald McCaig has been a philosophy teacher and an advertising executive.
Now he and his wife live on a farm in western Virginia, where they raise
sheep. As a farmer who makes his livelihood from the land, McCaig must
depend on the natural world and his own labor for his survival. He does
admit, though, that in some years he makes more money writing than he does
raising sheep. His best-known book is* Nop's Trials, *about the adventures
of a sheepdog. He has obviously lived in what many people call "the fast
lane," and he seems aware of the tensions between the city and the country
and of the need for balance in one's life.*

FEBRUARY IS THE LONGEST MONTH of the year. The old snow on
our remote West Virginia farm has changed to slush and gray ice and
mud that can suck a rubber boot right off your foot. Whenever there's
fresh snow, our dirt road is nearly impassable and we ferry feed and
groceries in our ancient four-wheel-drive pickup. With so many lambs
on the ground, feeding gets complicated and the free time between morning and evening chores gets short. We've been lambing since December,
and the marvel of new birth has become another routine job.

In the fall, we can take real pleasure in a full freezer, neat woodpiles,
the barn groaning with hay. We look forward to quiet winter evenings—
reading beside the fire, doing a jigsaw puzzle, perhaps hooking a new
rug for the living room. But, by February, we've done those things, and
the prospect of one more quiet country evening can set my teeth on edge.

That's when city life looks good. My wife, Anne, and I imagine
ourselves eating out in a nice little restaurant with wine and candlelight.
We want to see a movie on a screen bigger than nineteen inches, measured
diagonally. We dream about concerts, ballet, gallery openings, dancing.
We long for what Anne calls "life in the fast lane."

Harrisonburg, our shopping town, is only forty miles away, but bad
roads and mountains make for a slow trip: an hour and a half one way.
When lambs are coming, we rarely go there together, but this particular
morning we decided to chance it. The two ewes we'd been expecting to

341

lamb did so, considerately, at 6:30 A.M. A good single, and twins. Most of our ewes twin, some single, and occasionally a ewe will drop triplets.

The ewe due to lamb next was Bouncer, a big young Rambouillet, who had proved her mothering ability the past year. She wasn't showing any signs of hurrying into labor. She wasn't pawing herself a nest, or walking aimlessly about, or licking her lips, or separating herself from the flock. A neighbor promised to check Bouncer at noon, so we took off.

The trip in was pleasant; we made good time and stopped for chili dogs at Jess's Quick Lunch, not exactly the candlelit restaurant I had dreamed about.

We had a noontime appointment with our income tax preparer. Mrs. Peters is very sharp, but new to the area and to farm accounting. When we sat down, I was nervous, expecting the worst possible news. I chattered about the weather, which was supposed to turn cold and windy.

She asked if we had more lambs when the weather changed. She had been talking to a dairy farmer who always got his calves during sudden cold snaps. He claimed stress brought on labor.

I said, "That hasn't been our experience. Oh, when the weather's very bad, we check the ewes every couple of hours because newborn lambs are so fragile. When it's below zero, if a newborn isn't up and nursing within twenty minutes, he'll freeze to death. But I haven't noticed more lambs coming during bad weather."

Anne thought the dairy farmer was probably right. "It makes sense to me. Stress can start the contractions."

Pleasantries concluded, Mrs. Peters gave us the news about taxes. It wasn't as bad as I had feared. So I was in a pretty good mood as we did our shopping. We picked up groceries, milk replacer (for orphan lambs), and an order of vet supplies for a neighbor. Outside the Farmer's Co-op, I eyed a display of fruit trees: apple, pear, peach, and cherry trees with green plastic wrapped around their root balls. I'd been meaning to plant an orchard for years. Maybe this year . . .

It started to get colder as the truck ground up the steep curves of Shenandoah Mountain, but the scudding clouds overhead didn't look like snow. As soon as we got home, I checked the lambing yard. Bouncer stared at me placidly, a wisp of hay hanging out of her mouth.

I said, "Bouncer, you should probably go right ahead and lamb. You'll like it inside the barn. Besides, ewes with lambs eat better."

Bouncer didn't comment; she stuck her head back into the hay feeder.

The dozen ewes in the lambing yard were older commercial sheep. Some were Rambouillets (white-faced, long-wooled ewes), some had the black head and short fleece of the Suffolk breed, and some were crossbreds with dusky, speckled faces. They were big ewes—150 to 180 pounds—and all of them were experienced mothers.

We unloaded our provisions and started feeding the different groups of sheep. In the west, the sky was a pale, brilliant blue. The wind was starting to come up. I hauled water to the barn for the ewes with lambs and quickly checked all the lambs for health by sticking a finger in their mouths. If a lamb is healthy and nursing, the mouth is warm. But if a lamb's mouth is cold, you had better do something right away.

We feed hay off the back of a two-wheeled cart. As soon as I broke a bale open, the wind rolled and scattered it. It was work to pull the big field gates closed, but even when Anne said she had tied the barn doors with baling twine because of the wind, I didn't worry. Our farm lies across the bottom of a long, narrow valley. It's a natural wind tunnel and we've had high winds before. You get used to the tin roof shaking and rattling and the creak of house timbers.

The thermometer outside stood at ten degrees. No big deal.

I poured myself a cup of coffee and sat down to watch Walter Cronkite. Anne pulled off her high rubber boots and put on her slippers.

"The sheep hate that wind," she said. "Did you see how spooky the ewes were?"

The forecast was for gusts up to fifty miles an hour, but I pushed more wood into the stove and the house was very warm.

"I'll do the dishes if you cook," I suggested.

"Fair enough."

It was a good dinner, too: pepper steak, baked potatoes, and peas. The howling outside made the house seem especially snug, and we settled in for a quiet evening. Anne had her feet up, waiting for her favorite TV program, *M*A*S*H*, which came on at 8:30.

"I'm going to take a bath," I said. "I'll do a quick sheep check before I get in the tub."

"If you want to. I checked an hour ago and nobody was doing anything. Bouncer will probably wait until morning."

"Yeah, well . . ."

I put on my down vest and windbreaker and took the heavy sealed-beam flashlight. The lambing yard is only twenty feet from the house, and I had just stepped outside when I heard the familiar nicker of a ewe to her newborn lamb. It's a lovely sound, a soft *uh-uh-uh*, and it made me smile. I thought, "Well. We're not done for the night after all."

As soon as I opened the lambing-yard gate, I spotted her. The frantic mother, a big Suffolk, was trying to rouse her lambs—she'd had triplets—but they were all flat on the ground, motionless as boards. I ran back to the house and shouted, "Anne! Come quick!"

The ewe had done her best: she had cleaned each lamb as it came, and had tried to nudge them to their feet, but they were down now—

muddy, bloody, and stiff. I wiped the birth mucus of their faces and forced my finger into their mouths. Cold. Ice cold. One lamb's ribs heaved with breath, and he was using his last strength to lift his heavy head a few inches off the ground.

Anne was beside me now. We scooped up the filthy, frozen lambs in our arms, hurried back to the house, and laid them beside the wood stove, just six inches from the hot metal.

"Quick," Anne snapped, "get some warm water in the sink. Don't make it too hot." She was slapping at their sides, rubbing them down with a lambing towel. It looks a little rough, but you have to get the circulation going.

For triplets, they were very big: close to ten pounds each. Since multiple births are hereditary in sheep, these were very special lambs.

Anne was drawing medicine into a syringe as I plunged the worst lamb into the warm water. Its long, floppy ears were frozen into wings and I was afraid I might break them. When the lamb touched the water, it turned black and slimy. Anne was talking to the others as she injected them with AA1000 (a mixture of B vitamins, glucose, and electrolytes). As she slid the needle into their icy flanks, she was crooning, "Come on, honey. You can live. You can breathe now. *Hey, this one is breathing!*" And she brought both her lambs to the double sink. I was trying to fill the other side but couldn't find the stopper, and the warm water cascaded down my lamb's sides. Its eyes were half open, but slowly its eyelids slid closed.

"Quick. Give this one a hit." Anne's deft hands slipped the needle into the folds of loose skin over the ribs.

"I'm giving her three cc's," she said. "Is it a her?"

"I haven't looked. Yes. I can't use this sink."

"Use the sink in the bathroom."

The lamb overflowed the shallow basin of the bathroom sink. I cradled her head just above the filthy water and splashed water on her fine pointy nose to dissolve the strands of frozen mucus still clinging there. I held her up to my ear. Her eyes were closed and she wasn't breathing, but something tapped faintly inside the chest cavity.

"I'm done in here," Anne called. She swept into the living room with two thoroughly drenched lambs and an armload of the towels we use for lambing.

"I've got to try mouth-to-mouth," I said as I moved back to the deep sink again.

A lamb's muzzle will fit completely into a human mouth, so you can blow into the nostrils and mouth at the same time. Holding the lamb in the water, I enclosed its muzzle and puffed, took a breath, pressed its rib cage for the exhale, and puffed again. A lamb's lungs are smaller than a human baby's. It doesn't take very much air to fill them. Gently, gently.

Puff, breathe, press, puff, breathe, press. The lamb's muzzle was still icy cold. The air from her lungs tasted strange but clean in my mouth.

The warm water had brought my lamb's body temperature up, but she wasn't breathing on her own. Anne came in and added more hot water. "How is she?"

When I drew back, the tiny mouth opened. The bright red tongue came out a quarter-inch and retracted. "Can't tell. Either she's got some spark still left in her, or she's started her death spasms."

Puff, breathe, press, puff, breathe. No obstructions in her air passages, and it didn't feel as if I was pushing air into her stomach.

When I pulled her out of the water, her eyes stayed closed, she was totally limp, but her sides heaved convulsively, once, twice. She settled into a regular breathing pattern. "Hey! All right!" I yelled, and carried her in to lie on the towel beside her brothers. Two wet ram lambs and one wet ewe lamb. Anne and I knelt side by side, rubbing life into the newborn. Both of us were nattering heedlessly.

"Their mother can't raise triplets," Anne said.

"Why not? She's a big ewe."

"She had mastitis last year. She's got only one teat."

The two ram lambs were wriggling around, trying to sit up straight. The ewe lamb lay still. I slapped her face, rubbed briskly, and promised her the sun, moon, stars, and a good mother if she'd just open her eyes.

"I'll bet their mother is going bananas," Anne said. I pictured the mother, bleating and tearing around the yard searching for her missing babies. But when I stepped into the yard, I couldn't hear the ewe. Some sheep were peacefully pulling hay out of the feeder. A mother was nickering to a newborn.

Very quickly, I understood why the Suffolk wasn't hysterical about her lost lambs. She had found another one. That it wasn't hers didn't matter. I found two ewes nickering and nuzzling a big white single lamb who was sitting up comfortably, receiving the attentions of two mothers' tongues. When I checked the lamb's mouth, it was warm. He was in the lee of the feeder and the wind wasn't getting to him.

As I came through the kitchen, I said, "We've got another one. We can put him on hold for a while."

Anne had one lamb in her lap, trying it with a bottle. She had heated a mixture of colostrum and milk replacer, and was nudging the lamb's lips with the bottle.

My weak ewe lamb had her blue eyes open. I christened her "Lazarus."

Anne went outside and brought the other newborn back with her. When I'd seen him, he'd been as clean and white as a pearl. Now he was muddy, gasping, and half frozen. We got a fresh towel and went to work. Apparently, one of his mothers had got him up to nurse, but when he wobbled away from the windbreak, the wind had dropped him like a stone.

"He's big."

"Must go fifteen pounds."

One white lamb and three blackfaces, side-by-side on a crimson towel. Anne was working all of them, teaching them how to nurse. When a weak lamb first finds its suck, it's as though an electric shock passes through it. One can almost hear the lamb say, "Aha! So that's the idea." And it changes from a fumbling, passive creature into a torpedo, each muscle working to support the primary urge: *more milk!*

As they began to stand, we moved them into the front room, where the rug gave them better footing. They stumbled around, bleating and searching the corners. When they ran into each other, they would drop to their knees and try to nurse each other's ears. By 10:30, we had one lamb tangled in the fireplace screen, another trying to nibble a lamp cord, and enough noise for a zoo. Big White had a tremendous *baaa*, Lazarus a squeaky bleat.

It's always chancy pulling brand-new lambs off their mothers. The bonding process, in which the mother recognizes the lamb as her own, is fairly delicate, and sometimes, when the process is disturbed, the ewe will refuse a lamb and let it starve or even butt it to death in the lambing pen. You can raise lambs on bottles, but they never do as well as lambs raised by a good mother.

Ewes recognize their lambs by scent, but we had washed all the scent off the triplets. Anne eyed the clumsy, healthy lambs. "Fine," she said. "Now we have four lambs and two mothers that both want the big white one."

We would have to try and graft one of the triplets onto Big White's mother. The Suffolk could raise two lambs on one teat. Perhaps the ewes were so confused by now that they wouldn't know one lamb from another.

By 11:30, the lambs were strong enough to go outside. The wind had died down. We each carried two lambs. As soon as the ewes heard them, they went crazy, calling for the lambs, rushing back and forth. They were like woolly gunboats circling us, trying to get to the lambs, and when we stepped into the barn, all the other ewes, suddenly awakened and alarmed, started calling for their lambs. We laid the lambs in the straw of the lambing pens. The lambs found it hard to walk in the deep straw and weren't too certain of their direction, but they were in fine voice. The ewes fell silent. Reserving judgment, they extended their noses to sniff the lambs. With a soft nicker, and a swipe of her rough tongue, the Suffolk owned two lambs and resumed the job that had been so rudely interrupted. Big White's mother welcomed him right away but sniffed the grafted newcomer suspiciously. You could practically see her thinking, "Two lambs? But I'm almost sure I had only one lamb. Almost sure . . ." Then Lazarus let out a particularly lusty cry and the ewe accepted the stranger and nudged her back toward her milk.

When Anne checked at one A.M., the lambs on the Suffolk had learned to take turns on her one functional teat.

When I went out at three, all four lambs were asleep, banked up against their mothers. There's nothing so smug as a lamb with a full belly. When I put my finger in Lazarus's mouth, she bleated in outrage.

When Anne went out at five, all the lambs were fine and Bouncer promptly presented her with two new ones. An effortless, routine delivery. Bouncer's lambs were up and nursing while she was still cleaning them off.

Later, over breakfast, Anne laughed. "Life in the fast lane," she said.

QUESTIONS FOR CRITICAL READERS

Remembering and Understanding

1. In the course of his description of country life, McCaig provides a great deal of information about sheep farming and lambing. List this information and then incorporate it into a summary description.
2. In addition to telling a story of his life on the farm, McCaig is also making a point about country versus city living. Re-state that point in your own words and explain how McCaig's experience qualifies him to make that point.
3. What is McCaig's attitude toward city, country, and work? Identify the passages that reveal his attitude to you.

Analyzing and Discussing

4. McCaig provides a great deal of information that may not seem immediately necessary to his purpose. For example, he tells you what they had for lunch, the television programs they watched, etc. What does this information contribute to the essay?
5. What is McCaig's purpose? What effect does he want to produce in his readers?
6. What does McCaig mean by his title, "Life in the Fast Lane"? How does it apply to the story he tells and the point he makes?

Writing

7. McCaig has a specific vision of what a visit to the city—life in the fast lane—would be like. Select a place that you might like to visit and describe what you imagine that place is like and what you would do there.

Urban Density

A Defense

────────── **PETER SHAW** ──────────

In this essay, which originally appeared in the Antioch Review, *Shaw takes an unusual and possibly unpopular position in favor of population density (as well as other kinds of density) in cities. He argues that density is a positive influence, not only on individuals, but on civilization in general. Shaw is a lifelong resident of New York City, and this experience may have influenced his ideas about urban density.*

IN THE CENTER OF THE PLANNED COMMUNITY of Las Colinas, Texas, stands a twenty-six-story high-rise tower overlooking nearby Dallas. Why here, out on the plain, in a development conceived as an escape from the drawbacks of city life, would the builders imitate the skyscraper—an adaptation to the needs of crowded cities—instead of a low-rise model such as the Pentagon? Why replicate the parking problems, the elevator waiting and riding time, the lunchtime crush of people at restaurants and takeout stores, and above all the higher rentals for space in a structure of costly steel underpinnings and skeleton out of choice rather than necessity?

Las Colinas is one of several satellite cities built just outside older large cities over the past ten or more years. Referred to as "outtowns," "outer cities," or "urban villages," these developments offer new facilities suitable for high tech and computer companies, among others, along with relatively low home prices for employees, short-range automobile commuting, parking facilities, safety from street crime, and other advantages over aging cities. Besides Las Colinas, one of the newer and smaller examples, those most often cited by students of the new phenomenon are the City Post Oak-Galleria center on the west side of Houston; King of Prussia, Pennsylvania, near Philadelphia; and Tysons Corner, Virginia, near Washington, D.C.

In each of these communities the single greatest drawback is the absence of a true city ambience. Variously described as having to do with street activity, nighttime entertainment, neighborhood stores, or some other feature of large-city life, the desired ambience depends on concentrations of people. This is why every newly developed outer city has been willing to violate its aesthetic of convenience in favor of at least one tall building at its center capable of producing a crowd. As Paul Goldberger, architecture critic of the *New York Times,* put it in a discussion of the outer city phenomenon: "There is somewhere in all of this a desire to create some urban density; even as the building of a suburban outtown represents a turning away from the city, it also represents a search for concentration, activity and urban energy." In the older cities, meanwhile, an opposite impulse has been developing. Somewhere amid all their vibrant, crowded activity, there is a search for open spaces, lower buildings, and a diminution of urban energy.

Within the older cities, for example, the population density brought about by urban development, whether commercial or residential, has come to be regarded by some as at best a necessary evil. And it has come to be taken as axiomatic by nearly everyone that traffic, pollution, crowding, noise, and stress are all unavoidable accompaniments of urban density in the first place, and that each of these is an unmitigated evil besides. Accordingly, in the debate over development the advantages of density so evident to the new outer city planners are never advanced. Instead, virtually the only question put on the floor is that of how to scale down a given project so as to reduce its presumed social costs. Developers attempting to defend their projects at public hearings themselves accept the proposition that they are the producers of undesirable new density. Instead of talking about urban energy, they argue that the ills of density they are about to foist on the community will in some degree be offset by job creation, by keeping businesses in the city, or by additions to the tax rolls. Accepting the definition of their activity as socially deleterious, they feebly offer to balance the ledger with fiscal benefits.

Further in keeping with the anti-urban impulse within older cities, developers routinely offer additional compromises and compensations. We will introduce a little less density if you will let us keep operating, they say. We will build fewer stories high, reduce floor space, or cover less of our site. And then in compensation for the degree of density that we do introduce, we will provide middle- and lower-income housing units, public meeting rooms, public plazas, money for nearby projects such as mass transit improvements, and/or other concessions. No one thinks of defending development as *a good.* As for the notion that the density brought about by development might be the very source of that good—well, this would probably strike developers no less than their opponents as outlandish. Nevertheless, this proposition, which amounts to a working theory in the new outer cities, deserves to be reintroduced to the inner cities whence it came.

Inasmuch as "density" is a term denoting a relative condition, one would expect frequent disagreement over its exact meaning and application. But in practice it is rarely used except to describe a level of commercial or residential building that will supposedly concentrate people to the point of producing health and psychological harms. Oddly enough, it never seems to be noticed that "density" is applied almost exclusively to prospective buildings. Already standing large building projects, many of which would arouse opposition if they were presently being proposed, are not cited as illustrating the perils of density.

One such standing building is the first to have been criticized in its planning stage for threatening an undesirable level of density. This is New York's Pan Am building, erected in 1963 adjacent to Grand Central Station. It was predicted by its critics that when on the day the building opened, office workers would try to go to lunch, pedestrian chaos would ensue as they ran up against the crowds in the train station and the heavily used surrounding streets. In fact, on the Pan Am building's first day, no impact whatsoever of the additional people could be observed. Something was fundamentally wrong in the thinking of the anti-developers. Vastly more people could be located right near Grand Central Station, their point of arrival in the city, than logic seemed to dictate. Indeed, the new building went on paradoxically to *reduce* crowding twice each day at the rush hour by making it possible for thousands of those arriving at the station to walk directly to work instead of having to crowd onto public transportation within the city. Yet because no one seemed to know how to react to the absence of predicted crowding from the new building, instead of spurring an appreciation of the advantages of density, the advent of the Pan Am building left the matter up in the air.

In looking into the issues surrounding development, it is worth keeping in mind that because of this absence of analysis the Pan Am incident marked not the end but rather the beginning of a widely held belief in the dangers of density. Nowhere has that belief been more crucially operative than in the defeats in the fall and winter of 1987–1988 of proposals for two of New York City's largest projects. These were Mortimer Zuckerman's skyscraper on the site of the former New York Coliseum at Columbus Circle, and Donald Trump's Television City on a half mile of disused riverfront rail yards not far away.

As is currently the practice, the two projects were subject to complicated financial, zoning, and public-service arrangements before they could receive approval. These included improvements to the subway station below and a staggering sum to be paid to the city by the Coliseum developer. Objections to the projects came from local community boards, neighborhood activists, the Municipal Arts Society, the Parks Council, and a number of celebrities including Henry Kissinger, Norman Lear, Paul Newman, and Jacqueline Onassis. Once again it was asserted that too many people would be brought into the neighborhoods of the two projects, causing overcrowding and overburdening of the transportation system. But in the years since the Pan Am building opposition, anti-development issues had shifted from predictions of street overcrowding to the displacing of rental tenants and small businesses, and to the preservation of buildings said to be valuable to the city's heritage. These new issues could not be raised this time, though, since no removals of individuals or of desirable buildings were involved. Accordingly, the two projects were subjected to a broad range of criticisms, some of them still newer in concept.

Opponents of the projects themselves called attention to the uniqueness of their objections, arguing that these should be regarded neither as frivolous nor as desperate expedients coming from diehard opponents of all development. Instead, they were said to represent a new kind of civic consciousness. "This is not an anti-development effort," said Judith Spektor of the Parks Council in opposing Television City. And in a speech to demonstrators against the Columbus Circle building, television journalist Bill Moyers asserted: "We're not against growth. We're not against change. . . . We're against the forces of greed."

The new civic consciousness concerned itself largely with quality-of-life issues. These included what a *New York Times* headline termed "Rampant Growth" and one of its articles called "rampant construction." Aesthetics was another such issue: the proposed buildings were attacked as inferior in design and hence potentially damaging to the sensibilities of New Yorkers. Next, a soi-disant expert on skyscraper-generated air updraft was brought in from the West Coast to predict that Television City's proposed central tower, projected to become the highest building in the world, would generate winds of unacceptable velocity around its base.

Finally, there was the issue of "the most treasured of inner city resources." One wonders how many respondents in a random survey would have been able to name which resources were meant by this phrase before the campaigns against the two projects. The correct answer would be "air and light." Indeed, the most dramatic demonstration against the Coliseum building concerned one of these: light. The building would cast "a perpetual shadow" on Central Park, according to State Senator Manfred Ohrenstein; accordingly, demonstrators arranged themselves along the shadow's outline holding black umbrellas to signify its dread effect. But a *New York Times* editorial, even though against the project as planned, printed a diagram of present shadows on the park and pointed out, "All the buildings on Central Park West cast similar afternoon shadows on the park. . . . Even if the massive structure were built as already approved, it would add to them only marginally. The long, late shadows move fast and do not cover the same spot for more than an hour and a half." What bearing the absurdities of the anti-shadow demonstration had on the credibility of opposition to the Coliseum building was not explored by the *Times*.

At the very least, a sober consideration of these absurdities would have pointed to the movement's disingenuousness, especially about the environment. For as chance would have it, the shadowed strip of park in question was one regularly abandoned by ordinary citizens late each day to the derelicts who congregate there. A true concern for nature would have mandated comparing the loss of tree and grass growth from lack of late afternoon sunshine with the visible erosion and litter already being generated daily on the spot where the shadow would briefly pass.

Another kind of irony surrounded the aesthetic objections to the proposed Coliseum building. For it had been designed by Moshe Safdie, an architect of international standing, and was in the currently approved post-modernist mode. The preceding style, that of pure modernism's glass wall façades, had until recently been in favor, and of course remains visible throughout the midtown areas of most American cities. But that style is at present commonly referred to as "contemporary brutalism." If it is now deservedly out of favor, it had once been just as decidedly in favor. And at that time the Municipal Art Society critics of Safdie's drawings did not, so far as I know, put themselves on record as being against the spread of contemporary brutalism. We do know that years earlier the society championed a plan to cut diagonal boulevards through the Lower East Side and other poorer neighborhoods in order to improve traffic flow. "Hundreds of buildings would have been demolished and hundreds of thousands of people left homeless," writes Rebecca Read Shanor in *The City That Never Was*, "but at the time this was regarded as mere slum clearance." On its record the Municipal Art Society's opinion was at the least less than definitive. Certainly no one in the present unsettled state of architectural opinion was in a position to pronounce on the aesthetic worth of the Coliseum plan: least of all anyone with objections to the plan on other grounds as well.

As ever-new aesthetic and practical objections alike proliferate with each new project, it becomes difficult to keep up. Yet two practical objections that appear and reappear are worth examining for the light they throw on the nature of density. Both the Coliseum and Television City projects were opposed partly on the grounds that they would lead to overcrowding in the West Side neighborhood on which they abut. Supposedly affected would be buses, nearby subway stations, and the trains that run through them. Even with the sums paid over for subway station improvement, the transportation system would presumably remain overburdened.

To put these contentions in perspective, it is necessary in the first place to expose what might well be termed the dirty little secret of New York's anti-development drama. This is that the West Side neighborhood represented as direly at risk from density has in fact undergone a substantial *reduction* in density. Nor has this reduction been a minor one. Between 1950 and 1980, census figures show, the population of the West Side declined by fully one-third: from approximately 300,000 to 200,000. The implications of this secret are not limited to public transport. For insofar as the anti-development argument is based on density, it is virtually wiped away by the fact of decline.

The secret was certainly known all along to the leaders of opposition to the two projects, among whom can be included the reporters and editorial writers of the *New York Times*. Yet if one searches the *Times* coverage, which in the fall and winter of 1987–1988 included over thirty news stories, editorials, "sidelight" columns, op ed articles, letters to the editors, and an analysis by Paul Goldberger (plus an accompanying tattoo of development stories from around the country), one will get no idea of the true demographic state of affairs. The headlines affixed to the various accounts and opinions unremittingly conveyed the impression that density posed imminent danger to the West Side ("As Towers Rise, A Slow Fadeout of Sun and Sky"), that its opponents were no longer "just a few kookie naysayers" but sensitive, respectable, civic-minded, thoughtful, informed critics ("Don't Mock New Yorkers Who Want Air and Light"), and that the weight of evidence and argument had finally begun to turn a slumberous public opinion toward an enlightened opposition to development ("Two Big West Side Projects Fuel Anti-Development Sentiment"; "When the Tide Turned on Rampant Growth").

Later, after the projects had been shelved and the story had died down, the *Times*—which had itself never actually attempted to measure public opinion—duly reported the only survey taken during this period. Paid for by a real-estate group but conducted by an independent research organization, it found that even at the height of the anti-development agitation in which the *Times* had participated, 88 percent of respondents remained favorable to development. Not surprisingly, though, half of them had been swayed by the recent campaign over light and air to the extent of granting that loss of these was one of the costs of development.

But to return to transport overcrowding. In the first place some facts need to be understood. The same subway and bus system remains in place as in the years when the West Wide was one-third more dense than at present. The subways have been modified to make them more efficient: longer platforms can now accommodate longer trains making fewer stops and carrying more people. Yet it is true that the platforms and trains are sometimes more crowded than in the past. The explanation for this anomaly amounts to a lesson in the function of density in mass transportation. For the drop in subway usage attendant on the drop in West Side population has led to a drop in the number of trains per hour. This has meant longer waiting times and crowded platforms even as fewer people are being moved. It follows that the solution to the area's public transit difficulties is to increase population density, thereby adding riders who will justify restoration of the old schedule of frequency.

One immediate result will be a slight reduction in commuting time. Next, in addition to benefiting rush-hour travelers, increased density would put more people on the platforms at off hours, thereby making it safer to ride at those times. Just as the decline of the subway system has fed on itself, so would its revival thanks to increased density attract back some of its discretionary riders.

The larger lesson here has to do with the misrepresentation of transportation and street crowding as unpleasant, even frightening phenomena. Repeatedly conjured up is the jostling together of many bodies in an unhealthy closeness, producing stress that may at any moment break out into unpleasantness. Or else living at close quarters in large apartment complexes is said to produce a longer-term kind of stress that results in psychological damage and sporadic acts of violence. That ordinary people find safety rather than danger in numbers seems not to carry any weight with the theorists of density. Yet the most dangerous places to live in terms of psychological health and physical dangers are the least populated states of the United States. The safest places are those most dense: "The rates of violent death among youths in the most isolated parts of the West are higher than those in big-city ghettos, and studies show that residents of the underpopulated areas have worse health conditions and live shorter lives" (*New York Times* 12 Dec. 1987). Accidents, suicide, even infant deaths are all highest in the least populated states.

The reasons for these contrasts seem clear. Density of population, rather than breeding violence, tends to produce tolerant, acculturated individuals. Police protection in densely populated places is closer at hand, more experienced, more efficient. The same is true for fire protection and other kinds of rescue work, and for emergency medical care. The one undesirable product of urban density that cannot be denied is its tendency to produce a class of individuals who firmly believe that the minuscule blockage of light and turbulence of the air caused by a handful of tall buildings constitutes a health crisis.

The contemporary city alone among all of the institutions in the history of human culture could have produced the spectacle of its Henry

Kissingers, Paul Newmans, and Jacqueline Onassises demonstrating in their winter tans literally against shadows—arguably the least significant health hazard ever faced by the human race. In summer, of course, such people are away from the hot city altogether, so that it hardly occurs to them that the shade from tall buildings can be a positive benefit, making it easier to walk through the city than, say, a cornfield in Iowa.

If these luminaries genuinely felt a need for more light and air than they were getting in the city, they would soon notice that one of the most efficacious ways to secure even these items is through greater density. To understand how this is so, simply compare two methods of receiving urban light and air. The first is standing on the street where the shadow of a new building is going to fall when construction is completed. One would receive a certain amount of sunlight, along with the fumes from passing traffic. The second is lying high above the traffic on the sunroof of the same new building's health and swim club a few months later. Here is an area of far more preferable light and air newly created by density.

Neighborhood residents will soon notice other benefits of density provided by the high-rise building. Mailmen are delivering letters to hundreds of people without having to walk outdoors, security guards protect the residents at a low per capita cost, building repairmen are always on duty, packages can be left with building personnel, maid service is cheaply available since like the mailmen the maids save time by not having to travel between jobs, neighbors provide one another with services ranging from baby sitting to yoga classes, language and musical instrument instruction is available. The neighborhood had local piano and violin teachers, but now a brass and woodwind teacher is offering lessons in the new building.

But the leading concerns of those who oppose density are said to be cultural. And here, too, the realities are very nearly opposite to what has come to be accepted by residents of the older cities. Jane Jacobs has recently shown how a dense city economic environment spawns first small and then larger manufacturing operations, following which new suppliers and other support services develop to the point where an entire national economy may be said to radiate out from a country's dense urban cores. The performing arts especially—theater, opera, ballet, music—require similar concentrations of talent to survive. Painters and photographers, though they are capable of working on their own, also gravitate to the city center. The performing artists among them, given the intense training, rehearsal, and performance schedules they must follow, find it a necessity to live near the studios and theaters where they practice and perform. So do many of their teachers, along with the designers of costumes, sets, and lighting, as well as costume makers, managers, secretaries, publicity directors, and others. Once upon a time newcomers could hope to replace those moving out of the crowded neighborhoods in which they need to live. In the day of rent controls, though, city dwellers are no longer mobile. This means that new development alone can provide the needed new living space.

Other young people who come to the city to make their fortunes may not evoke the same aura of exalted purpose as their contemporaries in the arts. But they also have some claim to new space. They are partly drawn to the excitement created by the arts, whose future supporters they are, even as they are present supporters of the related popular entertainment industry. They, too, want to live near the crowded center—that is, right next to the anti-development activists who moved in, possibly for the same reasons, some time before them.

It is no exaggeration to say that modern civilization is largely the product of density, and that civilization depends on those who generate density for its health and forward movement. In this perspective development, rather than appearing as a necessary evil sometimes needed to accomplish other ends such as employment, emerges as a good in itself. The opposition to density is represented as including enlightened, environmentally sensitive, civically responsible people whose concerns need to be addressed through design compromises and special payments. Yet an examination of the protesters' rhetoric, such as Bill Moyers's opposition to "greed," exposes a dislike of business itself: most especially its profits, but also its dynamism. The opponents of development, furthermore, though they speak in the name of ordinary citizens—who happen to disagree with them—actually act to preserve their own privileged arrangements. After all, the very presence in the city of these cultural critics of density testifies to their own need for density. That these most vocal opponents of density should come from one of the groups that most benefit from it is an irony matched only by that of less affluent newcomers in the same fields resisting the enlightened conclusion that they should be located away from the dense urban center.

At a time when planners all around the country are trying to emulate the excitement of large cities by achieving concentrations of business and residential populations, within the big cities themselves influential elites are eschewing the very tendencies that have made their environments the cynosure of these other places. At the same time the businessmen responsible for erecting developments that sustain the dynamism and excitement of the older cities have grown apologetic about their role. It is as though the instinct responsible for the survival of a species were to begin withering away. For thanks to the anti-density movement, provinciality has changed places with urban sophistication. In the cities the talk is all of quiet and the absence of pressure, while in what used to be called the sticks the perspective is a sophisticated one of appreciation for the human activity, crowds, action, and dynamism that come from density. The point has been reached where if city dwellers are to be reawakened to the benefits of density, they are going to have to go to school to their country cousins.

QUESTIONS FOR CRITICAL READERS

Remembering and Understanding

1. Re-state Shaw's central point, and summarize the reasons and evidence he offers to support it.
2. Shaw makes much of what he calls a "true city ambience." Based on the information he provides here, what does he believe such an ambience consists of?
3. What are some of the advantages of density that Shaw points out? List them and then write a brief summary based on your list.

Analyzing and Discussing

4. Shaw says that modern civilization is largely the product of density. How would you go about evaluating that statement to determine its accuracy? Don't actually try to evaluate Shaw's statement; just describe how you would attempt to do so.
5. Shaw points out that developers are trying to achieve density at the same time that cities are attempting to reduce density. What does this contradiction suggest to you about contemporary society?
6. Shaw suggests that "density" is a relative term that has no single meaning. How would you go about defining the term? What factors would you consider in attempting to achieve a definition?

Writing

7. Research Shaw's contention that it is more dangerous to live in the least populated areas of the United States. Use reference works such as the *Statistical Abstract of the United States* to locate information. In addition to statistics, concentrate on giving *reasons* for the different rates of injury and death in different parts of the country.

The Solace of Open Spaces

GRETEL EHRLICH

Gretel Ehrlich went to north central Wyoming to make a film; she did not plan to stay. But through a variety of personal circumstances she did stay, and now ranches there with her husband. In recent years she has also established a considerable reputation as a writer. This selection is the title essay from her book The Solace of Open Spaces.

IT'S MAY AND I'VE JUST AWAKENED from a nap, curled against sagebrush the way my dog taught me to sleep—sheltered from wind. A front is pulling the huge sky over me, and from the dark a hailstone has hit me on the head. I'm trailing a band of two thousand sheep across a stretch of Wyoming badlands, a fifty-mile trip that takes five days because sheep shade up in hot sun and won't budge until it's cool. Bunched together now, and excited into a run by the storm, they drift across dry land, tumbling into draws like water and surge out again onto the rugged, choppy plateaus that are the building blocks of this state.

The name Wyoming comes from an Indian word meaning "at the great plains," but the plains are really valleys, great arid valleys, sixteen hundred square miles, with the horizon bending up on all sides into mountain ranges. This gives the vastness a sheltering look.

Winter lasts six months here. Prevailing winds spill snow-drifts to the east, and new storms from the northwest replenish them. This white bulk is sometimes dizzying, even nauseating, to look at. At twenty, thirty, and forty degrees below zero, not only does your car not work, but neither do your mind and body. The landscape hardens into a dungeon of space. During the winter, while I was riding to find a new calf, my jeans froze to the saddle, and in the silence that such cold creates I felt like the first person on earth, or the last.

Today the sun is out—only a few clouds billowing. In the east, where the sheep have started off without me, the benchland tilts up in a series of eroded red-earthed mesas, planed flat on top by a million years of water; behind them, a bold line of muscular scarps rears up ten thousand feet to become the Big Horn Mountains. A tidal pattern is engraved into the ground, as if left by the sea that once covered this state. Canyons curve down like galaxies to meet the oncoming rush of flat land.

To live and work in this kind of open country, with its hundred-mile views, is to lose the distinction between background and foreground. When I asked an older ranch hand to describe Wyoming's openness, he said, "It's all a bunch of nothing—wind and rattlesnakes—and so much of it you can't tell where you're going or where you've been and it don't make much difference." John, a sheepman I know, is tall and handsome and has an explosive temperament. He has a perfect intuition about people and sheep. They call him "Highpockets," because he's so long-legged; his graceful stride matches the distances he has to cover. He says, "Open space hasn't affected me at all. It's all the people moving in on it." The huge ranch he was born on takes up much of one county and spreads into another state; to put 100,000 miles on his pickup in three years and never leave home is not unusual. A friend of mine has an aunt who ranched on Powder River and didn't go off her place for eleven years. When her husband died, she quickly moved to town, bought a car, and drove around the States to see what she'd been missing.

Most people tell me they've simply driven through Wyoming, as if there were nothing to stop for. Or else they've skied in Jackson Hole, a place Wyomingites acknowledge uncomfortably because its green beauty and chic affluence are mismatched with the rest of the state. Most of Wyoming has a "lean-to" look. Instead of big, roomy barns and Victorian houses, there are dugouts, low sheds, log cabins, sheep camps, and fence lines that look like driftwood blown haphazardly into place. People here still feel pride because they live in such a harsh place, part of the glamorous cowboy past, and they are determined not to be the victims of a mining-dominated future.

Most characteristic of the state's landscape is what a developer euphemistically describes as "indigenous growth right up to your front door"—a reference to waterless stands of salt sage, snakes, jack rabbits, deerflies, red dust, a brief respite of wildflowers, dry washes, and no trees. In the Great Plains the vistas look like music, like Kyries of grass, but Wyoming seems to be the doing of a mad architect—tumbled and twisted, ribboned with faded, deathbed colors, thrust up and pulled down as if the place had been startled out of a deep sleep and thrown into a pure light.

I came here four years ago. I had not planned to stay, but I couldn't make myself leave. John, the sheepman, put me to work immediately. It was spring, and shearing time. For fourteen days of fourteen hours each, we moved thousands of sheep through sorting corrals to be sheared, branded, and deloused. I suspect that my original motive for coming here was to "lose myself" in new and unpopulated territory. Instead of producing the numbness I thought I wanted, life on the sheep ranch woke me up. The vitality of the people I was working with flushed out what had become a hallucinatory rawness inside me. I threw away my clothes and bought new ones; I cut my hair. The arid country was a clean slate. Its absolute indifference steadied me.

Sagebrush covers 58,000 square miles of Wyoming. The biggest city has a population of fifty thousand, and there are only five settlements that could be called cities in the whole state. The rest are towns, scattered across the expanse with as much as sixty miles between them, their populations two thousand, fifty, or ten. They are fugitive-looking, perched on a barren, windblown bench, or tagged onto a river or a railroad, or laid out straight in a farming valley with implement stores and a block-long Mormon church. In the eastern part of the state, which slides down into the Great Plains, the new mining settlements are boomtowns, trailer cities, metal knots on flat land.

Despite the desolate look, there's a coziness to living in this state. There are so few people (only 470,000) that ranchers who buy and sell cattle know one another statewide; the kids who choose to go to college usually go to the state's one university, in Laramie; hired hands work their way around Wyoming in a lifetime of hirings and firings. And despite the physical separation, people stay in touch, often driving two or three hours to another ranch for dinner.

Seventy-five years ago, when travel was by buckboard or horseback, cowboys who were temporarily out of work rode the grub line—drifting from ranch to ranch, mending fences or milking cows, and receiving in exchange a bed and meals. Gossip and messages traveled this slow circuit with them, creating an intimacy between ranchers who were three and four weeks' ride apart. One old-time couple I know, whose turn-of-the-century homestead was used by an outlaw gang as a relay station for stolen horses, recall that if you were traveling, desperado or not, any lighted ranch house was a welcome sign. Even now, for someone who lives in a remote spot, arriving at a ranch or coming to town for supplies is cause for celebration. To emerge from isolation can be disorienting. Everything looks bright, new, vivid. After I had been herding sheep for only three days, the sound of the camp tender's pickup flustered me. Longing for human company, I felt a foolish grin take over my face; yet I had to resist an urgent temptation to run and hide.

Things happen suddenly in Wyoming, the change of seasons and weather; for people, the violent swings in and out of isolation. But good-naturedness is concomitant with severity. Friendliness is a tradition. Strangers passing on the road wave hello. A common sight is two pickups stopped side by side far out on a range, on a dirt track winding through the sage. The drivers will share a cigarette, uncap their thermos bottles, and pass a battered cup, steaming with coffee, between windows. These meetings summon up the details of several generations, because, in Wyoming, private histories are largely public knowledge.

Because ranch work is a physical and, these days, economic strain, being "at home on the range" is a matter of vigor, self-reliance, and common sense. A person's life is not a series of dramatic events for which he or she is applauded or exiled but a slow accumulation of days, seasons, years, fleshed out by the generational weight of one's family and anchored by a land-bound sense of place.

In most parts of Wyoming, the human population is visibly outnumbered by the animal. Not far from my town of fifty, I rode into a narrow valley and startled a herd of two hundred elk. Eagles look like small people as they eat car-killed deer by the road. Antelope, moving in small, graceful bands, travel at sixty miles an hour, their mouths open as if drinking in the space.

The solitude in which westerners live makes them quiet. They telegraph thoughts and feelings by the way they tilt their heads and listen; pulling their Stetsons into a steep dive over their eyes, or pigeon-toeing one boot over the other, they lean against a fence with a fat wedge of Copenhagen beneath their lower lips and take in the whole scene. These detached looks of quiet amusement are sometimes cynical, but they can also come from a dry-eyed humility as lucid as the air is clear.

Conversation goes on in what sounds like a private code; a few phrases imply a complex of meanings. Asking directions, you get a curious list of details. While trailing sheep I was told to "ride up to that kinda upturned rock, follow the pink wash, turn left at the dump, and then you'll see the water hole." One friend told his wife on roundup to "turn at the salt lick and the dead cow," which turned out to be a scattering of bones and no salt lick at all.

Sentence structure is shortened to the skin and bones of a thought. Descriptive words are dropped, even verbs; a cowboy looking over a corral full of horses will say to a wrangler, "Which one needs rode?" People hold back their thoughts in what seems to be a dumbfounded silence, then erupt with an excoriating perceptive remark. Language, so compressed, becomes metaphorical. A rancher ended a relationship with one remark: "You're a bad check," meaning bouncing in and out was intolerable, and even coming back would be no good.

What's behind this laconic style is shyness. There is no vocabulary for the subject of feelings. It's not a hangdog shyness, or anything coy—always there's a robust spirit in evidence behind the restraint, as if the earth-dredging wind that pulls across Wyoming had carried its people's voices away but everything else in them had shouldered confidently into the breeze.

I've spent hours riding to sheep camp at dawn in a pickup when nothing was said; eaten meals in the cookhouse when the only words spoken were a mumbled "Thank you, ma'am" at the end of dinner. The silence is profound. Instead of talking, we seem to share one eye. Keenly observed, the world is transformed. The landscape is engorged with detail, every movement on it chillingly sharp. The air between people is charged. Days unfold, bathed in their own music. Nights become hallucinatory; dreams, prescient.

Spring weather is capricious and mean. It snows, then blisters with heat. There have been tornadoes. They lay their elephant trunks out in the sage until they find houses, then slurp everything up and leave. I've noticed that melting snowbanks hiss and rot, viperous, then drip into calm pools where ducklings hatch and livestock, being trailed to summer range, drink. With the ice cover gone, rivers churn a milkshake brown, taking culverts and small bridges with them. Water in such an arid place (the average annual rainfall where I live is less than eight inches) is like blood. It festoons drab land with green veins; a line of cottonwoods following a stream; a strip of alfalfa; and, on the ditch banks, wild asparagus growing.

I've moved to a small cattle ranch owned by friends. It's at the foot of the Big Horn Mountains. A few weeks ago, I helped them deliver a calf who was stuck halfway out of his mother's body. By the time he was freed, we could see a heartbeat, but he was straining against a swollen tongue for air. Mary and I held him upside down by his back feet, while Stan, on his hands and knees in the blood, gave the calf mouth-to-mouth resuscitation. I have a vague memory of being pneumonia-choked as a child, my mother giving me her air, which may account for my romance with this windswept state.

If anything is endemic to Wyoming, it is wind. This big room of space is swept out daily, leaving a bone yard of fossils, agates, and carcasses in every stage of decay. Though it was water that initially shaped the state, wind is the meticulous gardener, raising dust and pruning the sage.

I try to imagine a world in which I could ride my horse across uncharted land. There is no wilderness left; wildness, yes, but true wilderness has been gone on this continent since the time of Lewis and Clark's overland journey.

Two hundred years ago, the Crow, Shoshone, Arapaho, Cheyenne, and Sioux roamed the intermountain West, orchestrating their movements according to hunger, season, and warfare. Once they acquired horses, they traversed the spines of all the big Wyoming ranges—the Absarokas, the Wind Rivers, the Tetons, the Big Horns—and wintered on the unprotected plains that fan out from them. Space was life. The world was their home.

What was life-giving to Native Americans was often nightmarish to sodbusters who had arrived encumbered with families and ethnic pasts to be transplanted in nearly uninhabitable land. The great distances, the shortage of water and trees, and the loneliness created unexpected hardships for them. In her book *O Pioneers!*, Willa Cather gives a settler's version of the bleak landscape:

> The little town behind them had vanished as if it had never been, had fallen behind the swell of the prairie, and the stern frozen country received them into its bosom. The homesteads were few and far apart; here and there a windmill gaunt against the sky, a sod house crouching in a hollow.

The emptiness of the West was for others a geography of possibility. Men and women who amassed great chunks of land and struggled to preserve unfenced empires were, despite their self-serving motives, unwitting geographers. They understood the lay of the land. But by the 1850s the Oregon and Mormon trails sported bumper-to-bumper traffic. Wealthy landowners, many of them aristocratic absentee landlords, known as remittance men because they were paid to come West and get out of their families' hair, overstocked the range with more than a million head of cattle. By 1885 the feed and water were desperately short, and the winter of 1886 laid out the gaunt bodies of dead animals so closely together that when the thaw came, one rancher from Kaycee claimed to have walked on cowhide all the way to Crazy Woman Creek, twenty miles away.

Territorial Wyoming was a boy's world. The land was generous with everything but water. At first there was room enough, food enough, for everyone. And, as with all beginnings, an expansive mood set in. The young cowboys, drifters, shopkeepers, schoolteachers, were heroic, lawless, generous, rowdy, and tenacious. The individualism and optimism generated during those times have endured.

John Tisdale rode north with the trail herds from Texas. He was a college-educated man with enough money to buy a small outfit near the Powder River. While driving home from the town of Buffalo with a buckboard full of Christmas toys for his family and a winter's supply of food, he was shot in the back by an agent of the cattle barons who resented the encroachment of small-time stockmen like him. The wealthy cattlemen tried to control all the public grazing land by restricting membership in the Wyoming Stock Growers Association, as if it were a country club. They ostracized from roundups and brandings cowboys and ranchers who were not members, then denounced them as rustlers. Tisdale's death, the second such cold-blooded murder, kicked off the Johnson County cattle war, which was no simple good-guy-bad-guy shoot-out but a complicated class struggle between landed gentry and less affluent settlers—a shocking reminder that the West was not an egalitarian sanctuary after all.

Fencing ultimately enforced boundaries, but barbed wire abrogated space. It was stretched across the beautiful valleys, into the mountains, over desert badlands, through buffalo grass. The "anything is possible" fever—the lure of any new place—was constricted. The integrity of the land as a geographical body, and the freedom to ride anywhere on it, were lost.

I punched cows with a young man named Martin, who is the great-grandson of John Tisdale. His inheritance is not the open land that Tisdale knew and prematurely lost but a rage against restraint.

Wyoming tips down as you head northeast; the highest ground—the Laramie Plains—is on the Colorado border. Up where I live, the Big Horn River leaks into difficult, arid terrain. In the basin where it's dammed, sandhill cranes gather and, with delicate legwork, slice through the stilled water. I was driving by with a rancher one morning when he commented that cranes are "old-fashioned." When I asked why, he said, "Because they mate for life." Then he looked at me with a twinkle in his eyes, as if to say he really did believe in such things but also understood why we break our own rules.

In all this open space, values crystalize quickly. People are strong on scruples but tenderhearted about quirky behavior. A friend and I found one ranch hand, who's "not quite right in the head," sitting in front of the badly decayed carcass of a cow, shaking his finger and saying, "Now, I don't want you to do this ever again!" When I asked what was wrong with him, I was told, "He's goofier than hell, just like the rest of us." Perhaps because the West is historically new, conventional morality is still felt to be less important than rock-bottom truths. Though there's always a lot of teasing and sparring, people are blunt with one another, sometimes even cruel, believing honesty is stronger medicine than sympathy, which may console but often conceals.

The formality that goes hand in hand with the rowdiness is known as the Western Code. It's a list of practical do's and don'ts, faithfully observed. A friend, Cliff, who runs a trapline in the winter, cut off half his foot while chopping a hole in the ice. Alone, he dragged himself to his pickup and headed for town, stopping to open the ranch gate as he left, and getting out to close it again, thus losing, in his observance of rules, precious time and blood. Later, he commented, "How would it look, them having to come to the hospital to tell me their cows had gotten out?"

Accustomed to emergencies, my friends doctor each other from the vet's bag with relish. When one old-timer suffered a heart attack in hunting camp, his partner quickly stirred up a brew of red horse liniment and hot water and made the half-conscious victim drink it, then tied him onto a horse and led him twenty miles to town. He regained consciousness and lived.

The roominess of the state has affected political attitudes as well. Ranchers keep up with world politics and the convulsions of the economy but are basically isolationists. Being used to running their own small empires of land and livestock, they're suspicious of big government. It's a "don't fence me in" holdover from a century ago. They still want the elbow room their grandfathers had, so they're strongly conservative, but with a populist twist.

Summer is the season when we get our "cowboy tans"—on the lower parts of our faces and on three fourths of our arms. Excessive heat, in the nineties and higher, sends us outside with the mosquitoes. In winter we're tucked inside our houses, and the white wasteland outside appears to be expanding, but in summer all the greenery abridges space. Summer is a go-ahead season. Every living thing is off the block and in the race: battalions of bugs in flight and biting; bats swinging around my log cabin as if the bases were loaded and someone had hit a home run. Some of summer's high-speed growth is ominous: larkspur, death camas, and green greasewood can kill sheep—an ironic idea, dying in this desert from eating what is too verdant. With sixteen hours of daylight, farmers and ranchers irrigate feverishly. There are first, second, and third cuttings of hay, some crews averaging only four hours of sleep a night for weeks. And, like the cowboys who in summer ride the night rodeo circuit, nighthawks make daredevil dives at dusk with an eerie whirring sound like a plane going down on the shimmering horizon.

In the town where I live, they've had to board up the dance-hall windows because there have been so many fights. There's so little to do except work that people wind up in a state of idle agitation that becomes fatalistic, as if there were nothing to be done about all this untapped energy. So the dark side to the grandeur of these spaces is the small-mindedness that seals people in. Men become hermits; women go mad. Cabin fever explodes into suicides, or into grudges and lifelong family feuds. Two sisters in my area inherited a ranch but found they couldn't get along. They fenced the place in half. When one's cows got out and mixed with the other's, the women went at each other with shovels. They ended up in the same hospital room but never spoke a word to each other for the rest of their lives.

After the brief lushness of summer, the sun moves south. The range grass is brown. Livestock is trailed back down from the mountains. Water holes begin to frost over at night. Last fall Martin asked me to accompany him on a pack trip. With five horses, we followed a river into the mountains behind the tiny Wyoming town of Meeteetse. Groves of aspen, red and orange, gave off a light that made us look toasted. Our hunting camp was so high that clouds skidded across our foreheads, then slowed to sail out across the warm valleys. Except for a bull moose who wandered into our camp and mistook our black gelding for a rival, we shot at nothing.

One of our evening entertainments was to watch the night sky. My dog, a dingo bred to herd sheep, also came on the trip. He is so used to the silence and empty skies that when an airplane flies over he always looks up and eyes the distant intruder quizzically. The sky, lately, seems to be much more crowded than it used to be. Satellites make their silent passes in the dark with great regularity. We counted eighteen in one hour's viewing. How odd to think that while they circumnavigated the planet, Martin and I had moved only six miles into our local wilderness and had seen no other human for the two weeks we stayed there.

At night, by moonlight, the land is whittled to slivers—a ridge, a river, a strip of grassland stretching to the mountains, then the huge sky. One morning a full moon was setting in the west just as the sun was rising. I felt precariously balanced between the two as I loped across a meadow. For a moment, I could believe that the stars, which were still visible, work like cooper's bands, holding together everything above Wyoming.

Space has a spiritual equivalent and can heal what is divided and burdensome in us. My grandchildren will probably use space shuttles for a honeymoon trip or to recover from heart attacks, but closer to home we might also learn how to carry space inside ourselves in the effortless way we carry our skins. Space represents sanity, not a life purified, dull, or "spaced out" but one that might accommodate intelligently any idea or situation.

From the clayey soil of northern Wyoming is mined bentonite, which is used as a filler in candy, gum, and lipstick. We Americans are great on fillers, as if what we have, what we are, is not enough. We have a cultural tendency toward denial, but, being affluent, we strangle ourselves with what we can buy. We have only to look at the houses we build to see how we build *against* space, the way we drink against pain and loneliness. We fill up space as if it were a pie shell, with things whose opacity further obstructs our ability to see what is already there.

QUESTIONS FOR CRITICAL READERS

Remembering and Understanding

1. What is the dominant impression of Wyoming that Ehrlich creates? How does she create this impression? Identify the passages that produce this impression.
2. Ehrlich describes Wyoming (and her life there) in terms of opposites, extremes, and contradictions. For example, she says that Wyoming is "cozy." Identify several similar statements, and explain how they make sense.
3. Ehrlich provides a great deal of information, though she seldom arranges it in expository form. Choose one of her subjects (sheep, cattle, Wyoming, cattle, etc,), gather the information she provides, and write a summary or profile of the subject using that information.

Analyzing and Discussing

4. Ehrlich asserts some relationship between landscape and the character of the people who live there. What claims is she making? How do you believe landscape affects people and their relationships?
5. What is the "solace" that Ehrlich finds in open spaces? In what ways does her use of this word indicate her personal perspective?
6. Ehrlich says at one point that "space has a spiritual equivalent." What might this mean?

Writing

7. Ehrlich describes how the terrain and weather of Wyoming affect the people who live there. Consider the terrain and weather where you live, and write a paper in which you speculate about the effects they have on people and their behavior.

Field Corn

RICHARD RHODES

Richard Rhodes was born in Kansas and worked on a farm in Missouri when he was younger. He has written several books, including novels and The Making of the Atomic Bomb, *which won the Pulitzer Prize and other awards. Much of his work has been about the American Midwest, and one critic has called him "one of the few good Midwestern writers of his generation." The selection printed here is from* Farm, *in which Rhodes describes the year he spent visiting and working with a farm family in central Missouri. As you read, keep in mind that Rhodes is a partisan: he knows and loves the Midwest and its people.*

FIRST THING EVERY MORNING Tom checked his cattle and hogs. The holdout sow had farrowed during the night. Ten squeaking pigs, wrinkled and thin, climbed over each other scrapping along her teat lines, fighting to establish their claims. Two pigs had been born dead. One had died weeks earlier in the womb and was mummified, purple and shriveled. The other was a large, healthy pig that had probably smothered in the birth canal. On his way out, Tom picked both of them from the slatted floor at the back of the farrowing crate and dropped them into a five-gallon bucket that held earlier losses. "Seems like it's always the biggest pig that comes out last and gets smothered," he told Sally. Birthing as many as fourteen pigs at a farrowing, the sows tired, their contractions weakening. Once Tom would have set the alarm through the night for several nights running if necessary to midwife a sow. He had too much to do now to trade sleep for a pig. During waking hours when a sow began farrowing he injected it with oxytocin, a drug that strengthens contractions, to help the later pigs along. He'd saved a lot of pigs that way.

Except for Wayne, who was a sophomore off at college, the whole Bauer family sat down to breakfast together every morning before heading its separate ways. Sammi, the nine-year-old, still baby-plump, a child's tummy rounding her waist, was excited about the first meeting that Thursday of her special gifted class. She had her mother's dark eyes, large in her child's open face, and wore her dark straight hair cut bobbed. Last spring she'd tested out with the highest IQ of anyone in her grade in the entire Plymouth school district. She was a champion reader and a chatterbox with a quick smile. To ask a question she imitated a character from a book setting a finger to her cheek and cocking her head. Collecting ran in the family. Her brother Wayne collected Western-style belt buckles. She collected Barbie dolls and their endless accessories, buying them up for pennies at the garage sales she and her mother liked to shop. More than sixty of the skinny, platinum-haired dolls filled an entire room in the finished basement of the house, where Wayne and Brett had their bedrooms. It looked unreal, rows of identical dolls staring from shelves and chairs and daybeds, like a congress of cheerleaders assembled somewhere beyond the twilight zone.

In the backyard, under the big oak, Sammi had built a model countryside of dirt roads and twig fences. An assortment of plastic farm animals grazed her fields—small horses and giant chickens, hogs larger than cows—and a heavy traffic of battered steel toy trucks left over from her brothers' childhoods lumbered through the dappled shade. A combine had been her cradle. She'd slept through the harvests of her infancy in the cab beside her mother as Sally worked, corn and soybeans roaring lullabies.

Sally was off again to the ceramics shop. She was packing pieces to sell at the annual show in Kansas City in October, trying to get her overworked brother organized before Tom needed her to run the combine. Brett, a junior at Plymouth High School and a popular tackle on the junior varsity, would stay after school again for football practice. "You'll need to mix some feed when you get home," his father instructed him. The feed was for the hogs.

Tom planned to start the day by moisture-testing some corn, then clean out one of those backup storage spaces before carrying on with servicing the combine. There was also a corn test plot to visit down in the river bottoms that the Young Farmers Association was picking that day. It was cooler this morning after yesterday's storms, the sky blue and clear. Tom collected a broom, a scoop shovel and his portable moisture tester and drove off in the blue International work pickup rather than the GMC. The old truck coughed and stalled its way down the lane, warming up. Toolboxes built into its side panels and a seventy-five-gallon diesel fuel tank mounted behind the cab with a pump that ran off the engine battery allowed him to service and repair his farm machinery in the field. He'd nicknamed the truck Babe after the blue ox of the Paul Bunyan tall tales. Its odometer showed 147,000 miles, well along on the second hundred thousand.

The first field Tom planned to pick was a bottomland fifteen acres on the Ward farm. Field corn varieties differ by days and even weeks in the time they need to grow from planting to harvest. The corn Tom had planted in the Ward bottomland in April was an earlier-maturing variety, so it would be ready before some of his other fields. Since bottomland didn't drain as well as upland, he also wanted to get the field picked before autumn rains turned it into a mire. Tom made it a practice, a gift of goodwill to his landlords, to harvest his share crops before his own.

Field corn wasn't the sweet corn that city people ate. The individual kernels were bigger, longer in the tooth, dented at the top when they dried, and the ears were twice as big. They grew one and sometimes two to a stalk. They were picked ripe, when the meat of the kernel, the endosperm, had turned to starch and hardened, rather than green, when it was still mostly sugar paste and soft. The husks that protected the ears from the weather ripened too, toughening to the color of raw linen from sweet corn's unripened green. You could eat field corn when it was in the sugar stage just as you could eat sweet corn, but that wasn't the stage in which it was harvested. When it was ready for harvest the kernels were flinty. You had to wait for it to dry down below twenty-percent moisture unless you wanted to dry it in the bin with propane. It needed air blown through it once it was picked and in the bin to drop it on down below ten-percent moisture for long-term storage. Otherwise it could ferment and the heat of fermentation could kill it, pockets within the bin burning to a black carbon char. Each individual corn kernel was alive, a plant embryo in a state of arrested development packed with a starter supply of nutrients. If it died, chemical changes reduced its food value. Harvesting such living fruits by the billions meant paying close attention. It was anything but routine work.

Tom parked on the same road through the Ward fields that he'd driven earlier in the week when he'd brought out the combine. The Ward farm was located a mile west and south of his own. To get there he drove north to Devon, west on U.S. 24, south on the county blacktop. The road through the fields ran east off the blacktop, dividing the bottomland of the farm from the upland. It followed the rise of a low, weathered hill to the old fallen-down homestead collapsed within a grove of big oaks that looked north from the flattened crest. Beyond the homestead on the table of upland was the converted barn where Tom stored the combine. Beyond that, more corn and soybean fields extended south up a further rise that dictated their terracing. Back at the beginning again, at the northern limit of the farm, Little Cebo Creek meandering west formed the boundary of the bottomland. Tall rows of cornstalks standing shoulder to shoulder hemmed in the road, blocking the view of the creek, but the grass and weeds growing on the hill slope and the shallow pond at the western edge of the bottomland signaled drainage problems. Tom had only farmed the Ward place for one season. He had major plans for improving it.

He left Babe on the one-lane road and pushed his way into the bottomland corn. Five rows in he snapped off an ear, rustled a few feet farther down the row and snapped off another ear. He shucked the husks, carried the ears back to the truck, found a coffee can and shelled it full. The kernels were plump and rosy yellow. Tom chewed one to test it, nodded and spit it out.

His portable moisture tester looked like a high-tech coffee can. On the open tailgate of the truck he poured it full of kernels, set its scale and pushed a button. A battery sent electricity through the corn sample and a meter measured the sample's conductivity, which depended on its moisture. A rotating scale gave Tom the number he was looking for, twenty-one percent. That was still high, but it was getting there. With the sun out, even one day would make a big difference. The blower would work more efficiently on these first loads, before the bin filled up. It wouldn't be long now.

He hadn't used his moisture tester since the previous fall. It might be off. Tom decided to check it against a big state-inspected unit at an elevator. The Missouri Farmers Association cooperative elevator in Osage Station, four miles due south on the blacktop, was closer than Riverton. From MFA he could loop around the other county road to his brother's place. He backed Babe out to the blacktop and headed south.

Periwinkle-blue chicory bloomed at roadside. The soybeans had begun to turn. The leaves yellowed before they dropped. This early, the passing fields looked as if they were laid over with dark jade veined with gold. The countryside changed color from season to season, but at transitional seasons, spring and fall, it also changed color from day to day and you could tell exactly how things were if you knew what you were looking at. When the crops were harvested it opened up; when the crops were full grown it closed in. It breathed. There was life from horizon to horizon right down to the least small organism in the soil.

Two miles along toward Osage Station Tom passed an access road marked with a No Admittance sign. It led to a locked gate and beyond the locked gate to what looked like a small fenced lot. But the lot was surfaced with smooth gray concrete with streamlined curbs and a microwave communications antenna was mounted on the fence. Tom was used to the installation and hardly gave it a glance. It was a missile silo, blast-hardened and eighty feet deep, one of 150 punched into the central Missouri countryside on precise five-mile centers, insensible to the lay of the land. A three-stage Minuteman II missile was shock-mounted inside the silo, ready to fire, with a 1.2-megaton warhead.

In the scale room at the MFA office Tom gave the young clerk the coffee can of corn to test. The clerk weighed a 250-gram sample and poured it into his tester. The digital screen on his tester read out 23.7 percent. He poured the kernels back into the coffee can.

"How come you run that tester three percent high?" Tom asked, his voice going hard.

The clerk was surprised. "You're kidding."

"I'm serious. That old boy who used to work here said it ran high. There's a lot of talk about it."

"The state inspector always passes it," the clerk said. He turned back to the machine and ran another sample of Tom's corn. This time he got 23.9, well within tolerances.

"I don't know," Tom concluded as he picked up to leave, "it sure looks to me like it runs high." He made a mental note to send Brett to Comstock's with the coffee can to compare the two testers. Farmer against miller was a battle as old as the hills.

Tom pulled into the driveway of his older brother Warner's house and knocked on the back door. No one was home. A timid German shepherd came around from the front yard. She did her bows and Tom gave her a pat. His brother was making some changes. He'd decided to sell off most of his land. Lately he was driving a semi as an independent hauler, hauling corn down to Arkansas to the big Tyson broiler factories there. He was probably off making a run. The wife worked.

Tom crossed to the weathered gray barn behind the house and slid back the heavy door. Parked inside was his brother's silver pickup and, directly behind it, a small, open-seat New Idea tractor fitted with a scoop blade. The key was in the pickup's ignition but it wouldn't start. The battery was dead. Tom shifted into neutral, jumped down, pushed the truck out into the driveway and set the brakes. Back inside the barn he studied the two connected corncribs off the main aisle that he meant to clean. They'd been turned to storage, truck tires stacked in, pumps, lumber, pieces of angle iron, a quilt wadded into mouse nests on the floor, dust everywhere and cobwebs and chewed chunks of corncob. Tom counted four truck tires. They were new. He kicked one. "I bet old Warner bought these at a sale somewhere," he said. Out in the yard the German shepherd heard him and wagged her tail.

In the garage between the barn and the house Tom found an extension light. He strung it into the cribs to penetrate the gloom. Out came the junk, piece by piece. Tom loaded it into the tractor scoop. When the scoop was full he started up the tractor and drove around to the south side of the barn to an open cow shed. He stacked the junk neatly inside the cow shed by type, five-gallon oilcan with five-gallon oilcan, rags with rags, six-by-six oak beam leaned against the wall with its shorter twin. He made sure nothing metal was touching the ground where it might corrode. His brother wouldn't have to move his junk again for years.

Tom swept the cribs clean of trash, his black sideburns and eyebrows going gray in the process, then latched together the homemade wooden ducting that would channel air through the corn to dry it. When he was finished he could count six thousand bushels more capacity than he'd had before. "I sure as hell hate to haul that corn all the way over here, though," he told his brother later. "That combine's going to be just sitting out in the field waiting."

The Young Farmers Association corn test plot was laid out on good Missouri River bottomland. The test plot was an annual deal to face off the new varieties of hybrid corn that the corn companies came up with and see how they performed under real Missouri conditions. Different farmers donated the land in exchange for the free seed. Good hybrid seed cost around fifty-five dollars a bag. A bag weighed fifty pounds and contained about eighty thousand kernels. If you planted twenty thousand seeds to the acre you used about a fourth of a bag, so free seed saved that much expense. For the test they planted six rows of a standard corn and then six rows of a test variety. When they picked it they averaged the standard's yield across the entire twenty-acre field to give the test varieties a fair comparison across better and poorer patches of ground. This year's test plot was planted on April 17 with Jacques 7700, Jacques FX21, Coker 8391, Paymaster, Funk's, Super Cross, Garst, Pioneer 3901, MFA 4115, Cargill 893 and Asgrow varieties. Herbicides were Lasso and AAtrex.

Forty was the age cutoff for membership in the Young Farmers, so Tom was too old, but they allowed members who passed the age limit to stay on as associate members. Tom had been active in the organization when he'd had a real say. He only checked in once in a while now. The younger men were running it.

He'd gone by the house and cleaned up and picked up the GMC before driving over to the test plot, which was north of Plymouth a. few miles down a dirt road. It was nearly noon when he arrived. Pickups were parked fanned out in a ledge of tall weeds above the field. The broken-down weeds made the air acrid with their sap. Tom hiked down the ledge into the flat, open field—the outside rows had already been picked—and there was his older brother Dale. They grinned and shook hands, making a joke of it. "You old devil," Tom greeted his brother, "how you been?"

Like Tom, Dale was wearing a Funk's Hybrid G cap, showing the colors, the cap's light tan crown and bill set off by a good-looking patch with an ear of corn on it embroidered in green, red and gold. Dale sold Funk's seed to supplement his income from farming and his patch had an extension panel incorporating his name, address and phone. He was six feet tall, confident, heavier than Tom and balder, with cheeks like Santa Claus and a ruddy complexion. His eyes were the same blue, with the same twinkle. Anyone could tell they were brothers. He was retired after twenty years as a civilian aircraft mechanic for the Air Force, and sometimes Tom envied him that monthly retirement check. It made farming a lot less dicey proposition.

The combine picking the test corn was a Gleaner, finished in galvanized iron sheeting and angular and alien, the most insectlike of all the combine designs. The two brothers watched it make a pass-through, picking six rows at a time, then wheel off to one side of the field and dump the corn into a grain wagon, make another pass-through and wheel off to the other side and dump that corn into another grain wagon, separating the standard from the test plantings. Dale nudged Tom and they headed into the corn to look for corn borer damage, cornstalks broken at the joints and blown over where borer larvae had weakened them by eating out the pith. They found moderate damage, a stalk down every twenty or thirty plants. Out in the open again they walked up the stobble rows where the Gleaner had passed, following a trail of corn kernels the machine has failed to separate from the discharge. "He's got something out of adjustment," Tom said. "He ought to be picking that up." Dale nodded agreement.

They stopped to watch the farmer who owned the field trying to engage the gearshift on a rusty John Deere tractor hooked up to one of the loaded grain wagons. The gears wouldn't shift.

"Linkage is shot," Tom speculated.

"Hell," Dale said, "he's probably known about that for a year. Now, when he needs it, it breaks down." The Bauer boys took care of their machinery. "Then they come up to us when we're out in the field," Dale bragged, "and say, " 'You're lucky, you don't have breakdowns.' "

Jeb Hurder joined them to watch the comedy, one of Tom's neighbors, blond and handsome, another former Young Farmer. Like Tom, Jeb owned a red Case International combine. He knew Dale favored John Deere equipment, which was green. "Damn," he said, "I guess we could of brought some red paint. That would have helped that old thing." Farm machinery loyalties were always good for a laugh.

The men working on the tractor brought up a grain truck and tried to release the tractor's gears by towing it. It was seized up and wouldn't move. They unhitched the grain wagon then and hauled it away with another tractor. Behind them at the edge of the field, in the rich bottomland, sunflowers grew to twice a man's height in clumps where last year's seeds had fallen. They towered over bountiful stands of lacy marijuana. In the nineteenth century, hemp was an important Missouri crop, and volunteer marijuana grew everywhere in the state. Tom hitched a thumb in its direction. "That's probably worth more than the corn," he joked. It never would have occurred to him to smoke it. To all three men, weeds around a field, like a poorly maintained tractor, betrayed slovenly farming.

They hiked up to the barn for the free dinner. Two Plymouth banks this time had donated hamburgers and fixings. Young vice-presidents bulging from clean new blue jeans manned the charcoal grills. Forty or fifty farmers were on hand, the younger men in wash-faded jeans, the older men in grease-stained bib overalls. When they weren't Young Farmering, everyone was busy servicing machinery, getting ready to harvest.

The Gleaner worked on through dinner, eating up the rows, dumping the twenty-one- and twenty-two-percent-moisture grain into a batch drier set up at the edge of the field. The batch drier was a green cage of fine-mesh steel screen hooked up to a gas-fired blower that howled like a banshee. Below the blower's howl they could hear the deep growling of the combine. The growl changed in pitch as the machine worked toward them and away. After dinner Tom caught the Gleaner unloading, its iron auger gushing yellow grain. He climbed the ladder to the cab and rode a couple of rounds to check it out. "That booger hits into the rows, the RPMs don't drop," he told Dale afterward, a little surprised. "She can handle the corn." Gleaner made a good machine, but it wasn't a rotary. Rotaries were simpler. They wore better because they didn't have as many moving parts to get out of whack. International had a bunch of patents on the rotary design. He'd stick with them.

A couple of hours was as much time as Tom could stand hanging around watching someone else pick corn. He took off and drove back toward Devon. About half a mile west of town he turned in to a gravel driveway and followed it south past a one-story white farmhouse to a collection of weathered gray outbuildings. Parked in front on the gravel in the shade of a big elm was a rusty, four-row Gleaner F2 combine. Tom pulled up behind it.

His best friend, Clarence Galen, came sauntering out of the workshop gloom to greet him, his gray, grease-stained coveralls opened in the afternoon heat halfway to his waist. "Hey, boy," Clarence demanded, "get on over here. This old piece of crap needs that electrical expertise of yours."

"You mean you or that junk combine you bought?" Tom shot back, meeting Clarence halfway.

"Watch it, boy." They didn't shake hands; they got together nearly every day.

Tom had taught himself electrical wiring fixing up his own used machinery. Side by side on two sections of stump in the weeds outside the workshop the two men searched for the F2's wiring diagram in the shop manuals Clarence had assembled. He'd bought the old Gleaner at a bankruptcy sale for thirty-five hundred dollars. New, it would have cost sixty thousand but it wasn't nearly new. The bankrupt owner was a kid who'd inherited the family farm and run it into bankruptcy in just nineteen months. Tom didn't know how you could start with all your land paid off and run it into bankruptcy in nineteen months but the kid had managed it. The F2 was rusty because the kid had left it out in the field all year. Its electrical system was a mess because whenever the kid had an electrical problem he'd simply cut the wires.

The Galens were an old family in Crevecoeur County. Clarence's dad, Oliver Galen, owned a farm due north on the other side of the highway that ran back to the river bluffs. There were other Galens up and down the highway in orchards. Their descent was German, like Tom's family, but instead of lifelong Democrats they were solid Republicans. Clarence at sixty-three was pure gold, a lean, almost lanky man with a weathered, heavily lined face, full lips and bushy dark eyebrows. He was a Second World War infantry veteran, a tough survivor. He liked to clown as much as Tom did, but there was fatalism under the playfulness. Partly that was just his character. Partly it was the war. Partly it was circumstance. His only child, his son Gene, who operated a construction crane for a living and was running for city council in Plymouth, was fighting cancer.

Between them, Tom and Clarence couldn't find the wiring diagram. They went over to the combine and Tom climbed up into the cab and looked around. "This was all disconnected when you got it?" he asked Clarence.

"Hell, they was just tore out." Clarence pulled a pack of cigarettes from his breast pocket, set one in his teeth and cupped a Bic lighter to the tip.

"So you're just kind of having to guess at it?"

"Yeah."

Tom had brought along a pocket circuit tester, two wires forking from a glowlight. He began checking for lights and found a few still working, a utility light over the holding bin behind the cab and the rear flashers. He found the headlight wires and connected them within the cab. They worked, but the wire he hooked them to got hot.

"The two top lights should be on," he called down to Clarence.

"They are."

"Wire's getting hot. She's pulling a lot of ohms is what she's doing."

Clarence climbed the ladder and leaned into the one-man cab. "Let's see if we got a taillight." He worked a switch overhead.

"That could be the slow-moving-vehicle switch," Tom said.

Clarence clamped his cigarette between his teeth and hung off the platform. The smoke made him squint. "Nope. No taillights."

"We got to find that top wire is all," Tom said. "We ought to just run another pair of wires and bypass the problem."

Clarence looked back in. "You know why the priest wore his shorts in the shower?" he deadpanned.

Tom could deadpan too. "Reckon you'll tell me," he said.

"So's he wouldn't have to *look down* on the *unemployed*." Clarence laughed, loud and barking, and did a slow-motion parody of slapping his knee.

Tom laughed as much at Clarence's clowning as at his joke. "That the best they come up with down at the Liars' Club this morning?" The

Liars' Club was their name for a diner in Devon where farmers stopped for coffee.

Clarence wiped his eyes with the bent thumb of the hand that held his cigarette. "Yeah. Sure was. Like to died when I heard it." He barked another laugh. "Wouldn't have to be looking down on that old *unemployed*."

Tom went over the wiring while Clarence tried to figure out how to take a gear assembly apart. By the end of the afternoon they had all the lights working again.

QUESTIONS FOR CRITICAL READERS

Remembering and Understanding

1. Using the information Rhodes provides, list and then describe the various things a farmer needs to know in order to simply get through his day.
2. What is Tom Bauer like as a person? Use the information Rhodes provides to write a brief profile of Bauer and his personality.
3. Though the narrative here covers only part of a day, Rhodes provides a great deal of information about this farm family and its activities. Write a brief profile of the family.

Analyzing and Discussing

4. In what ways do the people and events described here confirm or depart from your notions of what farmers and farming are like?
5. What dominant impression does Rhodes create here about farmers and farming? Describe his tone and attitude. Identify statements that indicate how he wants you to feel about his subject.
6. What does the description of crops and farm machinery contribute to the overall narrative? How do they help you visualize or better understand Rhodes's subject?

Writing

7. Using someone you know (or someone who will let you follow them around), write a profile or description of a typical day or part of a day for that person. Take your readers through the person's activities, but also be sure to use details that disclose your subject's personality and your own attitudes toward your subject.

Synthesizing and Consolidating

1. Contrast the views of Ehrlich and Shaw on the value of open space.
2. Badger laments the loss of land to development, especially to RV parks and retirement villages. What would some of the other writers in this chapter (e.g., Shaw, Pasley, and Fairlie) say in reply to his concern?
3. Which of the writers in this chapter seem to romanticize the notion of place and the belief that it has some effect on people and their behavior?
4. How would Ehrlich and Hubbell respond to Shaw's ideas about population density?
5. Pasley discusses the long hours and hard work on farms. McCaig describes some of that work. How would McCaig and Tom Bauer (in Rhodes) respond to Pasley?

Suggestions for Research and Writing

1. Fairlie says that "work still gives meaning to rural life." Explore this statement. What could it mean? How would you explain it to someone else?
2. Badger says that the family farm is an anachronism in the age of "corporate agribusiness." Pasley says that corporations are not interested in farming. Begin with Pasley's statistics about farming, and gather other statistics about "corporate agribusiness." Who is right? Does corporate agribusiness dominate farming? What is the place of the family farm?
3. Ehrlich describes her surroundings in terms of landscapes rather than details. Describe your own surroundings using landscapes as the dominant focus, adding details only as they are necessary.
4. In contrast to question 3, describe your surroundings using details almost exclusively, ignoring the larger features of landscape.
5. Fairlie says that "urban life today is aggressively individualistic and atomized. Cities are not social places." Write a paper in which you respond to this statement, which might be taken as either a description or a value judgment. You may agree, disagree, or write about your own ideas and impressions. Your interpretation of the statement's intent will guide your response.
6. Write a paper in which you express your own ideas or beliefs about the relationship between people and their surroundings.

8

How Many Languages for America?

IN RECENT YEARS a number of groups have attempted to legally establish English as the official language of the United States. While these groups have had no success on the national level, almost twenty states have passed laws declaring English their official language. This movement is apparently a response to recent increases in Hispanic and Asian immigration to the United States, and the pressures for linguistic and cultural diversity that have followed that immigration. Many Americans believe that recent immigrants do not want to assimilate into American culture, and that they will continue to express their separateness from American culture by maintaining their native languages rather than adopting English.

Some Americans support English as an official language because they believe it is wrong to remain culturally separate while enjoying the economic and political advantages of living in the United States. Others support this movement because they fear that the United States will lose its sense of unity and cultural identity if it becomes a multicultural and multilingual society. They also fear that the English language itself might not survive in the United States if other languages are allowed to flourish, and that cultural and linguistic diversity will threaten the nation's survival. How, they ask, can a nation be united if its citizens do not speak a common language?

Those who oppose the official English movement believe that cultural diversity is the source of this country's strength, and that legislating an official language will deny important rights and services to those who speak languages other than English. These people point out that immigrants to the United States have always assimilated into American culture and adopted English, and that the present groups of Hispanic and Asian immigrants are following the usual pattern.

The reading selections gathered in this chapter survey the history of the official English movement and place it in the context of the history of cultural diversity in the United States and of efforts to regulate that diversity. James Crawford introduces the subject by providing a brief history of the U.S. English, one of the organizations in the official English movement. Stephen Wagner contributes a brief history of America's multilingual past in which he surveys how earlier groups of immigrants have assimilated into American language and culture. Mark Halton questions the value of forced assimilation, while George Will argues for a constitutional amendment to make English the official language of the United States. Diane Ravitch explores the ways in which the issue of bilingualism has politicized the schools. Abigail McCarthy expresses her approval of the English Only movement and her fear that multilingualism will fragment the United States. Richard Rodriguez writes about his experiences growing up with more than one language and culture.

Taken together, these selections suggest that discussions about language may not be about language at all, but about patriotism, the meaning of Americanism, and the preservation of individual and cultural identity. Reading about the official English movement thus becomes a way of examining one's own attitudes about language and culture.

Before You Read

1. Describe how you react when you meet someone from another culture or hear someone speaking another language (or in an accent that is unusual).
2. If you have had experiences with languages and cultures other than your own, or lived (even briefly) in another culture, describe your experiences and your reactions to them.
3. If you have had no experiences with other languages or cultures, explain the circumstances in your life that have prevented you from having these experiences.
4. Do you believe it is necessary to speak English to belong to or understand American culture? Explain why or why not.
5. How would you make yourself understood to people who do not speak your language? Choose a simple statement or request for information, and explain how you would communicate it to someone who does not understand your language.

6. Describe your family's language and ethnic background. What parts of this background does your family preserve? For example, does your family maintain sayings, customs, or food from its original culture? Describe these.
7. If you could go to another country to learn about its language and culture, which county would you choose, and why?
8. Summarize your present knowledge of the different linguistic and ethnic groups that live in the United States.

English Only or English Plus

———— JAMES CRAWFORD ————

James Crawford is a former Washington editor of Education Week. *In this selection, from his book* Bilingual Education, *he outlines the recent history of several organizations that have worked to have English declared the legal language of the United States. Crawford's primary interest is in bilingual education, which provides instruction in students' native languages, along with English, but does not attempt to replace native languages with English. The English Only movement is important to him because one of its goals is to eliminate or severely restrict bilingual education. As you read you will want to consider whether Crawford's perspective influences the way he presents information about the English Only movement.*

U.S. ENGLISH WAS ORGANIZED in 1983 as an offshoot of the Federation for American Immigration Reform (FAIR), a Washington, D.C.-based lobby that advocates tighter restrictions on immigration. Its founders were former Senator S. I. Hayakawa, the first sponsor of the English Language Amendment, and Dr. John Tanton, a Michigan ophthalmologist, environmentalist, and population-control activist. Tanton served as president of Zero Population Growth before launching FAIR in the late 1970s. By highlighting the cultural impact of increasing immigration, U.S. English has served to bolster demands for stricter control of the nation's borders. The fledgling group was an immediate success. Using sophisticated direct-mail techniques, U.S. English soon outgrew its parent organization, and by 1988 it was claiming a dues-paying membership of 350,000 and an annual budget of $7 million—roughly five times the size of FAIR's.

Language politics, formerly a minor theme in American history, has taken on a new urgency in the 1980s. U.S. English has crystallized a growing unease with bilingualism, or more precisely, with the perceived indifference toward English among recent immigrants. To many, these newcomers seem content to live in insular communities where they can work, shop, go to school, worship, watch television, and even vote in their native languages. Hispanics and Asians are transforming some cities to the extent that some English speakers feel like strangers in their own neighborhoods. Perhaps most galling to monolingual Americans, government is promoting programs like bilingual education that appear to encourage cultural Balkanization.

The U.S. English message is simple: our common language is threatened by the "mindless drift toward a bilingual society." In this nation of immigrants, the English language has been our "social glue"—not just "*a* bond, but *the* bond" that has held us together and allowed us to resolve our differences—asserts Gerda Bikales, the group's former executive director. Bilingual schooling and voting rights are beginning to weaken these ties, she charges: "They are the programs and symbols of a country which has chosen to divide itself, to adapt to and preserve division rather than to integrate and be whole."

Unless English is legally protected, Senator Hayakawa warns in U.S. English fundraising appeals, the country will find itself increasingly polarized "along language lines" and vulnerable to the kinds of social strife experienced by his native Canada. He argues that an English Language Amendment is necessary to head off a movement for official bilingualism—that is, coequal status for Spanish in the United States—and to "send a message" to immigrants that English-speaking ability is an obligation of American citizenship.

If U.S. English gets its way, that message will take a very practical form: federal, state, and local governments will be forced to curtail a range of services they now provide in minority languages. On specifics the group has been hard to pin down. At various times, leaders of U.S. English have advocated elimination of bilingual 911 operators and health services, endorsed English Only rules in the workplace, petitioned the Federal Communications Commission to limit foreign-language broadcasting, protested Spanish-language menus at McDonald's, and opposed Pacific Bell's *Páginas Amarillas en Español* and customer assistance in Chinese.

During the Proposition 63 campaign, U.S. English began to distance itself from the English Only label, denying any interest in interfering with nonpublic uses of other languages or in curtailing emergency services for non-English-speakers. Still, it has refused to repudiate the concept of language restrictionism, the idea that all Americans should be required to speak English in certain contexts. "There is a price to entering the social and economic and political mainstream," Bikales has insisted, speaking from her personal experience as a German-Jewish immigrant:

> In return for freedom and opportunity, one learns English. . . .
> Cultural displacement, cultural loss, is extremely painful. There is an emotional price to immigration. It doesn't come free. No one can be excused from paying it. Government should not stand idly by and let the core culture, the shared culture formed by generations of

earlier immigrants, slip away. [It] should not allow its own citizens
to feel like strangers in their own land. If anyone has to feel strange,
it's got to be the immigrant—until he learns the language.

This line of argument has found a receptive ear among Americans
of diverse backgrounds and political persuasions, liberal and conservative, Democrat and Republican. It has captured the imagination of pun-
dits, intellectuals, and assorted celebrities: Jacques Barzun, Bruno Bettelheim, Alistair Cooke, Walter Cronkite, George Gilder, Norman
Podhoretz, Arnold Schwarzenegger, W. Clement Stone, and Rosalyn Ya-
low, to name a few. At the same time, it has mobilized nativists who
make no secret of their animus toward language minorities.

In 1985–86, U.S. English generated the bulk of comments supporting the Reagan Administration's proposed regulations on bilingual
education. Along with arguments that immigrant children should be taught
English more quickly, for their own good, many of these letters expressed
ethnic fears and hostilities. Frequently, the latter came from areas with
growing language-minority populations:

> We here in Southern California are overrun with *all* sorts of
> aliens—Asian, Spanish, Cuban, Middle East—and it is an insur-
> mountable task if these millions are not required to learn English.
> Many are *illerate* [sic] in *their native language.* [Rolling Hills, Cali-
> fornia] . . . At the rate the Latinos (and non-whites) reproduce, [we]
> face a demographic imbalance if we do not change several of our
> dangerously outdated laws. Make English the official language every-
> where in the U.S.A. [Jersey City, New Jersey] . . . No other ethnic
> group has made the demands for bilingual education as have the
> Cubans. The more you give them, the more they demand. WHOSE
> AMERICA IS THIS? ONE FLAG. ONE LANGUAGE. [North
> Miami, Florida]

Such sentiments among its followers have proved an embarrassment
for U.S. English, and a rallying point for its opponents. Leaders of Hispanic and Asian communities, along with elected officials ranging from
Tom Bradley, the Democratic mayor of Los Angeles, to William Clements,
the Republican Governor of Texas, have denounced the English Only
movement as racially divisive. Attorney General James Shannon of Massachusetts, a Democrat, warned that enacting an official-English measure
in his state would intensify "bigotry, divisiveness, and resentment of
minority groups." Senator Pete Domenici, Republican of New Mexico,
called the proposed English Language Amendment to the U.S. Constitution "an insult to all Americans for whom English is not the first language. . . . It won't help anyone learn the English language. It won't

improve our society. It won't lead to a more cohesive nation. In fact, it will create a more divided nation."

CHARGES OF RACISM

Is U.S. English exploiting racism to advance its agenda? Is it using the official-English campaign as a stalking-horse for a new nativist movement? In a 1986 interview, Gerda Bikales rejected these suggestions as "a very vicious series of attacks. . . . I do not believe at all that we are responsible for any of this [racial animosity]. This is a mass movement. Anybody can and does join U.S. English. We do our very best to put out responsible ideas, responsible policies. We're not hate-mongers. There's no doubt that as long as our political leadership is going to continue to bury its head in the sand, we are going to have this kind of situation that's . . . somewhat out of control."

Stung by charges of anti-Hispanic bias, in mid-1987 U.S. English hired Linda Chavez as its president. Formerly staff director of the U.S. Commission on Civil Rights and director of public liaison in the Reagan White House, Chavez was sophisticated in the ways of Washington. Immediately, she began working to dispel the organization's exclusionist image and to replace it with a beneficent one. She championed official English as a way to bring newcomers into the mainstream. In frequent public appearances, she advertised the presence of immigrants on the U.S. English board of directors, including Senator Hayakawa, who had once been barred from this country under the Oriental Exclusion Act because of his Japanese ancestry. Finally, Chavez cited her own Hispanic roots dating back three centuries in New Mexico. "Contrary to any anti-immigrant sentiment pervading the official-English movement, quite the opposite concern motivates" U.S. English, she maintained:

> Unless we become serious about protecting our heritage as a unilingual society—bound by a common language—we may lose a precious resource that has helped us forge a national character and identify from so many diverse elements. I truly believe that the official English movement will help protect the future integration of new Americans, as it has helped make Americans of so many generations of immigrants in the past.

It was an effective argument, made by an effective spokesperson. Chavez boosted the credibility of U.S. English, especially on Capitol Hill. Representative Don Edwards, a liberal Democrat from California, convened the first House subcommittee hearings on the English Language Amendment. Leaders of language-minority communities continued to attack U.S. English as xenophobic. But such claims had limited force when a prominent Hispanic was leading the official-English campaign and portraying it as a civil rights measure.

For Linda Chavez and U.S. English, the honeymoon ended abruptly in October 1988. First came the publication of a memorandum by John Tanton that Chavez described as "repugnant" and "not excusable." In his paper the U.S. English chairman warned of a Hispanic political takeover in the United States through immigration and high birthrates:

> *Gobernar as poblar* translates 'to govern is to populate'. In this society, where the majority rules, does this hold? Will the present majority peaceably hand over its political power to a group that is simply more fertile? . . . Can *homo contraceptivus* compete with *homo progenitiva* if borders aren't controlled? . . . Perhaps this is the first instance in which those with their pants up are going to get caught by those with their pants down. . . . As Whites see their power and control over their lives declining, will they simply go quietly into the night? Or will there be an explosion? . . . We are building in a deadly disunity. All great empires disintegrate; we want stability.

Tanton's memo, written for a 1986 discussion on "the non-economic consequences of immigration to California," enumerated a range of cultural threats posed by Spanish-speaking immigrants: "the tradition of the *mordida* (bribe), the lack of involvement in public affairs"; Roman Catholicism, with its potential to "pitch out the separation of church and state"; low "educability" and high school-dropout rates; failure to use birth control; limited concern for the environment; and of course, language divisions.

The second damaging disclosure involved two large contributors to U.S. English and FAIR that had financed racist propaganda about immigrants and advocated policies of eugenic sterilization, respectively. Chavez expressed dismay to learn of these connections, explaining that she had been denied access to most of the U.S. English financial records.

Describing Tanton's written views as "anti-Hispanic and anti-Catholic," Chavez quit her $70,000-a-year job in protest. Walter Cronkite resigned from the advisory board of U.S. English and told the group to stop using his name in its fundraising. And Tanton himself stepped down, issuing a bitter statement in which he denied any racist intent and denounced the opponents of official English for their "McCarthyite tactics of guilt by association."

QUESTIONS FOR CRITICAL READERS

Remembering and Understanding

1. Summarize the reasons that U.S. English and other groups want to make English the official language of the United States.
2. According to Crawford, what evidence do English Only advocates present to show that English is threatened by other languages?
3. What evidence does Crawford present to support the charge that the movement to make English an official language is motivated by racism?

Analyzing and Discussing

4. Why should hearing people speak languages other than English make Americans feel like strangers in their own country? That is, what is it about hearing other languages that makes Americans uncomfortable?
5. Evaluate whether Crawford's presentation of information may be influenced by his position against the English Only movement.
6. What reasons might immigrants have for maintaining close ties with their native languages and cultures?

Writing

7. Many immigrants to the United States maintain close ties to their native languages and cultures. Write a paper in which you explain their reasons for this cultural and linguistic loyalty, and then explore what might would motivate them to abandon their native language and assimilate into American culture.

America's Non-English Heritage

—————— STEPHEN T. WAGNER ——————

In this selection Wagner takes a historical approach to the question of whether English should be the official language of the United States. Specifically, he examines the history of immigrant groups and their languages in the United States and explains how these groups have maintained their cultural identity and how they have assimilated into American culture. In addition, he looks at earlier attempts to provide for a multilingual society and to establish English as an official language.

In 1862, JUSTIN MORRILL OF VERMONT, later renowned as the father of the land-grant college system, spoke out in Congress against an attempt to require the printing of a German version of the government's *Report on Agriculture:* "I consider the proposition as unsound in principle, and as utterly subversive of the true doctrine of the country, and I hope we shall continue to hold to the sound and safe practice of printing in the English language." Despite Morrill's objections, the House of Representatives decided to print 25,000 copies of the report in German. The next day, however, Representative E. P. Walton reopened the matter, emphasizing the Printing Committee's concern with costs, and adding that he "would be willing to incur this expense for these German citizens if I would for anybody, but I submit the question whether we are to have a national language or not." After another congressman's inquiry as to "whether, in point of fact, we have any legal language or not" was ruled out of order, the House voted to print the report in English only. Though a defeat for those German-Americans who desired official recognition of their language, this decision did not settle for all time the larger question of the proper status of English and other languages in American law and government.

English was never the only language spoken by the American people. Spanish and French colonists brought their languages to the Southwest and Louisiana, where even today they are the mother tongues of many Americans. One of the first books printed in early Massachusetts was Eliot's translation of the Bible into the Algonkian speech of the local

Indians. Most of the English colonies attracted settlers from continental Europe in substantial numbers, and by no means all of these assimilated to an English-speaking culture as quickly as the half-mythical characters celebrated by Crèvecoeur. The Middle Colonies were especially mixed in language as well as national origins.

Before the Revolution Benjamin Franklin expressed alarm at the growth of the German element in Pennsylvania, which amounted to about a third of the province's population. In his *Observations on the Increase of Mankind* (first published in 1755), Franklin indignantly asked:

> Why should the Palatine [German] boors be suffered to swarm in our settlements and, by herding together, establish their language and manners to the exclusion of ours? Why should Pennsylvania, founded by the English, become a colony of *aliens*, who will shortly be so numerous as to germanize us instead of our anglifying them?

Yet within a few years Franklin eliminated this anti-German outburst from a reprint of his *Observations*. Indeed, during the War for Independence the Continental Congress sought support from American Germans by publishing for their convenience such important papers as the *Artikel des Bundes und der immerwaehrenden Eintracht zwischen den Staaten*— known in the original English as the Articles of Confederation. Franklin's fears of German domination proved groundless, and American statesmen felt comfortable enough about the Germans and other non-English-speaking minorities to refrain from attempting forcibly to anglicize them.

Neither the Articles nor the Constitution made English the "official" or "national" language of the United States, nor has any subsequent federal law explicitly done so. Individuals and groups wishing to use languages other than English among themselves have rarely encountered legal restrictions. Nonetheless, from the beginning, English has been used as the language of government, more or less as a matter of course. Requests for the official use of other languages have repeatedly been turned down; Congress in the 1790s, 1840s, and 1860s refused to publish German versions of public documents.

This approach to language issues paralleled the basic national policy which, with few exceptions, governed immigration to the United States for a century after independence: practically no restrictions on entering the country, but no favors to any particular group. As Secretary of State, John Quincy Adams explained to a German nobleman in 1819, "The government of the United States has never adopted any measure to encourage or invite emigrants from any part of Europe." Two years earlier, Congress had approved an extraordinary sale of Alabama lands to a company of French refugees who proposed to cultivate grapes and olives; but the ensuing land speculation prompted criticism of the lawmakers' judgment as well as of the immigrants' bad faith. *Niles' Weekly Register* expressed a representative opinion:

> I very much question the policy of any act of government that has a tendency to introduce among us a foreign national language or dialect, manners or character, as every large and compact settlement of emigrants from any particular country must necessarily occasion. . . . The people of the United States are yet wretchedly deficient of a national character, though it is rapidly forming, and in a short time will be as the vanguard of the national strength. Its progress, however, is retarded by the influx of foreigners, with manners and prejudices . . . repugnant to our rules and notions of right.

Although John Adams's proposal of 1780 for an American Academy along the lines of the *Academie Francaise* came to nothing, a number of his contemporaries did try to use language as a means of promoting national unity. While Noah Webster sought to standardize spelling and pronunciation, others urged immigrants to learn and use English. Edward Everett, for instance, in 1820 condemned the "inconceivable perversity" of those foreigners who thought it an advantage "to speak a language which your neighbor cannot understand, to be ignorant of the language in which the laws of the land you live in are made and administered, and to shut yourself out, by a Judaic nationality of spirit, from half the social privileges of life." Everett recommended that all immigrants "instead of wishing to cherish and keep their peculiarities of language and manners . . . get over and forget them as soon as possible; remembering, that from the days of the Tower of Babel to the present, confusion of tongues has ever been one of the most active causes of intellectual and political misunderstanding and confusion."

Immigrants themselves frequently urged their compatriots to learn English if they wanted to get ahead in America. A book of "advice and instruction for German emigrants," published in 1856 with German and English texts on facing pages, declared that "as it concerns our means of living, we must, above and beyond all, *rely upon a knowledge of the English language,* and the progress that we make therein has the most important and propitious influence upon our welfare. . . . Whoever does not understand or speak English . . . *continues a stranger here;* his employer entertains a kind of suspicion of him as long as he is unable to speak the language."

The noted political theorist Francis Lieber, an immigrant from Prussia, complained that Germans, Frenchmen, and other continental Europeans had more difficulty in obtaining government jobs than did Irish and other English-speaking immigrants. However, Adam de Gurowski, a Polish revolutionary exile, claimed in 1859 that the cause of the Germans' relative lack of success in American politics was their loyalty to their mother tongue.

American political leaders of the nineteenth century generally saw no need for efforts by the national government to hasten the assimilation of immigrants. Federal authorities showed a more active concern, however, about the continued use of non-English languages among three non-immigrant groups: the Indians, the French-speaking inhabitants of Louisiana, and the Spanish-speaking residents of New Mexico. Desire to "Americanize" these people was reinforced by fears that they might pose a political threat to the unity of the United States if they remained loyal to their own traditions, including their mother tongues.

From Jefferson's presidency onward, the U.S. government supported efforts to "civilize" the Indians. Early laws on the subject rarely mentioned language. In a treaty of 1828 the Cherokees did secure help in purchasing a press and type for printing in their own language; and several white missionary societies, evidently more concerned with spreading Christianity than with promoting the use of English, established bilingual schools that taught religion in the languages their pupils understood best. But government officials increasingly insisted that civilization required education in English.

Although in 1888 the missionaries won approval for the continued use of Indian Bibles, Arnold H. Leibowitz reports that by that time "there did not exist an Indian pupil whose tuition and maintenance was paid by the U.S. government who was permitted to study in any language other than English." Many young Indians were sent far from their reservations for years at a time to boarding schools, where they were forced to give up their traditional hairstyles, dress, customs, and languages—surely the most coercive attempt at cultural assimilation ever sponsored by the United States government. Not until the 1930s did federal authorities begin to encourage tribes to maintain their own languages and cultures.

American policy toward the French-speaking population acquired with the purchase of Louisiana in 1803 was also markedly pro-English, though not so anti-French as to provoke revolt. Jefferson attempted to conciliate the long-time residents of "Orleans Territory"; but many of his appointees there, including the governor and several judges, were recently arrived Anglo-Americans. This, as noted by Charles Gayarré in his famous *History of Louisiana,* caused some resentment, which was intensified by the confusion and injustice that attended the sudden introduction of the English language and common law into the courts.

Some New England Federalists had objected to the annexation of Louisiana, partly because of the French character of its people. Perhaps in an effort to mollify these critics, the 1811 act enabling the Louisianians to draft a constitution and apply for admission as a state specified that "the laws which such State may pass shall be promulgated, and its records of every description shall be preserved, and its judicial and legislative written proceedings conducted, in the language in which the laws and the judicial and legislative written proceedings of the United States are now published." The Louisianians accepted this condition for statehood.

The state constitution with which Louisiana entered the Union in 1812 stipulated that the language used for state laws, official documents, and judicial and legislative records had to be that "in which the Constitution of the United States is written." Such formulations, avoiding direct use of the term "English," may have reflected either hostility to the British government in a time of international tension or a desire to emphasize the political rationale for linguistic unity, or both. In any case, they were echoed in later justifications for the preservation of English as the de facto American national language.

Unlike Texas and California, New Mexico remained predominantly Spanish-speaking for decades after its acquisition from Mexico in 1848. Unlike Louisiana, which had been rather promptly admitted to statehood in spite of its Francophone majority, New Mexico was kept waiting for some sixty years. Not all of the factors contributing to the unusual delay related to the territory's Hispanic culture. But as late as 1902 a special Senate committee, led by Albert J. Beveridge, stressed its disapproval of the continuing widespread use of Spanish in schools and courts, arguing that New Mexico would not be ready for statehood until at least a majority of its people were assimilated to "American" language and customs. The enabling act that allowed New Mexico and Arizona to draft state constitutions passed early in 1910, the same year in which the census showed that, largely because of migration from the other states, "Anglos" had finally become a majority of New Mexico's population. In passing the enabling act, Congress insisted that the "schools shall always be conducted in English" and the "ability to read, write, speak, and understand the English language without an interpreter shall be a necessary qualification for all state officers and members of the state legislature." In 1911 Congress withdrew the second requirement but not the first; in 1912 New Mexico became a state.

STATE AND FEDERAL LAW

Throughout American history the language policies and practices of the individual states have been at least as important as those of the federal government, especially in the nineteenth century when state actions were much more likely than those of officials in Washington to affect the lives of ordinary people. English was, of course, routinely employed as the language of state and local government—and of the public schools— but at times other languages were also used. In general, languages of "old settler" groups, whose occupation of an area preceded or coincided with the arrival of English-speaking Americans, were more likely to be used in government than were those of new immigrants to long-settled places.

Old stories telling how German narrowly missed adoption as a (or even *the*) state language of Pennsylvania belong to myth rather than history. However, Pennsylvania did appoint an official German printer in 1843; and in the "Pennsylvania Dutch" region a great deal of the business of local governments and the lower courts was carried on in German. Likewise, Louisiana before the Civil War published its laws in both English and French and allowed the use of both languages in its legislature and courts; the language of government at lower levels was the language of the local population. Other states—and some territories besides New Mexico—quite commonly printed public documents in various languages. The constitution proposed for Minnesota in 1857, for instance, was issued in German, Swedish, Norwegian, and French versions.

Many early laws establishing public schools contained no language provisions. In 1836 Pennsylvania's Free School Superintendent explained that German-language schools could count as common schools. In 1840 Ohio, responding to considerable political activity among its German residents, explicitly sanctioned German-English schools, which led to the growth of a substantial bilingual school system in Cincinnati. Because of the American tradition of local control over public schools, non-English majorities in particular districts were often able to obtain tax-supported instruction in their own languages even where state laws were silent or hostile. Some Americans were very dubious about public schools in which, according to an 1873 *Atlantic Monthly* article, "the teachers are German, the moral atmosphere is German, the methods are German, and the language of the school, to say the least, as much German as English."

American suspicion of immigrants intermittently has found expression in politics, notably through the Know-Nothing clubs of the mid-1850s and the immigration restriction movement that flourished from the 1890s to the 1920s. Hostility toward the use of languages other than English has traditionally been regarded as a rather minor element in American nativism. Ray Billington's account in *The Protestant Crusade* focuses mainly on the role played by religious hatred in the pre-Civil War unrest, while John Higham's *Strangers in the Land* identifies anti-Catholicism, anti-radicalism, and Anglo-Saxon racism as the three major elements underlying the later agitation. When labor leaders have supported immigration restriction, their main objective has been to protect American wage rates, not the English language. Moreover, nativists' dislike of the Irish, which was very strong through most of the nineteenth century, shows that in their view the ability to speak English did not in itself entitle an immigrant to be considered truly American.

Nevertheless, many spokesmen for the English-speaking majority, considering full assimilation of the immigrants to be necessary and desirable, regarded the use of English as an almost indispensable means of Americanization. Theodore Roosevelt argued in 1888 that

> the man who becomes completely Americanized . . . and who "talks United States" instead of the dialect of the country which he has of his own free will abandoned is not only doing his plain duty by his adopted land, but is also rendering to himself a service of immeasurable value. . . . A man who speaks only German or Swedish may nevertheless be a most useful American citizen; but it is impossible for him to derive the full benefit he should from American citizenship.

Urging the newcomers to do themselves a favor by learning English, Roosevelt was still confident that the country could and would successfully absorb the immigrants.

However, even then the "new immigration" from southern and eastern Europe was increasing; and as industrialization and urbanization accelerated, cultural conflicts, including disputes over language, were becoming more important in American politics. As in earlier years, the use of languages other than English in the schools gave rise to controversy. Late in the 1880s Missouri's Superintendent of Public Instruction complained of the large number of districts in the state where school classes were conducted mainly or entirely in German. His report for 1889 urged that "the law should specify definitely in what language the instruction of our public schools is to be given. It is a shame and a disgrace to have the English language ruled out of our public schools and German substituted, as is done wholly or in part in many districts in this State. . . ." St. Louis and Louisville, among other cities, dropped the teaching of German from their public schools late in the 1880s.

Parochial schools that used German as the language of instruction found themselves threatened in 1889 when Illinois adopted the Edwards law and Wisconsin, the Bennett law. Both measures, originally passed with little controversy, were compulsory attendance laws which also required all schools to teach most subjects in English. German Lutherans and Catholics protested strenuously, administered severe defeats to the Republicans in the elections of 1890, and secured the repeal of the two laws in 1893.

Illinois Republicans blamed their defeat in the 1892 elections on continuing disaffection among Germans, Poles, Irish, and other immigrant groups. On January 20, 1893, Theodore Roosevelt assured the Hamilton Club of Chicago that Republican resistance to foreign languages in the schools had been correct:

> Those of foreign origin who come here must become Americans; they must become like us, and not seek to make us like them. . . .

> Americanism is primarily and in its essence a matter of faith, of belief, of spirit and purpose. . . . I want to make as strong a plea as I possibly can against hyphenated Americans of every kind, whether German-Americans, Irish-Americans, or native Americans. The word American is broad enough to cover us all. . . . I am an unflinching believer in and supporter of our common school system . . . a system of non-sectarian schools supported by the State, in which the exercises shall be conducted in English and the children are taught to speak United States.

Around the turn of the century immigrants were arriving in such numbers, and concentrating so heavily in certain urban areas, that many observers questioned whether they would in fact readily fit themselves into American society. Some openly denied that the United States could properly assimilate the throngs it was receiving. Beginning in the 1890s the Immigration Restriction League, supported chiefly by "old-stock" New Englanders and championed in Congress by Henry Cabot Lodge, sought to lessen the influx. The means proposed for doing so was a literacy test, which, it was assumed, would tend to exclude the "new immigrant" nationalities much more than the English, the Irish, or the Germans. Pseudoscientific racial theories now joined religious prejudice and fear of alien radicals in arousing dislike of the newcomers among well-established Americans, but linguistic differences also helped create negative impressions of the immigrants.

On returning to his native land in 1907 after many years of residence abroad, Henry James found himself fascinated by the operation of "the caldron of the 'American' character"—and also quite ill at ease. He objected to changes in the traditional "idea of the country": "Is not our instinct, in this matter, in general, essentially the safe one—that of keeping the idea simple and strong and continuous, so that it shall be perfectly sound? To touch it overmuch, to pull it about, is to put it in peril of weakening; yet on this free assault upon it, this readjustment of it in *their* monstrous, presumptuous interest, the aliens, in New York, seemed perpetually to insist." Boston proved just as unsettling to James. As he watched the Sunday crowd coming up Beacon Hill from the Common, he noted: "No note of any shade of American speech struck my ear, save in so far as the sounds in question represent to-day so much of the substance of that idiom. The types and faces bore them out; the people before me were gross aliens to a man, and they were in serene and confident possession." James was not always able to distinguish national origins according to appearance; repeatedly he was unaware of the "alienness" of people he met until he heard them speak. He was amazed when he learned that the young fellow he had asked for directions in the New Hampshire woods was an Armenian; the man whom he accosted when looking for the House of Seven Gables in Salem turned out to be another "flagrant foreigner." James did enjoy viewing the graceful old houses of the town—"the only thing was that I had never bargained for looking at them through a polyglot air."

However "alien" they seemed to sensitive natives, most of the immigrants did learn English, often quite willingly. Of course, as they used English, the immigrants also changed it. Israel Zangwill, whose popular success *The Melting Pot* Theodore Roosevelt called "a great play" in 1908, emphasized that "as to the ultimate language of the United States, it is unreasonable to suppose that American, though fortunately protected by English literature, will not bear traces of the fifty languages now being spoken next to it." Later research by H. L. Mencken and others has confirmed the accuracy of Zangwill's prediction.

In 1906 Congress, while attempting to bring order to the casual and often corrupt naturalization procedures that had prevailed in the states for many years, came closer than ever before to identifying American nationality with English speech. Except for those immigrants who had already applied citizenship, no more aliens were to be naturalized without demonstrating that they could speak English. The enforcement of this requirement doubtless varied considerably from court to court, and it seems unlikely that many judges insisted on near-native fluency in the language. English lessons did become an even more important part of the "Americanization" programs offered by numerous public and private night schools; but even so, for many years substantial numbers of naturalized citizens, let alone resident aliens, used little if any English.

Early in this century the United States government also pursued a pro-English language policy in the possessions it had acquired during the Spanish-American War. In Puerto Rico, for example, from 1905 until 1916 English was supposed to be the sole language of instruction in the schools. In 1916 the rules were altered so that Spanish was to be used through the fifth grade and English from that grade forward.

The greatest impetus toward the exclusive use of English in the United States came from the superpatriotism and suspicion of foreigners that swept over the country during the First World War. More than ever Theodore Roosevelt served as a militant spokesman for what became known as "one hundred per cent Americanism." No longer confident that immigrants who failed to assimilate were hurting only themselves, he declared in "America for Americans," a speech he delivered in 1916, that "unless the immigrant becomes in good faith American and nothing else, then he is out of place in this country and the sooner he leaves it the better." President Wilson and his supporters also joined in castigating "hyphenates." After the United States entered the war, national unity seemed even more imperative. In the autumn of 1917 Roosevelt drafted and circulated a statement which was signed by prominent Americans of various ancestries:

We must have but one flag. We must also have but one language. That must be the language of the Declaration of Independence, of Washington's Farewell Address, of Lincoln's Gettysburg Speech and Second Inaugural. We cannot tolerate any attempt to oppose or supplant the language and culture that has come down to us from the builders of this republic with the language and culture of any European country. The greatness of this nation depends on the swift assimilation of the aliens she welcomes to her shores. Any force which attempts to retard that assimilative process is a force hostile to the highest interests of our country. . . .

German-Americans, some of whom had been conspicuous—though hardly successful—apologists for Imperial Germany before American entry into the war, were the prime targets of the anti-hyphenate hysteria; much public pressure and some new state and local laws were aimed specifically at them. Both public and private schools eliminated instruction of and through German; whereas in 1915 about 324,000 students were studying German, by 1922 fewer than 14,000 were doing so. Some states, such as Nebraska, outlawed the use of any foreign language in elementary schools; Ohio singled out German for prohibition. The town of Findlay, Ohio, went so far as to impose a fine of $25 for using German on the street.

Foreign-language newspapers also came under attack. Theodore Roosevelt decried them as "our most dangerous foe." Government agents kept the foreign-language press, especially German and radical papers, under close scrutiny; in several cases they suppressed allegedly subversive periodicals by denying them the use of the mails.

Wartime suspicion of foreigners also contributed to the enactment, over President Woodrow Wilson's veto, of the first law forbidding the immigration of most adult illiterates. (However, literacy *in English* was not required; to pass the test a person merely had to read forty simple words in any language. Even for naturalization English literacy was not required until 1950.) After the end of the war this new restriction proved insufficient greatly to reduce the supposedly less desirable immigration from southern and eastern Europe. Accordingly, Congress in 1921 and 1924 enacted stringent quota acts which cut the total number of Old World immigrants to be admitted while favoring the peoples of the British Isles and northwestern Europe at the expense of other nationalities. No numerical restrictions were placed on immigration from Latin America, and the number of immigrants arriving from Mexico increased significantly in the 1920s. However, while the long-settled Hispanic population of New Mexico continued to educate its children largely in Spanish—often at the cost of isolation from the more dynamic "Anglos" of the state—Mexican newcomers in Texas and California were commonly segregated from Anglo children and not infrequently punished for speaking Spanish at school.

By the middle of the 1920s, with America seemingly once again safe in its isolation—and with immigration greatly reduced—the anti-foreign hysteria had largely subsided. In 1923 the Supreme Court, in *Meyer v. Nebraska* and other cases, struck down state laws it felt had unduly restricted the teaching or use of foreign languages. However, it allowed laws mandating the use of English as the sole language of instruction to stand; and by then 34 states had such requirements. The "Americanization" efforts which had peaked in 1918–1920 subsided, but their promoters' assumption that immigrants must be encouraged to learn English remained almost unquestioned orthodoxy. With the influx of Eastern Hemisphere immigrants diminished, the number of Americans unable to understand English dropped as well. Official use of any language other than English had come to seem unthinkable.

The influence of traditional American language policy is open to debate. Heinz Kloss has maintained that by and large the anglicization of non-English ethnic groups in the United States has been a matter of voluntary individual choices, not of governmental coercion. Arnold Leibowitz, however, has argued that English literacy tests and English-only requirements in the schools have served chiefly as a means of discriminating against members of minorities disliked by the dominant majority.

While arguing persuasively that American law and practice have accorded fewer linguistic rights to latecomers in settled areas than to groups who accompanied the English as pioneers, Kloss asserts that the languages which have received greatest protection from the state have been those of groups that were well established before the Anglo-Americans came to dominate them. This generalization hardly accounts for the fate of most American Indian languages; but it does apply to French in Louisiana and to Spanish in New Mexico—and, above all, to Spanish in Puerto Rico.

Puerto Rico has been the great exception to the usual language policy of the United States government. From 1900 on, Spanish has enjoyed legal equality with English in the island's legislature and local courts. (However, to facilitate appeals the federal district court's proceedings have been conducted in English.) Much more controversy has arisen concerning the language—or languages—of instruction to be used in the island's schools. Federal officials long hoped to make the Puerto Rican people genuinely bilingual, but their efforts had only limited success.

In the 1930s native Puerto Ricans in charge of the island's educational system sought to increase the use of Spanish in the elementary schools; they met opposition from Secretary of the Interior Harold Ickes and President Franklin Roosevelt. However, Puerto Rican nationalists strongly advocated primacy for Spanish in the island's schools; and, despite a veto by President Truman in 1946, Spanish has been the medium of instruction, even in the secondary schools, since 1949.

Unlike almost every other originally non-English-speaking area ruled by the United States, Puerto Rico never has attracted an Anglo-American "in-migration" large enough to make anglicization—or even true bilingualism—practical. In Kloss's words: "In Puerto Rico the nominal equality of Spanish, the language of the old, established settlers, and of English led in practice to the predominance of the former; the Anglo-Saxons in Puerto Rico play the role of a minority whose language does not enjoy full equality."

As U.S. citizens since the Jones Act went into effect in 1917, Puerto Ricans desiring to move to the continental United States have not been frustrated by the immigration laws. For the most part much more fluent in Spanish than in English, they have presented a special problem to educators and other public officials in places where they have settled in great numbers; as citizens they have, since the mid-1960s, been given government help in their native tongue, as in polling places (where New York's former English literacy test used to exclude many of them from voting) and in the schools.

Government agencies are now more willing to use languages other than English in dealing even with people who are not native-born citizens, but immigrants. The old faith in America as a melting pot has, to a considerable degree, been replaced by a belief—often rather vague—in "cultural pluralism" more or less as promoted in the 1920s by Horace Kallen; certainly the old assumption of Anglo-Saxon superiority is no longer respectable.

Changes in the immigration laws illustrate the shift in sentiment. "Refugee Relief" measures after World War II granted admittance to thousands of Italians, Poles, Jews, and others whom the national origins system would have kept waiting for years. The McCarran-Walter Act of 1952 was both more and less favorable to non-white would-be immigrants than its predecessors: it allowed more Asians but fewer West Indian blacks to enter the country. Since it retained the quotas favoring northwestern Europeans, it became law only over the veto of President Truman, who denounced the whole concept of using national origins as a selective principle: "The idea behind this discriminatory policy was, to put it boldly, that Americans with English or Irish names were better people and better citizens than Americans with Italian or Greek or Polish names. . . . Such a concept is utterly unworthy of our traditions and our ideals." By 1960 Congressman Walter's defense of the immigration laws seemed outdated: "Our quota system is based on the image of our own people. It is like a mirror held up before the American people, reflecting the proportions of their various national origins. The main purpose of it is to permit the speedy assimilation of the newcomer and his absorption into our social, political and economic system more readily than if the immigrants would arrive in numbers disproportionate to the national origins of the people who receive them and make them a part of their own." Despite Walter's objections, the Democratic party platform in 1960 called for scrapping the quota system. After Walter's death in 1963, President Kennedy pressed for such a change, which was signed into law—significantly, after the Civil Rights Act of 1964 was passed—by President Johnson in 1965. The new law by 1968 eliminated all preferential treatment of immigrants from English-speaking countries.

PRESENT AND FUTURE

Early in 1968 Congress passed the first major federal law favoring the use of languages other than English in the schools. Known as the Bilingual Education Act, Title VII of the Elementary and Secondary Education Act offered financial support for projects designed to meet "the special educational needs of the large number of children of limited English-speaking ability in the United States." Many of the act's supporters assumed that chief among those needs was the acquisition of proficiency in English; they regarded instruction using other languages mainly as a means to that end. However, others involved in implementing the law rejected this view of bilingual education as a "transitional" device; they sought instead to use the law to promote "linguistic and cultural maintenance efforts," for instance, by improving the Spanish-language skills of Hispanic students already quite capable of learning in English-language classes. The conflict between proponents of these two purposes for bilingual education continues.

Revisions made to the Bilingual Education Act in 1974 strengthened tendencies toward "biculturalism." Only those programs that employed non-English languages remained eligible for funding; moreover, educators were to teach "with appreciation for the cultural heritage" their students brought with them. On the other hand, changes made by Congress in 1978 attempted to reemphasize improvement in English-language skills.

Since 1974 the federal government has not merely encouraged schools to provide bilingual programs but, in many cases, has required them to do so. In its 1974 *Lau v. Nichols* decision, the United States Supreme Court determined that school districts receiving any federal aid were obliged to provide special help to students unable to benefit from ordinary classes taught in English; failure to do so would constitute national-origin discrimination and thus violate the Civil Rights Act of 1964. This finding upheld the position that the Office of Civil Rights within the Department of Health, Education and Welfare had taken in 1970. Federal officials have subsequently used guidelines derived from the *Lau* case, along with the incentive provided by greatly increased funding for Title VII projects, to stimulate adoption of bilingual methods and bicultural attitudes. Numerous other recent federal education laws provide money for bilingual programs or require, as a condition of continued eligibility for other federal aid, special efforts to educate persons who lack proficiency in English.

In August 1980 the Department of Education proposed to replace the "*Lau* remedies" guidelines with a more detailed and stringent set of rules. Responding to numerous objections, Congress required that the new rules not go into effect until it could debate them the following spring. But in February 1981 the new Secretary of Education, T. H. Bell, withdrew the proposed rules altogether, calling them "harsh, inflexible, burdensome, unworkable and incredibly costly." The 1975 *Lau* guidelines still remain in effect; however, Bell has announced that they will be rewritten to given individual school districts more flexibility.

Bell's action was apparently part of the Reagan Administration's overall plan to reduce federal activities and regulations while giving more scope to state and local governments. President Reagan himself charged on March 2, 1981, that bilingual education programs had been "distorted" by federal bureaucrats: "It is absolutely wrong and against American concepts to have a bilingual education program that is now openly, admittedly dedicated to preserving their native language and never getting them adequate in English so they can get out into the job market and participate."

State laws have, in recent years, become much more favorable to teaching in languages other than English than they had been since before the First World War. By 1976 only 11 states still required that all public school instruction, except for foreign language courses, be in English; and 10 states had mandated establishment of bilingual programs in districts with substantial numbers of students whose mother tongues were not English. However, in March 1981 the governor of Virginia signed a law designating English as "the official language" of that commonwealth and specifying that "school boards shall have no obligation to teach the standard curriculum in a language other than English." The effect of the new law is uncertain.

Senator Ralph Yarborough had sponsored the original Bilingual Education Act because of his concern about the poor performance of Mexican-American children in the schools of his own state, Texas. Although by the late 1970s Title VII was supporting instruction through the use of some seventy different languages and dialects, Hispanics—including Mexican-Americans, Puerto Ricans, Cuban-Americans and others—still constituted about eighty per cent of the students in bilingual programs. Hispanic leaders were prominent in the protests against Secretary Bell's revocation of the proposed bilingual education rules early in 1981.

The 1975 amendments to the Voting Rights Act of 1965 were also originally inspired by the situation of Mexican-Americans in Texas, where despite the absence of a literacy test only some 38 percent of the potential Chicano electorate voted in 1972. Deciding that English-language ballots and voting instructions placed improper burdens on non-English-speaking citizens, Congress determined that in certain districts election materials must be printed in Spanish or in the languages of various Asian-Americans, American Indians, or Alaskan Natives.

Resentment of seeming favoritism toward these alleged victims of discrimination (as well as toward blacks) helped prompt Americans of various European origins to seek benefits for their own groups. The resulting Ethnic Heritage Studies Act, first implemented in 1974, has done relatively little to stimulate the use of languages other than English, partly because of lack of desire among the groups concerned, partly because of low levels of funding.

Late in 1980 the Equal Employment Opportunity Commission proposed and then promulgated, with relatively minor changes, guidelines on discrimination because of national origin. These state that rules requiring employees to speak English at all times in the workplace will be presumed to violate the 1964 Civil Rights Act and will be closely scrutinized. However, "an employer may have a rule that employees speak only in English at certain times where the employer can show that the rule is justified by business necessity."

Although at least one advocate of bilingual/bicultural education has suggested that the United States may soon be compelled by the growth of its Hispanic population seriously to consider adopting Spanish as an "official" language alongside English, thus far there appears to be little support for such a step. Among other reasons, increasing awareness that several million of the aliens now in the country are here illegally—and that most of these are Spanish-speaking—may be reinforcing public hostility to further expansion of governmental use of Spanish.

The clearest case yet of a backlash against the increasing use of Spanish in public business—and probably against the latest influx of Cuban refugees, as well—came in a Dade County, Florida, referendum last November: Miami-area voters, by about a three-to-two margin, repealed a 1973 resolution that had made the county officially bilingual. The hard-fought campaign aroused fears of increased polarization between Anglo and Hispanic residents.

On April 27, 1981, S. I. Hayakawa (R., Cal.) introduced in the Senate a proposed amendment to the U.S. Constitution which would make English the official language of the United States and would prohibit the federal and state governments—specifically including the courts—from requiring the use of any language other than English. Himself a second-generation American and a semanticist, Hayakawa emphasized that he did not want to discourage the study of foreign languages and that transitional bilingual education programs would be unaffected by his proposal. His staff indicates that the Senator's mail, including that from Hispanics, has run heavily in favor of English as the official language; however, the issue has proved to be even more emotional than had been anticipated.

Nathan Glazer is probably right in asserting, in "Public Education and American Pluralism," that "it is still . . . part of the general expectation that a general American culture will prevail as the dominant one in our country, and one that does create national identity, loyalty, and commitment." But the role that English, as opposed to other languages, will play in American culture and government now seems less clearcut than it once did.

QUESTIONS FOR CRITICAL READERS

Remembering and Understanding

1. Summarize the political, social, and economic forces that contributed to making English the dominant language in the United States during colonial times and later.
2. Using the information Wagner provides, summarize the American attitude toward languages other than English from 1620 to 1900.
3. How and why did American attitudes toward languages other than English change after 1900?

Analyzing and Discussing

4. Identify and summarize the major reasons that Americans have discriminated against various languages throughout their history.
5. In what ways does a historical approach to the question of English as an official language provide insight into the present controversy?
6. What did Roosevelt mean when he said that those who could not speak English could not derive the full benefit from their citizenship?

Writing

7. According to Wagner, immigrants are expected to assimilate into American culture. Using Wagner's article and any other information you are aware of, including your own experience, describe what that culture is like.

In Defense of the Mother Tongue

—————— GEORGE WILL ——————

George Will is probably best known for his political commentary, for which he received a Pulitzer Prize in 1977. He customarily approaches his subjects from a conservative political perspective. The essay printed here is from Newsweek, *where Will's column appears regularly. Here Will argues in support of an amendment to the U.S. Constitution to make English the official language of the United States.*

ON THE FOURTH OF JULY the corn, rhetorical as well as agricultural, should be as high as an elephant's eye. But while enjoying the rhetoric of liberty, consider the connection between the English language and American liberty.

A proposed amendment to the Constitution would declare "the English language shall be the official language of the United States" and "neither the United States nor any state shall require . . . the use in the United States of any language other than English." It would prohibit governments from mandating multilingual publications and from establishing bilingual education as a general entitlement. It would end the pernicious practice of providing bilingual ballots, a practice that denies the link between citizenship and shared culture. Bilingual ballots, says Richard Rodriguez, proclaim that people can exercise the most public of rights while keeping apart from public life.

Rodriguez's autobiography, "Hunger of Memory," is an elegant and eloquent evocation of the modern immigrant's experience. A son of Mexican immigrants, he grew up in Sacramento in the 1950s. He was so "cloistered" by family sounds, so long "poised at the edge of language" that he was timid in public—too timid to be at home outside his home, in his community. Language is an instrument of intimacy, and Rodriguez's book is a hymn to the poignant bravery of immigrant parents. Such parents often launch children toward a cultural divide the parents cannot cross, the passage into linguistic fluency and social ease.

Urgent issues. Rodriguez's intelligent and unsentimental opposition to bilingual education makes his opposition to the constitutional amendment interesting. Writing today, he notes that bilingualism became part of the agenda of the left in the late 1960s, when there was "a romantic surrender to the mystique of the outsider." Those people who considered the culture diseased naturally thought the culture should be shunned. Bilingualism is an urgent issue because so much of current immigration comes from the Spanish-speaking Western Hemisphere and because of the availability of Spanish-language news and entertainment broadcasting encourages the notion that English is merely a marginally important option.

"Those who have the most to lose in a bilingual America," Rodriguez says, "are the foreign-speaking poor, who are being lured into a linguistic nursery." However, he considers the constitutional amendment divisive because many Hispanics will regard it as aimed "against" them. Such sensitivity should not be decisive, especially given the reasons, which Rodriguez gives, why bilingualism is injurious to Hispanics.

"Our government," he says, "has no business elevating one language above all others, no business implying the supremacy of Anglo culture." He is wrong, twice. The government has a constitutional duty to promote the general welfare, which Rodriguez himself says is linked to a single shared language. Government should not be neutral regarding something as important as language is to the evolution of the culture. Furthermore, it should not be bashful about affirming the virtues of "Anglo culture"—including the political arrangements bequeathed by the men of July 4, 1776, a distinctly Anglo group. The promise of America is bound up with the virtues and achievements of "Anglo culture," which is bound up with English. Immigrants, all of whom come here voluntarily, have a responsibility to reciprocate the nation's welcome by acquiring the language that is essential for citizenship, properly understood.

Citizenship involves participation in public affairs, in the governance and hence the conversation of the community. In ancient Greece, from which the political philosophy of "Anglo culture" directly descends, such participation was considered natural and hence essential to normal life. When government nurtures a shared language it is nurturing a natural right—the ability to live in the manner that is right for human nature.

Nowadays this nation is addicted to a different rhetoric of rights—including, for a few specially entitled minorities, the right to a publicly assisted dispensation from learning the language of public life. This age defines self-fulfillment apart from, even against, the community. The idea of citizenship has become attenuated and now is defined almost exclusively in terms of entitlements, not responsibilities. Bilingualism, by suggesting that there is no duty to acquire the primary instrument of public discourse, further dilutes the idea of citizenship.

Rodriguez wants America to "risk uncertainty" and "remain vulnerable," "between fixity and change." Obviously America cannot freeze its culture. But another way of saying that human beings are social animals is to say they are language-users. To be sociable they must share a language. America has always been (in Rodriguez's nifty phrase) "a marinade of sounds." But it would be wrong to make a romance of linguistic diversity. Americans should say diverse things, but in a language that allows universal participation in the discussion. Acceptance of considerable pluralism is a precondition of a free society; but so, too, is a limit to pluralism. Yes, *e pluribus unum*. But also: one national language is a prerequisite for the sort of pluralism that is compatible with shared national identity.

Linguistic unity.   Teddy Roosevelt's life was one long Fourth of July, a symphony of fireworks and flamboyant rhetoric. He embodied the vigor of the nation during the flood tide of immigration. He said: "We have room for but one language here and that is the English language, for we intend to see that the crucible turns our people out as Americans, of American nationality, and not as dwellers in a polyglot boarding house." American life, with its atomizing emphasis on individualism, increasingly resembles life in a centrifuge. Bilingualism is a gratuitous intensification of disintegrative forces. It imprisons immigrants in their origins and encourages what Jacques Barzun, a supporter of the constitutional amendment, calls "cultural solipsism."

On the Fourth of July, when we are full of filial piety toward the Founding Fathers, we should not lightly contemplate tampering with their Constitution. But a change may be necessary to preserve the linguistic unity that is as important as the Constitution to a harmonious national life.

QUESTIONS FOR CRITICAL READERS

Remembering and Understanding

1. George Will invites his readers to consider the connection between the English language and American liberty. Summarize his explanation of this connection.
2. What is Will's position about making English the official language of the United States, and what are his chief reasons for holding that position?
3. What is the effect of Will's extensive reliance on the ideas of Richard Rodriguez?

Analyzing and Discussing

4. At one point Will says, "When government nurtures a shared language it is nurturing a natural right—the ability to live in the manner that is right for human nature." What does this statement mean?
5. How is Will's understanding of the situation affected by his tendency to see it as a political issue rather than as a social or educational issue?
6. What is Will's definition of citizenship? Agree or disagree with it, and give reasons for your own position.

Writing

7. Will believes that a common language is essential to cultural unity. What other kinds of knowledge and behavior contribute to cultural unity? Select an activity, a body of knowledge, an attitude or belief, or something else that you believe members of your culture must share. Describe the item that you have selected, and explain its contribution to cultural unity.

Legislating Assimilation
The English Only Movement

——— MARK HALTON ———

Mark Halton is an assistant editor of The Christian Century, *where this article first appeared. He provides a brief overview of the English Only movement and of U.S. policies about bilingualism, and then he focuses on the question of how non-native groups usually assimilate into the United States. His special interest is in comparing the assimilation of recent immigrants with that of earlier immigrants.*

CONTENTION BETWEEN PEOPLE who speak different languages is as old as the story of Babel. The ancient Greeks referred to those who spoke in other tongues as "the babblers." Ancient Slavs called the Germans across their border "the mute" or "unspeaking" people. Today, U.S. residents whose primary language is other than English—especially Spanish speakers—are being regarded as "un-American."

A pitched battle is under way between those who consider that, for the sake of America's cohesion, English must be legislated the official language through state or federal constitutional amendments, and those who consider such attempts bigoted or xenophobic. The main goals of the English-only movement are to eliminate or limit bilingual education in the public schools; to prevent state or local governments from spending funds for translating road signs or government documents or for translators to assist non-English-speaking patients at public hospitals; and to abolish multilingual ballots—required in 375 jurisdictions by the 1965 Voting Rights Act. Florida, Colorado and Arizona—states with large Hispanic populations—voted in referendums last year to make English the official language, bringing the number of states with such laws to 17.

In contrast, New Mexico's legislature voted down an English-only law last spring and endorsed "English Plus," stating, "Proficiency on the part of our citizens in more than one language is to the economic and cultural benefit of our State and the Nation."

But what does "English only" mean? That question is being raised in California, where voters approved a language law four years ago. This year, a legislative committee rejected a bill that would have banned the use of languages other than English by state and local government agencies. Also, a state senate committee, responding to the U.S. Equal Employment Opportunity Commission, enacted a law prohibiting private companies from restricting their employees' use of non-English languages while at work, unless necessary for business reasons. In 1988 the Los Angeles federal appeals court, countering some companies' English-only rules, said such restrictions are not only a veiled form of discrimination but a way of increasing racism.

The groups that have led the fight "to protect English by declaring it the official language of the United States" are U.S. English (whose co-founder, S. I. Hayakawa, is a former U.S. senator from California and a retired professor of linguistics) and English First, part of the Committee to Protect the Family. These groups are on the offensive, claiming that they are trying to help non-English speakers get ahead economically and socially. U.S. English, which claims 350,000 members, cites the "political upheavals over language that have torn apart Canada, Belgium, Sri Lanka . . . and other nations" as a reason to ban the use of "many languages" for official purposes.

Seventy years ago Theodore Roosevelt expressed a similar resolve: "We have room for but one language here, and that is the English language, for we intend to see that the crucible turns our people out as Americans, and not as dwellers in a polyglot boarding house." He was reacting to the 5.2 million southern Europeans and the 8.8 million middle and eastern Europeans—the new immigrants—who had arrived on American shores in the two decades preceding the First World War. He was also expressing the nationalism that followed the war. By 1924 restrictive quotas were imposed to limit immigration from southern and eastern Europe, thus keeping out the people "not like us." Following World War I many communities banned the teaching of German and restricted its use in public meetings—and even on the telephone. The proponents claimed that they were only promoting unity, but anti-German feelings were evident. Striking down these laws, the U.S. Supreme Court ruled in 1923 that the "protection of the Constitution extends to all, to those who speak other languages as well as to those born with English on their tongue."

Most opponents of the English-only movement—such as the Mexican-American Legal Defense Fund and the U.S. Catholic Conference's Secretariat for Hispanic Affairs—are not against ethnic groups learning English, but against the us-versus-them rhetoric advanced by many English-only advocates. George Muñoz, writing in the *Chicago Sun-Times*, has said, "Opposition to English-only is not from a desire to stay apart; most

Hispanics want to integrate. But they don't want to be denied access to the mainstream while they're learning English." Muñoz argues that it's not the language of communication that should be important to the government but whether the government can make itself understood by all.

The recent English-only movement got its start in Miami—perhaps the most bilingual major city in the U.S.—in 1978, after Emmy Shafer was unable to communicate with any of the clerks at the Dade County municipal offices. They all spoke only Spanish; she, only English. Her protest led to passage of a 1980 county law stipulating that no funds could be used to translate public signs or documents into Spanish or other non-English languages.

But Miami is a special case. It contains the majority of the country's Cuban-Americans, who compose about 5 percent of the U.S. Hispanic population. They have largely avoided assimilating because they consider themselves exiles of Cuba, still awaiting the fall of the Castro government to return home. Puerto Ricans living in Miami, on the other hand, reportedly are learning English quickly, many of them vying for well-paying bilingual jobs.

On the whole, language assimilation in the U.S. has followed a four-generation pattern, according to Kenneth Wilson in *Van Winkle's Return: Change in American English, 1966–1986*. Between 1890 and 1920, for example, hundreds of thousands of Poles emigrated to the U.S. A typical Polish couple (call them the Pomykalskis) might have arrived in New York City in 1909 with an infant son and eventually settled in Chicago where they spoke only Polish at work, at mass, in the shops and, of course, at home. But in a few years their son spoke English at school, starting in first grade, while speaking Polish at home and at his after-school job. He and his Polish friends became bilingual and did not have an accent in either language.

He got married to his high school sweetheart in 1928—a Pole who had emigrated with her parents when she was 13 years old—and the two spoke English at home, she with a slight accent. With their parents they spoke Polish. Their children, the grandchildren of the immigrants Pomykalskis, spoke English at home and at school, and used Polish only when speaking to Grandmother in the kitchen. In each domain of language—school, social life, work, church and family—the use of Polish diminished.

The original Pomykalskis's great-granddaughter was born in 1956 in a suburb of Columbus, Ohio. She grew up speaking no Polish and has very little connection to her Polish heritage. She is thoroughly enculturated in American ways and language. As Wilson says, "Wistfully, this generation hopes to recover some linguistic access to a culture that now . . . they wish they knew better."

Some immigrants have defied assimilation. Hasidic Jews in Brooklyn speak Yiddish, and some Amish in the Midwest speak a German dialect; they have chosen to live on linguistic islands. Finnish and Scandinavian immigrants in rural communities in the northern Midwest did not quickly assimilate for geographical reasons. But the commercial and societal forces shaping Hispanic immigration over the past 35 years suggest a different scenario for these immigrants.

Social and economic constraints have cut off many Hispanics from mainstream American—that is, Anglo—culture. Hispanic women who work only in the home have had limited contact with U.S. culture, and language programs sponsored by local governments or businesses rarely reach them. Furthermore, in many of the largest U.S. cities one finds Spanish-language radio, TV and newspapers, and videocassettes, billboards and even grocery and department store labels in Spanish—not to promote Spanish but simply to sell goods. English-only legislation would not change these realities.

But despite the social and commercial forces leading Hispanics away from assimilation, recent studies have concluded that first- and second-generation Hispanics have learned English as fast as Italians, Russians, Greeks, Romanians or Japanese immigrants did at the turn of the century. An editorialist in the *Wall Street Journal* reports that an analysis of 1980 census data by professors at the Urban Institute and the University of Chicago reveals that while a great majority of Hispanics over the age of 25 speak Spanish at home, most also speak English with proficiency. And a study by the RAND corporation reveals that language-assimilation statistics for Hispanic immigrants are in line with the history of the Polish family discussed above. Nearly half the permanent Mexican immigrants living in California speak English well, and only about 25 percent speak Spanish exclusively. For the most part, their American-born children are bilingual and 90 percent are proficient in English. Over half of their grandchildren speak only English. David Lopez, a professor at UCLA, concludes that if immigration from Latin America dried up today (not likely to happen), language assimilation by Hispanics would be complete by the year 2030. Leonard Dinnerstein and David M. Reimers in *Ethnic Americans: A History of Immigration and Assimilation* believe that "with so much more public assistance available than had been given to immigrants in previous generations, it is possible that the newcomers may not need as long a time to move into the mainstream of American society."

The issue that most divides the English-only advocates and their opponents is bilingual education. Former President Reagan spoke against it. Congress has debated it. Newspaper op-ed pages and radio talk shows have discussed it. "Bilingual education" is really a misnomer, since the goal of such programs is not to produce bilingual students, but to make

Hispanic, Chinese or Vietnamese students proficient in English while drawing on their own native language as a transitional tool. U.S. English and other groups claim that bilingual education helps perpetuate adherence to non-English tongues. But the National Association for Bilingual Education points to research revealing the advantages of bilingual education: when students participate for an average of two to three years researchers notice "improved academic achievement test scores, reduced rates of school dropout and student absenteeism, increased community involvement in education, and enhanced student self-esteem."

Many older people who emigrated to the U.S. when they were in grade school were thrown into English-only classrooms and made to swim or sink. They claim that all their immigrant peers learned to swim, and quickly. However, no studies were done at the time to determine how many immigrant children sank—dropping out of school or never living up to their potential. Language acquisition can be a slow, arduous process for many. And there is more to education than learning a language. Learning math, science, music or art in one's native language gives a student skills readily transferable to the English-speaking world. A student does not need to relearn the subjects taught in Spanish when later reviewing them in English.

Though the U.S. has never had an official policy of introducing English to immigrants, language assimilation has always been startlingly rapid. Kenji Hakuta in *Mirror of Language: The Debate on Bilingualism* credits economic interests and "benign neglect" of one's own language as the leading causes of immigrants' forsaking their mother tongues. Another reason cited is that educational psychologists urged immigrant parents to avoid speaking a non-English language at home on the false premise that bilingualism stunts the academic growth of children. While no linguists tout this theory today, many proponents of the English-only movement still believe that there is room for but one language in a young person's mind.

When immigrants poured into America in the nineteenth century one of three scenarios could have played out. American culture could have transformed the immigrants (Americanization or assimilation); the culture could have been transformed by the immigrants (melting pot); or the culture could have split into separatist groups. For over 150 years the pattern has been one of assimilation, "a move," Dinnerstein and Reimers write, "into the mainstream of American life [requiring] the relinquishment of cherished cultural ties." Immigrants start in separate groups— as Hispanics do today by attending Spanish-language churches and marrying other Hispanics—but within four generations they assimilate, no longer calling themselves, for example, Polish-Americans but simply Americans.

Political unity, communication and transportation systems, and financial factors will keep the U.S. an English-speaking nation. English does not need to be legislated the official language; gentler forces than those proposed by English-only proponents will produce that end. As the U.S. enters the '90s, a new awareness of other cultures' music, language, customs, food, electronic goods and even political ways is transforming our life. There is a growing realization that Americans of northern European descent have much to learn from U.S. residents of Latin American or Asian backgrounds. Perhaps in the twenty-first century the strict assimilation patterns of the past will yield to more "melting"—the mixing of cultures in a way that changes the flavor of the entire society.

QUESTIONS FOR CRITICAL READERS

Remembering and Understanding

1. According to Halton, what motivates those who want to make English the official language of the United States?
2. What are Halton's reasons for opposing the English Only movement?
3. Halton gives examples of the experiences of several language groups in the United States. Use this information to summarize his view of how immigrants learn English.
4. What does Halton conclude about the necessity of making English the official language of the United States?

Analyzing and Discussing

5. Halton mentions several groups that have defied assimilation into American language and culture. Explain why these groups have been able to resist assimilation.
6. Much of the information that Halton provides is historical. How does this historical perspective contribute to understanding the present controversy?

Writing

7. Halton says that Americans are experiencing a new awareness of other cultures. To what extent are you experiencing this awareness personally? Write a paper in which you describe your personal experiences with foods, languages, customs, and products from other cultures. As part of your paper, explain how your life would be different without the influence of these other cultures.

A Common Currency

The Gift of a Single Tongue

ABIGAIL MCCARTHY

McCarthy is married to Eugene McCarthy, former senator from Minnesota, who ran for the presidency of the United States in 1968. In this article, which first appeared in Commonweal, *she argues in favor of making English the official and legal language of the United States.*

FOR THOSE OF US long addicted to public television, the face of Alistair Cooke is more familiar than that of many a relative. Only hear his name and the well-known face is there in the mind's eye—aristocratic, slightly horsy, with blue eyes a little protuberant—a very English face. And the voice and manner are with us once again—those of a confiding, avuncular, informative but never patronizing friend. Briton become American, he evokes what was most civilized in the country of his birth and his adopted one.

So, although the letter bearing his name was obviously a piece of promotional mail, I did not consign it to the wastebasket. I read it and found myself agreeing with Alistair. He and the organization for which he is spokesman, *U.S. English,* wanted to enlist my help in making English the official language of the United States.

That English is not our official language comes as a surprise to many Americans. Most of us have simply assumed that it was. As a letter writer to the *San Francisco Chronicle and Examiner* put it, "The Declaration, the Bill of Rights . . . (and on and on) are in English. Are these not clear enough [examples] as to our official language?"

That was probably how the framers of the Constitution saw it since they did not include a clause establishing an official language. They were without exception men for whom English was their native tongue and from colonies ruled by the English-speaking. Yet we are told that even in their time there was some dispute over language. There was some argument for making German the official language of the new country.

It was perhaps inspired by a post-revolutionary desire to separate from England in every way and, in part, because there were large German-speaking groups in Pennsylvania, New Jersey, and Maryland. But custom prevailed, and has prevailed, until recently. English was the language of the citizens of the United States. But not any more. Not exclusively.

"Until ten or fifteen years ago, there was never any doubt about it," writes Cooke. "But today we see cities and communities, with bewildered immigrant families, saying, 'Wouldn't it be simpler to let people stay with their native tongue? Print everything in two languages. Let them, in time, also learn English.' "

On further reading of material provided by *U.S. English,* the above seems a very temperate way of describing the highly politicized drive for bilingualism in significant sectors of the U.S. The drive has been largely fueled by the perceived needs of the Spanish-speaking immigrants, both legal and illegal, who have poured into the country from Central and South America. Hispanic community leaders, joined by some from other ethnic groups, have chosen to resist the use of English as the common language. They have claimed—perhaps with some justice—that to require English as a qualification for voting, or for being licensed to drive, or to enter certain occupations, is oppressive and discriminatory.

As a result of their pressure the federal government requires 375 U.S. jurisdictions to provide ballots for voting printed in other languages. In many jurisdictions special voter registration drives are conducted at taxpayer expense for those who wish to vote in their native language. De facto, without most Americans realizing it, English is no longer necessarily the language of the *citizen* of this country.

Evidently proponents of bilingualism intend to go further. The imposition of English (so viewed) is seen as a forced betrayal of ancestral culture, custom, and values. There are those who do not want to learn English, do not want to assimilate. As long as they pay taxes and obey the laws, say the leaders of the new ethnic blocs, why should they?

In a world torn by ethnic division the answer seems obvious. Language is unifying. The trend to bilingualism, argues Alistair Cooke, reverses the main American movement, over two centuries old, to meld many peoples into one. Cooke recalls that shortly after he himself came here as an immigrant, he visited a night class where immigrant parents of first-generation Americans were learning English. "It was a moving experience. It gave me a new appreciation of the foresight of the Founding Fathers in impressing on every American coin: *'E Pluribus Unum'*—Out of many, one."

The dream of "one nation, indivisible" could turn into a nightmare, a nightmare, Cooke warns, he has witnessed in countries in Asia, Africa, and the Middle East where nations struggle "to be united against the friction of competing languages."

We know that ethnic division based on language groups afflicts countries as disparate as Belgium and Indonesia and often leads to violence. It is rising as the Soviet Union crumbles and it is stirring in the newly free lands of Eastern Europe. To our north, Canada has never quite settled matters between its Francophone citizens and those who are Anglophone. As I write, once again Quebec is threatening to secede if the Meech Lake Accord (giving it special status) is *not* ratified, and New Brunswick, Manitoba, and Newfoundland threaten to do so if it *is*. It may not be too nightmarish to envision a time when a Spanish-speaking California or Florida threatens to secede from *our* union.

Such fears aside, most of us will agree that our two centuries and more of using English as our dominant language has been a practical way of knitting together a nation of diverse peoples. And it has not necessarily meant that they have thereby lost their roots, their folkways, or their festivals. If the common use of English is threatened now, it may be the time to affirm it as official, if not by constitutional amendment (as *U.S. English* proposes), then by a federal law.

QUESTIONS FOR CRITICAL READERS

Remembering and Understanding

1. What evidence does McCarthy give that the framers of the Constitution intended English to be the official language of America?
2. Re-state McCarthy's position, and give her major reasons for holding it.
3. How does to McCarthy characterize the purpose and function of an officially required or approved bilingualism? What is her attitude toward that policy?

Analyzing and Discussing

4. McCarthy says "it may not be too nightmarish to envision a time when a Spanish-speaking California or Florida threatens to secede from *our* union." Do you regard this as a realistic possibility? Discuss whether such a secession could actually take place, and what its consequences would be for all concerned.
5. Why would it be regarded as oppressive and discriminatory to require English as a qualification for voting? To what extent would the lack of English impede your ability to exercise the rights and responsibilities of citizenship?
6. Alistair Cooke is a well-known Englishman who has been a naturalized citizen of the United States since 1941. Based on what McCarthy says about him, what do you think he contributes to the goals of English Only? What is the effect of McCarthy's use of his name?

Writing

7. McCarthy clearly believes that the lack of a common language could fragment the United States and might even lead to attempts by some areas to secede. But are there other issues that might be as divisive as language, or even more so? Identify an issue that you believe is potentially divisive or harmful to the United States, explain what you believe might happen, and recommend actions that you believe will prevent the issue from getting out of control.

Politicization and the Schools

The Case of Bilingual Education

──────── **DIANE RAVITCH** ────────

*Diane Ravitch lives in New York and teaches at Columbia University's
Teachers College. She has written extensively about the history of American
education, often from a political perspective. In this essay she discusses bilingual education and its consequences in the context of other policies and
controversies that she believes have politicized the public schools.*

THERE HAS ALWAYS BEEN a politics of schools, and no doubt there
always will be. Like any other organization populated by human beings,
schools have their internal politics; for as long as there have been public
schools, there have been political battles over their budget, their personnel
policies, their curricula, and their purposes. Anyone who believes that
there was once a time in which schools were untouched by political controversy is uninformed about the history of education. The decision-making processes that determine who will be chosen as principal or how the
school board will be selected or whether to pass a school bond issue are
simply political facts of life that are part and parcel of the administration,
financing, and governance of schools. There is also a politics of the curriculum and of the profession, in which contending forces argue about
programs and policies. It is hard to imagine a school, a school system, a
university, a state board of education, or a national department of education in which these kinds of political conflicts do not exist. They are
an intrinsic aspect of complex organizations in which people disagree about
how to achieve their goals and about which goals to pursue; to the extent
that we operate in a democratic manner, conflict over important and even
unimportant issues is inevitable.

There is another kind of politics, however, in which educational
institutions become entangled in crusades marked by passionate advocacy,
intolerance of criticism, and unyielding dogmatism, and in which the
education of children is a secondary rather than a primary consideration.

Such crusades go beyond politics-as-usual; they represent the politicization of education. Schools and universities become targets for politicization for several reasons: First, they offer a large captive audience of presumably impressionable minds; second, they are expected to shape the opinions, knowledge, and values of the rising generation, which makes them attractive to those who want to influence the future; and third, since Americans have no strong educational philosophy or educational tradition, almost any claim—properly clothed in rhetorical appeals about the needs of children or of American society—can make its way into the course catalogue or the educational agenda.

Ever since Americans created public schools, financed by tax dollars and controlled by boards of laymen, the schools have been at the center of intermittent struggles over the values that they represent. The founders of the common school, and in particular Horace Mann, believed that the schools could be kept aloof from the religious and political controversies beyond their door, but it has not been easy to keep the crusaders outside the schoolhouse. In the nineteenth century, heated battles were fought over such issues as which Bible would be read in the classroom and whether public dollars might be used to subsidize religious schools. After the onset of World War I, anti-German hostility caused the German language to be routed from American schools, even though nearly a quarter of the high school population studied the language in 1915. Some of this same fervor, strengthened by zeal to hasten the process of assimilation, caused several states to outlaw parochial and private schools and to prohibit the teaching of foreign language in the first eight years of school. Such laws, obviously products of nationalism and xenophobia, were struck down as unconstitutional by the United States Supreme Court in the 1920s. The legislative efforts to abolish nonpublic schools and to bar the teaching of foreign languages were examples of politicization; their purpose was not to improve the education of any child, but to achieve certain social and political goals that the sponsors of these laws believed were of overwhelming importance.

Another example of politicization in education was the crusade to cleanse the schools of teachers and other employees who were suspected of being disloyal, subversive, or controversial. This crusade began in the years after World War I, gathered momentum during the 1930s, and came to full fruition during the loyalty investigations by state and national legislative committees in the 1950s. Fears for national security led to intrusive surveillance of the beliefs, friends, past associations, and political activities of teachers and professors. These inquiries did not improve anyone's education; they used the educational institutions as vehicles towards political goals that were extraneous to education.

A more recent example of politicization occurred on the campuses during the war in Vietnam. Those who had fought political intrusions into educational institutions during the McCarthy era did so on the ground of academic freedom. Academic freedom, they argued, protected the right of students and teachers to express their views, regardless of their content; because of academic freedom, the university served as a sanctuary for dissidents, heretics, and skeptics of all persuasions. During the war in Vietnam, those who tried to maintain the university as a privileged haven for conflicting views, an open marketplace of ideas, found themselves the object of attack by student radicals. Student (and sometimes faculty) radicals believed that opposition to the war was so important that those who did not agree with them should be harassed and even silenced.

Faced with a moral issue, the activists argued, the university could not stand above the battle, nor could it tolerate the expression of "immoral" views. In this spirit, young radicals tried to prevent those with whom they disagreed from speaking and teaching; towards this end, they heckled speakers, disrupted classes, and even planted bombs on campus. These actions were intended to politicize schools and campuses and, in some instances, they succeeded. They were advocated by sincere and zealous individuals who earnestly believed that education could not take place within a context of political neutrality. Their efforts at politicization stemmed not from any desire to improve education as such, but from the pursuit of political goals.

As significant as the student movement and the McCarthy era were as examples of the dangers of politicization, they were short-lived in comparison to the policy of racial segregation. Segregation of public school children by their race and ancestry was established by law in seventeen states and by custom in many communities beyond those states. The practice of assigning public school children and teachers on the basis of their race had no educational justification; it was not intended to improve anyone's education. It was premised on the belief in the innate inferiority of people whose skin was of dark color. Racial segregation as policy and practice politicized the schools; it used them to buttress a racist social and political order. It limited the educational opportunities available to blacks. Racial segregation was socially and politically so effective in isolating blacks from opportunity for economic advancement and educationally so devastating in retarding their learning that our society continues to pay a heavy price to redress the cumulative deficits of generations of poor education.

The United States Supreme Court's 1954 decision, *Brown v. Board of Education*, started the process of ending state-imposed racial segregation. In those southern states where segregation was the cornerstone of a way of life, white resistance to desegregation was prolonged and intense. The drive to disestablish racial segregation and to uproot every last vestige of its effects was unquestionably necessary. The practice of assigning children to school by their race and of segregating other public facilities by race was a national disgrace. However, the process through which desegregation came about dramatically altered the politics of schools; courts and regulatory agencies at the federal and state level became accustomed to intervening in the internal affairs of educational institutions, and the potential for politicization of the schools was significantly enlarged.

The slow pace of desegregation in the decade after the *Brown* decision, concurrent with a period of rising expectations, contributed to a dramatic buildup of frustration and rage among blacks, culminating in the protests, civil disorders, and riots of the mid-1960s. In response, Congress enacted major civil rights laws in 1964 and 1965, and the federal courts became aggressive in telling school boards what to do to remedy their constitutional violations. Initially, these orders consisted of commands to produce racially mixed schools. However, some courts went beyond questions of racial mix. In Washington, D.C., a federal district judge in 1967 directed the school administration to abandon ability grouping, which he believed discriminated against black children. This was the first time that a federal court found a common pedagogical practice to be unconstitutional.

In the nearly two decades since that decision, the active intervention of the federal judiciary into school affairs has ceased to be unusual. In Ann Arbor, Michigan, a federal judge ordered the school board to train teachers in "black English," a program subsequently found to be ineffectual in improving the education of black students. In California, a federal judge barred the use of intelligence tests for placement of students in special education classes, even though reputable psychologists defend their validity. In Boston, where the school board was found guilty of intentionally segregating children by race, the federal judge assumed full control over the school system for more than a decade; even reform superintendents who were committed to carrying out the judge's program for desegregation complained of the hundreds of court orders regulating every aspect of schooling, hiring, promotion, curriculum, and financing. In 1982, in a case unrelated to desegregation, a state judge in West Virginia ordered the state education department to do "no less than completely re-construct the entire system of education in West Virginia," and the judge started the process of reconstruction by setting down his own standards for facilities, administration, and curriculum, including what was to be taught and for how many minutes each week.

Perhaps this is as good a way of bringing about school reform as any other. No doubt school officials are delighted when a judge orders the state legislature to raise taxes on behalf of the schools. But it does seem to be a repudiation of our democratic political structure when judges go beyond issues of constitutional rights, don the mantle of school superintendent, and use their authority to change promotional standards, to reconstruct the curriculum, or to impose their own pedagogical prescriptions.

Now, by the definition of politicization that I earlier offered—that is, when educational institutions become the focus of dogmatic crusaders whose purposes are primarily political and only incidentally related to children's education—these examples may not qualify as politicization, although they do suggest how thin is the line between politics and politicization. After all, the judges were doing what they thought would produce better education. The court decisions in places like Ann Arbor, Boston, California, and West Virginia may be thought of as a shift in the politics of schools, a shift that has brought the judiciary into the decision-making process as a full-fledged partner in shaping educational policy. Reasonable people differ about the appropriate role of the courts as mediators among conflicting parties in educational disputes, even those involving questions of pedagogy and curriculum.

The long struggle to desegregate American schools put them at the center of political battles for more than a generation and virtually destroyed the belief that schools could remain above politics. Having lost their apolitical shield, the schools also lost their capacity to resist efforts to politicize them. In the absence of resistance, demands by interest groups of varying ideologies escalated, each trying to impose its own agenda on the curriculum, the textbooks, the school library, or the teachers. Based on the activities of single-issue groups, any number of contemporary educational policies would serve equally well as examples of politicization. The example that I have chosen as illustrative of politicization is bilingual education. The history of this program exemplifies a campaign on behalf of social and political goals that are only tangentially related to education. I would like to sketch briefly the bilingual controversy, which provides an overview of the new politics of education and demonstrates the tendency within this new politics to use educational programs for noneducational ends.

Demands for bilingual education arose as an outgrowth of the civil rights movement. As it evolved, that movement contained complex, and occasionally contradictory, elements. One facet of the movement appealed for racial integration and assimilation, which led to court orders for busing and racial balance; but the dynamics of the movement also inspired appeals to racial solidarity, which led to demands for black studies, black control of black schools, and other race-conscious policies. Whether the plea was for integration or for separatism, advocates could always point to a body of social science as evidence for their goals.

Race consciousness became a necessary part of the remedies that courts fashioned, but its presence legitimized ethnocentrism as a force in American politics. In the late 1960s, the courts, Congress, and policymakers—having been told for years by spokesmen for the civil rights movement that all children should be treated equally without regard to their race or ancestry—frequently heard compelling testimony by political activists and social scientists about the value of ethnic particularism in the curriculum.

Congress first endorsed funding for bilingual education in 1968, at a time when ethnocentrism had become a powerful political current. In hearings on this legislation, proponents of bilingual education argued that non-English-speaking children did poorly in school because they had low self-esteem, and that this low self-esteem was caused by the absence of their native language from the classroom. They claimed that if the children were taught in their native tongue and about their native culture, they would have higher self-esteem, better attitudes toward school, and higher educational achievement. Bilingual educators also insisted that children would learn English more readily if they already knew another language.

In the congressional hearings, both advocates and congressmen seemed to agree that the purpose of bilingual education was to help non-English speakers succeed in school and in society. But the differences between them were not then obvious. The congressmen believed that bilingual education would serve as a temporary transition into the regular English language program. But the bilingual educators saw the program as an opportunity to maintain the language and culture of the non-English-speaking student, while he was learning English.

What was extraordinary about the Bilingual Education Act of 1968, which has since been renewed several times, is that it was the first time that the Congress had ever legislated a given pedagogical method. In practice, bilingual education means a program in which children study the major school subjects in a language other than English. Funding of the program, although small within the context of the federal education budget, created strong constituencies for its continuation, both within the federal government and among recipient agencies. No different from other interest groups, these constituencies pressed for expansion and strengthening of their program. Just as lifelong vocational educators are unlikely to ask whether their program works, so career bilingual educators are committed to their method as a philosophy, not as a technique for language instruction. The difference is this: Techniques are subject to evaluation, which may cause them to be revised or discarded; philosophies are not.

In 1974, the Supreme Court's *Lau v. Nichols* decision reinforced demands for bilingual education. The Court ruled against the San Francisco public schools for their failure to provide English language instruction for 1,800 non-English-speaking Chinese students. The Court's decision was reasonable and appropriate. The Court said, "There is no equality of treatment merely by providing students with the same facilities, textbooks, teachers, and curriculum; for students who do not understand

English are effectively foreclosed from any meaningful education." The decision did not endorse any particular remedy. It said, "Teaching English to the students of Chinese ancestry who do not speak the language is one choice. Giving instruction to the group in Chinese is another. There may be others."

Despite the Court's prudent refusal to endorse any particular method of instruction, the bilingual educators interpreted the *Lau* decision as a mandate for bilingual programs. In the year after the decision, the United States Office of Education established a task force to fashion guidelines for the implementation of the *Lau* decision; the task force was composed of bilingual educators and representatives of language minority groups. The task force fashioned regulations that prescribed in exhaustive detail how school districts should prepare and carry out bilingual programs for non-English-speaking students. The districts were directed to identify the student's primary language, not by his proficiency in English, but by determining which language was most often spoken in the student's home, which language he had learned first, and which language he used most often. Thus a student would be eligible for a bilingual program even if he was entirely fluent in English.

Furthermore, while the Supreme Court refused to endorse any given method, the task force directed that non-English-speaking students should receive bilingual education that emphasized instruction in their native language and culture. Districts were discouraged from using the "English as a Second Language" approach, which consists of intensive, supplemental English-only instruction, or immersion techniques, in which students are instructed in English within an English-only context.

Since the establishment of the bilingual education program, many millions of dollars have been spent to support bilingual programs in more than sixty different languages. Among those receiving funding to administer and staff such programs, bilingual education is obviously popular, but there are critics who think that it is educationally unsound. Proponents of desegregation have complained that bilingual education needlessly segregates non-English speakers from others of their age. At a congressional hearing in 1977, one desegregation specialist complained that bilingual programs had been funded "without any significant proof that they would work. . . . There is nothing in the research to suggest that children can effectively learn English without continuous interaction with other children who are native English speakers."

The research on bilingual education has been contradictory, and studies that favor or criticize the bilingual approach have been attacked as biased. Researchers connected to bilingual institutes claim that their programs resulted in significant gains for non-English-speaking children. But a four-year study commissioned by the United States Office of

Education concluded that students who learned bilingually did not achieve at a higher level than those in regular classes, nor were their attitudes towards school significantly different. What they seemed to learn best, the study found, was the language in which they were instructed.

One of the few evidently unbiased, nonpolitical assessments of bilingual research was published in 1982 in the *Harvard Educational Review*. A survey of international findings, it concluded that "bilingual programs are neither better nor worse than other instructional methods." The author found that in the absence of compelling experimental support for this method, there was "no legal necessity or research basis for the federal government to advocate or require a specific educational approach."

If the research is in fact inconclusive, then there is no justification for mandating the use of bilingual education or any other single pedagogy. The bilingual method may or may not be the best way to learn English. Language instruction programs that are generally regarded as outstanding, such as those provided for Foreign Service officers or by the nationally acclaimed center at Middlebury College, are immersion programs, in which students embark on a systematic program of intensive language learning without depending on their native tongue. Immersion programs may not be appropriate for all children, but then neither is any single pedagogical method. The method to be used should be determined by the school authorities and the professional staff, based on their resources and competence.

Despite the fact that the Supreme Court did not endorse bilingual education, the lower federal courts have tended to treat this pedagogy as a civil right, and more than a dozen states have mandated its use in their public schools. The path by which bilingual education came to be viewed as a civil right, rather than as one method of teaching language, demonstrates the politicization of the language issue in American education. The United States Commission on Civil Rights endorsed bilingual education as a civil right nearly a decade ago. Public interest lawyers and civil rights lawyers have also regarded bilingual education as a basic civil right. An article in 1983 in the *Columbia Journal of Law and Social Problems* contended that bilingual education "may be the most effective method of compensatory language instruction currently used to educate language-minority students." It based this conclusion not on a review of educational research but on statements made by various political agencies.

The article states, for example, as a matter of fact rather than opinion: " . . . By offering subject matter instruction in a language understood by language-minority students, the bilingual-bicultural method maximizes achievement, and thus minimizes feelings of inferiority that might accompany a poor academic performance. By ridding the school environment of those features which may damage a language-minority child's self-image and thereby interfere with the educative process, bilingual-bicultural education creates the atmosphere most conducive to successful learning."

If there were indeed conclusive evidence for these statements, then bilingual-bicultural education *should* be imposed on school districts throughout the country. However, the picture is complicated; there are good bilingual programs, and there are ineffective bilingual programs. In and of itself, bilingualism is one pedagogical method, as subject to variation and misuse as any other single method. To date, no school district has claimed that the bilingual method succeeded in sharply decreasing the dropout rate of Hispanic children or markedly raising their achievement scores in English and other subjects. The bilingual method is not necessarily inferior to other methods; its use should not be barred. There simply is no conclusive evidence that bilingualism should be preferred to all other ways of instructing non-English-speaking students. This being the case, there are no valid reasons for courts or federal agencies to impose this method on school districts for all non-English speakers, to the exclusion of other methods of language instruction.

Bilingual education exemplifies politicization because its advocates press its adoption regardless of its educational effectiveness, and they insist that it must be made mandatory regardless of the wishes of the parents and children who are its presumed beneficiaries. It is a political program whose goals are implicit in the term "biculturalism." The aim is to use the public schools to promote the maintenance of distinct ethnic communities, each with its own cultural heritage and language. This in itself is a valid goal for a democratic nation as diverse and pluralistic as ours, but it is questionable whether this goal is appropriately pursued by the public schools, rather than by the freely chosen activities of individuals and groups.

Then there is the larger question of whether bilingual education actually promotes equality of educational opportunity. Unless it enables non-English-speaking children to learn English and to enter into the mainstream of American society, it may hinder equality of educational opportunity. The child who spends most of his instructional time learning in Croatian or Greek or Spanish is likely to learn Croatian, Greek, or Spanish. Fluency in these languages will be of little help to those who want to apply to American colleges, universities, graduate schools, or employers, unless they are also fluent in English.

Of course, our nation needs much more foreign language instruction. But we should not confuse our desire to promote foreign languages in general with the special educational needs of children who do not know how to speak and read English in an English-language society.

Will our educational institutions ever be insulated from the extremes of politicization? It seems highly unlikely, in view of the fact that our schools and colleges are deeply embedded in the social and political mainstream. What is notably different today is the vastly increased power of the federal government and the courts to intervene in educational institutions, because of the expansion of the laws and the dependence of almost all educational institutions on public funding. To avoid unwise and dangerous politicization, government agencies should strive to distinguish between their proper role as protectors of fundamental constitutional rights and inappropriate intrusion into complex issues of curriculum and pedagogy.

This kind of institutional restraint would be strongly abetted if judges and policymakers exercised caution and skepticism in their use of social science testimony. Before making social research the basis for constitutional edicts, judges and policymakers should understand that social science findings are usually divergent, limited, tentative, and partial.

We need the courts as vigilant guardians of our rights; we need federal agencies that respond promptly to any violations of those rights. But we also need educational institutions that are free to exercise their responsibilities without fear of pressure groups and political lobbies. Decisions about which textbooks to use, which theories to teach, which books to place in the school library, how to teach, and what to teach are educational issues. They should be made by appropriate lay and professional authorities on educational grounds. In a democratic society, all of us share the responsibility to protect schools, colleges, and universities against unwarranted political intrusion into educational affairs.

QUESTIONS FOR CRITICAL READERS

Remembering and Understanding

1. Explain the parallels Ravitch sees between *Brown vs. Board of Education* and bilingual education.
2. Why does Ravitch believe bilingual education is a political rather than an educational issue?
3. Summarize Ravitch's objections to bilingual education.
4. What assumptions does Ravitch make about the schools and their purpose? List as many as you can identify, and then write a summary of what Ravitch believes the schools are or should be like.

Analyzing and Discussing

5. How would you distinguish an educational goal from a political goal?
6. Make a list of the subjects you studied in public school. Can you determine

which ones are in the curriculum for political reasons and which are there for educational reasons?

7. Should subjects be included or excluded from the public school curriculum for political reasons? Identify a subject that is included or excluded from the curriculum for what you believe are political reasons and then explain those reasons.

Writing

8. Schools represent or express the values of the communities that they serve. Select some aspect of public education, such as a course or an activity, describe it, and explain the community values that you believe it expresses.

Aria

———— RICHARD RODRIGUEZ ————

*Richard Rodriguez grew up in Sacramento, California. His parents immi-
grated from Mexico, and as a small child he had to deal with the experience
of bilingualism. In this excerpt from his autobiography,* Hunger of Memory,
*Rodriguez describes his experiences growing up in Mexican and American
cultures and the pressures and conflicts he felt as he was drawn between
English and Spanish. As a result of his experiences, he reaches conclusions
about bilingual education that have implications for the English Only
movement.*

I REMEMBER TO START WITH that day in Sacramento—a California
now nearly thirty years past—when I first entered a classroom, able to
understand some fifty stray English words.

The third of four children, I had been preceded to a neighborhood
Roman Catholic school by an older brother and sister. But neither of them
had revealed very much about their classroom experiences. Each afternoon
they returned, as they left in the morning, always together, speaking in
Spanish as they climbed the five steps of the porch. And their mysterious
books, wrapped in shopping-bag paper, remained on the table next to
the door, closed firmly behind them.

An accident of geography sent me to a school where all my classmates
were white, many the children of doctors and lawyers and business executives. All my classmates certainly must have been uneasy on that first
day of school—as most children are uneasy—to find themselves apart
from their families in the first institution of their lives. But I was astonished.

The nun said, in a friendly but oddly impersonal voice, 'Boys and
girls, this is Richard Rodriguez.' (I heard her sound out: *Rich-heard Road-
ree-guess.*) It was the first time I had heard anyone name me in English.
'Richard,' the nun repeated more slowly, writing my name down in her
black leather book. Quickly I turned to see my mother's face dissolve in
a watery blur behind the pebbled glass door.

Many years later there is something called bilingual education—a scheme
proposed in the late 1960s by Hispanic-American social activists, later

endorsed by a congressional vote. It is a program that seeks to permit non-English-speaking children, many from lower-class homes, to use their family language as the language of school. (Such is the goal its supporters announce.) I hear them and am forced to say no: It is not possible for a child—any child—ever to use his family's language in school. Not to understand this is to misunderstand the public uses of schooling and to trivialize the nature of intimate life—a family's 'language.'

Memory teaches me what I know of these matters; the boy reminds the adult. I was a bilingual child, a certain kind—socially disadvantaged—the son of working-class parents, both Mexican immigrants.

In the early years of my boyhood, my parents coped very well in America. My father had steady work. My mother managed at home. They were nobody's victims. Optimism and ambition led them to a house (our home) many blocks from the Mexican south side of town. We lived among *gringos* and only a block from the biggest, whitest houses. It never occurred to my parents that they couldn't live wherever they chose. Nor was the Sacramento of the fifties bent on teaching them a contrary lesson. My mother and father were more annoyed than intimidated by those two or three neighbors who tried initially to make us unwelcome. ('Keep your brats away from my sidewalk!') But despite all they achieved, perhaps because they had so much to achieve, any deep feeling of ease, the confidence of 'belonging' in public was withheld from them both. They regarded the people at work, the faces in crowds, as very distant from us. They were the others, *los gringos*. That term was interchangeable in their speech with another, even more telling, *los americanos*.

I grew up in a house where the only regular guests were my relations. For one day, enormous families of relatives would visit and there would be so many people that the noise and the bodies would spill out to the backyard and front porch. Then, for weeks, no one came by. (It was usually a salesman who rang the doorbell.) Our house stood apart. A gaudy yellow in a row of white bungalows. We were the people with the noisy dog. The people who raised pigeons and chickens. We were the foreigners on the block. A few neighbors smiled and waved. We waved back. But no one in the family knew the names of the old couple who lived next door; until I was seven years old, I did not know the names of the kids who lived across the street.

In public, my father and mother spoke a hesitant, accented, not always grammatical English. And they would have to strain—their bodies tense—to catch the sense of what was rapidly said by *los gringos*. At home they spoke Spanish. The language of their Mexican past sounded in counterpoint to the English of public society. The words would come quickly, with ease. Conveyed through those sounds was the pleasing, soothing, consoling reminder of being at home.

During those years when I was first conscious of hearing, my mother and father addressed me only in Spanish; in Spanish I learned to reply. By contrast, English (*inglés*), rarely heard in the house, was the language I came to associate with *gringos*. I learned my first words of English overhearing my parents speak to strangers. At five years of age, I knew just enough English for my mother to trust me on errands to stores one block away. No more.

I was a listening child, careful to hear the very different sounds of Spanish and English. Wide-eyed with hearing, I'd listen to sounds more than words. First, there were English (*gringo*) sounds. So many words were still unknown that when the butcher or the lady at the drugstore said something to me, exotic polysyllabic sounds would bloom in the midst of their sentences. Often, the speech of people in public seemed to me very loud, booming with confidence. The man behind the counter would literally ask, 'What can I do for you?' But by being so firm and so clear, the sound of his voice said that he was a *gringo*; he belonged in public society.

I would also hear then the high nasal notes of middle-class American speech. The air stirred with sound. Sometimes, even now, when I have been traveling abroad for several weeks, I will hear what I heard as a boy. In hotel lobbies or airports, in Turkey or Brazil, some Americans will pass, and suddenly I will hear it again—the high sound of American voices. For a few seconds I will hear it with pleasure, for it is now the sound of *my* society—a reminder of home. But inevitably—already on the flight headed for home—the sound fades with repetition. I will be unable to hear it anymore.

When I was a boy, things were different. The accent of *los gringos* was never pleasing nor was it hard to hear. Crowds at Safeway or at bus stops would be noisy with sound. And I would be forced to edge away from the chirping chatter above me.

I was unable to hear my own sounds, but I knew very well that I spoke English poorly. My words could not stretch far enough to form complete thoughts. And the words I did speak I didn't know well enough to make into distinct sounds. (Listeners would usually lower their heads, better to hear what I was trying to say.) But it was one thing for *me* to speak English with difficulty. It was more troubling for me to hear my parents speak in public: their high-whining vowels and guttural consonants; their sentences that got stuck with 'ch' and 'ah' sounds; the confused syntax; the hesitant rhythm of sounds so different from the way *gringos* spoke. I'd notice, moreover, that my parents' voices were softer than those of *gringos* we'd meet.

I am tempted now to say that none of this mattered. In adulthood I am embarrassed by childhood fears. And, in a way, it didn't matter very much that my parents could not speak English with ease. Their linguistic difficulties had no serious consequences. My mother and father made themselves understood at the county hospital clinic and at government offices. And yet, in another way, it mattered very much—it was unsettling to hear my parents struggle with English. Hearing them, I'd grow nervous, my clutching trust in their protection and power weakened.

There were many times like the night at a brightly lit gasoline station (a blaring white memory) when I stood uneasily, hearing my father. He was talking to a teenaged attendant. I do not recall what they were saying, but I cannot forget the sounds my father made as he spoke. At one point his words slid together to form one word—sounds as confused as the threads of blue and green oil in the puddle next to my shoes. His voice rushed through what he had left to say. And, toward the end, reached falsetto notes, appealing to his listener's understanding. I looked away to the lights of passing automobiles. I tried not to hear anymore. But I heard only too well the calm, easy tones in the attendant's reply. Shortly afterward, walking toward home with my father, I shivered when he put his hand on my shoulder. The very first chance that I got, I evaded his grasp and ran on ahead into the dark, skipping with feigned boyish exuberance.

But then there was Spanish. *Español*: my family's language. *Español*: the language that seemed to me a private language. I'd hear strangers on the radio and in the Mexican Catholic church across town speaking in Spanish, but I couldn't really believe that Spanish was a public language, like English. Spanish speakers, rather, seemed related to me, for I sensed that we shared—through our language—the experience of feeling apart from *los gringos*. It was thus a ghetto Spanish that I heard and I spoke. Like those who lives are bound by a barrio, I was reminded by Spanish of my separateness from *los otros, los gringos* in power. But more intensely than for most barrio children—because I did not live in a barrio—Spanish seemed to me the language of home. (Most days it was only at home that I'd hear it.) It became the language of joyful return.

A family member would say something to me and I would feel myself specially recognized. My parents would say something to me and I would feel embraced by the sounds of their words. Those sounds said: *I am speaking with ease in Spanish. I am addressing you in words I never use with* los gringos. *I recognize you as someone special, close, like no one outside. You belong with us. In the family.*

(*Ricardo.*)

At the age of five, six, well past the time when most other children no longer easily notice the difference between sounds uttered at home and words spoken in public, I had a different experience. I lived in a world magically compounded of sounds. I remained a child longer than most; I lingered too long, poised at the edge of language—often frightened by the sounds of *los gringos*, delighted by the sounds of Spanish at home.

I shared with my family a language that was startlingly different from that used in the great city around us.

For me there were none of the gradations between public and private society so normal to a maturing child. Outside the house was public society; inside the house was private. Just opening or closing the screen door behind me was an important experience. I'd rarely leave home all alone or without reluctance. Walking down the sidewalk, under the canopy of tall trees, I'd warily notice the—suddenly—silent neighborhood kids who stood warily watching me. Nervously, I'd arrive at the grocery store to hear there the sounds of the *gringo*—foreign to me—reminding me that in this world so big, I was a foreigner. But then I'd return. Walking back toward our house, climbing the steps from the sidewalk, when the front door was open in summer, I'd hear voices beyond the screen door talking in Spanish. For a second or two, I'd stay, linger there, listening. Smiling, I'd hear my mother call out, saying in Spanish (words): 'Is that you, Richard?' All the while her sounds would assure me: *You are home now; come closer; inside. With us.*

'*Sí*,' I'd reply.

Once more inside the house I would resume (assume) my place in the family. The sounds would dim, grow harder to hear. Once more at home, I would grow less aware of that fact. It required, however, no more than the blurt of the doorbell to alert me to listen to sounds all over again. The house would turn instantly still while my mother went to the door. I'd hear her hard English sounds. I'd wait to hear her voice return to soft-sounding Spanish, which assured me, as surely as did the clicking tongue of the lock on the door, that the stranger was gone.

Plainly, it is not healthy to hear such sounds so often. It is not healthy to distinguish public words from private sounds so easily. I remained cloistered by sounds, timid and shy in public, too dependent on voices at home. And yet it needs to be emphasized: I was an extremely happy child at home. I remember many nights when my father would come back from work, and I'd hear him call out to my mother in Spanish, sounding relieved. In Spanish, he'd sound light and free notes he never could manage in English. Some nights I'd jump up just at hearing his voice. With *mis hermanos* I would come running into the room where he was with my mother. Our laughing (so deep was the pleasure!) became screaming. Like others who know the pain of public alienation, we transformed the knowledge of our public separateness and made it consoling—the reminder of intimacy. Excited, we joined our voices in a celebration of sounds. *We are speaking now the way we never speak out in public. We are alone—together,* voices sounded, surrounded to tell me. Some nights, no one seemed willing to loosen the hold sounds had on us. At dinner, we invented new words. (Ours sounded Spanish, but made sense only to us.) We pieced together new words by taking, say, an English verb and giving it Spanish endings. My mother's instructions at bedtime would be lacquered with mock-urgent tones. Or a word like *sí* would become, in several notes, able to convey added measures of feeling. Tongues explored the edges of words, especially the fat vowels. And we happily sounded that military drum roll, the twirling roar of the Spanish *r*. Family language: my family's sounds. The voices of my parents and sisters and brother. Their voices insisting: *You belong here. We are family members. Related. Special to one another. Listen!* Voices singing and sighing, rising, straining, then surging, teeming with pleasure that burst syllables into fragments of laughter. At times it seemed there was steady quiet only when, from another room, the rustling whispers of my parents faded and I moved closer to sleep.

Supporters of bilingual education today imply that students like me miss a great deal by not being taught in their family's language. What they seem not to recognize is that, as a socially disadvantaged child, I considered Spanish to be a private language. What I needed to learn in school was that I had the right—and the obligation—to speak the public language of *los gringos*. The odd truth is that my first-grade classmates could have become bilingual, in the conventional sense of that word, more easily than I. Had they been taught (as upper-middle-class children are often taught early) a second language like Spanish or French, they could have regarded it simply as that: another public language. In my case such bilingualism could not have been so quickly achieved. What I did not believe was that I could speak a single public language.

Without question, it would have pleased me to hear my teachers address me in Spanish when I entered the classroom. I would have felt much less afraid. I would have trusted them and responded with ease. But I would have delayed—for how long postponed?—having to learn the language of public society. I would have evaded—and for how long could I have afforded to delay?—learning the great lesson of school, that I had a public identity.

Fortunately, my teachers were unsentimental about their responsibility. What they understood was that I needed to speak a public language. So their voices would search me out, asking me questions. Each time I'd hear them, I'd look up in surprise to see a nun's face frowning at me. I'd mumble, not really meaning to answer. The nun would persist, 'Richard, stand up. Don't look at the floor. Speak up. Speak to the entire class, not just to me!' But I couldn't believe that the English language was mine to use. (In part, I did not want to believe it.) I continued to mumble. I resisted the teacher's demands. (Did I somehow suspect that once I learned public language my pleasing family life would be changed?) Silent, waiting for the bell to sound, I remained dazed, diffident, afraid.

Because I wrongly imagined that English was intrinsically a public language and Spanish an intrinsically private one, I easily noted the difference between classroom language and the language of home. At school, words were directed to a general audience of listeners. ('Boys and girls.') Words were meaningfully ordered. And the point was not self-expression alone but to make oneself understood by many others. The teacher quizzed: 'Boys and girls, why do we use that word in this sentence? Could we think of a better word to use there? Would the sentence change its meaning if the words were differently arranged? And wasn't there a better way of saying much the same thing?' (I couldn't say. I wouldn't try to say.)

Three months. Five. Half a year passed. Unsmiling, ever watchful, my teachers noted my silence. They began to connect my behavior with the difficult progress my older sister and brother were making. Until one Saturday morning three nuns arrived at the house to talk to our parents. Stiffly, they sat on the blue living room sofa. From the doorway of another room, spying the visitors, I noted the incongruity—the clash of two worlds, the faces and voices of school intruding upon the familiar setting of home. I overheard one voice gently wondering, 'Do your children speak only Spanish at home, Mrs. Rodriguez?' While another voice added, 'That Richard especially seems so timid and shy.'

That Rich-heard!

With great tact the visitors continued, 'Is it possible for you and your husband to encourage your children to practice their English when they are home?' Of course, my parents complied. What would they not do for their children's well-being? And how could they have questioned the Church's authority which those women represented? In an instant, they agreed to give up the language (the sounds) that had revealed and accentuated our family's closeness. The moment after the visitors left, the change was observed. '*Ahora,* speak to us *en inglés,*' my father and mother united to tell us.

At first, it seemed a kind of game. After dinner each night, the family gathered to practice 'our' English. (It was still then *inglés,* a language foreign to us, so we felt drawn as strangers to it.) Laughing, we would try to define words we could not pronounce. We played with strange English sounds, often overanglicizing our pronunciations. And we filled the smiling gaps of our sentences with familiar Spanish sounds. But that was cheating, somebody shouted. Everyone laughed. In school, meanwhile, like my brother and sister, I was required to attend a daily tutoring session. I needed a full year of special attention. I also needed my teachers to keep my attention from straying in class by calling out, *Rich-heard—* their English voices slowly prying loose my ties to my other name, its three notes, *Ri-car-do.* Most of all I needed to hear my mother and father speak to me in a moment of seriousness in broken—suddenly heartbreaking—English. The scene was inevitable: One Saturday morning I entered the kitchen where my parents were talking in Spanish. I did not realize that they were talking in Spanish however until, at the moment they saw me, I heard their voices change to speak English. Those *gringo* sounds they uttered startled me. Pushed me away. In that moment of trivial misunderstanding and profound insight, I felt my throat twisted by unsounded grief. I turned quickly and left the room. But I had no place to escape to with Spanish. (The spell was broken.) My brother and sisters were speaking English in another part of the house.

Again and again in the days following, increasingly angry, I was obliged to hear my mother and father: 'Speak to us *en inglés.*' (*Speak.*) Only then did I determine to learn classroom English. Weeks after, it happened: One day in school I raised my hand to volunteer an answer. I spoke out in a loud voice. And I did not think it remarkable when the entire class understood. That day, I moved very far from the disadvantaged child I had been only days earlier. The belief, the calming assurance that I belonged in public, had at last taken hold.

Shortly after, I stopped hearing the high and loud sounds of *los gringos.* A more and more confident speaker of English, I didn't trouble to listen to *how* strangers sounded, speaking to me. And there simply were too many English-speaking people in my day for me to hear American accents anymore. Conversations quickened. Listening to persons who sounded eccentrically pitched voices, I usually noted their sounds for an initial few seconds before I concentrated on *what* they were saying. Conversations became content-full. Transparent. Hearing someone's *tone* of voice—angry or questioning or sarcastic or happy or sad—I didn't distinguish it from the words it expressed. Sound and word were thus tightly wedded. At the end of a day, I was often bemused, always relieved, to realize how 'silent,' though crowded with words, my day in public had been. (This public silence measured and quickened the change in my life.)

At last, seven years old, I came to believe what had been technically true since my birth: I was an American citizen.

QUESTIONS FOR CRITICAL READERS

Remembering and Understanding

1. What is Rodriguez's position on bilingual education? Re-state it, and give his reasons.
2. Rodriguez explains that he regarded English as a public language and Spanish as a private language. How did these attitudes affect his language behavior as a child?
3. Describe Rodriguez's changing relationship with his parents, and explain the role of language in that relationship.

4. How was Rodriguez's experience with English and Spanish different from that of his parents?

Analyzing and Discussing

5. Because he spoke Spanish at home and English at school, Rodriguez experienced significant differences between his life at home and his life at school. How were your private and public worlds similar or different during your childhood? Did you associate special customs or foods or other experiences with one or the other?
6. How is the language you use in school different from the language you use at home?

Writing

7. Rodriguez associates speaking English with American citizenship. What do you associate with citizenship? Select one feature of American culture that you regard as central to citizenship; describe it, and explain why you believe it is so important to citizenship.

On Growing Up Bilingual

EINAR HAUGEN

Haugen was born in Sioux City, Iowa. His parents were Norwegian, and he grew up in a bilingual home. He has spent his career studying languages. In this selection from his book, Blessings of Babel, *he tells of his own childhood experiences with bilingualism and biculturalism. He draws on personal experience, and does not comment directly on the English Only movement or its motives. He forms an interesting contrast with Richard Rodriguez.*

MY INTEREST IN BILINGUALISM originated as an intensely personal concern. Born as I was in the state of Iowa of Norwegian immigrant parents, my earliest recollections are of the problems I encountered in keeping apart the Norwegian spoken at home by my parents and their friends and the English spoken on the streets by my playmates and at school by my classmates and teachers. The setting was urban and wholly American, with no immediately surrounding neighborhood to support my "foreign" language, contrary to the situation of many rural communities in the Middle West and the Northwest.

Thanks to my parents' adamant insistence on my speaking their native tongue at home, the threshold of the home became the cue to a code switch. As an only child I lacked the potential support of siblings to defy the will of my parents. When coming in from a lively period of play, I blundered many a time in violation of Norwegian idiom. My parents showed considerable tolerance in this respect. My mother, to be sure, being trained as a school teacher in Norway, tried to keep up standards of purity. For the most part, my errors, which I would now call "interferences," were not noted and corrected (Weinreich 1953:1). The Norwegian spoken by my parents in this setting was not only partly dialectal, but had also diverged considerably in the direction of English by adopting English words and phrases in a Norwegianized form.

We never used any other word for a "broom" than the English word, pronounced *brumm* in terms of Norwegian spelling. I recall the amusement and momentary consternation it caused when a visitor from

Norway used the Norwegian word *kost* to describe it. We never hesitated to say that we would *krosse striten* instead of *gå over gata* when we intended to cross the street. As travelers we might say *sette sutkeisen på saidvåaka* for "putting the suitcase on the sidewalk," instead of *sette kofferten på fortauget*, as our urban contemporaries in Norway would have done. My parents made some efforts to avoid such terms in speaking to well-educated or recent arrivals from Norway. But the words were so common in the usage of the people with whom they associated that they no longer excited any remark, aside from an occasional wry witticism. Historically, the English words were "interferences," or even well-established "loans." In our usage they were part of a new code, a partially merged language, an "interlanguage" if you will, a strictly American Norwegian.

At the age of eight I had the unusual experience of being conveyed by my parents to Oppdal, the rural community in Norway from which they had sprung. In view of the American urban neighborhood where I had lived so far, it was a traumatic experience. My parents were genuinely hopeful that they could "go back home," only to be disillusioned after two and a half years. This period coincided with the first two years of World War I. In this Norwegian interlude I had my first brush with dialect *diglossia*.

Even though I could communicate with the children of neighboring farms, who were my new agemates, my American Norwegian was not adequate. Not only did they use words and forms that I did not know, but they were baffled by my Americanisms. I had to unlearn the interlanguage of my American environment, not just "relexify" it by replacing its English loans with Norwegian terms, but also by adopting a stricter grammatical form of the dialect itself. I recall being bemused by the word for "tickle," pronounced as *kjåttå* /çot:o/ in the dialect, where standard Norwegian had *kile* /çi:lǝ/.

The pressure for linguistic conformity expressed itself in the usual way, through laughter and the unthinking cruelty of children to one another. They sometimes asked me to talk English, out of curiosity to hear what it sounded like (this was long before English had become a regular subject in the schools). But I refused from sheer fear of ridicule. In those years I hardly used English at all, except perhaps in solitary monologues. On our return it was noticed that I had acquired a perceptible Norwegian accent in my English. So once more I went through the process of overcoming deviations in language and bringing my English back to midwestern standards.

Once these problems were overcome, I had in fact internalized two codes for production: a relatively pure Norwegian dialect, and a relatively pure American dialect. I say "relatively" only because "pure" implies a perfection which I would be far from claiming. Perhaps I should say, "natively acceptable." These two were constantly reinforced by opportunities for use with native speakers. Among my parents' friends, and including particularly my father, I could count on an opportunity to show off my new Norwegian dialect. And of course, my English was quickly reestablished to the level of my agemates in the grammar school.

From my eleventh year forward life proceeded along two rather different tracks: on the one hand home and family, with friends and fellows in the Norwegian Lutheran Church to which we belonged and in which we were active; on the other hand, the American public school and friends I made there, along with such activities as scouting, which I shared with them.

But my parents were now pursuing their goal (especially my mother's) of enabling me to use also standard Norwegian, i.e. the literary language. Technically, this meant the Dano-Norwegian which has become the modern "Book Language" (*bokmål*) of Norway. In school I got no support for this endeavor, of course. My mastery of Norwegian was overlooked and if anything discouraged, at least until I got into high school. I can say with assurance that it did not hold me back in acquiring standard written and spoken English. I recall occasional interferences which had to be corrected in my writing, as when I wrote "on Iceland" (Norwegian *på Island*) instead of "in Iceland." In speech there were certain "hard words" that had to be mastered, as when I pronounced "horizon"/hoŕizən/ instead of /horaiźən/. But this was no worse than the illiteracies of most of my schoolmates, whose scholastic shortcomings could not be attributed to any "foreign" background. I took to English language and literature, even to grammar, with great avidity thanks to my realization of the linguistic possibilities that my Norwegian experience had implanted in me.

By the time of the generally recognized crucial threshold of puberty, I had in effect acquired six codes: a high and low register of American English, the literate and the vulgate; a local Norwegian dialect in two varieties, the native and the Americanized contact dialect; and an approximation to standard Norwegian: speech and writing. It is hard at this point to say to what extent each of them was productive or receptive. In any case I was clearly conscious of their existence and the problem of keeping them apart.

My reason for recounting this personal background is to illustrate the correlation of one's learning with the social experience of group living. American English grew out of my experience with playmates and teachers in an urban American setting. Dialect Norwegian came from immigrant parents and Norwegian playmates. Standard Norwegian stemmed from my parents and their friends as representatives of the community of cultivated Norwegians in America. In each of these settings I found satisfaction in performing functions that earned me acceptance and praise. Somewhere in this experience lies the key to the worries that many people have about making their children bilingual. No harm can result if the contexts are satisfying and supportive. In that case the problems of integrating two cultures and two languages are not overwhelming to the child. A satisfaction should result which, at least in my case, has never been equaled by the various languages I have learned later in life, mostly in school.

Of course there were problems. How could one be both a Norwegian and an American and identify with both countries? How could one be both a dialect and a standard speaker, identifying with a rural as well as an urban environment? Linguistically and culturally it involved a kind of tight-rope walking, a struggle against interference to achieve the norms of each social group. One remembers mostly the defeats, the lapses that tickled the funny bones of one's listeners. I once tried to explain to some contemporary Norwegian newcomers the difference between "soft" and "hard" water. I made up the word *hårdvann* for "hard water", which to the unbridled amusement of my listeners coincided in pronunciation with *hårvann* "hair tonic". After World War II, when I was Cultural Officer for the American Embassy in Oslo, I astonished a Norwegian committee by suggesting that a certain person "sit on" the committee (*sitte på*) instead of the correct "sit in" (*sitte i*). The phrase suggested that he would weigh the committee down with his physical presence. Such problems are part of being bilingual. But the reward of being accepted in two cultures outweighs the problems.

Having put in so much effort at learning these various codes, I was naturally drawn to the profession of language teaching, and on to linguistics, and eventually to a special concentration on bilingualism. Many had already written about this problem, especially in Europe, but the delimitation of it as a field of study was novel when I did my research, in the 1940's and 1950's. The problems and the rewards here sketched from my personal biography proved to have been shared by a multitude of people around the world. The problems were not peculiar either to me or to my contemporaries. There has nearly always been a conflict of interest between members of different language communities. Hence bilingualism is ultimately a political and social problem, made manifest in the minds and hearts of the persons who constitute these communities.

In thinking about the problem, it is important to keep the *individual* and the *social* aspects distinct. As we shall see later, one can locate individuals on a two-dimensional chart. On one parameter the various degrees of skill, from zero to native command, and on the other the language distance, from virtual identity to maximum difference. Both dimensions offer interesting themes of definition and research, and they give us some kind of a model to keep in mind.

The pressures exerted by society are of quite a different order. Here it is a question of the power differential between groups. We can think of a situation like that of Switzerland and describe it as "horizontal", a bilingualism without domination by one group over the other. The federalism and the loose-jointed relation of the cantons makes each one a monolingual unit, so that multilingualism becomes a problem only at the official, legislative level. Yet most Swiss speakers are not bilingual, at least not in the languages of their own country. A more explosive situation is the usual one, that we may call "vertical" bilingualism. Here one language group dominates the other in terms of access to power and the benefits that flow from such access. Here we may speak of a *dominant* and a *dominated* group. As social planners we would like to bring the dominant and the dominated together on a plane of equality.

The problem for the community is that of creating an atmosphere favorable to bilingual education both in the dominant and the dominated population. In our Southwest this means the Anglo and the Hispanic communities; in Canada it means the English and the French. Lambert has made the point that "priority for early schooling should be given to the language or languages least likely to be developed otherwise." He has in fact advocated a system of language immersion by the dominant group in the language of the dominated. The situation in our Southwest is just the opposite: the dominated are immersed in the language of the dominant. What we need is immersion programs in Spanish for American children.

To convince those who oppose such programs we need to show them that they are beneficial and in no way harmful to the children. We have to prove that such proposals are not un-American or unpatriotic, and that they make the United States a better place to live. Let us see this as a problem of *social ecology:* keeping alive the variety and fascination of our country, diverting the trend toward steamrollering everything and everyone into a single, flat uniformity.

To put such plans into effect we need more abundant materials at every level of education. Immersion calls for something more than just sampling a language for a few hours a week. Immersion requires living and thinking, even loving and feeling in the new language. It is like learning to swim: as long as one still thinks one will sink, one has not learned to swim. Swimming in a new language requires the provision of opportunity and the ability to communicate successfully with one's own as well the other group.

Now that laws for bilingual education have been passed by Congress and by the legislatures of many states, I can only say that this is an astonishing reversal for one who has experienced the hysteria against non-English teaching after World War I. Now even some ethnic groups that have been weakened with age, like the Germans and the Scandinavians, have awakened to their heritage and are making efforts to keep alive something of what their ancestors brought with them to this country.

What can we hope for as results from bilingual teaching? All depends on giving the dominated, weaker group an education that is equal in value to that of the stronger. In his article on the immersion programs of Canada, Lambert alludes to some of the problems, many of the same I have described above as occurring in my experience. He has noted something he calls an "immersion class French," an interlanguage in which literal calques on English appear, such as *Q'est-ce que c'est pour?* for "What's that for?" We need not take such lapses too seriously. Among other bilinguals such *gaffes* will be understood, even if they sound amusing. They will generally be ironed out when two populations have learned to speak to one another, just as my un-Norwegian or un-English idioms were counteracted by my further social experience.

Actually, it is the interlanguage of daily life, of the market place, that we want them to learn, not necessarily the languages of Racine or Shakespeare. Test scores are no ultimate proof of the success of a bilingual program. We look for a livelier, more vigorous group life, reduced discrimination, richer experience, and hopefully a more open society than the one we have.

QUESTIONS FOR CRITICAL READERS

Remembering and Understanding

1. Summarize the difficulties Haugen experienced because he spoke both English and Norwegian.
2. According to Haugen, what are some of the advantages of being bilingual and bicultural?
3. How has Haugen's professional knowledge about language influenced what he says here?

Analyzing and Discussing

4. Consider your own use of English. Do you speak it the same way in all situations? Select several social situations and explain how your language changes as you move from one to another.
5. Based on Haugen's descriptions of his experiences with Norwegian, explain what happens to a language when its speakers are isolated from their native language and culture.
6. Haugen suggests an immersion program in Spanish for English-speaking children in the Southwest. What would be the benefits of such a program?

Writing

7. Haugen recalls American and Norwegian children making fun of his language. Within your native language, are there sounds, pronunciations, words, or other features that people consistently find humorous or make fun of? Identify at least half a dozen of these and write a paper in which you explain why people react to them in this way, and what that reaction tells you about American attitudes toward language.

1. Explain the reasons for laws that have been passed against bilingualism, or in favor of an official language. What motivates those laws, and what do their authors want to accomplish? Make your explanations as specific and detailed as possible.
2. Summarize the arguments against laws that would make English the only or official language of the United States.
3. Explain the ways in which American culture might be threatened by having sizeable portions of the population of the United States speaking languages other than English.
4. How would Halton respond to George Will and Abigail McCarthy?
5. George Will appears to believe that "bilingualism" means a person need not learn English. Compare Will's statements with the understandings of bilingualism that emerge in the other selections in this chapter, particularly the pieces by Haugen and Rodriguez.
6. What evidence is available to suggest that earlier immigrants to the U.S. have not assimilated into American culture but have maintained their own cultures and languages?
7. Review George Will's column, "In Defense of the Mother Tongue." To what extent does the information presented in other selections in this chapter support Will's statements and assertions about assimilation and language minorities?
8. Haugen and Rodriguez both describe bilingual experiences. How were these experiences similar or different?

Suggestions for Research and Writing

1. Do a survey in which you ask people about their attitudes toward languages other than their native language. Take the time to decide what information you want to gather, and then design your questions carefully to obtain the information you need. Tabulate your results and write a paper in which you report the attitudes that you discover.
2. If American culture is the result of the combination of many cultures, then what is the distinctively American culture that several writers in this chapter refer to? Write a paper in which you identify and describe what is distinctive about American culture.
3. Some people support English as an official language because they fear Spanish or some other language will threaten the prevalence of English and even make it disappear. Write a paper in which you explain the social, economic, and cultural conditions that would have to exist before English could lose its position as the dominant language in the United States.
4. Many demographers predict that by the early twenty-first century the population of the United States will consist of a majority of minorities. Locate information about this trend, and write a summary. Then speculate

about the effects that this population shift might have on languages and language policy in the United States.

5. Using information from this chapter, identify several groups that have been the targets of cultural or language discrimination. Research the history of this group and explain the reasons for and results of the discrimination.

6. Find out as much as you can about the different languages that are spoken in the United States and the size of the group that speaks each one. Plot these languages on a map, and then write a description of America's linguistic and cultural diversity.

7. Investigate the history of one ethnic, cultural, or language group in the United States, and write a brief historical account of that group's experiences.

9

Taking Out the Trash

For most of the twentieth century Americans have disposed of their trash by burying it in landfills. While that has solved the immediate problem of getting rid of the trash, it has produced two other problems. Many cities are running out of space in their landfills, and finding new places to bury trash is proving to be difficult and expensive. Also, the landfills themselves have, in some cases, been identified as health hazards, sources of toxic pollution. Proposals to construct new landfills usually arouse strong opposition from those who live nearby. No one wants someone else's trash. Because of health risks, new landfills must be constructed and operated according to strict rules. For all of these reasons, disposing of trash has become increasingly difficult and expensive, and there is no hope that the problem will go away or become appreciably simpler in the near future.

The articles in this chapter examine the problem of solid waste disposal in a variety of ways. They look at the trash itself, the various methods of disposal, and the social, economic, political, and technological factors that influence consumption and disposal. In "Trash Can Realities" Jon R. Luoma provides a general introduction to the subject of trash production and various methods of disposal. In "The Technological Flaw,"

biologist Barry Commoner uses the concept of technological displacement
to explain why solid waste has become such a problem since World War
II. Bill Breen takes a close look at landfills. He explains what they are,
how they are constructed, how they could be made safer, and what can
be done with them after they are full. William Rathje, in "The History
of Garbage," reports about his research into historical methods of trash
disposal and also discusses the items he has found in his many excavations
of contemporary landfills. Ruth Norris and Mary Durant each look at
specific products that end up in landfills: plastic and bottles. In "The
Look is You" Blumberg and Gottlieb explore how changes in manufacturing and consumption since the 1940s have contributed to the production
of solid waste. Collectively, these writers suggest that technological solutions to the problem of trash disposal will work only if they are accompanied by social and political changes in the way that Americans consume.

   You will understand and retain more of what you read if you take
a few minutes now to become aware of what you already know about the
problem of trash disposal and of your own relationship to both the problem
and the solution. The questions in the next section, "Before You Read,"
will help you discover and review what you already know. Answer the
prereading questions as thoroughly as you can, and do it in writing. Later,
you can review the notes you make now and evaluate your present knowledge in light of what you learn from your reading.

Before You Read

1. Describe your attitudes toward trash and garbage. (What do you think of
   as you take out the garbage or watch garbage trucks go past your house?)
2. Most communities dump their trash and garbage in landfills. Explain as
   much as you know about landfills. What are they and how do they work?
3. What is your reaction to litter? Describe an experience you have had with
   litter or junk.
4. How would you react if someone wanted to put a landfill close to your
   house?
5. In your opinion, what are the five most important environmental problems
   facing the United States? List them in order of importance, and explain
   each one briefly.
6. Explain what you know about recycling.
7. What do you believe is the responsibility of the individual citizen in solving
   environmental problems? What should individuals do?

Trash Can Realities

———— Jon R. Luoma ————

Luoma is a freelance writer who specializes in environmental subjects and generally takes a position that might be described as "environmentalist." In this article, which appeared in the April 1990 issue of Audubon *magazine, he gives a general overview of the present methods of trash disposal in the United States. He also discusses alternative solutions, including recycling, discusses some of the problems associated with each potential solution, and offers suggestions for the future.*

Garbage is rife with symbols of wickedness and virtue, but conventional environmental wisdom may not be so wise after all.

MAYBE, AS AN EXERCISE in personal responsibility, each resident of Hennepin County, Minnesota, should visit once every year the place with the faint odor of rot and the agreeable name of "the tipping hall" in an immense beige building named HERC on the edge of downtown Minneapolis.

HERC is the Hennepin "resource recovery plant." The tipping hall is a cavernous room where garbage trucks dump their load into a cavernous pit, to be shoveled by huge scoops into a 2,000-degree furnace. There were three thousand tons of garbage piled in a mountain in and above the pit the day I visited, about an average day's output for the county of one million—about three days' capacity for the furnace.

To its builders and promoters, the plant, a high-tech "waste to energy" burner, represents a socially responsible exercise—a plant that uses trash as fuel to produce, virtually for free, some 35 million watts of electricity round the clock, reducing the trash to ash in the process. The plant is expected to pay for itself, using monies from both tipping fees charged to the garbage haulers and fees received from the sale of electricity to retire its $100-million-plus bonding debt.

But in the view of some critics, "resource recovery plant" is Orwellian Newspeak, designed to disguise the fact that such a facility is but a highly engineered version of the smoldering city dump of old. Say the critics, incinerators create as many problems as they solve. They toxify the atmosphere with traces of heavy metals and dioxins, and they produce an ash with such a high ratio of toxic metals to harmless substances that it often legally qualifies as a hazardous waste.

Better, the critics say, communities and business and government and individuals should learn to place far more vigorous emphasis on recycling wastes. Even better, this throwaway society—and surely we are that, generating roughly twice the junk per capita of even our affluent Western European counterparts—should turn to "source reduction." That means generating less of the stuff in the first place—less junk mail, less useless packaging, fewer disposable razors, disposable lighters, disposable coffee cups, disposable diapers, polyethylene bags for magazines. Even many of the milder critics of incinerators say that they discourage recycling and continue the illusion that citizens needn't ever recycle and reduce their waste output.

Garbage management is an issue rife with symbols of wickedness and virtue. Incinerators, in some minds, are the Greatest of Satans, even with the best air-pollution-control equipment available. Plastics run a close second. Virtuous paper, on the other hand, is at least a natural product, ideal for virtuous and continuous recycling. And recycling, or so the conventional wisdom goes, is a process that could reduce our waste flow to nearly nothing if Americans simply separated their wastes and saw that they got to a recycling center.

Yet a look into the realities of the American trash can suggests that, symbols and Satans aside, none of it is so simple, and even that much of the conventional environmental wisdom may not be so wise after all.

In the 1960s and 1970s so-called "sanitary" landfills were supposed to be the solution to America's garbage problems. Landfills, so the nation's engineers said, would be better than smoldering dumps, backyard burning-barrels, and apartment-building incinerators. Garbage, preferably packed into nice, clean, plastic bags, would be put out of sight. Out of mind. Sanitary.

Today, with hundreds of landfills nationwide leaching pollutants into groundwater aquifers, and many of those landfills now on the national register of Superfund sites, we seem to have learned a collective lesson: Dumping mixed wastes that include potential water pollutants into horribly designed landfills is a costly mistake.

Typically, we now may have overreacted. Some experts say that well designed landfills can be safe, provided the most noxious hazardous wastes are handled separately, and if the landfills are properly sited and engineered with a combination of clay and plastic liners and leachate collection systems so as not to leach pollutants into groundwater. But public perceptions run otherwise. "Landfill," in the popular American imagination, has become synonymous not with "sanitary" but with "hazardous." The result: The syndrome called NIMBY (Not In My Backyard) is more active in public policy than ever. Few landfills are being sited, anywhere. Permits for new landfills are snarled in regulatory or court hearings. And projections suggest that landfills are going to be closed in droves in the 1990s.

We've gotten into this fix because Americans are the unqualified champions of the dump. Each New Yorker produces about four pounds of garbage daily. Tokyo isn't far behind, at about three pounds. Parisians, however, produce only about two and a half pounds of garbage per capita. In Hamburg, unquestionably an affluent and industrial city, residents produce half the garbage of New Yorkers, about two pounds each day.

Cumulatively, Americans generate about 160 million tons of garbage each year, according to estimates from the U.S. Environmental Protection Agency. Of that, paper, leaves and grass clippings, pieces of wood, and food wastes are thought to make up about seventy percent of the total. In other words, the vast majority of our garbage is biodegradable, technically speaking. Of the remainder, nearly twenty percent is glass, metal, and cloth. Despite a widespread impression that plastics are at the core of the garbage crisis, EPA numbers suggest that plastics constitute less than ten percent of the garbage load by weight, although their relative volume is somewhat greater.

And it is volume, not mass, that is the greater public policy crisis. According to EPA, more than half the landfills in the United States will reach capacity in eight years. The problem is acute in the densely populated states of the Northeast. In Connecticut, state officials estimate that almost all the landfills will be full by next year. In New Jersey the number of landfills has declined from three hundred to one hundred since 1976, with twelve of them now providing more than 90 percent of waste disposal. In New York the State Legislative Commission on Solid Waste Management has predicted that all landfills in the state will be full by 1995— decreasing from five hundred in 1982 to 270 today.

Yet even while the landfills have been filling, some researchers have begun to challenge the conventional assumptions about what goes on inside them. William Rathje, an archeologist at the University of Arizona in Tucson, has spent the past several years specializing in the excavation of America's landfills.

Rathje, who describes himself as a "garbologist," and a team of students and helpers, once unearthed some 16,000 pounds of trash from landfills in the West, Southwest, and Midwest, weighing and cataloging each item. Their findings suggest that many of the symbols of our wasteful ways are, in fact, of far less consequence than most of us imagined. By weight, about one-tenth of one percent was made up of fast-food packaging. Disposable diapers amounted to less than one percent of the total. Plastics, Rathje reports, amounted to only about twelve percent of the volume in the landfills, less than five percent of the weight.

So what was the greatest constituent of the landfills? Paper in general, newspaper in particular, and also "layers of phone books, like geological strata, or layers of cake." (Newspapers, in fact, appear to be the number one disposable product in America. Each Sunday edition of *The New York Times* alone produces more than eight million pounds of wastepaper.)

But Rathje's most compelling contravention of conventional wisdom has been to show that biodegradation doesn't occur in a landfill. In the crush of compacted trash and soil little oxygen is available for decomposition, and the buried waste breaks down extremely slowly, if at all. Rathje reports that he has found copies of newspapers printed nearly forty years ago that "looked so fresh you might read one over breakfast." He has found hot dogs decades-old and still intact.

As we all knew, plastics can be expected to last virtually forever in the landfill. But so, it seems, will most of the supposedly biodegradable things. Each nicely brown, seemingly earthy, kraft paper bag chosen by the virtuous grocery shopper at the check-out line is, in fact, at least as polluting, and probably more so, than the polyethylene alternative. The brown paper sack is bulkier in landfills, much heavier, and, according to studies by National Audubon Society senior scientist Jan Beyea and the West German Federal Office of the Environment, produces more pollution, pound for pound, than polyethylene in its manufacture.

Of course, conventional wisdom suggests that paper might still be a better choice, since it can be recycled with relative ease. But once again, the issue is far from simple.

Tom Troskey is a professional supporter of recycling. As paper stock manager at one of the largest newsprint-to-paperboard recycling plants in the country, he'd have to be. These are, in some ways, good times for Troskey and the Waldorf Corporation, in St. Paul, Minnesota. Until last year Waldorf had to purchase the raw old newspapers for the company's immense manufacturing operation from the Boy Scouts and private collectors at up to twenty dollars a ton. Now he is happily getting the stuff for free, from communities that use tax monies to pick it up for him. He might get happier. The day may come when Waldorf gets paid to take old newsprint.

If you look inside the boxes of cookies and crackers and, especially cereal in your kitchen cupboards, you'll find that most have a gray interior. Those boxes are made of recycled newsprint and recycled office paper, likely produced and printed at one of Waldorf's two plants.

Standing at the end of an immense paper machine, where workers are nursing newly reconstituted paperboard onto a roll, Troskey suggests that despite a recent surge in efforts by communities all over America to recycle newsprint, little, if any, more recycling is actually occurring.

"This is not a supply-driven business," Troskey says. "Some people have this idea that no matter how much newsprint they bring to us, we can find a use for it. But this is a completely demand-driven business. It's as simple as that. Our ability to find markets for our recycled products has limits. And only the amount of paper that there's a demand for is going to find a home."

In the spring and summer of 1989 several large communities in Minnesota suddenly began curbside recycling pickups for the first time. The City of Minneapolis nearly simultaneously offered a reduction in garbage fees for residents who joined its existing curbside recycling program. Residents responded enthusiastically, and truckload after truckload of old newsprint began arriving at the Waldorf factory gate. Troskey stored whatever the Waldorf warehouses could hold, but he was forced to turn the rest away. Much the same was happening at paper recyclers all over the nation, as new communities suddenly discovered curbside recycling. Prices declined, then collapsed, throwing into disarray some communities' plans for recycling to help pay for itself.

Foreign markets have long helped support paper recycling efforts in the United States. Yet by last July prices that distributors of old newsprint could obtain from foreign markets had dropped to twelve dollars per ton. Since it costs more than that for brokers to clean up, store, and deliver the paper to a pier, dealers on the East Coast actually began charging municipalities to take newsprint off their hands.

In the end, despite the flurry of activity and tax monies being poured into paper pickup, despite the best intentions of good citizens convinced they were recycling their paper, virtually no extra recycling occurred. What happened, Troskey says, is that supply sources shifted while demand for paperboard boxes and for recycled newsprint, the limits of manufacturing, and capacity remained relatively constant.

In Minnesota, with the glut came high comedy: In the summer of 1989 some six thousand tons of newsprint that had been carefully separated by households, and dutifully picked up by recycling trucks, was shipped to the new Hennepin county incinerator to be remixed with household garbage and burned up in one of the facility's early test burns.

Meanwhile, prices for aluminum scrap cans have also begun to plummet. Jeff Connell, director of planning for Dakota County, south of Minneapolis, has watched scrap aluminum prices drop from $1,100 per ton to $900 per ton, and his budget assumes that will drop to $700 per ton. Currently, he says, officials of the county are finding a home for all of its newsprint, in part because Dakota is managing to market some of it, shredded like straw, for farmers and horse owners to use as animal bedding.

"Right now, two percent of the counties in the United States are recycling twenty percent or more of their wastes," he says. "If everyone gears up, where's all the newsprint going to go? Where's all the aluminum going to go? You can collect all you want, but you can only recycle what you can market."

Indeed, Margaret Fleming, an official of Canusa (formerly Cascades U.S.A.), a Baltimore pulp and paper broker, told Maryland municipal officials at a recycling conference last June to consider ceasing newsprint collection, at least for the time being, in part so that those who are already recycling won't have to pay more to get rid of the stuff as markets become even more glutted. Some new newsprint recycling mills are being built, and will someday absorb some of the excess capacity, but the plants won't begin operation for years.

However, there are some signs that the demand for recycled papers is about to rise. In 1989 California and Connecticut passed laws requiring newspapers published in those states to use much more recycled newsprint (over the objections of many newspaper publishers, who see the laws as discriminatory). Other states, including Wisconsin, a major paper maker, are considering similar laws. Under guidelines drafted by the Environmental Protection Agency, government agencies are increasingly required to turn to recycled papers, when costs aren't prohibitive.

Manufacturers, too, seem to have sensed a change. According to the trade newsletter *Recycling Times,* virtually all the major Canadian newsprint makers are conducting feasibility studies on the profitability of making recycled paper. And in what appears to be a major recycling breakthrough, Cascades Inc. of Quebec plans to build a new plant either in Quebec or upstate New York to begin making xerographic and computer paper from a combination of old newsprint and discarded glossy magazine paper. Glossy papers, like this page, contain varying amounts of clays that in the past have made recycling difficult. That problem is compounded by the poorly soluble glues used in magazine bindings. The new plant will be using a process invented in Germany by Cascades' partner in the venture, Steinbeis and Consorten, that actually takes advantage of the clay, as well as the long, strong fibers in quality papers. Using that process, Steinbeis is already making about fifteen percent of the copy paper in Germany. However, Cascades officials admit they face a marketing hurdle in North America. The paper tends toward gray instead of the clean, bright white to which most American businesses are accustomed. But the company hopes to peddle it as "comfort white." On the positive side, the paper might sell for as much as twenty percent less than photocopy and computer papers made from virgin pulp.

However, paper recycling has limits. With each repulping of the paper, fibers shorten and quality degrades. Thus, if paper has been recycled once or more, its value as a raw material to produce new pulp and new paper will decline. Better-quality recycled papers, even those using high-quality, long-fiber wastepaper, usually contain a significant fraction of virgin pulp.

And among printers and publishers, recycled stock has yet to live down a reputation for variations in quality and for breakage in large presses, problems that can dramatically increase printing costs.

There are related problems. At the Waldorf recycling plant, Tom Troskey spotted a tattered and smashed corrugated box in a large outdoor pile of corrugated pieces slated for the mill. "Look," he said, retrieving the box. "Japanese cardboard." The Japanese, according to Troskey, recycle their cardboard many times over. The cardboard, five plies thick, tore instantly, mushy and almost tissue-like in the hand. Yet another domestically produced piece next to it, only two plies thick, was more sturdy. To compensate, someone had wound the Japanese box with yards and yards of plastic strapping tape. Troskey heaved the box aside, muttering about the prospect of gummed-up machinery.

Historically, recycling processes for most products—paper, glass, metals—have evolved relatively slowly. But in 1989 progress in plastics recycling virtually exploded, an explosion ignited not by earnest citizens, not by responsible public officials, not even by hungry markets or smart entrepreneurial recyclers.

"Frankly," says one insider, "plastics producers suddenly got very interested in recycling because they got scared out of their wits."

The scare came from elected officials seeking a good scapegoat for the garbage crisis. Between the fall of 1988 and the fall of 1989, some 350 new laws and ordinances were proposed at various levels of government to ban or sharply curb the use of plastics. Hamburger fast-food boxes of polystyrene foam were a favorite target. At least nine communities banned the foam "clamshell" boxes outright.

"Essentially," says Leslie Legg, a spokesperson for the National Solid Wastes Management Association, "everyone blew the problem of plastics way out of proportion. It diverted a lot of attention from the difficult issues of recycling and disposal." Still, Legg agrees that all the furor encouraged major plastics producers to start looking rapidly for workable recycling processes and markets.

In 1988 several manufacturers of plastic-foam-type containers, many of them major petrochemical companies, rapidly formed the National Polystyrene Recycling Corporation, with an objective of recycling 25 percent of foam plastic wastes by 1995. Foam cannot be made into more foam but can be melted and reextruded into such non-throwaway products as food trays, garbage cans, fence and dock posts, memo holders, and even a kind of "plastic lumber." Last year the company purchased an existing plastics recycling plant in Leominster, Massachusetts, to which the McDonald's restaurant chain has promised to ship hamburger boxes from 450 restaurants (provided their customers heed signs telling them to separate the wastes into recycling bins). The company also plans to open four more recycling factories by the end of this year.

Meanwhile, Wellman Inc. of Allentown, Pennsylvania, claims it can't obtain enough waste two-liter soda bottles and other similar products, which are made of another kind of plastic—a polyester nicknamed PET. According to Daniel Brosey, recycling coordinator at Wellman, late in 1988 the company signed an agreement with Browning-Ferris Industries, one of the nation's largest waste haulers, to accept all the PET pop and other bottles as well as all the high-density polyethylene (HDPE) milk jugs the company can provide, including 80,000 pounds per month from a new recycling program in Cincinnati.

Wellman, which has been in the PET recycling business since the product hit grocery shelves about ten years ago, has developed a process that removes the HDPE bottom from the bottles, removes the metal caps and paper labels, and shreds the PET and reextrudes the plastic as a fiber. It sells the fiber on the polyester market for full price as fiberfill for sleeping bags and coats, as well as for carpet fiber. According to Brosey, the recycled fiber is indistinguishable from virgin material, and demand for it continues to run high. Although the process for recycling HDPE is not as well developed, that plastic can be mixed with virgin plastics to make some kinds of new containers, such as detergent bottles.

Nevertheless, the plastics recycling picture is far from a completely rosy one. Few towns and cities have collection sites for plastics, and although some communities are now looking into plastics recycling as a possibility, shipping and delivery systems generally do not exist. Some plastic containers, including squeezable ketchup bottles, are made from a multiple layer of different resins, making recycling nearly impossible. Another problem: Even the most earnest of home-recycling sorters don't know PET from HDPE from PVC (polyvinyl chloride—a plastic with bleak recycling possibilities whose manufacture causes particularly obnoxious air-pollution problems). Sorting the stuff for curbside pickup is thus a problem, unless communities limit the pickup to readily identifiable products, such as two-liter soda bottles and plastic milk jugs, and simply send the remainder to the landfill or incinerator. At least eighteen states now require that standardized codes be stamped onto plastic bottles to help people identify the type of plastic used.

The picture for aluminum is far from bleak. "We're ready to take all the aluminum beverage cans we can get our hands on," says John Van Devender, who is supervisor of marketing communication for Alcoa in Pittsburgh. Nearly 60 percent of the aluminum cans sold in the United States are being recycled, he claims, amounting to some 1.7 billion pounds of scrap aluminum, or 48 *billion* cans last year. Declining prices are largely the result of an overall price slump for aluminum on world markets, according to Van Devender. But since producing sheet aluminum for new cars from old cans consumes less energy, and is ultimately cheaper, and since there is already an effective and efficient system to "mine" aluminum from America's garbage (there are some ten thousand aluminum recycling collection centers and several large plants dedicated to making new aluminum out of old), there will always be a market for aluminum cans.

And there are further possibilities. Steel companies have long been heavy recyclers, according to David Jeanes, vice-president of market development for the American Iron and Steel Institute. About two-thirds of the scrap steel in the United States is recycled, most of that from junked cars and used appliances. In fact, virtually every car contains the ghosts of its ancestors. But according to Jeanes, steel makers are just beginning to realize the potential scrap supply that steel ("tin") cans could provide, especially since they can be separated magnetically—and hence easily— from garbage.

Even Procter & Gamble, a major manufacturer of disposable diapers, has found a way to leap onto the bandwagon. Once again, clearly the company was concerned at the prospect of losing profits from consumers alarmed by reports that diapers were overwhelming landfills. Last fall Procter & Gamble funded a study of composting the fiber interior and baby-waste in disposable diapers at a plant operated by Recomp Inc. in St. Cloud, Minnesota. The plant already makes compost from garbage (itself a technology that holds some promise in handling a portion of the garbage deluge). Although formal results of the study aren't in, the process appears to work, leaving behind a thin scrap of polyethylene that could be recycled into, say, garbage bags, as well as piles of compost that will be spread at a nearby Christmas tree farm. However, it seems unlikely that most communities will find it either economical or practical to set up separate composting facilities to handle disposable diapers.

But that seems to be a fact close to the heart of the garbage problem itself. There is no silver bullet. No single perfect solution free of consequences. There are instead, as Leslie Legg puts it, only "a lot of myths out there that don't provide any actual solutions."

Passing laws to ban plastics might satisfy the self-righteous among us, but it would have little real effect on the problem. Imagining that we are recycling because we are shipping our separated trash to a recycling center might mitigate some guilt. But again, as in the current case of newsprint, doing so might well be close to valueless. Surely an increased individual and business commitment to reducing the amount of wastes— from junk mail to shopping bags—generated in the first place would help. Making purchases that increase the demand for recycled products clearly would help, too.

But then what? The most level-headed answer to the question came from Janet Green, a botanist who sits on the citizen board of the Minnesota

Pollution Control Agency and chaired a 1988 Minnesota commission looking into the garbage issue. (Quite incidentally, Green sits on the board
of the National Audubon Society.)

"It boils down," she says, "not so much to a garbage crisis as a
crisis in individual responsibility. The public assumes it's a government
problem when it's really an individual problem. Nobody wants to deal
with the stuff. It's that kind of thinking that pushes politicians to want
to come up with a new solution, some kind of fix. That's how we got
pushed into big landfills. And that's how we're getting pushed into big
incinerators. But to solve this problem we need educators more than we
need engineers and politicians. We need people to accept responsibility
for their own wastes and to insist that their politicians look for a systems
approach. That means starting fresh—not being seduced by bond councils,
or by lawyers and engineers, but trying to look at an approach that calls
for us to reduce and recycle and compost. For what's left we have to
accept the fact that we are going to need incinerators or landfills but that
maybe they can be downsized."

In lieu of that, let's imagine a miracle. Maybe every North American
could cut his or her generation of wastes not by a small increment but
in half. After that, maybe every North American could find a market and
a means and the motivation to recycle about half of the remainder. (A
rate of recycling equal to the best achieved to date in the world, and that
in experimental, intensively managed programs in well-organized communities in Japan.) That level of miracle—a quartering of our current
output—would mean that Americans would produce "only" some 40 million tons of garbage annually.

No doubt about it. That order of miracle would mitigate part of the
problem. Communities could have smaller landfills and build fewer incinerators. But ultimately, and eventually, some more landfills or incinerators would have to be permitted. Somewhere. In the backyard of
somebody who makes garbage. But whose?

QUESTIONS FOR CRITICAL READERS

Remembering and Understanding

1. Give an overall summary of the solid waste disposal problem as Luoma
   describes it.
2. Using the information Luoma provides, list at least three solutions to the
   problem of solid waste disposal, and explain the advantages and disadvantages of each.
3. Explain the major barriers to a comprehensive recycling program.

Analyzing and Discussing

4. What should individuals, governments, and businesses be doing differently to solve or at least reduce the solid waste problem?
5. Many of the solutions Luoma describes are voluntary. What legal requirements do you think should be enacted to encourage solutions to the problems described here?
6. One of Luoma's informants says that solid waste disposal is a matter of individual responsibility. What can and should individuals do to encourage or find a solution?

Writing

7. Investigate trash disposal or recycling programs in your own community or at your college or university. Use what you learn to write a paper for your fellow citizens or students in which you either explain the present situation or urge some change.

The Technological Flaw

BARRY COMMONER

Commoner, a biologist, has written extensively about the relationship of science to public policy. He currently directs the Center for the Biology of Natural Systems at Queens College in Brooklyn. The present selection is from his 1971 book The Closing Circle. *In this discussion Commoner introduces the concept of technological displacement to explain why environmental problems have become so serious in recent years. Technological displacement is the process of one product or technological process being displaced by another, with a resulting increase in environmental costs or damage that may or may not be accompanied by social or economic benefits to society at large. Because it was written more than twenty years ago, you will want to evaluate whether the points made in this selection are still valid.*

WE HAVE NOW ARRIVED at the following position in the search for the causes of the environmental crisis in the United States. We know that *something* went wrong in the country after World War II, for most of our serious pollution problems either began in the postwars years or have greatly worsened since then. While two factors frequently blamed for the environmental crisis, population and affluence, have intensified in that time, these increases are much too small to account for the 200 to 2,000 per cent rise in pollution levels since 1946. The product of these two factors, which represents the total output of goods (total production equals population times production per capita), is also insufficient to account for the intensification of pollution. Total production—as measured by GNP—has increased by 126 per cent since 1946, while most pollution levels have risen by at least several times that rate. Something else besides growth in population and affluence must be deeply involved in the environmental crisis.

"Economic growth" is a popular whipping boy in certain ecological circles. As indicated earlier, there are good theoretical grounds why economic growth *can* lead to pollution. The rate of exploitation of the ecosystem, which generates economic growth, cannot increase indefinitely without overdriving the system and pushing it to the point of collapse.

460

However, this theoretical relationship does not mean that any increase in economic activity automatically means more pollution. What happens to the environment depends on *how* the growth is achieved. During the nineteenth century the nation's economic growth was in part sustained by rapacious lumbering, which denuded whole hillsides and eroded the soil. On the other hand, the economic growth that in the 1930s began to lift the United States out of the Depression was enhanced by an ecologically sound measure, the soil conservation program. This program helped to restore the fertility of the depleted soil and thereby contributed to economic growth. Such ecologically sound economic growth not only avoids environmental deterioration, but can even reverse it. For example, improved conservation of pasture lands, which has been economically beneficial in the western part of the Missouri River drainage basin, seems to have reduced the level of nitrate pollution in that stretch of the river. In contrast, further downstream, in Nebraska, agricultural growth has been achieved counterecologically by intensifying the use of fertilizer, which leads to serious nitrate pollution problems.

In other words, the fact that the economy has grown—that GNP has increased—tells us very little about the possible environmental consequences. For that, we need to know *how* the economy has grown.

The growth of the United States economy is recorded in elaborate detail in a variety of government statistics—huge volumes tabulating the amounts of various goods produced annually, the expenditures involved, the value of the goods sold, and so forth. Although these endless columns of figures are rather intimidating, there are some useful ways to extract meaningful facts from them. In particular, it is helpful to compute the rate of growth of each productive activity, a procedure that nowadays can be accomplished by committing the tables of numbers to an appropriately programmed computer. In order to compare one kind of economic activity with another, it is useful to arrange the computer to yield a figure for the percentage increase, or decrease, in production or consumption.

Not long ago, two of my colleagues and I went through the statistical tables and selected from them the data for several hundred items, which together represent a major and representative part of overall United States agriculture and industrial production. For each item, the average annual percentage change in production or consumption was computed for the years since 1946, or since the earliest date for which the statistics were available. Then we computed the over-all change for the entire twenty-five-year period—a twenty-five-year growth rate. When this list is rearranged in decreasing order of growth rate, a picture of *how* the United States economy has grown since World War II begins to emerge.

The winner of this economic sweepstakes, with the highest postwar growth rate, is the production of nonreturnable soda bottles, which has increased about 53,000 per cent in that time. The loser, ironically, is the horse; work animal horsepower has declined by 87 per cent of its original postwar value. The runners-up are an interesting but seemingly mixed bag. In second place is production of synthetic fibers, up 5,980 per cent; third is mercury used for chlorine production, up 3,930 per cent; succeeding places are held as follows: mercury used in mildew-resistant paint, up 3,120 per cent; air conditioner compressor units, up 2,850 per cent; plastics, up 1,960 per cent; fertilizer nitrogen, up 1,050 per cent; electric housewares (such as can-openers and corn-poppers), up 1,040 per cent; synthetic organic chemicals, up 950 per cent; aluminum, up 680 per cent; chlorine gas, up 600 per cent; electric power, up 530 per cent; pesticides, up 390 per cent; wood pulp, up 313 per cent; truck freight, up 222 per cent; consumer electronics (TV sets, tape recorders), up 217 per cent, motor fuel consumption, up 190 per cent; cement, up 150 per cent.

Then there is a group of productive activities that, as indicated earlier, have grown at about the pace of the population (i.e., up about 42 per cent): food production and consumption, total production of textiles and clothes, household utilities, and steel, copper, and other basic metals.

Finally there are the losers, which increase more slowly than the population or actually shrink in total production: railroad freight, up 17 per cent; lumber, down 1 per cent; cotton fiber, down 7 per cent; returnable beer bottles, down 36 per cent; wool, down 42 per cent; soap, down 76 per cent; and, at the end of the line, work animal horse-power, down 87 per cent.

What emerges from all these data is striking evidence that while production for most basic needs—food, clothing, housing—has just about kept up with the 40 to 50 per cent or so increase in population (that is, production *per capita* has been essentially constant), the *kinds* of goods produced to meet these needs have changed drastically. New production technologies have displaced old ones. Soap powder has been displaced by synthetic detergents; natural fibers (cotton and wool) have been displaced by synthetic ones; steel and lumber have been displaced by aluminum, plastics, and concrete; railroad freight has been displaced by truck freight; returnable bottles have been displaced by nonreturnable ones. On the road, the low-powered automobile engines of the 1920s and 1930s have been displaced by high-powered ones. On the farm, while per capita production has remained about constant, the amount of harvested acreage has decreased; in effect, fertilizer has displaced land. Older methods of insect control have been displaced by synthetic insecticides, such as DDT, and for controlling weeds the cultivator has been displaced by the herbicide spray. Range-feeding of livestock has been displaced by feedlots.

In each of these cases, what has changed drastically is the technology of production rather than overall output of the economic good. Of course, part of the economic growth in the United States since 1946 has been based on some newly introduced goods: air conditioners, television sets, tape recorders, and snowmobiles, all of which have increased absolutely without displacing an older product.

Distilled in this way, the mass of production statistics begins to form a meaningful pattern. In general, the growth of the United States economy since 1946 has had a surprisingly small effect on the degree to which individual needs for basic economic goods have been met. That statistical fiction, the "average American," now consumes, each year, about as many calories, protein, and other foods (although somewhat less of vitamins); uses about the same amount of clothes and cleaners; occupies about the same amount of newly constructed housing; requires about as much freight; and drinks about the same amount of beer (twenty-six gallons per capita!) as he did in 1946. However, his food is now grown on less land with much more fertilizer and pesticides than before; his clothes are more likely to be made of synthetic fibers than of cotton or wool; he launders with synthetic detergents rather than soap; he lives and works in buildings that depend more heavily on aluminium, concrete, and plastic than on steel and lumber; the goods he uses are increasingly shipped by truck rather than rail; he drinks beer out of nonreturnable bottles or cans rather than out of returnable bottles or at the tavern bar. He is more likely to live and work in air-conditioned surroundings than before. He also drives about twice as far as he did in 1946, in a heavier car, on synthetic rather than natural rubber tires, using more gasoline per mile, containing more tetraethyl lead, fed into an engine of increased horsepower and compression ratio.

These primary changes have led to others. To provide the raw materials needed for the new synthetic fibers, pesticides, detergents, plastics, and rubber, the production of synthetic organic chemicals has also grown very rapidly. The synthesis of organic chemicals uses a good deal of chlorine. Result: chlorine production has increased sharply. To make chlorine, an electric current is passed through a salt solution by way of a mercury electrode. Consequently, mercury consumption for this purpose has increased—by 3,930 per cent in the twenty-five year postwar period. Chemical products, along with cement for concrete and aluminum (also winners in the growth race), use rather large amounts of electric power. Nor surprisingly, then, that item, too, has increased considerably since 1946.

All this reminds us of what we have already been told by advertising—which incidentally has *also* grown; for example, the use of newsprint for advertising has grown faster than its use for news—that we are blessed with an economy based on very modern technologies. What the advertisements do not tell us—as we are urged to buy synthetic shirts and detergents, aluminum furniture, beer in no-return bottles, and Detroit's latest creation—is that *all this "progress" has greatly increased the impact on the environment.*

The displacement of natural products by synthetic organic chemicals and of lumber and steel by concrete has a similar effect, for both chemical manufacturing and the production of cement for concrete are intense consumers of electric power. Aluminum and chemical production alone account for about 28 per cent of total industrial use of electric power in the United States. Thus the expansion of power production in the United States is not an accurate measure of increased economic good, being badly inflated by the growing tendency to displace power-thrifty goods with power-consumptive ones. The cost of this inefficiency is heavily borne by the environment.

Another technological displacement is readily visible to the modern householder in the daily acquisition of rubbish, most of it from packaging. It is a useful exercise to examine the statistics relevant to some economic good—beer, let us say—and determine from them the origin of the resultant impact on the environment. We can begin the exercise by recalling that the relevant economic good is chiefly the beer, not the bottle or can in which it is delivered. The relevant pollutant is the nonreturnable bottle or can, for these, when "disposed of" in rubbish, cannot be assimilated in any natural ecological cycle. Therefore, they either accumulate or must be reprocessed at some expenditure of energy and cost in power-produced pollutants. The exercise consists in determining the relative effects of the three factors that might lead to an increased output of pollution, in this case, in the period from 1950 to 1967. In that time, the total consumption of nonreturnable beer bottles increased by 595 per cent and the consumption of beer increased by 37 per cent. Since the population increased by 30 per cent, the "affluence" factor, or the amount of beer consumed per capita, remained essentially constant (actually a 5 per cent increase). The remainder of the increased output of pollutant—beer bottles—is due to the technological factor—that is, the number of nonreturnable bottles produced per gallon of beer, which increased by 408 per cent. The relative importance of the three factors is evident.

It will be argued, of course, that the use of a nonreturnable beer bottle is more desirable than a returnable one to the individual beer drinker. After all, some human effort must be expended to return the bottle to the point of purchase. We can modify the earlier evaluation, then, by asserting that for the sake of whatever improvement in well-being is involved in avoiding the effort of returning the bottle, the production of beer in nonreturnable bottles incurs a 408 per cent intensification of environmental impact. No such subtlety is involved in comparing the environmental impacts of two alternative nonreturnable beer containers: steel beer cans and aluminum ones. The energy involved in producing the aluminum can—and therefore the amount of combustion and the resultant output of pollutants—is 6.3 times that required for a steel can.

Similar computations can be made for the added environmental impact incurred when extra layers of packaging are added to foods and other goods or when plastic wrappers (nondegradable) are substituted for degradable cellulosic ones. In general, modern industrial technology has encased economic goods of no significantly increased human value in increasingly larger amounts of environmentally harmful wrappings. Result: the mounting heaps of rubbish that symbolize the advent of the technological age.

It should be recognized that such computations of environmental impact are still in a primitive, only partially developed stage. What is needed, and what—it is to be hoped—will be worked out before long, is an ecological analysis of every major aspect of the production, use, and disposition of goods. What is needed is a kind of "ecological impact inventory" for each productive activity, which will enable us to attach a sort of pollution price tag to each product. We would then know, for example, for each pound of detergent: how much air pollution is generated by the electric power and fuel burned to manufacture its chemical ingredients; how much water pollution is due to the mercury "loss" by the factory in the course of manufacturing the chlorine needed to produce it; the water pollution due to the detergent and phosphate entering sewage systems; the ecological effect of fluoride and arsenic (which may contaminate the phosphate), and of mercury, which might contaminate any alkali used to compound the detergent. Such pollution price tags are needed for all major products if we are to judge their relative *social* value. The foregoing account shows how far we are from this goal, and once again reminds us how blind we are about the environmental effects of modern technology.

It is useful, at this point, to return to a question asked earlier: what are the relative effects of the three factors that might be expected to influence the intensity of environmental pollution—population size, degree of affluence, and the tendency of the productive technology to pollute? A rather simple mathematical relationship connects the amount of pollutant emitted into the environment to these factors: pollutant emitted is equal to the product of the three factors—population times the amount of a given economic good per capita times output of pollutant per unit of the economic good produced. In the United States all three factors have changed since 1946. By comparing these changes with the concurrent increase in total pollutant output, it is possible to assign to each of the three factors the fraction of the overall increase in pollutant output for which it is responsible. When this computation is carried out for the economic goods considered above—agricultural production (pollutant outputs: nitrogen fertilizer, pesticides), cleaners (pollutant output: phosphate), passenger car travel (pollutant outputs: lead and nitrogen oxides), and beer consumption (pollutant output: beer bottles)—a rather clear picture emerges.

The increase in population accounts for from 12 to 20 per cent of the various increases in total pollutant output since 1946. The affluence factor (i.e., amount of economic good per capita), accounts for from 1 to 5 per cent of the total increase in pollutant output, except in the case of passenger travel, where the contribution rises to about 40 per cent of the total. This reflects a considerable increase in vehicle miles traveled per capita. However, as already pointed out, a good deal of this increase does not reflect improved welfare, but rather the unfortunate need for increased travel incident upon the decay of the inner cities and the growth of suburbs. The technology factor—that is, the increased output of pollutants per unit production resulting from the introduction of new productive technologies since 1946—accounts for about 95 per cent of the total output of pollutants, except in the case of passenger travel, where it accounts for about 40 per cent of the total.

The foregoing conclusions are based on those instances in which quantitative data on pollution output of various productive activities are available. However, from the qualitative evidence on other pollution problems discussed earlier, it is already apparent that they follow a similar pattern: most of the sharp increase in pollution levels is due not so much to population or affluence as to changes in productive technology.

The overall evidence seems clear. The chief reason for the environmental crisis that has engulfed the United States in recent years is the sweeping transformation of productive technology since World War II. The economy has grown enough to give the United States population about the same amount of basic goods, per capita, as it did in 1946. However, productive technologies with intense impacts on the environment have displaced less destructive ones. The environmental crisis is the inevitable result of this counterecological pattern of growth.

QUESTIONS FOR CRITICAL READERS

Remembering and Understanding

1. Write a brief summary of the technological changes that Commoner describes, and their effects.
2. Explain the concept of technological displacement. Give an example of displacement that has occurred since Commoner wrote this selection.
3. Commoner suggests something called an "environmental impact inventory." Explain what such an inventory would do, and how it would help solve the problem of environmental pollution.

Analyzing and Discussing

4. Commoner asserts that many of the technological displacements he describes have occurred without improved welfare or benefit to society. How would you calculate such a benefit? For example, how would you decide whether the aluminum can actually produced a benefit or improved human welfare to a greater extent than the returnable glass container?
5. Using Commoner's statistics about postwar gains and losses for specific products, and the development of new products as your information base, describe the social changes that these technological and economic developments reflect. That is, what do these technological changes tell you about how American life changed after World War II?
6. Review Commoner's discussion of technological and production changes and then speculate about the effects of these changes on systems for trash disposal.

Writing

7. Use Commoner's observations and your own knowledge to write a paper in which you describe the changes that would have to take place in production, consumption, and technology to reverse what Commoner calls a "counterecological pattern of growth."

Landfills Are #1

———— BILL BREEN ————

Breen is senior editor of Garbage *magazine, where this article first appeared. His interest here is to understand landfills rather than simply condemn them. Thus, while he acknowledges the problems they present, he also explores the possibilities that exist for making them safer, more pleasant, and even reusable.*

BURDENED WITH NINETY cubic yards of garbage, the truck looks no longer than a Tonka Toy as it clambers up the 135-foot slopes of trash. At the landfill's summit, bulldozers squash and spread assorted detritus across 2,200 acres: mattresses, beer cans, tires, rugs, cleaning solvents. Seagulls swarm like black flies over the aromatic food waste.

These are the hills of New York City's Fresh Kills, the largest municipal garbage dump on the planet. Built on ecologically sensitive salt marshes on Staten Island's edge, the Fresh Kills Landfill is the final resting place for more than two-thirds of New York's trash. Each day, this vast garbagescape absorbs more than 34 million pounds of refuse from the city's households and businesses. At its present growth rate, the Fresh Kills Landfill will evolve into a 505-foot mountain of trash by 2005, when it is expected to reach its capacity (although no one can say when it will *really* close). In New York City, as well as the rest of the country, landfilling remains by far the predominant form of solid-waste disposal. (The U.S. Environmental Protection Agency estimates that 80 percent of the nation's municipal solid waste material is being dumped.) Most environmental groups will concede that until there's sufficient demand for recyclables, landfills will probably continue to be our number one garbage-disposal method, and will always be needed for the discards that can't be recycled and the bottom ash that remains after incineration. Yet Fresh Kills shows us, in a big way, why the town dump remains on every environmentalist's hate list:

• *Landfills consume precious municipal space.*
It's silly to suggest that landfill space is vanishing in a country as

vast as the U.S. Even so, some densely populated areas in the Northeast and Midwest really are running out of places to dump. So why does New York want more garbage for its primary landfill?

The city is planning to cut its dumping fee at the Fresh Kills Landfill from $40 to $25 a cubic yard for garbage that's been picked clean of recyclables. A spokesman for the sanitation department justified the move as a way to encourage private haulers to recycle. Critics say that the decreased fee is really meant to bring enough garbage back to Fresh Kills to increase city revenues by $17 million a year.

 • *Landfills discourage recycling and waste reduction.*

New Yorkers throw out more garbage (about six pounds per person, per day) and recycle less of it (about six percent) than many other city dwellers. (The national recycling average is around 13 percent, according to the EPA.) Environmentalists are concerned that Fresh Kills' yawning maw offers a convenient alternative to reducing, reusing, composting, and recycling waste. To critics, landfills foster an irresponsible attitude toward resource consumption.

"One way to prod decision-makers toward recycling is to point out the health and environmental problems associated with landfills like Fresh Kills," says Larry Shapiro, an attorney with the New York Public Interest Research Group.

 • *Landfills pollute groundwater and surface water.*

Each day, more than one million gallons of chemically contaminated leachate—runoff laced with such household hazardous wastes as the sulfuric acid in silver polish and the napthalene in drain cleaners—oozes into underground waterways beneath the high-rise garbage repository at Fresh Kills. The EPA has already identified over 100 potentially harmful substances in landfill leachate.

Researchers at the University of Southern California suggest that natural anaerobic processes convert even benign waste (such as the lignin in paper) into toxic chemicals like benzene and toluene. Yet only 25 percent of all municipal landfills have tested nearby waterways, even though drinking-water wells exist within one mile of 46 percent of the country's landfills. Fortunately, Staten Island residents do not rely on groundwater for their water supply.

 • *Landfills emit gases that threaten the atmosphere.*

The Fresh Kills Landfill lacks a comprehensive gas-collection system, so most of the methane, carbon dioxide, and trace levels of carcinogenic-organic chemicals (such as vinyl chloride, toluene, and benzene) produced by its decaying garbage escape directly into the air.

Gas emissions from landfills are a growing concern because methane traps about 25 times more infared energy than does carbon dioxide, the trace gas most often cited as the leading contributor to the possible heat blanketing of the Earth. Don Augenstein, a chemical engineer who's studied landfill methane, reports that methane emissions from U.S. landfills could contribute as much as two percent to the *entire* buildup of greenhouse gases. By comparison, landfill-methane emissions, in their greenhouse effect, easily exceed the amount of carbon dioxide expelled by 10 million automobiles.

Further clouding the landfill picture is the EPA's estimate that about 200,000 metric tons of volatile organic chemicals (VOCs)—which can affect atmospheric ozone and smog concentrations—are emitted from Fresh Kills and other U.S. landfills each year. "Fresh Kills has all of the problems of the rural, hole-in-the-ground dump," says Larry Shapiro. "Except now, it's a mountain."

• *Unsanitary, Sanitary Landfills*

Fresh Kills started accepting New York's waste in 1949, when a handful of city officials proposed that the "unsightly and unsanitary wastelands" in Staten Island could be filled with garbage, and eventually transformed into a beltway of parks. Of course, the planned operations at Fresh Kills would in no way resemble the malodorous, smoking, insect- and rat-infested dumps in other parts of the city. Fresh Kills, said the officials, would be a "sanitary" landfill.

Landfilling became the leading form of solid-waste disposal in the 1940s and 1950s, as government bureaucrats discovered inexpensive, undeveloped land on the outskirts of cities. To promote landfilling, proponents used the prefix "sanitary" as a catchword to distinguish the modern dump from open pits. As defined by the American Society of Civil Engineers, sanitary landfilling requires little more than covering the refuse "with a layer of earth at the conclusion of each day's operation." In design and practice, the new dumps were far from sanitary.

By 1971, more than 90 percent of the 14,000 communities using dumps failed to meet even the minimum requirements of the so-called sanitary landfill. "Only new legislation in 1976, an increasing scarcity of urban landfill sites, and growing public sentiment against contamination of the land and water finally placed real pressure on the open-dump system," write Louis Blumberg and Robert Gottlieb in their book, *War on Waste.*

Now, the EPA reports that of the 5,499 landfills currently operating nationwide, 4,265 will close in just 18 years. But closures do not necessarily predict future capacity. Consider Pennsylvania: At the same time that the state was losing 13 municipal landfills (between July 1986 and November 1987), its overall capacity was *increasing* because one new landfill had opened and two more were expanding. When you hear talk of declining landfill space, it's important to recognize that the scarcity has as much to do with politics (read "not in my backyard") as it does with escalating mounds of garbage.

Nevertheless, with 80 percent of the country's landfills due to close in the next 20 years, one of the looming challenges for solidwaste engineers will be the proper sealing, salvaging, and monitoring of some the nation's most contaminated dumps. Of the 1,777 sites included on the National Priorities List—a catalogue of hazardous waste sites eligible for the federal Superfund cleanup program—207 are old, unlined dumps.

As local governments, with limited federal assistance, shoulder the enormous costs of closing their dumps, siting new landfills will become even more difficult. Recognizing the public's growing intolerance, the EPA ranks landfilling last in its hierarchy of waste-disposal options (after source reduction, reuse and recycling, and incineration). Yet some experts argue that until the country makes significant strides in reducing waste and developing markets for recyclables, landfilling should be ranked at the *top* of the list. "There is no environmental objection to the landfill that I have heard of that cannot, for a cost, be controlled," argues Iraj Zandi, professor of resource management and technology at the University of Pennsylvania. "Landfilling of municipal solid waste can be designed so that all environmentally undesirable effects can be eliminated."

THE NEW, IMPROVED DUMP

No responsible solid-waste engineer will tell you that he can build a landfill that will *never* leak or bleed gases. "I wouldn't give anyone a 100-percent guarantee," says Thomas Marturano, a landfill designer and director of the division of solid waste at the Hackensack Meadowlands in New Jersey. "But yes, I can build a safe landfill." In 1982, the residents and politicians of southern New Jersey took Mr. Marturano and other engineers at their word when Cape May County accepted a 70-acre landfill.

Building the Cape May landfill presents special problems. The sandy soil in the county's pine barrens is porous and the water table is only about 11 feet beneath the surface, leaving residents' well vulnerable to rainwater that could seep through the landfill, leaching out organic chemicals and other compounds. A hole in the ground won't do. Landfilling in Cape May amounts to hill building, starting at ground level.

The Cape May facility must comply with New Jersey's strict environmental rules for landfills, which already exceed the tougher regulations expected in October from the EPA. (Although states set landfill standards, they will have to meet the minimums issued by the federal agency.) Cape May's Secure Sanitary Landfill Facility represents the updated version of the not-so-sanitary dump.

First, giant earth-moving machines compact and grade the topsoil. Workers then add two synthetic liners of high density polyethylene, sandwiched between alternating layers of clay and sand. The double-liner system is honeycombed with two levels of HDPE pipes, sloped so the rainwater that percolates through the landfill is drained into a central collection point. The upper network collects the leachate (about two million gallons per year), while the lower level detects and collects any breach in the liner system. The leachate is pumped into two concrete holding tanks and trucked to the county's wastewater-treatment plant for processing.

Some laboratory experiments indicate that volatile organic chemicals (such as toluene and xylene) can eat through synthetic liners. Engineers argue that under real landfill conditions, the chemicals are so diluted that they cannot breach the 60-millimeter liners used at the Cape May landfill. Of greater concern is the seaming of the liner segments. The huge rolls of polyethelene are laid down like carpet, overlapped, and welded with a heat gun. A poor seam, or a rip during installation, is a far more likely way for a liner to fail. "The manufacturer's guarantee on a liner is worthless," says Mr. Marturano. "Everything depends on the installation."

At Cape May, 16- and 18-acre cells of compacted trash are the landfill's basic building blocks. Once a cell absorbs its fill of garbage, its crown is capped with a 40-ml HDPE liner, one foot of topsoil, and 18 inches of sand, which keep the garbage in and the rainwater out. To monitor the performance of the leachate-containment system, the landfill's operators have drilled 18 wells down to the aquifers, enabling them to routinely check possible contaminants for up to 30 years after the operation is closed.

A WHOLE LOT OF HOT AIR

After leachate containment, the largest technical problem in landfill management is the control of gases. The methane from the Cape May landfill's decaying garbage is simply vented into the atmosphere, making this secure-sanitary facility, well, somewhat less than secure (even though it already complies with the upcoming EPA regulations on gas emissions). Why isn't the dirty methane tapped, cleaned of carbon dioxide and other contaminants, and sold as a low-grade fuel? Right now, the Cape May landfill is too small and too young to make gas collection economically viable, according to Charles Norkis, chief engineer for the Cape May County Municipal Utilities Authority.

Nationwide, about 1500 landfills deal with gas emissions by venting or burning gas as it escapes from collection pipes. The Office of Technology Assessment reports that if landfill methane was collected completely and processed for energy recovery, it could account for up to five percent of all natural-gas consumption or one percent of all energy demand in the U.S. Instead, between three to eight million metric tons of methane escape from the nation's landfills each year.

Owners of about 123 of the country's largest landfills, however, are finding that methane recovery can transform the town dump from a liability to an asset. The Pacific Energy company is collecting methane from 12 landfills in California and Maryland. "There are three ways to get energy out of landfill gas," says Tony Henrich, a spokesman for the Los Angeles-based company. "You can drop out the water and sell it over the fence to a nearby industry, or use it to produce electric power with gas, steam, turbine, or internal combustion. Or, you can remove the carbon dioxide and other trace compounds, and sell the purified gas as pipeline-quality methane. But unless a landfill emits enough methane to produce two megawatts of power, we're not interested. It just doesn't pay out."

PICNIC AT THE HACKENSACK DUMP

Decaying garbage can be recycled as an energy resource, so perhaps we should be thinking of landfills as more than just non-renewable, ever-expanding burial mounds. Some solid-waste engineers suggest that by entombing garbage to cut leachate and gas emissions, we are hindering the landfill from doing what it does best—biologically decompose our solid waste. Writing in *BioCycle* magazine, John Morelli of the New York State Energy Research and Development Authority argues that with enough water, a landfill can be a dynamic, anaerobic composter. Perhaps it's time to take a fresh look at the old dump.

Because dumps can take as long as 90 years to complete their process of decomposition, Mr. Morelli reasons that instead off trying to cut leachate by eliminating the moisture content in landfills, we should *add* water or even recirculate leachate through the landfill to speed degradation. In an interview, he estimated that leachate recirculation can degrade 90 percent of a landfill's organic wastes, enabling portions of the dump to be reused within 10 years. Reclamation projects already underway in Florida, Connecticut, Delaware, Massachusetts, and New York are refuting the long-held belief that garbage is supposed to remain buried forever.

Yet in most of the country's landfills, garbage *is* forever. Sometimes, municipalities convert their retired dumps into golf courses or amusement parks. Most of the time, when a dump is filled to capacity, it's simply abandoned. Never has a landfill site been returned to something resembling its natural state before it was buried under tons of trash; never, that is, until workers began restoring a landfill in New Jersey's Hackensack Meadowlands.

Here, landscapers are transforming six acres of a closed landfill into grass meadows and young woodlands. This "Experimental Park on a Landfill" is intended to test the adaptability of various plant species to the thin layer of unirrigated, unfertilized soil and the dry, windy conditions typical of a landfill; and provide food and shelter for the likes of songbirds and rabbits, mice and raccoons.

The six acres, containing 215,000 cubic yards of garbage, was capped with a synthetic membrane made with 440,000 recycled, PET-soda bottles that may otherwise have been buried. The one-liter bottles were processed into a fibrous material that looks and feels like a golf putting green, and bonded to a Hypalon liner. The mesh formed from the bottles prevents both the liner and nearly 15,000 cubic yards of topsoil from sliding off the landfill's steep slopes.

In a few years, groves of green ash and red cedar will canopy the landfill's crown. Now, a meandering footpath is edged with gray dogwood and fragrant sumac. The landfill offers sweeping views of the sky and surrounding waterways which are all too rare in this densely populated corner of New Jersey.

Eventually, the experimental park may point the rest of the country toward salvaging the thousands of acres of meadowlands and wetlands that shortsighted sanitation officials once dismissed as unsightly, unsanitary, and ultimately unusable—except for garbage dumping. "There's a tremendous untapped potential for landfills to become ecological oases," says Anne Galli, director of environmental operations at the Hackensack Meadowlands. "But we've got to assist the natural regenerative processes at landfills, not stand in their way."

QUESTIONS FOR CRITICAL READERS

Remembering and Understanding

1. Summarize the major points that Breen makes about landfills.
2. Methane gas and leachate are two major products of landfills. What are they, how are they produced, and why are they problems?
3. Describe the major changes that will make landfills safer.

Analyzing and Discussing

4. What do you think would be the best way to deal with the prevailing public attitudes about landfills?
5. How do you react to the suggestion that landfills can be made into parks where people can have picnics? Do you think people might resist this idea? How could that resistance be overcome?
6. Most people do not want landfills located near their homes, and the choice of a location is often a political decision as well as a technical one. What criteria would you use for deciding where to locate a landfill?

Writing

7. Assume that your local government has announced that a landfill will be built approximately one mile from your home. Write a letter or report for your neighbors in which you explain why they should support or oppose the landfill.

The History of Garbage

———— WILLIAM L. RATHJE ————

Rathje, founder of The Garbage Project, *describes himself as an anthropologist and garbologist; he teaches anthropology at the University of Arizona. From his perspective as a social scientist he asks three questions about solid waste disposal: What is its history? How much garbage does the United States actually produce? And what is the role of human behavior in producing and reducing the amount of garbage?*

GARBAGE IS NOT MATHEMATICS. To understand garbage you have to touch it, feel it, sort it, smell it. You have to pick through hundreds of tons of it, counting and weighing all the daily newspapers, the telephone books, the soiled diapers, the Styrofoam clamshells that briefly held hamburgers, the lipstick cylinders coated with grease, the medicine vials still encasing brightly colored pills, the empty bottles of scotch, the cans of paint and turpentine, the forsaken toys, the cigarette butts. You have to count and weigh all the organic matter, the discards from thousands of plates: the noodles and the Cheerios and the tortillas; the hardened jelly doughnuts bleeding from their wounds; the pieces of pet food which have made their own gravy; the half-eaten bananas, mostly still with their peels, black and incomparably sweet in the embrace of final decay. You have to confront sticky green mountains of yard waste and slippery brown hills of potato peels and brittle ossuaries of chicken bones and T-bones. And then finally there are the "fines," the vast connecting soup of indeterminable former nutrients, laced with bits of paper and metal, glass and plastic, which suffuse every landfill like a kind of lymph. The fines, too, must be gathered and weighed.

To an archaeologist like myself, garbage trails mankind in an unbroken line from the first flakes of flint left by tool-makers a million years ago to the urine bags left by astronauts in outer space.

For most of the last two million years, human beings left their garbage where it fell. This disposal scheme functioned adequately because hunters and gatherers frequently abandoned their campgrounds. When modern hunter-gatherers, like the aborigines of the Australian outback, are provided with government housing, one of the immediate problems they face is that of garbage disposal. Aborigines typically begin their settled lives by trashing their houses, leaving debris in all the rooms and throwing it out the windows and doors. As such behavior suggests, man faced his first garbage crisis when he became a sedentary animal.

That brings us to the first important truth about garbage: There are no ways of dealing with it which haven't been known for many thousand of years. As the species has advanced, people have introduced refinements, but the old ways are fundamentally still the only ways, and they are four: dumping garbage, burning garbage, turning garbage into something that can be used again, and minimizing the volume of material goods (future garbage) produced in the first place ("source reduction," it's called).

Given the choice, a human being's first inclination is always to dump. From prehistory through the present day, dumping has been the means of disposal favored everywhere, including the cities. Archaeological excavations of hard-packed dirt and clay floors usually recover a multitude of small finds, suggesting that a great deal of garbage was just left on the floor where it fell, or was brushed into a corner. In 1973 a civil engineer with the Department of Commerce, Charles Gunnerson, calculated that the rate of uplift due to debris accumulation in the ancient city of Troy was about 4.7 feet per century. If the idea of a city rising above its garbage at this rate seems quaint, it may be worth considering that "street level" on the island of Manhattan is fully fourteen feet higher today than it was when Peter Minuit lived there.

At Troy and elsewhere, of course, not all trash was kept indoors. The larger pieces of garbage and debris were thrown into the streets where semi-domesticated animals (usually pigs) ate up the food scraps while human scavengers, in exchange for the right to sell anything useful they might find, carried what was left to vacant lots or to the outskirts of town, where it was sometimes burned but more often simply left. The image of sulfurous "garbage mountains" in the Third World is repelling and almost a cliché, but the people who work these dumps, herding their pigs even as they sort paper from plastic from metal, are performing the most thorough job of garbage recycling and resource recovery in the world. What's an enlightened, right-thinking environmentalist to say? The garbage mountains point up another important truth about garbage: Efficient disposal is not always completely compatible with other desirable social ends—due process, human dignity, economic modernization. In a liberal democracy, these other ends compete for priority. In the United States, a garbage problem is in some respects just the modest price we pay for having done many things right.

It was the threat of disease, finally, that made garbage removal at least partially a public responsibility in Europe and the U.S. In the United

States, the path was pioneered by Colonel George E. Waring, Jr., the "Apostle of Cleanliness," who became the Street Cleaning Commissioner of the City of New York in 1895 and set up the first comprehensive system of refuse management in the country. Col. Waring and his 2,000 uniformed White Wings cleared the streets of rubbish and offal and carted off the refuse to dumps, incinerators, and, until the affluent owners of shorefront property in New Jersey complained, the Atlantic Ocean. Waring's powerful image as protector of the public health influenced communities everywhere. Taking the long view reminds us of one more important fact about garbage: Ever since governments began facing up to their responsibilities, the story of the garbage problem in the West has been one of steady amelioration, of bad giving way to less bad and eventually to not quite so bad.

How Much Garbage?

It stands to reason that something for which professionals have a technical term of long standing—*solid waste stream*—should also have a precisely calibrated volume attached to it. But the fact is that estimates of the amount of garbage produced in the United States vary widely.

During the past 15 years, The Garbage Project has handsorted and recorded modern household refuse in Tucson, Phoenix, Milwaukee, New Orleans, and Marin County (Calif.). By some happenstance, our sample neighborhoods—white, Hispanic, black, low income, middle income, upper income—all discarded less than the prevailing national averages for residential refuse. As a result, I became interested in the way national averages are calculated. I found that there are limits on the accuracy of material measurements because of the biases of the researchers and the logistical constraints involved in data collection, analysis, and reporting.

Since there is no way to measure or weigh more than a fraction of what is actually discarded, all studies take short cuts. Some have tried to measure refuse in ten or 20 cities and then extrapolate findings to the nation as a whole. These studies suffer from acknowledged biases in data collection: Their informants were garbage haulers who had a vested interest in high figures. And sample sizes were small.

Another estimation technique, the "materials-flow" method, doesn't examine garbage at all. Instead, it looks at industrial production, distribution, and sales records and applies assumptions about discard patterns to determine the rate at which materials enter the solid waste stream. The problem here is that the assumptions are largely untested. The study most quoted for current generation rates, for example, assumed that the maximum uselife of major household appliances is no more than 20 years, after which time the appliances are discarded. That assumption ignores the substantial trade in used durables, which supplies many low-income households with appliances and is a source of parts no longer carried by standard dealers. Such untested assumptions abound.

Perhaps it should not have been a surprise that hands-on sorts produced figures consistently below accepted estimates. Nor should it be shocking that over the past two decades many incinerators were oversized beyond their actual refuse intake, or that a 1981 column in *Public Works* asked, "Where has all the refuse gone?"

Even though today most of us believe we are in the midst of a "Garbage Crisis," we don't really know how much garbage we actually generate every day or every year. We don't even seem to know if the quantities discarded are growing or shrinking. My own view is that the higher estimates of garbage generation (frequently reported as five to eight pounds per person per day) significantly overstate the problem. Garbage Project studies of actual refuse reveal that even three pounds of garbage per person per day may be too high an estimate for many parts of the country. A weight sort of garbage in Milwaukee in 1978–79 yielded a weight of one-and-a-half pounds per person per day, a result that has been roughly corroborated by weight sorts in other communities. Americans are wasteful, but to some degree we have been conditioned to think of ourselves as more wasteful than we truly are—and certainly as more wasteful than we used to be. The evidence of our senses reinforces such perceptions. Fast-food packaging is ubiquitous and conspicuous. Planned obsolescence is a cliché. Our society is filled with symbolic reminders of waste. What we miss is what is no longer there to see. We do not see the 1,200 pounds per annum of coal ash which every American generated at home at the turn of the century and which was dumped usually on the poor side of town. We do not see the hundreds of thousands of dead horses which once had to be disposed of by American cities every year. No, Americans are not suddenly producing more garbage. On a per capita basis, our record is, at worst, one of relative stability.

THE ROLE OF BEHAVIORS

The root problem in assessing the true magnitude of garbage accumulation is in the nature of garbage itself. Unlike the evidence of other social problems, be it a human one such as poverty or an aesthetic one such as bad architecture, the evidence of specific pieces of garbage disappears from one day to the next. People put their garbage in the can under the sink and then someone TAKES IT OUT. The garbage that is taken out is eventually left at the curb and then IT IS GONE. Garbage passes under noses virtually unnoticed, the constant turnover inhibiting perception.

With the permission of the sanitation division of the city of Tucson, my students and I have during the past 15 years examined the garbage of thousands of households. The Project has conducted studies designed to compare how people say they behave with how the garbage they discard says they behave; or, to put it another way, to compare what people say they throw away with what they actually throw away. Such detailed studies require that the interview responses of any household be matched against its garbage over a period of several weeks.

As you might suspect, people are an utterly unreliable source of information. What people claim in interviews to have purchased and used, eaten and drunk, recycled and wasted, almost never corresponds directly to the packaging and debris in their garbage bags.

If a behavior has a generally positive public image, it is over-reported. People report eating far higher quantities of high-fiber cereals, vegetable soups, and skim milk than the boxes, cans, and cartons they throw out would suggest. By the same token, if a behavior is seen in a negative light, it is under-reported. Informants drastically deflate the volume of alcoholic beverages, breakfast pastries and desserts, and high-fat foods they consume. One common form of distortion results from what might be called the Good Provider Syndrome: Heads of households usually estimate that their families go through a great deal more food and other goods than one can actually find evidence for in the family's garbage. On the other hand, when asked to report their own diets, most people succumb to the Lean Cuisine Syndrome and report smaller portions and fewer fats and sweets than their garbage indicates. If you want to know how much alcohol people drink at home, don't ask them. They will typically under-report *by 40 to 60 percent.*

People's unpredictable behavior can have a direct impact on any attempt to change their discard patterns. For example, in California's Marin County, 88,000 households produce about 64,700 tons of hazardous materials each year. The county began sponsoring "collection days" when residents are encouraged to bring household hazardous wastes to a centralized location. To determine the efficacy of the Toxics Away! Day held in 1986, The Garbage Project sorted Marin household refuse for one month before and two months after the event. The results were not at all what we (or the County) expected. The refuse discarded *after* the collection day contained more than twice the quantity of hazardous materials which we had found discarded in refuse samples examined before the collection day. Why? The collection was held on only one day with no future collections announced. Most likely some citizens, who had been made aware of their household toxic products through publicity but had missed the actual collection, decided to get rid of their hazardous wastes through normal channels—at the curb.

Or let's look at the realities of changing behaviors that would facilitate, say, recycling. Let's say that the demand for recycled paper, plastic, aluminum, and glass was insatiable. How much garbage would Americans be prepared to recycle? If Americans were Germans or Japanese, the answer might be a lot. Germans are furnished by local governments with three different trash containers, and they "source separate" their garbage to make recycling easier. In Japan, citizens are required to separate their garbage into at least seven and in some places as many as twenty categories to expedite re-use. In America, the only factor that could conceivably drive a systematic recycling effort is money. Money is the reason why junk dealers pay attention to some kinds of garbage and not to others, and it is the reason why most people return bottles and cans to supermarkets, and newspapers to recycling centers, instead of just throwing them away. If recycling does not make economic sense to the actors at every link along the great garbage chain, it simply won't happen.

I belabor this point because it is so often overlooked, and because there are studies that seem to suggest—erroneously, I think—that for noble motives alone people would go to considerable lengths to make recycling an integral part of American life. Barry Commoner, the biologist and environmentalist, recently conducted a study of a hundred households in Easthampton, Long Island, in which participants were asked to separate their garbage into four containers: one for food debris and soiled paper (to be made into fertilizer), one for clean paper, one for metal cans and glass bottles, and one for all the rest. Mr. Commoner found that, because it was rationally discarded, a stunning 84 percent of the garbage from these households could be sold or recycled. Only 16 percent had to be deposited in a landfill. Of course, this experiment lasted only a few weeks, and the households surveyed had actively volunteered to take part. Recognizing that his results were perhaps a little skewed, Mr. Commoner conducted a telephone survey in Buffalo, New York, and ascertained that a reassuring 78 percent of all respondents said sure, they'd be willing to separate their garbage into four containers. However, only 26 percent of the respondents said that they thought their neighbors would be willing to do so. This "What would the neighbors do?" question has a special resonance for Garbage Project researchers. We have found over the years by comparing interview data with actual trash that *the most accurate description of the behavior of any household lies in that household's description of the behavior of a neighboring household.* Americans have a pretty firm understanding of human nature; they just don't want to admit that it applies to themselves.

There have been studies that claimed that the people most likely to recycle are those with the most money and the most education, but all of these studies are based on people's "self-reports." A look through household garbage yields a different picture. Between 1973 and 1980, the Project examined some 9,000 refuse pickups in Tucson from a variety of sample neighborhoods chosen for their socioeconomic characteristics. The contents were carefully sorted for newspapers, aluminum cans, glass bottles, and tinned-steel cans (evidence that a household is not recycling), and for bottle-caps, aluminum pop-tops, and plastic six-pack yokes (possible evidence, in the absence of bottles or cans, that a household *is* recycling). A lot of statistical adjustments and cross-referencing had to be done, but in the end we made three discoveries. First, nobody recycles as much as they say they do (but they do recycle just about as much as they say their neighbors do). Second, patterns of recycling by household vary over time; recycling is not a consistent habit. Third, high income and education and even a measure of environmental concern did not predict household recycling rates. *The only reliable predictor was the price paid for various commodities at buyback centers.* When prices rose for, say, newsprint, the number of newspapers found in local garbage suddenly declined as service groups and charities found it worth their time to collect and recycle.

Every Garbage Project study seems to prompt the same conclusion: Our world is composed of two realities, one mental and one material. I personally believe that today's "Garbage Crisis" is largely the result of significant differences between the real world and the mental worlds which revolve around common household refuse. On one side there are still very few quantitative studies that physically measure the constituents of refuse. On the other side are all of the unique experiences each of us has had and the resulting set of personalized attitudes, beliefs, and ideas stored in our minds about garbage. These two sets of information—material measurements and mental perceptions—are equally "real," and both are constantly summoned by government officials, businessmen, environmentalists, and concerned laymen into evaluations of our solid-waste dilemma.

As an archaeologist, I further believe that an even bigger problem with what our society recognizes as a garbage problem is that human *behavior* is systematically ignored. Today, garbage is perceived as a kind of primordial ooze, spontaneously generated. The material view usually reports "x" percent of plastic by weight, while the mental view often depicts plastics as materials to be eliminated from refuse because they are "unnatural" and "harmful to the environment" (usually in some unspecified way). But neither view identifies the role of specific plastics in our lifestyles or social order. As a bathroom products company, would you rather transport your product in glass containers or in much lighter, unbreakable plastic? As a consumer, would you purchase a glass container for the tiled bathroom or a lighter, safer container that won't shatter and cut? Because of the consistency of business *and* consumer choices, it is now difficult to find bathroom commodities in glass.

For good, for bad, or for ugly, garbage cannot be successfully understood or managed or legislated separate from the behaviors that produce it.

THE FUTURE OF CRISIS

The garbage problem in the United States today is indeed serious, but I believe that the most critical issue is not landfill closings or incinerator emissions, collecting recyclables or mandating source reduction. To me, the central issue is obtaining accurate, objective, scientific data on each of these issues in all three of their dimensions—material, mental, and behavioral.

Politicians, city officials, municipal and private haulers, the municipal engineering industry, environmental groups, and more all have elegant plans to reduce, collect, recycle, reuse, and dispose of solid wastes by means both efficient and environmentally appropriate. In contrast, the physical reality is a mess of immense proportions and complexity. At present, our knowledge and attitudes are out of sync with both behaviors and material realities. *That* is the real garbage crisis.

QUESTIONS FOR CRITICAL READERS

Remembering and Understanding

1. Write a brief summary of the historical information Rathje provides about garbage.
2. Why does Rathje believe estimates of the amount of garbage produced in the United States are usually inflated?
3. What is Rathje's major conclusion about "the garbage crisis," and what evidence does he offer to support this conclusion?

Analyzing and Discussing

4. What does Rathje mean when he says that "garbage is not mathematics"?
5. Rathje says that garbage cannot be understood, managed, or legislated separate from the behaviors that produce it. Choose two or three objects or products that you use, and that you would be reluctant to give up. Explain how these objects are related to your lifestyle and why they should or should not be replaced with other products that might produce less trash or be otherwise less harmful.

Writing

6. Keep track of the products you buy and the trash you produce for at least a week. List exact quantities and items. At the end of the period, write a description of your lifestyle as it is reflected by the products you consume and the trash you produce.
7. Rathje says that only money would motivate a systematic recycling effort in the United States. If you agree with him, explain why. If you do not agree with him, explain the other incentives that you believe might motivate people to participate in recycling.

A Tide of Plastic

──────── RUTH NORRIS ────────

Not all solid waste finds its way into landfills or incinerators. Many people simply throw trash onto the ground or into the water, and much of this litter eventually finds its way into the oceans. In this article, which originally appeared in Audubon *magazine, Norris, a free-lance writer who specializes in environmental issues, describes what happens when birds and marine animals encounter plastic trash adrift in the ocean.*

THE SEA TURTLE, a hawksbill, died two days after it was found stranded on a Hawaiian beach. It was a young turtle, its shell only a foot long, and when found it was emaciated and unable to dive.

"This is what I found in its gut," says George Balazs, a National Marine Fisheries Service sea turtle biologist, handing over a plastic Ziploc bag about eight inches square. It contains a mass of garbage. There are a few pieces of pumice stone, but most of it is plastic—a golf tee, shreds of bags and sheeting, bits and pieces of monofilament line, a plastic flower, part of a bottle cap, a comb, chips of Styrofoam and hard plastic, dozens of small round pieces. "The intestine was completely blocked with this stuff, all matted with fecal matter. That's eight-tenths of a kilogram of plastic. The animal weighed less than five and a half kilograms, so it's no wonder it couldn't dive."

The western Hawaiian island where this turtle was found is one of the more remote places tracked by the biologists who study creatures of the sea—a tiny speck in a huge ocean, two thousand miles from the American mainland and from the nearest island group to the south. Visitors, however, don't escape constant reminders of those distant worlds. Their litter fills the sea and accumulates daily on the beaches. There are scraps of ropes and lines, strapping, containers, sometimes a whole fishing net weighing hundreds of pounds. Hawaiian monk seals as well as sea turtles have become entangled in plastic lines and nets, which sometimes snag on rocks or reefs and drown their captives. As the carcasses of dead albatrosses decompose on the beaches, the nondecomposing contents of their stomachs remain: plastic fragments, pellets, cigarette lighters, toy cars and soldiers. A recent U.S. Fish and Wildlife Service study of albatross chicks on Laysan Island found 90 percent with some quantity of plastics in their digestive systems.

Almost anyone who treasures remote beaches can tell of discovering some isolated spot littered with fishing gear, plastic sandals, detergent bottles, bags, and assorted debris. Participants in a "coastwalk" cleanup of Oregon beaches two years ago picked up twenty-six tons of garbage in just three hours. Plastic pellets—the raw material of which all those utensils, containers, and toys are made—have washed up on New Zealand beaches in such quantities that the beaches seem coated with plastic sand. Some Alaskan beaches are so littered with lost and discarded monofilament fishing nets that any animal hauling ashore risks entanglement and death.

More than 50,000 ships sail the seas, with crews numbering one and a half million. Since very few ports provide adequate facilities for collecting ship-generated garbage, it's not surprising to find the oceans serving as a giant dump. More than five million plastic containers are chucked overboard every day. Plastic cargo nets, sheeting used to protect cargo, strapping bands, and utensils all get the same treatment. Garbage ships haul city refuse out into the ocean to be dumped. Commercial fishermen alone, the National Academy of Sciences estimates, dump more than fifty million pounds of plastic packaging into the sea each year and lose some 300 million pounds of plastic nets, lines, and buoys. Raw plastic particles—nibs, pellets, and beads—find their way into the oceans from the outfalls of manufacturing plants, by spilling as they are loaded for shipping, or by being dumped or hosed off the decks of ships.

Unlike old-time fishing nets of hemp or flax, unlike tin cans and cardboard containers, which sink and eventually disintegrate, plastic garbage is buoyant and nearly indestructible. It collects in huge masses wherever wind and currents take it. It snags and kills wildlife. Plastic banana bags thrown from docks in Costa Rica wind up in the digestive tracts of sea turtles, perhaps because the turtles mistake them for a favorite food, jellyfish. Lost fishing nets continue to capture fish, even though their owners will never return to claim them. They also capture seabirds that dive to catch the fish, unable to see the transparent netting until it is too late. In the North Pacific, netting has been recovered with one hundred dead seabirds and two hundred dead salmon entangled in a single piece.

This tide of plastic garbage began to surge just after World War II, when disposable, durable, inexpensive polymer materials came into wide use. The 1960s brought a tremendous increase in commercial fishing, with an attendant loss and abandonment of more and more gear. Each year brings new and stronger plastics and yet more uses: oxygen-barrier bottles that can keep the fizz in soft drinks, plastic containers tough enough to be reheated after packing perishable foods. Unfortunately, products made more durable for supermarket shelves are also more durable after disposal. But "upscale convenience products" continue to replace bottles and cans. Plastic packages can go from microwave to table, and plastic containers are lighter and take less energy than metals to manufacture. "Almost everything that's in other packaging now is apt to find itself in plastic eventually," declares a spokesman for the Society of the Plastics Industry.

Something similar could be said for the creatures of the sea. They find themselves in plastics, and plastics in themselves, accidentally. Seabirds may mistake plastic pellets for the tiny crustaceans they normally feed on. One part of the problem, notes George Balazs, is that "tides and currents tend to concentrate plastics in the same way they normally concentrate food items. If it's where food is supposed to be, it gets eaten."

Seals and sea lions are in particular danger because they tend to cozy up to nets, strapping bands, and lines. At the National Marine Fisheries Service lab in Honolulu there are pictures of Hawaiian monk seals—among the most endangered marine mammals occurring in U.S. waters—entangled in nets, encircled by packing bands, muzzled by container rings. One seal is easily recognizable by a scar around its neck left by a strapping band. For years the seal carried the band, which became tighter and tighter as the seal grew around it.

Anecdotal evidence from other areas is even more gruesome. "I observed a sea lion with a net fragment so deep in its tissues that the net had cut through skin, blubber, and muscle and had actually cut open the trachea," Rich Tinney of the Center for Environmental Education told a congressional committee two years ago. "The animal was incapable of diving for food because water would enter its throat through the opening cut by the net."

The best evidence of the plastics pollution problem, and perhaps the most devastating effect on a single species, can be found in the North Pacific. There, each night, Japanese, Taiwanese, and Korean fishermen set out their eight-mile-long, twenty-six-foot-deep nets, with weights at the bottom and floats at the top. In all, the night's work stretches 20,000 miles of invisible curtains of net. Because their gills catch on the nets, fish too large to make it all the way through the mesh become caught when they attempt to back out. Each morning, when the nets are retrieved, an average of ten miles of netting escapes detection. And thousands of miles of deteriorated nets are abandoned or dumped overboard each year. These "ghost nets" continue to fish until they wash ashore or sink from the weight of their catch.

This fishery has been controversial since its inception. Native Alaskans have objected to the Asians' interception of anadromous salmon that otherwise would return to Alaskan waters. Although an agreement with

Japan has recently been signed, it will have little effect beyond moving the fishery to inshore waters, and it postpones a planned phaseout for five years.

A few of these nets, and a great many more from the bottomfish trawlers that ply the Bering Sea, are a major threat to northern fur seals. Fur seals have themselves been a subject of considerable controversy: Their population has declined dramatically, and reauthorization of the treaty that protects them was held up because of protests by animal-rights groups against the hunting of seals by Pribilof Islanders. But, according to National Marine Fisheries Service researchers, ten times as many seals are killed each year when they become caught in plastic fishing nets as are killed in the hunt. On at least four separate occasions, floating balls of netting and debris containing eight to twelve dead fur seal pups have been sighted. Since the area inhabited by fur seals is vast, these few sightings undoubtedly represent only a tiny fraction of actual occurrences.

What is to be done about a problem whose dimensions can only be guessed at, whose consequences appear only as its victims happen to be washed up by winds and currents, whose sources encompass the whole of factories on land and ships at sea? Although there are laws and treaties prohibiting the disposal of persistent plastics at sea, they are not binding on all ships, and detection and enforcement have not been high on any country's priority list. The unintentional loss of fishing gear is not criminal. In the United States, the National Oceanic and Atmospheric Administration is responsible for preparing five-year plans for the control of oceanic pollution. But the agency has barely begun to address the plastics problem. Until 1985, notes Michael Bean of the Environmental Defense Fund, it was possible to read the national marine pollution plan from start to finish without even finding mention of entanglement.

Those who study the problem have several items on their action agenda. Existing legal authorities could be used to pursue research. Current laws could be enforced and aid programs administered in such a way as to minimize dumping. Development of more biodegradable plastics could be encouraged, and additional international treaties could be brought into force.

It was by congressional directive—a million-dollar appropriation specifically designated for work on marine debris—that a NOAA agency, the National Marine Fisheries Service, came up with a plan. The overwhelming majority of the funds have been put into research and education, however. Less than fifteen percent are for measures actually aimed at reducing the amount of garbage in the sea, and even here, the emphasis is on encouraging the shipping fleet not to litter and on studying potential alternatives. Only five thousand of the million dollars are earmarked for developing strategies to enforce existing prohibitions on disposal of plastics at sea.

Two treaties currently regulate the dumping of plastics at sea: the London Dumping Convention (implemented in the United States by the Ocean Dumping Act) and MARPOL, diplomatic shorthand for the 1973 Marine Pollution Convention. The former regulates trash-hauling ships, the latter other vessels. MARPOL's prohibition against dumping persistent plastics, though, is contained in an "optional" section known as Annex V. It has been signed by twenty-four countries but will not be put into effect until it has been signed by countries representing half the gross tonnage of the world shipping fleet. If the United States and Britain, each with about five percent of the world tonnage, were to sign, Annex V would acquire force of law.

"There are a number of laws enacted for other purposes that might be brought to bear, assuming a creative and aggressive desire on the part of agencies to address the entanglement problem," adds Michael Bean. For example, the Endangered Species Act, Migratory Bird Treaty Act, and Marine Mammal Protection Act prohibit the killing of marine birds, turtles, and mammals. Negotiations with fishermen might produce agreements on precautionary measures to be taken in return for immunity from prosecution for accidental kills. Then there are programs that compensate fishermen for lost gear. Fishermen who wished to participate in those programs could be required to mark their gear, dispose of it safely, report inventories and disposition of all gear, and notify authorities when they spotted concentrations of debris. (Presently, foreign fishermen operating in U.S. waters are required to mark gear with their radio call signals, and they have U.S. observers on board who at least theoretically could enforce the Fishery Conservation and Management Act's prohibition on discarding gear into the ocean. But there are no such requirements on U.S. ships.)

Some states have made attempts to attack the problem at its source, enacting laws and creating incentives for the use of biodegradable plastics. Although it is too soon to rely on these products as a solution, their hazards at least are shorter-lived than those of what's out there now.

Eight states now require the plastic yokes that bind six-packs to be made of biodegradable materials, and similar legislation has been proposed in two dozen other states. These plastics remain strong while kept inside stores and homes but become brittle and decompose into tiny flakes when exposed to sunlight. Since the ultraviolet rays that do the job don't penetrate seawater, a different tack would have to be taken for plastics used by ships—perhaps disintegration when exposed to saltwater.

Firms that have specialized in biodegradable plastics (Good 'n Tuff garbage bags, for example) have found their products to be price-competitive with standard-issue plastics, but the real question is whether consumer demand will lead to an expanded array of degradable products. One of plastics' prime selling points has been their durability, and many firms fear that degradables will hurt plastics' overall reputation for reliability.

And so the masses accumulate. The same currents and tides that shift and deposit sands on shorelines also bring their daily loads of oceanic litter. In the northwestern Hawaiian Islands, observers have begun gathering the trash, hauling it off or burning it, and they have seen a decrease in the number of monk seals entangled. But the fur seals, whales, sea otters, manatees, turtles, and all the birds—murres, puffins, shearwaters, auklets, albatrosses—are not so closely concentrated or so carefully tended. Each species has its band of dedicated researchers. All of these monitors have ideas about the extent to which their charges are being harmed by plastic debris, and about the strategies that might bring the problem into focus and under control. What is missing is that creative and aggressive desire, fuel to turn agencies that *could* be doing something into partners in pollution control.

QUESTIONS FOR CRITICAL READERS

Remembering and Understanding

1. Write a summary of Norris's article in no more than one hundred words. Be sure you include information about the specific kinds of damage caused by drifting plastics.
2. Why do drifting plastics create more problems for marine animals than other kinds of litter?
3. In what ways do drifting plastics create problems for humans?

Analyzing and Discussing

4. Explain and evaluate the various solutions that have been proposed or attempted.
5. What are the most compelling reasons for solving the problem of plastics dumped into the oceans?

Writing

6. Much of the dumping that Norris describes appears to be accidental, inadvertent, or done without a full realization of the magnitude of the problem. Write a paper in which you explain how you would devise a solution that relied on changing human behavior rather than law enforcement or technology.
7. Litter exists everywhere, not just the oceans. Look closely at your own surroundings, and identify the various kinds of litter you find there. Write a paper in which you identify the hazards this litter might pose to animals or people, and then alert people to the dangers.

Here We Go A-Bottling

—————— Mary Durant ——————

Durant is a professional writer who has written novels, short stories, and dictionaries of animals and wildflowers. With her late husband, Michael Harwood, she wrote On the Road with John James Audubon, *an account of their retracing of Audubon's journeys. In this article, which was first published in* Audubon *magazine (May 1986), Durant focuses on a specific trash problem: bottles that become litter. She approaches this issue from several perspectives: first she gives historical information; then she demonstrates her skills as a close observer; finally, she considers what can be done to solve this particular problem with incentives and laws.*

THE ART OF BOTTLE-MAKING began in the Near East more than 3,000 years ago, and the first American bottles are thought to have been produced in the Jamestown colony in 1608. The first patent on the almighty tin can was registered in England in 1810, and five years later a New England entrepreneur named Ezra Daggett took out a patent of his own for canned salmon, lobster, pickles, jams, and sauces. With that, we were off and running. In no time at all, North America was awash in castaway bottles and cans from sea to shining sea, and we've been complaining ever since.

A gold-rusher's wife, writing home from California in the 1850s, made particular mention of diggings on the Feather River that were "thickly peppered" with bottles and oyster and sardine cans. Owen Wister later delivered the same message in his novel *The Virginian*. He described the town of Medicine Bow as surrounded by a rampart of discarded cans, "the first of her trophies that Civilization dropped upon Wyoming's virgin soil," and though the wind had blown away the white ashes of the cowboys' campfires, wrote Wister, the empty sardine can "lies rusting over the face of the Western earth."

There's no record of exactly what those bottles along the Feather River contained—whiskey, gin, patent medicine, or liniment—but they would be collectibles today. The gold-rusher's wife would be amazed at the prices nineteenth-century glass fetches, whether it's a bottle of Cathedral Peppersauce ($15), a bottle of Drake's Plantation Bitters ($45), or a commemorative flask (as much as $35,000). As far as I know, the venerable sardine can is not a collector's item, but beer cans, which were introduced in 1935, *are*, with price guides published annually. If this makes you anxious to start digging for buried treasures in old trash heaps and cellar wells, take your time. They'll keep.

The aluminum can, technology's gift to the North American landscape in the 1960s, takes 500 years to biodegrade, and glass a million years. Plastic, the bane of the twentieth century, does not naturally biodegrade, *ever*. And there goes your town dump, already full to overflowing. One of the prime reasons these days is those blasted throwaway beverage containers. Americans drink more beer and soda pop than all other soft drinks combined—coffee, tea, fruit juice, or whatever—and it's been estimated that if you stacked a year's collection of our empties end to end, you could build twenty towers to the moon. Or, if you'd rather, you could circle the Earth with them 200 times. These statistics remind me of the time I crossed the Great Salt Lake Desert three years ago, the shimmering barrens on either side of the highway laced with names, initials, and religious slogans written in giant letters made from empty cans and bottles. An infinity of empties.

Connecticut, where we live, is one of nine states blessed with bottle bill legislation. This means (in case you've been living in a cave for the past decade) that the consumer pays a deposit on each container—glass, plastic, or aluminum—in which carbonated beverages are sold. And bottle bills work. There's a 90 percent return rate wherever such legislation is on the books, though, sad to say, bottle bills do not necessarily transform the entire citizenry into saints overnight. There are always the diehards and dunderheads who wouldn't redeem an empty if their lives depended on it. Never. Toss 'em out. Any old place.

But as fast as they toss them out, there's usually someone who will pick them up, turn them in, and collect the refund—a nickel apiece in these parts. For the poor in our urban areas, it's found money, and you'll see the homeless asleep at night in parks, in doorways, and on church steps with bags and carts they've filled with empties. Out here in the country, we have no homeless, but we have plenty of picker-uppers, and they're not just schoolchildren on bicycles. The most colorful of our local scavengers is a jaunty old gent who works the side roads, throwing the empties into a cardboard carton strapped to his back. On his shoulder he carries a long stick decorated with his insignia of office: a fluttering red bandanna and, atop the stick, a red, white, and blue Budweiser can. Not only is he death on litter but also on ragweed, which he pulls out by the roots as he tramps along.

For sheer volume, I recently heard about a young man who scours the countryside in his Chevette, filling it to the gunwales with empties.

He claims to have collected enough refund money—since 1980, when Connecticut's bottle bill was enacted—to buy a bass-fishing boat complete with aerated fish tanks and a depth gauge.

The hot spots for empties around our little town are the lilac bushes across the street from the liquor store, lover's lane at the cemetery, the parking area next to the beaver pond, and just about any downhill curve. There's something about those downhill curves, a magnetic pull, and empties are sent flying out the window of passing vehicles.

What's more, pitching cans and bottles is a year-round phenomenon. An amazing number of people are evidently unable to drive from Point A to Point B without a six-pack of ice-cold beer, even in zero-degree weather. And an amazing number toss out beer cans that haven't even been opened. General opinion has it that these are underage beer drinkers getting rid of the evidence before going home with the family car. I don't agree. I think it's just another example of litter lust.

Sometimes the diehards scratch the refund labels off bottles so no one else can redeem them, and sometimes they rip aluminum can to shreds with their bare hands. Another flourish is to put the bottom of the can against your forehead and smash it flat with one blow. Very macho. But in Connecticut, for one, this sort of bravado is a waste of time, because accordionized cans are returnable under the law. Across the border in New York State, however, redeemable cans have to stand on their own two feet. Otherwise, no nickel.

Within my immediate circle, the picker-uppers include our appliance repairman, my dentist, a biology professor, a retired house painter, and one of my old friends, who for years has played a game of hide-and-seek with the groundskeeper of a local school. He stows his empty beer cans behind a lonely stretch of stone wall, and she faithfully picks them up on her daily walk. My husband, too, is a devout picker-upper and collects any empties in his path when he's out birding. One of his particular hot spots is at a nearby lake, where migrating waterbirds throng the coves and picnickers, boaters, and fishermen throng the wooded shoreline. Most of us are moved by an esthetic outrage that here in our pretty New England town there should be any litter whatsoever, with or without nickel refunds. One soda pop can on the village green or in an open meadow has more shock value than five hundred of them in a vacant city lot.

I've had my own adventures in the field, of course. On two occasions, deep in a nearby forest preserve, I've stumbled upon that rare and little-known botanic species, the beer can tree—sparkling new aluminum cans impaled on the branches of head-high saplings and positively dazzling on a sunny winter day. Yes, I took them off and turned them in. But these are the litterbugs who anger me the most, the ones who romp into the forest because it's quiet and beautiful and then merrily trash it up.

One of my favorite places within the preserve is the crest of River

Ridge, with a sweeping view that I think of as mine: Iron Mine Ridge to the west, where a Revolutionary War shot tower still stands, and Painter Ridge to the east, its name given in colonial days, when mountain lions were known as panthers or "painters." There's not a house to be seen, only the wide corridor through the hemlocks with a couple of pastures, a cornfield, and acres of mountain laurel and azalea on the rocky slopes. Not the acid-hot, acrylic colors of hybrid azaleas but nature's own, in pink and peach. On a bright afternoon last November, I went up that way to pick a winter bouquet of sweet everlasting, *Gnaphalium obtusi-folium*, which has a delicious smell—vanilla and cinnamon with a whiff of pecan, like coffee cake in the oven. The witch hazel trees were in bloom—spidery yellow flowers that close when the temperature drops, then open again when it warms up. The resident blue jay flew screaming along a brook, to give warning of my arrival, and the juncos chattered their little alarm calls.

And then—splat. In the clearing where the wood lilies bloom in July was a sprawl of Coors golden-yellow beer cans, all clearly marked "Refund 5¢." Twenty-four of them. Once more, the nature lovers had been there and gone. I find their leavings in that clearing at least three times a year, yet I've only once seen anyone else up there, a solitary cross-country runner whom I'd first spotted a mile away as he dropped down off Painter Ridge. A few minutes later he whirled through—steady pace, steady breathing, and no greeting as he passed. (Running, I've noticed, tends to be a serious business.) However, I will swear to this—he was not carrying a case of Coors. Who the devil does trek in with all this beer? Very well. I took off my jacket and tied the sleeves together to make an impromptu tote bag for the cans, threw in the pizza boxes also left behind by our nature lovers, and added one empty nonrefundable bottle of Peachtree Schnapps. River Ridge was mine again.

The cans, by the way, were clean and dry, and that was a plus. Under the law, you may not return dirty containers. No mud inside, for example, no cigarette butts, and no slugs. Slugs love beer, and many gardeners put out saucers of it to protect their vegetables. The slugs crawl into the saucers, sample the beer, get drunk, and drown, which they also do if a beer container is not entirely empty. Sometimes you'll find a dead shrew that crawled in after the slugs and perished similarly, and sometimes carrion beetles (fingernail-sized, black carapace, an orange band on the back of the neck) that have crawled in after the shrew. Thus, an ecological kingdom unto itself in one discarded beer container, and you'll be forgiven if you bury it under a rock or drop it in the nearest trash barrel.

Besides Connecticut and New York, the states with bottle bills are Massachusetts, Vermont, Maine, Delaware, Michigan, Iowa, and Oregon, which in 1972 became the first to pass such legislation. It's been an uphill battle all the way, with howls of pain from the beverage and container industries. From where they stand, it's a whale of a lot easier to manufacture throwaways, raise the price to cover the cost, and let the garbage collectors figure out what to do with the mess. This is a reckless waste of recyclable resources: In a can of beer, the aluminum container is worth 55 percent of the price, and the beer a mere 12 percent. (The remaining 33 percent goes for distribution, advertising, and such.) But aluminum can be melted down to make new containers, glass bottles refilled, and plastic reprocessed into such items as plastic "peanuts" for packing breakables and filler for sleeping bags and winter coats.

Meanwhile, the beverage industry spends millions in its continuing fight against bottle-bill legislation. One of the goofiest attacks came from the National Soft Drink Association, which announced that many people have become bottle-bill activists to escape "the intolerable boredom and humiliating insignificance of their private lives." Among the beverage industry's scare tactics are dire warnings about the high cost of handling and storing empties at redemption centers and infestations of vermin, yet none of the store owners I've talked to have a word of complaint. Sure, space had to be made for the empties, but the only "vermin" mentioned were ants, which are attracted by the sugary residue in pop cans and are easily controlled by occasional fumigation. Hereabouts store owners approve wholeheartedly of our bottle bill. They like to see the countryside clean and neat. "After all," said one, "I live here too."

The Environmental Action Foundation, in Washington, D.C., says that when a few more states have come into the fold—and 1986 looks to be a good year—it will have the ammunition to push once again for a federal bottle bill. What a pity we haven't had one all along, as Norway does, for example. The Norwegians smelled trouble ahead and banned throwaway beverage containers before they even came on the market.

In closing, may I offer a few suggestions in case you feel shy about picking up empties. Try carrying a pair of binoculars, and if you're caught wading into the underbrush after a six-pack of Coke cans, you can always pretend you're out birding. Or try one of my masterful ploys. Shade your eyes with your hand and stare fixedly into the trees, as though you'd just discovered a raccoon snoozing on a branch. Or you can brazen it through. That's what my husband does. This morning, he found two cans on the roadside across from our house and waved them aloft as he brought them in, on his face the classic expression of the devout scavenger—one part triumph, two parts dismay.

QUESTIONS FOR CRITICAL READERS

Remembering and Understanding

1. Explain what a "bottle bill" is and summarize Durant's position on them.
2. Does anyone benefit from litter? Who and why?

Analyzing and Discussing

3. Why do people throw bottles and cans away, even when they could claim a refund on a deposit? See how many reasons you can come up with for this behavior. Once you have your own list, talk with people who litter (they should be easy to find) and see if their reasons are the same as the ones you thought of.

4. What would prevent people from littering? Would you stress incentives, penalties, or education? Explore each one of these and attempt to develop a plan.

5. Durant's objections to bottle and can litter are mostly aesthetic; that is, the litter ruins her view or her experience of favorite places. What are some other reasons that litter might be harmful?

Writing

6. Observe and document the existence of litter in your own community or on campus very carefully, and describe the extent of the litter problem. Be sure to include, as Durant does, the kinds of items you find and the location in which you find them.

7. Research and write a brief account of at least one anti-litter campaign.

The Look Is You

────────── LOUIS BLUMBERG ──────────

and

ROBERT GOTTLIEB

This excerpt is from War on Waste, *a book that gives a comprehensive overview of the problem of solid waste disposal in the United States. The original study that led to the book was conducted in the Urban Planning Program at UCLA. The authors take what might be called a social-science/ planning approach to the problem of waste disposal. That is, they do not see the problem as technological, but as social and human. This selection surveys the dramatic changes that have taken place in packaging, advertising, and marketing since World War II, and the effects these changes have had on the production of solid waste.*

IN 1960, A PROLIFIC AND POPULAR WRITER named Vance Packard produced yet another in his string of exhortative best-sellers criticizing the system of values and choices that had come to characterize post–World War II American society. Entitled *The Waste Makers,* Packard's book opened with a poignant quote from novelist Dorothy Sayers, who wrote: "A society in which consumption has to be artificially stimulated in order to keep production going is a society founded on trash and waste, and such a society is a house built upon sand." Elaborating on this theme, Packard proceeded to discuss such key marketing and production-related practices as planned obsolescence and "throwaway" products. As a result of these changes in product design and packaging, Packard warned, a waste crisis was in the making.

Packard's analysis, though substantially integrated into the popular discourse about waste, tended to be dismissed by both policy-makers and academics as an overly dramatic popularization of themes and a misstatement of issues. The rapid changes in the industrial base and the patterns of consumption that had developed in the post–World War II era were still being celebrated as contributing to America's national prosperity and dominance in international markets. The notion of waste, Vance Packard's best-selling books notwithstanding, was rejected in favor of the concept of "productivity" to describe a system based on producing more goods

497

and expanding consumer markets. The related concept of "consumerism" highlighted, for both marketing experts and economists, the presumption that the system could meet "human needs" by offering a wide range of differentiated products.

The period from the Progressive Era to the 1960s that Packard focused on can be seen as a prologue to the contemporary period of crisis and contention around solid waste issues. During this period, the per capita generation of wastes increased significantly while the composition of the waste stream changed as well. New, potentially hazardous consumer and industrial products and processes entered the marketplace, coinciding with a major revolution in packaging and materials use. These changes were tied to the rise of the petrochemical industry, which in turn substantially influenced this transformation of the waste stream (see table).

The growth of advertising with its impact on production decisions and consumer habits also played a critical role in restructuring the waste issue. Advertising became responsible, in part, for the system's tendency toward overproduction and the elevation of waste generation into an essential by-product of economic activity. With the advent of television, advertising's "perfect medium," advertising mushroomed into a billion-dollar industry and a central facet of production.

The expanded level of advertising and marketing activities was most pronounced in influencing the role of packaging in the production system. Previously, packaging had been basically a subset of the manufacturing

MATERIALS DISCARDED INTO THE MUNICIPAL SOLID WASTE STREAM
(IN MILLIONS OF TONS AND PERCENTS)

MATERIALS	1970		1984		2000	
	TONS	%	TONS	%	TONS	%
Paper and paperboard	36.5	33.1	49.4	37.1	65.1	41.0
Glass	12.5	11.3	12.9	9.7	12.1	7.6
Metals	13.5	12.2	12.8	9.6	14.3	9.0
Plastics	3.0	2.7	9.6	7.2	15.5	9.8
Rubber and leather	3.0	2.7	3.3	2.5	3.8	2.4
Textiles	2.2	2.0	2.8	2.1	3.5	2.2
Wood	4.0	3.6	5.1	3.8	6.1	3.8
Other	—	0.1	0.1	0.1	0.1	0.1
Food wastes	12.7	11.5	10.8	8.1	10.8	6.8
Yard wastes	21.0	19.0	23.8	17.9	24.4	15.3
Miscellaneous inorganics	1.8	1.6	2.4	1.8	3.1	2.0
Totals	110.3	100.0	133.0	100.0	158.8	100.0

SOURCE: "Characterization of Municipal Sold Waste in the United States, 1960–2000." Franklin Associates, EPA, Office of Solid Waste, PB-178323, 1986.

process. There were no trade associations, no consulting firms nor discrete spheres of activity such as packaging design. Nor were there specific organizational or financial operations distinct from the manufacturer itself. Packaging was functional, not a strategic element in a successful sales campaign, as it eventually evolved.

The shift in packaging's role during the post–World War II era, when both advertising and petrochemicals became dominant factors in the production system, was thorough and profound. The concentration of production and distribution in the food and consumer products industries meant that small firms serving local markets were supplanted by a few companies serving national and international markets. These trends were encouraged by the changes in packaging, while at the same time they helped precipitate the shift in packaging's role. Packaging, for example, had direct bearing on the rise of supermarkets and the demise of the general store. And, with the elimination of the salesclerk, the package became, as Walter Stern, a packaging industry figure, pointed out, the producer's "sole representative at the sales decision point." Relying on advertising messages and product claims, the package, Stern continued, conveys "the message he wants to communicate. Look. This product is different. This product will satisfy, benefit, totally respond to your need. It will really do what it says it will do. You won't like it only now. You'll like it in your home. Even weeks from now."

By the 1960s, packaging had been elevated to equal status with manufacturing itself, and was considered an essential component in the movement of goods from producer to consumer. The era of the "growing package," as one *Time* magazine article put it, had emerged, associated with such production innovations as "disposable," "one-way," or single-use products and "convenient living." Packaging now vied with advertising for a lion's share in the costs of production, and the two activities became so fully intertwined that most of the technical and instrumental capabilities of the package, such as its ability to extend product life, had become secondary to its marketing role. "Today," one industry speaker pointed out at a 1969 conference on packaging wastes, "packaging is recognized as too important to be assigned anything less than a specific responsibility and strategy in the goals and management procedures of most companies. . . . Packaging is too closely related to the company's profit and loss picture," the speaker concluded, "and it is too definitely connected to a firm's growth potential to be left to chance."

This 1969 conference billed itself as the first of its kind and was largely dominated by industry interests such as package users, designers, and producers, as well as the plastics, glass, paper, and ferrous metal companies and trade associations. The meeting was instructive for both its representations of the problem and its recommendations for possible solutions. Industry-related groups with such names as the California Anti-

Litter League ("People, Not Materials, Create Litter" was its motto), the Foundation for Conservation of our Environment, the Package Design Council, Package Engineering, and Flexible Plastics Corporation, as well as major producers such as Dow Chemical, Crown Zellerbach, Continental Can, and Monsanto, all argued that while waste disposal had indeed become a problem, in part because of packaging growth, government intervention was not the answer.

The growth of packaging wastes, in fact, at least in terms of measurement by weight, had peaked by this period. Though increases during the 1940s and 1950s of the per capita generation of container and package discards had been substantial, there developed a veritable explosion of packaging wastes in the 1960s, coinciding in part with the dramatic rise in the use of petrochemical-related materials, especially plastics, for packaging materials. According to a 1986 EPA waste stream analysis, packaging wastes jumped from 0.73 pounds per capita per day (pcd) in 1960 to 1.05 pounds pcd in 1970. Today, packaging represents more than one-third of the entire waste stream.

In the same vein, the petrochemical industry in general and plastics in particular were transformed from nearly nonexistent industries in the 1920s to multi-billion-dollar operations by the 1970s, with most of that growth taking place in the late 1940s, 1950s, and 1960s. The use of plastic, in both packaging and a wide range of consumer products, became particularly attractive in this period because of its versatility and price. The market for plastic products first developed during the World War II years, when government funding and subsidies for the potential military application of plastics also laid the groundwork for its future use. While government policy focused on the use of plastic as a substitute product in order to save other raw materials, a natural market was established among veterans, who, for example, became familiar with the use of a broad range of plastic materials, including the plastic can. The development of the industry, moreover, was strengthened during the Korean War with its increases in new products and industry subsidies.

The market for plastic products took off most dramatically during the late 1950s and 1960s when the prices for plastic compounds such as polyethylene began to drop significantly as production levels increased. The plastics industry moved aggressively to expand its markets in several different directions, especially in substituting for other materials. Plastic materials were lighter and tended to cost less during this boom period for chemical and petroleum products, and this versatility allowed them to be made into an unending variety of forms and textures. As a result, the proportion of plastic materials in a wide range of manufactured products increased dramatically in a relatively short period of time. In 1960, for example, less than 1 percent by weight of an average passenger car consisted of plastic materials; by 1984, that figure had increased to 6.4

percent, which translated into about 200 pounds of plastic per automobile, or 1 million tons of plastic wastes in the waste stream! This amount of plastic waste from automobiles, moreover, was expected to triple by the year 2000. Diaper backings, made from linear low-density polyethylene (LLDPE)—also used in the production of plastic bags, sacks, and a variety of other plastic packaging products—was another example of a product transformed in part after 1960 by the introduction of plastics as a key raw material.

This industry growth, in turn, had direct bearing on the waste stream. "Solid wastes are produced at essentially every step in the manufacture of plastics," two EPA consultants wrote in 1981, and that was particularly true regarding its end use or "postconsumer segment." Furthermore, the largest single end use that had evolved in the 30 years since plastics began to saturate the market was in packaging: plastic bags, plastic wrapping, foam containers, plastic bottles, and so forth. From literally no impact on the waste stream prior to World War II, plastics had come to represent, by the 1970s, its fastest-growing segment, with predictions of future growth at the same accelerated rates.

The advent of plastic products in turn helped to reshape waste disposal issues. The glass container industry, for example, responding partly to the pressure of a competitive product, helped engineer the decline of the returnable bottle, long a fixture in the marketplace. As late as 1947, refillable bottles maintained a nearly 100 percent market share of the glass container business. But with the advent of the plastic and glass "one-way" nonrefillable bottles, as well as the metal beverage can, the share of the market for refillable bottles rapidly declined over the next 30 years. Meanwhile, single-use disposable products captured literally all of the extensive overall growth in the beverage container industry that occurred in this period. Not only did its market share decline, but there also was an actual decline in the total production of refillables, while disposables were making enormous gains.

Plastic bottles especially turned out to be the prototypical single-use, nonrecyclable product. As late as 1977, one EPA study estimated that there was still no calculable measure of recycling and recovery of the various kinds of plastic containers on the market. And more than ten years after that, despite protracted battles over container recycling and reuse in more than a dozen states, more than 99 percent of all plastic containers continued to be discarded as one-way products.

The decline of the recyclable product was by no means limited to either plastics or glass containers. The paper products industry, facing strong competition from a range of new petrochemical-based product alternatives, successfully marketed a range of its own "convenience" items, including paper diapers and other chemically treated paper goods. One paper goods manufacturer that witnessed rapid increases in sales and income during the late 1950s began to describe itself as a "totally integrated" producer of packaged goods with its emphasis on disposable paper products.

By the 1950s and 1960s, the proliferation of new consumer products, product design modifications that focused on style changes while reducing a product's use life, and the continuing drive to develop and secure new markets for such products were all encouraged by the rapidly expanding share of advertising and promotion as a cost of production. The rise of television especially contributed to the prominent role of advertising in the decision-making structure of production. Within less than a decade after its introduction on a large scale, television had achieved a level of consumer penetration that "no other advertising medium has ever approached," as one marketing analyst noted. Given its ability to reach the entire family and establish "captive audiences," television became advertising's most successful means of "indoctrinating" and creating new sets of preferences, or what some analysts called "invented" or "artificial" needs. To consume, according to this television/advertising environment, became an essential form of self-expression. "The Look," as two critics of the 1960s scathingly wrote, had become "You."

This consumer goods revolution of the post–World War II era was fueled by the expansion of markets both here and abroad, and the increase in income levels that lasted for an unprecedented two decades. Advertising helped transform the American family and the American public into captive audiences to be delivered to the buyer of advertising time. Marketing and advertising personnel spoke of this creation of artificially stimulated needs as a form of "forced consumption," converting the purchase of goods into a set of rituals and a form of induced satisfaction. This revolution in consumption, furthermore, framed the changes in the generation of solid wastes. "We need things consumed, burned up, worn out, replaced, and discarded at an ever increasing pace" in order to alleviate the pressures of overproduction, an article in the *Journal of Retailing* proclaimed in the spring of 1955. Yet even with the severe recessions of the 1970s and early 1980s, which slowed down both consumer spending and waste generation levels, the changes wrought by petrochemicals and other new products, as well as advertising with its emphasis on continually expanding markets and packaging's role in differentiating products, a major permanent niche for disposable products had been secured in the contemporary industrial order. The evolving patterns of production and consumption had set the stage for the contemporary solid waste dilemma.

QUESTIONS FOR CRITICAL READERS

Remembering and Discussing

1. Summarize the ways packaging and its functions have changed since the end of World War II.
2. Why has a change in the function of packaging resulted in more packaging? That is, how has the change in purpose resulted in more packaging?

Analyzing and Discussing

3. Visit a store and look specifically at the way products are packaged. Find examples of packaging used as a container as opposed to packaging used as advertising. How are the two kinds of packaging similar and different?
4. Does television advertising create artificial needs in order to encourage consumption? Make a list of products that appear to exist only because an artificial or invented need has been created for them. For three or four of these, explain why you believe their existence is the result of an invented need. Compare your list with those of your classmates, and discuss your agreements and disagreements.
5. The authors say that consumption has become a form of self-expression. Explain what this means, and give examples.

Writing

6. What influence does packaging have on your own buying habits and preferences? Select several products you have purchased lately and compare their packaging with that of similar products that you decided not to buy. Write a paper in which you describe the different kinds of packaging and discuss the extent to which the packaging may have influenced your decision.
7. Survey your house, apartment, or room (or a single room in your house, such as the kitchen or bathroom). Make a list of the single-use items you find (such as plastic, disposable razors). How many of these products could you replace with reusable items? Choose three or four of these pairs and explain the advantages and disadvantages of buying the single-use or reusable one.

Synthesizing and Consolidating

1. Discuss or explain the problems presented by plastics and disposable or single-use products in terms of the technological displacements Commoner explains.
2. Rathje and Luoma appear to cover the same information, but in fact there are important differences in their approaches. Identify the points at which these two writers agree and disagree, and also compare the tone and the sense of urgency with which they present the problem.
3. Several of the writers in this chapter provide statistics for various aspects of waste production and disposal. Collect and examine comparable statistics from several sources in this chapter and then evaluate them in terms of Rathje's criticisms.
4. Summarize the various points of view about landfills presented in this chapter. Identify the different positions, explain each one briefly, and then attempt to evaluate each one.
5. Use the information provided by Rathje, Commoner, and Blumberg and Gottlieb to summarize the social factors that influence the production of trash.
6. Write an overall summary of the issue of solid waste production and disposal, drawing on the selections in this chapter for your information.

Suggestions for Research and Writing

1. Keep track of your personal or household trash for at least a week. Make a detailed list and be sure to include the trash you create outside your own house or apartment, such as in restaurants. At the end of the week write a report that describes the trash you have produced and relates that trash to your lifestyle.
2. How would you reduce your waste generation by half, as Luoma suggests? Write a description of the changes you would have to make in your lifestyle and patterns of consumption and disposal. Comment on whether these would be easy or difficult changes to make.
3. The trash problem has been variously described as a matter of individual, business, or government responsibility. How would you apportion this responsibility? Write a paper in which you explain what each group should be doing to help reach a solution to the problem of solid waste disposal.
4. Choose a specific solid waste issue, such as disposable or single-use products, bottle bills, plastics, or biodegradability. Summarize the information available in this chapter about that issue, and then update that information through library research. Write a summary of that information.
5. Make a list of the disposable products that you use. Are there reusable alternatives? Match the alternatives to the disposables and then make detailed comparisons of at least three pairs. You should consider such factors as environmental hazards, convenience, relative costs, and any others that you believe will help you produce a thorough comparison. Based

on your study, recommend which product other people should use, and explain why.

6. Using the information in this chapter about changes in technology and in the kinds of waste produced, write a description of the major changes in U.S. society since World War II.

7. Speculate about whether the most effective solutions to the problems described in this chapter are technological or social. As the focal point of a paper, select a single problem and describe the different approaches that technological and social solutions might take.

10

Sociobiology

Science and Values in Conflict

SOCIOBIOLOGY FIRST ATTRACTED national attention in 1975 when Harvard entomologist Edward O. Wilson published his controversial book *Sociobiology: The New Synthesis*. In this book, Wilson argued that human social behaviors such as aggression, altruism, and division of labor are biologically based, the result of natural selection operating on human genetics, rather than the product of human culture or learning. This view turns what is thought to be the normal cause-and-effect relationship on its head. Instead of asserting that the social environment shapes human behavior, sociobiology insists that the environment itself is a product of biological forces.

Wilson's ideas drew immediate criticism from those who saw them as an argument for biological determinism and a justification of existing social, economic, and political conditions. According to these critics, sociobiology presented social ills such as racism, poverty, and inequality as the inevitable results of a biological process rather than as the products of human social and political decisions. The implication, of course, was that the victims of discrimination and poverty deserved their condition because it was their genetic or evolutionary destiny. Some critics were further upset by the suggestion that it would be possible, even desirable, to manipulate human genes to encourage certain traits and behaviors and eliminate others.

The reading selections gathered here explain sociobiology and some of the controversy that has surrounded it by placing it in social, intellectual, and scientific contexts, and showing the connections between science and society at large. Historian Donald Fleming's article, written in 1969, describes the social, intellectual, and scientific atmosphere in which Wilson developed his ideas about sociobiology. Wilson himself, and Charles Lumsden, one of his frequent co-authors, provide a clear explanation of sociobiology's major ideas. Loren Graham, a historian of science, shows how Wilson's ideas about sociobiology developed from his earlier research into ants. David Barash, a zoologist like Wilson, points to specific aspects of sociobiology that have produced controversy or misunderstanding. Barry Schwartz examines the problems involved in applying animal research to the study of humans. Sarah Blaffer Hrdy is a primatologist and a student of Wilson's. Her perspective on sociobiology stems from her interest in the ways that women are often victims of social policies that seem to have the force of natural law. Stephen Jay Gould, a paleontologist who disagrees with Wilson, focuses on the distinction between biological potential and biological determinism. Finally, the editors of *Consumer Reports* write very specifically about some of the ways that genetic research has led to unpleasant social and economic consequences for individuals.

Before You Read

1. Make a list of the facts that you know about genetics.
2. Separate the statements you made in question 1 into lists as follows:
   a. Statements you know to be true and can verify.
   b. Statements you believe to be true but cannot verify.
   c. Statements you cannot classify as true or false using the knowledge you now have.
   d. Statements you believe to be false.
3. To the best of your ability, explain what genes are, what they do, and how they work.
4. Explain the scientific method to someone who does not understand it.
5. What does the phrase "genetic engineering" mean?
6. Explain what you know about the effects of heredity and environment on human development. Which do you think is more important?
7. Select a human trait, characteristic, or behavior that you have observed, and speculate about the roles of heredity and environment in shaping it.

The Sociobiology Controversy

—————— Charles J. Lumsden ——————

and

Edward O. Wilson

In 1983, eight years after the publication of Sociobiology, *Wilson and his co-author published the following explanation of Sociobiology in their book,* Promethean Fire. *Their purpose in this book was to explore the origins and development of the human mind. Because it was written some time after the original controversy, and presumably with the benefit of much reflection, we are probably justified in taking this explanation as accurately representing Wilson's ideas and his responses to his critics. It has the added virtue of being one of the clearer explanations of sociobiology, as it was written specifically for nonscientists.*

WHY HAS THERE BEEN a controversy over sociobiology? Nothing about this extraordinary episode makes sense until the subject itself is accurately characterized. Contrary to its usual popular image, sociobiology is neither a particular theory of behavior nor a politically defined doctrine on human nature. It is a scientific discipline and as such is defined as the systematic study of the biological basis of all forms of social behavior (including sexual and parental behavior) in organisms, up to and including man. General sociobiology, covering the facts and theories for all living creatures, can be usefully distinguished from human sociobiology, which addresses the topics peculiar to man. Most public interest and the bitterest disputes have centered on human applications. But the great majority of sociobiologists are only marginally concerned with this part of the discipline. They are principally zoologists, students of animal behavior who work on various social animals from colonial jellyfish to ants and chimpanzees.

Sociobiology is closely allied to ethology, which can be defined loosely as the study of whole patterns of behavior under natural conditions. Both disciplines pay close attention to the evolutionary history of species and the manner in which behavior (instinct in particular) adapts organisms to their environment. But where ethology focuses on the details of individual behavior, including the activity of the nervous system and the effects of hormones, sociobiology concentrates on the most complex forms of social behavior and the organization of entire societies. Ethology consists to a substantial degree of the study of physiology and anatomy, where sociobiology is grounded in population biology: in the genetics, ecology, age structure, and other biological traits of whole aggregates of individuals.

EVOLUTION BY NATURAL SELECTION

Most of biology is concerned with "how" questions: how cells divide, how protein is digested, how genes prescribe information. Sociobiology concentrates more on "why" questions: why cells divide in a certain way or why parents behave altruistically toward their offspring. The query "why?" can be answered only by the study of history. And the history of biological process is by definition evolution. Its creative process is natural selection, sometimes referred to as Darwinism.

As a consequence, much but not all of sociobiology consists of evolutionary explanations of such forms of social behavior as altruism, cooperation, and aggression, with special emphasis on the role of natural selection. Evolution by natural selection occurs through the following steps.

• Individuals vary in a certain trait, for example the ability to taste a particular poison, owing to differences in genes at one or more locations on the chromosomes. Let us suppose that one kind of gene (located, say, on a particular spot on chromosome number 6) confers the ability to taste the poison, while the opposing gene provides no such competence.

• The presence of the poison in food or water is the selection pressure. Individuals with taster genes detect the substance, avoid it, and survive. Those possessing nontaster genes consume the poison and die. As a result, the frequency of taster genes increases, and a larger percentage of the population has the hereditary ability to avoid the poison. This change from one generation to the next constitutes evolution by natural selection. Individuals able to taste the poison are said to have "superior genetic fitness." The taster trait is spoken of as "adaptive."

• New kinds of genes can arise suddenly in the population by means of mutations, which are either random changes in the chemical composition of preexisting genes or rearrangements of the genes by alterations in the structure or number of the chromosomes. Suppose that in the beginning a population consists exclusively of individuals with nontaster genes. Taster genes might then originate in the population by means of mutations in one or a few individuals. If the poison occurs in food or water, natural selection would ensue, causing the taster genes to increase relative to the nontaster genes throughout the population. In a word, mutations produce the raw materials of evolution, while natural selection gives direction to evolution by determining which mutations will prevail. Incidentally, when man deliberately selects certain genes over others to produce desirable traits in plants and animals, the process is called artificial selection. When he tries to do so with himself, it is called eugenics.

Evolution sometimes proceeds by means other than natural selection. Mutations can occur at such a high frequency as to push up the percentage of mutants in the population without the aid of natural selection. Alternatively, immigrants can bring new genes into the population at a high enough rate to change the overall genetic composition of the population. These auxiliary phenomena occur and are occasionally important, but most biologists agree that they are much less potent than natural selection in directing evolution over long periods of time. In other words, natural selection is the dominant mode of evolution.

Sociobiology has extended this basic model of evolution, which is generally accepted among biologists, into the realm of social behavior. The procedure has been very successful in analyzing and explaining certain complex and previously little understood phenomena in animals. When the method is applied to human beings, the results are much less clear-cut, and they tend to provoke emotional responses. The purpose of the theory of gene-culture coevolution is to permit a deeper and more satisfactory expansion of biology into the domain of the social sciences. We will return to the relation of this theory to general sociobiology, but it would be better first to examine the classic explanations of several of the universal forms of human social behavior.

THE SELFISH GENES

Individuals do not duplicate themselves during the process of reproduction. They duplicate their genes and then scatter them like seeds through the population. This strange process can be clearly visualized with the help of the following arithmetical argument. You receive one half of your genes from each parent, one fourth from each grandparent, one eighth from each great-grandparent, and so on back in a regular geometric progression. An ancestor from the late eighteenth century has bequeathed only about 1 percent of his genes to you by direct descent. Thus our individual set of genes, the hereditary material that makes each one of us biologically distinct, dissolves into smaller and smaller packets as it is traced back into history. And in a perfectly symmetrical pattern, that same set will dissolve again as it is spread among our descendants.

Each child gets one half of its genes from a given parent, each grandchild receives one fourth, and so on. The only unit not ultimately divided in this manner is the gene. At each moment of the continuing present, individual human beings are of course the precious be-all and end-all, but over many generations they can be seen in a different light—as the temporary vehicles by which genes are multiplied and disseminated. From the viewpoint of evolutionary theory, and hence sociobiology, all of the traits of individuals are potential enabling devices for the expansive replication of the hereditary material that prescribes the traits. Color vision, pulse rates, insulin production, linguistic competence, the tendency to enjoy music, and tenderness toward children are creations by which the body and mind may grow strong and spread the genes through future generations. In this special sense, the genes compete in an ultimate race. Those that prescribe full color vision are matched against the various forms that cause color blindness. If color blindness declines in the population due to the handicap it imposes, so do the genes that underwrite it.

The genes come together in new combinations in each generation. Your father may have had blue eyes, the ability to roll his tongue into a tube (30 percent of the population lacks the hereditary ability to do this), AB blood type, and so on across thousands of categories of human traits controlled by particular combinations of genes. But this distinctive combination—your father—was broken into genetic fragments and reassembled into new combinations during the process of sperm production that led to your own creation. As sperm are formed, pairs of chromosomes resembling each other exchange genes and then pull apart to reduce the number of chromosomes by one half. Following insemination, a sperm cell unites with an egg to restore the original chromosome number (two of each kind), thus creating a new individual. In summary, the father's hereditary material undergoes the two basic processes of Mendelian hereditary: segregation, in which the pairs of similar chromosomes are pulled apart and placed in different sperm cells, and recombination, in which matching chromosomes from the father and mother are joined to restore the original double number.

THE MEANING OF SEX

The processes of sex-cell formation and fertilization are not primarily devices for reproduction. In order to replicate themselves, the genes are not required to separate from each other in a way that destroys the integrity of individual heredity. Nature has far more direct and efficient means of reproduction that preserve the entire ensemble of genes intact, such as the production of embryos from unfertilized eggs. Furthermore, sex does not merely serve the purpose of giving pleasure. The exact reverse is the case: the feeling of pleasure in the brain makes the performance of sex more likely and allows the packets of genes to be taken apart and put together again.

The primary role of sex is more subtle than straightforward reproduction: it is the creation of genetic diversity among offspring. An organism that reproduces without sex, say by hatching unfertilized eggs, can replicate itself exactly, gene by gene, without wasting time on courtship. But if all the offspring are identical, they are less likely as a group to withstand important changes in the environment. Suppose that a disease sweeping through the area kills all individuals with the mother's hereditary makeup. If the mother had reproduced in a nonsexual manner, she and all of her offspring would perish. But if she had mated with a male bearing disease-resistant genes, at least some of her offspring would survive. Also surviving would be the tendency to reproduce sexually; sex itself can be said to be favored by natural selection. Sex is slower than nonsex, but it provides a balanced array of genetic combinations to present to the world. It spreads the hereditary investment, including all the time and energy that go into reproduction, in a way that copes more consistently with harsh and constantly changing environments. Most biologists agree that adaptability, the general ability to adapt, is just as important as adaptiveness, the actual set of responses made by organisms to the environment that keeps them alive and allows them to reproduce. This long-term property is what has given sex an edge through eons of evolution and fixed it in the biology of most kinds of organisms.

We come now to the question of the differences between the sexes. When sexuality is examined in various types of organisms, from lower plants and animals to man, the fundamental distinction between males and females is seen to be based not on any set of outward anatomical traits but on the more basic character of the sex cells. Simply put, females produce large sex cells (eggs) containing yolk for the nourishment of the embryo, while males produce small sex cells (sperm) designed exclusively for the fertilization of the eggs. There is a cooperative division of labor: the female typically nourishes the embryos and sometimes goes so far as to carry them in her body or to build a nest for added protection. The male fertilizes the eggs and in a few species stays around to help care for the young. At the absolute minimum, the female and male create various combinations of their personal genes to face the unknown rigors of the future environment. Further commitment to the young is an option in evolution chosen by a minority of species, of which one happens to be *Homo sapiens.*

Because females contribute more to each fertilization, they are able to participate in fewer procreations. The average woman launches only about 400 eggs into her uterus during her lifetime, but every physiologically normal man releases millions of sperm each time he ejaculates. As a result, one male has the capacity to participate in a vastly greater number of fertilizations than a female.

Evolutionary theory predicts that several important consequences will follow from this elementary difference between the sexes. Perhaps the most basic is that males as a rule have a good deal more to gain by competing for mates. A Don Juan can theoretically become a father every night. But if he succeeds in achieving many fertilizations, a corresponding number of males must fail to become fathers. Throughout the animal kingdom, and in most human societies as well, males in fact compete aggressively with each other for territory, status, and above all access to females. There is a strong selection pressure to acquire, in Darwin's words, both "the power to charm the ladies" and "the power to conquer other males in battle." This is sexual selection, a special form of natural selection. As a result males are typically more reckless and ostentatious than females, and extremely intolerant of being cheated. Yet in many species, including the human, they are equally capable of forming close and affectionate bonds with their mates and offspring, as well as friendly alliances with other males.

In most higher animal species, females also participate in sexual selection, but in a qualitatively different manner. They can be inseminated in a given reproductive cycle by only one male, and they usually have the greater burden of looking after the young. Therefore it is to their advantage to be more discriminating: flirtatious, to attract many suitors, but also hesitant, socially skilled, and perceptive in order to mate with the best of the males. By "best" in this case is meant the most competent in dealing with other males and, among those species in which males help to rear the young, the male most likely to devote himself cheerfully to that task.

In view of these circumstances it is not surprising that most animal species are polygynous—males prefer to mate with more than one female. And relatively few are polyandrous, with females forming a bond with more than one male.

ALTRUISM

In its narrowest conception, evolution by natural selection—Darwinism—seems to imply survival of the fittest, the triumph of some individuals over others and the perpetuation of their genes in the next generation. But surrounding this unappealing image is a soft glow of altruistic behavior. We know that parents are willing to sacrifice a great deal on behalf of their children, even their own lives. Such behavior still conforms to Darwinism in the strict sense, because so long as children are preserved the parent's genes are passed on. If the self-sacrificing behavior of the parent is prescribed by some of the favored genes, then that particular form of altruism will be spread through the population.

Altruism of a broader kind can evolve by essentially the same mechanism. Note that brothers and sisters are just as closely related to each other as parents and offspring. Put another way, any two siblings share half their genes through common descent—the same fraction as that shared by a given parent and child. If a man makes a sacrifice on behalf of his brother or sister, and as a result of his act the sibling has more children, the man's altruistic act will cause an increase in the number of genes that are identical to his own. This form of natural selection is called kin selection, and it can cause a spread of altruistic behavior toward close kin other than direct offspring. Suppose that an individual either dies or gives up any chance to have children in order to perform an altruistic service. The biological result is the same for both cases—no direct transmission of genes to the next generation. Suppose also that variations in the prosperity for altruistic behavior result from corresponding changes in certain of the genes. The question is: how much good must the beneficent act do the relatives in order for such genes to spread? The answer is that the number of offspring must be increased by a factor that is the reciprocal of the fraction of genes that are identical through common descent. The relation is simple. A brother has half of his genes identical to those of the altruist. So the sacrifice of the altruist must result in at least a doubling of the number of the brother's offspring for the altruism-causing genes to be spread (the reciprocal of 1/2 is 2). A first cousin has one eighth of his genes identical; if the altruism is directed at first cousins alone, their offspring must be increased at least eightfold for the altruism genes to spread. And so on.

We can see why hard-core altruism, given freely and without thought of reciprocation, is usually confined to the closest relatives, in both animals and human beings. Outside the circle of first cousins, only a spectacular increase in the success of the benefited relative is sufficient to compensate for a unilateral sacrifice. In human beings and a few of the most intelligent monkeys and apes, the circle of altruism is broadened by reciprocal altruism. In this soft-core form of giving, the altruistic act is performed with the expectation that the beneficiary will repay in kind at some future date.

Sociobiology is often said to take the goodness out of altruism. This characterization, which refers to the hard-core version of the behavior, means that while an individual may give up an advantage, perhaps even his life, the genes that prescribe such behavior give up nothing; on the contrary, they gain in number and influence. This difference is not really a contradiction. It is simply natural selection working simultaneously at two levels, that of the gene and that of the individual organism. The individual can behave in a moral and unselfish manner toward others, but his conduct results in an even greater proliferation of his genes than if he acted with consistent selfishness.

AGGRESSION

Aggression consists of a diversity of behaviors united only by the common feature of harmful action or the threat of harm to others. Some animals display several different stereotyped forms of aggression. When facing most larger enemies, a rattlesnake coils, draws its neck and head into an S-shaped striking posture near the center of the coil, and vibrates its rattle. If the adversary is a kingsnake, a particularly dangerous predator on other kinds of snakes, the rattlesnake pulls its head beneath the coils and slaps at the intruder with an extended loop of its body. When pursuing prey of its own, such as a mouse, it neither coils nor rattles but strikes silently from any convenient position. Finally, two male rattlesnakes fighting over access to females engage in neck wrestling. Although one could kill the other with a single venomous strike, they do not. The two snakes settle the dispute with a ritualized form of fighting that usually gives the advantage to the larger and stronger contender.

The rattlesnake illustrates several important features in the evolution of aggression. First, a great deal of the behavior consists of threat and ritual. Animals expend large amounts of time and energy persuading their adversaries that they are powerful and dangerous. When fighting does occur between members of the same species, it is most commonly in the form of ritualized combat. In such exchanges the contender who is thrown to the ground, pushed out of the arena, or otherwise bested usually accepts his defeat. He leaves the field uninjured and tries his luck elsewhere. Sometimes the exchange is limited to purely visual displays. In the great majority of cases the contest is won by the individual who is being pressed on his own territory by an invader. When no such initial advantage exists, as when the contenders meet on neutral ground, it is usually the large individual who prevails. Only when an individual is trapped and physically endangered is he likely to resort to escalated fighting, an all-out attempt to destroy the opponent.

Rattlesnakes are also typical of most kinds of animals in the opportunism displayed by their evolution. Each of the four forms of aggression they employ is clearly shaped to serve a particular function. This circumstance leads to an interesting question in evolutionary theory. If no relevant function existed in a given species, would the absence of a need result in the absence of aggression? The answer is yes, so far as we can tell. Species of animals are known that appear to lack all forms of such behavior. Aggression, apart from the seizing of prey and defense against predators, is a device to deal with competition for limited resources. When competition is lacking, the capacity for aggressive behavior is absent. Some plant-feeding insect species are kept at moderate population levels by predators, disease, and emigration. They rarely become abundant enough to run out of food, shelter, or places to lay their eggs.

Such species do not "rely" on competition to regulate their numbers, and aggressive behavior has not been added to their repertory. Another way of putting the matter is that there is no generalized instinct of aggression that permeates animal behavior, as implied in the earlier writings of Sigmund Freud, Robert Ardrey, and Konrad Lorenz. Aggressive behavior is opportunistic, tending to evolve into certain forms that appear and are shaped genetically according to the particular needs of the species.

Ecologists and sociobiologists have made substantial progress in defining the circumstances under which the varieties of animal aggression evolve. Territoriality, the defense of a space by means of threats of fighting, is most likely to appear when some part of the living space of the animal contains a resource that is both in short supply and predictable in occurrence. Thus if a location contains a regular supply of food or a superior roosting site, and either of these resources is scarce enough to limit population growth, animals are likely to try to preempt that part of the space. But in addition this territory must be defensible in an economic sense; the risk of life and the energy spent to maintain it must be outweighed by the benefits gained through owning exclusive rights to it. In fact, animals tend to defend areas that are just large enough to provide them with their minimal needs on a year-round basis.

SOCIAL BEHAVIOR

When the full sweep of social evolution is examined from bacteria to man, the following paradox emerges. As we ascend the evolutionary scale arranged on the basis of anatomy, physiology, and brain size, we descend in the quality of the traits intuitively associated with sociality, namely cooperation, altruism, division of labor, and integration.

For convenience we can recognize four pinnacles across this array, represented by the colonial invertebrates (corals, sponges, colonial jellyfish); the social insects (ants, bees, wasps, termites); monkeys, apes, and other social mammals exclusive of man; and man himself. The members of coral colonies and similar tightly clustered groups of invertebrates originate from a single fertilized egg and multiply by the simple fission and budding off of entire new organisms. As a result the individuals living together are identical in hereditary composition. So kin selection can easily overcome strictly individual selection: looking after a neighbor is just the same as looking after oneself so far as replicating genes are concerned. This circumstance clears the way for the evolution of extreme forms of social organization. The members of the advanced colonies are fitted together into a superorganism almost indistinguishable from a single, well-knit organism. Thus the Portuguese man-of-war resembles a large jellyfish but is actually made up of a cluster of many very specialized individuals.

One at the top forms the bladderlike float, others farther down are bell-shaped structures that propel the colony through the water, while still others at the bottom are shaped into tentacles and odd receptacles for the receipt and digestion of food. Only a few individuals contribute sex cells for the production of new colonies.

The same considerations hold for the social insects, but to a lesser degree. Colonies of bees, wasps, and ants comprise mostly sisters. Because of peculiarities in the way in which sex is determined in these hymenopterous insects, sisters are more closely related to one another than are mothers and daughters. On the average, three quarters of their genes are identical by common descent instead of the usual one half. It is also true, probably as a partial result of the genetic similarity, that most of the females in a colony are sterile workers, who are often further modified into specialized castes such as nurses and soldiers. The insect society is far less well integrated than that of the Portuguese man-of-war and other colonial invertebrates, but it is still much more so than mammal and human societies. Its members live in a state of impersonal intimacy. The individual worker is almost always in close touch with other colony members, and virtually everything it does is directed to the welfare of the colony. Hence it can be truthfully said that one ant is no ant. On the other hand, the workers do not recognize each other as individuals. Their entire behavior is conducted with reference to the colony population as a whole, or at the very most to the queen and various castes, and not to other individual workers.

The mammalian societies represent a radical departure. The members of a monkey troop or an elephant herd are less intimately associated than are the colonial invertebrates and insects. They also recognize and treat each other as individuals. They create dominance hierarchies, pair off to mate, and form into kin groups. Whereas the worker ant always acts for the good of the queen, the individual mammal only marginally serves the welfare of its group. In fact the opposite relation holds: social life is exploited for the improvement of individual survival and reproduction. In comparison with ant workers, the members of a mammal society are extremely self-centered, strife-ridden, and preoccupied with sexual roles.

Then (and here we encounter a real paradox) the downward trend leading from the social invertebrates to the mammals is partly reversed in *Homo sapiens*. Human beings are unique in their possession of a fully symbolic language, an enlarged memory, and long-term contracts upon which elaborate forms of reciprocity can be based. They have attained relatively high levels of cooperation, altruism, division of labor, and social integration. All this has been accomplished without surrendering the ancient mammalian heritage of personal identity and welfare. But how? And where do the mind and culture fit into the picture? We have come at last to the root of the sociobiology controversy—or, more accurately, the sociobiology controversies, for there were two that flared up in rapid succession in the late 1970s.

QUESTIONS FOR CRITICAL READERS

Remembering and Understanding

1. Summarize Lumsden and Wilson's explanation of sociobiology.
2. Explain the advantages of genetic diversity.
3. Explain the connection between natural selection and sociobiology.

Analyzing and Discussing

4. Lumsden and Wilson make it clear that sociobiology does not address individual behavior, but "the genetics, ecology, age structure, and other biological traits of whole aggregates of individuals." Why is this distinction important?
5. How might Wilson's training as an entomologist have influenced his view of the origins of human behavior?
6. What are the similarities and differences (to the best of your present knowledge) between human society and an invertebrate colony or an insect society?

Writing

7. The extension of the principles of natural selection into the realm of social behavior, especially in humans, has provoked a number of negative reactions. Choose one of the concepts of sociobiology explained here, and write a paper in which you explain why some readers might object to it. At the same time, explain how Wilson might respond to those objections.

On Living in a Biological Revolution

—————— DONALD FLEMING ——————

Fleming, a historian, wrote this essay in 1969. His purpose was to assemble the biological discoveries of the previous fifteen years in one place and argue that those changes amounted to a revolution, a fundamental change in biological science and its effects on the way humans live. Much of what Fleming describes is no longer startling or new, and some of his predictions about the future were probably too timid. He does, however, give a clear account of the scientific and intellectual climate in which Wilson developed his ideas about sociobiology.

HERE ARE A DOZEN THINGS that we have discovered in the last fifteen years.

1. We have discovered the structure of the genetic substance DNA—the double helix of Watson and Crick—the general nature of the process by which the chromosomal strands are replicated.

2. We have discovered in viruses how to achieve the perfect replication of DNA molecules that are biologically effective.

3. We have discovered the code by which DNA specifies the insertion of amino acids in proteins.

4. We have discovered how to produce hybrid cells between the most diverse vertebrate species, including hybrids between man and mouse; and some of these hybrids have gone on multiplying for several (cellular) generations.

5. We have discovered the power of viruses to invade bacterial and other cells and to insert the genes of the virus into the genome of the host; and we have good reason to conjecture, though not yet to affirm, that this phenomenon is involved in cancer.

6. We have discovered hormonal contraceptives and grasped in principle the strategy for devising a contraceptive pill for *both* sexes, by knocking out certain hormones of the hypothalamus, the master sexual gland of the body.

7. We have discovered on a large scale in the livestock industry that deep-frozen mammalian sperm, suitably mixed with glycerol, can be banked indefinitely and drawn upon as desired to produce viable offspring.

8. We have discovered in human females how to produce superovulation, the release of several eggs into the oviduct at the same time instead of the customary one, with the possibility on the horizon of withdrawing substantial numbers of human eggs for storage, culture in test tubes, or surgical manipulation, without destroying their viability.

9. We have discovered in rabbits how to regulate the sex of offspring by removing fertilized ova from the female before they become implanted in the wall of the uterus, "sexing" the embryos by a technique entailing the deletion of some 200 to 300 cells, flushing embryos of the "wrong" sex down the drain, and then in a substantial minority of cases, successfully reinserting in the uterus embryos of the desired sex that proceed to develop normally.

10. We have discovered drugs, above all the hallucinogens, that simulate psychotic states of mind; and have thereby rendered it plausible that the latter are the product of "inborn errors of metabolism" and as such remediable by the administration of drugs.

11. We have discovered in principle, and to a certain extent in practice, how to repress the immunological "defenses" of the body.

12. We have discovered a combination of immunological and surgical techniques by which the kidney, liver, or heart can be transplanted with fair prospects of the recipient's survival for months or even years—the first constructive proposal for turning our death wish on the highways to some advantage.

Each of these is a major discovery or complex of discoveries in itself, but they add up to far more than the sum of their parts. They constitute a veritable Biological Revolution likely to be as decisive for the history of the next 150 years as the Industrial Revolution has been for the period since 1750.

Definitions of what constitutes a revolution are legion. An undoctrinaire formulation would be that every full-scale revolution has three main components: a distinctive attitude toward the world; a program for utterly transforming it; and an unshakable, not to say fanatical, confidence that this program can be enacted—a world view, a program, and a faith.

In this sense, Darwinism did not usher in a full-scale biological revolution. Darwinism was a profoundly innovating world view, but one that prescribed no steps to be taken, no victories over nature to be celebrated, no program of triumphs to be successively gained. Indeed, one of the most plausible constructions to be put upon it was that nothing much *could* be done except to submit patiently to the winnowing processes of nature.

This defect was not lost upon Darwin's own cousin Sir Francis Galton, who tried to construct an applied science of eugenics for deliberately selecting out the best human stocks. But Galtonian eugenics was sadly lacking in any authentic biological foundation. Once the science of Mendelian genetics came to general notice about 1900, a more promising form of eugenics began to commend itself, the effort to induce artificial mutation of genes in desirable directions.

This was long the animating faith of one of the most extraordinary Americans of the twentieth century, the geneticist Herman J. Muller. He was the actual discoverer, in 1927, of artificial mutation through X rays. But this great achievement, for which he got the Nobel Prize, was a tremendous disappointment to Muller the revolutionary. There was no telling which genes would mutate in which direction, and he came to suspect that the vast majority of mutations were actually harmful in the present situation of the human race.

Muller at the end of his life—he died in 1967—was thrown back upon essentially Galtonian eugenics. He did bring this up to date by his proposal for sperm banks in which the sperm of exceptionally intelligent and socially useful men could be stored for decades and used for artificial insemination. He also envisioned, in the not too distant future, ova banks for storing superior human eggs. But none of these modern touches, these innovations in technique, could conceal the fact that this was still the old eugenics newly garbed, but equally subjective and imprecise.

BIOLOGICAL ENGINEERING

The Biological Revolution that Muller failed to bring off was already in progress when he died, but on very different terms from his own. There is a new eugenics in prospect, not the marriage agency kind, but a form of "biological engineering." When this actually comes to pass, chromosomes, segments of chromosomes, and even individual genes will be inserted at will into the genome. Alternatively, germ cells cultured in laboratories will be enucleated and entire tailor-made DNA molecules substituted. Alternatively still, superior genes will be brought into play by hybridization of cells.

The detailed variants upon these general strategies are almost innumerable. They all have in common the fact that they cannot be accomplished at present except in viruses and bacteria or in cell cultures. But it would be a bold man who would dogmatically affirm that none of these possibilities could be brought to bear upon human genetics by the year 2000.

That is a long way off for the firebrands of the Biological Revolution. The Nobel Prize winner Joshua Lederberg in particular has been pushing the claims of a speedier remedy, christened by him "euphenics," and defined as "the engineering of human development." The part of human development that fascinates Lederberg the most is embryology, seen by him as the process of initially translating the instructions coded in the DNA into "the living, breathing organism." Embryology, he says, is "very much in the situation of atomic physics in 1900; having had an honorable and successful tradition it is about to begin!" He thinks it will not take long to mature—"from 5 to no more than 20 years." He adds that most predictions of research progress in recent times have proved to be "far too conservative."

The progress that Lederberg has in mind is the application of new embryological techniques to human affairs. He is at once maddened and obsessed by the nine-months phase in which the human organism has been exempted from experimental and therapeutic intervention—such a waste of time before the scientists can get at us. But the embryo's turn is coming. It would be incredible, he says, "if we did not soon have the basis of developmental engineering technique to regulate, for example, the size of the human brain by prenatal or early postnatal intervention."

SEX CONTROL

Nothing as sensational as this has yet been attempted, but the new phase in embryology that Lederberg heralded is undoubtedly getting under way. The most conspicuous figure at present is Robert Edwards of the physiology laboratory at Cambridge University. In 1966 Edwards reported the culture of immature egg cells from the human ovary up to the point of ripeness for fertilization. He made tentative claims to have actually achieved fertilization in test tubes. The incipient hullabaloo in the newspapers about the specter of "test tube babies" led Edwards to clamp a tight lid of security over his researches in progress.

In the spring of this year, however, he and Richard Gardner announced their success in "sexing" fertilized rabbit eggs before implantation in the wall of the uterus and then inducing 20 percent of the reinserted eggs to produce normal full-term infants. The aspect of these findings that attracted general attention, the prospect of regulating the sex of mammalian offspring, is not likely to be of permanent interest. For this purpose, Edwards and Gardner's technique is obviously a clumsy expedient by comparison with predetermining the "sex" of spermatozoa—

presently impossible but certainly not inconceivable within the next generation.

The real importance of Edwards and Gardner's work lies elsewhere. They have opened up the possibility of subjecting the early embryo to microsurgery, with the deletion and "inoculation" of cells at the will of the investigator, *and* the production of viable offspring from the results. The manufacture of "chimeras" in the modern biological sense—that is, with genetically distinct cells in the same organism—is clearly in prospect.

Work in this vein has just begun. The only branch of euphenics that has already become something more than a promising growth stock in science is the suppression of immunological reactions against foreign tissues and the accompanying, highly limited, successes in the transplantation of organs.

BIOLOGICAL REVOLUTIONARIES

The technical details and immediate prospects in eugenics and euphenics, however fascinating, are less important than the underlying revolutionary temper in biology. The most conspicuous representatives of this temper are Lederberg himself, the biochemical geneticist Edward L. Tatum, and Francis Crick of the model—all of them Nobel Prize winners, with the corresponding leverage upon public opinion. Robert Edwards, though slightly singed by the blast of publicity about test tube babies, is clearly in training for the revolutionary cadre.

One of the stigmata of revolutionaries in any field is their resolute determination to break with traditional culture. For a scientist, the most relevant definition of culture is his own field of research. All of these men would angrily resent being bracketed with biologists in general. Biology has always been a rather loose confederation of naturalists and experimentalists, overlapping in both categories with medical researchers. Today even the pretense that these men somehow constitute a community has been frayed to the breaking point.

At Harvard, for example, the revolutionaries have virtually seceded from the old Biology Department and formed a new department of their own, Biochemistry and Molecular Biology. The younger molecular biologists hardly bother to conceal their contempt for the naturalists, whom they see as old fogies obsequiously attentive to the world as it is rather than bent upon turning it upside down.

In one respect, the molecular biologists do overlap with the contemporary naturalists and indeed with most creative scientists in general— in their total detachment from religion. In a way, this is a point that could have been made at any time in the last seventy-five years, but with one significant difference. Herman Muller, for example, born in 1890, had no truck with religion. But he was self-consciously antireligious.

The biological revolutionaries of today are not antireligious but simply unreligious. They give the impression not of defending themselves against religion but of subsisting in a world where that has never been a felt pressure upon them. They would agree with many devout theologians that we are living in a post-Christian world, to such an extent that some of the most doctrinaire biological revolutionaries are able to recognize without embarrassment, and even with a certain gracious condescension, that Christianity did play a useful role in defining the values of the Western world.

The operative word here is in the past tense. Francis Crick says that the facts of science are producing and must produce values that owe nothing to Christianity. "Take," he says, "the suggestion of making a child whose head is twice as big as normal. There is going to be no agreement between Christians and any humanists who lack their particular prejudice about the sanctity of the individual, and who simply want to try it scientifically."

This sense of consciously taking up where religion left off is illuminating in another sense for the revolutionary character of contemporary biology. The parallel is very marked between the original Christian Revolution against the values of the classical world and the Biological Revolution against religious values.

All the great revolutionaries, whether early Christians or molecular biologists, are men of good hope. The future may or may not belong to those who believe in it, but cannot belong to those who don't. Yet at certain points in history, most conspicuously perhaps at intervals between the close of the Thirty Years' War in 1648 and the coming of the Great Depression in 1929, the horizons seem to be wide open, and the varieties of good hope contending for allegiance are numerous. But the tidings of good hope don't become revolutionary except when the horizons begin to close in and the plausible versions of good hope have dwindled almost to the vanishing point.

For the kind of good hope that has the maximum historical impact is the one that capitalizes upon a prevalent despair at the corruption of the existing world, and then carries conviction in pointing to itself as the only possible exit from despair. Above everything else, revolutionaries are the men who keep their spirits up when everybody else's are sagging. In this sense, the greatest revolutionaries of the Western world to date have been precisely the early Christians who dared to affirm in the darkest days of the classical world that something far better was in process and could be salvaged from the ruins.

Both of these points are exemplified in the Biological Revolution that has now begun—despair at our present condition, but infinite hope for the future if the biologists' prescription is taken. Anybody looking for jeremiads on our present state could not do better than to consult the new biologists. "The facts of human reproduction," says Joshua Lederberg, "are all gloomy—the stratification of fecundity by economic status, the new environmental insults to our genes, the sheltering by humanitarian medicine of once-lethal genes."

More generally, the biologists deplore the aggressive instincts of the human animal, now armed with nuclear weapons, his lamentably low average intelligence for coping with increasingly complicated problems, and his terrible prolificity, no longer mitigated by a high enough death rate. It is precisely an aspect of the closing down of horizons and depletion of comfortable hopes in the second half of the twentieth century that conventional medicine is now seen by the biological revolutionaries as one of the greatest threats to the human race.

Yet mere prophets of gloom can never make a revolution. In fact, the new biologists are almost the only group among our contemporaries with a reasoned hopefulness about the long future—if the right path is taken. There are of course many individuals of a naturally cheerful or feckless temperament, today as always, but groups of men with an articulated hope for the future of the entire race are much rarer. The theologians no longer qualify, many Communists have lost their hold upon the future even by their own lights, and the only other serious contenders are the space scientists and astronauts. But just to get off the earth is a rather vague prescription for our ills. Few people even in the space program would make ambitious claims on this score. In a long historical retrospect, they may turn out to have been too modest.

This is not a charge that is likely ever to be leveled against the new biologists. It is well known by now that J.D. Watson begins his account of his double-helix double by saying that he had never seen Francis Crick in a modest mood. But after all, modesty is not the salient quality to be looked for in the new breed of biologists. If the world will only listen, they *know* how to put us on the high road to salvation.

CUSTOM-MADE PEOPLE

What exactly does their brand of salvation entail? Perhaps the most illuminating way to put the matter is that their ideal is the manufacture of man. In a manufacturing process, the number of units to be produced is a matter of rational calculation beforehand and of tight control thereafter. Within certain tolerances, specifications are laid down for a satisfactory product. Quality-control is maintained by checking the output and replacing defective parts. After the product has been put to use, spare parts can normally be supplied to replace those that have worn out.

This is the program of the new biologists—control of numbers by foolproof contraception; gene manipulation and substitution; surgical and biochemical intervention in the embryonic and neonatal phases; organ transplants or replacements at will.

Of these, only contraception is technically feasible at present. Routine organ transplants will probably be achieved for a wide range of suitable organs in less than five years. The grafting of mechanical organs, prosthetic devices inserted in the body, will probably take longer. Joshua Lederberg thinks that embryonic and neonatal intervention may be in flood tide by, say, 1984. As for gene manipulation and substitution in human beings, that is the remotest prospect of all—maybe by the year 2000. But we must not forget Lederberg's well-founded conviction that most predictions in these matters are likely to be too conservative. We are already five to ten years ahead of what most informed people expected to be the schedule for organ transplants in human beings.

The great question becomes, what is it going to be like living in a world where such things are coming true? How will the Biological Revolution affect our scheme of values? Nobody could possibly take in all the implications in advance, but some reasonable conjectures are in order.

It is virtually certain that the moral sanctions of birth control are going to be transformed. Down to the present time, the battle for birth control has been fought largely in terms of the individual couple's right to have the number of babies that they want at the desired intervals. But it is built into the quantity-controls envisioned by the Biological Revolution, the control of the biological inventory, that this is or ought to be a question of social policy rather than individual indulgence.

Many factors are converging upon many people to foster this general attitude, but the issue is particularly urgent from the point of view of the biological revolutionaries. In the measure that they succeed in making the human race healthier, first by transplants and later on by genetic tailoring, they will be inexorably swamped by their own successes unless world population is promptly brought under control. The irresponsible Malthus is springing from his lightly covered grave to threaten them with catastrophic victories.

LICENSED BABIES

The only hope is birth control. The biologists can contribute the techniques, but the will to employ them on the requisite scale is another matter. The most startling proposal to date for actually enforcing birth control does not come from a biologist but from the Nobel-Prize-winning physicist W.B. Shockley, one of the inventors of the transistor. Shockley's plan is to render all women of childbearing age reversibly sterile by implanting a contraceptive capsule beneath the skin, to be removed by a physician only on the presentation of a government license to have a child.

The mind boggles at the prospect of bootleg babies. This particular proposal is not likely to be enacted in the near future, even in India.

What we may reasonably expect is a continually rising chorus by the biologists, moralists, and social philosophers of the next generation to the effect that nobody has a right to have children, and still less the right to determine on personal grounds how many. There are many reasons why a couple may not want to be prolific anyhow, so that there might be a happy coincidence between contraception seen by them as a right and by statesmen and biologists as a duty. But the suspicion is that even when people moderate their appetite in the matter of babies, they may still want to have larger families than the earth can comfortably support. The possibility of predetermining sex would undoubtedly be helpful in this respect, but might not be enough to make people forgo a third child. That is where the conflict would arise between traditional values, however moderately indulged, and the values appropriate to the Biological Revolution.

This issue is bound to be fiercely debated. But some of the most profound implications of the Biological Revolution may never present themselves for direct ratification. In all probability, the issues will go by default as we gratefully accept specific boons from the new biology.

Take, for example, the role of the patient in medicine. One of the principal strands in Western medicine from the time of the Greeks has been the endeavor to enlist the cooperation of the patient in his own cure. In certain respects, this venerable tradition has grown much stronger in the last century. Thus the rising incidence of degenerative diseases, like ulcers, heart trouble, and high blood pressure, has underscored the absolute necessity of inducing the patient to observe a healthful regimen, literally a way of life.

This has been the whole point of Freudian psychiatry as a mode of therapy, that cures can be wrought only by a painful exertion of the patient himself. We often forget, for good reasons, how traditional Freudianism is after the one big shock has been assimilated. In the present context, it actually epitomizes the Western tradition of bringing the patient's own personality to bear upon his medical problems.

Where do we go from here? The degenerative diseases are going to be dealt with increasingly by surgical repair of organs, by organ transplants, and later on by the installation of mechanical organs and eventually by the genetic deletion of weak organs before they occur. The incentive to curb your temper or watch your diet to keep your heart going will steadily decline.

As for mental illness, the near future almost certainly lies with psychopharmacology and the far future with genetic tailoring. Though the final pieces stubbornly decline to fall into place, the wise money is on the proposition that schizophrenia and other forms of psychosis are biochemical disorders susceptible of a pharmacological cure. If we are not presently curing any psychoses by drugs, we are tranquilizing and anti-depressing many psychotics and emptying mental hospitals.

Neuroses, the theme of Freudian psychoanalysis, are another matter. It is not easy to envision a biochemical remedy for them. But even for neuroses, we already have forms of behavioral therapy that dispense with the Freudian tenet of implicating the patient in his own cure. For the *very* long future, it is certainly not inconceivable that genetic tailoring could delete neurotic propensities.

Everywhere we turn, the story is essentially the same. Cures are increasingly going to be wrought upon, done to, the patient as a passive object. The strength of his own personality, the force of his character, his capacity for reintegrating himself, are going to be increasingly irrelevant in medicine.

GENETIC TAILORING, BOON OR BANE?

This leads to what many people would regard as the biggest question of all. In what sense would we have a self to integrate under the new dispensation? The Princeton theologian Paul Ramsey has now been appointed professor of "genetic ethics" at the Georgetown University Medical School, presumably the first appointment of its kind. He thinks that genetic tailoring would be a "violation of man." To this it must be said that under the present scheme of things, many babies get born with catastrophic genes that are not exactly an enhancement of man. Our present genetic self is a brute datum, sometimes very brutal, and anyhow it is hard to see how we can lose our identity before we have any.

As for installing new organs in the body, there is no evident reason why the personality should be infringed upon by heart or kidney transplants per se. Brain transplants would be different, but surely they would be among the last to come. States of mind regulated by drugs we already possess, and obviously they do alter our identity in greater or lesser degree. But even here we must not forget that some identities are intolerable to their distracted possessors.

We must not conclude, however, that the importance of these developments has been exaggerated. The point is that the immediate practical consequences will probably not present themselves as threatening to the individuals involved—quite the contrary. Abstract theological speculations about genetic tailoring would be totally lost upon a woman who could be sure in advance that her baby would not be born mentally retarded or physically handicapped. The private anxieties of individuals are likely to diminish rather than increase any effective resistance to the broader consequences of the Biological Revolution.

One of these is already implicit in predicting a sense of growing passivity on the part of patients, of not participating as a subject in their own recovery. This might well be matched by a more general sense of the inevitability of letting oneself be manipulated by technicians—of becoming an article of manufacture.

The difficulty becomes to estimate what psychological difference this would make. In any Hegelian overview of history, we can only become articles of manufacture because "we" have set up as the manufacturers. But the first person plural is a slippery customer. We the manufactured would be everybody and we the manufacturers a minority of scientists and technicians. Most people's capacity to identify with the satisfactions of the creative minority is certainly no greater in science than in other fields, and may well be less.

The beneficiaries of the Biological Revolution are not likely to feel that they are in control of the historical process from which they are benefiting. But they will not be able to indulge any feelings of alienation from science without endangering the specific benefits that they are unwilling to give up.

The best forecast would be for general acquiescence, though occasionally sullen, in whatever the Biological Revolution has to offer and gradually adjusting our values to signify that we approve of what we will actually be getting. The will to cooperate in being made biologically perfect is likely to take the place in the hierarchy of values that used to be occupied by being humbly submissive to spiritual counselors chastising the sinner for his own salvation. The new form of spiritual sloth will be not to want to be bodily perfect and genetically improved. The new avarice will be to cherish our miserable board of genes and favor the children that resemble us.

QUESTIONS FOR CRITICAL READERS

Remembering and Understanding

1. According to Fleming, what will be the major social consequences of the biological revolution that he describes?
2. What kind of world does Fleming envision from his vantage point of 1969? What are his hopes? What are his fears?
3. Describe Fleming's idea of a biological revolutionary. What are such people like? What do they want to accomplish?
4. What is Fleming's attitude toward the biological revolution he describes? What specific words and phrases in his essay convey that attitude to you?

Analyzing and Discussing

5. Choose one of the discoveries Fleming describes, and explain specifically how it challenges traditional values.
6. To what extent were Fleming's speculations about the future correct or incorrect? What has not happened that he predicted? What has happened that Fleming did not anticipate? How has the biological revolution influenced society during the past twenty to twenty-five years?

Writing

7. Assume that it were possible to manipulate human genetics to produce any kind of person. Write a paper in which you describe what the ideal person would be like.

Sociobiology

——— LOREN GRAHAM ———

Edward O. Wilson has called the discussion printed here a "balanced account of the history and political implications of sociobiology." This selection is from Graham's book, Between Science and Values. *Graham is a historian of science, and in this selection he examines sociobiology within the context of other types of research into animal and human behavior.*

THE MOST COMPREHENSIVE and authoritative delineator of social and human significance in biology in the 1970s was the Harvard entomologist, E.O. Wilson, whose 1975 book *Sociobiology* provoked a great controversy that entered into the pages of many general-interest publications. Wilson was praised and criticized, hailed and condemned. In some quarters the discussion became primarily political, and Wilson was castigated for advancing conservative, establishment views that potentially could hinder social reforms.

I will give my view of the validity of these criticisms below, but first I wish to approach the problem of interpreting Wilson's work from quite a different direction, as I think this avenue is the most fruitful one. Instead of initially concentrating on the place of this one book in an ideological context, I would like to consider the development of Wilson's views over time and some of the main interests and motives that brought him to his major topics. The later analysis will then be built on this foundation.

A helpful approach to understanding Wilson's work is to examine his three major works of the seventies together, the 1971 *The Insect Societies*, the 1975 *Sociobiology*, and the 1978 *On Human Nature*. The 1971 book is important for understanding the 1975 and 1978 publications, and, indeed, for appreciating the overall direction of Wilson's intellectual development. And Wilson himself spoke of the "momentum left from writing *The Insect Societies*" which helped him "to attempt a general synthesis."

Although the books differ greatly in the comprehensiveness of the material covered, they have in some respects organizational or "morphological" similarities. Each book discussed a certain topic in great detail

531

and then in its last chapters issued a call for extension of the analysis into a much larger area. Thus, *The Insect Societies* was almost entirely a discussion of the social insects, but the last chapter addressed a much more ambitious task, "The Prospect for a Unified Sociobiology," and contained in embryo the plan for the 1975 book. *Sociobiology*, in turn, was almost completely a description and analysis of invertebrate and vertebrate zoology and behavior, but the last chapter was entitled, "Man: From Sociobiology to Sociology." It contained an ambitious expansionist call for the "biologicization" of ethics and sociology. *On Human Nature* dealt to a large degree with ethics and values, but the last chapters were on "religion" and "hope." If the logic of the trilogy were continued, the next book would be on religion. And, indeed, Wilson stated in the third book that "religion constitutes the greatest challenge to human sociobiology and its most exciting opportunity to progress as a truly original theoretical discipline."

In the research that led to these books, Wilson grounded himself in theoretical conceptions about the significance of the animal world for larger, ultimately human problems, but the nature of these conceptions changed in an essential way during the work. Indeed, I will speak of two different models that served as frameworks for his work, although they can be placed on a conceptual continuum on which the discrete two models are merely convenient points of analysis. What did *not* change was Wilson's desire to have such a model as a goal for his work, that is, as an illustration of the relevance of his work for large human concerns.

Entomologists have often been considered by other scientists, even by other biologists, as somewhat narrowed empiricists, people who collect and classify a staggering variety of insect forms, but who have not made many theoretical contributions to the science of biology as a whole. In this century geneticists and molecular biologists have usually considered themselves much closer to the theoretical core of biology.

It seems likely that this perception of entomologists has strengthened the desire of many of them, including several of the most talented, to illustrate the theoretical relevance of their work. Wilson's illustrious predecessor at Harvard, William Morton Wheeler, wrote fascinating articles and books that are best described as "biological philosophy" as well as many classical, rigorous studies of ants and social insects. One of Wheeler's philosophical ideas, to be discussed below, had a strong influence on Wilson, even though Wilson eventually abandoned it. But Wilson always emulated his predecessor in requiring that his work have comprehensive, theoretical impact.

The very first sentence in Wilson's book *The Insect Societies* is the question, "Why do we study these insects?", and his answer refers to the principles of organization of social insects and the utility these principles may have outside the field of entomology:

> The biologist is invited to consider insect societies because they best exemplify the full sweep of ascending levels of organization, from molecule to society. Among the tens of thousands of species of wasps, ants, bees and termites, we witness the employment of social design to solve ecological problems dealt with by single organisms. The insect colony is often called a superorganism because it displays so many social phenomena that are analogous to the physiological properties of organs and tissues. Yet the holistic properties of the superorganism stem in a straightforward behavioral way from the relatively crude repertories of individual colony members, and they can be dissected and understood much more easily than the molecular basis of physiology.

This quotation says a great deal about Wilson's early work; the words and phrases "ascending levels of organization," "superorganism," and "holistic properties" can be unpacked to reveal whole chapters of biological thought that were important to Wilson's background.

The single most important influence on Wilson's early research was probably Wheeler, who was also a specialist in ants, and also the author of several books on insect societies. Wheeler was a proponent of the concept of "emergent evolution," the belief that "the whole is not merely a sum, or resultant, but also an emergent novelty, or creative synthesis." Wheeler saw in insect societies the emergence of qualities that transcended the individual members of the society. Indeed, as time went on, Wheeler began to regard ant colonies as superorganisms that could be regarded as single, living entities in a real, not merely metaphorical or analogous, sense. In a well-known article written in 1911 Wheeler wrote of the ant colony as an organism, and by 1928 the social insect colony was a *super-organism*. He wrote in the latter year: "We have seen that the insect colony or society may be regarded as a superorganism and hence as a living whole bent on preserving its moving equilibrium and integrity."

Wheeler's views sound romantically speculative today. And Wilson wrote in *The Insect Societies* that "seldom has so ambitious a scientific concept been so quickly and almost totally discarded." And yet Wilson also claimed that the superorganism concept had a "major impact on current research," that it was "the mirage that drew us on." He noted that "the idea was inspirational and . . . as originally formulated by Wheeler had just the right amount of fact and fancy to generate a mystique. . . . It would be wrong to overlook the significant, albeit semi-conscious role this idea has played." One gains the clear impression that Wilson is admitting that much of his intellectual drive in the study of social insects had been after a goal that proved to be illusory, a mirage indeed.

Why was this mirage so attractive, and how did it appear? The appeal of the superorganism project was the potential it had for providing explanations of broad biological significance. If an ant colony was analogous or identical to whole biological organisms, as Wheeler claimed, then one might be able to get at the principles of organization of whole biological organisms by studying the principles of organization of ant colonies. One can take apart and examine the individual functioning parts of an ant colony much more successfully than one can dissemble the parts of a living organism. As Wheeler wrote:

> Another more general problem is suggested by the insect society, or colony as a whole, which . . . is so strikingly analogous . . . to any living organism as a whole, that the same very general laws must be involved. But the biologist, with his present methods, is powerless to offer any solution of the living organism as a whole. . . . We can only regard the organismal character of the colony as a whole as an expression of the fact that it is not equivalent to the sum of its individuals but represents a different and at present inexplicable "emergent level."

Wilson later said that Wheeler's use of words such as "powerless" and "inexplicable" here represented a challenge which his generation accepted. They wished to test their analytical powers against this riddle. How was it possible to explain the apparent "emergent levels" of insect societies? Wilson and his colleagues took on that task and worked on it so successfully that they abolished the superorganism concept itself.

A central question for early students of insect societies was how to explain the organizational, homeostatic or self-regulatory powers of the communities they examined. Honeybees, for example, maintain a remarkably constant internal temperature in the hive, fanning their wings and regurgitating water drops on hot days, and clustering in swarms on cold ones. Ants occasionally move from one nest site to another, carrying their eggs and larvae with them. Many social insects, such as termites, build nests of intricate architecture. All this activity would seem, at first glance, to require some sort of conscious coordination, and, indeed, some early specialists even spoke of the "spirit of the hive." One such writer, Maurice Maeterlinck, described bee and ant colonies in detail and then asked, "What is it that governs here, that issues orders, that foresees the future?" A slight leap of anthropomorphic thought, and one can easily conceive an architect-termite, plans in hand, directing the construction of the complex system of passageways and ventilating shafts of a termite nest.

The results of the work of a generation of entomologists have revealed that the most fruitful approach to this problem was that of behavioral genetics, a path that eliminates the necessity of postulating anything approaching conscious coordination. Communication exists in complex forms in insect societies, but it is made up of individual responses based on genetic control. Pioneer ethologists, such as Konrad Lorenz, played important roles in illustrating to entomologists the importance of concepts such as fixed action patterns and innate releasing mechanisms (FAP, IRM) in explaining the behavior of organisms. As Wilson commented, "They [the ethologists] convinced us that behavior and social structure, like all other biological phenomena, can be studied as 'organs,' extensions of the genes that exist because of their superior adaptive value."

Yet the behavior of insects was certainly not "fixed" in every instance, but seemed instead to be based on probabilities. Consider, for example, Wilson's description of "mass actions" among ants and bees:

> An important first rule concerning mass action is that it usually results from conflicting actions of many workers. The individual workers pay only limited attention to the behavior of nestmates near them, and they are largely unaware of the moment-by-moment condition of the colony as a whole. Anyone who has watched an ant colony emigrating from one nest site to another has seen this principle vividly illustrated. As workers stream outward carrying eggs, larvae, and pupae in their mandibles, other workers are busy carrying them back again. Still other workers run back and forth carrying nothing. Individuals are guided by the odor trail, if one exists, and each inspects the nest site on its own. There is no sign of decision-making at a higher level. On the contrary, the choice of nest site is decided by a sort of plebiscite, in which the will of the majority of the workers finally comes to prevail by virtue of their superior combined efforts. . . . The same process occurs in the construction of comb cells by honey bees. In order to obtain pieces of wax for cells of their own, the workers regularly tear away walls that are in the process of being constructed by other nestmates. . . . Although these various antagonistic actions seem chaotic when viewed at close range, their final result is almost invariably a well-constructed nest that closely conforms to the plan exhibited throughout the species.

The clue, then, to the understanding of many mass actions of insects that appear to be coordinated "from above" is the concept of "the emergence of statistical order from competing elements," an order which in the final analysis derives from genetic programs that have evolved during natural selection. Probabilities for certain behaviors under certain environmental conditions and stimuli grow or decrease as selection pressures change. In "cooperative labor" among insects the most important stimulus for the future behavior of the insects is "the product of work previously accomplished, rather than direct communication among nestmates.

Once this approach to the study of insect societies had been formulated, the appeal of Wheeler's superorganism concept rapidly faded.

Differences between insect societies and higher organisms, in which over-all coordination on the basis of central nervous systems definitely does occur, became ever more apparent. Wilson further observed, "It is not necessary to invoke the concept in order to commence work on animal societies. The concept offers no techniques, measurements, or even definitions by which the intricate phenomena in genetics, behavior, and physiology can be unraveled."

The decline of the superorganism concept was a result of the achievements of Wilson and his generation, and yet one has the clear sense that Wilson, at least, found the passing of that era somewhat saddening. He stated quite clearly that the concept "drew them on," gave them a goal. Furthermore, the concept of the superorganism bestowed upon entomology the promise of making a special contribution to theoretical biology, of revealing the unique regularities that govern the social insects and simultaneously whole organisms. The new affirmation of the overwhelming importance of the genetic base of insect behavior, and the assertion that mass effects can be explained as the probabilistic meshing of individual actions was a de facto denial of unique regularities. In the final analysis, the reductionist biologists, even the molecular geneticists, held the promise of the ultimate explanation of the social behavior of insects.

Wilson asked rhetorically in *The Insect Societies*, "What vision, if any, has replaced the superorganism concept?" What goal could draw him on now? The answers to these questions are, in my opinion, the essential factors for explaining his next ambitious venture, the writing of *Sociobiology*.

Wilson was certain that no new holistic conception would replace the old one. Rather, the new goal consisted of taking new, higher levels of biological complexity and trying to apply similar analysis there, i.e., "the continuing quest for precise evolutionary, that is, genetic, explanations of the origin of sociality and variations among the species in details of social structure." This quest, said Wilson, is "the exciting modern substitute for the superorganism concept." If insect biology could not provide clues to the unique principles of whole organs or "higher" organisms, since upon examination it turned out there were no such unique principles, then perhaps the very demolition of the appearance of unique principles could serve as a model for an attack on the allegedly unique principles of "higher" social behavior, including human behavior.

WILSON'S MAIN WORK ON SOCIOBIOLOGY

Sociobiology is not a book devoted to the study of human beings, and, indeed, is much more cautious about extending biological speculations to humans than a host of earlier works by ethologists and ethology popularizers. True, one chapter out of twenty-seven does concern man, but the book can easily stand alone without that chapter. Wilson made some ambitious and foolish expansionist claims in chapters 1 and 27 about the eventual absorption of ethics and sociobiology by biology, but the significance of the book is something quite different: the attempt to formulate the main theoretical problems and analytical categories of a sociobiology based almost entirely on the nonhuman animals.

The most important concept behind *Sociobiology* was that of kin selection. As Arthur Caplan later observed, "It is the theoretical models of kin selection . . . that provided the theoretical spark for sociobiology." The importance of kin selection was, first, that it provided a theoretical answer to the question of how complicated social behavior, especially cooperation and altruism, could evolve in Darwinian terms, and, second, it provided by extension a base for what in humans might be called moral behavior. To some biologists kin selection seemed a means for showing how normative behavior can develop out of material evolution.

The original problem was that classical Darwinian evolution was heavily based on the individual. Any individual of a species that sacrificed itself for another, and therefore had fewer progeny, seemed to be a loser in the Darwinian struggle. Surely its inheritance would not spread in the population. Yet it was known in Darwin's time that altruistic acts occur in the animal world. Bees protect the hive by stinging intruders and killing themselves in the process. In fact, among social insects the Darwinian ultimate in cooperation and altruism occurs, since the specialized castes of workers are completely sterile. How can this phenomenon be explained in strict Darwinian terms?

As is often the case in the history of science, the first great figure in the field sensed the later difficulty more fully than many of his immediate followers. Darwin called the problem of social insects "one special difficulty, which at first appeared to me insuperable, and actually fatal to my whole theory." Darwin pointed toward a possible solution by saying that natural selection may occasionally act on levels higher than the individual, such as the family. If sterile worker-insects increased the fitness of the family as a whole, their sterility would be an adaptation of biological significance that might be preserved by natural selection.

With the development of population genetics in the twentieth century Darwin's suggestion could be examined in a more rigorous way. In the 1960s William D. Hamilton developed a formal and mathematical statement of kin selection based on the concept of *inclusive fitness*. He defined inclusive fitness as the sum of an individual's own fitness plus the sum of all the effects it causes to the fitnesses of its kin. A reciprocal relationship thus arose which can be stated in the following way: if the reduction of gene contribution to succeeding generations by the sacrificing individual is more than compensated for by increased similar gene contributions of its relatives, a self-sacrificing act can be considered biologically adaptive.

Wilson placed Hamilton's idea of inclusive fitness at the base of this sociobiological scheme. Wilson gave the following example of a simplified network consisting only of an individual and his brother, and proposed that it was legitimate to speak of "altruistic genes" (meaning genes for altruism):

> If the individual is altruistic he will perform some sacrifice for the benefit of the brother. He may surrender needed food or shelter, or defer in the choice of a mate, or place himself between his brother and danger. The important result, from a purely evolutionary point of view, is loss of genetic fitness—a reduced mean life span, or fewer offspring, or both—which leads to less representation of the altruist's personal genes in the next generation. But at least half of the brother's genes are identical to those of the altruist by virtue of common descent. Suppose, in the extreme case, that the altruist leaves no offspring. If his altruistic act more than doubles the brother's personal representation in the next generation, it will *ipso facto* increase the one-half of the genes identical to those of the altruist, and the altruist will actually have gained representation in the next generation. Many of the genes shared by such brothers will be the ones that encode the tendency toward altruistic behavior. The inclusive fitness, in this case determined solely by the brother's contribution, will be great enough to cause the spread of the altruistic genes through the population, and hence the evolution of altruistic behavior.

On the basis of this sort of analysis, Wilson hypothesized that in humans social and moral values may be influenced by genes. In addition to "altruistic genes," he spoke of possible "conformer genes," and he said that "human beings are absurdly easy to indoctrinate—they seek it." He thought that religious belief and other types of conformity further the welfare of their practitioners and may well have acquired a genetic basis. He thought it likely that many other forms of human social behavior are genetically influenced, and he named as possibilities the cooperative division of labor between males and females, incest taboos, sexual activity, language acquisition, artistic impulses, maternal care, aggression, dominance, territoriality, and group cohesiveness.

We should remind ourselves that in speculations of this sort nearly any kind of human conduct can be "explained" by postulating a genetic foundation. But when one does so, one may be committing the "dormitive virtue in opium" fallacy, that is, one may convert what should be an empirical investigation into a dance around tautologies. The verification procedures applied to such hypotheses may, if one is not careful, contain the original hypothesis in disguised form.

Wilson was aware of these dangers and he did not draw many conclusions from his speculations about the genetic bases of human values. Instead he postulated possibilities. He pointed in the direction of genetic explanations of human behavior, but he cited few specific examples of universal culture traits that he believed were genetically determined. Instead, he emphasized how labile human traits are, and how flexible human behavior is. He criticized the ethologists who drew parallels between animal rituals, such as the mating "ceremonies" of birds, and similar human rituals. He even observed:

> During the past ten thousand years or longer, man as a whole has been so successful in dominating his environment that almost any kind of culture can succeed for a while, so long as it has a modest degree of consistency and does not shut off reproduction altogether.

Wilson later said that he was surprised by the controversy which his *Sociobiology* caused, and we have no reason to doubt him. The academic reviews were largely laudatory, but he was sharply attacked by a group of Cambridge, Massachusetts, academics in the "Sociobiology Study Group," who maintained that Wilson was a biological determinist whose arguments amounted to a justification of the existing social order by implying that it was an inevitable genetic product.

Wilson's most vocal critics often distorted his viewpoints and certainly overreacted to a book that was much less biologically determinist than many previous writings on man's animal origins. Yet the criticism probably had a beneficial effect, for it forced Wilson to face more directly than he had earlier the political and moral implications of his work. If one compares Wilson's 1975 *Sociobiology* with his 1978 *On Human Nature* several important differences become apparent, and it is highly likely that the criticism he received after publication of *Sociobiology* was a factor accentuating the changes. In *Sociobiology* Wilson speaks little of the moral goals to which man's future evolution should be, in his opinion, directed. Instead, he spoke of the past biological determinants of that behavior. In the last sentences of *Sociobiology* he quoted Camus on the alienation of man by his loss of illusions and "the hope of a promised land;" Wilson continued that "when we have progressed enough to explain ourselves in these mechanistic terms . . . the result might be hard to accept." In *On Human Nature,* on the other hand, the pessimism of Camus is abandoned for a call for a "mythopoeic drive" that "can be harnessed to learning and the rational search for human progress."

QUESTIONS FOR CRITICAL READERS

Remembering and Understanding

1. Summarize Graham's account of the development of Wilson's thought from *The Insect Societies* to *Sociobiology*.
2. What was Wilson's overall goal in studying social insects?
3. Explain the concept of understanding social insect colonies as organisms or superorganisms. Why did Wilson's generation of scientists abandon this concept?

Analyzing and Discussing

4. What are some of the limitations of applying the results of research into animal behavior to humans?
5. What are the implications of Wilson's analogy of studying behavior and social structures as though they were organs, and thus "extensions of the genes?"
6. Why would Wilson be criticized for ideas that support the existing social order?

Writing

7. Write a paper in which you explain how the study of social insects forms a background for the study of human behavior and social structures.

Science and Human Nature

———— BARRY SCHWARTZ ————

In this excerpt from his book The Battle for Human Nature, *Schwartz, a behavioral scientist, discusses whether there can be a science of human nature. He places Wilson's work in the context of the goals and methods of science in general and the progressive enlargement of the domain of science in the past several hundred years.*

WE HAVE SEEN THAT RULES-OF-THUMB about human nature are built out of everyday experience together with the guidance provided by social institutions like the family, the church, and the school. Indeed, traditionally, these have been the principal sources of knowledge about the world in general. But over the last three hundred years or so, tradition has given way to a new authority: the authority of science. People no longer seek their priests or grandmothers to find out how to treat a rash or a stomachache. Nor do they turn to them to find out why the sky is blue, or how cows turn grass into milk. It is firmly understood by virtually all citizens of industrial societies that the ultimate authority in certain domains is neither the priest, nor the parent, but the scientist.

As science has developed over the last three centuries, the domains over which it has sought authority have expanded. The initial achievements of modern science were in its ability to explain the behavior of nonliving things, like the planets and other heavenly bodies. This was the concern of the physics ushered in by Galileo and Newton in the seventeenth century. But even as people were willing to defer to the authority of the scientist with respect to the physical world, it was believed that physics went only so far, that living things shared some special characteristics that inanimate things did not possess and that physical principles could not explain. Thus, the authority of science stopped at life. With the emergence of scientific biology in the eighteenth century, however, the explanatory domain of science was extended. At least some characteristics of all living things could be understood scientifically. Indeed, perhaps all characteristics of nonhuman living things were susceptible to scientific analysis. But still, people were thought to be special.

The human capacity for reason and the human soul placed human beings outside the bounds of physics or biology. In the last one hundred fifty years or so, this last barrier to scientific authority has come under steady attack. The "human sciences"—economics, sociology, anthropology, and psychology—are attempting to show that no aspect of human life can resist the power of scientific scrutiny. As these disciplines progress in explaining people in the same way that physics has succeeded in explaining planets, they come to replace the family and the church as the sources of our conception of human nature. Our everyday conception of human nature comes to approximate the scientific one.

To examine what a "scientific" conception of human nature is, we must first look at what characterizes scientific conceptions more generally. For most people, the first encounter with "science" is as a subject in school. Somewhere around the fourth grade, a portion of the day gets set aside for science lessons. These may be lessons in nature—folksy, Disneyesque accounts of exotic creatures living in exotic lands, or perhaps nowadays, discussions of food chains, pollution, endangered species, and ecology. Or they may be lessons in "chemistry"—discussions of atoms and molecules and of what happens when different elements are combined or when substances are heated. Or perhaps they may be lessons in "physics"—in how flashlights work, or how airplanes stay in the air, or how ships manage not to sink. The impression that this regimen of science lessons engenders is that "science" is a body of knowledge, that what sets it apart from "history" or "English" is what it is about. As schooling continues, people learn that just as there are different kinds of history (world history and American history) and different kinds of English (grammar, vocabulary, poetry, novels), there are different kinds of science. The scientific monolith of early schooling is differentiated into domains like biology, chemistry, and physics. Still, however, science is understood to refer to some domain of information.

Although most people never move beyond this understanding, it is fundamentally mistaken. What is distinctive about science is not so much the things that science is about as it is a set of procedures, or methods, for finding out about those things and a set of standards, or criteria, for deciding whether anything has actually been found out. In other words, "science" is really a process for finding things out about the world. It is a process that, *in principle*, could be applied to any set of phenomena. There could be a science of cooking, or pole vaulting, or gardening, just as there are sciences of biology, chemistry, and physics.

One of the most distinctive qualities of human beings is their persistent effort to make sense of the world around them. Whether children or adults, farmers or professors, members of highly technological or of primitive cultures, a substantial part of people's daily activity involves attempting to understand the events that affect their lives. Science is just one particular approach to seeking an understanding of the world. The reason it commands special attention is that it has been so powerful in enabling people to intervene effectively in their environments. Every aspect of life in modern, highly technological society is testimony to the explanatory power of scientific modes of understanding. Every time someone flips on a light, drives a car, takes a photograph, turns on the television, photocopies a letter, or computes his income taxes with the aid of a calculator, he is presenting himself with evidence that science has delivered the goods. The kind of understanding that characterizes science is what has led to all of these technological innovations. To the extent that technology enables people to control their environments better than they could before, it validates the scientific conception of the world. But what is the scientific conception of the world? What does it mean to understand something scientifically?

In attempting to understand a given phenomenon, the scientist searches for some other event or phenomenon that caused it. To understand what causal explanations typically involve, consider an example: Suppose someone drops an expensive, antique vase, and it falls to the floor and breaks into a hundred pieces. What caused the vase to fall and shatter?

A first response to this question might be, "He dropped it. That's why it fell and shattered." This "causal" account has several important properties. First, the cause identified was such that, under the circumstances, had the cause not occurred, the phenomenon would not have occurred. Thus, if the vase had not been dropped, it would not have fallen and broken. In short, dropping the vase was *necessary* for it to fall and break. But this cause was only necessary *under the given circumstances*. Had the circumstances been different (for example, an earthquake), the vase might have fallen without anyone's intervention. Second, under the circumstances, the cause identified was *all* that was required to bring about the phenomenon. Thus, once the vase dropped, nothing else had to happen for it to fall and break. Dropping the vase was *sufficient* for it to fall and break. But of course, this cause was only sufficient under the circumstances. If the vase had been dropped while it was over a mattress, it would have fallen, but it wouldn't have broken. Finding causes of a phenomenon, then, involves finding influences that are necessary and sufficient for its occurrence, under a given set of circumstances.

Does this mean that "He dropped it" counts as an appropriately scientific explanation of the behavior of the vase? Not quite. For what is perhaps the most significant feature of scientific explanations is that they relate the specific phenomenon to be explained to other, similar phenomena. At the heart of scientific explanation is the search for *generalizations*, or *laws*. While the fact of the matter is that this particular vase may have fallen and broken after a particular person dropped it, it would have fallen and broken no matter who dropped it. Indeed, the fact that it was dropped is not essential to its falling and breaking. No matter what is responsible for setting a vase in free fall, it will move toward the center of the earth. Furthermore, the object needn't be a vase. Any object in free fall will move toward the earth, and any object composed of certain sorts of materials will break when it contacts the hard ground. Finally, the cause of the behavior of the vase is the same as the cause of the motions of the planets. For when it is said that the vase fell and broke because someone dropped it, what lies beneath this explanation is a wealth of knowledge from physics about gravity and its effects on objects in free fall. It is this knowledge of physics that tells us that the vase would not have fallen and broken if it had been dropped on the moon. It is this knowledge of physics that tells us to what general class of phenomena the behavior of the vase belongs. Without knowing this, someone might still be able to say that the vase fell and broke because it was dropped. But he would not necessarily be able to use this knowledge to help understand other phenomena, or perhaps predict or control events in the future.

How we generalize a particular phenomenon has a lot to do with what we do about it in the future. Science is an attempt to discover which kinds of generalizations will provide the broadest and most powerful guidance about what to do in the future. In suggesting that science has delivered the goods, what I meant was that the generalizations it has provided have enabled people to predict and control the world in which they live with unparalleled success. That is why the kind of understanding reflected by science's search for general, causal laws has become a model of what understanding should be in the technologically advanced world.

That scientific understanding involves generalizations, or laws, is important for another reason. It is only because scientific explanations of particular events are really explanations of classes of events that people are able to evaluate their causal judgments. Consider again the fallen vase. We believe the vase fell because someone dropped it, and gravity took over. Someone else believes the vase fell because a demon in the center of the earth wanted it to. Still a third person believes the vase fell because its owner had done something to anger the gods. Which explanation is right, and how does one know? In fact, any of these explanations might suffice to account for the fact that this *particular* vase fell to this *particular* floor at this *particular* time. And so might dozens of other explanations.

Or consider another example. Suppose a baker follows a recipe to make a cake and the cake comes out heavy and dry. Is it because he didn't beat the eggs enough, or because he baked it too long, or because the oven was hotter than the thermostat setting indicated, or because the recipe was bad? There is no way of telling in the case of this one cake. It could be for any or all of these reasons that the cake was a flop.

The way to sift through this plethora of possible explanations is to make more observations—to gather more data. In the case of the fallen vase, someone might walk around with a careful eye open to note other vases falling, or other objects falling. In the case of the cake, the baker might take note of how other things made in the same oven turn out, or how other people following the same recipe do. Repeated, systematic observation of a phenomenon helps to weed out the implausible candidates for causes and focus on the likely ones. If other cakes baked in the same oven come out fine, it is unlikely that the failed cake was the oven's fault. If vases dropped by other people also fall and break, it is unlikely that this vase fell and broke because its owner angered the gods.

Systematic, repeated observation allows one to begin to separate the wheat from the chaff as far as causal accounts are concerned, but it has its drawbacks. It may be necessary to wait and watch for a long time before collecting enough examples of broken vases to be confident about what caused them to fall and break. This takes time and patience. What if one has neither? Science has provided an alternative. Instead of waiting for vases to fall, we can make them fall ourselves. We can try to *create* additional observations that relate to the phenomenon under investigation. This intentional creation of observations is what scientists refer to as *experiments*. An experimenter might drop other vases, or other objects, and have other people drop them, and she could do this repeatedly, at different times and places. If she did, she would discover that no matter what the time or place, no matter what the object, and no matter who dropped it, it fell. Or the baker might try other recipes in the same oven, the same recipe in different ovens, and so on to determine whether there were any circumstances in which the cake came out all right. In this way, by appropriate observations via experimentation, one could move rapidly and surely to an accurate causal analysis. With such an analysis in hand, it would be possible to produce good (or bad) cakes on demand, or make objects fall, or keep them from falling.

There is no question that systematic observation and experimentation are what have given science its extraordinary explanatory power. But it is important to realize that the logic of these methods rests on a very significant assumption. The assumption is that other falling objects belong to the same class as the vase and that future cakes belong to the same class as this first failure. Without this assumption, there would be no reason to treat the phenomena observed or created by experiment as relevant to the ones the experimenter initially set out to explain.

This is no small assumption. Every phenomenon or event is in some respects unique. It occurs at a particular place and a particular moment, and once that moment has passed, it can't be recaptured. Even if other cakes come out dry, the baker can't be sure that what makes them fail is what made the first one fail. Maybe there was something special about the butter and eggs used in the first cake. It can never be proven that there wasn't. By asserting that the cake failed because the recipe was bad, the baker is saying that for all the uniqueness of that first cake, made with those ingredients at that time, it was just like any other cake would be that was prepared according to the same recipe. Said another way, when science formulates the sorts of generalizations that it is after and that justify doing experiments, it is engaged in a process of abstraction. It looks at the unique phenomenon, place, and time and abstracts from it those features or elements that it has in common with other phenomena, places, and times.

What this discussion reveals about scientific understanding is that in pursuing causal laws, science tells us in what categories individual phenomena belong. In doing this, science ignores the many features that make each and every object or event unique and focuses on essential properties they have in common. It is just this feature of scientific understanding that allows for the prediction and control of aspects of the future on the basis of what is understood about aspects of the past.

Now the search for causal laws presupposes that the phenomena of nature are sufficiently orderly and repeatable that laws are there to be found. Without this belief in the orderliness of nature, scientific activity would not make much sense. When talking about falling vases, this belief seems quite straightforward and uncontroversial. That their uniqueness as objects that fall can be disregarded is hardly a surprise. But as we move into other domains, uncertainty arises. Consider, for example, the claim that people cheat on their income taxes because it is human nature to pursue self-interest, without regard for the welfare of others or for one's responsibilities to the larger community. An account like this says that for purposes of causal analysis of tax cheating, the uniqueness of individuals can be disregarded. All people can be treated as members of a single class that has in common the pursuit of self-interest. Clearly, in a domain like this, treating unique individuals simply as members of larger classes is not so straightforward.

Indeed, even treating human actions as phenomena, like the motions of vases, that *have* causes is not so straightforward. Most people hold the view that the appropriateness of scientific understanding stops at phenomena that are essentially human. In their everyday lives people do not seek to understand their own behavior and that of their friends, loved one, employers, and political leaders in terms of necessary and sufficient causal laws. They think of others and themselves as having control over their actions, as exercising discretion and choice, and not as being pushed around, like vases, by necessary and sufficient causes. Are human actions caused? Are human actions reliable and repeatable in the way that the action of the falling vase is?

In general, when the attempt is made to understand human action rather than the behavior of inanimate objects, notions of purpose, belief, expectation, and deliberation replace notions of necessary and sufficient causes. People are comfortable with explanations of human action in these terms and uncomfortable with explanations that have a scientific character. People assume that there are *reasons* for what they do, and the task in understanding is to discover those reasons. And because how we understand something has practical consequences for what we do about it, the commitment to explanations of human action based on reasons is reflected in many customary social practices and cultural institutions. For example, it is common to try to influence people by *reasoning* with them, by giving them reasons to change their minds. It is common to hold people responsible for what they do. They are praised or blamed when appropriate, their actions are regarded as moral or immoral, they are sent to prison, or elected to high office. But no one would consider holding the vase responsible for falling. This reflects a commitment to the belief that vases can be understood in terms of causal forces, but that people cannot be understood in the same way. Thus in our everyday understanding of human action—of human nature—we are usually content to bypass the explanatory power offered by the sciences.

A SCIENCE OF HUMAN NATURE

Despite our reluctance to replace our everyday explanations of human action with scientific ones, the power of science has been engaged in a relentless assault on the human barricades. If physics can give us the power to fly, if chemistry can give us food preservatives and life-saving drugs, if biology can give us the means to detect and prevent birth defects, who knows what a science of human nature can deliver? Our everyday conception of human nature may soon be regarded as nothing more than a superstition, which the methods of science will allow us to peel away.

What might a science of human nature look like? Remember that the goal of science is to discover causal laws, generalizations that apply to a wide range of different phenomena at different times and places. The goal of a science of human nature would be to discover generalizations that were true of all people. At first glance, the task of discovering universal generalizations about human nature seems positively daunting. Even the most sheltered observer of human nature must be struck by the wealth of human diversity. People living in cities behave differently from people living in the country. Europeans are different from Asians. Adults are different from children. Men are different from women. It is hard to believe that science could cut through all this difference to find underlying similarity. It is tempting to conclude that there is no human nature, that there is no set of characteristics that all people, in all places, at all times share. What people are, and how they act, will differ enormously from time to time and culture to culture. Human behavior is dramatically affected by the particular circumstances in which people find themselves. The physicist knows that a rose is a rose is a rose. But it just isn't so that a person is a person is a person. Pursuing general laws of human nature is sheer folly. Or is it?

It isn't really true that all falling rocks are the same. In the ideal world of a vacuum, with no air or wind resistance, every rock, no matter what its size or shape, will fall at the same rate. So will leaves, feathers and pianos. But in real life, size and shape make a difference. What the physicist does in arriving at a generalization about falling rocks is treat them as abstract objects falling in an abstract universe. Factors like wind are regarded as a nuisance, giving the impression that each object falls in its own unique way and obscuring what all falling objects have in common. While it is true that the wind and the air resistance will combine with the size and shape of every particular object to give it its own distinctive motion as it falls to the ground, these idiosyncrasies are only part of what determines the way an object will fall. The rest is determined by gravity, which affects all falling objects in the same way.

So a complete understanding of the falling of rocks has two parts. There is first the general part, the laws of physics that apply indiscriminately to all falling objects. And then there is the specific part, which takes account of the interaction of each unique object and the environment in which it is falling. Perhaps the same story can be told about people. The explanation of human action may also require two parts: one part that consists of the universal characteristics of human beings; and a second part that accounts for the way in which these universal characteristics are affected by the influence of particular times and places.

When a physicist wants to get at the general laws that are involved when an object falls, he eliminates the specifics. He eliminates the effects of air and wind by creating a vacuum and studying how objects fall in the absence of extraneous influences. By analogy, to get at human nature, one would want to study people in a "vacuum," an environment free of the various particular influences that give people their uniqueness. While the physicist's vacuum eliminates air and wind, the human vacuum would have to eliminate culture. So the question would become, what are people like in the absence of culture? How does a person act in the state of nature? What is "natural man"?

These questions cannot be answered by doing experiments. We cannot take babies, put them by themselves in the woods, and see what they come out like as adults. That is, cultural vacuums can't actually be created. However, this practical limitation does not leave the scientist without resources. He can observe and experiment with other animals in the state of nature. He can see what they are like and extend his findings, by analogy, to humans. And he can speculate. He can construct hypotheses about what sort of human nature *would* be revealed if people were forced to fend for themselves, without the support and influence of a social environment. The logic underlying this attempt to uncover what natural man would be like is the same logic that underlies the physicist's experimentation. Neutralize or eliminate the forces that make for individual uniqueness, and what is left is universal. What is left—what is natural—is human nature.

Among those who have asked what people would be like in the state of nature—what human nature divorced from the influence of culture is—the person whose ideas have had perhaps the greatest influence on the modern conceptions that will concern us in this book is Thomas Hobbes. Hobbes lived in the England of the seventeenth century, at a time when modern science was just taking root. In *Leviathan*, he offered a theory of human nature that was at the same time a defense of a particular kind of political organization. Hobbes thought that each human machine "endeavors to secure himself against the evil he fears, and procure the good he desires." Moreover, the human machine never rests in this pursuit. "Felicity of this life consists not in the repose of a mind satisfied. . . . Nor can a man any more live, whose desires are at an end. . . . Felicity is a continual progress of desire."

In other words, people are moved to action so as to satisfy their desires, and their desires can never be fully satisfied. They will always want something. The reason for this unlimited desire, Hobbes asserted, is that while it is fixed and universal human nature to try to satisfy desires, what people actually desire is neither fixed nor universal. What people want is conditioned on what others around them have. Value and worth "consist in comparison. For if all things were equally in all men, nothing would be prized." Thus, to satisfy desire is to have more than the people around you have. But because satisfaction of desire will mean this to everyone, there will be endless competition among people to outdo one another. And the competition will be ugly. For the best way for one person to outdo another is simply to take what is his. And the best way to do that is by being powerful. Thus, there is in men "a perpetual and restless desire for power that ceases only in death." It must be perpetual and restless, requiring eternal vigilance, for if one person lets down his guard, even for an instant, someone else will be there to take what is his. All men must therefore endeavor, "by force, or wiles, to master the persons of all men he can, so long, till he see no other power great enough to endanger him."

The result of this human nature, according to Hobbes, is a never-ending war of all against all. A life of perpetual warfare and destruction is obviously undesirable, but it is inevitable if human nature is given free reign. The only sensible alternative, Hobbes argued, is for all people to surrender their power to some common authority (the state) that is larger than any individual and that can and will "keep them all in awe," that is, keep human nature in check.

What Hobbes meant when he said that it was human nature to pursue the satisfaction of unlimited desires is that one could not be a person and act any other way. People had no more control over their natures and actions than falling rocks did over theirs. People were machines, set in motion by external, causal forces. They could be influenced by influencing the forces acting on them. But they could not exert self-restraint; restraint would have to be imposed from without, by a powerful state, the Leviathan.

Hobbes's views about human nature may seem a little extreme, but there is a distinctly modern ring to them. Hobbes regarded people as isolated individuals, with their own individual interests. It is the hallmark of modern, liberal democracy to regard people in just this way, as isolated individuals, in pursuit of their individual interests. Hobbes acknowledged that the precise nature of these interests would vary from person to person and from place to place, but he argued that everyone will have them and will do whatever can be done to satisfy them. Hobbes thought that people would be in constant competition, trying to outdo one another. Most of us certainly experience the reality of "keeping up with the Joneses"— that luxuries become necessities when everyone has them. We may differ from Hobbes in supposing that there are limits to what people will do. We may believe, unlike Hobbes, that even without a state policing the behavior of individuals, people will not indiscriminately try to steal from one another, that it is wrong for people to engage in ruthlessly aggressive competition, and that many people, if not all, will think twice before doing what is wrong. Hobbes might agree that it is wrong to pursue one's interest no matter what. But he would argue that good or bad, right or wrong, it is simply the way people are. Deceive yourself into thinking they are otherwise, and you will be swallowed up.

It is possible to agree that Hobbes's description of human nature has a ring of truth to it but put a very different interpretation on it than Hobbes did. One possible interpretation—the one Hobbes intended—is that people are selfish by natural law. They couldn't be, and never have been, otherwise. But another possible interpretation is that people are selfish only under certain conditions, conditions that could be different. It makes an enormous difference which of these interpretations one has in mind in claiming that it is human nature to be selfish. Consider two people, both of whom agree with Hobbes to the last detail that people are selfish, endlessly acquisitive, competitive, and aggressive. One person also believes that it is in the nature of the species to be this way. The other person attributes it to the peculiar conditions of a competitive, free-market capitalist society, in which every person is expected to fend for himself. The first person might, like Hobbes, seek some kind of social organization that could keep ruthless selfishness in check. The second person, unlike Hobbes, might seek some kind of social organization that would create people who were not so acquisitive, competitive, and aggressive. The first person might, again like Hobbes, see the need for an authoritarian state. The second might argue for some form of social democratic, welfare state. Thus two radically different prescriptions for social, economic, and political organization could arise from an agreed upon view of what people are like, if there is a disagreement about why they are like that.

And views like the hypothetical ones of our anti-Hobbesian have almost as long a tradition as the Hobbesian view. The French philosopher Rousseau argued for what is sometimes called a "noble savage" view of human nature. On this view, people in the state of nature are cooperative rather than competitive. They show care and concern for their fellows and are altruistic rather than greedy. This benevolent innocence is corrupted by the social institutions within which the person grows, institutions that demand competitiveness and beat down cooperation.

The conflict between these two views has been played out often, in scholarly argument, in literature, and in late-night, beer hall conversation. It is a conflict whose resolution is enormously important, since it bears on the kind of society one aspires to create. But it is also a conflict whose resolution is enormously difficult. For both parties to the conflict agree about the facts—that people are selfish, competitive, and aggressive. They disagree about interpretation; incorrigibly evil human nature on the one hand; and corrigibly evil social institutions on the other. And it is not at all clear how to decide between these interpretations.

QUESTIONS FOR CRITICAL READERS

Remembering and Understanding

1. Summarize Schwartz's explanation of science.
2. How are scientific conceptions of animate and inanimate phenomena different from non-scientific conceptions?
3. Schwartz asks: "What does it mean to understand something scientifically?" Summarize his answer to this question.

Analyzing and Discussing

4. Why is the ability to generalize important to science?
5. Why do people resist applying scientific explanations to human actions?

Writing

6. Contrast the roles of tradition and science in solving problems. Do some situations require scientific solutions and others require traditional solutions? Write a paper in which you identify one of each type of situation and explain the differences between them.

Evolution as a Paradigm for Behavior

Areas of Controversy and Difficulty

——— DAVID BARASH ———

David Barash is interested in the evolution of behavior. In this selection, which first appeared in Sociobiology and Human Nature *(Jossey-Bass, 1978), he explores the political and scientific objections to sociobiology.*

AREAS OF CONTROVERSY AND DIFFICULTY

LIKE ALL REVOLUTIONS, sociobiology has met considerable resistance (Allen and others, 1976). The objections can be divided for convenience into two groups, political and scientific. Some of the political objections and a brief response to each are summarized as follows (interestingly, nearly all the controversy centers around extrapolations of sociobiology to human behavior).

1. "Sociobiology is racist and sexist and represents a return to Social Darwinism." Insofar as sociobiology assumes genetic influences on behavior, this concern is understandable. However, there have been no sociobiological treatments of racial issues. Furthermore, with its emphasis on underlying biological "universals," ostensibly shared by all *Homo sapiens* from Bushman to Wall Street businessman, sociobiology appears instead to be a cogent antidote to racism. Yet much sociobiological theory relies heavily on male-female differences in behavior; and, indeed, if the identification of evolved behavioral differences between males and females is sexist, then so is sociobiology—but so is "Mother" Nature! Alternatively, the term *sexism* seems more appropriately reserved for preferential societal treatment or valuation of one sex over the other, and sociobiology is innocent on this score. Like the *yin* and *yang* of Taoism, an evolutionary

553

approach to sexuality recognizes female and male as complementary forms, each defining the other and achieving unity. Neither is better; both are essential, and both "win" every time a new generation is successfully produced. The specific implications for male-female differences in human behavior are unclear and, indeed, hardly explored.

As for Social Darwinism, it was an unfortunate misstatement of evolutionary biology, due especially to efforts by successful turn-of-the-century capitalists to justify their exploitation of others, including imperialism and colonialism. It was an effort in which social science readily joined and for which it has been doing penance ever since by taking a virtually monolithic stand behind environmental determinism of all behavior. Social Darwinism was a travesty of biological theory, based on the mistaken notion that "survival of the fittest" referred solely to the outcome of aggressive competition. We now recognize that natural selection proceeds by differential reproduction, and Social Darwinism accordingly has no place in sociobiology or, indeed, anywhere else.

2. "Sociobiology is a doctrine of biological (genetic) determinism." This formulation confuses genetic determinism with *genetic influences* on behavior (Dobzhansky, 1976). Behavior can be genetically influenced while still retaining a wide range of flexibility. Indeed, it is no less "genetic" if susceptible to environmental influences—notably (in humans) early experience and social learning. Geneticists know that phenotypes are not magically enclosed within a gene, like the tiny homunculi of medieval medicine. Rather, genes code for a range of potential phenotypes; they are blueprints of varying flexibility, depending on the species and the behavior in question. The difference between genetic determinism and genetic influence is like the difference between shooting a bullet at a target and throwing a paper airplane—on a windy day. Julian Huxley has warned biologists against "nothing but-ism," the mistaken notion that since humans are animals we are nothing but animals. His warning is well taken, but it can also be turned around with equal cogency: Even though humans are unique in their behavioral flexibility, it is inaccurate to assume that they are "nothing but" *tabulae rasae*, blank slates on which experience can write as it will. Nonetheless, genetic determinism is a red herring, nowhere implied in the interaction principle or elsewhere in sociobiology.

Accordingly, sociobiology does not necessarily imply that humans have surrendered their autonomy to the despotism of DNA. And yet, insofar as genes influence our behavior, inclining us to do what maximizes our fitness, sociobiology may provide real insights to the deep structure that underlies our everyday behavior. It may tell us nothing of why we chose a red tie today instead of a blue one, but it may say a great deal about why we choose to adorn our bodies in the first place. Similarly, our choice of particular presidential candidates may say much about our inclinations to have leaders at all. Does evolution mean the death of free will? All scientific theories of behavior must of necessity be relatable to natural laws, and certainly conditioning theory does not offer our species any greater freedom or dignity (Skinner, 1971). I suggest that free will is at a maximum when individuals are able to behave in accordance with their inclinations, whether these derive from early experience, social learning, cultural traditions—or evolutionary biology. Sociobiology is simply a concerned effort to understand the contribution of natural selection to behavior.

3. "Sociobiology implies support for the status quo." The idea is that an evolutionary perspective implies a Panglossian view that "all is for the best in this best of all possible worlds." There are several misunderstandings here. First, this view suggests that what is "biological" is necessarily "good" as well. The goal of sociobiology is to better understand behavior, not to legitimize our foibles. Similarly, we study pneumococci to understand them better, not because we approve of pneumonia! (A similar argument can be applied to sociobiology's purported sexism.) Second, the conception of behavior as adaptive does not imply perfection in any system; in fact, it implies quite the opposite: Evolution is notoriously opportunistic, often selecting short-term success at the cost of long-term fitness. The eventual consequence, of course, is extinction. Sewall Wright's (1969) image of "adaptive landscapes" further emphasizes the less-than-perfect nature of adaptions: Populations may get stuck on minor adaptive peaks, with the constituent individuals unable to achieve greater fitness because they cannot cross a valley separating them from a higher peak. Wright's conclusion was that a certain frequency of random movements (genetic drift), combined with the blind upward momentum of selection, is necessary for adaptation. The moral for sociobiology and its detractors is that nothing in nature is perfect. The existence of a social system is *de facto* evidence that it is at least minimally adaptive. However, this does not imply that something better cannot be found.

Finally, evolution is by its nature a doctrine of change. For that reason, in fact, it was strongly resisted by the early nineteenth-century European establishment, which had recently been shaken by the American and French revolutions and was understandably apprehensive of ideas that the natural world was mutable. Such notions tended to undermine the establishment's own claim to special position by virtue of divine will and the rigid structuring of nature implied in the doctrine of special creation. It would therefore be ironic if an evolutionary paradigm for behavior should now be seen as supportive of establishment values!

4. "Culture is so important to human behavior that genetic factors (and hence sociobiology) may be considered irrelevant." It is undoubtedly true that genetic factors are less influential in the behavior of *Homo sapiens*

than they are for any other species. But this does not mean they are irrelevant. Anthropologists and sociologists often point to the enormous cultural diversity shown by our species. But that is just the point. Insofar as certain cross-cultural universals emerge as truly *human* traits, despite the enormous cultural overlay, then the evidence for biological underpinnings is all the more cogent. Cultural diversity is like the icing on the cake. Thus far, anthropologists in particular have studied the icing, while psychologists and psychiatrists have concerned themselves with how the icing is put together. Sociobiology urges us to look at the human *cake* that underlies the icing—at the basic human patterns of behavior toward kin versus nonkin, parent-offspring conflict, male-female differences in reproductive strategies, and the fundamental organization of human families. Because of ethical constraints, our hands are tied concerning direct experimentation on the genetic basis of human social behavior. But we can use sociobiology to predict the existence of certain cross-cultural universals. And then, if the shoe fits. . . .

The following scientific criticisms of sociobiology may well be more cogent than the preceding political concerns. They warrant further attention from both opponents and proponents of the new revolution.

1. "There is no evidence for specific genes influencing specific behaviors in humans beyond simple inherited metabolic and structural traits." This is true. There is abundant evidence for non-human animals, but, since no experimental manipulation can be performed on humans, we are reduced to extrapolation and speculation. But, unless we are willing to posit a qualitative discontinuity between the biology of human and of nonhuman animals, the interaction principle should apply to *Homo sapiens* as well. Nonetheless, it will be very difficult to disentangle biological from cultural factors in the etiology of any given human behavior, since in many cases both processes lead to the same phenotype. For example, among certain Eskimo societies old people are the first to commit suicide during famine. This is consistent with sociobiological theory, since inclinations toward altruism should increase as personal reproductive potential decreases. It is also explicable by kin selection, group selection, parental manipulation, and even reciprocal altruism, extended across generations. But geriatric self-sacrifice could also be due to cultural traditions that celebrate people who behaved that way in the past. In a sense, successful cultural traditions are those that have withstood a process analogous to natural selection (Campbell, 1975); accordingly, they tend to be adaptive, at least for societies, if not for individuals. But, unlike organic evolution, cultural evolution is Lamarckian, not Darwinian. However, the results of these two very different phenomena can be disquietingly similar and will be a challenge to assess.

2. "Natural selection is not the only factor responsible for the distribution of genes in a population; in particular, stochastic processes may be important." This also is true. At present, however, most evidence supports the role of selection as the primary, although not sole, determinant of gene distribution (Ayala, 1975). Furthermore, stochastic processes can be modeled and included in sociobiological theory—in certain areas, a start has already been made (Cohen, 1971).

3. "Sociobiology explains everything. It is too easy to generate untestable theory." Again, this is a serious objection. It is easier to produce theory than to test it—in fact, this is a continuing problem with other aspects of evolutionary theory as well (Peters, 1976). But this difficulty is not insurmountable; in particular, adroit use of the predictive approach should keep sociobiology on a firm empirical footing. There are additional, related problems. For example, we simply do not know how much "adaptiveness" genes can store. Theory suggests that individuals should behave toward each other as a function of cost-benefit fitness considerations, in which genetic relatedness figures prominently. Indeed, much theory turns on the ability of animals to respond to subtle differences in fitness considerations; yet we do not know whether most behavioral predispositions are literally capable of such fine tuning: "How do I love thee? Let me count thy genes." Still, by making the expectations of theory as explicit as possible, they can eventually be susceptible to confirmation or refutation, just as with any science (Barash, 1976b).

In the current flush of theoretical enthusiasm, there is certainly a danger that sociobiologists are constructing unsupported bridges, until, like cartoon characters, they may look down one day only to discover they are building on air! With a discipline so ripe for theory and simultaneously so resistant to the acquisition of pertinent data, such expeditions are perhaps inevitable. The sociobiological imagination may ultimately require weights rather than wings, but even now there are enough hard data to restrain excessive light-footedness.

FUTURE DIRECTIONS

As to the future, some limited predictions can be made with confidence. There will certainly be further theoretical insights and, hopefully, vigorous attempts to consolidate past gains by gathering appropriate data on free-living populations. Sociobiology may be about to enter a period of "normal science" (Kuhn, 1962) in which the dizzying advances of the past ten years will be evaluated, solidified, and perhaps extended into new realms. We hope to learn the precise adaptive limits of which organisms are capable; that is, it is one thing for theorists to suggest behavioral tactics that would ultimately serve the strategic goal of fitness maximization—it is another to see whether animals *really do* behave optimally. Studies assessing the predicted correlation between altruism and genetic relatedness, for example, would go far toward this goal, and accurate field techniques permitting measurement of genetic relatedness between individuals would be extremely valuable. On the one hand, sociobiology will almost certainly expand with further extrapolations to human behavior, perhaps providing a new perspective on the data of anthropology and the theories of sociology. Kin selection in particular may provide a means of evaluating human family structure in biological terms (van den Berghe and Barash, 1977). I doubt very much that evolutionary biology, in itself, will provide ethical or moral guidelines. On the other hand, it is very likely that new light will be thrown on the bases of our own human morality. The Golden Rule, incest taboos, patterns of inheritance and of interaction between old and young—all these are interpretable through natural selection. And the end is not in sight. Indeed, we are barely glimpsing the beginning!

Prophesying more boldly now, the evolutionary paradigm may provide considerable fresh insight to old problems. For example, sociobiology's concern with genetic relatedness suggests a new perspective on multicellular organisms, such as that their physical and functional integrity may be due to the genetic identity of the participating cells. (Why else would liver cells labor altruistically to detoxify dangerous substances, leaving reproduction to the gonadal cells?) In this sense, senescence may be explicable as the necessary consequence of accumulated somatic mutations, increasing the genetic distinctness of individual cells and therefore decreasing the payoff that otherwise selects for cooperation. Certainly, cancer is associated with dramatic cellular mutation, and, appropriately, it is characterized by a breakdown of susceptibility to normal regulatory restraint.

In more general terms, sociobiology suggests a perspective of health. Considerations of adaptive significance suggest a functional value to phenomena that might otherwise be viewed as pathological, or, at best, neutral. An evolutionary paradigm suggests the existence of hitherto unappreciated biological strategies for fitness maximization. For example, "spontaneous" abortion may well represent one such strategy, mediated through gametic altruism, fetal altruism, and/or parental manipulation, rather than simple incapacity of fetus or mother (Bernds and Barash, in press). Similarly, the regular loss of neurons with increasing age may indicate a strategy of redundancy combined with progressive jettisoning of incompetent cells. Recent studies of the apparent value of low-grade fever (Bernheim and Kluger, 1976) reflect a similar world view, in that any consistent physiological response, such as fever in warm-blooded animals, is likely to be one that contributes to fitness, or else it would have been selected against.

A sociobiological perspective may provide numerous unexpected insights to human behavior. It holds the promise of profound insight to our innermost behavioral inclinations—those inclinations should perhaps be distinguished from the final outcomes, which derive from complex interactions between genotype and experience and which are more properly the concern of social science. For example, Dostoyevsky's ([1864] 1972) *Notes from Underground* is a profoundly disturbing work, in large part because the narrator's underlying motivation is "spite." Defined sociobiologically, *spite* refers to an interaction in which both initiator and recipient lose fitness. Accordingly, it should not be found among animals, and so far it has not been. True spiteful behavior may be unique to humans, among whom it is nonetheless generally recognized as somehow inappropriate and bizarre, perhaps because of our own unconscious application of the central theorem. Sociobiology may be more relevant to normal behavior than to psychopathology, but even here the possibility exists that further insight to neuroses and psychoses may be gained by viewing them as the adaptive consequences of individual inability to follow a behavioral course of fitness maximization. We may well have been selected to follow such courses, just as we have been selected to seek food, rest, appropriate mates, and so on.

At this point, the crystal ball grows dim. However, it seems increasingly obvious that no paradigm approaches natural selection in its ability to explain a wide range of behavioral phenomena among animals and that none offers equivalent promise of cutting a clean swath through the morass of data and theory currently surrounding research on human behavior. One thing is perfectly clear: The future of the sociobiological revolution will be neither more nor less than what we make it. When Faraday was asked about the value of his new discovery, electricity, he responded, "What good is a baby?" For good or ill, sociobiology is just such a baby.

QUESTIONS FOR CRITICAL READERS

Remembering and Understanding

1. Write a summary of Barash's explanation of the political objections to sociobiology and his responses to those objections.
2. Summarize Barash's explanation of the scientific objections to sociobiology and his responses to those objections.
3. Explain the difference between genetic determinism and genetic influence on behavior.

Analyzing and Discussing

4. Which of the political objections to sociobiology seems strongest?
5. Which of the scientific objections seems strongest?

6. Barash says he doubts that evolutionary biology will provide ethical or moral guidelines. In your opinion, what is the role of science in providing moral or ethical insights?

Writing

7. Barash frequently mentions the concepts of fitness and adaptation. Using his statements as a starting point, and using any other sources that you need, write an explanation of these terms.

Some Women That Never Evolved

SARAH BLAFFER HRDY

Hrdy, a biologist, did her graduate work with E. O. Wilson at Harvard. The selection printed here is the first chapter of Hrdy's book, The Woman That Never Evolved. *Hrdy's interest here is to examine the popular and widespread notion that the typical social roles of men and women are biologically determined. In particular, she wants to challenge the idea that women are evolutionarily determined to be weaker than men. She draws on anthropology and primatology for background and information about her subject, and uses evolutionary theory to understand the social position of women.*

Natural selection is not always good, and depends (see Darwin) on many caprices of very foolish animals.

—GEORGE ELIOT, 1867

BIOLOGY, IT IS SOMETIMES THOUGHT, has worked against women. Assumptions about the biological nature of men and women have frequently been used to justify submissive and inferior female roles and a double standard in sexual morality. It has been assumed that men are by nature better equipped to conduct the affairs of civilization, women to perpetuate the species; that men are the rational, active members of society, women merely passive, fecund, and nurturing. Hence, many readers will open a book about the biology of female primates with considerable apprehension.

Feminists in particular may rebel at the thought of looking to the science of biology for information that bears on the human condition. They may be put off by the fact that among our nearest relations, the other primates, the balance of power favors males in most species. Yet, if they persist, readers may be surprised by what else they learn concerning their distant cousins and, by inference, their own remote ancestresses. They will find no basis for thinking that women—or their evolutionary predecessors—have ever been dominant over men in the conventional sense of that word, but they will find substantial grounds for questioning stereotypes which depict women as inferior to men—as naturally less assertive, less intelligent, less competitive, or less political than men are.

For at least two reasons, feminists have tended to reject biological evidence about females of other species in their thinking about the human condition. First, there is a widespread misconception that "biology is destiny." According to this view, if even a portion of the human male's dominance is ascribed to evolutionary causes, an intolerable status quo will have to be condoned as fundamentally unalterable. Second, biological evidence has been repeatedly misused to support ideological biases, and field studies have been designed and executed in the thrall of such biases. Certainly, this has been the case in the study of other primates. Research has focused on the way adult males maneuver for dominance while females attend to the tasks of mothering; it has neglected the manifestations of dominance and assertiveness in females themselves, behavior that some-times brings females into conflict with males and with each other.

Primatology is a rapidly expanding field. The most accurate infor-mation about female primates has only been collected in the last decade. Much of is confined to Ph.D. theses and technical accounts and has yet to find its way into the mainstream of the social sciences. Disastrously, experts writing about sex differences among primates have relied upon stereotypes of the female primate constructed in the early sixties. Pretend this is a quiz. Which of the following recent statements about primate social structure, all made by eminent social scientists, also happen to be obsolete?

> "The dominant male is obviously the central figure in the group's persistence over time."
> "Competition is peculiar to the male sex."
> "There is reason to believe that the female hierarchies are less stable. A female's status tends to change when she is in estrus, and to reflect the status of her male consort while she is in the mating phase of her cycle."

The answer is that all three are out of date. Yet such stereotypes have led to the widespread impression that "primate females seem bio-logically unprogrammed to dominate political systems, and the whole weight of the relevant primates' breeding history militates against female participation in what we can call 'primate public life.' " As we shall see in the course of this book, few statements about the biological origins of sexual asymmetries could be quite so far from the truth.

An occasional voice has warned that there was another side to this story—the work of the anthropologist Jane Lancaster comes to mind—but the reports about competitive males and mothering females continue to roll out of the textbook mills and are currently entrenched in college curricula and in popular literature. By comparison, more accurate accounts are technical and less accessible. Not surprisingly, otherwise broadminded writers and policymakers in psychology and the humanities (particularly those sympathetic to feminist goals) have ignored the primate record or chosen to reject it altogether. As a curious result, today we find that theories explaining the nearly universal dominance of males fall into two categories: hypotheses that are either biologically oriented and informed by stereotypes (that is, views which contain a kernel of truth but are, on the whole, quite misleading), or those that eschew the primate evidence altogether and thereby ignore much that is relevant to understanding the human condition.

When I refer to dominance among humans, I mean the ability to coerce the behavior of others. Among nonhuman primates, a simpler definition is often feasible because dominance hierarchies can be recognized from observations of one-on-one interactions between individuals competing for the same desired resource. When speaking of nonhuman primates, then, I use "dominant" to describe the animal that usually wins in a one-on-one encounter, the animal that typically can approach, threaten, and displace another. No one is particularly satisfied with the concept of dominance. Typically, dominance is difficult to assess and highly dependent on context; furthermore, dominance is not necessarily related among different spheres of activity. Hence, the publicly acclaimed emperor may be ruled by his wife at home; a sated tyrant may lose a wedge of meat when matched against a particularly hungry minion; and the richest or most powerful male may not beget the most children if his wives are routinely unfaithful. Nevertheless, the ability of one individual to influence or coerce the behavior of others, usually by threatening to inflict damage but also by promising to give (or withhold) rewards, remains a real phenomenon, and a term for it is useful. Even the most ardent critics of the concept do not advocate total expurgation of the term.

Whatever definition we might choose, though, there seems to be a general consensus among anthropologists that for most human societies, sexual asymmetry appears in dominance relations, and it gives the edge to males. Hence,

> Whereas some anthropologists argue that there are, or have been, truly egalitarian societies . . . and all agree that there are societies in which women have achieved considerable social recognition and power, none has observed a society in which women have publicly recognized power and authority surpassing that of men . . . Everywhere we find that women are excluded from certain crucial economic or political activities . . . It seems fair to say, then, that all contemporary societies are to some extent male-dominated, and that although

the degree and expression of female subordination vary greatly, sexual asymmetry is presently a universal fact of human social life.

The obvious question is, Why?

Psychologists and anthropologists have proposed a variety of explanations for male domination among humans. The following is not an exhaustive list, but it includes the major current theories.

Following Marx and Engels, one scenario begins with an egalitarian species. Only when an economic transition facilitated the accumulation of surpluses and trade, which in turn led to warfare in the defense of material goods and trade routes, did women lose out. As valuable producers but inferior warriors, they yield their autonomy to male capitalists.

Post-Freudian theory holds that subordination of women results from conditions of socialization. Long periods of close association between mother and offspring foster close identification of daughters with their mothers. Whereas daughters fail to form any strong sense of separate identity, boys must struggle to define their own gender role, and in the process not only deny but also devalue all that seems feminine.

Anthropologists from the structural school tell us that people associate women and their procreative functions such as menstruation and childbirth with Nature and natural processes. By contrast, men are identified with Culture and civilized processes. Because people perceive Culture to be superior to Nature, females by analogy are perceived as inferior.

For many "biobehaviorists," it was Man the Hunter who usurped the independence of women: big-game hunting, a peculiarly human adaptation, led to social inequality between the sexes. In one widely cited version of the theory, as hunting became important, the strength of males combined with their freedom from encumbering babies quickly permitted them to monopolize the chase and the distribution of meat. Success depended on special male skills: visual-spatial capacities, stamina, stalking abilities, and especially cooperation. According to a now notorious extension of this scenario, "our intellect, interests, emotions, and basic social life—all are evolutionary products of the success of the hunting adaptation." (Curiously, few anthropologists have asked why intelligence never became sex-linked or why—if intelligence evolved among males to help them hunt—Nature should have squandered it on a sex that never hunted.) The hunting hypothesis was later refined to emphasize the importance of male predispositions to bond with other males: such bonds provided the power base for subsequent political preeminence achieved by men. Furthermore, male hunters were able to cement reciprocal relations with an even wider network of allies through the presentation of meat. Men engendered obligations and gained recognition by such gifts. Once male preeminence was established, females themselves became objects of exchange and were given in marriage by brothers or fathers who received wives for themselves in return.

Although essentially male-centered and to some tastes "sexist," these theories rely on traditional anthropological tenets. Feminist reconstructions of this stage in human evolution are based on the same assumptions about early human ecological adaptations; they also focus on division of labor, sharing, the right to allocate resources, and the importance of ritual bonding. (Theory has even found its way into practice. Feminist educators, for example, have absorbed the notion that in order to compete successfully for power, women's socialization must begin to incorporate the lessons and social reflexes to be learned from teamwork. In a recent book on managerial women, the authors advocate competitive team sports so that women leaders-in-training may participate in this contemporary analogue of hunting and tribal warfare.) In developing a new perspective, revisionists highlight female contributions to subsistence, tool manufacture, and cultural traditions, but they leave the basic outlines of early human ecology unchanged. For example, the feminist anthropologists Adrienne Zihlman and Nancy Tanner concur with the conventional view that people diverged from other primates around five million years ago, and they hypothesize that as early humans shifted from forest to savanna they increasingly shared resources, differentiated assignment of task by sex, and relied on tools. Zihlman and Tanner regard these changes as central to the transformation of our primate ancestors, but they also emphasize that women were gathering a large proportion of the food, that the vegetables women gathered were crucial to subsistence, and that it was women who tended to invent new food-getting technologies and to transmit this information from generation to generation. It is different wine in the same bottle: now woman is the toolmaker. From this perspective, male "superiority" is simply an impression conveyed by biases in data collection and analysis.

Here, then, are five theories to explain male dominance, each highly informative in its own right. But they all share one striking deficiency. Each focuses upon the human condition and lays the burden of sexual inequality, real or mythical, at the doorstep of specifically human attributes: the production of surpluses and the subsequent rise of trade economies; the discovery of the "self" and the formation of ego boundaries; binary conceptualizations of the universe which engender oppositions such as Nature and Culture; big-game hunting; and a sexual division of labor related to subsistence. Each of these theories may contribute to our understanding of the human case, but even taken together, they are insufficient to explain the widespread occurrence of sexual inequality in nature, inasmuch as they account for only a small portion of known cases. They cannot explain sexual asymmetry in even one other species. Yet male dominance characterizes the majority of several hundred other species that, like our own, belong to the order Primates. Save for a handful of highly informative exceptions, sexual asymmetries are nearly universal among primates. Logic alone should warn us against explaining such a widespread phenomenon with reference only to a specialized subset of human examples.

It is of course completely appropriate in some respects that theories to explain the peculiar status of women relative to men should focus as they do on uniquely human attributes. We do differ from other animals in our use of language, in our creation and transmission of value systems and advanced technologies, and, most importantly, in our capacity to formulate and articulate conscious decisions. Other creatures simply fall into place within social systems that persist because they happen to be evolutionarily stable. We, by contrast, exhibit an insatiable desire to imagine or bring about novel social systems, some of them idealistic or even utopian in character.

So our idealism—and our ability to consciously change our society— sets us apart from other creatures, but that does not give us license to devalue the facts about other primates. Indeed, awareness of the differences, when combined with knowledge of our close relation by common descent with the other apes, ought instead to make us wonder out loud how we could have come to be the way we are. Although opinions differ as to whether chimpanzees or gorillas are our closest living relatives, it is clear that we are more closely related to these two species of great apes than either chimps or gorillas are to the third great ape, the orangutan. By current estimates, only five million years have elapsed since the nearest common ancestor we share with chimps. The genes of humans and chimps are biochemically almost indistinguishable—a fact which has led scientists to suspect that a relatively small number of genes governing the timing of development make all the difference between speaking, culture-bearing humans and our less talkative cousins.

There is an impressive degree of continuity in the experience of humans and other higher primates (this includes both monkeys and apes) that goes far beyond similar anatomy and biochemistry, fingernails, and stereoscopic vision. We and the other higher primates perceive the world in a similar fashion, and we process information in similar ways. For example, we share striking neuroanatomical patterns in those portions of the brain concerned with memory. Expressions of emotion, such as the smile, can be traced from species to species and identified in very rudimentary form in the "open-mouth display" of other primates. Under appropriate conditions female primates, from hamadryas baboons living in a harem to women living in college dormitories, tend to synchronize their menstrual cycles. At the beginning of the school term, young women arriving from all parts of the country are cycling on different schedules; by the end of the school year, close friends menstruate around the same time of the month. Several recent studies have shown that women, like other primates, are more likely to initiate sexual activity around the time of ovulation, and there is increasing evidence that other aspects of woman's sexuality, such as her capacity to experience orgasms, are shared by other primate females. Most importantly, it is competition among individuals of the same sex (not just competition among males, but also among females) that has permitted reproductive exploitation of one sex by the other to evolve and be maintained (that is, a member of one sex manipulating another to his or her own reproductive advantage). In this respect, humans may be far more similar to other primates than we are different from them.

On the other hand, by refusing to talk about biology, we effectively hide the fact that there are important ways in which human females are in a worse position than are females in other species. (One of the justifications, after all, for ignoring the animal evidence is that supposedly it paints a picture prejudicial to the aspirations of women.) Among humans there is a universal reliance on shared or bartered food. In many societies, a woman without a man to hunt or earn income, or a man without a wife to do the cooking, is at considerable disadvantage. By contrast, among all nonhuman primates each adult is entirely responsible for supplying his or her own food. The only exceptions involve occasional meat sharing among chimpanzees, but even here males tend to monopolize meat from cooperatively hunted prey (small ungulates and other primates); females rely for animal protein on termites and other individually obtained small prey. Among chimpanzees there is a rudimentary division of labor by sex, but in no case does one sex depend on the other for any staple.

In this respect, female primates (and also, one could argue, the males) enjoy greater autonomy than do either men or women. In roughly 80 percent of human societies, fathers or brothers exercise some control over adolescent and adult females. Such *authority* does not exist among other primates. The Marxists have a point: patriarchy tends to develop where women produce commodities and not just offspring. We have a uniquely elaborate division of labor by sex, and a unique reliance on sharing. But more basic asymmetries between the sexes, based on reproductive exploitation of one sex by the other, long predate the human condition. The fact that males are almost universally dominant over females throughout the primate order does not mean that males escape being used! But dominant they are, with only a few (very important) exceptions. Since we are typically primate in this respect, it seems foolish to continue to focus our attention exclusively on those features of our way of life in which we are *untypical* of other primates. Male authority is indeed uniquely human, but its origins are not.

Primatologists tend to see the world a bit differently from other people. Not surprisingly—it's an odd occupation, after all, crawling under brambles to keep a monkey or an ape in view. Primatologists pay attention to what animals do, not to what they say they do. And primatologists tend to be excessively curious about ancestry. What sort of ancestor did the creature at hand evolve from? And why? What social and environmental pressures made it advantageous for an individual to possess a certain trait? Because of the taxonomic relationship between us and the other primates, few primatologists can resist the temptation to combine an anthropocentric concern for *Homo sapiens* with this urge to understand origins. A peculiar perspective, no doubt, but it is my contention that a broader understanding of other primates is going to help us to expand the concept of human nature to include both sexes, and that it is going to help us to understand the problems we face in attempting to eliminate social inequalities based on sex. In the process, we will also find out why some current notions of what it means to be female depict natures that never did, and never could have, evolved within the primate lineage.

For example, the belief that women once ruled human affairs still enjoys some currency among some feminists, particularly those who work in a Marxist tradition. They inherit the notion, by way of Friedrich Engels, from a Swiss jurist and student of Roman law, Johann Bachofen. Supporting his ideas with copious references to ancient mythology embellished with bits of archaeology and pre-Hellenic history, Bachofen in 1861 published an outline of human history entitled *The Law of the Mother (Das Mutterrecht)*. In it, he proposed that people first lived in a state of cheerful promiscuity which then gave way to a more orderly society controlled by women. Matriarchy was supplanted, gradually, by systems in which men were dominant, and those have persisted until the present. Bachofen believed that a matriarchal phase was universal in the history of human societies and was not a special adaptation to environmental or political circumstances.

Yet the weight of evidence from anthropology and archaeology since Bachofen's time has not favored his view. To be sure, there have been societies in which property was passed through the female line and children were identified primarily as their mother's offspring rather than their father's. Such matri*lineal* (not matri*archal*) arrangements are far from rare among human societies. About 15 percent of the world's cultures reckon inheritance through mothers, and in about half of these a man goes to live with his wife's family when he marries. (As a rule these societies are horticultural, and the property in question is a garden plot passed from mother to daughter.) Yet even in these circumstances men tend to become the administrators of the family's wealth and retain the governing voice in collective affairs. It is certainly possible that some groups of women banded together to live like Amazons, but such societies were never a universal stage in human evolution.

Myths about women ruling the world usually come linked with a theory about the true nature of women. The prototypical matriarchs, the Amazons, were believed to be on the whole aggressive and warlike—masculine spirits in drag. At the other extreme, the idealized women of *Herland*—Charlotte Perkins Gilman's marvelous 1915 utopian novel about an all-female society—were even-tempered and utterly rational creatures whose solidarity dumbfounded a male spy into exclaiming, "Women can't cooperate—it's against nature." Both traditions have recent exponents. Valerie Solanis revived the Amazonian ethos in her 1967 manifesto for the Society for Cutting Up Men (SCUM), while Elizabeth Gould Davis refurbished Gilman's vision in her book *The First Sex*, which averred that there once was a "golden age of queendoms, when peace and justice prevailed on earth and the gods of war had not been born."

The matriarchal fallacy and the myths linked with it about the nature of women are not merely a misreading of the anthropological and paleontological records. They have also provided a refuge from and a defense against another, more popular nineteenth-century belief about the nature of women: that they are sexually passive creatures devoted to the tasks of mothering and that they are devoid of political instincts. This doctrine of female inferiority has disfigured several ostensibly impartial realms, particularly the study of human evolution. Such ideas have predisposed biologists to some curious conclusions about women and female animals in general. For example, it is often assumed—most often implicitly—that only males gain an evolutionary advantage from being competitive or sexually adventurous. To the extent that female behavior contradicts these assumptions, it is dismissed as merely a by-product of the masculine character.

I am scarcely the first person to point out that the evolution of female traits is no less subject to the rigors of competition than that of males. Just four years after Charles Darwin published *The Descent of Man and Selection in Relation to Sex* (1871), Antoinette Brown Blackwell published a polite critique of the book. She made no bones about her commitment to both feminism and to Darwin's theories about natural selection. But Blackwell wished that she could broaden his perspective.

> Mr. Darwin, also, eminently a student of organic structures, and of the causes which have produced them, with their past and present characters, has failed to hold definitely before his mind the principle that the difference of sex, whatever it may consist in, must itself be subject to *natural selection* and to evolution. Nothing but the exacting task before him of settling the Origin of all Species and the Descent

of Man, through all the ages, could have prevented his recognition of ever-widening organic differences evolved in two distinct lines. With great wealth of detail, he has illustrated his theory of how the male has probably acquired additional masculine characters; but he seems never to have thought of looking to see whether or not the females had developed equivalent feminine characters.

In accepting the theory of natural selection, Blackwell firmly rejected the doctrine of female inferiority and the idea that females are somehow incomplete versions of males—beliefs which "need not be accepted without question, even by their own school of evolutionists." But the evolutionists were not listening.

In the late nineteenth century the popular understanding of evolution became permeated by social Darwinism, a philosophy most closely identified with Herbert Spencer, who was energetically adapting Darwin's theories to fit his own political views. Spencer thought females never had been inherently equal to males and could never be; subordination of women was not only natural but, in his view, desirable.

Social Darwinism has, almost indelibly, tainted most people's understanding of evolutionary theory—certainly as it applies to human beings. Yet social Darwinism differs from Darwinism-without-adjectives in one all-important way, and ignoring this distinction has been one of the most unfortunate and long-lived mistakes of science journalism. Darwinism proper is devoted to analyzing all the diverse forms of life according to the theory of natural selection. Darwinists describe competition between unequal individuals, but they place no value judgment on either the competition or its outcome. Natural-selection theory provides a powerful way to understand the subordination of one individual, or group of individuals, by another, but it in no way attempts to condone (or condemn) subordination.

By contrast, social Darwinists attempt to *justify* social inequality. Social Darwinism explicitly assumes that competition leads to "improvement" of a species; the mechanism of improvement is the unequal survival of individuals and their offspring. Applying this theory to the human condition, social Darwinists hold that those individuals who win the competition, who survive and thrive, must necessarily be the "best." Social inequalities between the sexes, or between classes or races, represent the operation of natural selection and therefore should not be tampered with, since such tampering would impede the progress of the species. It is this latter brand of Darwinism that became popularly associated with evolutionary biology. The association is incorrect, but it helps to explain why feminists have steadfastly resisted biological perspectives.

Blackwell's informed dissent was drowned out in the wake of popular acceptance of social Darwinism. Her contribution to evolutionary biology can be summed up with one phrase: the road not taken. This turning point, over a century ago, left a rift between feminism and evolutionary biology still not mended. Historically and politically, there was obvious justification for the split. There has been a prevailing bias among evolutionary theorists in favor of stressing sexual competition among males for access to females at the expense of careful scrutiny of what females in their own right were doing. Among their recurring themes are the male's struggle for preeminence and his quest for "sexual variety" in order to inseminate as many females as possible. Visionaries of male-male competition stressed the imagery of primate females herded by tyrannical male consorts: sexually cautious females coyly safeguarding their fertility until the appropriate male partner arrives; women waiting at campsites for their men to return; and, particularly, females so preoccupied with motherhood that they have little respite to influence their species' social organization. Alternative possibilities were neglected: that selection favored females who were assertive, sexually active, or highly competitive, who adroitly manipulated male consorts, or who were as strongly motivated to gain high social status as they were to hold and carry babies. As a result, until just recently descriptions of other primate species have told little about females except in their capacity as mothers. Natural histories of monkeys and apes have described the behavior of males with far greater detail and accuracy than they have described the lives of females. Small wonder, then, that audiences sensitized to both the excesses of social Darwinism and conventional sexism have found this emphasis upsetting.

Yet evolutionary biology, and its offspring, sociobiology, are not inherently sexist. The proportion of "sexists" among their proponents is probably no greater than the proportion among scientists generally. To be sure, contemporary analyses of mammalian breeding systems can cause even a committed Darwinian like myself to contemplate her gender with foreboding. Yet, it is all too easy to forget, while quaking, that sociobiology, if read as a prescription for life rather than a description of the way some creatures behave, makes it seem bad luck to be born either sex.

The purpose of this book, then, is to dispel some long-held myths about the nature of females, and to suggest a few plausible hypotheses about the evolution of woman that are more in line with current data. Throughout the discussion, it will be well to keep in mind a central paradox of the human condition—that our species possesses the capacity to carry sexual inequality to its greatest known extremes, but we also possess the potential to realize an unusual social equality between the sexes should we choose to exercise that potential. However, if social inequality based on sex is a serious problem, and if we really intend to do something constructive about it, we are going to need a comprehensive understanding of its causes. I am convinced that we will never adequately understand the present causes of sexual asymmetry in our own species until we understand its evolutionary history in the lines from which we descend. Since we cannot travel back in time to see that history in the making, we must turn to those surrogates we have, other living primates, and study them comparatively. Without the perspective such a study affords, we will remain ignorant of the most fundamental aspects of our own situation, in part because of a diminished ability to ask interesting questions about it.

QUESTIONS FOR CRITICAL READERS

Remembering and Understanding

1. Explain why, according to Hrdy, women are reluctant to enter into biological discussions about the status or role of women.
2. Summarize at least two of Hrdy's specific comparisons between women and female primates.
3. Identify and restate Hrdy's central point, and give the major reasons she offers in support of that point.
4. List and explain at least three of the long-held myths about women that Hrdy wants to dispel.

Analyzing and Discussing

5. Why should women be uncomfortable about comparisons between human and primate societies?
6. Hrdy says that, "sociobiology, if read as a prescription for life rather than a description of the way some creatures behave, makes it seem bad luck to be born either sex." Why would she say this?

Writing

7. Hrdy's concern is primarily with women. Write a paper in which you explain how Hrdy's insights might be equally true of some group other than women, such as men, blacks, Native Americans, or some other easily identifiable group.

Biological Potentiality vs. Biological Determinism

STEPHEN JAY GOULD

Gould, a paleontologist and geologist by profession, is professor of Zoology at Harvard and writes a monthly column for Natural History *magazine. He was one of the early critics of Wilson's attempts to apply sociobiology to humans. In this essay he explores the distinction between biological determinism (which holds that specific features and behaviors can be genetically caused), and biological potentiality (which holds that genes produce the potential for a wide range of features and behaviors, but do not compel them).*

IN 1758, LINNAEUS FACED the difficult decision of how to classify his own species in the definitive edition of his *Systema Naturae*. Would he simply rank *Homo sapiens* among the other animals or would he create for us a separate status? Linnaeus compromised. He placed us within his classification (close to monkeys and bats), but set us apart by his description. He defined our relatives by the mundane, distinguishing characters of size, shape, and number of fingers and toes. For *Homo sapiens*, he wrote only the Socratic injunction: *nosce te ipsum—"know thyself."*

For Linnaeus, *Homo sapiens* was both special and not special. Unfortunately, this eminently sensible resolution has been polarized and utterly distorted by most later commentators. Special and not special have come to mean nonbiological and biological, or nurture and nature. These later polarizations are nonsensical. Humans are animals and everything we do lies within our biological potential. Nothing arouses this ardent (although currently displaced) New Yorker to greater anger than the claims of some self-styled "ecoactivists" that large cities are the "unnatural" harbingers of our impending destruction. But—and here comes the biggest *but* I can muster—the statement that humans are animals does not imply that our specific patterns of behavior and social arrangements are in any way directly determined by our genes. *Potentiality* and *determination* are different concepts.

The intense discussion aroused by E. O. Wilson's *Sociobiology* (Harvard University Press, 1975) has led me to take up this subject. Wilson's book has been greeted by a chorus of praise and publicity. I, however, find myself among the smaller group of its detractors. Most of *Sociobiology* wins from me the same high praise almost universally accorded it. For a lucid account of evolutionary principles and an indefatigably thorough discussion of social behavior among all groups of animals, *Sociobiology* will be the primary document for years to come. But Wilson's last chapter, "From Sociobiology to Sociology," leaves me very unhappy indeed. After twenty-six chapters of careful documentation for the nonhuman animals, Wilson concludes with an extended speculation on the genetic basis of supposedly universal patterns in human behavior. Unfortunately, since this chapter is his statement on the subject closest to all our hearts, it has also attracted more than 80 percent of all the commentary in the popular press.

We who have criticized this last chapter have been accused of denying altogether the relevance of biology to human behavior, of reviving an ancient superstition by placing ourselves outside the rest of "the creation." Are we pure "nurturists?" Do we permit a political vision of human perfectibility to blind us to evident constraints imposed by our biological nature? The answer to both statements is no. The issue is not universal biology vs. human uniqueness, but biological potentiality vs. biological determinism.

Replying to a critic of his article in the *New York Times Magazine* (October 12, 1975), Wilson wrote:

> There is no doubt that the patterns of human social behavior, including altruistic behavior, are under genetic control, in the sense that they represent a restricted subset of possible patterns that are very different from the patterns of termites, chimpanzees and other animal species.

If this is all that Wilson means by genetic control, then we can scarcely disagree. Surely we do not do all the things that other animals do, and just as surely, the range of our potential behavior is circumscribed by our biology. We would lead very different social lives if we photosynthesized (no agriculture, gathering, or hunting—the major determinants of our social evolution) or had life cycles like those of the gall midges discussed in essay 10. (When feeding on an uncrowded mushroom, these insects reproduce in the larval or pupal stage. The young grow within the mother's body, devour her from inside, and emerge from her depleted external shell ready to feed, grow the next generation, and make the supreme sacrifice.) But Wilson makes much stronger claims. Chapter 27 is not a statement about the range of potential human behaviors or even an argument for the restriction of that range from a much larger total domain among all animals. It is, primarily, an extended speculation on the existence of genes for specific and variable traits in human behavior—including spite, aggression, xenophobia, conformity, homosexuality, and the characteristic behavioral differences between men and women in Western society. Of course, Wilson does not deny the role of nongenetic learning in human behavior; he even states at one point that "genes have given away most of their sovereignty." But, he quickly adds, genes "maintain a certain amount of influence in at least the behavioral qualities that underlie variations between cultures." And the next paragraph calls for a "discipline of anthropological genetics."

Biological determinism is the primary theme in Wilson's discussion of human behavior; chapter 27 makes no sense in any other context. Wilson's primary aim, as I read him, is to suggest that Darwinian theory might reformulate the human sciences just as it previously transformed so many other biological disciplines. But Darwinian processes can not operate without genes to select. Unless the "interesting" properties of human behavior are under specific genetic control, sociology need fear no invasion of its turf. By interesting, I refer to the subjects sociologists and anthropologists fight about most often—aggression, social stratification, and differences in behavior between men and women. If genes only specify that we are large enough to live in a world of gravitational forces, need to rest our bodies by sleeping, and do not photosynthesize, then the realm of genetic determinism will be relatively uninspiring.

What is the direct evidence for genetic control of specific human social behavior? At the moment, the answer is none whatever. (It would not be impossible, in theory, to gain such evidence by standard, controlled experiments in breeding, but we do not raise people in *Drosophila* bottles, establish pure lines, or control environments for invariant nurturing.) Sociobiologists must therefore advance indirect arguments based on plausibility. Wilson uses three major strategies: universality, continuity, and adaptiveness.

1. Universality: If certain behaviors are invariably found in our closest primate relatives and among humans themselves, a circumstantial case for common, inherited genetic control may be advanced. Chapter 27 abounds with statements about supposed human universals. For example, "Human beings are absurdly easy to indoctrinate—they *seek* it." Or, "Men would rather believe than know." I can only say that my own experience does not correspond with Wilson's.

When Wilson must acknowledge diversity, he often dismisses the uncomfortable "exceptions" as temporary and unimportant aberrations. Since Wilson believes that repeated, often genocidal warfare has shaped our genetic destiny, the existence of nonaggressive peoples is embarrassing. But he writes: "It is to be expected that some isolated cultures will escape the process for generations at a time, in effect reverting temporarily to what ethnographers classify as a pacific state."

In any case, even if we can compile a list of behavioral traits shared by humans and our closest primate relatives, this does not make a good case for common genetic control. Similar results need not imply similar causes; in fact, evolutionists are so keenly aware of this problem that they have developed a terminology to express it. Similar features due to common genetic ancestry are "homologous"; similarities due to common function, but with different evolutionary histories, are "analogous" (the wings of birds and insect, for example—the common ancestor of both groups lacked wings). I will argue below that a basic feature of human biology supports the idea that many behavioral similarities between humans and other primates are analogous, and that they have no direct genetic specification in humans.

2. Continuity: Wilson claims, with ample justice in my opinion, that the Darwinian explanation of altruism in W.D. Hamilton's 1964 theory of "kin selection" forms the basis for an evolutionary theory of animal societies. Altruistic acts are the cement of stable societies, yet they seem to defy a Darwinian explanation. On Darwinian principles, all individuals are selected to maximize their own genetic contribution to future generations. How, then, can they willingly sacrifice or endanger themselves by performing altruistic acts to benefit others?

The resolution is charmingly simple in concept, although complex in technical detail. By benefiting relatives, altruistic acts preserve an altruist's genes even if the altruist himself will not be the one to perpetuate them. For example, in most sexually reproducing organisms, an individual shares (on average) one-half the genes of his sibs and one-eighth the genes of his first cousins. Hence, if faced with a choice of saving oneself alone or sacrificing oneself to save more than two sibs or more than eight first cousins, the Darwinian calculus favors altruistic sacrifice; for in so doing, an altruistic actually increases his own genetic representation in future generations.

Natural selection will favor the preservation of such self-serving altruist genes. But what of altruistic acts toward nonrelatives? Here sociobiologists must invoke a related concept of "reciprocal altruism" to preserve a genetic explanation. The altruistic act entails some danger and no immediate benefit, but if it inspires a reciprocal act by the current beneficiary at some future time, it may pay off in the long run: a genetic incarnation of the age-old adage: you scratch my back and I'll scratch yours (even if we're not related).

The argument from continuity then proceeds. Altruistic acts in other animal societies can be plausibly explained as examples of Darwinian kin selection. Humans perform altruistic acts and these are likely to have a similarly direct genetic basis. But again, similarity of result does not imply identity of cause (see below for an alternative explanation based on biological potentiality rather than biological determinism).

3. Adaptiveness: Adaptation is the hallmark of Darwinian processes. Natural selection operates continuously and relentlessly to fit organisms to their environments. Disadvantageous social structures, like poorly designed morphological structures, will not survive for long.

Human social practices are clearly adaptive. Marvin Harris has delighted in demonstrating the logic and sensibility of those social practices in other cultures that seem most bizarre to smug Westerners (*Cows, Pigs, Wars, and Witches*. Random House, 1974). Human social behavior is riddled with altruism; it is also clearly adaptive. Is this not a prima facie argument for direct genetic control? My answer is definitely "no," and I can best illustrate my claim by reporting an argument I recently had with an eminent anthropologist.

My colleague insisted that the classic story of Eskimos on ice floes provides adequate proof for the existence of specific altruist genes maintained by kin selection. Apparently, among some Eskimo peoples, social units are arranged as family groups. If food resources dwindle and the family must move to survive, aged grandparents willingly remain behind (to die) rather than endanger the survival of their entire family by slowing an arduous and dangerous migration. Family groups with no altruist genes have succumbed to natural selection as migrations hindered by the old and sick lead to the death of entire families. Grandparents with altruist genes increase their own fitness by their sacrifice, for they enhance the survival of close relatives sharing their genes.

The explanation by my colleague is plausible, to be sure, but scarcely conclusive since an eminently simple, nongenetic explanation also exists: there are no altruist genes at all, in fact, no important genetic differences among Eskimo families whatsoever. The sacrifice of grandparents is an adaptive, but nongenetic, cultural trait. Families with no tradition for sacrifice do not survive for many generations. In other families, sacrifice is celebrated in song and story; aged grandparents who stay behind become the greatest heroes of the clan. Children are socialized from their earliest memories to the glory and honor of such sacrifice.

I cannot prove my scenario, any more than my colleague can demonstrate his. But in the current context of no evidence, they are at least equally plausible. Likewise, reciprocal altruism undeniably exists in human societies, but this provides no evidence whatever for its genetic basis. As Benjamin Franklin said: "We must all hang together, or assuredly we shall all hang separately." Functioning societies may require reciprocal altruism. But these acts need not be coded into our consciousness by genes; they may be inculcated equally well by learning.

I return, then, to Linnaeus's compromise—we are both ordinary and special. The central feature of our biological uniqueness also provides the major reason for doubting that our behaviors are directly coded by specific genes. That feature is, of course, our large brain. Size itself is a major determinant of the function and structure of any object. The large and the small cannot work in the same way. The study of changes that accompany increasing size is called "allometry." Best known are the structural changes that compensate for decreasing surface/volume ratios of large creatures—relatively thick legs and convoluted internal surfaces (lungs, and villi of the small intestine, for example). But markedly increased brain size in human evolution may have had the most profound allometric consequences of all—for it added enough neural connections to convert an inflexible and rather rigidly programmed device into a labile organ, endowed with sufficient logic and memory to substitute nonprogrammed learning for direct specification as the ground of social behavior. Flexibility may well be the most important determinant of human consciousness; the direct programming of behavior has probably become inadaptive.

Why imagine that specific genes for aggression, dominance, or spite have any importance when we know that the brain's enormous flexibility permits us to be aggressive or peaceful, dominant or submissive, spiteful or generous? Violence, sexism, and general nastiness *are* biological since they represent one subset of a possible range of behaviors. But peacefulness, equality, and kindness are just as biological—and we may see their influence increase if we can create social structures that permit them to flourish. Thus, my criticism of Wilson does not invoke a nonbiological "environmentalism"; it merely pits the concept of biological potentiality—a brain capable of the full range of human behaviors and rigidly predisposed toward none—against the idea of biological determinism—specific genes for specific behavioral traits.

But why is this academic issue so delicate and explosive? There is no hard evidence for either position, and what difference does it make, for example, whether we conform because conformer genes have been selected or because our general genetic makeup permits conformity as one strategy among many?

The protracted and intense debate surrounding biological determinism has arisen as a function of its social and political message. As I argue in the preceding set of essays, biological determinism has always been used to defend existing social arrangements as biologically inevitable—from "for ye have the poor always with you" to nineteenth-century imperialism to modern sexism. Why else would a set of ideas so devoid of factual support gain such a consistently good press from established media throughout the centuries? This usage is quite out of the control of individual scientists who propose deterministic theories for a host of reasons, often benevolent.

I make no attribution of motive in Wilson's or anyone else's case. Neither do I reject determinism because I dislike its political usage. Scientific truth, as we understand it, must be our primary criterion. We live with several unpleasant biological truths, death being the most undeniable and ineluctable. If genetic determinism is true, we will learn to live with it as well. But I reiterate my statement that no evidence exists to support it, that the crude versions of past centuries haves been conclusively disproved, and that its continued popularity is a function of social prejudice among those who benefit most from the status quo.

But let us not saddle *Sociobiology* with the sins of past determinists. What have been its direct results in the first flush of its excellent publicity? At best, we see the beginnings of a line of social research that promises only absurdity by its refusal to consider immediate nongenetic factors. The January 30, 1976, issue of *Science* (America's leading technical journal for scientists) contains an article on panhandling that I would have accepted as satire if it had appeared verbatim in the *National Lampoon*. The authors dispatched "panhandlers" to request dimes from various "targets." Results are discussed only in the context of kin selection, reciprocal altruism, and the food-sharing habits of chimps and baboons—nothing on current urban realities in America. As one major conclusion, they find that male panhandlers are "far more successful approaching a single female or a pair of females than a male and female together; they were particularly unsuccessful when approaching a single male or two males together." But not a word about urban fear or the politics of sex—just some statements about chimps and the genetics of altruism (although they finally admit that reciprocal altruism probably does not apply—after all, they argue, what future benefit can one expect from a panhandler).

In the first negative comment on *Sociobiology*, economist Paul Samuelson (*Newsweek*, July 7, 1975) urged sociobiologists to tread softly in the zones of race and sex. I sees no evidence that his advice is being heeded. In his *New York Times Magazine* article of October 12, 1975, Wilson writes:

> In hunter-gatherer societies, men hunt and women stay at home. This strong bias persists in *most* [my emphasis] agricultural and industrial societies and, on that ground alone, appears to have a genetic origin . . . . My own guess is that the genetic bias is intense enough to cause a substantial division of labor even in the most free and most egalitarian of future societies. . . . Even with identical education and equal access to all professions, men are likely to continue to play a disproportionate role in political life, business and science.

We are both similar to and different from other animals. In different cultural contexts, emphasis upon one side or the other of this fundamental truth plays a useful social role. In Darwin's day, an assertion of our similarity broke through centuries of harmful superstition. Now we may need to emphasize our difference as flexible animals with a vast range of potential behavior. Our biological nature does not stand in the way of social reform. We are, as Simone de Beauvoir said, "l'être dont l'être est de n'être pas"—the being whose essence lies in having no essence.

QUESTIONS FOR CRITICAL READERS

Remembering and Understanding

1. Explain the difference between biological potentiality and biological determinism.
2. Explain Gould's interpretation of the special/not-special distinction as he applies it to humans.
3. Why do altruistic acts defy Darwinian explanation?

Analyzing and Discussing

4. Explain Gould's statement that flexibility may be more adaptive (and thus more important) than direct genetic programming of behavior.
5. Review Gould's description of the panhandler experiments. How would "urban fear [and] the politics of sex" alter the results of those experiments?
6. Why does Gould say that aggression, social stratification, and differences in behavior between men and women are the "interesting" properties of human behavior? What makes these more interesting than other kinds of behavior?

Writing

7. Write a paper based on Gould's assertion that "the range of our potential behavior is circumscribed by our biology." Explain what Gould means, and also give examples of how human behavior is limited by human biology. At some point, provide an example of how a different biology could alter human behavior.

Forging a New Underclass

────────── THE EDITORS OF ──────────
CONSUMER REPORTS

In this selection, the editors of Consumer Reports *explain how recently developed genetic tests can be used to discriminate against people who have the genetic potential to develop health problems.*

AS IT BECOMES POSSIBLE to decode our genetic secrets, certain outsiders will find it profitable to tune in. Even without predictive tests, some employers and insurance companies have seized on genetic information as a means of forecasting an applicant's future health.

"Genetic discrimination is present now and will continue, driven by economic considerations," states physician and attorney Philip R. Reilly, executive director of the Shriver Center for Mental Retardation in Waltham, Mass. "Organizations tend to shy away from people whose problems may be costly."

The extent of such bias can only be guessed. When Harvard geneticist Paul Billings ran a medical-journal ad asking for reports of genetic discrimination, 29 respondents met study criteria. They'd been turned down for auto, life, health, mortgage, or disability insurance, turned away from adoption agencies, or denied employment, all on the basis of their genes. Yet most were neither disabled nor certain to become so. Some were excluded because their family history put them at risk, though their personal genetic status was unknown. Others were treated as if they were ill, despite therapy that kept them symptom-free.

Individuals with a genetic disorder were assumed to be severely affected, though that wasn't always the case. "There can be extreme variability in how a gene is expressed," says Billings. "That's true even within a family, with the same gene and essentially the same environment. Yet the presence of a genetic trait carries an aura of predestination. Once you're labeled with a genetic disease, insurers don't want to know that you're barely affected."

LIMITED POWERS OF PREDICTION

Predictive tests only partially illuminate future events. A positive test rarely reveals the severity of a disorder and whether or when it will appear. And if genetic-disease prognosis can be an uncertain business with simple, single-gene inheritance, disorders influenced by multiple genes and environmental factors will be even harder to sort out.

But perfect prediction may be unimportant to institutions eager to minimize costs, says Dr. Neil A. Holtzman, professor of pediatrics at the Johns Hopkins University School of Medicine. "In times of ample labor, employers might welcome a test for something like manic-depressive illness, even if it screens out some people not really at risk."

Corporate interest in genetic testing is already on record. In 1982 the U.S. Office of Technology Assessment (OTA) surveyed leading companies and utilities to determine the extent of genetic testing in the workplace. Twenty-three of the 366 respondents were using genetic tests or had previously done so; 59 were considering the possibility. At the time, screening focused on workers' susceptibility to certain occupational hazards, despite the OTA's finding that the genetic tests then in use didn't meet "established scientific criteria for routine use in an occupational setting."

Some observers believe that using valid genetic tests to exclude workers sensitive to certain toxins can be reasonable protective measure. The danger is that industry may try to screen out the most vulnerable rather than clean up an environment that places all workers at increased risk. Some industries, for example, have barred women from jobs involving exposure to lead (which affects the fetus) rather than reduce the exposure levels.

The most likely emphasis of future screening, however, will be to hold down corporate health-care costs, which have been climbing some 20 percent annually. Premiums for group health insurance, a benefit offered by almost all medium and large firms, are based on the group's actual health expenses. So it pays for employers to avoid hiring anyone with serious medical problems—or anyone likely to develop them. In addition, half of all employers are self-insured: Every dollar in health claims comes directly from company coffers.

SIGNS OF THE TIMES

The role of genetic tests in pre-employment screening is probably still small (an OTA survey to be released this fall will detail current practices). But several signs suggest the tests will be used as soon as they're technically feasible, says Mark Rothstein, director of the Health Law Institute at the University of Houston Law Center. For one, increasing numbers of companies are refusing to hire people who smoke, even if only at home, because smokers statistically have higher health bills. And last year the Northwestern National Life Insurance Company found that 15 percent of 400 employers surveyed plan to screen the dependents of potential employees for pre-existing conditions.

The insurance industry is also grappling with the implications of genetic testing. Insurers depend on risk classification to assess applicants' eligibility, set premiums, and protect against heavy losses. Pre-existing conditions are often grounds for higher premiums or specific exclusions from coverage. Individuals with certain disorders—diabetes, emphysema, epilepsy—may be turned away completely.

Many experts expect genetic screening to seep into the underwriting process. From the industry's point of view, it will be a necessary defense against people who purchase extensive coverage knowing they're at risk for a serious disease. For applicants, however, the danger is that uncertain or highly variable disease probabilities will be treated as gospel. If predisposition to disease is viewed as a pre-existing condition, many people could be subject to higher rates, limited coverage, or no coverage at all.

FEW LEGAL SAFEGUARDS

For now, only a few states have laws prohibiting unfair genetic discrimination by insurers. Even in those states, however, many people work for self-insured companies, which are exempt from state insurance law. Without further safeguards, predictive testing could push additional millions into the ranks of the uninsured.

Employees are specifically protected from being fired for their health-care costs, but safeguards for job applicants are ambiguous. Laws designed to prevent employers from discriminating against candidates with disabilities—including a new law passed by Congress—could be interpreted by the courts to cover people with disease-encoding genes. Even so, predicts attorney Rothstein, discrimination in hiring will prevail so long as economic incentives are strong and candidates can be tested and rejected without explanation.

The danger of discrimination casts a troubling pall over the new genetic tests. Unless society can devise ways to protect the rights of individuals, say sociologist Dorothy Nelkin and attorney Laurence Tancredi in their book *Dangerous Diagnostics,* "we risk increasing the number of people defined as unemployable, untrainable, or uninsurable. We risk creating a biologic underclass."

QUESTIONS FOR CRITICAL READERS

Remembering and Understanding

1. Summarize the role of genetic screening in employment and health insurance decisions.
2. What are the limitations on genetic screening?
3. What provisions haves been made to protect people from a discriminatory or unfair use of information from genetic screening?

Analyzing and Discussing

4. What legal safeguards do you believe should be available to people who have genetic disorders?
5. Should people be refused insurance coverage if they have a genetic predisposition to develop a specific health problem?
6. Based on your knowledge of what is happening now, what other abuses of genetic screening might occur in the future?

Writing

7. To say that some uses of genetic screening are unfair suggests that other uses might be fair. Write a paper in which you describe or identify types of genetic screening that you believe would be fair or beneficial, and explain why you believe they would be fair.

Synthesizing and Consolidating

1. Carefully compare what the other writers in this chapter say about socio-biology with the explanation Lumsden and Wilson provide. What similarities and differences (points of agreement and disagreement) do you find? Based on your review, write a comprehensive explanation of sociobiology as a scientific discipline.
2. Wilson has been criticized because of the perception that his ideas about sociobiology support political positions and ideologies that favor racism, sexism, and the economic and political status quo in the world. Evaluate this accusation, using what Wilson and the other writers here say as your evidence.
3. Draw on the information in this chapter to explain how concepts from sociobiology might be used to support racist, sexist, or social Darwinist policies.
4. Some critics have challenged sociobiology because they believe its ideas can be used to support the political, social, and economic status quo. What parts of the status quo do they find objectionable? That is, what is it about the status quo that they believe should be changed?
5. If it could be proven that the present situation of the world could not be other than it is, how would that knowledge affect public policies? (i.e., If we could prove that the poor are biologically destined to be poor, what policies would that knowledge justify?)
6. Summarize the major objections to sociobiology.
7. Summarize the major concepts of sociobiology.
8. Using the information provided by Fleming and Graham, describe the scientific context in which E. O. Wilson developed his ideas about sociobiology.

Suggestions for Writing and Research

1. In recent years scientists haves frequently claimed to have found genetic links with specific kinds of behavior (e.g., crime, homosexuality, and so on). Using newspaper and magazine indexes (and specialized indexes if possible) attempt to locate stories in the popular press about specific genetic links to traits or behaviors. Summarize the stories that you find.
2. Some public officials have proposed programs of genetic screening for desirable or undesirable traits or behaviors, such as criminal behavior. Research this question. Summarize the proposals that have been made, and comment on whether you believe they are reasonable and fair.
3. If someone proposed that society should actively pursue programs of selecting for or against specific genetic features, much the way we breed animals to emphasize certain traits and eliminate others, how would you respond to this proposal? What questions would you ask? What information needs to be considered? What are the ethical issues involved?
4. A number of writers in this chapter use terminology from computer tech-

nology to refer to humans. What is the effect of discussing people as though they were machines? (Some scientists talk about nature and genetics as though they were machines, too). Explore the mechanistic metaphors common in biology.

5. If behaviors and traits are genetically based, and if scientists can manipulate genes to eliminate undesirable traits and increase the occurrences of desirable traits, how would this be done in a manner consistent with the provisions for freedom and the protection of individual rights in the U.S. Constitution?

6. If you could make the kinds of changes in society that some sociobiologists envision, what changes would you make?

7. Locate a copy of Wilson's *Sociobiology* and read the last chapter, "Man: from Sociobiology to Sociology." This is the chapter that has drawn the greatest criticism from scientists and others. Summarize Wilson's major points, and explain what statements some readers might find objectionable.

8. If human social behavior is biologically based, then what are we to do with concepts of personal responsibility for one's actions, the teaching of values, and the role of learning in social behavior?

Page 193. Reprinted by permission of Greenwood Publishing Group, Inc., Westport, CT, from *Young, Black, and Male in America*, by Jewelle T. Gibbs. Copyright © by Auburn House, 1988.

Page 199. Reprinted by permission of Harry Edwards, Department of Sociology, University of California, Berkeley.

Page 208. From *Black Masculinity* by Robert Staples, "Race, Masculinity and Crime." Reprinted by permission of the author.

Page 216. From *Blacks in College*, Jacqueline Fleming, "Differences by Race and Sex." Reprinted by permission of Jossey-Bass, Inc., 1988.

Page 222. Copyright © 1990 by Shelby Steele. From the book *The Content of our Character* and reprinted with permission from St. Martin's Press, Inc., New York, NY.

Page 232. From *Brothers & Keepers* by John Edgar Wideman. Copyright © 1984 by John Edgar Wideman. Reprinted by permission of Henry Holt and Company, Inc.

Chapter 6

Page 244. From *Harrowsmith*, July/August 1988, Jack Connor, "Empty Skies." Reprinted by permission of Camden House Publishing, Inc.

Page 258. From *Audubon*, the magazine of the National Audubon Society, September 1989. David Wilcove, "In Memory of Martha and Her Kind." Reprinted by permission of the author.

Page 264. From *Birder's World*, January/February 1989. Kim Harris, "Fuel Efficiency." Reprinted by permission of the author.

Page 269. From *Audubon*, the magazine of the National Audubon Society, July 1986. Bernd Heinrich, "Why Is A Robin's Egg Blue?" Reprinted by permission of the author.

Page 278. From *One Day At Teton Marsh* by Sally Carrighar. Copyright 1947 by the Curtis Publishing Co. Copyright 1945, 1946, 1947 and renewed 1975 by Sally Carrighar. Reprinted by permission of Alfred A. Knopf, Inc.

Page 288. With permission from *Natural History*, September 1983; Copyright the American Museum of Natural History, 1983.

Page 296. From *The Land of Little Rain*, Mary Austin, "The Scavengers." Houghton Mifflin, 1903.

Page 301. Excerpt from *The Peregrine* by J. A. Baker. Copyright © 1967 by J. A. Baker. Reprinted by permission of HarperCollins Publishers.

Page 309. Copyright © 1980 by the University of Georgia Press. Used by permission.

Chapter 7

Page 316. From *A Country Year: Living the Questions* by Sue Hubbell. Copyright © 1983, 1984, 1985, 1986 by Sue Hubbell. Reprinted by permission of Random House, Inc.

Page 320. From *Audubon*, the magazine of the National Audubon Society, November 1989. Curtis J. Badger, "We're Selling the Family Farm." Reprinted by permission of the author.

Page 326. From *The New Republic*, December 8, 1986. Jeffrey L. Pasley, "The Idiocy of Rural Life," reprinted by permission of *The New Republic*.

Page 334. From *The New Republic*, January 5 and 12, 1987. Henry Fairlie, "The Idiocy of Urban Life," reprinted by permission of *The New Republic*.

Page 341. From *The Atlantic*, February 1981. Donald McCaig, "Life in the Fast Lane," reprinted by permission of *The Atlantic*. Copyright © 1981 Donald McCaig.

Page 348. Copyright © 1989 by The Antioch Review, Inc. First appeared in the *Antioch Review*, vol. 47, No. 2 (Spring, 1989).

Page 358. From *The Solace of Open Spaces* by Gretel Ehrlich. Copyright © 1985 by Gretel Ehrlich. Reprinted by permission of Viking Penguin, a division of Penguin Books USA Inc.

Page 368. From *Farm* by Richard Rhodes. Copyright © 1989 by Richard Rhodes. Reprinted by permission of Simon & Schuster, Inc.

Chapter 8

Page 382. James Crawford. From *Bilingual Education: History, Politics, Theory, and Practice.* Trenton, N.J.: Crane Publishing Co., 1989. Copyright © 1989 by James Crawford. Reprinted by permission.

Page 388. Published by permission of Transaction Publishers, from *Society*, vol. 19(1). Copyright © 1981 by Transaction Publishers.

Page 404. From *Newsweek*, July 8, 1988. Copyright © 1988, Newsweek, Inc. All rights reserved. Reprinted by permission.

Page 408. Copyright 1990 Christian Century Foundation. Reprinted by permission from the November 29, 1990 issue of *The Christian Century*.

Page 414. From *Commonweal*, May 4, 1990. Abigail McCarthy, "A Common Currency: The Gift of a Single Tongue," reprinted by permission of the Commonweal Foundation. 1990.

Page 418. From *The Schools We Deserve*, Diane Ravitch, "Politicization and the Schools: The Case of Bilingual Education." Reprinted by permission of American Philosophical Society.

Page 429. From *Hunger of Memory* by Richard Rodriguez. Copyright © 1982 by Richard Rodriguez. Reprinted by permission of David R. Godine, Publisher.

Page 438. From *Blessings of Babel*. Reprinted by permission of Mouton de Gruyter, a Division of Walter de Gruyter & Co.

Chapter 9

Page 449. Copyright © Jon R. Luoma, 1990. "Trash Can Realities." Reprinted from *Audubon*, the magazine of the National Audubon Society, March 1990. Reprinted by permission of the author.

Page 460. From *The Closing Circle: Nature, Man and Technology* by Barry Commoner. Copyright © 1971 by Barry Commoner. Reprinted by permission of Alfred A. Knopf, Inc. Originally appeared in *The New Yorker*.

Page 468. Reprinted with permission from the September/October 1990 issue of *Garbage* Magazine, Brooklyn, New York.

Page 476. William L. Rathje, "The History of Garbage," from *Garbage* Magazine, September/October 1990, reprinted by permission of author.

Page 485. From *Audubon*, the magazine of the National Audubon Society, September 1986. Ruth Norris, "A Tide of Plastic." Reprinted by permission of the author.

Page 491. From *Audubon*, the magazine of the National Audubon Society, May 1986. Mary Durant, "Here We Go A-Bottling." Reprinted by permission of author.

Page 497. "The Look Is You," by Louis Blumberg and Robert Gottlieb, Island Press, a Division of The Center for Resource Economics, (1989) from the book *War on Waste*.

Chapter 10

Page 508. Reprinted by permission of the publishers from *Promethean Fire* by Charles J. Lumsden and Edward O. Wilson, Cambridge, Mass.: Harvard University Press, Copyright © 1983 by the President and Fellows of Harvard College.

Page 519. From *The Atlantic Monthly*, February 1969. Donald Fleming, "On Living in a Biological Revolution." Reprinted by permission of the author.

Page 531. From *Between Science and Values*, Loren Graham, "Primatology and Sociobiology." Reprinted by permission of The Columbia University Press.

Page 541. Reprinted from *The Battle for Human Nature, Science, Morality and Modern Life*, by Barry Schwartz, by permission of W. W. Norton & Company, Inc. Copyright © 1986 by Barry Schwartz.

Page 553. From *Sociobiology and Human Nature*, David Barash, "Evolution as a Paradigm for Behavior." Reprinted by permission of Jossey-Bass, Inc.

Page 561. Reprinted by permission of the publishers from *The Women That Never Evolved* by Sarah Hrdy, Cambridge, Mass.: Harvard University Press, Copyright © 1981 by the President and Fellows of Harvard College.

Page 573. "Biological Potentiality vs. Biological Determinism" is reprinted from *Ever Since Darwin, Reflections in Natural History*, by Stephen Jay Gould, by permission of W. W. Norton & Company, Inc. Copyright © 1977 by Stephen Jay Gould. Copyright © 1973, 1974, 1975, 1976, 1977 by The American Museum of Natural History.

Page 581. Copyright 1990 by Consumers Union of United States, Inc., Mount Vernon, NY 10553. Reprinted by permission from "The Telltale Gene," *Consumer Reports*, July 1990. Reprints of the entire article are available for $3 each directly from Reprints/CU, 286 Washington Street, Mount Vernon, NY 10553.